The Negro Leagues Revisited

ALSO BY BRENT KELLEY

They Too Wore Pinstripes:
Interviews with 20 Glory-Days
New York Yankees 1998

Voices from the Negro Leagues:
Conversations with 52 Baseball Standouts
of the Period 1924–1960 1998

The Early All-Stars: Conversations with
Standout Baseball Players of the 1930s and 1940s 1997

In the Shadow of the Babe: Interviews
with Baseball Players Who Played With
or Against Babe Ruth 1995

Baseball Stars of the 1950s: Interviews with
All-Stars of the Game's Golden Era 1993

The Case For: Those Overlooked by
the Baseball Hall of Fame 1992

The Negro Leagues Revisited

Conversations with 66 More Baseball Heroes

by
BRENT KELLEY

McFarland & Company, Inc., Publishers
Jefferson, North Carolina, and London

For Daniel

A great fan of the Negro leagues.

Library of Congress Cataloguing-in-Publication Data

Kelley, Brent P., 1941–
    The Negro leagues revisited : conversations with 66 more
baseball heroes / by Brent Kelley.
        p. cm.
    Continues: Voices from the Negro leagues. c1998.
    Includes bibliographical references (p.) and index.
    ISBN 0-7864-0875-8 (illustrated case binding : (50# alkaline paper)
    1. Baseball players — United States — Interviews.   2. Afro-
American baseball players — Interviews.   3. Negro leagues —
History.   I. Kelley, Brent P. Voices from the Negro leagues.
II. Title.
GV865.A1 K435   2000
796.357'0973 — dc21
                                                        00-22198
British Library cataloguing data are available

Manufactured in the United States of America

*McFarland & Company, Inc., Publishers
    Box 611, Jefferson, North Carolina 28640
    www.mcfarlandpub.com*

Contents

A Note on Statistics

The statistics that appear on the pages that follow, as in my previous book *Voices from the Negro Leagues*, are probably incorrect and I'm sorry. I'm not sorry because what I report is wrong, but rather because we just don't have the true statistics to report.

Complete, correct statistics for Negro league baseball do not exist today. They may never have. Some have been unearthed in recent years by researchers, and some more undoubtedly will be in the future, but it's safe to say that there will always be a gap — we'll never have them all. And that's too bad. Baseball lends itself to statistical analysis like no other sport, but that's only a part of the reason. There are people who will tell you that Negro baseball was inferior, and one of the reasons they say this is the lack of hard, black-and-white, statistical proof.

(One of my favorite arguments by those who put down Negro baseball as inferior is the one that goes something like this: "They only played against other blacks." Well, the whites only played against other whites, so what's the point?)

Sure, Ted Williams has great career "numbers," but even without them, anyone who ever saw him swing a bat knew he was a marvelous hitter. You could tell Rickey Henderson was fast without checking his stats. Stand at the plate for a Nolan Ryan fastball and you didn't need a list of his strikeout victims to know he could bring it.

And so it is with men such as Buck Leonard, Cool Papa Bell, and Bill Foster. Stats only verify what all who saw them already knew. Unfortunately, not enough saw them and those who did are, all too literally, a dying breed.

With that said, some statistics are presented on the following pages. For some seasons and for some players, we have nothing; for others (seasons and players), we have something, but it's likely incomplete. Statistics from Latin America and Canada are likewise incomplete; in fact, we don't even have records of years played and teams played for in many cases, but what we do have is included here.

For some players in some years, there may be only a few numbers. There may be stats from some league games but not all, or there may be stats from games against all competition. There may be complete totals in some categories but only partial in others; for instance, a pitcher may have a correct number of innings in a season, but only a partial total of strikeouts.

Also confusing are the sources of the stats. One source differs from another frequently and both claim to be accurate. Perhaps they both are, perhaps neither is. And some of what you see here is hearsay, based on the memories of the men themselves.

With all those disclaimers, the statistics we have are presented.

Introduction

A few years ago, *Voices from the Negro Leagues* was written because there was a need for information about the Negro leagues and the players who performed in them. The most reliable way to get this information was, of course, to go to the players themselves.

As I said in the introduction to that book, the average fan has heard of Satchel Paige and Josh Gibson, but for all he knew, those two stood out there and tossed the ball back and forth to each other. No one (of any color) may have played baseball as well as they did, but for that ability to be recognized there had to be someone to compare them to: other pitchers and other hitters.

And there were—thousands of them over the years—and just as mere mortals were dwarfed by the likes of Cobb and Ruth and Mathewson and Grove, so were they dwarfed by Paige and Gibson and Stearnes and Foster.

Those who wanted to keep baseball divided along racial lines said then, and some still say today, that black ballplayers were inferior to white ballplayers. The fact that in head-to-head competition between black teams and white teams the black teams won the majority of games doesn't sway them. They respond by saying the white players had nothing to prove and weren't trying as hard. One must feel, however, that the white players didn't like to lose, so that alone should have given them the proper incentive.

Larry French, an excellent major league pitcher in the '30s and early '40s, was a regular member of the white teams that played each fall against black teams. After years of trying, he finally won a game in these competitions. "Now I can retire," he said, and did. He never pitched again against anyone.

Voices contained interviews with 52 former players, of which more than a dozen have now passed away. This book has interviews with 66 more, and some of them have already gone as of this writing. Between the two books, more than a third of the Negro league veterans who were alive at the time of the 1995 75th anniversary of the founding of the Negro National League tell their stories: how they began, who helped them, what they faced, how they coped. The early ones tell how they never thought their race would play in organized ball; the later ones tell how even though they could, advancement and acceptance were difficult or impossible.

So this book, along with the previous one, is a history of our country and of our national pastime as told by those who made it. It is important to record these remembrances now because in a few years there will be no one left who remembers. With an average age of almost 80, the remaining living Negro league veterans represent an endangered species, one that no legal restriction can save.

And when they're gone, they're gone. And when they go, their stories will go with them. These books are a modest effort to preserve a marvelous portion of our (America's) legacy, albeit one that never should have been.

PART ONE
The 1920s and the 1930s

Prior to 1920, Negro baseball was loosely organized, but in 1920 the Negro National League (NNL) was formed. Over the next dozen years, other leagues of major league stature (Eastern Colored League, East-West League, Negro Southern League, Negro American League) came and went, some quickly. In fact, the NNL did not play in 1932; instead, it was replaced by the NSL, its only year of major league play, and the EWL, which died an early death in June of that year. The ECL began earlier and lasted longer, from 1923 through 1927. The unstable and short-lived ANL appeared in 1929, but did not play in 1930 and consisted of only four teams in 1931, then folded.

With the reappearance of the NNL in 1933, a level of stability was reached for a few years before the Negro American League began operations in 1937. The two leagues presented good baseball and strong competition and black baseball entered its heyday.

William "Bobby" Robinson
"The Human Vacuum Cleaner"

BORN OCTOBER 25, 1903, WHISTLER, AL
HT. 6', WT. 170 BATTED AND THREW RIGHT

Negro Leagues debut: 1925

There are few people around today who saw him play, but those who did say he may have been the best third baseman ever to play the position. And there are testimonials to the same effect left by those who are no longer with us: Bobby Robinson was a great third baseman. Vacuum cleaners were still relatively new when Robinson played, but nonetheless he was dubbed "the human vacuum cleaner" by his fans and peers.

Talking to Robinson is a lesson in baseball history. He played with 11 Negro leagues teams and against many major leaguers from 1925 through 1942, and he has a wonderful memory. He can speak with authority on legends of the game, men such as Oscar Charleston, Pop Lloyd, Cannonball Dick Redding, Cool Papa Bell, Ty Cobb, Jimmie Foxx, and most of the other stars of an era from which few witnesses are still around.

I've heard you were the best third baseman ever to play. Is that true?

[Laughs] That's what most of the people said. I had to have good range to be what I was. Matter of fact, I'll put it like this: I seldom made an error, I know that.

How did you come to join Indianapolis?

They got me by seein' me play with another team. Semi-pro. I was with Pensacola Giants and they hired me to make a trip with 'em. I made the trip and we had made it to Birmingham and that's where I was scouted. Matter of fact, I was scouted before I got to Birmingham; this scout told me he had been scoutin' me for the last couple of weeks or so. He was from Indianapolis ABCs and he asked me would I want to sign a professional contract to play professional baseball. I told him I would, but I said since it's late up in the season I said I'd probably rather wait until next spring to go to spring training.

You played everywhere.

[Laughs] That's the way it looks. I played all over. When you said "everywhere," you just about hit it. [Laughs] All the different states, different places. I played so many places until I don't know where I played myself.

Were there any problems in your travels?

Well, when we first started we traveled mostly by train. They chartered a Pullman car. We traveled like that for a while, then later on we started traveling by buses.

Accommodations were pretty rough, in a way of speakin', because, number one, you couldn't stop and eat food in nice places 'cause you couldn't be served. It was just rough gettin' food.

I didn't know what a hotel was when we were down in the South. It was rough in the South, I'm tellin' you. And when I say rough, I mean *rough*. They had hotels in the North, but you couldn't just stop in any hotel you wanted to then. All the big hotels around Indi-

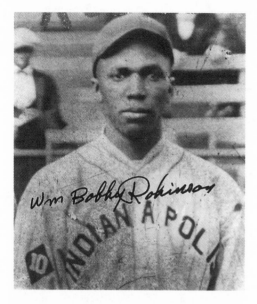

Bobby Robinson, 1925 (courtesy of William Robinson).

anapolis, you couldn't stop in 'em. I remember once I stopped in the Booker Cadillac Hotel. You ever hear of that one? That was about the first major hotel I stopped in. That was a nice one.

You must have spent a lot of time sleeping in the bus.

I sure did. [Laughs] You can bet I did. It was rough, too.

You played against a lot of good ballplayers.

I sure did. Oscar Charleston was probably the greatest outfielder I played against in my time. Then I also played *with* him, too. He was with the ABCs when I went there. He didn't stay there long, but he was there when I first go there. He left shortly and went to Baltimore to play with the Baltimore Black Sox.

I remember, he talked to me after I got there; he told me about the type of third baseman I was. He told me I was gonna get the job. There was a couple of other guys there tryin' to get the job and he told me that I didn't have to worry about them. He said they was just there, that I was gonna get the job as the regular third baseman 'cause there wouldn't be no way for 'em to outplay me.

You remember Bingo DeMoss? I played for him and I played against him, too. Great second baseman.

Did you see much of Josh Gibson?

He wasn't around them. He was around later. *Way* later.

Pop Lloyd was playin' then. He was an outstanding player. A class by hisself. He could do it all. [Laughs] Pop Lloyd was really a great ballplayer.

It took a while to get him into the Hall of Fame.

Yeah. He should've been there long ago. Like Oscar Charleston and a number of players I know should've been in the Hall of Fame.

Smokey Joe Williams. Bill Wright. He was a great one. He should've been in the major leagues without question. I played with him at Baltimore.

What kind of hitter were you?

Pretty good hitter. I was a little weak on curveballs but finally they kept throwin' me curveballs, throwin' me curveballs and finally I got to where I could hit curveballs pretty good.

I didn't have too much power. The biggest thing I hit was like singles, doubles — like that. I wasn't a guy that hit a lot of home runs. I did hit a home run here and there, but I didn't hit home runs like most average guys that was on that team. There were some terrible hitters on that team.

Which team do you consider yourself to be a part of?

I guess I would have to say the Indianapolis ABCs. That was my first stop.

Who was the best pitcher?

Did you ever hear of Bill Gatewood? He was one. Dick Redding. I hit against Redding. I did pretty fair; I didn't get nothin' but a single off him. [He] oughtta be in the Hall of Fame.

Do you remember one game or incident in your career that stands out?

Yes, I sure do. I think it was 1930. I was playin' with Detroit Stars and we were playin'

St. Louis Stars in order to decide who was gonna play in the World Series at that time. In that series in St. Louis, we beat 'em the first part of the series, but they had a great team. I mean, a *great* team.

The greatest thrill in my career would have to be against St. Louis Stars in St. Louis. I think we were leadin' St. Louis, 2–1, in the bottom of the eighth innin', I think. St. Louis came to bat and first up was Cool Papa Bell. He could *fly*. Look like to me he could take three or four steps from home plate and he was fast as he was gonna get. He was extra fast.

But anyway, Cool Papa got on, then next hitter behind Cool was [John Henry "Pistol"] Russell. I was captain of the team at that time, and I walks up to the pitcher and I told him, I said, "Whatever you do, make sure you don't throw nothin' high inside to this hitter 'cause he's a very dangerous man. He'll break the ballgame up."

The first pitch he threw to this guy, he threw him an inside pitch like I asked him not to throw. He [Russell] hit a bullet to right field but it was a foul just about three feet. It scared me, I'm tellin' you. [Laughs]

When we get things settled and got ready to go again, I walks up to him just before he got ready to start pitchin' and I told him, "Whatever you do, don't throw nothin' high inside to him. He's one of the most feared hitters in the game today."

I never played deep like most third basemen I see today, even in the major leagues. I never played that deep. I always played about five feet behind third and second base line. I never played deep like lots of third basemen. Lots of 'em almost play as deep as the shortstop. Lotta guys used to tell me, "I don't see how in the world you can field like you can field to play as close as you do." I played that same way on most hitters, unless they're lefthand hitters. On lefthand hitters, I played them a little bit different.

Gettin' back to that play, Cool Papa was on third, Pistol Russell was on second base — never will forget it — and I didn't hardly know what to do right then. I called time and I talked to the pitcher and the catcher. Mitch

Murray, he was a *great* catcher, he told me, he said, "Robinson, I'll tell you what. Nine times out of ten this guy hits your way." I said, "I know he do. I'm playin' him to hit my way." And sure 'nough, he did. He hit my way *hard!*

Cool was on third and Russell was on second base and Cool had a pretty big lead off of third base. I was playin' him in kinda short. I never will forget that ballgame. The hitter hit a low line drive to me and the catch was on my right side, and I speared that ball righthanded with my right hand, and I stepped on third base and caught Cool divin' back to third base and fired to second base for a triple play.

That was the greatest play in all my career and I never forgot that. Different people ask me about that same play now in different places.

Did you win the game?

Yeah, we won the game. We beat 'em, 3–2, but St. Louis beat us in the series. They had a *very* good team.

Was there any thought in those days of playing in the white leagues?

It wasn't too much at that time. As a matter of fact, durin' that time nobody never did

Bobby Robinson, 1998 (Lesa Feder photograph).

think that black players would be in the majors.

I had a number of players to tell me that if things was right, I would be playin' in the major leagues. I'll tell you one guy told me that: John McGraw. He was manager of New York Giants. He was a great one. He saw this triple play that I made. They were on their last swing west and were playin' in St. Louis. Willie Wells was St. Louis shortstop at the time, and he sent Wells over to the dugout to get me. He wanted to compliment me on that play, so I ran across the field and met him.

By the time I got there, he got up and give me a hearty handshake and he told me right away, he said, "Bobbie, I'll tell you. I have read of your playin' third base lots of times, but this the first time I've seen it. I think you're probably one of the greatest ever." I said, "Thank you." He said, "If things were right, today you would be playin' third base for me and the New York Giants." He told me that.

Another guy told me that. He was a personal friend of mine; he was *tough*, too — tough to get along with. Lots of people didn't like him. Ty Cobb. He was a great outfielder and he could hit it. I met Cobb; he was with the Tigers and I was with the black team in Detroit — the Detroit Stars.

He came down to the dugout one time and he started talkin' with me. He was tellin' 'bout what a great pair of hands I had. He told me to stretch my hands out. I stretched my hands out and he looked and said, "Look what big hands!" [Laughs] He told the other players that. He told me right then and there, he said, "One thing, today if things were like they should be, you'd be playin' third base for my team." I know one thing: He was a *great* one.

Did you play many games against white teams?

Quite a few. [Rogers] Hornsby and lots of 'em. I played against [Jimmie] Foxx. Boy, he could hit it and he was a great guy, too. Nice person. Buck Weaver was a friend of mine. He was a good third baseman and a good hitter, too. Very nice person.

Lots of old ballplayers tell me today around different places I go, they say, "I don't see how you can remember about them different guys that you played with. Man, them guys was *way* back there." I say, "I know they are, but I remember 'em."

Did you have any regrets from your career?

I don't think I did really. I can't think back of nothin' that I regret 'cause most all the games that I played in I enjoyed. I played great baseball all the way through.

It looked like to me I was a gifted guy. I could field — play third base. I was just gifted to play third base. I had a very good throwin' arm. They say I was one of the best ever did it. [Laughs] I never brag much, but I know that I was a good one.

Would you go back 75 years and be a ballplayer again?

If I had it to do over again, I think I would like to do the same thing over again. I enjoyed it just that much.

BATTING RECORD

Year	Team, League	Pos	G	AB	R	H	2B	3B	HR	RBI	SB	BA
1925	Indianapolis, NNL	3b										
1926	Ind.-Clev. Elites, NNL	3b										.129
1927	Chi.-Birm.-Mem., NNL	3b										.251
1928	Memphis, NNL	3b										
1929	Detroit, NNL	3b										.309
1930		3b										.260
1931		3b										
1932	Balt.-Clev. Stars, EWL	3b										
1933	Clev. Giants, NNL	3b										
1934	Clev. Red Sox, NNL	3b										

Year	Team, League	Pos	G	AB	R	H	2B	3B	HR	RBI	SB	BA
1934	St. Louis, ind.	3b										
1935	St. Louis, ind.	3b										
1936		3b										
1937	St. Louis, NAL	3b										.277
1938	Indianapolis, NAL	3b										
1939	St. Louis, NAL	3b										
1940	St. Louis, ind.	3b										
1941	St. Louis, NAL	3b										

Ted "Double Duty" Radcliffe
"One of a Kind"

BORN JULY 7, 1902, MOBILE, AL
HT. 5'10", WT. 190 BATTED AND THREW RIGHT

Negro Leagues debut: 1926

There probably aren't enough pages to list all the accomplishments of Double Duty Radcliffe, but here are a few.

He earned his nickname when he pitched the first game of a doubleheader and then caught the second game, something he did several times in his career. He is the only man at any level of professional baseball to have been both the starting pitcher and the starting catcher in All-Star games. All together, he played in six East-West All-Star games. In the 1944 game, with his mother in the stands, he hit a two-run home run and his brother, Alec, added a two-run triple. In 1943, he was chosen as the American Negro League's Most Valuable Player.

Full statistics don't exist for most of his career, but he is credited with about 500 home runs, a batting average in the .340 neighborhood, and somewhere around 500 wins as a pitcher. He was still an active player in his mid–50s, and he managed for many years. He is an amazing man who had an amazing career. And now, nearing the age of 100, he's still going strong.

Did you consider yourself a pitcher or a catcher?

It didn't make no difference, just so we won. I was a good hitter, too.

Do you belong in the Hall of Fame?

I haven't been in yet. I think they got mad with me when we were down in Cuba and we beat the American League All-Stars in 1939. Satchel and I pitched and we shut 'em out. They had a meetin' there that night in that auditorium and they asked me to speak, and they asked me why I wasn't in the big league. I say, "You'll have to ask the two Grand Dragons of the Ku Klux." They asked me who was it and I said, "J. Edgar Hoover and your Judge Landis," and he said, "You're right." I think they hold that against me, but it don't make no difference now. I'm gettin' a pension.

I played long as Satchel. I did everything I's supposed to do. I managed 28 years; I played 37 years. What more could I do? I had a good battin' average. They say my lifetime battin' average was .343 and I hit 507 home runs and all that. What more could I do?

They got some white boys should be in. You know Pete Rose should be in.

You played on some outstanding teams. Which one do you think was the best?

In 1930, I was with the St. Louis Stars. We won it. Nineteen thirty-one I was with the Homestead Grays. We won it. Nineteen thirty-two Satchel and I both, and Josh, was with the Crawfords. But the 1931 team of the Homestead Grays — we had George Scales on second, Oscar Charleston on first, Jake Stephens at short, Boojum Wilson on third; we had Vic

Harris in left, Billy Evans in center, and Ted Page in right, Josh Gibson and me catchin', Bill Foster, Smokey Joe Williams, Lefty Williams, Oscar Owens, and George Britt and Roy Williams [pitching]. That was the best team I ever been on. The 1931 Homestead Grays.

I'll tell you another team that was a great team — the team we had at Bismarck, North Dakota [in 1935]. We had me and Satchel and Quincy Trouppe with that white team, but we had a couple of boys that could play anywhere. They were white, but they couldn't play in the major leagues 'cause they drink. That was [Billy] Oberholzer and Moose Johnson. They could hit good as anybody I've ever seen, and they helped us win the tournament in Wichita and we won 41 straight tournaments up in Minnesota and Canada, until they barred us out. In 1936, they barred us out. They said at the tournament in Wichita, "Double Duty and Satchel are niggers, but they're big league niggers and we can't beat them." So we didn't go back.

What was the attendance for your games?

Everywhere I went, attendance was good in those days. When I went to Homestead Grays in St. Louis, we used to outdraw the

Double Duty Radcliffe (courtesy of Ted Radcliffe).

Cardinals and the Browns 'cause back in those days the Browns stayed on the bottom for 21 years. We outdrew 'em.

I'll show you how good we was. You remember in 1939, Clark Griffith tried to get us in the big leagues with Washington 'cause we made that one of our home grounds. In 1941, you know Bill Veeck tried twice but they didn't do nothin' until Branch Rickey spoke up. He got it because they wasn't drawin' and they had to do somethin', didn't they? Baseball was *bad* back in the early '40s.

As long as Judge Landis was the commissioner, you guys weren't going to be able to play.

Well, if Judge Landis and Hoover hadda lived, there wouldn't have been any in there now 'cause they were dyed against blacks.

Ford Frick and one of the greatest men I ever knowed, a Southern man, Happy Chandler, helped. He told 'em to go ahead and play or go to the cotton fields. You know that Dixie Walker and his brother and a few more tried to keep 'em out. That boy what caught for the Cardinals, he's on our committee now — he swore he didn't do it but he's one of 'em. The boy on TV — [Joe] Garagiola. He's changed quite a bit. He treats me like a king now. That shows you there's some good in everybody. I don't have nothin' against him. I got nothin' against none of 'em; what's gonna be gonna be 'cause after they start to givin' me a pension that helped me a lot.

When did you start playing?

I had one year in 1926. Rube Foster sent a team to New Orleans called the Creoles 'cause that was their name down in New Orleans — the Milwaukee Creoles. Me, and my brother was the shortstop. He didn't wanna pay but a hundred dollars a month, but I was playin' with a white man — Gilkerson's Union Giants — and he was givin' me a hundred and fifty, and then every time I pitched a game he'd give me ten dollars extra. That was a lotta help in those days, so I stayed out there with him until I went to the Detroit Stars [in 1928]. They was always after me, but Bingo DeMoss was in my neighborhood, and he was a good friend of mine and he baited me up. He took

Double Duty Radcliffe tags out Josh Gibson at home in the 1944 East-West Game (courtesy of Ted Radcliffe).

me down to the tailor shop they called Eli and had me two suits made up and that got it. I went with him. [Laughs]

You played into your 50s.

I managed 'til '56. I stopped playin' in '56. I played altogether 36 years in America and 18 in foreign countries, so I played 54 years altogether. Ain't nobody ever did that. And pitchin' and catchin' I never had a sore arm. If I hadn't got my fingers hurt...

I never will forget. We were playin' the World Series against the Homestead Grays and I was catchin'. Saperstein went and got a special rubber thing to put over my hand, and I caught with two broken fingers and I hit as good as I ever hit in my life. I throwed out everybody that ran. They got some t-shirts with me and it says, "Thou shalt not steal, not on Double Duty's arm." [Laughs]

. I wanna go up there and see that man in

Milwaukee. I'm gonna throw out the first ball for him. [Bud] Selig. He went to bat for us, him and the man with the White Sox. I threw out the first ball for them this year twice. I told Dennis [Biddle] to tell him I'd like to come up there for the openin' game. He's due my respect.

I got a letter from a man in Colorado. He's a writer for a paper. He said, "Double Duty, I been readin' up on your record and I don't know what the hell they're thinkin', they haven't put you in [the Hall of Fame]." He said, "They don't put you in, they ought to burn the son of a bitch down."

They might do somethin'. I don't care, but I'm not gonna lose no rest, you know.

I used to manage Cincinnati. I had a good team. To show you how the black leagues ran, we won the championship and we were barnstormin' with the House of David, and the American Giants and Kansas City said

Double Duty Radcliffe (left) and Candy Jim Taylor (courtesy of Ted Radcliffe).

they were playin' for the championship. Neither of 'em didn't win it. [Laughs]

Who was the best player?

One of the best was Oscar Charleston. Willie Mays — I played against him. The greatest was Turkey Stearnes. There was Willie Wells. All those fellas was super. I played against so many I could talk all night.

Pitchers like Satchel Paige, Smokey Joe Williams, and that Steel Arm Dickey. They can't throw that ball a hundred miles in the big leagues like *they* did. If they get one up can throw 90, they're lucky. Baseball's a joke now. They're gettin' all those teams and they ain't got no players.

How many home runs would Josh Gibson hit against today's pitching?

Oh, it would have been murder.

You know, the first year we got him — don't nobody know how we got him. Satchel and all those was in Hot Springs takin' baths, and a white guy was there — a Coca-Cola man, a salesman — and he heard about us. We was sittin' up there where you play the horses for fifty cents and a dollar. He come up and he talked to me and he said, "There's a boy, there's a bright boy down in Rome, Georgia, can really hit that ball." So we got in touch with him [Gibson], and we went and picked him up in 1931.

He hit 75 home runs the first year. Nineteen-thirty-nine he hit 84. I'll tell you how good he was. When we played in the big ol' stadium in Washington [Griffith], the whole [American] league only hit 29 that year in '39, and he hit 42 in that park. He's the only man I ever read of hit one outta Yankee Stadium. I know one time he hit a ball down in Cuba

Bismarck (ND) Giants, 1935. Back row (l-r): Hilton Smith, Red Haley, Barney Morris, Satchel Paige, Moose Johnson, Quincy Trouppe, Double Duty Radcliffe. Front row (l-r): Joe DeSiderato, Bill Leary, Neil Churchill (owner), Bill Oberholzer, Ed Hendree (courtesy of Ted Radcliffe).

over the park out in the ocean. They never did find it. He could hit.

I get a pension every three months. It's pretty good. It comes to about 900 a month. It's better than nothin'. I get my social security and I make good money signin' autographs and speakin' at colleges. They keep me busy.

I'm gonna leave Chicago. I've been here 80 years. I came here in 1918. I'm goin' back home, but I gave my home in Mobile to my two sisters ten years ago. But I'm goin' down there. They like me so well the mayor said they'll give me a home, but I don't want that. I want to look out for myself. If you take too much gifts, you got to do what they say. I'm expectin' to go down there at Thanksgivin' and stay 'til March. I want to rest a while.

The weather's better, and I got four or five nieces and they take care of me so good. What I like about it, I like oysters and I like red snapper. And they got that gumbo.

When I was with the American Giants and Pittsburgh Crawfords, we used to play four games a day and that was really rough. Catchin' one, pitch one, play first base or right field or somewhere and give another fella a break. Then go home and your wife fix you dinner and [you] lay across the bed, and when you wake up the dinner's still there the next mornin'. You're too tired to eat.

[Leo] Durocher, when he was managin' the Cubs in 1969, he had me come up and have lunch with him in the clubhouse and talk to the president. Billy Williams is from my hometown, you know; he [Durocher] put him in the Hall of Fame.

Baseball was so bad. They thought Jackie had a hard time. I never will forget. We were goin' from Birmingham, when I managed Birmingham in '42, we were goin' to Jacksonville to play the Red Caps, and we stopped in Waycross, Georgia, to get some gas at a Sinclair station. The boys jumped outta the bus and grabbed the hose and the man hollered, "Put that hose down, niggers! Them's white folks' hose! Get you a Coca-Cola bottle."

So I pulled out. I wouldn't buy no gas. We got on the road five miles out and run outta gas. We had to push the bus ten miles. But them boys was laughin' and havin' fun. They was glad I didn't buy the gas.

Another time, we was *way* up in Wisconsin where they had a resort somethin' like down near Philly where the rich white folk used to go all the time. They didn't allow Negroes up there, only the ones was maids or chauffeurs or somethin' like that.

We went up there to play and a big white man was police captain or somethin' and he told us, "If you niggers beat us, we gonna run you out of town."

So I told the boss — that was my second year of managin' — a white guy was the boss, I told him, I said, "Go down there and get two of them state police to give us some protection." We run 'em, 20–0, then, and the police brought us ten miles out on the road and stood there 'til we got outta sight.

We went to Lansing, Michigan, 90 miles away, and we get hotels there all the time. All over Michigan mostly. But some places — southern Illinois and all them other places — you couldn't get a room.

Sometime you couldn't take a bath for three or four days. When we got in a town where they had a barber shop, I would ask could I use the restroom. They say, "Yeah." While I was in there I'd take a short nap and take a short hot bath, get up and wash myself off, and when I got back in the bus I'd change clothes so I'd be presentable. We had a hard time, boy.

Nineteen-forty-four I was managin' the Birmingham Black Barons, and we won the championship and played the Grays. We went to Kansas City and we beat Kansas City a doubleheader, 2–1, each game. I beat Satchel and Porter Moss beat [Booker] McDaniels. Two to one, each game. The people in Kansas City was mad.

We went down to Columbia, Missouri, on our way to St. Louis to go across the river to play the Belleville, Illinois, team and Abe Saperstein was with us and we stopped at a barbecue place — a steak house.

T-bone steaks back in those days wasn't but a dollar to a dollar-and-a-half, you know. We told him to get us 18 steaks and we was gonna cook 'em. We was all sittin' at the bar and waitin' and the man come up and say,

"Y'all can't stay in where the white folks is. They'll be mad with me." So we said, "Sell 'em the steaks," and we left.

He called the police and told 'em we had stole some cigars. None of us didn't smoke. Police came, but he said, "Go on. He ain't nothin' but a trouble-maker." He wanted us to sit out under the tree where the birds could sit on our food. I wasn't fixin' to do that.

You met all kind of people that helped you. Sometime I like to sit back and talk to the great guy from Washington, Judge Carver, and them. We'd sit there in the hotel and talk to 'em. It's just like goin' to school. It's a education for you, travelin'.

Look at Lena Horne. When I was playin' with the Grays, she was nine years old, goin' to school, but when she got up I was honored by her at her home one time in Hollywood.

I was fortunate enough to been at the White House three times, with Carter, Reagan, Clinton. Clinton asked me a lot of questions. He said, "Double Duty, Satchel said you was a ladies' man." He asked me how many children did I have. I said, "Four." He said, "I don't mean at home. I mean on the road." I said, "Now that's a $64 question." He said,

Ted Radcliffe, 1999 (Lisa Feder photograph).

"Why?" I said, "I was a hit-and-run man. I didn't like no double plays." [Laughs]

Then he said, "Double Duty, Helen, my maid, is dyin' to meet you. She heard Satchel and Buck Leonard and them talk about Double Duty so much she's dyin' to meet you." I said, "How old is she?" He says, "69." I said, "No." He said, "Why?" I said, "What's a Frigidaire gonna do with a ice box?" He said, "That's enough." [Laughs]

He said, "I want you to come back Christmas 'cause I enjoy your company." He say, "You're in a class by yourself, Double Duty." But I'm not goin' back. He's too good to the black people and the Republicans don't want him in there. He's good for the world. I think he's the best president we ever had. Do you see what he did for all them old men — white and black — in the World War? Give 'em a pension. My brother's 103; they're sendin' him $350 a month.

My sister died at 104, four years ago. We do pretty good. None of us never drinked that whiskey stuff. Only thing, I ain't never had enough women, but I had to turn 'em loose because the doctor told me my resistance has got low. They come now and worry you 'cause they think you got money, you know that. But I told 'em I'm in hibernation with the black bear.

I remember when I was in the South, when I was 15, 16 years old — we had to work ten hours to get a dollar. That's ten cents a hour. That's the reason I left. I left on an excursion goin' to Newark, Ohio, to work in a brickyard plant. I got over there and I was a pretty good dice shooter and I won 40-some dollars shootin' dice the first night. I worked two nights and I went to the man — me and my brother was with me — and we got drawed ten dollars and next day we caught the freight train and come to Chicago 'cause my brother was here. I been here ever since 1918. I been here 80 years. I'm tired of it. It's cold as hell. The wind was 40 miles per hour last night.

Would you play baseball today if you were a young man?

The money they're payin', I'd love to.

BATTING RECORD

Year	Team, League	Pos	G	AB	R	H	2B	3B	HR	RBI	SB	BA
1926	Gilkerson's Union Giants, ind.	c-p										
1927												
1928	Det. Stars, NNL	c	67	256	68	13	4	8			1	.266
1929		c	32	126	39	7	2	3			4	.310
1930	St. Louis, NNL	c-p	55	180	51	11	2	6			4	.283
1931	Det. Wolves, ind.											
	Homestead, ind.	c-p	17	47	14	3	1	1			0	.298
1932	Pittsburgh, ind.	c-p	15	47	11	3	0	2			0	.234
1933	Homestead, ind.											
	Columbus, NNL											
	Clev. Giants, NNL	c-p	12	47	15	1	1	0			1	.319
1934	Chicago, NNL	c-p	1	2	2	0	0	0			0	1.000
1935	Brooklyn, NNL	c-p	16	42	11	2	0	0			2	.262
1936	Bismarck, ind.	c-p										
1937	Cincinnati, NAL	c-p-m	24	87	31	3	2	0			0	.356
1938	Memphis, NAL	c-p-m	11	31	7	0	0	0			2	.226
1939		c-p	13	26	8	0	0	0			0	.308
1940	Vera Cruz, MxL	c-p										.247

Year	Team, League	Pos	G	AB	R	H	2B	3B	HR	RBI	SB	BA
1941	Memphis, NAL	c-p	6	6	2	1	0	0			0	.333
1942	Birmingham,											
	Chicago, NAL	c-p	13	39	11	1	0	0			0	.282
1943	Chicago, NAL	c-p		52	13	1	0	0			0	.250
1944	Birmingham, NAL	c-p	26	93	20	4	0	0			1	.215
1945	Kansas City, NAL	c-p										
	Harlem, ind.	c-p										
1946	Homestead, NNL	c-p										.222
	Mx. City Reds, MxL	c-p										
1947	Mx. City Reds, MxL	c-p										
1948	Chicago, NAL	c-p										
1949												
1950												
1951	Elmwood, MnDkL	c-p-m										
1955		c-p-m										

(Radcliffe played in several Latin and semipro leagues throughout the years and those statistics are unavailable. He is credited with around 500 home runs and a batting average of about .340.)

PITCHING RECORD

Year	Team, League	G	IP	W	L	Pct	H	BB	SO	ERA
1930	St. Louis, NNL	30	94	9	3	.750	89	24	40	
1931	Det., Homestead, ind.	17	106	9	5	.643	22	15	39	
1932	Pittsburgh, ind.	24	156	13	5	.722	60	14	17	
1933	Homestead, ind.									
	Columbus, NNL									
	N.Y. Blk Yanks, ind.	1		0	1	.000				
1934	Chicago, NNL	2	6	0	1	.000	3			
1935	Brooklyn, NNL	13	58	4	6	.400	59	9	19	
1937	Cincinnati, NAL	1		0	1	.000			4	
1938	Memphis, NAL	8	38	3	2	.600	20	0	3	
1939		10	49	4	3	.571	45	26	9	
1940	Vera Cruz, MxL			5	6	.455				5.93
1941		7	35	1	2	.333	38	1	7	
1945	Kansas City, NAL			3	0	1.000				
1946	Birmingham, NAL									
	Homestead, NNL	14	32	3	2	.600	45	3	12	

(As with his batting records, pitching statistics from everywhere he played are not available. He is credited with more than 200 wins.)

William "Red" Lindsay
"Did McGraw See Him?"

BORN APRIL 15, 1905, SPARTANBURG, SC
HT. 5'11½" WT. 170 BATTED AND THREW RIGHT

Negro Leagues debut: 1931

How many members of the old Bacharach Giants are still around? With the passing of Gene Benson in early 1999, there may be only one: William Lindsay. William is not listed in some recent Negro leagues literature, but "Charles Lindsay" is. Charles, like William, was also a stalwart shortstop, but he is not the same person as William.

Charles did play for the Bacharach Giants in 1929, and because of this and the position they played, they have been confused. William joined the team from Johnson C. Smith University in 1931 on the recommendation of a friend and played with the Bacharachs intermittently through 1934.

He found the transition from college pitching to professional pitching to be a little challenging — neither the first nor the last man to experience this phenomenon — but he described himself as "a good .250 hitter," and his steady glove kept him in the lineup until he found he needed glasses. Unbreakable lenses were not available 60 to 70 years ago and bad hops were the rule rather than the exception, so he left baseball in 1934.

Once, a poster advertising a game claimed John McGraw had proclaimed him as "the greatest shortstop ever seen." Lindsay himself doubts that McGraw ever saw him, but there is no way to disprove it.

I went to school at Charlotte, North Carolina, at Johnson C. Smith University. At that time, it had a high school department. Being born in the South, we had no high school for Negroes. I started at John C. Smith in the first year of high school and I spent the whole eight years there — four years of high school and four years of college.

I went out for the baseball team my first year of high school and I did so well they wanted me on the varsity team, but I wasn't too keen on that then. I wanted to kind of get my feet wet. [Laughs] So I started playing on the varsity my second year of high school and I played on the varsity team seven years.

My best year as a hitter was my second year. I batted .434 during the college season, but I never amounted to that again. My six-year batting average combined was .366. I was pretty good at college. [Laughs] I'm in the Hall of Fame at John C. Smith University.

I played a long time. I was All-CIA shortstop my second year and, far as I know, I kept that position all of that time.

I have a degree in French and English. English was my major and French was my minor. I graduated in 1931.

I had a friend on the baseball team; he had been there almost as long as I had. He came to Philadelphia because he had relatives here, and, of course, being 1931, it was the midst of the Depression and you could not get a job any kind of way.

A team came from Detroit and they were

going to be stationed here in Philadelphia because you could play around town all the time and make a living. Not a good one, but a living. So he went out to try out for the team and they took him over to New Jersey to pitch his first game. He did so well and they were so impressed with him — this was on Thursday — that they saved him for Sunday and had him pitch against a team in Camden, New Jersey, that had two former big leaguers on it. He pitched so well that he beat them, 2–1.

They were so impressed with him that they asked him if there were any more good ballplayers down South. He said, "Yes." They said, "Well, what does it take to get him up here?" He said, "Sixteen dollars." That was bus fare for me. [Laughs]

So I came here. The team was named the Bacharach Giants. I came here and I became a big hit and I did so well, the following year — 1932 — they decided to have a team in Washington, D.C., called the Washington Pilots. I had been there in 1931 [with the Bacharachs] to play *against* the Washington Pilots and they had fliers — you know, a big sheet — advertising what the ballplayers was doing.

We were going to play the New York Black Yankees. I think it was part-owned then by the dancer Bojangles Robinson. His name was on that as part owner of the Yankees. They featured four players further down on the page and one of 'em was Pop Lloyd, one was Nip Winters, and they included my name. The note was "Lindsay — proclaimed by John McGraw as the greatest shortstop ever seen." I had sense enough to know that John McGraw had never seen me play. I was pretty sure of that, but I thought it was pretty nice of them to pick me out as a featured ballplayer. [Laughs]

I don't think I was that good because that guy Pop Lloyd, they tell me that he was great. And then Dick Lundy. I played against him, and Dick Lundy told me that he got possibilities of becoming a manager the following season and he wanted to keep in touch with me because he wanted me to play shortstop for him.

I recall a game at Bradley Beach, New Jersey, and he was managing that team. Somebody hit me a line drive that I caught on one hop. There was one man on first base and, 'course, it was a double play and that kind of impressed him, I think. That was the only time I recall him seeing me.

I played four years, from '31 through '34. The '31 team was the Bacharach Giants and '32 was when I told you about this new team in Washington. They wanted me to come down there to play and they offered me $135 a month. The former manager — the one I had the previous year — he was the one dickering because he thought that it would be a good thing for me to play on a team that paid a salary rather than a co-plan. I went down to Washington and they had *all kinds* of ballplayers there with various positions, and one shortstop, which was myself. [Laughs]

During the spring training, we were going to play against a team in Camden, and the pitcher that was going to pitch against us had been in the big leagues and he knew how to take a rough ball and make it do tricks. As the game progressed, the guy batting in front of me was named Tom Dixon — he had a brother named Rap Dixon — and he singled, so when I came to bat, they gave me the bunt sign. I bent over to bunt on a ball I thought

William "Red" Lindsay (courtesy of William Lindsay).

was medium low and that ball just all of a sudden exploded up in my face. It hit the bat, but my finger was between the ball and the bat, so I broke my finger.

So it didn't take them too long to get rid of me because, you know, Negro baseball wasn't that rich to afford to carry somebody that wasn't going to play. I came back home and played with the Harrisburg Giants, and we went up in Canada and various places.

When I came home the second time, I went back to the Bacharach Giants, which was the team I started with. I played with them the balance of '32, '33, and '34.

Out in Fort Wayne, Indiana, one night, we were playing a night game and the lights were furnished by Dynamo on the sidelines and they were pretty poor lights. [Laughs] Someone hit a ball up in the air above my position and I think I probably did every kind of dance you ever saw [Laughs] and finally I lunged and luckily I caught it. It wasn't from ability; it was just luck. I told the manager I did not want to play at night anymore.

When we came back home, I went to have my eyes examined and the doctor gave me glasses. In those days, glasses were made out of glass. They didn't have plastic or anything. I was afraid to play on the rough grounds that we played on with glasses, so I quit playing.

It so happened that the man who owned the ballclub—the Bacharach Giants—had a sporting goods store and I started working at the store from 1933 'til 1983. That was the end of my job and it wound up now that I live alone with my cat. They're company; I tell people if someone offered me a thousand dollars for this cat I wouldn't take it.

I worked there so long, now I'm reaping the benefits of it. I get pretty good social security. Uncle Sam gives me $1511 every month. I jokingly tell people, I say, "I got more money than I got time." [Laughs]

The major leagues send me a couple of checks a year—small checks, like a hundred bucks. They have the insignia of the major leagues on the envelope.

One of the things that I'm proud of more

than anything else is I have a Jewish friend. We became friends at the basketball games—the 76ers—and he took me to Cooperstown. It was great. The only thing I could not understand was people kept coming to me for autographs, and I was wondering how did they know I was an old-time ballplayer. But I found out. This fellow that took me there, he had written an article when he had me throw out the first pitch at the Judy Johnson game. He was a friend of mine. Every year they honor him and every year I'm invited there.

I kept wondering why people were coming to me for autographs. I said, "They don't know me from Adam." I didn't know he was standing around the corner passing out the articles he wrote. [Laughs]

I went over big there and the people asked me to come back and make a second trip there, and they gave me just about everything that I wanted. I told 'em they had seven people in the Hall of Fame there that I had played with and against. They went and got me pictures of every one of those. That included Satchel Paige, Roy Campanella, and a lot of 'em.

I played two games *with* Roy Campanella when I was like 26 years old, maybe older, and he was about 14. We had two catchers and both of 'em were injured, so someone said, "How 'bout that kid?" They were talking about Roy Campanella. So we went there [to his house] one Sunday morning, but his mother didn't want him to play because it was Sunday. She finally relented when we told her we couldn't play unless we had a catcher. [Laughs] So I played a doubleheader with Roy Campanella. [Laughs] We became pretty good friends after that.

I had another close friend named Jackson who was a real *close* friend of Campanella, so naturally we became a pretty good group.

You mentioned some great ballplayers. Who was the best, in your opinion?

I guess the player that most people would say was the best would be Satchel Paige, wouldn't they? That's the only bad part about my playing against Satchel Paige: Josh Gibson was doing the catching. [Laughs] I finally met his son last year at the Judy Johnson event.

Satchel was the most renowned, but there were others. Cool Papa Bell—I played against him and he hit a single and a little bit later he tried to steal second and, by me being shortstop, I covered and we got him out. He says he wasn't out, but the umpire called him out. That's one of the highlights of my career.

Josh and Satchel were the people most known. I enjoy now having seen them play, but I didn't enjoy batting at Satchel's pitches. I kept hitting the ball back to the second baseman and back to the pitcher. He used to throw it so hard I couldn't pull it. [Laughs] Finally, it looked like he must have made a mistake or figured I was such a nonentity that he could do it. He threw me a slow ball high and I hit that son of a gun. I said, "You sucker, I got you now!"

I hit it to right field and it hit the bottom of the fence about four to six inches foul, so I wound up with nothing. I got no hits off of Paige. [Laughs] I would've had a good triple 'cause I could run so fast in those days. I get to thinking 'bout that now. I can barely walk. [Laughs]

My name got around somewhere because I'm always getting something from strange places. People will send me cards to autograph. 'Course, the pleasure's all mine.

Do you know any of your professional statistics?

The first year up here, I hit .279. I would say I was a pretty good .250 hitter. I didn't have much power in the Negro leagues, but at John C. Smith I hit 20 home runs in one year. I told you my batting average there for the seven years was .366. That's the difference between college and professional. [Laughs]

Playing in the East as you did, you didn't have a great deal of travel, but how was it?

You traveled in automobiles and sometime you could ride all night and play a doubleheader the next day. [Laughs] I managed a team in North Carolina in 1930, and we used to drive all night and try to sleep on the hooks and then play a doubleheader the next day. When I came up here, the mode of travel was the same, but we would play five or six games during the week. We'd play 'bout every day and then one game on Sunday where we would make 'bout ten dollars apiece. Ten dollars was a lot of money in those days. You could buy a loaf of bread for seven cents. [Laughs]

During my career, I played down in Delaware and on the way back we had an automobile accident. The shortstop—the guy was playing shortstop 'cause we had gotten him and I could play third, so I played third base and he played shortstop—on the way back from that game he got killed. His name was [Benny] Brown. I knew him pretty well; I think I got a flier around here now with both our names on it.

That was like on Friday, and on Saturday I played a doubleheader in New York and I was the only one in that car that was able to play. I was lucky that I was able to play. The only thing I got was a little scar on top of my head. In those days, the automobiles had shades in them, and naturally the shades got some metal, and my head hit that metal frame on the shade.

Any regrets from baseball?

No. I think that's the best thing I ever did because if I hadn't been in Philadelphia where they have great hospitals, I think I would've probably been dead long ago had I gone back to South Carolina to live. I have had an operation for prostate cancer and if I had been in the South where it wouldn't be found out, I probably would've been gone.

Would you do it again?

Yes, I would. I was crazy about it. 'Course, anything that you can do pretty well, you like. [Laughs] This should make you laugh. At college, I played basketball two years, but I was a lousy basketball player. The thing about it, we didn't have these seven-foot guys playing and I could jump high and I was on the track team; I was a high jumper. In basketball in those days, after every basket you jumped center again, so if that hadn't been I'd've never been on that team. I could outjump most guys five or six inches taller than

I was. A guy 6'5" was a monster back then. [Laughs]

I still try to go to sports. I have season tickets for the 76ers. It costs me $4,000. [Laughs]

During the time I was working at the store, I ran the sporting goods department and I was involved with the Sixers and I got a call one day. He said, "Lindsay, I want to tell you something nobody in Philadelphia knows." I said, "What's that?" "We just signed Dr. J. Julius Erving. The Wilson Company will bring you a jersey tomorrow morning." This was like Monday; the season opened on Wednesday. He said, "I want you to put number six on the back."

I knew about Erving. I said, "Erving wears 32." He said, "Yeah, but 32 is [Billy] Cunningham's number and besides, we just gave Erving six million dollars." [Laughs]

So I got the jersey and got it fixed and Wednesday came and it was snowing. The trainer called me again, said, "Lindsay, how about that jersey?" I said, "I have it ready." He said, "I don't have anybody to come get it. How about bringing it down here? I know you're coming to this game tonight anyway, but we need it before that time."

So I agreed. I'd worked at the store so long that all that I had to do to leave was just tell 'em when I'd be back. About 4:30 that afternoon, I told 'em I was going and I wouldn't be back anymore today, so I went to the parking lot to get my car and there was a guy stuck in the snow. I had to sit there about 35 minutes before I could get out.

I finally got out and went to the Spectrum where Erving was and when they saw me coming, they started wiping sweat off their brows. Six million dollar man and no uniform. [Laughs]

He was a real nice guy. I recall, I used to be in the clubhouse every night because there was always somebody wanted something from the store and I'd bring it, even back in the Wilt Chamberlain days.

Erving was always the last one to shower because the reporters kept him busy, so he finally got through and dressed and went to the door. I thought he'd forgot something, you know, and what he forgot, he came back and hit me on the shoulder and said, "See you Friday." [Laughs] I thought that was very nice of him.

We became pretty good friends. He ran a shoe store here, so I asked him one day, I said, "Hey, Doc. You think I could buy a pair of your shoes?" He said, "I don't see why not." [Laughs] He was a nice guy.

Recognition has been slow in coming to you fellows.

Some guy from Detroit called me and said he was coming to Philadelphia and he wanted to interview me. He finally came and the day he came, there was a basketball game and I missed him, but he called me the next day and he came 'round. He came in a van and he parked his van and he brought stuff in here for the next half an hour. I bet I must've signed a hundred fifty, or maybe two or three hundred, articles that he had. But he was nice about it and when he left, he gave me a hundred bucks.

This past summer, somebody called from Detroit, but this time they were colored people. They came and I signed a couple of hundred things and they gave me nothing. [Laughs]

I wasn't looking for money. As I told you, I'm not wealthy, but I have a son and when I pass away, I will leave him a goodly amount. As long as I live, I guess, Uncle Sam will keep giving me the $1500 every month.

BATTING RECORD

Year	Team, League	Pos	G	AB	R	H	2B	3B	HR	RBI	SB	BA
1931	Bacharach, ind.	ss										.279
1932	Washington, EWL	ss										
	Harrisburg	ss										
	Bacharach, ind.	inf										
1933	Bacharach, ind.	inf										.249

Andy Porter
"Pullman"

BORN MARCH 7, 1911, LITTLE ROCK, AR
HT. 6'3½" WT. 190 BATTED AND THREW RIGHT

Negro Leagues debut: 1932

Even if Andy Porter hadn't been one of the premier pitchers in the Negro leagues, he would be remembered today because he had one of the great nicknames of all time: "Pullman."

But Porter *was* a top pitcher and, with Bill Byrd and Jonas Gaines, gave the Baltimore Elite Giants one of the strongest pitching staffs in baseball. Well into his 30s by the time the color barrier was broken, the big righthander was never considered for the major leagues, but had the door opened a few years earlier, he most certainly would have made it.

He pitched in the 1949 East-West All-Star Game and combined with two other pitchers to hold the West squad to only two hits as the East won, 4–0. Bob Griffith of the Philadelphia Stars started for the East and tossed three hitless innings, then Porter held the West hitless for the middle three innings. Finally, Pat Scantlebury of the New York Cubans allowed two singles in the final three frames. This gave the East a measure of revenge, as they had been shutout, 3–0, on a three-hitter by the West the previous year.

Andy Porter pitched professionally for more than 20 years. Today he is retired and living in Los Angeles.

I started out playing baseball in 1932. My hometown is Little Rock, Arkansas, and in 1932 they organized a team in the [Negro] Southern League. I had pitched around Little Rock all my young days — I was still a young man then — and I thought I was a pretty good pitcher. When they assembled this team, they had a manager from San Antonio. He brought four pitchers with him and I didn't get a job and that almost killed me. I felt so bad.

About a week later, a team came through there from Chicago called the Chicago Memorial Giants. They told 'em about me and they picked me up. The first place we went to was Monroe, Louisiana. I pitched there I believe on a Thursday and lost, 4–3, and I come back on that Sunday and pitched again against one of their top pitchers, Barney Morris, and lost,

2–0. He pitched a one-hitter against us. That was the first two games I pitched.

Then we left Monroe, Louisiana, and went to Memphis. I won a game in Memphis, and on the way back to Chicago, right out of Louisville, Kentucky, that old car we was in broke down. We were in a little old town in Indiana about two days, then one day a big car pulled up over there and took four or five players off this Chicago team to Louisville. Tom Wilson had a team — the man that I finally played with for 14 years — and we went back to Louisville and played two or three games over there and I did pretty good.

Then we went to Nashville, where his main team was, and we played against this team. On our team, we had guys from Birmingham — Sam Bankhead, Nate Oliver, myself,

Andy Porter (author's collection).

and a guy named Rolls. And they had taken us on that team in Nashville after we had gone down there and beat Nashville two out of three. That's where my career was really taking off then.

I played from '32 to '53 and I played in South America, Cuba, Mexico, Canada — everywhere you could play, other than the major leagues. And I played in the minor leagues in the United States for a while as a coach and player.

You played with the Elite Giants in every city they called home, but you left and went to Mexico for a while.

During the time I was playing with them, a lot of players would go to Mexico during the playing season. One thing about it, when we went to Mexico and come back they'd always take you back on the club that you played for 'til the latter years.

I went to Mexico in 1939 and played down there. Quite a few of us were down there, but I come back and played with my home team, the Elites.

Some players have mentioned the differences in the way a player was received in the United States and Mexico.

In Mexico, we stayed at, not the best hotels, but at *nice* hotels; but here in the United States, blacks didn't have no heck-fired hotels, and we didn't stay in the white hotels. We had to stay wherever they had hotels. A lot of cities, like New York, where we stayed at the Woodside Hotel, and Baltimore had different hotels, but most cities didn't. But in Mexico, we had nice hotels to stay in.

You made more money down there.

Oh, yeah. That's why we would leave and go down to Mexico, but if you played down there all the year and you think about the Fourth of July here in the States and all like that, you'd wanna come back.

We had a regular schedule, more so than we did in the black leagues. We played maybe three games or five a week, whatever the schedule was — just like the schedule in the minor leagues. We traveled the best way; we had buses and trains, sometimes planes when you had to be at a certain place and had a distance to go. It was like the minor leagues here in the United States.

You led the league in Mexico in strikeouts a couple of times. Did you ever lead in the States?

Not that I know of. We didn't have very accurate statistics [in the Negro leagues] because we played in so many different places during the week, where people wouldn't even know about it. We didn't have sportswriters everywhere we went.

The Elites there in Baltimore had some awfully good teams, and you had some awfully good teammates along the way. One was Wild Bill Wright.

He was with the team before I went to Nashville. That's where he started out at. He was a great ballplayer. Big guy — about 6'3", weighed about 190 pounds. But he was fast. Outfielder — hit from both sides. He could do everything.

Another teammate was Henry Kimbro.

Kimbro came to us about '36 or '7. He's

from Nashville. He was good. Fast. Bill Wright went to Mexico and stayed down there a long time, but they might've played together for a while. Maybe somewhere in the '40s. Kimbro was a great outfielder. Good ballplayer, good hitter. Lefthanded hitter.

Wright went down there [Mexico] in '39, the same year I went down there. I came back in '41 for a while, then I went back in '42, '43.

Do either Wright or Kimbro belong in the Hall of Fame?

Oh, yeah. Bill Wright, especially. Maybe not in my lifetime, but someday he'll probably be inducted into the Hall of Fame.

Bill Byrd was one of your pitchers.

He was a good pitcher, but I'll tell you, he pitched different. Well, I won't say "different," but he was a spitball pitcher. They outlawed that later on, but they let him do it as long as he played. He and another guy named [Neck] Stanley. They both was spitball pitchers and I don't think they kept them from doing it. They let them use it all during their career, but the major leagues banned it.

A lot of times Byrd pretended he was throwing spitballs and he wasn't. He was a good pitcher *and* a good hitter. Hit from both sides; played outfield, too.

Who was the best player you saw?

Oh, that's hard to say. According to what position? When I played, most every guy that played it was very hard for them to lose that job because they were great themselves and they'd take a long time to get that way. Guys then would play five, six, seven years on the same team and nobody else could play that position. Just like Bill Wright. If they had two right fielders, he played all the time and unless they felt like he needed a rest the other player didn't get to play.

Bill Wright, Cool Papa Bell, Bankhead — all them guys — it was hard to get a job when they were on a team.

Who was the best pitcher?

Oh, that's hard, too. Now you take when Satchel Paige was pitching. He would play maybe only on Sundays or a holiday, so you wouldn't see him like you'd see Bill Byrd or me or Stanley or Leon Day. We had so many good pitchers. Hilton Smith, Ford Smith, Theolic Smith, Gene Smith. All them guys were great pitchers, good hitters. We had good ballplayers.

Would you have made it in the major leagues if they had opened the door earlier?

I believe so. I remember, I was playing in Mexico — Laredo, Mexico — and I would go across the Rio Grande River over in Laredo, Texas. The Texas Rangers would be around all the time and one of 'em said, "Ain't you that so-and-so that pitched over there in Laredo?" I said, "Yeah." He said, "If you wasn't a nigger, you'd be in the major leagues."

That's the way it was then. Yeah, there was a lot of us could've played in the major leagues.

How was the travel in the United States?

We had our private bus. First, we had an old bus with straight-up seats. Later on, when buses came out with reclining seats, we had

(L-r) **Jose Gonzales, Andy Porter, Cool Papa Bell with Alijadores, MxL, 1939 (author's collection).**

them. We didn't have air-conditioning like maybe the minor leagues, but I doubt if they had it, either. All the teams mostly had private buses.

How many miles would you cover in a day?

Like we were in Baltimore and we were gonna play in Philadelphia — well, that's about 80-some miles. To play in New York, we'd leave in time, say, eight o'clock, to play that night or afternoon. That's a hundred-and-some miles. Maybe we'd play in Pittsburgh and go play in Harrisburg. That's about 200 miles. It used to take us from eight o'clock to that evening to get from Pittsburgh to Harrisburg, but after they built the turnpike it'd take about three or four hours 'cause the mountains that we'd been going over, we went *through*.

We did a lot of traveling, but mostly on the East Coast, like around New York, Pennsylvania, Delaware, Maryland. We'd go to Chicago at times. Chicago was about the farthest west we would go from Baltimore. We went there maybe once a year.

Is there a game that stands out in your memory?

Quite a few of 'em. When Monte Irvin, Larry Doby, [Jimmy] Wilkes, [Bob] Harvey, Leon Day were all with Newark; I used to pitch against 'em. I used to beat Newark pretty easily, but I remember one night I pitched a game against 'em. The first seven men up, I struck 'em out. I had some good games — a lot of good games — and some bad.

I remember when Jim Taylor was our manager. Candy Jim Taylor. We were sitting out in front of the hotel one day and he said, "You know somethin', Porter. You throw as hard as Satchel." I said, "You think so?" He said, "I *know* so."

When he said that, I thought, gosh, how is it that the guys that Satchel strikes out hit me? So I was walking down the street just saying to myself, "Now why did he tell me that?" So I said later, "Candy, you say I throw as hard as Satchel," then I asked him that question: "Why is it that some guys he can strike out I can't strike 'em out?"

He said, "Satchel's ball looks *small*. He throws a small ball." His ball looked smaller than mine. That's a fact.

You take Bill Byrd. I used to hate catching with him 'cause his ball was so heavy. Some pitchers throw balls that are real heavy, some pitchers throw balls that are light. You watch some of these pitchers pitching today. You can see the fastball how they break. And some pitchers throw and it seems like they're straight, it don't seem like they move. Some just go in and out. I don't know if it's the grip or what it is.

We had a pitcher name of [Bill] Harvey — a lefthander. I used to watch him warming up, and when he threw his ball it had a big bend in it. I wondered why his ball would do that and other pitchers' didn't. He couldn't tell us.

You played a long time. Were there disappointments along the way?

Oh, yeah. Some times during my career I'd have a sore arm. You'd have disappointments there because things you *did* do you *couldn't* do. I had a sore arm, but it came back.

How did you come to play in the minor leagues?

They had a league out here and they put a team in there and Chet Brewer was the manager and he wanted me to help him with the younger players and that's when I played there.

I had a opportunity to go in the Arizona-Texas League [earlier], but I didn't go. I was older than most of the guys that would be on the team and I just didn't go. It wasn't for just but two weeks at the end of the season. A guy that used to be with the St. Louis Browns asked me 'bout going down there 'cause they was in contention for the league championship.

Would you do it again?

Oh, yeah!

There ain't but one thing different now than when I was playing. They got better fields. And don't say nothing 'bout the equipment because the gloves — and we used the same gloves the major leagues used — somebody hit the ball — a line drive back to you — and you try to stop it and it'd go through the webbing of your glove. Today that won't happen.

The fields are in better condition, the players are much larger. One thing, we didn't have players catching as many cramps as these of today. I look at these players today, running and grabbing their legs. We used to have cramps from riding the bus from the way we'd sit or something like that, but not like the players today.

PITCHING RECORD

Year	Team, League	G	IP	W	L	Pct	H	BB	SO	ERA
1932	Nashville, Louisville, Cleveland, NSL									
1933	Nashville, NNL									
1934										
1835	Columbus, NNL									
1936	Washington, NNL									
1937										
1938	Baltimore, NNL									
1939	Baltimore, NNL									
	Tampico, MxL	22	146	10	7	.588	117	35	111	2.28
1940	Nuevo Laredo, MxL	*42	*296	21	14	.600	268	*125	*232	3.34
1941	Mexico City, MxL	37	235	11	*16	.407	261	116	*133	4.47
1942	Vera Cruz, MxL	19	103	5	8	.385	125	81	47	5.66
	Baltimore, NNL			8	0	1.000				
1943	Vera Cruz, MxL	3	3	0	0	—	17	7	0	30.00
	Baltimore, NNL									
1944	Baltimore, NNL	8	43	3	1	.750	54	19	14	
1945		11	82	8	0	1.000	82	18	30	
1946	Baltimore, NNL	9	69	2	4	.333	72	16	31	
	Nuevo Laredo, MxL	9	39	2	2	.500	50	24	13	5.12
1947	Newark, NNL									
1948	Indianapolis, NAL	12	77	4	5	.444	47	21	54	*4.68
1949		20	139	10	6	.625	143	30	61	3.63
1950		3	17	2	0	1.000	15	5	6	3.71
1952	Porterville, SWIntL	12	78	3	5	.375	92	35	47	4.27
1939–40	Santa Clara, CWL	9		3	4	.429				
1940–1	Almendares, CWL	14		6	5	.545				

*Led league

Earl Wilson, Sr.
"His Namesake Made It"

BORN DECEMBER 5, 1915, NEW ORLEANS, LA
HT. 5'11" WT. 185 BATTED AND THREW RIGHT

Negro Leagues debut: 1934

Earl Wilson is a name that should be familiar to baseball fans from the 1960s. It belonged to one of the top pitchers in the American League. In 1967, he led the league in wins with 22 and compiled a record of 121–109 over an 11-year career. He was also one of the top hitting pitchers in major league history.

But this was Earl Wilson, Jr. Thirty years earlier, another Earl Wilson — Sr. — played professional baseball and played it very well, too. His career was short because he couldn't support his young family on what he was being paid, but he loved it while it lasted, and he would do it all again.

In his short time in the Negro leagues he had a couple of marvelous highlights: He once hit a ball where only Babe Ruth had ever hit one before, and he broke up a no-hitter by none other than Satchel Paige. It's too bad he wasn't able to play longer.

The elder Wilson is a private man and one not fond of giving interviews, but, whether he likes it or not, he does a very good job at it.

I played from 1932 to '36. I played with different teams; we traveled around.

I got into baseball through a cousin named Percy Wilson. He was playing with the New Orleans Black Pelicans and he got me in there. I was very young, but I set my age up. I was big for my age, but I was about 16-and-a-half or 17 years old.

I played with the Pelicans, and after I left the Pelicans I went to Birmingham. I played with them and I left them and went to Memphis and played a little bit there. Not too long, not a whole season. Then I went back to Birmingham and played there 'til 1936.

I got married and Earl was born. I wasn't making enough money to support a family; that's why I quit. Earl was born in 1935 — October 2, 1935. I got married in 1934.

What did you do when you left baseball?

I got a job and I started barnstorming just for the pleasure of it. The girl I married, she lived in a little small town and my home was in New Orleans. She was going to school in New Orleans and I met her there and we got married, and she wanted to go stay where she was born. I got me a job and moved there. I stayed there 'til I come to San Diego in 1939. I started working here and then the war started and I got a job in aeronautics.

I tried to get on a team here and they refused me 'cause I was black. They invited me to practice, but wouldn't nobody throw the ball to me. They wouldn't let me in the restroom 'cause it was a hundred percent white.

That was Bob Billings. He ran the aeronautical team. So that was the end of my career. I was still young, but I couldn't hook on with anybody. During that time, a black man just didn't have a chance.

The funny part, the same man that set me down was the one that started my son out. And I reminded him of it, too. [Laughs] He was very good to my son; he helped him a whole lot. Bob Billings. This was up in the '50s [when Billings helped Earl Jr.]. Things really changed.

When I was playing in the Negro leagues, I never could make enough money to support a family. I think the most money I got was $100. When it was rained out, you didn't make no money, you didn't get anything out of it. It rained a whole lot, it looked like to me. [Laughs]

For meals, what happened, we had to stay in a boardinghouse. Couldn't stay in them hotels like they're doing now. They would just pay for your meals. They paid whoever was cooking.

Sometimes we had to get off the bus fully dressed. If we had to play ball the next day, when we got through playing we had to just jump on the bus and hop it on. A lot of times, we just got off the bus and went on the field. The same ol' funky clothes. [Laughs] They knew I was coming before I got there.

Those are the things we had to go through with. Some of the parks wouldn't let us play in 'em. We run into that. When we got there, they'd say they had it rented for something else, so we had to cancel the game. We wasn't making no money there.

It was real tough. The little money you'd get, you'd try to squeeze it so you can live. That's why I said when I got married I couldn't do it. They'd give you $100 or $75; it was good money at that time, but it still wasn't enough to take care of a wife and a child. Most of the time, I had to support myself while I'm gone and then I had nothing left for the family.

Do any games stand out?

All my games was pretty good, but I had some bad days. I ain't gonna tell you about the time I struck out so many times. I remember I struck out six times in a row. That's when you get in one of them slumps.

Earl Wilson, Sr. (courtesy of Earl Wilson, Sr.).

The biggest highlight I ever had in my life was when we played in a place called Bogalusa, Louisiana. The funny thing, years ago I guess when he was with the Yankees, Baby Ruth was the only one that ever hit a ball across that dance hall out there in the corner of the center field, and I hit one there. That was the highlight that really excited me because Baby Ruth had done it. That was a great thing with me. I smiled for a whole week. [Laughs] I hit a ball as far as Baby Ruth did.

I remember when I broke up a no-hitter. I hit a bleeder down between third and short. Satchel Paige was pitching; he had a no-hitter going and he promised me that I'd never get another hit on him the rest of my life, and he fulfilled that promise. [Laughs] I did not. I faced him six times. One for six. Some guys didn't get that. He told me — they used to call me the kid 'cause I was so young-looking — says, "Hey, kid, you'll never get another hit as long as you live." [Laughs] I didn't believe it, but he made a believer out of me.

I had some good games. I played against some good ballplayers. I got hurt. Murray Gloster hit me up the side of the head. He was a pitcher for the Pittsburgh Crawfords. I kept my head up there too long. Instead of ducking, I was standing there looking. At the time we called 'em in-shoots and out-shoots. He throwed the in-shoot and I didn't think it was gonna break yet, but it did. Knocked me out. That was the worst injury I ever had. He was a very good pitcher.

Who was the best pitcher you faced?

Other than Satchel Paige? This guy Murray Gloster, he was good, and we had one called Hilton Smith. He was with Kansas City. He was *good*. Matter of fact, the only thing between him and Satchel Paige, Satchel Paige got more publicity than he did. As far as the pitching, he was just as good.

Some players have told me he might have been better.

That's true. I agree with 'em. Satchel was just being a clown; that's what made him look better. He made his life.

Earl Wilson, Jr., with Boston Red Sox, early 1960s (author's collection).

Bill Dickey, he was a good pitcher, too. We had a lot of good black pitchers, but Satchel Paige just had it going. It was just like Buck Leonard. He was a good first baseman, but I'll put Goose Tatum up there just as much as anybody.

I wasn't a flashy guy. I was just a regular player. And I wasn't the greatest one, but I was good.

I went to the Homestead Grays for a couple games. They just wanted me for two games and I didn't know that. Papa Bell got hurt and when he got well, they didn't need me anymore. They heard I was pretty fair then. I was better defense than I was offense, so they got me to take his place. I thought I was in then, but he come back and they told me I was through. Just like that. You didn't sign no contract. It really hurt me. I had left the team 'cause I thought I was gonna make it. When they said, "Homestead Grays," why, hell, I jumped out of my shoes. That was some of my bad luck.

The sleeping wasn't too good. Like I said, we slept on the bus a lot of time. If we didn't have far to go, we used to drive. Four or five or six would get in the car. The bus was expensive and we weren't making no money.

We made more money playing in towns that didn't have a league — a team — than we did in some of the ballparks. When they'd know we was playing, they'd close the sawmill down and come see us play. We didn't know 'til we got there that they'd closed everything. It was packed — black and white in there.

We made more money like that than we did if we went to the city because they're used to us. "We saw him the other day," or, "They played here the other day," or something like that. A lot of teams did a lot of barnstorming. That's where we made our money.

How many games did you play in a season?

I guess we played about, oh, sixty to seventy. I don't remember playing no hundred games.

Earl Jr. is a big man. Were you big?

I never was as big as him. I weighed 185 pounds. I was 5'11". He was 6'3", some people say 6'4". When he started playing, he weighed 215 pounds. He's living good, I guess; he's picked up weight and he went up to about 240. [Laughs] Still, he has no fat on him at all.

He could hit. Did you teach him?

I didn't teach him anything. He started out as a catcher, caught most of his minor league [career]. He went to El Paso, Texas; Boston sent him there. Sid Cohen, a guy I knew in New Orleans — used to play with New Orleans, pitched with New Orleans — give the ball to him and said, "This is your day. You're gonna pitch today."

He got out there and pitched and won his ballgame. His arm was dead for a whole two weeks. He said, "Oh, Lord, my career's over with." That's when he started pitching; he never did catch no more. He turned out to be pretty good; he could throw pretty hard.

Who was the best player you saw?

The best player — we all know Papa Bell was a hell of a good outfielder, you know that, so I would bypass him.

This guy Chester Williams — he was a shortstop — was good, and Dandridge was a hell of a good player, but he wasn't a good hitter. I would say, as all-around, Josh Gibson was about the best. He could hit, throw, and run, but he drank a hell of a lot, too. He could hit and he could throw.

We had another catcher 'bout as good as he was called Pepper Bassett. He used to sit in a rocking chair and clown once in a while. He could hit, too. And Piper Davis was a good ballplayer, too.

There was another catcher. I don't recall his name now; he used to live up in Compton. He could hit, but he couldn't run. He'd almost have to hit a ball off the wall to get to first. That's true. The biggest highlight he had was he stole a base once in his life. He helped me a lot. He tipped me off on pitches.

When we played, we had to use each other's bats. We couldn't afford to buy a bat. [Laughs] We'd say, "Don't break my bat!" We used to take them bats and almost sleep with 'em.

During those times, you had to keep up with your glove 'cause some guys would steal. Take your bat, glove, shoes — anything they could. You'd have to go to bed with 'em [the equipment].

If you were a young man again, would you play baseball?

Yes, I'd do it all over again 'cause I loved it. I loved baseball. I used to go to bed with it. I sure would. Even with the trouble we went through, I'd do it again.

Do you have any regrets?

No, I have no regrets. I wish I was young enough to play it now. I'd do the same thing over again if I was young. I'm 84 years old now.

Life has been good to me. Even when I was young, I enjoyed what I was doing. I don't have no problems. I'm living pretty good and I'm doing very well. I travel a lot. I go to a lot of conventions. I stay active with that, but when it comes down to working, I don't do no more than I have to and very little of that. Work ain't good for anybody.

BATTING RECORD

Year	Team, League	Pos	G	AB	R	H	2B	3B	HR	RBI	SB	BA
1934	Birmingham, NSL	of										
1935	Memphis, ind.	of										
	Birmingham, NSL	of										
1936	Birmingham, NSL	of										

Percy Reed
"Umpire"

BORN MAY 10, 1910, MOBILE, AL
HT. 5'3" WT. 100 BATTED AND THREW RIGHT

Negro Leagues debut: 1935

Josh Gibson loved to play in Cincinnati because of Percy Reed. "Now we'll get the corners," he told his pitchers.

Percy Reed was small in stature but large in composure. Raised in an orphanage in Cincinnati from the time he was a baby, he left high school after his third year to get married and shortly thereafter he began playing semipro baseball.

After the games, the teams were supposed to be paid. Watching the stands, a guess could be made as to how much money would be divided among the players, but the individual shares would often come up less than anticipated. He wanted to be in baseball, but he wanted to earn money, too. He saw that the umpires didn't have to worry about the split; they were paid regardless of how many people may have been in attendance.

So he studied the rules of baseball and took the umpiring test, which he passed with flying colors. He began umpiring in 1929, and from 1935 through the integration of the major leagues in 1947, he called Negro leagues games in Cincinnati every Sunday, weather permitting. Through the years he saw the best black ballplayers in the world and remembers them well.

In addition to umpiring, Reed worked 20 years for the Cincinnati Recreation Commission as director of the Ninth Street Boys' Club and later served as a probation officer before being appointed Commissioner of the Ohio State Lottery, from which he retired in 1988 at the age of 78.

Along the away, he had two marriages, the second one still going strong after nearly 50 years. He had a son from each marriage, a stepdaughter, five grandsons, and two great-grandchildren, at last count.

Today he lives in a nursing home as a result of recent failing eyesight, but his mind is far from failing: he recalls the plays and players he saw 50 and 60 years ago as vividly as if he saw them yesterday.

My mother brought me to Cincinnati on a pillow after her and my father separated. We stayed with friends until my mother got sick and then they placed us in the home. I don't remember the date. There was three of us: My brother Johnny was oldest, my sister Teresa was the second child, and I was the third. I was young; I was a baby.

How did you get into umpiring?

I got into umpiring because I was a pretty good ballplayer. I knew a man in Walnut Hills named Boss Parker and he had a baseball team called the Excelsior club. Excelsior A.C. Every boy in Walnut Hills wanted to be an Excelsior ballplayer. That was in the years between the '20s and the '30s. I played second base. I was leadoff man.

Back in them days you needed a little

change in your pocket if you wanted to go to the movies. We'd go out to Lockland and places where we played baseball and I'd look up at the crowds up in the stands and I'd see quite a few people in there, but when it would come time to pay off, it seemed there weren't too many people up there. In other words, the rats ate up the silver and I just got tired of 'em eating up *my* silver, so I took me a book and just studied.

A man named DeHart Hubbard—he was the first Olympic athlete, I think, from Cincinnati; he was a broad-jumper; he went to Walnut Hills High—was the recreation manager for the Cincinnati Recreation Commission in charge of all colored activities. Back in those days, the colored had one activity and the whites had their own activity. They didn't mix 'em like they do now. [DeHart Hubbard was the Olympic running broad jump Gold Medal winner in 1924.]

I asked him to put it in the paper that they wanted umpires. They were gonna start a league there—eight or nine teams—and they wanted umpires, so I studied that winter and I took the examination and I was third on the list. I made 92. So I turned to umpiring to make some money. That was back in '29.

DeHart Hubbard and a lot of doctors here in the city, they formed the clubs. They would sponsor a team and bring all the other Negro teams in here to play. They used to play exhibition games and then they formed a league. This all happened between '32 and '40.

They formed a league of Negro baseball players and they'd bring players in here like Josh Gibson of the Homestead Grays and Buck Leonard and all these fellows. They'd bring all the teams in here: Kansas City Monarchs, Chicago American Giants, Indianapolis Clowns, Memphis Red Sox.

Our pay increased because we signed up as umpires for amateurs, but they worked us in with the pros. They said I was a pretty good umpire, that I gave the corners. All the catchers said they liked me because I gave the corners and they kept me there.

Percy Reed, 1999 (author's photograph).

You traveled with the Cincinnati Tigers.

Only when I could get away. See, I had a civil service job and I couldn't be gone over three days. I went on short trips, like up to Dayton.

My fellow umpire was Harry Ward, a.k.a. "Wu-Fang," a great athlete from Wilberforce University. We had two umpires and we alternated between home plate and the field.

Was there a game that stands out?

All of 'em was important to me. I called what I seen and seen what I called. A man named Bill Carpenter—he used to train the umpires for the International League—he was the instructor and he said, "Call what you see and put yourself in a position to see it."

You stood behind a lot of great catchers. Who was the best?

Josh Gibson.

Who had the best arm?

Josh Gibson.

Gibson really liked your umpiring.

I liked the way he got back there in the box, too. He'd sit back there and he was about six-three, about 225 pounds; he was a good athlete, but he loved alcohol.

As you say, he was a big man and so were many of the other catchers. Did you have trouble seeing around them?

No. You see how the umpire behind the plate takes his position: over the left shoulder of the catcher. You put yourself in that position, you can see everything inside, outside, upside down — any way you want to see it.

You saw all the great pitchers, too. Who was the best?

Satchel Paige.

How hard could he throw?

Oh, he couldn't throw *that* hard. He had control. He had a good curveball; he had a good spitter. He just had control. He could work the inside, the outside corners. Very seldom did he hit the middle of the plate.

Josh Johnson caught for the Tigers.

He was pretty good. See, the average ballplayer that was in the Negro National League, they couldn't have made the professional [Cincinnati] Reds team because they didn't have no training — previous training — because they wasn't letting 'em in the colleges at that time and they wasn't playing on the high school teams, so they had to just pick 'em up off the street and they played themselves in condition. They didn't go to no training camp because they didn't have no buses; they didn't have no money. They had to use the revenue from each game to pay the brass.

How about Double Duty Radcliffe?

He was just about what they called him: he'd pitch one game and catch one game on doubleheader days. He was good — better than average, I'll put it that way. He had a baseball mind. He came here as a player and left here as a manager. He had that baseball mind, he and his brother both.

Do you remember Willie Simms, an outfielder?

Average ballplayer. Clean cut.

Who was the best hitter?

Josh Gibson.

Who was the next best?

Buck Leonard.

Even great hitters have some weakness. What was Josh's weakness?

Change up, if you caught him off-balance. You'd better catch him off-balance because if he hit it, it's gone.

What about Buck Leonard?

He was just a natural hitter. I didn't see no weakness. There was quite a few of 'em didn't have no weakness. We had a boy that worked for DeHart Hubbard: [Howard] Easterling. He was a pretty good hitter, played shortstop. He went down South to play on one of them teams.

A lot of people think that Branch Rickey signed Jackie Robinson to a major league contract because he was the best ballplayer. He wasn't. The only reason Jackie Robinson was signed, he was the most educated, and Branch Rickey knew what he [Robinson] was going up against — the slurs and the slams — when he graduated from UCLA, and that's why he took him. The rest of 'em couldn't have stood that jazz thrown at 'em.

Who else who played in those days could have made it to the major leagues?

Satchel went straight to the major leagues. He could've gone younger. I think Buck Leonard and them could've done it, too.

See, there was another team that didn't get no publicity that was very good. They came up here as the [Ethiopian] Clowns out of Florida and they were the Indianapolis Clowns. They didn't get much publicity behind them because the wrong man had 'em, Abe Saperstein, the man that owned the Globetrotters, and they didn't want him to make all the money. The man helped 'em all; half of 'em couldn't have lasted if it weren't for him. He had a booking agency; he booked the teams all over the world.

You saw everyone from the mid '30s on. Who was the best defensive player? Any position.

Cool Papa Bell. I can't leave San Jethroe out. And this boy that was with the Newark Eagles that signed up with Cleveland. Larry Doby. He was a good ballplayer. Cool Papa Bell could've played on anybody's team. He was fast.

Did you ever call him out on a steal?

Oh, yeah. See, he was the kind of ballplayer who wouldn't steal just to say, "I'm Cool Papa Bell." If you needed a run, he'd put himself in position. They were very smart. They knew their baseball smarts.

In those days, the guys loved it, the umpires loved it. They smiled all the time; they don't smile now. Back in them days, it was a sport. Today, it's a business. Today, they got billionaires against millionaires. The millionaires are your ballplayers, the billionaires are your owners.

How did you handle arguments?

They believed in me and I believed in them. I used to quote 'em the rule book; I'd take the rule book out of my pocket and let 'em read it.

All of 'em used to say, "Put the watch on 'em." I kept me an old Ingersoll watch; I'd wind it up every Sunday, then I'd go play and I'd give 'em one minute. I'd say, "You got one minute to get the game going. You're here to play ball, not to argue." And I'd walk right behind the plate and when that minute was up, I'd put it back in my pocket and they'd go out and take the field. They believed in me and I believed in them.

Did you have to eject many players?

I never throwed nobody out.

When did you stop umpiring?

I took a position in 1949. I umpired off and on when I'd get a chance because I worked with the Recreation Commission. I actually stopped when Jackie Robinson went in the major leagues [in] '47.

How many games a year would you call?

Oh, every Sunday that it didn't rain. Two games every Sunday, then during the week I had softball games.

If you went back to the late '20s, would you go into umpiring again?

Yeah. That's a good life, good pay. See, you have to enjoy the sport in order to be a good supervisor, and an umpire's nothing but a supervisor. Baseball's a kid's game.

Joe Burt Scott
"The Missing Career"

BORN OCTOBER 2, 1920, MEMPHIS, TN
HT. 5'8" WT. 170 BATTED AND THREW LEFT

Negro Leagues debut: 1936

There are not many reference works on the Negro leagues. James A. Riley's *The Biographical Encyclopedia of the Negro Baseball Leagues* is a marvelous work, but it is incomplete and contains errors of both commission and omission. *The Negro Leagues Book,* produced by the Society for American Baseball Research and edited by Dick Clark and Larry Lester, is probably more complete, but still is missing information and contains less individual information.

There are others, but those are the two biggies.

The reason, of course, is that the records — the stats, the rosters, even the teams — were not kept. The black players — those in teams and leagues — were playing baseball for the sake of baseball, for the love of the game. Box scores were kept, but no one saw a reason to write down, say, that Pop Lloyd batted .500. They *knew* he could hit, and they pitched accordingly.

I suppose that in the volumes of reference works on major league baseball there are two or three players whose names are missing or maybe a handful whose records are incomplete or erroneous. From Negro baseball, there are probably dozens (hundreds?) of names missing and hundreds (thousands?) of incomplete records.

This is not a knock on the literature of black baseball. Without it, there would be a cavernous void. This is a challenge to those who have the time, energy, and interest in baseball history — black baseball history specifically — to find what's missing. Good luck.

In the available references, Joe Burt Scott is credited with, depending on the reference, a three-year, a five-year, a six-year, or a 12-year career in baseball. In actuality, it was 20 years. Available stats give him perhaps a .260 lifetime batting average. It was probably well over .300. He is listed as playing with only one team in most works, but he may have played with as many as a dozen or more.

The records say you began playing around 1945. Is that correct?

No. I began to play earlier than that. I started in 1936. I played with grown men then. I played in Chicago; I played with more teams than anybody ever played with, I imagine. I played with the Zulu Giants, the Chicago American Giants, the Bacharach Giants — that's around Chicago in the '30s. I played under an alias name durin' those days because I was in [high] school. And I only played then when school was out in the summertime.

I played at New York — New York Black Yankees; Pittsburgh with the Pittsburgh Crawfords. This was in the '40s now. Then I came to Memphis to play.

The Negro leagues literature doesn't credit you with all that.

36

They don't have me credited even with a battin' average worth nothin'. They just put somethin' at random down, not talkin' to me or talkin' to the older fellas I played with, like Satchel Paige and Turkey Stearnes. I played with Cool Papa Bell, Bubba Hyde — he's the only one livin' now from the early days. We were just as close as you can get to ballplayers. I played with Willie Wells. I played with all of them and they gave me a A-rating-plus 'cause I could do everything. I played against a whole lot of great guys that have gone on. Even Double Duty Radcliffe. He had a brother that could outplay him. Alec Radcliffe. I played with Alec with the Chicago American Giants.

Nobody talk about me hittin' or nothin' else. You can go back to when we barnstormed when I was with Satchel. Bob Feller, Warren Spahn — all these guys could tell you. "How can you hit that ball like that and stay up all night and hit that ball? And ride in the buses and whatnot." I said, "Well, it's just part of the game."

Verdell Mathis said you could hit.

If he won 25 games, I won 15 for him with my bat. He's dead now. It just took the run outta me; he was just as close to me as a brother. When he died, I was in Chicago for my high school reunion. I went to Tilden Tech High School in Chicago and I played on the championship team in high school in Wrigley Field in 1937.

What name did you play under in the early days?

Sandy Thompson. Satchel give me that name. I had to do that because I had a good career in high school.

I could play with any team at 15 years old. In fact, I played on four white teams in my career. If those people were still livin,' they could tell you I could hit the ball.

Do you know any of your batting averages?

I don't have complete records, but I led the Provincial League up in Canada in 1950 or '51. I hit about .390 one year up there. I have a trophy that I got playin' around Chicago; in 58 ballgames — that's all I played

Joe Burt Scott (courtesy of Joe Burt Scott).

that summer — I hit .714. I played on all-service teams — the Wright Field Kittyhawks outta Dayton, Ohio — I hit .621 in 22 ballgames playin' against major league teams.

I don't fret over people talkin' about hittin' or nothin'. I used to tell people, I said, "When I was playin', I made pitchers duck." They would tell you they're gonna throw at you. It didn't bother me. I had pitchers say *every* night I played, "I'm knockin' you down." I said, "Okay. Go ahead and knock me down."

And I tripled and tell the catcher, I say, "I'm comin' home." Pepper Bassett — you heard of him? — Pepper would back up off home plate and let me have all of it many a day.

My career in baseball has been over and I enjoyed my career. I played 20 years. I talk to some of the guys now. The fella that played with the Detroit Tigers, we talk religiously sometimes. I played against him once in Great Lakes with the great ballplayers up there, like Mickey Cochrane, Charlie Gehringer, Red Rolfe. Virgil Trucks. He belongs in the Hall of Fame. That's the trouble with the Veterans Committee — half of 'em don't know him. I wrote 'em already; Verdell *and* Virgil Trucks belong in the Hall of Fame. I hope he gets in there before he dies.

In those 20 years, is there one incident that stands out?

Oh, a whole lot of 'em. The most important game that stands out in my memory, I played against the Pittsburgh Pirates. That's when I was in service. Pittsburgh's manager was the Fordham Flash [Frankie Frisch]. We played in Muncie, Indiana. I got a copy of the box score. I think I had 2 out of 4 in hits, but I was on base all four times. Frankie Frisch asked my manager this: "Who's leadin' off?" And he told him me and he went back to the dugout right quick and told [Rip] Sewell — he was pitchin' that ballgame — he said, "Knock him down." But he didn't know how many times I been knocked down. I tripled and slid into third. Didn't have to slide, but I did. When I got up, he said, "We done woke him up."

After the ballgame, Frisch come over and said, "What you gonna do when you get out of service?" I said, "Well, I got $500 in 1944 to play with the New York Black Yankees out East, whenever I get out. If I don't get out in 20 years, I still have to go to the Yankees."

He said, "Well, you're a so-and-so ballplayer." I said, "Thank you."

I don't back up off any ballplayer that played against me. They'll tell you that. Sam Jethroe, all of 'em. You've heard of him. I threw him out three times one night in Dayton. Don't run on me. I was playin' center field that night with the [Memphis] Red Sox. Larry Brown was catchin'. Maybe you can get the box score on that: the Red Sox playin' the Buckeyes.

The reason I could throw him out, I was gonna throw him out because the man hittin' behind him was nothin' but a singles hitter. That was Willie Grace. I threw Jethroe out three times, two times goin' from first to third and one time goin' from second to home. Those stand out in my memory because I always knowed Jethroe was a real speed demon and *loved* to run.

Jethroe was probably the fastest man in baseball then.

Yes, but we had another man that was fast. Bubba Hyde. He could look back and run faster than a lotta guys that was playin' then. He was my roommate for a while, and teammate. I told Cool Papa Bell's granddaughter that Bubba Hyde could outrun Cool Papa Bell. When they played on the West Coast, like All-Star games, Bubba Hyde followed Cool Papa and he could outrun him. I'm nothin' but a kid then.

You must have learned a lot from Bubba Hyde because he had been around for several years before you started playing.

Yes, but you know who I learned a lot from? Believe it or not, the greatest hitter in baseball — *all* baseball. Not in the Negro leagues. I say in *all* baseball. Do you know who that is?

Some say Ted Williams; some say Josh Gibson.

Josh Gibson was a basher. He could hit a lotta home runs, but I'm gonna tell you who the greatest hitter is. The greatest hitter was a fella by the name of Rogers Hornsby. He was my teacher in hitting. He taught me a lot about hitting.

I met him in Hot Springs, Arkansas. He had a baseball school over there. I was the only black over there in the school at one time. My classes was after the white boys' in the mornin.' They went from nine to one; I went from one to three, for two days, and then Rogers Hornsby told me to come out with the rest of 'em.

All this is history. A lot of people don't know this. One man could tell you about this; he's still livin' and you can call him up — and that's Superman. Art Pennington.

I have a book and I have nine chapters written and I'm not leavin' out no outstandin' ballplayers, like Superman. I can name a host of ballplayers that should've been playin' major league baseball way before time. I wasn't nothin' but a kid then, a teenager.

Travelin' with Satchel was my greatest adventure for six years. From 1939 to 1945, I played with Satchel. Satchel would come to my house and get me in '39 when he heard about me around Chicago. This was before the Luke Easter days. I played with Luke Easter; I played with a lotta great ballplayers.

Does Easter belong in the Hall of Fame?

I would say yes. He could hit off anybody and as *long* as anybody. I played with him and he'd laugh about it. I think he belongs in there. He'll eventually get in there, I hope.

Who else from the Negro leagues belongs?

Bubba Hyde should be in there. Double Duty. Above all, Double Duty should be in there for his tenure in the Negro leagues. I would say Lester Lockett. I played with all these guys. They don't remember nothin', but they remember me. I played with Lester Lockett one year; this was '39. I played with Palmer House, the hotel in Chicago. We won the championship in a semipro league. Nobody talks about that. We had ballplayers then that wouldn't play in the Negro leagues, wouldn't leave home. They could really play.

Pitchers we had, pitchers that could hit fourth. One of 'em—I can't recall his name now; it's been over 60 years ago. There's a lotta guys that deserve to be in the Hall of Fame that played in the Negro leagues. We had a ballplayer here—he's dead and gone—Neil Robinson.

Then they had another player before my time that I seen play and talked with was named Cunningham. They'll never get in the Hall of Fame.

Some owners should be in the Hall of Fame in Cooperstown. Number one—he'll never get there—was Gus Greenlee. Dr. W. S. Martin—he did a lot for the Negro leagues; he did more for the Negro leagues as owner than any other Negro league owner because he had money and he loved baseball. I played for him after I finished my career. I just played a couple of weeks for him; he wanted somebody to travel with him. I traveled through Birmingham, Nashville, Chattanooga, Knoxville, and back here.

The greatest story about me, I used to get whippin's for playin' baseball as a teenager.

My mother and father separated when I was nine years old. I'd get out and bat handball and all that until I got to Chicago and around here in Memphis. She was whippin' me because she said baseball was gamblin'. You was tryin' to win, and playin' with the grown men. My mother was very religious; she belonged to the Church of God and Christ. She's been dead for about 14 years now, but I always remember her teachin's.

I did all of my chores around the house. I had to get in the wood and coal, every two weeks wash the windows in the house, every Saturday scrub the kitchen floor. I had to hustle coal and wood for my mama because we didn't have much money then. I had to go on the railroad tracks and the man would hump the train so I could get a sack of coal off there and carry it home.

And then I'd go play ball. She'd call home and my sister and my brother'd say, "He's on the ballfield." Thursdays and Sundays were the only days she would come home from work and she'd say, "Get your clothes off. I know you been on the ballfield," and whip me until she was satisfied. And I didn't cry, either. But before she died, she always commended me on bein' a good boy.

Who was the best ballplayer you saw?

W. W. Willie Wells. I played with him; he was my roommate and he'd sleep baseball. He'd get up and talk about what he was gonna do the next day on the field. Hittin' pitchers and things. And the Chicago American Giants had some good pitchers and some good ballplayers.

There's some more I didn't name. A fella pitched for Chicago by the name of [Ted] Trent. And Subby Byas; he was a catcher and first baseman for the Chicago American Giants. All these guys were much older than I; I mean double my age at that time. I was 15 and 16 and they was 32 and 34 and 40 years old, but I loved to play baseball.

Who was the best pitcher?

Satchel. The second best pitcher was Trucks. Virgil Trucks. I wish you'd talk to the Veterans Committee.

I played against big Bill Wright, I played against [Roy] Campanella before he left and went up, and Joe Black.

I played to bat. I could hit any pitcher. I played against Satchel one time. This is a good story. Satchel and Dizzy Dean was travelin'; they come through Dayton, Ohio. Satchel called me at the camp and my commandin' officer told me to go on in and play.

Satchel told Dizzy Dean, "You can use Scott today, but you can't use him after today." He said he'd never played against me; he said, "But I'm gonna show the kid somethin'." [Laughs] Satchel called me "kid."

Satchel said, "Kid, you're playin' against me tonight and I'm gonna show you somethin'." The first time up, Satchel struck me out. The next time I come up, he was puttin' on a show and he walked Dizzy Dean to pitch to me. I said it was the worst thing that he could do. I tripled and got to third base and Satchel was over there after I was gettin' up — I had to slide into third. He said, "Kid, what did you hit?" I said, "That fire you throwed." He laughed; he said, "I always knowed you could hit."

I told Dizzy Dean, "Don't you be so slow

Joe Burt Scott, 1999 (Lisa Feder photograph).

roundin' them bases." Dizzy was ahead of me; I caught up with him between second and third.

I've had lots of fun. I could play with anybody in my teenage years. Just call me and I'd be ready to go and didn't want no money. Didn't think about money. I played a lotta days and the man give me 50 cents. I played all over the country, played in a lotta tournaments and the semipro leagues and didn't get three dollars. The most money I got was in the town of Ottawa, Illinois. We were playin' I think the second leg of the tournament. I won, for gettin' the most hits, 19 dollars worth of quarters. [Laughs]

We had a wreck comin' back from Ottawa. I'll tell you who was on that team with me. Lester Lockett. Lester Lockett had a 1939 brand-new Buick and we had a wreck comin' back. That was the most money I ever made in semipro.

What was your salary as a pro?

My most professional money was made when I went to the Black Yankees. I didn't make no money playin' with the Chicago American Giants or Zulu Giants. I didn't get no money. Number one, like I say, I was in high school then and I couldn't accept no money, but the manager of the team would always give my mother somethin' for me to leave home, like five dollars, two dollars. I just got out there and played; I wasn't even thinkin' about no money 'til I started professionally with the New York Black Yankees.

Like Candy Jim Taylor managed the Chicago American Giants and he told my cousin that he'd give me $35 a month when I was in Chicago, and my cousin said, "I'll give him more than that on Saturday nights if he'd come down to my place and just sit up on the bar and talk to the people." That's the reason I never got any money other than when I started playin' with the Black Yankees.

They gave me $750 a month. I got out of service in 1946 — January the 26th. I called the Black Yankees' office and told 'em I was out of service and Sep [Black Yankees' owner James Semler] sent me a contract for $350 a month. I sent it back and Sep said, "You got to come to Miami for spring trainin' and you got to show me that you need it. You're just a rookie."

I said, "Man, I been playin' for ten years. No rookie plays for ten years nowhere."

So when I got to Miami, a lot of young ballplayers was down there with 'em, includin' Willie Wells. Sep said, "We got eight ballgames with the Homestead Grays all up and down the Florida coast. If you prove to me in those eight games, I'll give you a better contract." And I said, "Well, okay," and I wore that ball out down that west coast in Florida.

Got to New York, Sep called me in the office and said, "I'm gonna give you more money than I sent that contract for. What do you really want?"

I said, "Somethin' so I can live in the winter after the ball season." Our season was short, you know.

He said, "What about 600?"

I said, "I got to live through the winter. If you'll pay my way home and give me seven-fifty, I'll play. Or else I'll go back home and do somethin' else." I had a job at the stockyard playin' with Armour and Company and they would give me a lotta money; not a lot, but all the year 'round.

He said, "Well, come on, sign this." I signed a contract and I played with the Black Yankees.

Then I went with Gus Greenlee. Gus asked Sep for me durin' the season of '46. Gus told Sep, "I gave you Satchel Paige and I gave you Josh Gibson and two limousines. You mean to tell me you won't give me Joe Scott?" [Laughs] And Sep said, "We got to ask him. You know he's a high-paid player." Gus called me in his office at 1401 Wiley Street, Pittsburgh, P-A, and told me, "You're gonna have to come over here and help us get the United States League started."

I went over there. Gus Greenlee give me $750 a month, paid my way home, and gave me two credit cards to go to the department store and the sporting goods store to buy whatever I wanted. I never shall forget Gus.

That same month, I went to Louisville,

went in there and got six bats with my autographed name on 'em. Gus paid for 'em. I rode with Gus on a lot of trips. I used to ride with him instead of ridin' in the bus.

You mentioned several managers. In your opinion, who was the best one?

I say Larry Brown, right here with the Memphis Red Sox. He wasn't a real violent manager with players. Larry would tell you what he want done and it was done without any problem. All the ballplayers liked Larry.

Barker outta New York was a good manager. Hank Barker. He was a quiet manager. All he'd want you to do is stay in shape to play ball. I'd go to bed early at night. We really didn't have a curfew, but you was supposed to be ready to go whenever they said go. [Laughs] Even if you'd been up all night and I know a lotta ballplayers stayed up all night, walked the streets all night and played the next day.

You traveled all over this country and Canada. Did you have any problems?

No, no problems. I didn't have any. The only problem that come up that anybody spoke about was in Muncie, Indiana, when I was playin' with the Wright Field Kittyhawks. The waitress wouldn't wait on me. This was at the largest hotel in Muncie. I won't forget these dates; it was April the 12th, 1945. The waitress wouldn't give me a menu and my roommate and teammate was Sal Yvars. He'll tell you I could hit that ball.

Sal said, "Roomie, they're not servin' you?" I said, "No." He called McGill over and McGill called the waitress and told her, "Bring him a menu." She said, "I can't." He said, "Well, go get the manager."

The manager come over and McGill said, "This is a soldier — Air Force — and he's on this team, and I demand that you serve him or else we'll all walk out."

They brought me a menu. That was the only thing that people refused me anywhere.

I've had people after games say, "You ought to be with the White Sox," "You ought to be with the Cubs," when I was playin' around Chicago. And I played against two teams there — semipro teams — which were castoffs for the Cubs and White Sox and Boston. They were Duffy's Florist and the Mills. You heard of those names? This goes way back in the '30s. I played against those guys. Major league players would come down and they would import players to play against our team. The Bacharach Giants or the Zulu Giants. It was a 60-40 thing then; winner gets 60 [percent], loser gets 40.

What is the one biggest thrill you had in your career?

I remember most games because I was playin' against outstandin' athletes, you know?

I say in Chicago, playin' against the Chicago American Giants, playin' with the Memphis Red Sox. I was in the service and Dr. B. B. Martin sent me $200 to get from Dayton to Chicago. He wanted his brother, W. S. Martin, to take a look at me. When I arrived in Chicago I went to my mother and stepfather and I said, "I want you all to come out to the ballgame." My mother said, "I ain't goin'." [Laughs] So my stepfather said, "You're goin' to see this boy play one time." They come out to see me play.

I had suited up and hit the field and practiced. I didn't start the game. Neil Robinson was the outstandin' star on Memphis at that time, as far as hittin' and everything. In the fourth innin', Gentry Jessup was pitchin' for the Chicago American Giants. You heard of that name? He was my teammate once upon a time around Chicago.

I come up to hit for Neil Robinson. They announced me as hittin' for Neil Robinson in about the fourth innin'. The bases was loaded and I doubled off the left field wall at Comiskey Park. That was the biggest thrill I got because my mother was watching me play.

Did she understand what you had done?

No. [Laughs]

Then another time, in high school, my mother seen me play. My stepfather had to get her out because the headlines said, "Tilden and Scott defeat Linden," "Tilden and Scott defeat Hyde Park." My stepfather said, "We got to go out and see him play."

In this game, I was playin' against a team,

Wendall Phillip High School; it was all black. My mother got out there and we had a new coach then. This coach said, "I heard you like to run," and I said, "Yes." He said, "Look. You don't run until I tell you to run."

But we were losin' this game by one run and I come up and singled and stole second and stole third and went home on a fly ball and tied the ballgame up. When the side was retired, the coach told Bunny Horner to go to center field. After the game was over, he said, "You know how come I took you out of the ballgame?" I said, "Yes." He said, "I told you not to run." That was a lesson for me: Listen to the coach.

Those were the great memories of my baseball.

After you left Memphis, you played in the minor leagues for a few years.

A short time. I didn't play too long. I went to Knoxville; I went to Hot Springs.

In '48, I was with Hot Springs for a short time but they didn't want me to travel with the team. They wanted me to stay right there in Hot Springs and play.

Then after my career was over — this was in '56 — Dick Bartell wanted me to help him get in the playoffs at Knoxville. I went up there and the fans give me all kinds of noise. They announced that I was comin' to Knoxville and I had a good contract. I don't want to quote the price I got; I got double what the minor leaguers was gettin'.

I got up there and Dick said, "You got ten days to get in shape." Okay, the first night I had to get in a ballgame. Dick and the center fielder got in an argument over the center fielder missin' the signal and Dick asked me to go up and hit for this fella. I don't know his name now; this was 1956, in July. I went up there and the fans started chanting, "Strike that nigger out! Strike that nigger out! Strike that nigger out!"

I had a pretty good at-bat. I think I doubled the first time I come up and stole third. We won two of the three ballgames that I played in up there and every night that I played I heard, "Strike that nigger out! Strike that nigger out!"

But I had a job waiting for me back here in Memphis with the teamsters, so I told Dick, "Here's your money and here's your check." He give me money and a check. He said, "You keep it, Scott." He said, "Maybe we'll work out somethin' for next year." So I left Knoxville and came back to Memphis and went to work. I was with the teamsters seven years.

Would you play baseball again if you were a young man?

Yes, sir. Sure.

And number one, I wouldn't get a lawyer to get my money. No, sir. And wouldn't want no ten million. Or no million. I'd just wanna make a livin.' And I wouldn't fret because another man's gettin' ten million, either. I'll say this to all the millionaire ballplayers: They're not worth that kinda money. They

don't show me anything and I'll put it like that.

As a fan, I go out religiously to see different ballplayers play. They don't show me that they're worth that kinda money. They can't do nothin' for it. They'll be lookin' up in the sky and the ball's hit to right center that they should catch, they miss it. I watch all of this. No ballplayer's worth that kinda money.

If somebody offers it to them, they'll take it.

That's what I say. I'll use this quotation quite a bit: A monkey'll take money and can't spend a dime. I use that quotation to people when they refuse money.

I wouldn't confront 'em tryin' to earn that kind of money. I wouldn't care what the other players would get. I wouldn't confront 'em; I'd just go out there and play ball 'cause I love baseball.

BATTING RECORD

Year	Team, League	Pos	G	AB	R	H	2B	3B	HR	RBI	SB	BA
1936	Zulu Giants, ind.	of										
1937	Ethiopian Clowns, ind.	of										
	Chicago, NAL											
1938	Ethiopian Clowns, ind.	of										
	Nuevo Laredo, MxL	of										
	Bacharach Giants, ind.	of										
1939	Bacharach Giants, ind.	of										
	Ethiopian Clowns, ind.	of										
1940	Pittsburgh, ind.	of										
	Philadelphia, NNL	of										
1941	Pittsburgh, ind.	of										
1942–43	military service											
1944	Memphis, NAL	of										
1945	Memphis, NAL	of										
	Philadelphia, NNL	of										
1946	N.Y. Blk. Yanks, NNL	of										
	Pittsburgh, USL	of										
1947	Memphis, NAL	of										
1948		of										.261
1949		of										.289
Early to mid–1950s	ProvL	of										
1938–39	Mex. City Reds, MxL	of										
1945–46	San Juan, PRWL	of										

Willie Simms
"Top of the Order"

BORN DECEMBER 23, 1908, SHREVEPORT, LA
HT. 5'9" WT. 160 BATTED LEFT, THREW RIGHT

Negro Leagues debut: 1936

The baseball career of Willie Simms was over before the color line was officially broken, and therein lies his big regret: he never had the chance to find out if he was good enough to play in the major leagues.

He says that he may not have been, but that's probably modesty speaking. He was the quintessential leadoff batter: an excellent eye, patience at the plate, a good base stealer, and the speed to take an extra base if the opportunity was presented. There have been many teams throughout baseball history that certainly could have used a man with his talents.

And there were teams that could have used the likes of Paige, Bell, Gibson, Charleston, Porter, Mackey — the list is too long to continue it here. It is not only baseball's loss; it is America's loss.

The team with which Willie Simms played the most, the Kansas City Monarchs, was a perennial champion and he helped it attain that position. He may have been able to help move a major league team up a notch or two in the standings, also. We'll never know and, unfortunately, neither will he.

I got started when I was a kid 15 years old on the sandlot. We played on Sunday. The kids didn't have nothin' to do when I was like 14, 15, and there was a carpenter that had a young kid that loved baseball like I did and he was only a couple of months older than me. There was a lotta kids around there playin' baseball every day, so he took it on hisself and he called us to pick out the best of us and he organized a little team of kids like 14 to 15 years old.

From there, the guys was askin' me to go around and they were puttin' up money, bettin' on us. The guys used to bet when I was 15, 16 years old.

I lived in Shreveport, Louisiana, and that town at that time was in the Texas League. All the rest of the teams in that league was out of Texas; Shreveport was the only oddball. I used to go to the ballpark every day and watch them play ball when they were in town, when they were at home. If they was on the road, I listened on the radio. I learned a lot that way.

I kept baseball on my mind all the time when I was that age as I grew up from 15 to 17, 18, 20, and by the time I was 21 — no, a little older than that; I guess I was about 22 — the guys wanted me to leave and go and play on the little organized teams that they had around. The Sawmill League, they called it. That was still in Louisiana. So I started to playin' on those Sawmill League teams for about a couple of years.

I went to a little town like Leesville, Louisiana; a little town called Boley and that's down around Mansfield. I liked what I was doin'; I just loved to play baseball. I could play all day. My energy didn't never run out, didn't seem like.

When I knew anything, there was a guy come to Shreveport and he wanted to organize a travelin' team that he could take on the road. By that time, I was up in my 20s, like 24 or somethin' like that. I'd fooled around for a long time. I didn't start goin' away from home — I mean, goin' to play on big teams — until I was around 23 or 24, somethin' like that.

Anyway, this guy organized a team and he took us on the road and we went all up through Canada. It was a devil of a trip that we went through. Quite a trip. In going around like that, don't you think that I wasn't takin' it in because I said, "Shucks, I like this. I'm gonna make a career outta this." I said, "One day, I might get a chance to play some big league baseball," but I never did. I was thinkin', that was in my mind, "One day it will happen," but by being born too early, like way back in nineteen hundred and eight, I didn't make it.

The only thing that was available to me was the Kansas City Monarchs, the Pittsburgh Crawfords — at that time they had a awful good baseball team, they could've beat anybody — and the Homestead Grays, Philadelphia Stars, and the New York Black Yankees — teams like that. They had a league organized and that was the black major leagues. Chicago American Giants.

I finally played with them before I was too old. I was around 30 and the guy — everybody knew about him — Jim Taylor, Candy Jim Taylor they called him — he come to my house in Shreveport, Louisiana, and he says, "How about comin' to Chicago with me?" And I said, "Well, I don't know. I can't say that I wouldn't enjoy it, but what kind of a deal can we make?"

He made a proposition and I went along and I played about three years in Chicago, but before I went to Chicago I landed in Cincinnati, Ohio, on another one of the big teams that was in the league. I didn't play there but one year because I wanted somethin' bigger. That was one of the league teams, but it wasn't good enough for what I thought it should be.

I took a run over to Kansas City. I stayed

Willie Simms (courtesy of Willie Simms).

over there a year and things didn't look too rosy there, but Kansas City was, at that time, one of the better teams. I had a spot there where I played sometime and sometime I didn't. I wanted to play every day, so I got out of there after one year, 1937.

I went up to Chicago for three years and next thing I know, why this guy in Kansas City, he wanted me back. [Laughs] So I went back to Kansas City and I stayed there 'til 1943.

In the spring — well, it was still wintertime, February 12 — I left for Los Angeles and I says, "I think I'm gonna put down everything and I'm gonna see what California's like," and I came out here and I got me a job and I went to work. The guys in Kansas City said, "What's the matter — you not comin' back with us?" I says, "Well, I'm working now." "Aw, what are you talkin' 'bout, workin'."

So I put down the job for a while and I said, "What'll you do? You wanna send me a ticket, you wanna send me some train fare and some money in my pocket?" He say, "Yeah, because we need you."

So I went back to Kansas City some-where around the last part of May or some-thin' like that. I was already in pretty good condition because they had a lotta teams around Los Angeles—a lotta semipro teams. There was a guy that had a semipro team that played on Saturdays and Sundays, and I played with him and I stayed in pretty good shape while I was working five days a week.

Then this guy, he calls up in Kansas City—J. L. Wilkinson. He was the owner of the Kansas City Monarchs—big guy, had all the money in the league, and he did as he wanted to. He was *Mister* Wilkinson in that league.

So I went out there and I played until I got ready to come back home. California was what I was callin' home at that time. I no longer wanted Louisiana for a home. I says, "Well, fellas, this is it. I've had enough of it. I'm gonna stay in one place."

I got me a job and went to work and in two or three years I was able to put a little money on me a home, and I started buyin' me a home and I stayed here. I said, "That's the end of my runnin' around." I spent, let's see, from 1944 until 1974 in Los Angeles, then I moved to Perris in 1974.

Sometime I says, "Why in the world didn't I get me a job managin' before I put the game down?" Some of these fellas—even a coach—I could've taught some of the kids that needed to know a lotta things.

Is there a game that stands out in your memory?

Yes. I was thinkin' about this game just last night. It comes to my mind sometimes. There's *one* game that we played in Washing-ton, D.C., against the Homestead Grays and in that ballgame, we lost it, 2–1. I can't look at it no other way but say that I lost it myself.

I cost 'em that ballgame that night because I was leadoff man for Kansas City and had been every time I'd go to play at Kansas City. I was not a slugger at 160 pounds, and I had to fit in somewhere. I could run, steal bases, throw, and hit, but I couldn't hit for distance because I was too little against them big boys. I just figured I had to hit someplace

else, so I started to hittin' in second place. That's what moved me towards the top. The next thing the guys wanted me to lead off.

But in this one game that we're speakin' about, we played before a sellout crowd. It must've been 35-, 40,000 people in Griffith Stadium. I opened up the ballgame with a three-base hit into left–center field. The next guy comes up to hit a short fly ball. Nobody was tellin' me to go home, but at the catch the center fielder had to come in a few steps to catch the ball and, knowing this guy as much as I'd played against him, I says, "I'm gonna score. I'm not gonna wait on the next guy to drive me in."

With nobody out, I should've stayed at third base on a short fly ball and I went home and was thrown out, oh, by six feet. I was tagged before I started my slide. The catcher had the ball and that was the best throw that this guy ever made. Jerry Benjamin was his name, a good outfielder but he couldn't throw; his arm was so sad and everybody pitied his throwin' arm and so this is why I took a chance and went. I said, "This guy's gonna limp the ball in and I should beat this throw."

But he put everything he had on that throw and, of all things, I was tagged out six feet away from home plate because I had no room to slide. Just as I was ready to start my slide, the catcher put the tag on me up the line between third and home.

And I never was so give out about that, and just last night that thing rolled across my mind. I still think about that. We lost that ballgame, 2–1, before all them people, and nobody hates losin' any worse that I did with a crowd of 35- or 40,000 people lookin' at you.

At that time, the Kansas City Monarchs could draw crowds everywhere they went. We had a pretty good ballclub. Everywhere they went, people wanted to see us and they didn't care; we could go off and stay two weeks and come back and draw another big crowd. It was a drawing card; that ballclub could draw ever-where we went.

But, anyway, that's a ballgame that will never go out of my mind until they get ready to put me away. I thinks about that because I said, "This guy couldn't throw." I knowed that his throwin' arm was bad, but now on this one time he throws a one-hop. The ball hopped off the turf in the infield when it hit the ground and it just skidded, it looked like — it just took off and skidded. We were playing nights and you know the ball skids on a good soil like that, like they have in the big league diamonds. The ball just takes a skid and it's in the glove.

We just couldn't pick up another run, and these guys beat us, 2–1. In the eighth innin' they picked up the winnin' run. When I come up again the next time, I was out. I think I come up with two hits outta that ballgame — a triple and a single — but this triple that I got to open the game with, I just can't forget that and I couldn't score. That hurt my heart for a long time. And I still remembers it. That's one game I will never, never, never forget.

I wasn't one of those guys could hit a lotta home runs and I didn't hit a lotta home runs, but I could pick out good balls and strikes and pitchers had to get the ball down in there or else they had walked me. That's why they kept me hittin' in the leadoff spot for as long as I played. I could see the ball real good and if it was off the plate two or three inches away, I didn't go after it. Same way if it was high or low. That made me get a lot of walks, so I was on base every time you looked around. If I wasn't hittin' you had to throw strikes to get me out or else I'd be walking.

I was a guy that liked to steal bases and that was in every game. If I get on base, why, I'd be going anytime because they knew that I could run. I wasn't the fastest guy out there. Cool Papa Bell was just about the fastest guy I ever seen on bases. I tried to imitate some of those other guys that could do a lot of good things, like running, dragging — drag bunt. It kept me busy tryin' to get on base because I hated to go back to the dugout. Nobody hated that any more than I did.

There were times when I had my nights and my days and I'd be able to come up with three and four hits in a ballgame, or two, and a lotta times I'd come up with none. I'd get my share to stay in that top spot. You know a guy don't lead off doin' nothin' when they're on a good ballclub like the Kansas City Monarchs. You don't lead off for a club like that. They know when you're gettin' on base and when you're not. That was my position.

I've got my name in a lotta lineups in my scrapbook. I was a pretty good hustler when it came to gettin' on base.

Do you know any of your seasonal batting averages?

I'm gonna tell you the truth. That's something that they really didn't take. They didn't take care of that in our big leagues. They wasn't concerned about it. They would put a write-up in the paper, like the *Chicago Defender* and things like that, that so-and-so is hittin' .340. It was mostly these owners. When they wanted to try to make stars out of certain fellas, they would put averages in.

This will make a star out of this guy because they got to have somebody that they push before the public that can get people to come to the gate and buy tickets. This is what they're after. I didn't have them big high averages advertised in the paper all the time — "Simms is hittin' .400," and all like that — but they knew how Simms was gettin' on base every time they looked up. Either I'd come up with a base hit or I got four balls or somebody make a error in handlin' the ball, and by me bein' fast enough to get down to first base, which I could do pretty good, I was just a ideal guy for a leadoff spot. That's all that I could do.

As far as hittin' home runs, I couldn't do it and I hated that because I would like to be able to hit the ball and trot around the bases without sweatin'. [Laughs] But, no, I could not. I had to sweat.

Before I got with the big boys, yes, I hit a few home runs, but when I got with the big boys, those fellas knew how to pitch on you and you had to be up there sweatin' and tryin' to pick out a good one to hit and you wasn't gettin' it, well, I got to the place that I was chokin' the bat up. I used to use a 34-inch bat

Cincinnati Tigers, 1936. (L-r): Marlin Carter, Frank Edwards, Charlie Miller, Harvey Robinson, Turkey Smith, Jelly Taylor, Willie Simms, Neil Robinson, Jess Houston, Virgil Harris, Wolf Childers, Porter Moss, Sonny Harris, Josh Johnson, Ewing Russell, Arthur Maddox, Jerry Gibson. Kneeling: Jim Glass, manager (author's collection).

and I would choke up on that sometime; I wouldn't swing that from the end. Most times I was chokin' up on a 34-inch bat.

I never used the 33s, I never used 35s. I wanted to buy myself some bats that was 34-inches long and when I choked up, my hand wouldn't be too far away from the knob. If I got the pitch down there where I could get ahold to it, I'd hit the ball between the outfielders and go racin' around the bases. I didn't care if I didn't hit a home run so long as I hit two or three base hits like that. I didn't care about a home run.

Today they like to hit the ball over the fence and look good trottin'. In my day, I liked to look good runnin'. [Laughs] If I hit one between the outfielders and stopped at second base, good. Very good. I was happy with that.

I'll tell you. We got a bad break in my day when I came along. When I say "bad break," some of the boys that's playing now, they wasn't quite as good as the boys was that we had. They don't know the game too well, and I look at some of them now and the things

that they do I would have got chewed out.

Andy Cooper was my manager; he was one of the smartest guys about the game of baseball that you ever looked at, and in his day he was a lefthanded pitcher, and a good one, too. He knew how to get the pitch on hitters inside and out. Away. And he knew how to get it in on their hands and make 'em break up their bats and he'd laugh at 'em.

He'd draw 'em up to the plate by throwin' away from 'em a little bit. If they move up to the plate, you better get ready to hit one right in on your fingers. You couldn't stand up and take it because it would be a strike. He was just that slick. He'd throw the ball outside a couple of times, hopin' to draw you up to the plate, and then he'd say, "Now I'm gonna mash his fingers." [Laughs] And he would do it. He'd get one right down in there, right close up to you, and you'd take a cut at it and you couldn't do nothin' with it. He was a big guy, weighed 220. He could fire that ball down in there.

I tried to do the best I could with what

I had. I knew that a guy weighin' 160 pounds like me couldn't hit many home runs, so I didn't try. I tried meetin' the ball. Never no hard cuts, just try to meet the ball and get it in there. If you hit the fastball and hit it down on the line, it's gonna go to the fence if it gets by the outfielders, but you gotta be able to hit it down the line. You gotta be lucky enough to hit it down the line because I *know* that there's such a thing as hittin' a line drive right at somebody, so every time you hit a line drive it don't mean that you're runnin' the bases. You can be out.

I learned all that when I was goin' to the Texas League in Shreveport, Louisiana. I saw many a hard hit ball and the infielders catch it and you ain't got nothin'. I'd say. "Ain't that a pity." [Laughs]

When I started playin', it happened to me the same way: tryin' to hit line drives by the infielders, and part of the time you'd hit right at them.

Who were the best players you came across?

Well, I'll tell you. Paige was still the best man out there. Satchel. And you know what? I told you I didn't hit many home runs 'cause I couldn't, but I remember back in the year 1934. We were playing an exhibition game in a little town called Monroe, Louisiana. Satchel started that game and finished it. They finally beat us. As hard as he could throw — that man could throw a hundred miles an hour for nine innin's when he'd get warmed up. From the first inning when he went out there, he wouldn't be throwin' no harder in the first innin' than he would be throwin' in the ninth. He could throw nine innin's showin' you nothin' but little shirt buttons. He could throw that ball so hard it looked like shirt buttons.

But on this day, I had two hits on this guy. One, I happened to rake it between the second baseman and the first baseman into right field. A grounder. But in the eighth innin' it was, I come up. I never will forget this. I come up in the eighth innin' with a man on base and they were leadin' us, 3–1. I hit the ball over the right field fence on this guy and I mean he didn't let up on me at all. He was

pourin' down as hard as he could and I got ahold of that fastball and that thing jumped about, I'd say, 420 feet without me even swinging. I wasn't takin' a cut; I was just tryin' to meet it.

I hit that ball about 420 feet and we had a pretty good little crowd down there in Monroe and people went crazy, They said, "Oh, I think they're gonna beat the Crawfords. I think they're gonna beat the Crawfords." And they beat us, 6–4, anyway, even after I tied 'em up with the home run.

But I had two hits on Satchel that day. I was a young kid then and I had my good eyesight. I could see real good and him throwin' so hard, it didn't matter to me. I could see the ball real good, and if it wasn't a strike I wouldn't go for it. He was a guy with good arm strength and he had good control. He could go nine innin's just as hard as he was throwin' in the first. He could throw that ball outta sight.

Dizzy Dean would pick him a major league All-Star team. It was when Dizzy Dean was playin' with the St. Louis Cardinals and Dean would get a bunch of his boys and Satchel would get a bunch of his boys and he wouldn't care who he had because he said, "I can have anybody. Ain't gonna be much hittin' goin' on." [Laughs] He was the chesty kinda guy that he believed that he could get anybody out, and he'd figure, "Oh, well. If I don't strike 'em out, they ain't gonna hit it far and anybody gonna be able to catch it 'cause they ain't gonna hit it that hard." And he believed that. He'd go out there and do it.

He did a lot of barnstorming after the season had closed, and he'd get them major leaguers together and they made a lotta money.

The best hitter was the guy that used to catch Paige. I hated to see that guy come to the bat. Josh Gibson. He was a catcher, but the guy could hit the ball against anybody. He could hit home runs, he could hit doubles against the fence, and he was so cocky that he would do all this and make the pitcher look small. He'd run bases laughin' at 'em. "I'll show you, throwin' that dinkiness up there, that rinky-dink stuff. I'll kill somebody out there in the stands. You're gonna get somebody hurt yet." He'd just be laughin' and pointin' at you.

If I had been a pitcher, he would have made me mad and I would have been throwin' at him more than he would have got a chance to hit. They did believe in throwin' at you, but nobody didn't throw at him because they didn't want him hurt. Nobody around the league wanted him hurt 'cause he was the biggest drawin' card in the league. Well, I don't say the biggest, 'cause Satchel was the biggest drawin' card we had.

He used to catch Satchel, and then Satchel left Pittsburgh and they started playing against each other. Josh could hit the ball over the fence on Satchel just like he did on anybody else.

They wasn't countin', but he had to hit around 75 or 80 home runs a season because of the little papers—and I don't think they would be lying—he would always be hittin' two or three home runs sometimes. He could hit home runs if you didn't walk him, and the people didn't like for you to walk him because they wanted to see him hit. If you started puttin' him on every time he'd come up, they'd start booin' you and this would make you feel kinda cheesy-like, so you'd go ahead and throw it in there and he'd go on and hit it outta there.

I think he was about the best hitter I played against. There were a few other guys, like this guy that played first base along with him. He was a good hitter. Buck Leonard. They had a good ballclub and they had other guys on there could hit, too.

I think that the major leagues lost a whole lot of money back in those days by not lettin' the colored boys move in to the major leagues. I think they lost a *whole* lot of money they could have been picking up because if they had let some of the colored boys come in to that league then, they'd've had big crowds and more people would've been playing baseball because there was a lotta kids that had a little bit of ability to play the game.

They say, "Shucks, you all go out and play before maybe 10-, 15,000 people. How come they don't let y'all in the big leagues?" Well, we didn't have no answer to that. We'd have to tell 'em, "Well, they don't want us." That's all you could do.

I don't say that all of us could've played in the big leagues. Maybe I couldn't've played in there myself. In order to be on the best there is in baseball, you should be good yourself. I wouldn't doubt that I wouldn't've been one of those that was good enough to play in the big leagues, but I would like to have had a chance to see. Then I would've come away saying, "I couldn't make it. The big leagues was too fast for me. I couldn't cut it." And I would've laughed at myself and went ahead, but just to think I got to close my eyes and forget the whole thing because I didn't get a chance in the time that I put into baseball. I hated it, but there was nothin' I could do about it. It's gone by the boards.

You know, I was thinkin' about it just a couple of days ago. I said all the teams that they got now—I don't know how many teams are in the big leagues no more; I used to tell you just in a second, eight teams in the National League and eight in the American League. But now how many do they have? Twice as many as they had for a hundred years it looked like, playing with eight teams in a league. More of us could've played at that time when they were callin' ourselves the best. There was a whole lot of us that could have played at that time, but they wouldn't stand for that because they didn't want the black faces to play then.

So they got money-thirsty, I guess, and they decided, "We'll pick up a few black boys." So they started pickin' up one here, one there. Pretty soon every team in the league had at least two or three.

And the money now. The first baseman [Mo Vaughn] with the Angels—come from Boston—they say he's gettin' $80 million.

In my time, $80 million would have put too much pressure on us. We had to sweat— I mean *sweat*—for the few dollars we got.

Thank God things are different for our boys today. I am 90 years old and many changes have been made.

BATTING RECORD

Year	Team, League	Pos	G	AB	R	H	2B	3B	HR	RBI	SB	BA
1936	Cincinnati, ind.	of										.280
1937	Kansas City, NAL	of										
1938	Chicago, NAL	of										
1939		of										.258
1940		of										
1941	Kansas City, NAL	of										.182
1942		of										.206
1943		of										

Jeff "Bo" Campbell
"Semipro Hired Gun"

BORN MARCH 26, 1907, WYATT, LA
HT. 6' WT. 160 BATTED AND THREW RIGHT

Negro Leagues debut: 1937

Jeff "Bo" Campbell played baseball for close to 20 years, yet only one was spent as a professional. He made a good living playing in the semipro leagues around Louisiana and the surrounding area.

It wasn't a lack of opportunity that kept him there. He was asked to join Negro leagues teams more than once, but he was a very big fish in his own area.

Semipro ball was huge back in the 1930s, and as his reputation grew, the demand for his services grew. Teams would ask him to pitch for them. When a big game was scheduled, a team would go get him to pitch it for them.

Along the way, he faced many professional teams and many professional players, and he more than held his own. Witness his performances against none other than Satchel Paige, which he recounts in the following interview.

There is no record of how many games he won, but in nearly 20 years it was a lot. 200? Maybe. But it could be closer to 300.

To give an idea of his ability, at the age of 30 he finally gave in to an offer from a professional team. He joined the Homestead Grays for part of 1937, posting a 5–1 record. The illness of his pregnant wife caused him to leave the Grays before the season was over, and he chose to stay closer to home after that.

When did you begin playing baseball?

I began playing baseball when I was 'round 16 years old. I went on to high school and I played in high school on the team there, and then I would play with the men during the summer. I had a scholarship to go to college, but I turned it down to play baseball because, during that time, I could make more money playing semipro baseball than I could in college. I chose that for my profession.

I played semipro I'd say, off and on, until '40 or '41. I had a long career. I played in Louisiana, Arkansas, Texas, and Oklahoma. I was put up to be one of the best pitchers in the South during those times — through Arkansas, Oklahoma, Louisiana, and Texas. I had plenty opportunities to go professional.

During that time, Louisiana was populated with big sawmills and paper mills. Every big sawmill had their own ballclub and they paid pretty good. You would always have a contract; they would pay your room and board, then about $15 a week. Then you got other little gimmies, you know, like clothing and things like that at a reduced price. The temptation to go pro wasn't that great.

I played against them. I had an opportunity to go with Memphis in 1930. I was playing in Shreveport, Louisiana, and they came through there. I played against all the big clubs down South.

I did go to the Homestead Grays. I was there a year. I did good. My time was short in '37 because when I left Texas — I was staying in Texas then — and when I left, my wife was pregnant. We was on a road trip in Virginia and when we got back to Homestead, I had a telegram that my wife was sick, and that was my priority. I left and came back to Texas.

They didn't keep too much of a record, but I had a pretty good record. I think I lost one game out of six.

You played against a lot of good ballclubs. Which was the best one?

I think the Pittsburgh Crawfords was the best club we played against then. That was in the Negro leagues in the early '30s.

Who was the best player?

During that time, Gibson and Satchel Paige. Gibson was a catcher, Satchel Paige was a pitcher. They had some good ballplayers, but the ones that got the publicity, that was Satchel Paige and Josh Gibson. They were good, but there was others that were, too. It goes when you get their attention, you know.

The thing with Satchel, he started off with the Pittsburgh Crawfords, too, then when he went to the islands, they kind of blackballed him from the Negro National League. Then he came to the American League in Kansas City. That's where he really made it.

Is there one game that stands out in your career?

In Alexandria, Louisiana, he beat me, 1–0. They got their run on a bunt. They got a man to third and they bunted him home. I think I gave up five hits; Satchel gave up more than I did.

We played against each other about three times. He came out, two to one.

How were the traveling conditions down there through Louisiana and Texas?

The condition was pretty good during that time down in there. I played on different ballclubs, and when they wanted me, they would come and get me. Send for me. The transportation was pretty good there, but when I was in Homestead, we had good transportation there, but the hours that you traveled — that was the hard thing. You may play this morning and this evening you catch a bus and go to someplace and have to play that night. We drove all night sometimes.

Just like you would go from Homestead to Philadelphia, well, you may get a hotel in Philadelphia and then you're playing in Morristown and you leave there and go to Ohio. It's a round-the-horn. When you get there, you may stay, say, in Toledo, that night, then you go from there to Indianapolis, Indiana, and from Indianapolis back into Homestead. You may be there two or three days and you're off again, going into Virginia or Wheeling, West Virginia. That's where I was when I went back to Homestead and got the telegram that my wife was sick.

Were there lodging problems?

You had lodging problems out East and in the Midwest, but it wasn't as bad as it was in the South. The fact that you were traveling, they always made preparations for you to stay with different families.

Mostly they served meals at the cafes and places like that. Eating wasn't a problem within the Negro community, but in the white restaurants they didn't serve you unless you went back to the back. There were lots of 'em that wouldn't serve you at all. In the Midwest, it was the same way in some places, some parts of Ohio.

What did you do after baseball?

After baseball and during baseball, I worked. When I quit playing baseball in the '40s, I went to work for civil service. I was in administration; I was a foreman over sandblasting and painting. I stayed there 30 years.

Any regrets from baseball?

No. I regret that I didn't have a chance to go to the majors — the major leagues. We played against a bunch of the guys and I'll say this, there was lots of white players that wasn't against Negroes coming into the major leagues. But the majority was against it. Even some of the guys from the South, they always said that they wished the best Negro league ballplayers could play in the majors.

The fact of it, if you take out East [for instance] where we was making our money, it was playing semipro white clubs. Lots of times, they'd have a day and they would pay the club so much money to play the game. 'Course, it was guaranteed, rain or shine. That's where the Negro leagues made most of their money, playing semipro whites. We'd draw good, good crowds.

If you were a young man, would you do it all again?

Yes, I would. I think a man should follow his talent, regardless. I enjoyed playing baseball. During that time, it was just fun. It was lots of fun playing baseball. You got the publicity. It was just fun.

PITCHING RECORD

Year	Team, League	G	IP	W	L	Pct	H	BB	SO	ERA
1937	Homestead, NNL			5	1	.833				

James "Big Train" Dudley
"Stuck Behind the Greats"

BORN MAY 12, 1910, BALTIMORE, MD
HT. 5'10½" WT. 198 BATTED AND THREW RIGHT

Negro Leagues debut: 1937

James Dudley is one of many players who has been shorted in the Negro leagues baseball literature. The references either don't mention him at all or have the years he played listed incorrectly. In truth, he had nine years in professional ball, all with the Baltimore Elite Giants. He was a catcher, but he had the misfortune to play behind two of the greatest catchers in baseball history — Biz Mackey and Roy Campanella — and a third, Eggie Clarke, who could play with anybody.

Perhaps if he had begun playing professionally earlier — he was 27 when he joined the Elites from the semipro ranks — he may have been better known because he was an excellent athlete. He was very fast — as a teenager he ran sub-10-second 100 yard dashes — and today may have been of Olympic caliber, but the country didn't want black Olympians in the 1920s.

Since his retirement from baseball, Dudley has worked for the World Wrestling Federation and today is a member of the WWF Hall of Fame. A man of many talents, he just came along at the wrong time.

How did you get started in professional baseball? You were nearly 30.

Just about.

The Elites were originally the Nashville Elite Giants and they moved from Nashville and came to Washington. They were in Washington for a year and, by the Senators playing there, the teams came through and they couldn't play the games they were supposed to play 'cause everytime there was something for them, the Senators was home, so they made arrangements with a guy named Mackey in Baltimore that had a field over there called Bugle Field.

Then, I think, in '37 they moved over there. It didn't hold as many people and it wasn't a first-class place, but it was somewhere they could play when they got ready. They were the boss there.

I was pretty good with all the semipros. I played with all the semipro teams in Baltimore then and they used to stay at the York Hotel at Madison Avenue and Dolphin Street in Baltimore. Across the corner on Madison Avenue, there was a hotel called the Clark Hotel and a famous black ballplayer had a shoeshine parlor there — [he was] named Norman Yokeley. All the guys used to come over there and play cards down there in the basement and I got to playing with 'em. One day, I went over there and was warming up the pitcher and that was the beginning of it. I think this was '37.

I didn't travel then. When they came home, I was the bullpen catcher. I didn't start traveling with 'em 'til around the first of '38. I was with 'em 'til about '45 or '46. That's when I stopped.

James Dudley receiving his James Dudley induction plaque to the World Wrestling Federation Hall of Fame (courtesy of James Dudley).

You played with some awfully good ballplayers with the Elites: Wild Bill Wright, Henry Kimbro, Bill Byrd.

Bill Byrd — that's my man, until he'd throw that spitball. [Laughs] Kimbro was the center fielder; Wright was out there, too.

I was there before Campanella. Campanella's father brought him down from Philadelphia one Sunday, and then after that his father would come every time we was home on Sunday and he'd have a bag full of fruit for everybody. He'd say, "Look out for Camp while you're gone away." So everybody was on the job. Everybody had a job looking out for Camp. [Laughs] He wasn't but 16 or 17, but he had a arm like a rifle. He just couldn't throw straight at that time.

We had a great black catcher named Biz Mackey. He was managing the team and he was on Camp for throwing and getting foul tips. He'd pick that fungo and hit that ball up in the air and make you go get it. If we was playing a night game we had to go out to the park about five o'clock and he'd start. When the team got there, we'd be soaking wet. He

could run you to death. Biz Mackey deserves to be in the Hall of Fame.

Many people say he was the best catcher they ever saw, better than Gibson.

Well, see, that's where people get the wrong impression. When you start to talking about catchers, they talk about Josh, but Josh was a hitter, not a catcher. But the way he could hit the ball, how could you keep him out of the lineup? When you're making the lineup, you had to put him in there. We had a whole lot of catchers better than Josh, as far as receiving from the pitcher.

He was a pretty good catcher, but we had some terrible catchers. A guy name of Lasses come out of Newport News, Virginia, and Pepper Bassett with the Birmingham Black Barons. That guy lay down in the dirt like a little child playing. He'd tell the pitcher, "Throw hard 'cause you can't throw bad." [Laughs] It didn't make no difference where the ball went in that dirt, he got it.

Another guy that played with Cleveland was named [Quincy] Trouppe. Oh, we had a whole lot of good catchers. Catching was a terrible job.

How good were you?

[Laughs] Oh, I was just about the average. Then, being there, I was with Mackey, [Eggie] Clarke out of Richmond, Virginia, and then Campanella come. Being there with that kind of stuff, you didn't even get a chance to show what you got. [Laughs] I'd go right straight to the bullpen. I know where I was going.

Did you see much action?

During the week I did.

Campanella could catch, he could throw, and he could hit. I know one time, the man that run the team — he became the owner, we called him Fat Pappy, his name was Vernon Green — he told Camp, "You ain't gonna be able to run at all." He [Campanella] said, "When you hit the ball as far as I do, you don't have to run fast." [Laughs]

Who were the best overall players you saw?

I think the best — I have to name two

players. The best players I ever seen was a little boy named Tommy Bunch playing shortstop and Cool Papa Bell.

Was Cool Papa as fast as everyone says?

[Laughs] When he said he'd shut out the lights and be in bed before the room get dark, he was just about right. He set us catchers crazy. "You ain't got no trouble today. Those bones have got the old man," [Bell would tease] and you squat down there and stay down and give the signal and when you look he's standing on first base. No play, the old man's safe. [Laughs] And he'd do the same thing when he got on third base. You better keep your eyes open 'cause he'd run right over top of you.

Who was the best pitcher?

Well, that's a terrible thing. The best pitcher — you have to say it — was Satchel Paige for all the things he got, but he only pitched three innings.

Now the best pitcher I ever seen pitching nine was Norman Yokeley. The sportswriter for the *Baltimore News* — his name was Rogers Pittman — and at the end of the season he would bring a major league All-Star team after the World Series to Baltimore to play the Baltimore Black Sox, and Yokeley pitched every Sunday. Lefty Grove, who went to the Philadelphia Athletics, pitched and he [Yokeley] beat Grove, 1–0. Grove told Pittman, "He beat me because I didn't have my regular catcher." Mickey Cochrane was the catcher for the Athletics, so the next Sunday, Rogers Pittman brought Mickey Cochrane down to catch Lefty Grove and Yokeley beat him, 3–0.

He messed his arm up over in Cuba. That was the biggest thing for black ballplayers then — to go play winter ball. Go to play in Cuba and Puerto Rico in the winter, and that's what messed up Josh's life, too. That's what happened to Leon Day over there, too. It messed up a whole lot of guys' arms. I don't know whether it was the climate over there or what, but it always took the effect mostly on pitchers. But a whole lot of guys drank over there and they ruined their career with

drinking. That's what Josh did. He drank whisky like he was drinking water.

When he'd leave there, coming down to the boat, you'd think it was a parade coming. Wasn't no airplane then, you know; they'd go by boat.

Talk about wrestling.

Oh, I been with the WWF that was started by Vince McMann. I was with Jess McMann — that's the oldest one — and then he went into boxing. He was the matchmaker for Mike Jacobs and then his son, Vince McMann, went into wrestling. Me and him was hand-in-hand. "You stay with me and every time I go up two steps, I'll pull you up one." And I stayed with him 'til he died. Then when he died, now I'm with the son, with Vince McMann, Jr.

In the promotions, I ain't bragging on me. I learned from Vince McMann, Sr. I can do *every*thing from carrying the water bucket to counting the money.

Back to baseball. Did you encounter problems as you traveled around the country?

When you went south, you had a hard time finding someplace to stay, but up this away we stayed in the black hotels. We rode in buses, you know, and sometime they didn't want to sell you gas or didn't want you to get no drink of water. But as it went on, that wore off.

One morning, we woke up in Benton, Mississippi. The bus had stopped in the station and the man come in and said, "What can I do for you?" He give us first-class service. I said, "Man, there's gonna be hell here when he finds out we're black." [Laughs] When he come to collect the money, he said, "Be sure to stop on your way back." I say, "He don't care what color he is if he's got that money." [Laughs]

How much were you paid?

I got $150 and I would've done the same thing for nothing, just to be with the team, to say you played professional ball. I'd been getting seven or eight dollars, so when I started getting 150 I was getting big money. We were

Baltimore Elite Giants, early '40s. James Dudley is fourth from left in back row (courtesy of James Dudley).

playing that 74 ball; you get seven, eight dollars and if you get ten dollars, oh Lord, you thought the world was coming to an end. [Laughs]

Any regrets?

I would say I was just a little too early. I was a little too early for track *and* baseball.

In 1924, when they was having the Olympic trials, there's a place here in Baltimore called Homeland—Homeland Field, that's Johns Hopkins' field. They were having trials here in the morning and 'bout ten of us went out there. We said we were going to be in the meet. They said, "Not here, you won't." And then after that, they wouldn't let us buy a ticket to come in.

They had that meet there in the morning and that evening in the other section of Baltimore—which is south Baltimore, they called it Carol Park—they had a track meet down there they called the Colored Municipal Games.

Now this might sound like a fairy tale: I run the 100 yard in ten flat down there with my sailor pants on. I was mad about what happened that morning and I didn't even take off my clothes. I just rolled the sailor pants up and run the 100-yard in ten flat down there and got a trophy. The boy that won the 100

out to Homeland ran in 11-something and went to Bordentown, New Jersey, to the semifinals.

I didn't have on no shirt. I just had my spikes on and my pants and I turned my pants up.

In 1925, if you'll look up the records, you'll see they used to have a big track meet in Baltimore called the Johns Hopkins Track Meet. During that time, in the 100 yards you had a guy named Frank Hussey, Jackson Schultz, and Lockey. All them were with the New York Athletic Club. We had a guy named Louis Clark, just graduated from Johns Hopkins, and he joined the National Guard. And I lived right across the street at 216 Huffman, and they were training, getting ready for this meet.

Somebody told the coach 'bout the boy lived 'cross the street. On the corner of Huffman and Bolton, there was a grocery store there and we used to get custard pie; a slice of pie cost ten cents. He sent for me and I come over there. He said, "Can you run?" I said, "A little bit." "You like custard pie?" They told him 'cause I used to get pie every day. I say, "Yes, sir!" He said, "All right. You run with him [Clark]."

So we started. Clark was giving me five yards. He said, "Now don't let him catch you." I say, "Okay."

Every evening, we'd go over to Cohen's — a man named Max Cohen had the store — and he'd get me a pie and ice cream cone.

The last week — the meet was going to be that Saturday — that Monday I was giving Clark five yards and he was keeping me from catching him. [Laughs] He run the 100 that night indoors in nine and four-fifths.

His father called and told me, said, "You meet me at the armory Monday morning," and that Monday morning I met him and he carried me down to the clothing store and I got everything brand new — underclothes, socks, necktie, shoes, and a suit, coat, hat.

So on Sunday, we all used to hang out at Park Avenue and Huffman Street, right down the hill from the armory. That Sunday, I come with my stuff on and the guys said, "Goldarn! Look at Dudley! Look at that overcoat he got on!" 'Course, the meet was held in February, see. I said, "These guys must be crazy. Keep on talking 'bout the overcoat and they ain't said nothing 'bout my suit." And it was cold as the devil and I took my overcoat off and folded it up so they could see my suit. [Laughs] "Don't keep on talking 'bout no overcoat and don't say nothing 'bout my suit." I nearly froze. [Laughs]

BATTING RECORD

Year	Team, League	Pos	G	AB	R	H	2B	3B	HR	RBI	SB	BA
1937	Baltimore, NNL	c										
1938		c										
1939		c										
1940		c										
1941		c										
1942		c										
1943		c										
1944		c										
1945		c										

Byron "Mex" Johnson
"The Best Shortstop in the League"

BORN SEPTEMBER 16, 1911, LITTLE ROCK, AR
HT. 5'8" WT. 160 BATTED AND THREW RIGHT

Negro Leagues debut: 1937

That's what they called Byron Johnson: the best shortstop in the league. Someone said perhaps the best shortstop in *any* league.

Over the last 50 or 60 years, baseball has seen the likes of Omar Vizquel, Ozzie Smith, Mark Belanger, Phil Rizzuto, Marty Marion, and so on. At some point, someone has called each "the best shortstop to ever wear a glove." But most, if not all, of these praise-givers never saw Byron Johnson.

It was hard to see him. For one reason, those who heaped praise were heaping it in white newspapers; Johnson was a Negro leaguer. For another reason, he only played a few years of professional baseball: 1937–40. Unlike the vast majority of his contemporaries — black or white — he did not need baseball to make a good living. He was a schoolteacher, so he could rely on a good job where he wouldn't have to put up with the conditions black ballplayers in the late '30s had to endure.

As poor as the conditions were, though, he loved the game and in his short stay, he proved that he could play as well as any. And field better.

I was born in Little Rock, Arkansas, and just like here in Denver, nearly every alley has a basketball hoop for the kids to go play. I guess you see that where you are. But in my day, remember, we didn't have that. We had vacant lots. Now, that's where I got started in baseball. Just about every vacant lot, just like about every alley with a basketball hoop, you find a game.

So that's the way I got started, and then I worked up in school and then I joined up on a little city team there in Little Rock, Arkansas. I played just about — well, I don't remember *not* playing baseball, really.

As I worked up, I began to develop a name in sports because I played football in high school, and baseball and ran track, but baseball was always my better game and I kind of leaned that way. I later managed a team there in Little Rock, which exposed me to the public and some cities near there and a few out of state, like New Orleans. I went to New Orleans and I went to Omaha, Nebraska, with my team. I played with what we called the Dubisson Tigers; Dubisson was a mortuary and somehow the owner figured out a way we could ride the Missouri-Pacific train.

As I played longer, my name kind of became known throughout, just like football at the high school. Later on, I was asked to play in Shreveport, Louisiana, and that's where the scouts saw me first, I think — somewhere in there.

Anyway, they began to call me and ask me about coming to play on different teams. The Memphis Red Sox, over in Memphis, Tennessee, 150 miles from my home, wanted me to play, but at that time I didn't see them paying like they should so I wouldn't go.

But as a result of playing in Shreveport, I got a scholarship to go to college to play football. I was a small man [Laughs], but fortunately for me, the coach saw me in all those baseball pads and he thought I was a much larger man. Anyway, he had committed himself to get me down to Wiley College in Marshall, Texas.

Now, I did go down there and he was a very *rough* coach and he liked large men. He let it be known he was very disappointed in my size, so I had a hard way to go, *but* I toughed it out and got my college degree, which I'm thankful for.

In all this process, the Kansas City Monarchs heard about me, too. Then one day in early '37, I got a call from them. Keep in mind, at that time I was teaching at my old alma mater high school in Little Rock — Dunbar High. I talked to them about playing with the Monarchs and I wasn't too sure, but I finally left to go to Kansas City because my dad told me, "You got a brother and a sister there. You could at least see them if you don't want to play." They sent me a roundtrip ticket, so I didn't have anything to worry about.

I got up there and, to make it short, they were playing, I believe, the Birmingham Black Barons. About the fourth or fifth inning — somewhere in there — we got ahead and the owner, J.L. Wilkinson, came down and said, "I know you've been riding most of the night, Johnson, but do you feel like going out and trying out? This is a good time."

Well, at that time, I didn't care because I'd kind of made up my mind, when I saw who was playing shortstop for them, that I *might* be heading back to Little Rock. It was a man that I had played against in Shreveport, Louisiana, and Monroe, Louisiana, whose name was Willard Brown. He later went with Hank Thompson to the [St. Louis] Browns.

I knew what this man could do. I had played against him. He hit home runs all the time. I knew at that time I was *not* a home run hitter, and I said, "Here I am, being asked to run Brown out of shortstop?" 'Cause that's what he was playing.

Byron Johnson (courtesy of Byron Johnson).

Anyway, I got a chance to go out and play. They gave me a uniform and I went out. As luck would have it, I made a double play soon after I got out there and the double play I made was kind of routine to me. It was a ball hit right near second base and I just loved to go over, going one way, and flip that ball to the second baseman. And we did that; we made a double play and the fans just roared. I can never forget that moment because I *could not* understand why they were doing all that hollering and clapping when I'd been making double plays like that for a long time. I didn't think I'd done anything unusual for a shortstop.

But what I didn't know was that the Monarchs had been looking for a shortstop for over a year, they said, that could *make* the double play. To make it short, I played in the seven-inning game, which was then true of doubleheaders [that is, the second game was only seven innings], and when I got another chance to make a double play, I made that one.

When I came in then, the old manager, Andy Cooper, he came in and he looked at Brown; he said, "Well, Brown, get your glove. You're going to the outfield 'cause I finally found me a shortstop." [Laughs]

That's the way I made the Kansas City Monarchs. I played with them in '37 and '38, but even at that time we were talking about going in the big leagues. If I remember correctly, and I think I do, the St. Louis Cardinals did not want us; well, lots of teams didn't want us, but the Cardinals were very vocal about it.

So I didn't see where I had much of a chance, even though that year — '38 — was my best year and I was voted to represent the West in the East-West Game, which was similar to the All-Star Game. It was held every year in Chicago, at Comiskey Park. I was voted from the West by the players and the coaches and everybody, I guess, at that time to play shortstop in that East-West Game.

I had an added incentive. Turkey Stearnes was one of our greats. He was very particular about his bats [Laughs], but I'd always slip and get one somehow or another. He was an older player, but he liked me. I never shall forget when I was voted to go represent the West, he told me one day, "Well, little fella, here. I'm gonna let you use one of my bats to go to the East-West Game." And he did.

He said, "Now, *if* you get a hit, it's yours. If you don't, bring my bat back to me." That was the agreement.

As luck was, I got my hit. Now you might not know it, but at that time, a *whole* lot of the stars went to the East-West Game and it was common knowledge that, for some reason, all the good hitters had a hard time getting a hit. I got mine the second time at bat.

I had that bat and kept it all through the years until I gave it to the museum in Kansas City. It says on that bat, "Given to Byron Johnson for getting a hit in the East-West Game in 1938 at Comiskey Park." I donated that to the museum, the Negro leagues museum.

I don't remember the pitcher. I really don't. It's in the books, who was pitching for the East in the third inning. [It was Edsall "Big" Walker of the Homestead Grays.]

And I had my hands — Hitter's Hands — they were made in wax here in Denver and I'm one of the few that had that, I understand. A few of the big leaguers had it, but my hands are there, also, right at the Kansas City museum.

That was my best year, but I couldn't see where I was going to improve because they wouldn't let us in the big leagues. The next year, Wilkinson, who was the owner of the Monarchs, decided he wanted another team to feature Satchel Paige. Keep in mind, he was a businessman and he knew Satchel Paige would draw the people, so he formed another Monarchs team and this team took some of us with it and got new players.

We headed out to play strictly on the West Coast, which we did featuring Satchel Paige. I played with them two years and we had a good time. It was much easier than playing in the league because we didn't face the pitchers that we did in the league.

I did that for two years and then I got tired of the traveling — afraid, really, of all that high-speed up and down the mountains — so I decided I was going back home. I had a job; I was teaching school. I went back to Little Rock and I stayed there.

That was how I made and how I played with the Kansas City Monarchs.

Who was the best player you saw?

The best player? Oh, Lord, that's a hard one. I saw so *many* good players.

I can put it this way: *Some* of the best players that I played with, I'll give you those first. I think Hilton Smith, who was a pitcher for the Kansas City Monarchs, and I think Bullet Rogan were two of our greats. I think if *any*body should be in the Hall of Fame — and I'm speaking of the whole world — those two people should be there, but they're not.

I played with some good ones. Keep in mind, I played with Satchel Paige and I played against Bob Feller and his All-Stars from the big leagues in '38. Oftentimes they ask me, "What about this? Did you face Satchel?" I say, "I told you. I was one of the lucky ones. I was on his side."

But now, going over to the East, I did play against Josh Gibson, who was one of the greats, you know that; Buck Leonard, who was also one of the greats at that time; Cool Papa Bell; Double Duty Radcliffe — just to name a few. I think all those fellas were great, I really do. They were great ballplayers.

Which pitcher gave you the hardest time?

Oh, boy! I can answer that because when I went to the Monarchs first, I could hit anybody's fastball, but I was weak on curves. Chicago American Giants in Chicago had one of the best curveballers at that time. His name was [Ted] Trent, and I don't remember his first name, but he was one of their ace pitchers. He made me know that I was not a hitter, because he made me look *bad* several times.

I was disgusted with myself, but the manager said to me, "Byron, don't worry about that because as long as you can play shortstop and complete those double plays for me, you got a job. I've got hitters." [Laughs]

That made me want to hit. Bullet Rogan, in addition to being one of the greatest pitchers of all time, was an *excellent* hitter. He saw how interested I was in hitting; he took me several mornings, when everybody else was asleep, out to pitch to me to show me how to hit curveballs.

That was the greatest riddle of my life until he showed me. I told him, "The test will come whenever I can meet Trent again."

That did come months later. [Laughs] I laugh about it now. When I walked up to the plate, Trent struck me out again, but you know what he struck me out on? The fastball! [Laughs] My favorite.

Bullet laughed. He said, "Well, that's why I had you to do this, Byron. I wanted to let you see the difference between great pitchers and just regular pitchers. When Trent saw you come up there with a different stance, your determination, he knew that I, or somebody, had taught you." He knew what they taught me because of the way I used to bat. He said, "He knew you weren't ready for the fastball, that's why he threw it to you." That helped me a whole lot.

So later, the next time I faced him, I got a triple off him, hitting the ball up against the right field fence. That was the greatest thrill I had then, when I hit Trent on that curveball. I got where I was a good curveball hitter; in fact, that started me to hitting down that right field line. I got several doubles and triples down that right field line because that's the way I was going.

I loved to hit lefthanders anyway. Always did. That curveball didn't bother me because, you know, it was coming *in*, but the ones that had me were the righthanders.

Talk about the problems and the conditions.

Oh, Lord. That was rough, my man. It was really rough.

I had to make a talk in my church last night with young people. They were just thrilled; I went through all the problems for them. [Laughs] They said, "I don't see how you took all of that." I said, "Well, you learn to take a whole lot when you want to do something."

One of the young ladies said, "I don't see how you took all that and then went out there and played baseball. Why?"

I said, "Let me ask *you* a question. Do you have any sport that you like to do?"

She just told me, "I just *love* to dance."

I said, "Oh, you love to dance. Let me ask you this. Suppose there was a big dance coming up and you find out it's in an old building and they say the floor is bad and not smooth. Would you go?"

She said, "Oh, yeah. I'd go because I love to dance."

I said, "Now that's your answer why I took all this to play baseball. The answer is simply that. I *loved* to play baseball just like you love to dance. And that's why I stayed with it."

I said, "I have played when I *knew* I would not get a single cent or dime for playing, but I loved the game and that's why I think I was able to take all this and keep on wanting to play baseball, even though I didn't have a decent place to sleep or a decent place to eat." I had to pass them up because all of them were for whites. We had a few decent ones in some places.

I was not treated like a man. It worried me then and sometimes people say, "How did you take it?"

I said, "Well, I loved it, I guess. That's the only answer I can give."

But when I went up in Canada, I was treated like a man and most of the fans were white. They treated us like kings because they loved baseball. I enjoyed that and I saw that there was a different life; all I had to do was get out of the South, but I never did that because I was a family man. I wanted to go back to be with my people, and I did.

What were you paid with Kansas City?

I was paid, at my top salary — my basic salary — $125 a month plus a dollar a day eating money. Every day, the man came and gave you a dollar to eat.

I told the kids that last night and they said, "A dollar!" [Laughs] "For breakfast and lunch?"

I said, "Yeah. I could get so much to eat for 15 cents it was pitiful." They got a big kick out of that. I said, "That was my salary, but at the same time, we were paid differently. Satchel Paige was making around $450 a month, but don't you forget, he was one of the greatest ballplayers of all time, regardless of color." In my opinion, he was one of the greats.

I did fairly well for myself, considering.

Do you have any regrets from baseball?

Well, the big regret, naturally, is they wouldn't let me play in the big leagues. I think I could've taken care of my family. My kids came on later.

Don't get me wrong. I've had a *wonderful* life. I didn't have everything I wanted, but if I had been able to make all that money, I'm *sure* I would've built my people a big home.

I loved baseball. I did. No question about it. I got lots of experience traveling. It was a wonderful lesson, but it could've been much easier. The color of my skin made the difference. That was hard to take, but so was everything else. [Laughs]

But I've had a good life, don't get me wrong.

BATTING RECORD

Year	Team, League	Pos	G	AB	R	H	2B	3B	HR	RBI	BA
1937	Kansas City, NAL	ss									
1938		ss									
1939	Satchel Paige's All-Stars	ss									
1940		ss									

John "Buck" O'Neil
"Spokesman"

BORN NOVEMBER 13, 1911, CARABELLE, FL
HT. 6'2" WT. 190 BATTED AND THREW RIGHT

Negro Leagues debut: 1937

Buck O'Neil is probably the most recognized ex–Negro leaguer alive today, but that recognition does not come from his baseball-playing days. Without question, he was the star of Ken Burns' great baseball special on PBS a few years ago, and from this came a much-belated acknowledgment of Buck's contributions to the game. But even now, the average fan knows little about him other than he played baseball.

He was a first baseman and a manager for the Kansas City Monarchs from the late '30s through the mid '50s, a three-time All-Star, and a batting champion (.351 in 1946). His lifetime batting average is just shy of .300 from the records that exist. He was the first black coach for a major league team (Chicago Cubs, 1962) and he scouted for the Cubs and Kansas City Royals. He's a member of the Hall of Fame Veterans Committee and is the chairman of the Negro Leagues Baseball Museum.

Just as Jackie Robinson was the right man for the job in 1947, Buck O'Neil is the right man for the job today, the job of promoting and representing the hundreds of Negro ballplayers who were all but forgotten.

Before you joined the Monarchs, you had played all over. How did you get started?

In Sarasota, I started with the Sarasota Tigers, which was the local ballclub. I must've been about 14, 15 years old. I was a big kid, and that's the way I got started in baseball and just kept going. With the Sarasota ballclub we traveled. We would go to Tampa, West Palm Beach, Miami, so this is the way the Miami Giants saw me and that's why, in 1934, I started playing with the Miami Giants, which was a semipro ballclub.

Later I played with a semipro team in Shreveport, Louisiana; that was the Shreveport Acme Giants. They were like kind of affiliated with the Kansas City Monarchs. Just like a farm team for the Kansas City Monarchs. I played with them in 1936, and in 1937 the Monarchs trained in Shreveport and the Acme Giants trained right along with the Monarchs.

They saw me play, they liked me, and the owner of the ballclub said that he wanted me to play with them, but they had a first baseman — his name was [Eldridge] Mayweather — and he broke his leg the year before. He said he wanted to give Mayweather a chance in 1937 to see if he could come back, but what he would do, he would send me to Memphis 'cause the Memphis Red Sox needed a first baseman. He talked to the Martins [the Red Sox owners] and I went over to Memphis in '37.

Mayweather played, but they wanted me as a first baseman, so in 1938 I go to spring training with the Kansas City Monarchs, and Mayweather, too; but they traded Mayweather to St. Louis and I was the first baseman from then on.

You played for at least 20 years and saw a whole lot of players. Who was the best one?

Buck O'Neil (courtesy of Buck O'Neil).

The best player for me was Oscar Charleston of the Indianapolis ABCs. Then there was Cool Papa Bell, Josh Gibson, Buck Leonard.

Run down your all-time All-Star team.

Oh, yeah. For my catchers, I would take two; I would take Josh Gibson and Johnny Bench.

My first baseman would be Lou Gehrig. My second baseman, I would take Jackie Robinson. Shortstop — hmmm — that's a pretty good one, but for the power I think I'd take Ernie Banks. Third base, I would take [Mike] Schmidt with Philadelphia.

And for my outfield — there's just so many great outfielders. I'm gonna take Oscar Charleston. Oh, man! This is hard to do. Willie Mays. Oh, man! Cool Papa Bell. There's just so many great outfielders there. You got to think about Ruth for his hitting ability. Oh, man! You got DiMaggio. Williams, Aaron. You got so many great ballplayers.

You know, with this ballclub I'm gonna pick, I could pick another one that would be just as great.

Pitching staff. I would start with Satchel. [Laughs] Oh, man! There's so many great pitchers. Satchel as a righthanded starter, Smokey Joe Williams as a righthanded starter, Walter Johnson, righthanded starter. I would put Dizzy Dean, a righthander, there, too.

Lefthanders: Koufax. [Laughs] And Carl Hubbell. Oh, man! I need another lefthander. Willie Foster.

What about the bullpen? You wouldn't really need one with those guys.

But I would take one. You're right; I really wouldn't need much of a bullpen. [Laughs]

Oh, man! Damn! You know I left out the guy going into the Hall of Fame, the big righthander. Nolan Ryan. I don't know about that bullpen.

I'd take Lee Smith and Rollie Fingers.

Hey, I would go with that. That's two *good* stoppers.

You picked Ernie Banks. There was criticism about his range at shortstop.

Range! Oh, excellent range! He was *so* smooth, he never would be diving for the ball like you see a lot of shortstops do and then can't throw somebody out. He was always in front of the ball. People writing about range — no, no!

Ernie Banks was *smooth* and had the truest arm I've *ever* seen. I never saw him, in all those years, make a bad throw to first base.

In your career, is there one game that stands out above all the others?

I believe 1943; we opened in Memphis, Tennessee, and in that ballgame, first time up I doubled, next time up I singled, next time up I hit the ball over the left field fence.

The next time up, I hit the ball to left-center. It looked like it was going out of the park. I said, "Hit the fence! Hit the fence!" And it did hit the fence and come back between the center fielder and the left fielder and I got to third base and the coach is telling me to come on, I could have a stand-up home run, but I said, "No, no," and I stopped at third. [Laughs] I hit for the cycle that day.

It was a close ballgame. That's why this guy wanted me to run on home. [Laughs]

What do you think was the best Kansas City team you either played on or managed?

One that I played on might've been the 1942 ballclub. Outstanding ballclub.

Catching I had Frank Duncan and Joe Greene. I played first base, Newt Allen played second base, Jesse Williams played shortstop, and at third base we had Herbert Souell. In the outfield, in left field we had Bill Simms, center field we had Willard Brown, right field we had Ted Strong — great athlete, Globetrotter basketball player.

My pitching: Satchel Paige, Hilton Smith, Jack Matchett, Booker McDaniels, Connie Johnson, and Lefty LaMarque.

Willard Brown had some age on him when he went to the St. Louis Browns, but did he get a fair shot?

No! Of course not. He nor [Hank] Thompson neither one. It proved that they didn't get a fair shot when you see what happened to Thompson; when he went to the Giants he was an outstanding player.

But one thing about it is, they thought when they hired Brown and Thompson that the people would come just like they were going to see the Dodgers, to see Jackie. That's just what they thought. But St. Louis didn't have a good ballclub. People didn't turn out, so we said, "Send 'em back to us."

They were going to pay us a certain amount for 'em if they kept 'em, so they didn't keep 'em. They would've performed if they let 'em perform. They could do the job, but they were just an attraction. If they had people start pouring in the ballpark to see them like they did to see Jackie, they would've kept them and they would've played.

In 20-plus years of playing, you went everywhere in North America and a lot of places in Latin America. Talk about the travel and the situations.

Here in the United States, we didn't come up with too many hard times because we knew in our circuit where to go. When we played in the South, like in Atlanta, we stayed in some of the best hotels in the country. They just happened to have been black hotels. We knew the places to go, the places you couldn't go.

The only problem we had was like in the North. We would go to places and we would go in the place and there wouldn't be nobody to put you out, but nobody would serve you. That was the North, but in the South we knew. We ate at all-black restaurants, stayed at all-black hotels. In the North, we made reservations to the hotel and when we got there they'd say they didn't have any rooms.

How about Canada?

Oh, wonderful. No problem at all. Canada, Cuba, Mexico. Oh, no, man, you were just a ballplayer in those countries. You were a ballplayer here, but you were a *black* ballplayer.

What was your starting salary and what was your best salary?

My starting salary was a hundred dollars a month. A dollar a day meal money. My best salary was $700 a month. That was here managing the Monarchs after the war.

You've basically been associated with baseball all your adult life — player, manager, coach, scout — but did you ever do any other kind of work?

Well, yes. I've been in baseball all my life, still in it. I worked a couple of years here; I worked at the post office. That was during my managerial stint when I did that.

See, before I married I always would go home. I could've played in Cuba or Mexico long before I did, but I had a little business in Florida and I'd go home every winter.

Speaking of Cuba, did you ever see Martin Dihigo?

Yes, Lord. I saw him over here. He could play, do *every*thing. Best *all-around* ballplayer, could play *every*where. He played all the positions but catcher. I never saw him catch, but he played all other positions and he played them like a champion. You know, a lot of guys fill in in different places. He wasn't never a fill-in *no*where.

Kansas City Monarchs, 1953. Buck O'Neil's last champion team as manager (l-r): Delberto Nunez, Juan Armenteros, Dick Phillips, Hank Bayliss, Joe Douse, Sherwood Brewer, A.B. Holder, Gene Richardson, John Jackson, Duke Henderson, Willie Steele, Ernie Banks, Tom Cooper, Bill Dickey, Pancho Herrera, Ernest Johnson, Buck O'Neil (author's collection).

Do you have any regrets from your baseball days?

No, of course not. Nothing from my baseball days. My regret would be I couldn't attend Sarasota High School; I couldn't attend the University of Florida. Those would be *my* regrets, not baseball. I had a wonderful career in baseball.

One thing about it now, a lot of black ballplayers might've had regrets because of things that happened. Just say, for instance, a Satchel Paige or Josh Gibson, and we had ballplayers like Willie Wells — you know, they could've played major league baseball, but integration came just too late for 'em. When people tell me, you know, they were mad because they picked Jackie first. No, the only thing, they didn't start it [the integration of the major leagues] sooner when *they* [Paige, Gibson, and Wells, among others] were in their prime. If they had done it ten years before,

you would've seen Josh Gibson; you would've seen a *great* Satchel Paige; you would've seen Buck Leonard, Willie Wells, Cool Papa Bell. If it just happened ten years earlier.

We say the greatest ballplayer was Oscar Charleston. The greatest major league ballplayer I ever saw was Willie Mays. I think DiMaggio — great player — but DiMaggio couldn't beat you as many ways as Willie beat you. He [Mays] could beat you any way there was to beat you.

DiMaggio's name brings to mind Wild Bill Wright, called the "Black Joe DiMaggio." I think he belongs in the Hall of Fame. What do you think?

Of course. I think so, too, and I think one day he will make it.

See, I'm talking with you and what you did know, he was a great ballplayer, *but* what happened to people for being nice. That doesn't get you in the Hall of Fame. *Can you play?* [should be the question whose answer determines induction]. And I'm on the Veterans Hall of Fame Committee and I know guys wouldn't vote for a guy 'cause he wasn't nice.

This is the same thing that happened to a lot of guys now I think should be in the Hall of Fame. They aren't there because they didn't get in there with the writers because there was something the writers didn't like about him — his personality or something like that.

I think I had more to do with Enos Slaughter going in the Hall of Fame than anybody. The thing they had on Enos Slaughter was the fact that he was prejudiced. They would say that Enos Slaughter was one of the guys that didn't want to play because of Jackie, or things like that. I say, "Could he play? You got a whole lot in the Hall of Fame now. During their era, they felt the same way as Enos Slaughter felt."

While we're on the subject of the Hall, why isn't Hilton Smith in there?

It's going to take time and Hilton Smith will be in it. I think he'll be in before it's over. I hope so. He could pitch.

Okay, one last question, and this is a silly question, but I always ask it anyhow.

It's not silly if you don't know the answer.

Wait 'til you hear it. Would you do it again?

That *is* a silly question. [Laughs] Of course.

BATTING RECORD

Year	Team, League	Pos	G	AB	R	H	2B	3B	HR	RBI	SB	BA
1937	Memphis, NAL	2b-of	3	11		1						.091
1938	Kansas City, NAL	1b	27	89	23	5	3	1			7	.258
1939		1b	30	101	26	7	2	2			3	.257
1940		1b	30	113	39	5	3	1			6	.345
1941		1b	25	95	25	4	3	0			3	.260
1942		1b	39	137	36	3	1	2			1	.263
1943		1b		99	22	0	2	2			1	.222
1944	military											
1945	service											
1946		1b	58	197	69	1	1	2			1	*.351
1947		1b	46	162	58							.358
1948		m-1b	42	162	41	6	1	1			3	.253
1949		m-1b	40	109	36							.330
1950		m-1b	31	83	21	5	2	1			5	.253
1951		m-1b										
1952		m-1b										
1953		m-1b										
1954		m-1b										
1955		m-1b										

* Led league

Herbert Barnhill
"Red Cap"

BORN JULY 12, 1913, HAZELHURST, GA
HT. 6' WT. 175 BATTED AND THREW RIGHT

Negro Leagues debut: 1938

Herbert Barnhill began and ended as a Red Cap. He played for the Jacksonville Red Caps throughout that franchise's existence as a member of the Negro American League, except for the years they played in Cleveland as the Bears. In the winter months, he worked at the railroad in Jacksonville as a redcap.

Jacksonville had been a member of the Negro Southern League, a minor league that gained major league status in 1938, the year Barnhill joined the Jacksonville club. The team spent '39 and '40 in Cleveland, but returned to Jacksonville for '41 and '42, its last season as a member of the NAL.

With the Red Caps no longer having major league status after '42, the better players from the roster were picked up by established teams. Barnhill spent the rest of his career (four years) as the number one or platooned catcher for the Kansas City Monarchs and the Chicago American Giants before returning to Jacksonville to continue his career as a red-cap.

How did you come to play professional baseball?

That's a *long* story. I was playin' ball around my little hometown [Hazelhurst, GA], so this team came from Florida and they got stranded in my hometown. I made up a baseball team to play 'em and I went down there to the sheriff's 'cause we put signs on the sidewalk and [asked him] would he help us out. He says, "Yeah, we'd like to see a ballgame."

We didn't have a ballpark but we had a open field, so he went and got a plowline and we charged 25 cents for the people to come in and see us. We went store to store, pickin' up money to buy some baseballs. That night we had a dance and had all of 'em come out and we made enough money from the dance to get the boys some tires to go on the car and some gas to get to Jacksonvile.

They wanted to take me from my hometown to Florida. I went with 'em and the sheriff run the car down. We was ridin' in a seven-passenger car; we had two cars. The sheriff take me out and brought me back and put me in jail. The next mornin' I asked why he'd do that and he said 'cause my mother had passed. He said, "Lucy"—her name was Lucy—"Lucy wouldn't want you to leave here. You don't know where you're goin', boy. She wouldn't want you to leave and we don't want you to leave, either."

I cried all the way back home. I went home and sit on the porch with my head down and I heard a horn blow. There was two railroads there, Georgia and Florida and the Southern Railroad. The guy was from the Georgia and Florida Railroad, the one that go where the ballteam was playin' down in Fitzgerald, Georgia. Douglas, Georgia, 'cause the train ain't goin' to Fitzgerald.

70

He asked why didn't I go with the ball-team and I told him what happened. So he say, "Where was the team goin'?" I told him Fitzgerald. He say, "Do you know the manager's name?" I told him, so he say, "Get your bag and get in the car." He carried me down to the station and he teletyped and got the manager on the teletype and told him that he was puttin' me on the train to Douglas and for him to meet me at the Douglas station.

The manager did and had a uniform in the car and I put on the uniform and went on to Fitzgerald. Everybody was there; the ball-game was fixin' to start.

So I had to go over and warm up to pitch. [Laughs] I mean, I was throwin' that ball! I didn't have but one pitch and that was a fastball and I was throwin' it. I looked like Satchel Paige out there 'cause I was throwin' so hard. And I hit a home run myself.

We left and we come through Hilliard, Florida, and we had a flat tire. We was ridin' on the rim, and the little ol' sheriff run us down and put the car and everybody in jail in a cow pasture over there. At dark, one of the boys got away and hitchhiked to Jacksonville and got the owner. The owner come and got the driver outta jail and brought some stuff to get the car back to Jacksonville.

So we come back to Jacksonville. I didn't have any money. I was hungry and tired and didn't have no money, didn't know where I was gonna stay 'cause they hadn't got around to that. It was on a Sunday mornin'.

My profession in my hometown was a shoeshine boy. I asked this fella could I shine his shoes and he said yeah. So I shined his shoes. It wasn't but a dime, but the guy give me a quarter. So I offered the quarter to the guy who the shoeshine stand belonged to and he said, "No. You can have that." So I said, "Thank you."

I walked around with the quarter and I didn't know what to do with the quarter. I went around where they were shootin' dice. I was pretty good at that in my hometown, so I waited 'til the dice got to me and I run that quarter up to 13 dollars.

They asked me where I was from. I told

Herbert Barnhill, 1996 (courtesy of NoirTech Research, Inc.).

'em, "From Georgia." So they said, "Well, you can't shoot no dice here." I said, "Thank you."

I went in the place I was gonna live and I paid the lady two dollars for a foot tub with some hot water, so I went in there and take me a bath. She didn't have no bathtub, so I taken me a little wipe-off. I had pretty good clothes and I put my clothes on and I come to town.

I had to cross the bridge to come over into the town — to Jacksonville. I come on Davis Street and there was a steam table there and there's some pigtails and rice for 15 cents. Everything was cheap then. I went to the theater, then I was scared to go back over where I lived because it was nighttime and I didn't quite know where I was, so I got me a room in the hotel.

Well, the Atlanta Black Crackers come through my hometown lookin' for me. They knowed about me. I was a catcher then. The manager of the Black Crackers was a catcher and I run into him in the hotel. He said, "Barnhill, I been lookin' for you in your hometown. What about catchin' for us today? I got athlete's feet and my feet is hurtin' me so bad I won't be able to play."

I said, "Sure. I'll be glad to. You got a car can run me over there where I'm livin' over in Nixontown?" He said, "Yeah," so he run me over there and I got my catcher's mitt and shoes and everything and I come back.

We played the Red Caps and beat the Red Caps, 1–0. Eighteen innin's and I caught the whole 18 innin's. Tagged the guy out at home plate at the end of the eighteenth innin'.

The owner of the Red Caps wanted me. He asked me to come down to the station to get a job and he told me what the rules were. He said, "You have a railroad job here. You have a chance to grow and get a pension. You have a job as long as you do the right thing. You can play baseball. There won't be no salary for doin' the railroad. Everything will be tips." We worked on tips 'til 1939, when the salaries started. I liked that because we could file for our pension.

I continued to play with 'em. They wanted to branch out, so they went to Cleveland, Ohio — the team did. The owner couldn't sell the Red Cap name, so they had to call 'em the Bears. The Cleveland Bears. I played with them for a while 'cause I was the extra man on the board. It went by seniority then on the railroad. I was on the extra board; I wasn't a regular man on the railroad.

I didn't do much playin' with the Cleveland Bears; I was the backup catcher. That was in 1939, I think. I finished up that year and I come back to Jacksonville and I worked around the station for a while, then I went to Canada for a year and I came back.

Then the Kansas City Monarchs wanted me in 1943. They wanted to know how much I make down at the station in tips. I didn't know so I asked one of the older fellas; he said, "You tell 'em you make around about $250 a month. That was good money, but they was makin' more that that at the station, though,

'cause them movie stars and Babe Ruth and all of 'em — celebrities — come through there.

When I was ready to go, I wouldn't leave my job less'n I got a leave of absence for at least six months. The team that wanted me had to pay my boss man for my leave of absence; I don't know how much that was but it didn't make no difference.

They put me on the train and I got off in 30th Street Station. Buck O'Neil met me there; he was secretary at the time for the Monarchs. I told him who I was, he told me who he was, so he give me my first eatin' money there at Philadelphia or Baltimore, one.

We went out and played that night. We played against [Roy] Campanella and all them guys. He let me play left field. Campanella hit a ball over my head, so I run it down like Willie Mays used to do and I caught it on the hop with my back to the home plate and I turned around and threw it as far as I could and as hard as I could — one hop to the third baseman — to keep it from bein' a home run. When I got in, all of 'em cheered me.

They wanted me to be a catcher. I had caught here in Jacksonville, but it didn't count 'cause it was syndicated. They had guys that they wanted to play. By me leavin' the Red Caps and goin' to the Monarchs, it was just like leavin' a farm and goin' to the major league.

The owner of the Monarchs was a white fella named Mr. Wilkie [J. L. Wilkinson], and he called me in and questioned me and asked my name and how old I was, did I have any bad teeth or anything. He had his own dentist. I told him no. "Now, Mr. Barnhill," he say, "you're ready to come here for $250 a month. I'm willin' to offer you more than that, but here's the details. We'll be outta Kansas City most of the time. I'll give you $350 a month and you take care of your expenses while you're in Kansas City, or I'll give you $250 a month and I'll take care of you while you're in Kansas City."

So I said, "I'll take the $250 a month." By doin' that, I was smart 'cause we stayed in Kansas City most of the time.

1937 Jacksonville Red Caps. Herbert Barnhill is front row, left (courtesy of Herbert Barnhill).

That was durin' the wartime, so we had to ride the train wherever we'd go 'cause they was rationin' gas. So like we played in New York or someplace, he would give us tickets and meet us at the Woodside Hotel there in New York.

I was catchin' Satch and we played the Homestead Grays in Washington, 'cause the Homestead Grays was playin' outta Washington, D.C. We got to the ballpark early — playin' a night game — so we was goin' inside the ballpark and there was a sportswriter. She was the editor of a paper — a nice-lookin' young woman, black woman — and she wanted to know where Satchel Paige was. I said, "He's back there. He's comin' up now."

She said, "Wait a minute. I wanna talk to you."

[Laughs] I said, "I'm nobody. Satchel Paige, he's the great one. You talk to him."

She said, "No. You wait."

So Satchel came and she interviewed him and then she interviewed me, asked me why did I play baseball. I told her I just loved baseball. She asked where I was from. I told her where I was from in Georgia. She asked me what I was gonna be doin' after the ballgame. We played a night game.

I said, "I don't know. I'm goin' to the hotel and go out to eat."

She said, "I'll come by and get you and I'll take you out to eat and you can tell me all about yourself."

Satchel didn't like that. I didn't know he didn't like that. We went to play that night and I wasn't lookin' to catch Satchel that night because I had never caught him a night game. We was sittin' there waitin' for the ballgame and the announcer said, "This is the lineup for tonight for the Kansas City Monarchs. Barnhill will catch and Paige will pitch."

I was nervous as I could be. I couldn't hardly get my shin guards on. [Laughs] I went out there and warmed Satchel up. I was excited. We got together on our signals and all. He always liked to show out against the Homestead Grays. The first hitter up was a lefthand hitter, so Satchel throw his knuckleball and his curveball, which he never did try to throw for strikes. He messed around and walked the first man.

So I kinda cut my eyes down the third base line and I saw the coach down there. It looked like it was a hit-and-run sign. I give my pitchout to Satchel, he nodded his head, he threw back over to first. He nodded his head and throwed back over there again. I still had it on. It was a lefthanded hitter up to the bat again.

When he got ready to pitch, I shift over to my left side to get the pitchout and he throwed one of the prettiest curveballs I ever seen. He fooled the hitter; he buckled the hitter's knees. I blocked the ball and the runner was off and I throwed him out at second base.

I told the umpire, "Time," and I went to Satchel. I said, "Gates" — we called one another nicknames — "you crossed me up there."

He said, "You go on back there and catch. You don't know what the hell you're doin' no how."

I said, "Man, that's not right. I'm a rookie, I'm tryin' to make it; it don't make sense to make me look bad."

He said, "Well, that's the way it is."

I said, "No, that *ain't* the way it is, Paige. It don't make sense for you to cross me up and break my fingers and make me look bad. If you don't want me to catch you, you tell the manager. He got another catcher. You hurt my fingers and break me up like that. You might be the great Satchel Paige to other ballplayers, but you're another man to me."

So when I got back to Kansas City, Mr. Wilkie told me, "Satchel is gonna leave if you don't leave, but I got you a place to play with the Chicago American Giants." So that's what it was. Satchel wasn't gonna play ball with me anymore, so he had the man to fire me.

I went over to the Chicago American Giants and I started playin' with them. You had Candy Jim [Taylor] as manager. I played there through 1946. We would barnstorm and we played Kansas City in Detroit.

We were in Detroit and we played the Monarchs there and Satchel was on second and the next hitter come up and hit a line drive to center field. We had a center fielder who could throw the ball well. He throwed it in there to me, one hop to home plate. Satchel was roundin' third base comin' home and I met him up the line, thought he was gonna let me tag him and go and sit down. He's takin' those big shoes he had and he kicked me down and was gonna kick me while I was

down on the ground. The umpire run between us. We had about 45,000 there and they booed us. "Boooo!" [Laughs]

I said, "What's wrong with you, man? I never did anything to you." I found out he got mad because the girl liked me and didn't like him. [Laughs] That's what it was all about.

Same thing happened in Chicago. I was playin' against the Memphis Red Sox. The center fielder for the Red Sox was named Neil Robinson. I had the same offer as I did in Kansas City: take care of my expenses while I was in Chicago or they'd take care of my expenses while I was outta Chicago. I decided to take care of my expenses while I was in Chicago 'cause we was gone most of the time.

It got so it was rainin' and we had to stay in Chicago most of the time. There was a kinda middle-aged lady watched the ballgames all the time and she asked me how I was gettin' along. She was a baseball fan. I said, "Pretty rough now 'cause I have to pay my expenses while I'm in Chicago." I told her what the situation was.

She said, "I got a extra room in my apartment. You can live there." I said, "Won't be no trouble?" She said, "No, it won't be any trouble. I'm out most of the time. I work over there for a rich family."

So I moved in there. I didn't know she was goin' with this Memphis guy. There wasn't nothin' goin' on with me and her.

In the meantime, when Memphis came to Florida, I got him as a guest goin' out to my house. I was married and he was married, so I got somethin' to drink for us and we fixed a nice supper and he told me and my wife — he lived in Cincinnati — if we ever go to Cincinnati he wanted us to meet his wife and his child. He had a little daughter.

We had four games there. [While in Cincinnati, Barnhill discovered his landlady and his friend were having an affair.] I said, "Look, Neil, I didn't know that was your girlfriend. We're not anything; I'm just livin' there to cut expenses."

"I know. I know. That's all right. I met your wife and all and I'm married. I know there's nothin' goin' on. I love my wife and you love yours. She's just a girl I like to be with when I come there to Chicago."

I said, "Okay. When you all're in town, I can move out and go to a hotel."

He said, "No, you stay there."

So after the ballgame, me and him'd go out to the bar and we'd have a beer or somethin' with her and come back. I'd go up to my room and get a book and start readin'.

The next night we had a ballgame. We had to go to their dressin' room to go to the ballpark. He's there sharpenin' his spikes with a file.

We're out there playin' and he messed around and got on third base. The next hitter got up and he was a right field hitter. I pulled in my infield — the right side — and the hitter hit two hops to the second baseman and he throwed it home to me. I pulled off my mask to tag him and he leaped up in the sky to smack me in the face. I ducked and he hung up in my wrist, cut my artery in two. Blood was everywhere.

They tried to stop the blood and carried me to some hospital. They took it off and it started bleedin' again, so they called the doctor and the doctor was late comin'.' I said, "Tie me up. I'm gettin' weak. I'm gonna bleed to death." They tied the thing back up and I had to ride a good ways back to the company doctor — the baseball team doctor.

He was gonna put some stitches in there. He was gonna put me to sleep and I said, "No, I lost too much blood." They sewed it up and I went to the hotel there.

Next mornin' the owner of the ballclub wanted me to come into the office. One of the fellas said, "He's gonna try to get rid of you. We're gonna get some of the ballplayers to go with you because he's gonna want to get rid of you 'cause you're no more good to the team for a while."

So I did. I got six of the ballplayers; they went with me. I went into the office and he spoke to me. He said, "Good morning, Mr. Barnhill." I said, "Good morning, Dr. Martin."

He said, "Mr. Barnhill, I'm sorry, but you got hurt and it'll be a good while before you get ready. I can't pay you for sittin' down

like that. The contract says you got to be able to play a certain length of time and you're not able. I got to get someone to replace you and I can't pay two people."

I said, "I know, Doc, but I got hurt in the line of duty. If you're not gonna do that for me..." Then I said, "Come here, fellas." They said, "Yeah, Doc, we heard what you said. No, you're supposed to take care of Barnhill. We don't feel like playin' ball for you. If one of us gets hurt, you'd do us the same way. You take care of Barnhill or we won't play any more ball."

He looked at me and said, "Well, you got me, Mr. Barnhill. What's on your mind?"

I said, "Doc, you got a son in Detroit who's a doctor. He could take care of me up there. My wife's in Detroit with her cousin. I can go to Detroit while I'm recuperatin' and I can go to your son and he can take care of me."

He said, "All right. What you need?"

I said, "I need about $150." He said okay and told his secretary to get me $150 and a train ticket. I went into Detroit and I stayed there until I got well and I come back to Chicago and finished the regular season.

I'm just showin' you how they treated us. Negro baseball was pretty rough then.

I came back to Jacksonville. I was a regular man [on the railroad]. While I was off playin' ball those many years, guys were gettin' old or they retired, so my seniority went up, see. I retired from the railroad in 1975.

I grew up with a white boy. We was about the same age and he was a ballplayer, too. He was a pitcher and I was tryin' to catch. He'd bring a glove and a mitt and a ball and he'd come back in the alley where I was workin' and we'd make a plate there like a pitcher's mound and walk it off. He would throw the ball and I would catch it.

He'd throw the ball and he didn't know what it was and I didn't know what it was. It was a knuckleball he would throw and it would dance and I had to block it down. He said, "You can't catch it, Herbert." I was afraid to put both hands up; I might break my fingers on my right hand.

He said, "You wanna do somethin' with the mitt? Take it home." I take it home with me and takin' some of the paddin' out and made a squeezer outta it and then I could catch him good. He was good at it; he could throw it and I could catch it.

Come the time for them to play. They had a little league there. So he asked the manager, "Can Herbert catch me 'cause none of the other ballplayers can catch me?" He said, "No. Herbert's a nigger. You know we can't let no niggers play ball with us. It'll cause a riot."

"Barnhill's not a nigger! He's a person!"

He said, "No. Niggers and white people don't play ballgames together."

So he cried and I said, "Go 'head on. Don't do that. I understand."

He wouldn't play. He give 'em back the uniform. He eventually left and went to California and I left and came to Jacksonville. That's the way it was in them days. It was kinda rough.

When I came back from Kansas City to work, a [radio] station come down to interview me and the station manager run 'em off the premises. He said, "This nigger's got to work. He ain't got time to be interviewed."

Monte Irvin and I, we used to play ball against one another. He was with the Newark Eagles and they had a heck of a ballclub. Had Leon Day and Monte Irvin and Doby and a bunch of good ballplayers. He told me in Kansas City in '95, he said, "Barnhill, you know what? When I went to the major leagues it was a piece of cake."

I said, "What do you mean?"

He said, "Man, it's just like me goin' from a sandlot team to a major league team. I was over-qualified when I got to the major leagues. Anybody who can play Negro baseball is *over*-qualified to play major league ball. You ain't got the uniform to bother with, you got a good place to sleep, you ain't got to worry 'bout no travelin' and all like that. You don't have to worry 'bout gettin' your uniform up."

We had to play in wet uniforms. We didn't have a chance to dry 'em. We didn't have but one uniform. I didn't have no equipment

to catch with; I had an old mask that would put wrinkles in my face 'cause it was so heavy. Everything was so bad. The chest protector I had was so thin, when the ball hit me there I could feel blood runnin' down inside me. Man, it was rough. That's why I got arthritis and bad legs and can hardly walk now. They call it rheumatoid arthritis. I have to sleep on a hospital bed to keep my legs up. I played hard. That's why I'm hurtin' now.

You talked some about Satchel Paige. Who was the best pitcher you saw?

A little fella playin' with Kansas City named Hilton Smith. He was the greatest. He had the best curveball. He could throw it on three-and-nothin'. He would start that curveball at the hitters and hitters had to duck and it would go right over the heart of the plate.

You take these pitchers that pitch in the major leagues, just like [Tom] Glavine, that pitcher for Atlanta; he wouldn't be in there one innin' against a Negro ball team because the next hitter would see that outside, outside. They'd be waitin' for the outside pitch and they'd hit it to right field. You got to pitch inside to let the hitters know you know they're there.

We would bunt. We'd sacrifice. I don't see no major leaguers doin' their job. The first two men get up, they get on base. Nobody out. The next man come up, he has him swingin' away. Pop up, that's one out. The next man come up, he'll hit into a double play. That's the innin'. They don't put no hit-and-run or squeeze or all that stuff. Some do, but not all of 'em.

Another thing, I would pay a guy to throw me balls in the dirt. I would learn myself blockin' them balls in the dirt. A pitcher could throw the ball over my head, but not down in the dirt. If they throw it in the dirt, I would slap it.

And the catchers are flat-footed back there when they got mens on base and that's not the way to be. A pitcher can't control that ball all the time. Be back there so you can pivot from one side to the other but, no, they're flat-footed. That ball gets away and you know what they're gonna say? A wild pitch by the pitcher.

All the pitchers liked to pitch to me because they know I can trap those balls. They know their confidence in me catchin' their curveballs. If they throw it in the dirt, I can block it. You take those major leaguers. The catchers don't wanna catch no curveballs with a man on third base.

Baseball is not like football. Football, it takes strength; but you play baseball tryin' to outsmart the other fella.

That's why I liked Jackie Robinson. Jackie Robinson could out-think the other ballplayers. He wasn't the greatest ballplayer, but he could out-think the average ballplayer. I saw Jackie on first base and a ball be popped up behind first base. The first baseman go out there to field that ball with his back turned to Jackie. Before he could turn around, Jackie's slidin' into second base.

The same thing. He'd be on second base and the guy'd sacrifice down to third, the third baseman come up the line to field that ball and throw to first base. Jackie ain't stopped runnin.' He's slidin' into home plate.

We played the Homestead Grays in the Cub ballpark and the White Sox played the Yankees in the White Sox ballpark, and we had 45,000 fans seein' us play and the Yankees and the White Sox had 20,000.

They told us we couldn't play in the same town that a major league team played in. We didn't have no ballpark. The only team that had a ballpark was the Birmingham Black Barons and the Memphis Red Sox. They wouldn't let us play in St. Louis; we had to play in East St. Louis. They wouldn't let us play in that ballpark.

The Kansas City Monarchs were the only ones they let play in Boston in that ballpark. We played in Boston back in '43; we played a semipro white team there. They had one colored boy on the team, played shortstop, and he was great. After the ballgame, they asked Satchel what'd he think about Negroes goin' to the major leagues. Satchel would tell 'em he was the best pitcher they ever seen. He said, "You really wanna know what I feel about it?

I think you should put a whole Negro team in one league and let 'em fight for the pennant. That's the way I feel about it. Put a whole Negro team in each league — the American League and the National League — and let 'em fight for the pennant just like the white boys."

They didn't like that and after that they started callin' all the good Negro ballplayers from the Negro leagues. They was breakin' up the Negro leagues. They called Campanella; they called Jackie Robinson; they got Larry Doby and Hank Thompson and Willie Mays and Hank Aaron. They got 'em all. So nobody would come to see us play anymore because they waited for the major leagues to come there so they could see the Negroes on the major league team. They took all the stars. The broke up the Negro teams.

I played ball pretty good. I had a good solid career and I was pretty smart. I could think pretty good. If I can say it myself, I must've been a pretty good ballplayer 'cause of all of the teams I played for.

And I give my heart. I went out there and if the other team wasn't givin' a hundred percent it make me mad. It would hurt me if a team wasn't strong as we was would whip us 'cause the other guys let down. You know, when a pitcher let down or somethin' like that. I could tell when a guy's not givin' all he's supposed to give out there.

Me, I wasn't supposed to warm up my pitchers but I would go down in the bullpen and warm up my pitcher to see what he had, then we would work with that pitch.

We didn't have scouts like the major leagues has; we had to scout ourself. Like if we was playin' a team that got through playin' another team, I would get with that catcher next night and ask him what this guy hit we're gonna play against. He'd tell me and I would write it down and I would give it to my manager. Like this guy's a good fastball hitter or a right field hitter or all that and I knowed how to play my outfield. That's the way we got along playin' Negro baseball. We didn't have a scout.

When I went to Chicago I was weak on hittin' curveballs, so he [manager Candy Jim Taylor] got his best pitcher to warm up like it was a ballgame and he put a catcher back there. That pitcher could curve that ball on that corner. I think his name was Charlie Shields. He put some bats behind me in the batter's box and told me to hit that ball to right field. Stand there and hit that ball to right field. I didn't like it when I first started up, but I started battin' that ball to right field.

Who was the best ballplayer you saw?

Let me see. The best ballplayer that I came across was my teammate Jesse Williams, shortstop for the Monarchs. He was a great shortstopper. Hank Thompson was the second baseman and we had a third baseman named Herb Souell, Buck O'Neil playin' first base. He was a great first baseman; he was a sure-'nough first baseman. He was smart; he knowed his hitters, he knowed which way the hitters was gonna hit. He studied 'em; he *knowed* which way a hitter was gonna hit. He knew where to play.

I think between Jesse Williams and Buck O'Neil was the two greatest ballplayers I ever played ball with. Williams was the best I seen at shortstop.

If you were a young man again, would you be a baseball player?

Yes, sir. That was my gift I was born with. That was my God's gift.

I didn't get much education. I can read and write my name pretty good. It hurt sometimes that I didn't get enough education 'cause when I was workin' at the station I had to refuse jobs 'cause I wasn't qualified. When it got so I could go to the ticket office and make that big money, I couldn't do it.

I tell these kids now, I say, "Now you need education because you need education to dig a ditch now. Everything is computerized now and you got to have a education to get a job." I try to tell all the young kids I meet about that. Stay in school. I suffered. I been through that.

I had my granddaughter with me when my wife was livin'. She's handicapped. We had to raise her. She'd sit on the porch with me and she'd have her book and she'd say, "Granddaddy, what's this say?" I had to go in the bathroom and cry 'cause I couldn't tell her. I couldn't help her.

BATTING RECORD

Year	Team, League	Pos	G	AB	R	H	2B	3B	HR	RBI	SB	BA
1938	Jacksonville, NAL	c										
1939	Cleveland, NAL	c										
1940		c										
1941	Jacksonville, NAL	c										
1942		c										
1943	Kansas City, NAL	c-of										
	Chicago, NAL	c										
1944	Chicago, NAL	c										.270
1945		c										.259
1946		c										.198

Bernard Fernandez
"Charleston's Find"

BORN MARCH 5, 1918, TAMPA, FL
HT. 6'1" WT. 200 BATTED AND THREW RIGHT

Negro Leagues debut: 1938

Bernard Fernandez was an intimidating figure on the mound. A righthander, his size (6'1", about 200 pounds) helped, but he threw hard and from time to time had control problems. A big fastballer who didn't necessarily put the ball where he wanted to all the time would cause a batter to think twice before digging in too deeply.

Born in Tampa of Cuban ancestry, he spent most of his playing days in the North and, indeed, adopted the North as his home when he left baseball after the 1948 season. Completing eight years as a professional ballplayer, he had his career interrupted when he went to work for the war effort at an airbase in the early '40s.

He enjoyed his days in baseball and still thinks about games of 50 and 60 years ago and how things could have been done differently to affect the final scores. Win or lose, he'd do it all again.

How did you get started in baseball?

I got started around Tampa, like young kids get up a baseball club and we traveled to different parts of the city to play and stuff like that. I got a lotta interest because we used to go out and watch the Cincinnati Reds durin' spring training in Tampa, my hometown. My father used to take me out to watch them. I just got interested in baseball and that's where I started from.

And then, as time got on, when I got so I was able to pitch in the league, I went to Jacksonville Redcaps. I played with them, then I played with Atlanta for a little while. I was real young then and I was away from home and I stayed homesick, so I came back.

Then a fella named Oscar Charleston — he's in the Hall of Fame — he had a baseball club and he came to Florida and I played against his team and fortunately I beat them. He said, "Well, if you can win with this team

you got here against the team I got, I could give you a job."

My first job was $100 a month. That was in 1941. This was with a team called Sandblast Indians in Indianapolis, where he was from. It didn't last long. He moved on to Philadelphia and became manager of the Philadelphia Stars; that's when he sent for me and a couple of more players. We joined him in Philadelphia. That was in 1941.

Then, after the season was over, I went back to Florida. Then the war broke out and so I got a job. I was workin' at a air base in Florida. We used to play teams in spring training. Then I left again in 1943 and I came back to Philadelphia and I played with the Philadelphia Stars and New York Black Yankees. I played around eight years total. I retired in 1948; '48 was the last year I played, and I played down in Richmond with the Richmond Giants.

Bernard Fernandez (courtesy of Bernard Fernandez).

At that point, you were still a young man.

Well, yeah. I think I was in my early 30s when I retired. What made me really get away from baseball — I may coulda had a few more years in there — I was married and my wife, she was tired of an apartment and stuff. She wanted a home and she wanted me to be here with her, you know. I gave it up and I went into buildin' construction. I stayed with that until I retired in 1979.

Do you know any of your seasonal records?

I can tell you my highest total of winnin'. I think I won around about 10 games in a season; I appeared in 14 games. That's a fairly good season. That was in '46.

How was the travel?

We traveled by bus and a couple of times we had to travel in station wagons. Some of the buses was pretty rickety, but fortunately I can say the bus we had for the Philadelphia Stars and New York Black Yankees, they was updated. They were pretty nice.

I didn't travel the whole country, but at different times with different clubs, we used to travel out West. We'd hit Pittsburgh and Dayton, Ohio, and places like that, and on into Chicago and out from Chicago out to Iowa. That was about it. I never went no further west than that. And we went all over the Southern states — Birmingham, Memphis, North Carolina, South Carolina.

It was a lot of fun. [Laughs] We didn't make a whole lotta money, but it was a lot of fun. I enjoyed it. I really did.

Did you encounter any problems as you traveled?

Personally, I'll tell you the truth. There were very few problems that I came into. I understand a lotta the other fellows came into some problems. You know, I heard them refer to it. My only problem was like not bein' able to be served at places, but that was about it. I didn't have no other problems with nobody.

That was the only difficulty, like if you wanted to eat somethin', you were denied the privilege of comin' in that restaurant or whatever. But all in all, I enjoyed it. When we was hungry, we'd stop over and buy bread and baloney and stuff like that — cheese — make sandwiches and eat. [Laughs]

A lotta times we had to travel all night long to get to our destination the next day. I was involved in two games one day; we played a mornin' game in Philadelphia and then went over that evenin' to Camden and played over there that night.

Did you play any position other than pitcher?

No, not really. I was in the outfield two or three times, but not for no great length of time.

Who were the best players you came up against?

I'll tell you somethin'. You know Satchel Paige? Well, outside of Satchel, there was Ray Brown from the Homestead Grays. He was a pitcher I admired. I mean, I think he should be in that Hall of Fame. He was great. In fact, I used to talk with him when we played them. I'd see him down in the hotel and we'd sit and talk a little bit. He was a great guy to be around to talk with. He showed me things.

We used to go on tours with each other. Sometimes we'd go on a six-game tour, or a four- or five-game tour. Then we'd pick up the Newark Eagles. They had Monte Irvin over there, and Larry Doby. And then we'd go on a tour with the Elite Giants — Baltimore — and hit different parts of the country.

Our other games used to be close by. Sometimes we'd just play white teams that wasn't too far distant. They had to be exhibitions for us because the other team wasn't in the league like we were, you know. We had Baltimore Elite Giants, Philadelphia Stars, Newark Eagles — those were the teams out here in the East. New York Cubans and Black Yankees. We had six teams out here in the East.

In the other — the Negro American League — there was Chicago American Giants, Atlanta Black Crackers, Birmingham [Black] Barons, and Memphis Red Sox, Cleveland Buckeyes. They was in the other section of the country.

We went to Memphis and all. In fact, I played in just about every stadium in the country. You know what I mean — baseball.

Who was the best hitter you saw and who was the toughest on you?

Well now, I got to think. Gibson was a power hitter. He was real strong and he got his hits and his home runs. Just about every pitcher feared his hittin'.

I think Monte Irvin was a pretty consistent hitter. He was good. Doby — he was consistent, but he was a power hitter, too.

The hardest one on me — let me see. To be truthfully speakin', I didn't have too many home runs hit offa me, but there was plenty of line drive singles and doubles. [Laughs]

Not Campanella, because I didn't face him too much. I think Larry Doby was. He was tough for me.

Do any games stand out in your memory?

There was a game over in Yankee Stadium. I was pitchin' against Birmingham Black Barons; I don't know why this game stands out like it did, but I was leadin' 'em, 2-nothin', goin' on to the seventh innin' and

Oscar Charleston, Hall of Famer who signed Bernard Fernandez (courtesy of Bernard Fernandez).

I happened to get a little wild and a couple of errors was made. We wound up losin' the ballgame, 4–2. That game stood out; I had a lotta regrets about that one.

I felt good when I won. One particular game I was proud of was one I won from the Newark Eagles. We were down there in Richmond. That game was outstandin' for me because Newark was the world champions in 1946. They had all the power and everything and I was lucky enough to beat 'em.

Most of your pitching was to two real good catchers, Bill Cash and Stanley Glenn. This question may get you in trouble, but who was your favorite catcher?

I enjoyed pitchin' to Cash, but then again, too, Glenn was nice. But the fellow I *really* enjoyed pitchin' to was a smart catcher and he called most of the shots. His name was Robert Clarke. He used to be manager of the Richmond Giants, but he played with the Baltimore Elite Giants. I pitched to him in Richmond when I was down with Richmond. That was my last year I played.

Do you have any regrets about leaving baseball?

Yes, I think about it all the time and I think about games we played that I thought we should have won and different things like that.

If I could do it all over again, I believe I would [play again]. [Laughs] I really enjoyed it.

PITCHING RECORD

Year	Team, League	G	IP	W	L	Pct	H	SO	BB	ERA
1938	Jacksonville, NAL									
	Atlanta, NAL									
1941	Philadelphia, NNL									
1943	Philadelphia, NNL									
1944	Philadelphia, NNL									
	N.Y. Blk. Yanks, NNL									
1945										
1946		14		10						
1947	N.Y. Blk. Yanks, NNL									
1948	Richmond, NSL									

Dick Powell
"Executive"

BORN NOVEMBER 29, 1911, BALTIMORE, MD

Negro Leagues debut: 1938

Dick Powell never played professional baseball, but that didn't stop him from loving the game. He was the force behind the selection of Baltimore as the home for the nomadic Elite Giants. The franchise had tried Nashville, Columbus, and Washington, D.C., over the years, and no city had worked out satisfactorily. But Baltimore did, and the Elites were a factor in black baseball from 1938 through the early 1950s, and Powell was with them the whole time.

Powell points out early that many teams in the Negro leagues were run by men in the number racket, and he mentions bookies. In those days, these were illegal activities, but it is interesting to note that today we have state-run lotteries and off-track wagering.

Powell served in just about every front office capacity in his time with the club and he was still there at the end, when the team was sold and black baseball became a memory in Baltimore.

A baseball executive is a busy man. What was it like to try to run a team back 50 and 60 years ago?

Well, it wasn't easy, and yet at the same time, it gave you sort of a pleasure to be doing something which afforded people some entertainment.

So often, to be honest with you, it took fellows in, well, we will call it a number racket at the time. But I want to say this about the number business, or if you're a horse race bookie: you have got to have a fair record for honesty with the people with whom you're dealing because otherwise they wouldn't trust you with their money. They have to have a feeling that they're going to get paid.

Aside from that, they were the ones that more or less had, say, a few extra dollars on hand. Were it not for some of these fellows, there perhaps would have been no Willie Mayses, Roy Campanellas, or Jackie Robinsons because they kept the thing going. When

the time presented itself, we had some fellows that were ready.

It wasn't easy. We had a salary scale that was comparable with that of most of the minor leagues, I would say, below Triple-A. It was sort of in keeping with, say, Double A.

We had to rely upon booking agents and they did a good job and they made some money, too, in keeping us active. There were a few [teams], not too many, who did their own booking, but most of us would rely on the agents, depending upon what area of the country you were in. We were in the East; I don't know too much about the situation in the West — the teams around Chicago and Kansas City and whatnot — but in the East, we relied largely upon Ed Gottlieb out of Philadelphia and Bill Leuschner out of New York.

The team traveled by bus. Was it your responsibility to see that it was maintained?

Oh, yes. That was our responsibility, same as the team's salaries. If we prevailed upon a fellow to, say, leave his home in California, Alabama, or wherever, we felt, and he did, too, secure that he was going to get his money.

What was the typical starting salary for a player?

Well, maybe at 200 a month. You have to take into account that that was fairly decent money at that time.

You know of Junior Gilliam. We started him with 250 in the mid '40s. You know the rest of his story. Then we had the fellows who reached 500 to 700, fellows like Josh Gibson and several others. Lennie Pearson. Campanella got in the three-something bracket before he went up. There weren't too many on our teams in that bracket.

What about someone such as Henry Kimbro, who was with the team for a long time?

Kimbro was in the 350-400 range. He didn't reach the 500 range.

I'm glad you mentioned that because it brings to light how some of the fellows used to go to Latin American countries and play. Those fellows were *not* out-and-out jumpers; they would come to the fellow who operated the team and say, "These people are offering me 450, 500 and you're paying me 350."

We'd say, "Well, we can't pay you any more." The object was "You go and play this season, but you still belong to us," so to speak. That was an understanding between a player and team owner. But most of the onlookers took for granted that he was jumping without rhyme or reason because he was offered a few more dollars and he went to Puerto Rico or Cuba.

Wild Bill Wright came and went a couple of times.

Bill was an exceptionally good ballplayer and he was that type of fellow. He would come to the man named Vernon Green; he was kind of heavyset and the fellows would call him "Fats"; that was acceptable.

Although Tom Wilson owned the team, Green handled the business. He handled the team when it was on the road or if they were representing some other city. But in a pinch, say we ran into rain for several days and needed a few extra dollars to pay the hotel where we might be staying, then you would call on the money man. [Laughs]

Bill was that type of fellow. He would say, "Hey, Fats, these people offered me 650. I need it." Fats would say, "All right, go ahead. If things don't work out for you, you can always come back with us."

You were instrumental in bringing the Elites to Baltimore.

As a boy, my dad had taken me to the ballgames and I just got set on it. Of course, we didn't have all the things like pro football or basketball. We had no competition along that line. Therefore, I just loved the game of baseball.

We had a man here in town named George Rossiter, who was a white fellow who owned the Baltimore Black Sox. The fact that he was a saloon owner, I don't think he was allowed to operate a team in organized baseball, so he decided he would have his own team. He and a couple of fellows named Joe Lewis and J. B. Hairstone organized this team with players from Washington [D.C.] and Maryland and came up with this name of Black Sox just before the famous World Series scandal.

When the Depression hit, Rossiter had to give it up. Joe Cambria, who had been operating the Bugle Coat and Apron Company, had a few dollars, so he decided to take over the Black Sox. The word got around that Joe was kind of tight with a buck, so fellows started drifting off to Philadelphia and New York and other places to the point that he didn't have much of a team.

Then a fellow name Douglas Smith tried to establish a team in Washington called the Black Senators. They didn't last very long. That was primarily because, in Washington, all the people there were accustomed to seeing a major league team.

So, anyway, Smith was fortunate enough to get the Oriole baseball park. The team was in the International League. He promoted a couple of games there and I noticed that there was this enthusiasm in myself as well as in many others.

I understood that this team had tried to establish itself in other places, as well as D.C., after Smith had to give up the Black Senators. I ran across Smith on the street one day and I said to him — I thought he was the number one man — "Why don't you try to establish yourself in this city, in Baltimore?"

He said, "I'll take you to the fellow who's in charge," and he carried me to Mr. Green. I think he probably just saw me as an interested spectator; he was just more or less not taking it seriously.

He carried me to him [Vernon Green] and I chatted with Mr. Green with the same words: "How about trying to establish a team here?"

He said, "If you can get enough publicity and create enough interest, sure, we'd be happy to."

I went to our paper, the *Afro-American*, and asked Leon Hardwick, the sports editor, why these fellows weren't being given more notice because if they did, they would try to stay here. So, after a few words were exchanged, he said to me, "Do you think you can do something about it?"

I said, "Yeah!" [Laughs] Just like that.

So I took it upon myself. I was fairly well known around my area. There was a fellow who had been a bookmaker and he had asked me to go to certain people, like doctors and professional people that he felt were responsible, and collect his monies for him. I didn't want to run that risk because there was the risk of the police arresting you, so I started going around places — nightclubs, barber shops, hairdressers — and I started off with, "What is wrong with colored baseball in Baltimore?"

From that point on, things began to build up. In fact, I agreed to go with the team on a promise of pay. There was no set salary. He said, "If we make some money, we'll give you some money."

I said okay because still there was that

love of baseball within me. I didn't have any responsibilities of any consequence at that time. I owned my own little home.

Then I started traveling with the team and sending the results of how they were doing, and it just mushroomed from there.

You stayed with the team for a long time, until the end. What capacities did you hold?

You name it. I was traveling correspondent, business manager, scout, confidante for Mr. Green. If we had a player who seemed to be having some kind of problem, I was the one who would approach him and say, "Hey, look. What the hell's going on? You don't have to do thus and so," and tone him down. That went well with other players on the team, particularly if this fellow was one whom they were relying upon.

Did you handle the hotel bookings?

We handled that. Wherever we played, we had a list of the acceptable hotels and we would inform them weeks ahead of time that we expected to be in, say, Detroit April the fifth and we're going to be there for two or

Dick Powell (courtesy of Dick Powell).

three days and let us know what your rates are. That sort of thing.

Did you keep a list of the eating places that would accept black ballplayers?

That was a sort of word-of-mouth thing that was generally known. When we went into a town, the hotel might say, "There's a nice little restaurant you fellows can go to down on the corner," and that sort of thing.

How much did you give the players for meal money?

[Laughs] That's a good question. Well, I'll tell you; theirs was a dollar a day. That wasn't bad. I was given 75 cents since I didn't play. We could go to restaurants in the morning and we could have bacon and eggs and coffee and then have money to go to a matinee show.

Also, during that period, men with families — maybe a wife and three or four children — were receiving seven dollars a week. You could buy a dozen eggs for a dime. They were good times, particularly for us because we were doing what we enjoyed doing and being paid for it, and you eked out enough to send a few dollars home.

What was the biggest difficulty you faced as a baseball executive?

The weather. [Laughs] No one has ever asked me that before, but that's truly the answer.

Of course, we had very little night ball until someone came up with the idea of using ladders and floodlights. We played most of our games during the day and it wasn't too difficult to get games, particularly in the Philadelphia and New Jersey–New York area. The big day was always Sunday at home. That's when we made our payroll.

What was the admission for a Sunday game?

I think about a dollar and a half was tops at the time. You can't get a hot dog for that today. [Laughs]

After Jackie Robinson and Larry Doby and those fellows left the Negro leagues, the general consensus today is that the Negro leagues ceased

to play a decent level of baseball. That's not true, but what happened?

I'll give you a simple explanation. The fans deserted us. Not in their hearts they didn't desert us, but it was something that had been kept from them for, what — 50 years? There was a feeling, even among the team owners — there was very little resentment from the team owners, although they were losing something that they enjoyed and maybe making a few extra dollars. They felt all the while our fellows should have been given an opportunity to play.

Talk about those opportunities. If you were a Doby or a Robinson or a Campanella, who were outstanding ballplayers, you were given the opportunity, but if you were a good ballplayer but black, you still didn't get the opportunities that were afforded white ballplayers of equal or lesser ability.

That is quite right. There was virtually no resentment among the players because they could only say, "I wish I had had the opportunity and I'm glad for you."

From 1948 on, then, the situation was approaching hand-to-mouth for the teams?

Yeah, you might say that. Actually, it just fell apart like the stock market in '29. It was that type of thing.

Organizations began to run excursions. Maybe a busload would go into Philadelphia to see Jackie Robinson, or we're going to New York and stay overnight.

Unfortunately for Baltimore, the ballpark that we were using — and perhaps we still would have drawn fairly well — was sold. Two women owned the ballpark. They were what we called spinsters, but, nevertheless, someone made them a good offer and they sold the land. That hurt us more than perhaps anything else. But the teams were hurt all over.

The Elites final demise and the move of the St. Louis Browns to Baltimore were less than a year apart. Did one influence the other?

It wasn't too much of a surprise because the Browns were faring very poorly and this had been a good team in the International

League. It was considered a good move for the Browns and for some of the people around here who had the means.

We had a young mayor here at that time, Tommy D'Allesandro. He, of course, went out for it and that was just about it. But it wasn't a factor in the end of the Elites.

What did you do with the franchise?

Wilson died. Green bought the team from Wilson's son and when he passed away, his wife became the owner. All the league members knew what my status was with Green and the team and I think there was hardly anyone else who would have gotten league approval without my being in the front, so to speak.

I sold the franchise to a fellow named [William] Bridgeforth. There was the thought at the time that the teams could possibly retrench south because they didn't expect that type of movement to occur too quickly in those areas. But it did.

We got $10,000 for the team. That was considered a good figure.

You were part of the Elites for about 15 years. Who was the best ballplayer you saw?

Oh, now let's see. Martin Dihigo, the Cuban. Charleston was outstanding, too, but actually Dihigo could do more things on the ballfield than Charleston. Dihigo could play first base, he could give you some third base, and he could pitch. I mean, *pitch!* Actually, he defeated John McGraw's team back in the mid '30s [in Cuba] as a member of Batista's team. McGraw carried his Giants there.

McGraw loved baseball and he didn't see any color. All he wanted to see was how well you played baseball. He was an advocate long before Rickey came on the scene. There was a Chinese fellow who was a pretty good ballplayer—a third baseman—and McGraw didn't care whether you were Asian or Jewish or black, white, green, or gray. He was just interested in your ability to play baseball and he could see that *in* you. He didn't see you as a person of some particular race, he saw your ability to play the game of baseball.

Also, I might mention, Jackie was not the first to play in organized ball. Fleetwood Walker and his brother played in, at the time, what was recognized as a major league way back in the 1880s.

Oscar Estrada of the St. Louis Browns only hung around for maybe about a year [in the major leagues]. He came to Baltimore in 1924 with Alex Pompez's Cuban Stars and someone convinced him to get away from that group and sit tight and he'd be picked up later. He went back—I think he may have stayed with Pompez's team as far as '25—but in '29, he was signed by the St. Louis Browns. As I say, he only played one year.

Then there was a tremendous shortstop named Pelayo Chacon. The Boston Braves were interested in him, but they said he was just a *little* too dark. Adolf Luque, he jumped in the stands in Cincinnati at someone who made a derogatory remark to him. He was quite a pitcher.

Speaking of pitchers, as Luque and Estrada were, who was the best?

I'd have to say Laymon Yokeley. He didn't last long. Yokeley had the opportunity to prove it in a way that perhaps Smokey Joe Williams or a few others didn't. That was through this man Rossiter.

He operated a place where they sold bootleg whisky because the stuff wasn't legal at the time. It was located in Lansdowne, Maryland, and the Washington Senators—Goose Goslin and all the others—as well as the senators who were representatives of various states, would come in and have their nips. [Laughs] Naturally, the subject of baseball would come up and Rossiter said he had the best team in the world and he set out to prove it.

After the end of the minor league season—after Labor Day—he had his contacts through a well-known sports editor at that time in the city, and they started recruiting fellows to play against his team.

In 1926, I think, he brought in Yokeley from a black school in North Carolina called Livingstone and Yokeley had the opportunity to perform against the best. When I say "the best," Rossiter brought in the best after the World Series. I recall so well how he brought in the St. Louis Cardinals' double play combination of Tommy Thevenow and Frankie Frisch, and Jimmie Foxx seemed to *delight* in coming here and being a participant against those fellows.

Clark Griffith usually brought his entourage over and, particularly if he had a youngster that he was high on, he had *him* to participate in the series and let him know, "If you don't play well against these fellows, you aren't going to make it with us."

Mickey Cochrane had the same experience with the fellow that played for Newark, a fellow named [Jimmy] Hill. This was happening in Florida. And Campanella went through the same thing. Camp, having gone to a school in Philadelphia which was an integrated school, had no qualms about playing with or against white boys. When we were going into the Philadelphia area for three or four days, Campanella had the privilege of staying home. He would go out to Shibe Park and work out with the Athletics.

Coming to Hill, Mickey Cochrane was then manager of the Detroit Tigers and Hill was just one of the curious kids that loved to play baseball and could throw hard. Cochrane probably said, "Let's use him as a batting practice pitcher. Let him throw."

And when one or two players grumbled about batting against him, Cochrane told them, "If you can't hit him, you aren't going to be able to hit anyone in the majors. Get up there and try to hit him." [Laughs]

Many incidents happened like that. I'll give you one more final tip. Well-to-do whites — the Vanderbilts, etc., etc. — every year in the winter had the top black baseball players to perform for them under the guise of the Royal Poinciana and the Breakers hotels. Their job was to come out and play a game of ball at one or two o'clock. If they wished, some of them could hustle as waiters to make some extra money.

What did you do when you left baseball?

I went back with the Federal Government. I had worked with the Federal Government at the outbreak of the war, then I came back to baseball when I got out of the service at the end of '45, New Year's Eve. I put in 20 years there.

MANAGERIAL RECORD

Year	Team, League	
1938–48	Baltimore, NNL	Richard Powell served as a front office executive for
1949–52	Baltimore, NAL	the Baltimore franchise until it ceased to operate.

William "Jimmy" Barnes
"Escape from Birmingham"

BORN FEBRUARY 20, 1921, BIRMINGHAM, AL
HT. 6'1" WT. 195 BATTED AND THREW RIGHT

Negro Leagues debut: 1939

As a youth, William Barnes wasn't happy living in Birmingham. The racial situation was more than he could tolerate, and he wanted out.

He found that way out through baseball. The Baltimore Elite Giants signed him in 1939 as a third baseman, but immediately moved him to the mound because of his powerful throwing arm. Other infielders complained because he threw so hard. It was a good move. He became a member of a pitching staff that annually kept the Elites in the first division of the Negro National League, and in 1942 the team won the pennant.

Then the Army took him for three years, but he came back to play a couple more seasons before he retired.

When and how did you start playing professionally?

I just tried out for a little city league team. Dan Bankhead and I were trying out for third base and we were throwing the ball across the infield so hard. The Baltimore Elites took me and the Memphis Red Sox picked him up that day. This was in 1939.

I wasn't a pitcher then, but they made a pitcher out of me 'cause I had such a strong arm. From third base to first base, that's a long throw, but we was zipping it over there with so much fire on it, they said, "Well, damn, we need these fellas to pitch."

They were heading to spring training then and they took me right away — to New Orleans for six weeks every year — and taught me the fundamentals of toeing the mound and so forth. I just barely had turned 18 years old.

Was the switch difficult?

Not really because I wanted to do something anyhow, any opportunity that came

along. I was trying to get out of the South *bad*. I didn't like the South.

Birmingham, my home, was the most prejudiced place. They talk about Mississippi; they don't know about Alabama. I was just trying to get away, that's all. Anything that took me away was fine.

How long were you with Baltimore?

From, let's see, 1939 'til '42, when I went in the Army. I stayed in the Army three-and-a-half years and came back in '46 and played the '46 season with Baltimore. They were breaking the ballclub up 'cause Campanella had left and Junior Gilliam was gone and Joe Black, my roommate, they was taking him up, so they wanted everybody else to take pay cuts and I wouldn't take that.

A friend of mine, Willie Wells, they had offered him a job managing the Clowns and he offered me a $100 raise over what Baltimore was paying me, so I went to the Clowns with him and got hurt.

I was pitching against the Monarchs one

William "Jimmy" Barnes (courtesy of William Barnes).

night and fouled a ball down on my instep. I didn't come out of the ballgame, and tried to make a delivery and my foot gave out on me and I just snapped my arm. I finished the season out with Birmingham Black Barons.

They got a little team up in Chattanooga and the next year, which was '48, I went up there. We brought Willie Mays out of Birmingham. We went down there and played this little high school team; we played 'em a scrap game once and everybody liked the way he looked, so we brought him out.

He was my roommate because he couldn't hit me. He didn't know why. [Laughs] But I knew, so I taught him. I taught him a lot of things and then turned him over to Birmingham Black Barons and the Giants got him.

Do you know any of your seasonal records?

No, I don't have any. My first wife had all of those credentials and I don't know what she ever did with 'em. I called her and tried to get all the pictures and things that we had taken by the team and so forth and evidently she had destroyed 'em. My sister's kids destroyed a bunch of 'em. I got one picture left, a picture of the pitching staff of Baltimore Elites in 1941.

I had some nice roommates. Me and Roy Campanella, we were roommates all before the war, but we were so young they had to break us up. [Laughs] We was kids and the rest of the guys was grown men, 30, 35 years old. We did too many crazy things. We liked the girls. They couldn't keep us in the hotel. [Laughs] We had an 11 o'clock curfew and we'd get in the bed with our clothes on. Felton Snow was the manager and he'd come and check us in and, no sooner than he left, we was out of the bed and gone. [Laughs] We did a lot of things. We had a lot of fun; it was good. A lot of experience.

Who was the best ballplayer you saw?

I would say, all in all, Josh. Josh Gibson. He was a thing to see. He was a very egotistical person, but he knew that he was good and he didn't mind telling the world that he was good. And he *was* good. [Laughs] No doubt in my mind.

Who was the best pitcher?

There was a lot of pitchers. People don't know anybody but Satchel Paige and Josh Gibson. There was Terris McDuffie, there was

1941 Baltimore Elite Giants pitching staff (l-r): Roy Williams, Bill Byrd, "Jimmy" Barnes, Bob Griffin, Jesse Brown, Jonas Gaines, Ace Adams (courtesy of William Barnes).

Leon Day, there was Henry McHenry, there was Barney Brown, there was Roy Partlow, there was John Wright, there was Bill Byrd, there was Jonas Gaines. I could name you pitchers. Impo Barnhill. I could name 'em from now on, but people only know Josh Gibson and Satchel Paige.

People don't understand, too, that the reason you got major league baseball today is because they tore up our league to get players to go into their league because they wasn't making money. Wherever we played, we filled ballparks. We filled the ballparks to their capacity. Three [major league] teams, I would say, was making money: the St. Louis Cardinals, the New York Yankees, and the Brooklyn Dodgers. But the rest of the teams was starving.

They had most of the ballplayers off the Phillies and the Athletics over with the Brooklyn Bushwicks. They had a major league ballclub right there and they didn't play nothing but black ballclubs. They didn't play no white teams at all; they didn't play *nothing* but black ballclubs and their park was full all of the time.

They were tough and they were cheaters, too. They taught you a lot of things that you didn't know. They would freeze the baseballs that we hit. You can hit it on the nose and it barely makes it over shortstop. [Laughs] It's what you had to do; they was paying good money for the entertainment.

We'd go over there. We beat 'em double-headers 'cause we had good pitching. They'd hit live balls, but they wasn't getting it off the infield no-how. [Laughs]

They mostly played Eastern teams or teams from out West, like Kansas City, that were on tour in the East. They had a two-weeks break in the middle of the season and, like the Chicago American Giants and the Kansas City Monarchs, Birmingham — them teams would come East and they would go out and play them every now and then.

How much were you paid?

I was making 450 a month in '46. Just like everybody else, when you're at home you have to pay your own expenses. On the road, the team paid your expenses. It wasn't a lot of money, but you could live off it. It was more than people could make in the foundries.

How was the travel?

I enjoyed the travels when we was out East because the travels wasn't too far in between cities, like Philadelphia was 90 miles from Baltimore and New York was another hundred miles and Newark was right there. Pittsburgh was probably the longest trip that we made.

But now I got with the Clowns and it was a nightmare. Man, you was out through Texas from one end to the other. [Laughs] I just couldn't understand that. It was a horrible thing for me playing with the Clowns anyhow, because they didn't want to win ballgames. All they wanted to do was make people laugh. It was very frustrating if you were used to being on ballclubs that was trying to win.

Baltimore was a *good* ballclub. They didn't have the real great big stars, but they had a kind of a team that was a team, you know what I mean? They had players like Bill Wright. You could've considered him as a big star. Henry Kimbro, Bill Hoskins, Johnny Washington, Sammy Hughes, Tommy Butts, Felton Snow. Biz Mackey was there when I first went there, but he left and Robert Clarke came and Roy Campanella. They had a good ballclub.

You just named three great catchers. Who was your favorite?

Clarke. I think Eggie Clarke was the best receiver in the game. Listen, man, he was a *marvel.* He could work hitters. That's a great help to a pitcher, especially when you got good control, if you got good control and you got a catcher that knows what's happening. Clarke could watch the hitters' feet and when they moved their feet a certain way, he'd know what they were looking for and he'd do just the opposite.

Who was your favorite manager?

Felton Snow. Felton Snow, he was a nice man, he knew baseball, he wasn't harsh, he never screamed at anybody. If you didn't have it today, you just didn't have it. He was a beautiful man. He was one of the best third basemen, too.

What did you do when you left baseball?

I came here to Detroit and got a job. I had people here. You could get a job anywhere then. You could go across the street and get a job and if you didn't like it, you quit and come across the street and get another job that you do like and stay on it. I worked in the foundry at Ford. It was dirty, but it was good. Good pay and if your job was done, you could sit there all day unless there was some repair needed. Then you had to get up and work. The foundry wasn't bad.

I retired in '86. I love it. I wish I had never had to work. [Laughs]

You mentioned the racial problems in Birmingham. Did you encounter any overt racial problems elsewhere?

Oh, yeah. There were a lot of times we made those Southern tours when you stop at a restaurant — a little sandwich place on the highway — and they'd want you to go to the back door. I didn't want to eat those sandwiches anyhow 'cause I didn't want people spitting on my sandwich. I know how they did colored people. We had to stop at grocery stores and get some baloney, cheese, and stuff, and keep riding.

Racism is just as big now as it's ever been. They've got the skinheads, and the Ku Klux Klan is coming back. There's very little to do about it. Nobody's trying to do anything about it anyhow. Unless the government takes these things over, then there ain't going to be nothing done about it.

Do you have any regrets from your baseball career?

No. I cherish that. I cherish the experiences that I ran across, the people that I met. I met some great people, some beautiful people. The fans and so forth.

At the time, we were like the basketball

players are now. We could go in New York —
anywhere we'd go — and there'd be crowds and
crowds of people just to get your autograph
and to talk to you and so forth.

Would you go back and be a ballplayer again?

I would be a ballplayer. I kind of cracked
myself up playing football when I was young.
[Laughs] I advise all kids now to let that football alone. "Can you do anything else?" "No,
I can't." "Okay, go ahead and play football if
you can't do nothing else, but if you can play

baseball or tennis or anything, do that in pref-
erence to football."

I gave it up to take this baseball job. If
I'd've finished one more year in high school,
I'd've got a scholarship to Xavier University in
New Orleans. But I'd have had to play football. I had this knee operated on and I said,
"They'll never hurt this one again." I was
quarterback, but at that time quarterback was
just like a running back — run and block and
do everything else everbody else did.

But I'd play baseball.

PITCHING RECORD

Year	Team, League	G	IP	W	L	Pct	H	BB	SO	ERA
1939	Baltimore, NNL									
1940										
1941				4	2	.667				
1942				2	2	.500				
1943–45	military service									
1946	Baltimore, NNL									
1947	Indianapolis, NAL									
	Birmingham, NAL									

Charlie Biot
"Center Fielder Par Excellence"

BORN OCTOBER 18, 1917, ORANGE, NJ
DIED MARCH 10, 2000, EAST ORANGE, NJ
HT. 6'2" WT. 180 BATTED AND THREW RIGHT

Negro Leagues debut: 1939

Charlie Biot could chase a fly ball. He did it so well that, in 1940, when he played on a black All-Star team in a winter exhibition series in Los Angeles, he played center field and Henry Kimbro and Wild Bill Wright, two of the greatest fielding outfielders in baseball history, played the corners.

And Biot could hit a little, too. In 1940 with the New York Black Yankees, he batted .305. After the 1941 season, he was drafted into the army, where he played ball, but he chose not to return to the professional game when he was discharged in 1946.

How did you come to join the Newark Eagles in 1939?

I came with Monte Irvin. We played together on the Orange [New Jersey] Triangles — me and the Irvin boys. There was Monte and Bob. Monte was the oldest, then Bob, then came Calvin. There was one in between there; I forgot his name. We played with Orange Triangles and when Monte went and another guy named Lennie Pearson, we all followed them.

You were only with Newark one season.

Part of a year. Not quite a year. She [Effa Manley, Eagles' owner] had enough outfielders, so she said, "I'll let you go to the Black Yankees because you're a good center fielder and you're just what they need." So I went to the Black Yankees and I played two years with them — part of '39 and '40. My last year I went to the [Baltimore] Elite Giants.

The word is you were an outstanding outfielder.

Yeah, I was pretty good. I played three years and I only missed one ball. Dim lights, poor conditions — the parks were not kept up wherever we were playin'. We only got to a major league park once or twice a year — like Yankee Stadium and Polo Grounds and Forbes Field out in Pittsburgh.

Trying to remember is hard. From '39 to '99, that's 60 years. [Laughs] That's a long, long time.

But I was one of the best outfielders in baseball. Me and [Henry] Kimbro.

We went out to California — a group of us, mixed team — and played against Babe Herman's All-Stars in Los Angeles. They won the first game of a doubleheader and we played them 11 more games, and we beat them 11 games. Babe Herman, Bob Sturgeon, Lou Novikoff, Andy Pafko. Those were the players we played against, and we beat them so bad. Gerald Priddy played second base and shortstop and he was later a New York Yankee. Damn good ballplayer. He played every game against us. We beat them 11 out of 12 games. There should be some kind of record on it.

I bet the papers didn't play it up too much at the time.

They didn't. Nah.

A couple of us are still livin' that played. Henry Kimbro and another fella named Moore. Red Moore. From Atlanta. He played first base. We had one of the best fieldin' teams in baseball. [Kimbro has passed away since this interview.]

You and Kimbro were both great center fielders. Who played center out there?

He played left and I played center. And we had another guy — Wild Bill Wright. He played right. Kimbro said, "You play center; you're more used to it than I am." So Kimbro went to left field.

Babe Herman said it was the best outfield he ever saw in his life. No balls would drop. [Laughs] He said, "You guys don't let a ball drop between you at no time." We had *some* outfield.

All of us were great outfielders. Matter of fact, Wild Bill was the fastest man in baseball at that time. Cool Papa Bell was gettin' older; I never saw him play, he never played in the East when I was playin'. He was 12 or 13 years older than I was; I think he died a few years ago. [Bell died in 1991.] They say he was somethin' to see. I knew he was fast.

But speed isn't everything. There's judgment, too. You gotta have the judgment and take the shortest route to the fly ball. You can run like the devil, but you can run by the ball if you're not careful. [Laughs]

That's the best team I was ever with at one time. We had some team.

Who were your pitchers?

A fella named Barbee — Bud Barbee — and another little fella named Adams. His name was Ace Adams. We played on Sundays, a doubleheader every Sunday.

Jackie Robinson came to the hotel and a fella that knew me very well was on the team. Nate Moreland. Nate brought Jackie to the hotel; Jackie was still in school, his second year of college, I think.

And Nate said, "I got a friend of mine, Charlie, named Jackie Robinson." I said, "Oh, I've read about him playin' football out here. Wonderful halfback."

Charlie Biot (courtesy of Charlie Biot).

Jackie was standin' right there and he said, "You have a pass for me?" I said, "Oh, sure. I've got a pass upstairs." We were allowed one pass a person and I didn't know nobody out there at the time, so I gave Jackie the pass. So the next 11 games he sat right behind home plate. When I did see him, I could only see him for three or four minutes. I didn't take time to go over and watch him when he was with the Dodgers, him and [Roy] Campanella.

Campy was my roommate for a little while with Baltimore and Campy said, "You know, Charlie, you are the best outfielder in baseball. You are better than Joe DiMaggio. I don't wanna swell your head, but Joe can't catch those balls you get to. I've watched Joe play" — Campy hadn't been to the big leagues yet — "a few times, but he couldn't get to the balls you get to. Nah, he's not that fast."

You're a tall man. You must have covered a lot of ground.

Six-foot-two and about 180 pounds. I could run like a jackrabbit. You got Bill Wright and me and Kimbro, it's a wonder we didn't run into each other out there. [Laughs]

But we had our signals straight to make sure we didn't do that. Make sure if you had the ball, you call it and you go for it. Don't go for a ball that you're not gonna catch 'cause it would cause a collision. We had the best outfield Babe Herman said he'd ever seen. He said, "I never saw one like it." Gerald Priddy, too. He said the same thing, "I never saw three guys play the outfield like you three."

I'll never forget. We played in old White Sox Park—Chicago used to train there—and I didn't know any of the white ballplayers at the time. We played there 12 games and they won the first game of a doubleheader and the only ones I know that will remember that is Kimbro and Red Moore. There's only three of us still livin' that played in that 12-game set against the Babe Herman All-Stars.

They had a pretty good team—minor league ballplayers and major league ballplayers. DiMaggio used to come out there and play every year, but he didn't come out the year I was out there. I was out there in 1940. Joe never did come out. Gerald Priddy was there, Bob Sturgeon was there. Babe Herman played first base every game. He tried to pitch a little bit, too. Most all the guys are dead and gone. You're talkin' to a fella that's one of the very few that's still left. Campanella's gone. Kimbro and me and Red Moore—we're the only three I know that's still livin.'

Bill Wright—oh, he could run. If he hit a ball to the shortstop or second baseman—a slow roller—they could put it in their pocket 'cause he's down to first base before you could say boom, you know. He'd bat both ways—right- or lefthanded. Kimbro batted lefty and I batted righthanded. That was the best outfield I was ever on.

Do Kimbro and Wright belong in the Hall of Fame?

I would say Bill Wright belongs in the Hall of Fame. We called him Wild Bill, and Wild Bill was a terrific two-base hitter. He hit

a lot of singles and doubles, not many home runs. Kimbro was the same way; he hit a lot of doubles. I think Kimbro might have made it [in the major leagues]. He was a fine outfielder. Me and Kimbro, we were better outfielders than Wright.

There was another player—I think his name was Brown. Home Run Brown, with Kansas City. Willard Brown. He hasn't been dead too long. He had Alzheimer's disease. I didn't get to know him too well because he was out West playin' and I was always in the East. I knew most all the Eastern ballplayers at the time. The Homestead Grays, a team called the Washington [Black] Senators. Is that right? I don't want to get it mixed up with Cal Griffith's team. Philadelphia Stars—they had a good team. The [New York] Cubans were very good fielders, but not too much as hitters.

The greatest ballplayer they say was a Cuban. All-around. His name was Martin Dihigo. He was a little older than me. I saw him play, but when I saw him he was gettin' old. Played first base, just messin' around. He come over and shook my hand and said, "You know, you're a better outfielder than anyone." [Laughs] That guy was some ballplayer. He could do it all.

The best one I saw was Martin Dihigo and he'd slowed down. Martin Dihigo was better than Oscar Charleston. I didn't see Oscar because he was slowed up by the time I come up to the league. Oscar was coachin' and pinch hittin' once in a while. He could hit, though. He was coachin' the Homestead Grays, with Josh Gibson and Buck Leonard and Sam Bankhead and that bunch.

Sam Bankhead was a fine ballplayer, too. He had brothers, but Sam was an all-around ballplayer. He could catch, play third—anywhere. Outfield. You need a center fielder, put him out there. You need a left fielder, put him out there. He was some ballplayer. It's hard to play all the positions—pitch and catch, too.

Campanella was a fine catcher. Campy wasn't anything but a catcher, but he was a beautiful catcher. One thing about him, he could throw true. He could almost hit second base at times. All the second baseman or shortstop had to do was get there and put the glove on the bag. He'd knock the glove off your hand, that's how good he was.

Josh couldn't catch as good as Roy. No, he couldn't touch Roy. He could outhit Roy. Josh had slowed down when I come up. He started having those headaches and he died from it. They wanted to operate and he said, "No, ain't nobody cuttin' my head open." He wouldn't take the chance and it kept gettin' worse and worse and the tumor just kept growin'. Finally, he was almost blind before he died. But I saw Gibson and I saw the greatest black ballplayer hitters.

Irvin was a fine young ballplayer. Monte Irvin could've made the big leagues as a young player. I'll tell you who was crazy about him: a pitcher who used to be with the [New York] Giants. His name was Harold Schumacher. He was crazy about Monte. He said, "Monte, you should've been up here when you was 19 and 20 years old."

There were some great ballplayers in them days. I saw DiMaggio play; I saw Babe Ruth play in an exhibition. He was with Boston [Braves] at that time. Over the hill then, you know. First team he came to was Boston [Red Sox] as a pitcher and they'd write him up as a great pitcher, too, but he hit so many damn home runs. I didn't see Babe Ruth when he was young; I wish I could have.

DiMaggio could do it all. He had a beautiful arm. I always wanted to play against him, but he never came out. He was quiet, didn't have much to say to nobody, kept to himself.

The old Yankees team — I don't think this team today could beat them, not when Ruth and Gehrig and all them were there. They had some pitchers in them days, too. They had [Lefty] Gomez and [Red] Ruffing — I remember those two. Herb Pennock. Waite Hoyt was there. They had *some* team.

Bill Dickey caught all the games. If you were playin' behind him you didn't get a chance to play. He could hit so well. He was one of the best catchers, and there was another boy — Cochrane, his name was. Mickey Cochrane. They were great ballplayers, but

they played at the wrong time. They'd have all been millionaires if they played today. Babe Ruth could've told George Steinbrenner, "I'm your partner." [Laughs]

In the old days, there were only three or four guys that hit 50 home runs. Ruth, Hack Wilson, Hank Greenberg hit 58, Jimmie Foxx. Now everybody's doin' it. Greenberg would've made it [to 60], but they started walkin' him. They wouldn't pitch to him. Foxx, the same thing. And they played 154 games in them days. That makes a big difference.

When I was young, I'd make the lineup. My father would say, "What are you doin'?" "I'm makin' up the lineup for the Yankees." "Don't you know there's more teams in the league?" I said, "Sure. There's the Philadelphia A's." They had a hell of a team. Connie Mack, Al Simmons, Cochrane. [George] Earnshaw. [Lefty] Grove. I used to make up my own lineups and keep track, especially when they played against New York.

The Yankees had [Frank] Crosetti, [Tony] Lazzeri. They had a boy couldn't hit with much power named Earle Combs. He was a good outfielder. They're almost all gone now. Crosetti's still out in California. Lazzeri was a sick man; he had epilepsy. That's what he died from; he was still a young man.

What was travel like when you played?

Travel was very rough. A lot of times the teams we were with didn't own a bus. My team eventually got a bus. The Newark Eagles had a bus. The lady had the team, and her husband. Manley. They bought a bus in 1938, I think, or '37.

They had one of the finest teams in the East. They had a fella named Mule Suttles who hit a lotta home runs. Big guy. I don't think there was no team any better at that time. They finally won the championship, but most of those years they couldn't beat the Homestead Grays, even when they had that real fine team.

That damn Josh, Buck, the Bankhead brothers — they had some team. They had some pitchers, too. Lefties, righties. [Roy] Partlow, Raymond Brown, Edsall Walker.

1941 Baltimore Elite Giants outfield (l-r): Goose Curry, Bill Hoskins, Charlie Biot (courtesy of Charlie Biot).

Them guys was great pitchers, too. That damn Josh caught every game 'til he got older and he got sick. I don't know how many home runs Josh would've hit if he could've stayed well. They said he hit one outta Yankee Stadium. The pitcher was Henry McHenry of the old Philadelphia Stars. He was still pitchin' when I came up. Damn good pitcher.

Who was the best pitcher?

I think as far as I was concerned, Raymond Brown was the best pitcher. He had control; he had a number of different type pitches. Raymond Brown was about the best pitcher in baseball at that time. I mean, he could've made it in the big leagues, too, but he didn't get the chance. A lot of guys that were real good, they never got a chance when they were in their early 30s or 20s. Some of 'em could've walked right into the big leagues.

Max Manning's still living. I see him at old-timers gatherings that we have two or three times a year. We meet at different places, especially at Shea Stadium. They're nice to us

old guys. They give us $500 apiece and all we do is sit at a table and talk. Max was quite a pitcher. Him and Leon Day — there are two beautiful pitchers up there.

Leon could do everything: pitch, run, play center field, go to right field — anywhere. And he wasn't a big guy. About 170 pounds.

Ray Dandridge was on that team. He was the third baseman and Willie Wells, he was one of the best shortstops I've ever seen. He had a weak arm, but he was a fielding gem. I never saw him boot a ball — miss a ball, let it go through his legs. And all them bad diamonds we played on with lumps and dirt on 'em, Willie Wells would pick up the dirt and the ball and all and make the throw to first base. You know, he couldn't throw hard but he always beat the runner. He had a quick release, that's what it was, 'cause he couldn't throw from deep short. I don't think his ball would've got to first base. He was a beautiful hitter. Beautiful fielder and hitter. He belongs in the Hall of Fame. Monte Irvin belongs there. They might eventually put Manning in. Awfully nice fella.

You entered the service after three years in base-ball.

I went in in 1942. I played '39, '40, and '41, and '42 I was called to go in the Army. I stayed 'til '46. I captained the Army baseball team: 369th Infantry baseball team, 93rd Division.

I played one or two games when I got out. Some of the players wanted me to come back. The money wasn't there, you know. Three hundred dollars a month. It was a long time before they made 500 a month. Larry Doby, when he came in — him and Don Newcombe — they started makin' 500 a month. That was '43 or '4 [1944]. Nineteen forty-five.

Doby was a great hitter. He could hit when he was with the Eagles. He hit a lot of home runs. He was a good ballplayer. I wonder why it took them so long to put him in the Hall of Fame. He led the [American] league in home runs. I don't know why it took them so long [to elect him to the Hall of Fame]. I think he was hurt by that, too.

Who was the one best player you saw?

Willie Wells. I saw a lot of Willie. I think he was the best all-around player at the time I came up. Him and Dandridge. They were on the same team, but I didn't see Dandridge much 'cause Dandridge played in Mexico when I was in the States. Him and Wild Bill Wright.

I saw Willie Wells, Monte Irvin. Josh was the best all-around hitter I ever seen. If he didn't hit a home run, he hit a double or a triple. It was hard to strike Josh out. Anything near the plate, he just had beautiful timing. He didn't hit many fly balls, most of 'em were straight out and over the center field wall or left field fence. He was just a natural-born hitter. Josh was the best I ever seen.

Then Buck, of course. I don't think the Eagles had hitters that could've passed either one of them. That's why they won all the championships — Buck and Josh.

They had a good infield and outfield, too. Dave Whatley played right field, [Jerry] Benjamin in center, Vic Harris in left. Vic Harris later became a manager. When I came

up, he started managing. He was some ballplayer. He was about finished when I come up; he'd slowed down. Oscar Charleston, he'd quit. He'd come in once in a while and pinch hit. He coached first base.

Is there a game or a play that stands out in your memory?

Yeah. It was in Nashville, Tennessee, and the fella that hit the ball was named Goose Curry. He hit a ball over my head — I was playin' a little shallow — and I went back and I turned around once; I went back again for the second time and I said, "Damn, I still gotta go back!" so I went back one more time and the ball almost hit me in the face. I caught it right in my face.

And Goose Curry said, "You're the only damn player in the world could've made a catch like that! You spun once, you spun twice, and the third time you went back the ball almost hit you in the face."

He come down in the outfield and picked me up to hug me. He said, "I ain't never saw a player like you in my life." It was right at the base of the wall; I couldn't go back any further. He hit a floater; it was the best catch I ever made in my life. I made some good ones, but I think that was the best one I ever made. I had a good glove, I could catch the ball one hand or two hands. I had deadly hands — good hands for fieldin' balls.

I only missed one fly ball in three years of play, and you know how many games we played every year. Lenny Pearson hit it in Newark's Ruppert Stadium. He was a good ballplayer. He hit it and I caught it and I thought I had more room behind me, but as soon as I caught it I backed into the fence and dropped the ball.

He said to me, "Charlie, I never saw you drop a fly ball." I said, "Lenny, I really didn't miss it. I caught it, but my shoulders jarred against the fence. I didn't know I was that close to the fence."

I dropped one fly ball in three years — that's pretty good, right? I considered myself one of the best outfielders in baseball. Talk to Monte Irvin and he'll tell you the same thing.

He was 31 years old when he went to the Giants. He played third, he played in the outfield — left field. They put him everywhere. He didn't have no *one* position that he was real excellent at. He played short a little bit. He could catch if he wanted to. He was a damn good ballplayer.

Bobby Thomson played with him on the Giants. He was a good ballplayer. They still show that home run he hit [in 1951] on television. It beat the Dodgers and put 'em in the World Series. Andy Pafko was playin' left field [for Brooklyn].

What kind of field conditions did you encounter in the ballparks as you traveled?

Oh, broken-down fences, rough infields. We played nights, and Saturdays and Sundays were the only time durin' the day we played because nobody could come out and see the game durin' the week. We played mostly Saturday and Sunday and one or two games durin' the week, but very few. If we did, it was a twilight game, started at around 5:30 or 6:00. We didn't have no lights when I first came up.

Orange had a pretty good team up there, too. All them fellas used to come from New York and played against the black teams — Smokey Joe Williams and some of the great old ballplayers in those days. Cool Papa Bell. Cool Papa Bell would be a hundred years old or close to it. Ninety-six or -seven. I know he was way older than me 'cause when I came up he wasn't what he once was. I didn't see much of him 'cause I think he played out West when I was up. He played a lot of his games with the Pittsburgh Crawfords. They had a good team. A great team.

Did you bat against Satchel?

No. Let me tell you somethin'. I'm glad you mentioned that. I never saw Satchel Paige. He never came back durin' those three years I played. He was in Mexico or either in Puerto Rico. Him and Dandridge. I saw Dandridge play a few games when I was much younger. I told Dandridge I never saw him play but one game with the Newark Eagles and he played in East Orange. All those guys are gone now.

Did you see John Beckwith?

Yeah, I saw Beckwith play. He played in Orange. Great righthand hitter. They say he was one of the best hitters in baseball. Weighed about 230, 225. Big guy. They say there was no hitter no better than him. They often spoke of him to us young guys when we came up. Beckwith was one of the greatest hitters of all time. He belongs in the Hall of Fame.

In a doubleheader in my hometown where I was born — Orange, New Jersey — they had a team called the Orange AA. Wore real dark blue uniforms. They got all their best players, like the Eastside BBC, outta New York, like the Bushwicks. They'd come over and make $20 on the side. That's a lotta money then. [Laughs] The most I ever made for one game back then was about $10, $8. Somethin' like that.

What was your salary when you played professionally?

I made $160 a month. That was the most I ever made. That's one reason why I didn't come back. When I came back, baseball was still only payin' $200 a month. I said to hell with this. A top ballplayer only got $250 a month when I played. Campy was makin' 175. I remember Campy said, "I got $15 more a month than you." [Laughs]

Now they're makin' one million, two million dollars. And they want more money. [Laughs] Ain't no player worth two million dollars.

People can't afford to go to the games now. I never go. It'll cost a family $100 or more. That's a lotta money to go see a ballgame. They can't keep payin' 'em like that 'cause people won't be able to afford to go.

What's your all-time All-Star team, black and/or white?

That's a tough question.

During my time, I have to go along with Gibson. He'd be your main man. And Buck Leonard. And I'd put a young man out there named Stan Musial. He was a very good one. Ted Williams. Let's see, in center field there'd be DiMaggio. They were top ballplayers. Ruth would be a sub. They tell me he was a hell of an outfielder, but he had slowed down when I saw him.

I would take Sam Bankhead at second base. He was one of the finest second basemen I ever seen. And the shortstop, I'd say Willie Wells. The third baseman — I didn't see a lot of him, but they say Dandridge was the best. Ray Dandridge. Judy Johnson was before my time; I don't remember seein' Judy. When I came into the Negro leagues, he was gone. He was out West, but he was too old to be any more threat. I actually saw Josh when he was still in his prime — 1939.

Pitcher, I would say Leon Day was one of 'em. I didn't see many of the white pitchers, but from what I hear, Carl Hubbell was one of the greatest. Red Ruffing was real good, too. Raymond Brown was the best of the black pitchers, I think, but I didn't see Satchel so I can't comment on how good was Satchel. He jumped from team to team. He went wherever the money was. If he could get $300 to pitch three innin's, that's where he went. [Laughs] I never saw him, I never met him.

Those were about the best players I ever seen in my time. I didn't see too much of Babe Ruth. They say when Ruth was young, he was the greatest. He could throw; he was a pitcher at first.

Lou Gehrig was just about near the end of his time. Ty Cobb was way before me. They say he was a ballplayer, the best ballplayer of all time. He could hit three-somethin' every year. You can't leave Cobb out. He could hit. He must've been somethin'.

Would you be a ballplayer again if you had it to do over?

I imagine I would. I thought it was a good thing to be in the Negro leagues, but my father discouraged me. He said, "You're never gonna make no money in baseball." He came and saw one doubleheader. I was a pitcher with the Orange Triangles against the East Orange Red Sox. He saw that game. He said, "Everybody's cheerin' you, but you ain't makin' no damn money." And my papa would never go to another game. He never saw one of the big colored games, the Eagles.

PITCHING RECORD

Year	Team, League	G	IP	W	L	Pct	H	BB	SO	ERA
1939	Newark, NNL	of								
	N.Y. Blk. Yanks, NNL	of								
1940	N.Y. Blk. Yanks, NNL	of								.305
1941	Baltimore, NNL	of								.278

Thomas "Monk" Favors
"Family Man"

BORN DECEMBER 29, 1920, ATLANTA, GA
HT. 5'7" WT. 165 BATTED AND THREW LEFT

Negro Leagues debut: 1939

As has been pointed out before, the literature of the Negro leagues contains both incomplete and erroneous information. It's understandable, as records were kept either partially or not at all, and there were few chroniclers whose works were preserved.

Today we have very few statistics, but we also have a lack of information on most of the players beyond statistics. Names are spelled incorrectly, the players are listed on wrong teams in wrong years, career lengths are incorrect, positions are in error.

In the major Negro leagues reference works, Thomas Favors is listed as a pitcher in one — he never pitched — and as having played but one year, 1947, in another. In truth, he was an outfielder and first baseman who played initially in 1939. World War II took him for a few years in the '40s, but he returned to play in '46 and '47.

He retired after the 1947 season. He was not yet 27 and probably had not reached his peak, but a growing family and the needs for a regular paycheck and to be home so he could be a father to his children led to this decision.

How did you get started in baseball?

It came from playing softball on the playgrounds. I was 12 or 13 and they had a junior and a senior team. I started playing with the big boys when I was actually just 12 years old. On another side of town, they had baseball teams, so they said I might could play baseball; that's the way I got started.

I started playing semipro first. I went to Baltimore in '39. I was just 19 then. I played first base and outfield. In Baltimore, they had me listed as a pitcher but I never did pitch.

Do you know any of your statistics?

At the time, we didn't keep records. The only time they started to keep records was when I went with Kansas City. It's hard to say; my figures wouldn't be right.

Is there a game along the way that stands out?

With the Black Crackers [in 1946] in New York; being from the South we'd always go out to New York City and play a doubleheader. They might have teams from the South to play each other before the big game, a league game. So we was playing Montgomery in the Polo Grounds. I 'member that game real well. That's when I hit a home run with the bases loaded. I'll never forget that.

I don't recall the pitcher's name. What happened, the bases was loaded and the manager went to take him out and he told him, "I can get Favors out." They let him stay in.

In the Polo Grounds, to right field I think it was less than 295 or something like it. It looked like the second baseman jumped at the ball and the ball just kept rising. It was a line drive.

You traveled all over the country. How was it?

We traveled by bus. It was something else. The buses sometime would break down.

We were in the hills up in Kentucky. I never will forget that. I always had seen the shows about hillbillies and that's the first time I ever run into any, but they treated us real nice. They even fixed our bus. We had fellas that sang quartet and some of the fellas was singing and they brought out jugs of corn whiskey. They was real nice.

Were there any racial incidents?

Oh, yeah, plenty of that in that time. Not only in the South, but in the North. Indiana — I'll never forget Indiana. We stopped there to eat. We figured, well, we're up here in the North, we can go in and eat. They didn't say we couldn't come in; they didn't wait on us. We sit there and they went all around us. We finally got the message.

A lot of places, they'd tell us, "You have to go around to the side window." They'd serve us like that, but you couldn't go in and eat. Even in Hartford, Connecticut — the same thing.

Who were some of the players you faced?

Well, you name 'em. I played against Lemon, Newcombe. I never played against Jackie, but I played against Wild Bill Wright, Monte Irvin. The Clowns — Goose Tatum; he's well-known most as a hell of a basketball player, but Goose played a lot of baseball.

At the time, Jackie Robinson wasn't the *best* of the black players but I guess he was the most qualified. He knew how to carry hisself. But there was a bunch of 'em could've made it. They picked the right man.

Who was the best player you saw?

Dandridge — I don't know how come he didn't make it. He played in the Giants' chain.

Let me see. It's kinda hard to say who *was* the best player. I'll say Josh Gibson and Buck Leonard. I liked Luke Easter. He did make it; he wound up in the big leagues. Most of 'em were up in age when they went. A lot of 'em put their age back. Cool Papa Bell — he was something else. By my standards, he was old but he still could play and could run.

Thomas Favors (courtesy of Thomas Favors).

Oscar Charleston — the old captain. Turkey Stearnes — that cat could play and could hit. He could've made it.

Who was the best pitcher?

The best pitcher I ever seen was Leon Day. And I played with one: Hilton Smith — he was up in age but he could pitch. Hilton Smith ought to be in the Hall of Fame. And Mathis, too. He passed. He could pitch.

What was your top salary?

The most I ever made was $450 a month. That was with Kansas City.

My last year was '47. I promised my wife if I passed the post office exam I would quit baseball so I could be at home. You know, you played baseball in the summer but you still had to go to work when the season was over.

And I had a family, too. I wound up with six children.

I put 30 years in the postal service. I retired from there.

If you were a young man again, would you be a baseball player?

I would be a baseball player. I could play baseball all day and all night. I wouldn't get tired; it was not like working. I'd rather play baseball any time.

And the kind of money a ballplayer makes now? Even if I didn't make the big league, the players in Triple-A, they make good salaries.

BATTING RECORD

Year	Team, League	Pos	G	AB	R	H	2B	3B	HR	RBI	SB	BA
1939	Baltimore, NNL	1b-of										
1940		1b-of										
1942		1b-of										
1943–46	military service											
1947	Kansas City, NAL	1b-of										

Alton King
"Job Security"

BORN AUGUST 14, 1922, THOMASTON, GA
HT. 5'10½" WT. 170 BATTED AND THREW RIGHT

Negro League debut: 1939

Alton King says he doesn't take his baseball career seriously today. He doesn't talk about it with friends and neighbors, and he avoids the public appearances made by Negro leagues players. That's too bad; he is a very congenial man and has some great stories to tell.

Though he retired early he says he would play again. He had a growing family and had the foresight to see down the road a few years, so he chose job security and the benefits that accompany it. It must have been a tough decision at the time, but it was the right one, and it has worked out well. Today his children are an accomplished group of adults.

I left Georgia when I was six months old and my parents brought me to Detroit. I've been here ever since.

I first started off playing baseball when I was about 15 years old. I started playing with a few pickup teams, you know, sandlot teams. We played local ball, and then in 1942, I started playing with the Motor City Giants; that was a team in Detroit that was affiliated with the Negro National League. The other team was the Detroit Wolves; it came after the Motor City Giants.

I played from '41 to '44; I went in the service then. I stayed in the service a year and I come out in '45 and I played with the Wolves from '45 'til they went in extinction. [Laughs] They didn't last long after Jackie come in.

We played exhibition games with Jackie Robinson in 1947 against his barnstorming team. We won both games. [Laughs]

Some teams traveled a lot. Did your teams?

No, we didn't travel that much. We played most of our games on Saturdays and

Sundays. We traveled a few times, like out in New York and Louisville and Atlanta. We'd go down and play Atlanta Black Crackers in Ponce de Leon Stadium before they tore it down. And Nashville and Knoxville and places like that.

I also played when I was about 16, 17 with the Zulu Giants. [Laughs] They was at the end of the road then.

Does a game stand out?

We were playing Satchel and his All-Stars with the Motor City Giants several times. We beat Satchel three or four times. [Laughs] Satchel would only come in in the seventh or eighth in real close games and close it out. And we got him in the first game of a doubleheader. He was so mad, he started the second game. [Laughs]

Who were some of your teammates?

There was Ron Teasley and Cecil Kaiser, Red House, the Dean brothers, Wilbur King. He played second base and I played shortstop. At one time, they rated us one of the best com-

1943 Semipro League Champions, Detroit. Back row: Alton King (fifth from left), Marshall Williams (uncle of Hall of Famer Billy Williams, seventh from left, later played with Homestead Grays). Front row: Buddy Brown (third from left, played with New York Black Yankees), Cecil Kaiser (fifth from left, played with Homestead Grays), Wilbur King (sixth from left, later played baseball with Cleveland Buckeyes and basketball with Harlem Globetrotters) (courtesy of Alton King).

binations in the Midwest. [Dave] Hoskins, the guy who pitched for the Cleveland Indians, played outfield for us, but he never pitched.

Who was the best player you came across?

You might as well say Satchel. [Laughs] We played the Grays, too. They had Buck and Josh, [Sam] Bankhead, and that group. That was the best team I think I ever played against.

I was with Peanuts [Davis] — used to pitch for the Clowns — on an All-Star team. We played 'em up in Hamilton, Ontario — up in Canada — and I saw Josh hit one one night off of Peanuts. He hit it about 450 feet and it started rising. At the 450 mark, it started going up. He could play. We had 'em beat 'til the seventh inning and we run out of gas.

You remember a fella named Charley Justice? I played with him, too, but he was more known for softball. He played with Tip Top Taylor [a softball touring team].

What were you paid?

First they started paying us by percentage baseball. We would probably knock down sometimes 45 to 50 dollars a day. We had good crowds. When Satchel come in, we'd knock down maybe 185 to 190 dollars a day. When Jackie come in, they got slick; they paid us a regular salary: $50 flat a game. [Laughs] And pocket the rest. Jackie, he got 2500.

After that, they started paying us by the games. They'd pay us $30 a day, but back then $30 a day was a lot of money. You were only making $40 a week in a factory.

We got meal money only when we went out of town. We didn't go that often with the teams out of Detroit. Most of our games were played here in Detroit. We could draw good crowds. We beat Birmingham Black Barons; they had just won the Negro championship.

We traveled mostly by cars. We traveled by train several times. The only reason we traveled by train, the bus broke down. [Laughs] We was going up to Buffalo and the bus broke down somewhere between there and [St.] Catherine's, Ontario, and we were stranded out there on the highway. No buses were running up that way then. A guy come by in a cattle truck and he had some manure and stuff on it in the back. He took us all the way into Buffalo.

We got into Buffalo and the people were standing outside the stadium wondering where in the heck we've been 'cause we were late. We explained and they started laughing—you know, these fools coming in in a cattle car. We beat 'em a doubleheader. [Laughs]

That's when we started riding the train from there. We went into Pittsburgh and we beat the Crawfords a doubleheader, too.

You spent most of your playing days up North. How were the conditions up there for black teams?

It was not bad. The only time that we had it bad was in 1943, I think. We wasn't playing in the league then; they had a league here called the Federation and the Recreational League. You go in the tournament and you advance and play for the World's Tournament in amateur baseball.

The team that we was playing was supposed to beat us. They were all white and we had a mixed team. That's the first time they ever had a mixed team here in Detroit. We beat the white team.

They were so sure the white team was going to beat us that they made reservations ahead of time for the hotel for the white team. We got there and we couldn't stay in the hotel. This was in Battle Creek, Michigan. We ended up staying in a house of prostitution. [Laughs] That's the truth. That's the only place we could get because the war was going on.

One year we were going from Detroit down to Nashville and Kentucky and we got on the train and the conductor asked us, "How come you niggers ain't in the Army."

Down in Knoxville—I had never been in the deep South since I was a little kid—we stopped in a bus station and I went in the restaurant and the people asked where the hell was I going. I said, "I'm gonna get me a sandwich." They said, "No, you can't eat in here.

You go 'round to the back." There was a little hole in the wall and they served the food out there. I said, "Hell, I don't want none. I ain't hungry." But we didn't have no trouble in the North.

I was one of the first Negroes that played in Wrigley Field. We couldn't change at the park. We couldn't change in none of the parks that we played in; we had to change in the hotel or some people's house that we knew. Couldn't use the showers, couldn't use the locker room.

When I was with the Zulus, we were going to Farmington, Missouri, and one of the cars broke down, so we had to double up in the car. We got down to Farmington and we were playing one of the New York Yankees farm teams. It was a white team, of course.

Soon as we got out of the car—I never heard this before in my life—the people said, "Where in the hell you niggers been?" [Laughs] We got in the park and it was crammed and I looked for the black people. They was *way* down the right field foul line.

I played against some minor leaguers and major leaguers in Toledo. We would go over to Toledo quite a bit and play. We'd go over there and play teams like Cleveland Buckeyes and the Clowns and teams like that because Toledo didn't have a good team. At that time, we had one of the better teams in the Midwest because of the war and most of the people that wasn't in major league baseball were working in the factories.

How did the team stay together during the war?

It was easy. The bad part about it, in 1943 or '4, Kansas City raided us. Did you ever hear of a fella named Bob Johnson? He's dead now. They took him and the two Deans. Thomas Dean, he used to play with the Chicago American Giants. They took Wilbur [King] and Kaiser and that broke up the team.

Why didn't you go?

I had a family. I had a chance to go with Atlanta, Pittsburgh, and several other teams. Even Saperstein wanted me to go up in Manitoba, but the catch was, he wanted ten percent of what I made. [Laughs] They was going to pay 300 a month and Sap wanted ten percent of that. I had a family — two kids. I married young.

One of my kids is a schoolteacher, one is a vice-president of a bank, one works for the purchasing department at General Motors, and I have two sons out in California. My oldest boy was drafted for professional basketball. He played with Long Beach State when Tark [Jerry Tarkanian] was the coach. He was drafted in his junior year. He got cut the last day with Denver. He only scored 30-some points a game in junior college. His first name is Lamont.

What did you do when you left baseball?

I worked in the factory for General Motors. I called it a "professional babysitter"; I ended up being a production supervisor. [Laughs] I retired after 30 years. That's more than 20 years ago now.

How long did you play ball in all?

Well, they say when they give you over two dollars, that's professional baseball. I started when I was 15; at 15, I was making 'bout three or four dollars a game. [Laughs]

I'd've played for nothing because I didn't know any better. I played about ten to 12 years.

Any regrets?

Yeah. I was born about ten years too soon.

I'm glad I stopped chasing that little white ball when I did. Most of the fellas stopped playing ball when they was about 35 or 40 years old and when they got through playing, they didn't have no job security. I was lucky; I quit early and went into the factory and at least I have paid insurance and a pension and stuff like that. I'm glad that I stopped playing that early.

I played a little amateur ball after that, but there was no more games on the road or going out of town or nothing like that.

If you went back, would you play baseball again?

Yeah. If I could've come along even maybe five years later, I could've gone to the minors or even to the majors. Teasley, when he went up, he was playing with us. He's about three or four years younger than I am. They were mostly interested in kids 18 or 19 years old then.

BATTING RECORD

Year	*Team, League*	*Pos*	*G*	*AB*	*R*	*H*	*2B*	*3B*	*HR*	*RBI*	*SB*	*BA*
1939	Zulu Cannibals, ind.	inf										
1942	Motor City Giants, ind.	ss										
1943		ss										
1944		ss										
1945	Detroit Wolves, ind.	ss										
1946		ss										
1947		ss										

Albert "Buster" Haywood
"An Eye for Talent"

BORN JANUARY 12, 1910, PORTSMOUTH, VA
HT. 5'8" WT. 160 BATTED AND THREW RIGHT

Negro Leagues debut: 1940

Buster Haywood was a good defensive, strong-armed, hustling catcher for more than a decade in the Negro leagues, primarily with the Clowns in that club's nomadic tenure (Miami, Cincinnati, Indianapolis), but, although he was an occasional All-Star and batted .300 or better a couple of seasons, his place in history is reserved for an incident in his managerial career.

At the helm of the Indianapolis Clowns from 1948 through 1954, Haywood fielded some good teams. From 1950–52 and again in 1954, his teams had the best record in the Eastern Division of the Negro American League. In seven seasons as the Clowns' manager, he compiled a 252–215 record in league play.

Even so, Haywood's claim to fame lies not in anything he did, but in what he recognized. In 1952, while the Clowns were playing in Mobile, Alabama, he brought a scrawny, teen-aged shortstop to the team. The kid wasn't with them long, though, because scouts from major league clubs soon saw and recognized what Haywood had already seen as Hank Aaron's first manager.

You started with the Birmingham Black Barons in 1940 at the age of 30. Where had you been before that?

Playing ball in my hometown. Portsmouth, Virginia. Semipro.

How did the Black Barons acquire you?

A guy came around and saw us play and he signed me for Birmingham. A guy from Memphis, Tennessee, had the team in Birmingham. An undertaker.

I only stayed a short time. I left and went to the *Denver Post* tournament 'cause they wasn't payin' no money. I wanted to stay there but they wasn't payin' me nothin'.

I went to the *Denver Post* tournament and played with the Indianapolis Clowns — the Miami Clowns at that time. We won it. I was voted Most Valuable Player out there.

You were essentially a Clown for most of the rest of your career. How long were you with them altogether?

I don't know. Quite a while. I can't remember now. The Miami Ethiopian Clowns. They moved a lot and I just went with 'em when they moved.

You were not a big man for a catcher.

I had a good arm, though. I could catch, too. I caught Satchel, caught Don Newcombe, caught Joe Black. Sad Sam Jones. I caught all of 'em.

How did you handle it when a big man — say a Wild Bill Wright or a Luke Easter — was coming home?

If you don't get the ball in time, it's stupid to even block the plate. When you get the ball in time, let him come. If he slides, you jump on top of him.

A small man can hurt you at home plate

Buster Haywood (courtesy of Albert Haywood).

if you don't get that ball in time. He's got the force to hit you and you're standin' still. I didn't have no trouble.

Who was the best baserunner you came up against?

Cool Papa Bell. Sam Jethroe. I threw 'em out, but if they get the jump on the pitcher, you can't throw 'em out. Then there's nothin' you can do. They can't outrun that ball — I don't care how fast they can run.

If you got a good arm, you can get 'em, but if they get a big lead on you ain't no use to throw if he can fly like Jethroe. He could run and if he's got a big lead there ain't no need to throw. If you hold him close to that bag, there's a chance 'cause he can't outrun that ball.

You were selected for the All-Star game a couple of times. How did you do?

They had Quincy Trouppe and all them big guys, but I was bullpen catcher.

There were a lot of good catchers in the Negro leagues when you played.

Oh, yeah. Bill Cash was playin' with the Philadelphia Stars. Larry Brown played with the Memphis Red Sox. He didn't have a good throwin' arm, though, but he got rid of the ball real quick.

There was Cash and myself and Quincy Trouppe. We had better catchers in our league than there was in the major leagues. Black ballplayers did a lotta runnin' and if you didn't have a good arm you wouldn't do nothin'.

Who was the best catcher when you played?

Larry Brown was a good catcher. Quincy Trouppe was a good catcher, but he was big — he couldn't move around good. I could catch as good as any of 'em. I was voted Most Valuable Player of the *Denver Post* tournament.

Black teams played All-Star teams out here on the [West] Coast. We had Satchel Paige pitchin', and Sad Sam Jones. We had a good ballclub.

Who was the best pitcher?

They all were good, but Satchel was the best pitcher — there ain't no 20 ways about that.

If you had to choose four starting pitchers, who would they be?

Well, you have to take Satchel, and Sad Sam Jones and Joe Black. Joe Black was a good pitcher. We had good teams, we had top-notch teams with good pitchers. They had to be to play in that league. Verdell Mathis was the best lefthander.

Who was the best hitter?

You had some guys could hit long balls, some guys could hit singles and steal bases, so it's pretty hard to judge that.

How were the travel conditions?

It was rough. Some teams had good buses, some teams had raggedy buses. We had a good bus.

What were the conditions like as you traveled through the South?

You stayed in black hotels, boardin' houses. You couldn't stay in no white hotel down there. At that time, we had nice colored hotels down in the South; we had good hotels down there. In small towns, we stayed in boardin' houses or people would take you in for $2 a night or $3 a night a man.

There weren't no racial problems 'cause you know what's gonna happen. Just abide by the rules and regulations of the area; you didn't go there to try to change nothin'.

How much did you get for meal money?
Two dollars a day.

What were the salaries like?
Oh, it was accordin' to the ability of the ballplayer, accordin' to your status on the team. Are you a good ballplayer? You see, like Sam Jethroe and Quincy Trouppe — guys like that. My top salary was about $350 a month. At that time, that was pretty good.

How many games did you play in a season?
We played every day it didn't rain. All summer long. Sometime we'd have a off day, but very few.

You remember Abe Saperstein? He was bookin' us, so we had a schedule. He'd send a schedule so we'd know where we were gonna play the next day.

You eventually became a manager. How did you like that?
I enjoyed it. That ain't no problem. I had Hank Aaron; I had good ballplayers.

You were Hank's first manager.
Right. Seventeen years old. He could hit. When it came to hittin' that ball, there weren't no learnin' him nothin', either. When we had him down South in Mobile, Alabama — when we got him he was ready. He was a skinny kid but he had good wrists. I never had no trouble with him at all.

Is there one game that stands out in your memory?
When we won the *Denver Post* tournament, that stands out in my mind. We was playin' a team from Oklahoma. They had a couple of major league ballplayers, and minor league, too.

Other than that, does anything stand out?
We played the white major league All-Star team out here in California. Bob Feller and Bob Lemon and them. We cut 'em a duster — Satchel and Don Newcombe. We had a good ballclub. It don't make no difference 'cause you're in the majors; we had a good ballclub.

I played with Jackie Robinson's All-Stars. Jackie played with us on the Coast. He was great. Great, great. No 22 ways about it. We were playin' and Jackie was stealin' bases and them guys said, "You act like you're playin' in the World Series," and Jackie said, "That's what I want to do."

When you started playing, did any of you think the major leagues would open the doors to you?
No. See, we used to play a lotta white ballclubs in the South and they saw the drawin' card they had, so they say you gotta do somethin'. So then we started playin' against the major league All-Stars.

We beat 'em two-thirds of the time. We had Satchel. Satchel said if we didn't get no runs, they wasn't gonna get none. He was amazin'.

I was the smallest catcher in baseball. I'd throw to second base like my arm was sore in practice, then when they'd get on base it was a different story. You had to jive them ballplayers so they'd think you couldn't throw. In our league, if you couldn't do nothin' you wouldn't play.

Me and Buck Leonard played ball against one another. He lived in Rocky Mount [North Carolina], I lived in Portsmouth, Virginia, and we played 'em every holiday. Rocky Mount and Portsmouth Black Swans. Then Buck went up, then I went up, too. Buck went up before I did.

Was he the best first baseman?
He was a good one, but you had Jim West and another — I forget his name now. They had good ballplayers in the league — Cool Papa Bell playin' outfield, Ray Dandridge, Bus Clarkson.

King Tut was with the Clowns.
He didn't play no ball. He was a clown. I was there when he was there; he was clownin' when he played first base. He came there with

Miami. He could play first base, but it got to where he was just doin' the clownin' on the team.

You ended your career with Memphis in 1955. What kind of ballplayer was Bubba Hyde?

He was a good ballplayer. Red Longley played with Memphis, and Casey Jones. He was a catcher, but he couldn't throw good. He was a good catcher.

I had a good arm. I didn't care nothin' 'bout runnin' on me. Cool Papa Bell — you couldn't catch him, I don't give a damn who you were. Cool Papa Bell could run like a deer. If he got a jump on the pitcher, there ain't nothin' you could do.

Do you know your lifetime batting average?

Two-fifty, -forty-five, or somethin' like that.

Every ballplayer thinks he's a hell of a ballplayer. He wants a lotta publicity. If he was a hundred-and-fifty hitter, he'll tell you he batted .300. I could throw, I was a good catcher. I caught Satchel, caught Sad Sam Jones, caught Don Newcombe, caught Joe Black — I caught all of 'em. Every ballplayer's gonna build himself up and he didn't do

nothin.' I was a .240–.250 hitter. That's all. There were some .300 hitters, like Cool Papa Bell.

People read what these ballplayers say — they want to give themselves a big name — and the people who read it don't know no different. I read it and I know the good ballplayers and them that couldn't play. Like Sam Jethroe, Cool Papa Bell, Josh, Buck Leonard, Satchell — they were outstandin' ballplayers.

Like me. I was a .250 hitter, but I was a damn good catcher. I could catch and I could throw.

Don't nobody know, that's why they say it. Nobody kept scores. You play in Chicago, a sportswriter'll be there, but you play in the other towns — the smaller towns — no sportswriter'd be there. The sportswriters were in the cities like Chicago, Cincinnati, New York, Philadelphia, but after you get outta that you ain't got none.

Would you be a ballplayer again if you were a young man?

Sure, I'd play it again. I loved it.

BATTING RECORD

Year	Team, League	Pos	G	AB	R	H	2B	3B	HR	RBI	SB	BA
1940	Birmingham, NAL	c										
	Ethiopian Clowns, ind.	c										
1941	Ethiopian Clowns, ind.	c										
1942	N.Y. Cubans, NNL	c											.211
1943	Cincinnati, NAL	c										
1944	Cinc./Ind., NAL	c										.270
1945	Cinc./Ind., NAL	c										.152
1946	Indianapolis, NAL	c										.223
1947		c										
1948		c–m										.267
1949		c–m										.300
1950		c–m										.307
1951		c–m										
1952		c–m										
1953		c–m										
1954	Memphis, NAL	c										

Clinton "Casey" Jones
"Quite an Arm"

BORN JULY 19, 1918, MISSISSIPPI
DIED NOVEMBER 17, 1998, MEMPHIS, TN
HT. 6'2" WT. 195 BATTED LEFT AND THREW RIGHT

Negro League Debut: 1940

How many catchers can you name who threw out *eight* baserunners in one game? Until you read that title up there, you probably couldn't name any, but now you can. In one game, Casey Jones of the Negro American League's Memphis Red Sox threw out eight members of the Brooklyn Bushwicks as they attempted to steal.

The Bushwicks weren't just a bunch of middle-aged men having a little fun on weekends. The team was probably the best semipro club ever assembled, being made up of players just out of professional ball or, in a couple of cases, players who were on their way *to* professional ball. Year after year, the Bushwicks lineup was dotted with former major leaguers.

And the Bushwicks thought they could run on Jones's arm. He showed them they couldn't.

Jones spent 16 years (1940–55) in the Negro leagues, all with Memphis. During that time many baserunners fell to his strong arm. He also did damage to the opposition with his bat. He was a powerful, dead pull hitter who had a .635 slugging average one season and played in the 1950 and 1953 All-Star games.

I started from school playin' — rag ball, you might say. I could run faster than anybody on the team and throw the ball out of sight. My daddy was the manager of the ball team in The Plant, Mississippi, which was called the First Nine. I played with the second team — the Second Nine. It had to be in the '30s.

I played infield, outfield, catcher — everything but pitcher. I never felt like I needed to pitch; I didn't want to. I figured there was a lotta work in it. I liked catchin'.

My first catchin' job was with the farm team down in The Plant where I was raised at. One Sunday we went to the ballgame where my dad was playin' and there wasn't but one catcher on the team and he came out there in a bleached white suit and said he wasn't gonna get his clothes dirty. My daddy asked me if I wanted to catch and I said yes. I had been messin' around with catching.

Later I come over here to Memphis from Mississippi and started playin' around the town. I was recommended to the minor league ballclub in '40. The owner of the Red Sox sent me to Cleveland, Ohio, to meet the team on the All-Star weekend and I caught my first game.

You couldn't guess how we lost the ballgame. On a passed ball. My first day and I let a passed ball get by me. I let that ball get by me and I will never forget I missed that ball in my first minor league game.

Larry Brown was the manager and the

Casey Jones (courtesy of Clinton Jones).

catcher. There were some home boys that played when we were at home but mostly I was behind Brown 'til he retired. Brown never took his mask off to catch foul balls.

I was with the team the whole time, except during fall seasons. I played 'til '55. I played with one team for 16 years. I played all around through the States and during off seasons I played in Puerto Rico, Cuba, Mexico, and Dominican Republic.

We played the boys up in Bushwick — them young boys outta New York. I had an arm like a bullet. I threw out eight one night there. They tried 'til they couldn't. I got every one of 'em — eight in a row. All the boys, they trapped me and gathered around me after the game was over, touched my fingers and arm and wanted to know what did I have to throw with. That ball was goin' down there just like a bullet. I got a thrill outta that.

Another thrill I got, I got it out in Chicago in '53 in the All-Star Game. I hit two home runs. [Earl] Bumpus, a lefthanded

pitcher, was pitchin' — a big lefthander, a sidewinder. He'd come down the first base line like he was gonna hit you in the back. I hit from the left side. He threw down that line and my right foot went outta the box toward first base and I waited up there with my bat. I had power in that bat up there and that ball went up in the upper deck.

The next innin' I was up, they put his righthander in — Bobbie Fields. He throws me a line drive and it went in the lower deck.

We left the '53 All-Star Game in Chicago on the Fourth of July. I had made connections with a team down in South America. They sent me a ticket and money. I couldn't get away from the team in Chicago. I was gonna leave in Minnesota but I couldn't get away there, either, and I went on to Winnipeg, Canada. I got up there and first time up, I hit a line drive over the fence for a home run. That week I was hittin' pretty good.

I went to New York from Winnipeg, Canada, and from New York I went to South America. I played down there all of September. I didn't hit a home run. Couldn't get the ball level enough. I stayed down there about 20 days. I couldn't hit the ball level enough; I hit the ball high — up above the stand. The wind would take the ball and bring the ball back, like that park they had out in Denver. I hit several home runs out of the park in Denver. But there was no wind. There was a big, deep hole there and the fence was built down around in there.

I had a good time down in Dominican Republic. Went down there and stayed a month and got $1500 a month. That was pretty good change. That was '53-'54.

Who was the best pitcher you caught?

Verdell Mathis. Oughtta be in the Hall of Fame. I don't know why he couldn't get in the Hall of Fame. He had superb control and he was an all-around athlete. He could hit. He stayed in the game for his hittin'. When he wasn't pitchin' he played in the games a lotta times. Or if a game was really needed, he would go out and relieve somebody. The only thing, he used his arm too much and hurt it.

Who was the best pitcher you batted against?

Well, let me see now. We had some good pitchers. Satchel Paige and Hilton Smith were good. Kelly Searcy was good, and Verdell Mathis.

They were signin' 'em in the major leagues then. Dan Bankhead and I were fixin' to go to South America at the same time to the same place, but he didn't go to South America. I went down there and played.

Dan Bankhead and Jehosie Heard signed. Willie Hutchinson would have been a good one to go up there to the major leagues. Big righthander, but he had a temper. Good fastball. Good curveball. He was just in the wrong place at the wrong time.

Reuben Jones was managin' back in the '40s. Hutchinson wouldn't throw what was called. You call one thing and he'd shake it off and throw another one. Reuben Jones told him, "Don't shake another sign off or you're on that train." He had a good fastball, a terrific swingin' curveball, and his knuckleball was useful.

Charley Pride was one of your teammates.

Charley Pride was a good man. He didn't stay in the game long enough to play the way he'd like to. He was in there for a good little while but he ran off with his career — singin'.

What about Charlie Davis?

He was a lefthanded pitcher. He was all right, too. He didn't have the zip on the ball like Satchel Paige, but he could throw the ball where he wanted it at. That means more than three or four fastballs, when you can throw it where you want it. I saw him in Kansas City 'bout four or five years ago. He's a fine fella.

Who were some of the best players you saw?

Neil Robinson, Bubba Hyde, Fred McDaniel. They were with the Red Sox. Willie Mays, Herbert Souell, Ed Steele — all of them in Alabama. With the Clowns was the boy who went on to play basketball — Goose Tatum. His hands were long as your arm from your elbow down to your fingers. It was just like he had a mitt for his hand. He could catch that ball any sorta way.

Henry Kimbro was a good one, too. I saw him up in Milwaukee just recently.

They had one boy over there with Kansas City, he coulda played with anybody. Willard Brown. And Earl Taborn, the catcher, this boy that went to the Yankees [minor league system]. Taborn was a good man but he couldn't stop 'em from runnin'. He couldn't throw nobody out. Every time we'd play together, we'd throw together, you know. Make our line and throw down to second, but he had to be outside [a few steps in front of] the base [home plate] before he could throw. By the time he'd throw, the man's there. When he'd jump up he had to run a step or two to throw. When I raised up, I raised up throwin'. When my left foot hit the ground, the ball was gone.

Kansas City had several good ballplayers over there. I can't think of all their names now. There were a *lot* of good ballplayers that could have gone to the majors if they would have taken 'em.

I played ball against Bob Feller in the winter leagues. He went to California most every year. I'd go down to Mexico 'bout every September and October and make 'bout $1500 and then I'd come back home. That's when they'd go to California to play. I could have played with all of them but I didn't. I wanted to stay home. I wanted to be with my kids while they were growin' up.

You retired after 1955. Why?

I wasn't makin' no money. I couldn't take care of my family. I had a growin' family then.

Would you be a ballplayer again if you were a young man?

I wouldn't take nothin' else for it.

BATTING RECORD

Year	Team, League	Pos	G	AB	R	H	2B	3B	HR	RBI	SB	BA
1940	Memphis, NAL	c										
1941		c										

Year	Team, League	Pos	G	AB	R	H	2B	3B	HR	RBI	SB	BA
1942		c										
1943		c										
1944		c										.194
1945		c										.237
1946		c										
1947		c										
1948		c										.265
1949		c										
1950		c								11		.267
1951		c										
1952		c										
1953		c										
1954		c										.277
1955		c										

Ulysses "Hickey" Redd
"Surviving the Cut"

BORN NOVEMBER 13, 1914, BATON ROUGE, LA
HT. 5'10½" WT. 162 BATTED AND THREW RIGHT

Negro Leagues debut: 1940

A lot of fine ballplayers, especially Negro leagues ballplayers, have come out of Louisiana. One of those was Ulysses Redd, a line-drive hitting shortstop with great range and a strong arm.

But, like so many of his time, World War II interfered with his career. He was actually drafted before the U.S. entered the war, and he was looking forward to his discharge when the Japanese attacked Pearl Harbor. Redd had to spend four more years fighting for his country — four years when he may well have been at his peak as an athlete.

And he was an athlete. After the war, in addition to baseball, he played professional basketball. He loved it all and hated to see it end.

When did you begin playing professionally?

In 1940 with Birmingham. I was playing up in Shreveport, Louisiana, with a team — the Black Sports — and the manager [Winfield Welch] knew people in the leagues. He had played in the leagues a little bit himself. He came here to Baton Rouge and got me to go to Shreveport with him to play up there. I was 26.

Every year, some of the teams used to come down durin' the spring and we would barnstorm with 'em, or at least play 'em a game or two as they passed through on their way down to New Orleans. Like the Homestead Grays would come through there, and the Monarchs sometime, but mostly he was well-acquainted with the Homestead Grays than any other teams out there. They used to always come. First they would come to Gramblin', and Welch and the president of Gramblin' was good friends. When they played over at Gramblin' they would come over here to Baton Rouge and played Welch's team. Welch was my manager. Birmingham was lookin' for

Ulysses Redd (courtesy of Ulysses Redd).

117

ballplayers. They was goin' down to New Orleans to get a pitcher and the man from Birmingham knew Welch and he stopped by to see him.

One of my neighbors played in the league — Pepper Bassett. Pepper used to live about three blocks from me and Welch knew Pepper. Pepper told Welch about me. Welch brought me to Shreveport and from there he sent me to Birmingham. He didn't go with me at first, but he finally came over there and managed Birmingham the next year. When he sent me to Birmingham, Uncle Jim — Jim Taylor — was managin' there at that time.

We went to spring trainin' and had a bunch of guys out there — a bunch of shortstops, anyway — and I just knew I would be goin' back to Shreveport pretty soon. Even Dan Bankhead wanted to be a shortstop at that time, but he was throwin' so hard they said they would make a pitcher outta him. [Laughs] They did the right thing.

When I got to Birmingham and went to spring trainin', I was ready to come back here. They had *so* many guys. When I went to Birmingham, I didn't know a soul, not a ballplayer there that I knew. Everybody else there had friends, somebody they had played with or they knew.

They had one little fella from North Carolina — [James] Mickey. He and the second baseman were buddies. They had played together. And Mickey, to me, was gonna be Birmingham's shortstop.

I tried so hard and I hurt my arm. It was cold over there; we trained in Jackson, Mississippi. It got cold down there and, oh, man, I caught a cold and I'm feelin' bad, but I didn't want the man to know. And Uncle Jim never would say anything to me. That's my manager. My roommate's name was Paul Hardy. Paul told me, "Don't worry about that." So *every*time I looked around, I missed somebody. They'd sent him home.

They moved Dan over to the pitcher's mound and that left just the two of us, Mick and me. That was a Friday and we was openin' up with Kansas City that Sunday in Birmingham. I was out in the outfield shaggin' balls

while they were takin' their battin' practice. Paul took his and he come runnin' out there. "Roomie, you better go take your knocks!"

I said, "What's the matter?"

He said, "Go up there and look at the lineup."

And I walked in that dugout and saw my name in the lineup, hittin' in sixth place. I looked around for Mickey and I didn't see him. I went up to the battin' cage then and I didn't see Mickey nowhere around. Somebody was standin' there waitin' to take his turn at bat. I said, "Where's Mickey?"

"That man sent Mickey home last night."

I got the shakes then. I couldn't do nothin'. [Laughs] But after the game started, I got all right.

After that I was there in Birmingham in 1940 and '41, then I got drafted in the service. I was drafted for a year but the Japs attacked Pearl Harbor. I was countin' down, on my way to come out, 'til the Japs attacked Pearl Harbor, then they made it indefinite. Then I went to Saipan, Okinawa, Guadalcanal. Every time we secured an island, then we'd start our recreation program. We'd play baseball, basketball — everything but golf. I like to play golf.

You have a reputation for having a lot of range in the field.

Well, I thought I did, anyway. I played my position pretty well. I had a strong arm and I was good and quick at the time. I played all the infield positions other than first base. I played second and I played third, also.

They classed me as a pretty good hitter — line-drive hitter. I wasn't no home run hitter. I batted around sixth, but there was a few times I batted in second place, too. I could hit the ball often; I'd put it in play and I could hit to any field. I had that teachin' from Welch when I played down here in Shreveport. He taught us all that. I hit most of my balls to right field.

When you finally left the service, you didn't return to Birmingham.

I'll tell you what. That was Welch again. I was on my way back and he told me don't go back, hang around a couple of weeks. He had somethin' different.

They organized the Cincinnati Crescents team, which eventually got to be the Seattle Steelheads. Mr. Welch came here and got me and promised my grandmother that he would look after me and he did look after me while I was with him.

He said they was goin' to Cincinnati to play with the Cincinnati Crescents. I went on with him and from there a little while with the Steelheads. In the meantime, Welch was the business manager on the road for the Harlem Globetrotters and they had a baseball team, so that made me go with him to the Harlem Globetrotters.

The travel was rough at times and it was good at times, but it wasn't as bad as a lotta people thought it was. We had our good times, but the main thing was we had trouble findin' lodgin' and places to sleep and eat sometimes.

I used to help drive the baseball bus, too. When I got with the Globetrotters, when the baseball season was over, Abe Saperstein, the owner of the Globetrotters — we had so many good basketball players could play baseball, so he kept most of the good ballplayers there because he's gonna have a baseball team. Some of the basketball players was on the baseball team, but instead he just made him a basketball team and he played outta Kansas City. Our name was the Kansas City Stars but we all traveled together on the basketball bus, and I helped to drive the basketball bus, also.

What happened, when they left Cincinnati, I went to the Harlem Globetrotters baseball team, and after baseball season was over I stayed there with the basketball team.

I played with the Trotters three or four years. I was with the American Giants I think in '51. My uniform shirt is in the Kansas City museum.

What did you do for a living when you left baseball?

I didn't intend to leave it, to be frank with you, but my wife and I was raisin' a family and my wife said I was gone too long from home. Winter and summer. Baseball in the summer and basketball in the winter. Never

home for the holidays — Christmas, New Year's, and all that stuff.

She told me that I oughtta go down to the post office and put in an application. I used to tell her all the time, "If I could find anything worth stayin' home for, I will." And, sure 'nough, I went down there and put in the application and a few days later they called me down there to take the test. Next thing I know, I was hired as a letter carrier, so then I did that until I retired in '82. Twenty-six-and-a-half years.

Who was the best player you saw?

I've had that question asked me quite a few times. I've seen a lotta guys play, but I couldn't just pinpoint the *best* player I ever saw. But I could tell you what: the man that I admired most was Willie Wells, Sr. He was the best all-around ballplayer I ever saw. I saw Marty Marion, Pee Wee Reese — I saw quite a few of 'em — but he was the one I admired most.

Who was the best pitcher you saw?

Now there you go again. I can tell you who gave *me* the most trouble. You hardly hear of him. His name was Hilton Smith.

I had a couple of pitchers on my team that I thought was pretty good, too. Dan Bankhead was a teammate of mine, but we had a fella there named Alvin Gipson from Shreveport. We played together in Shreveport. He was a good pitcher. You *never* hear of him: Alvin Gipson. He came to Birmingham that one year, I believe. We always called him "Bubba," but I don't know what happened to him. I went in the service and lost track of him.

Does one game stand out?

Yeah. It was the second game of a doubleheader. We played Kansas City in Birmingham. Hilton pitched against us the first game and Satchel pitched against us the second game, and we beat Satch, but he was foolin' around. They beat us the first game and Satchel was out there foolin' around.

Welch, our manager — he and Satch go *way* back, he used to tell us Satch used to

Harlem Globetrotters Baseball Team, late 1940s (l-r): Unidentified player, Herb Simpson, Luke Easter, Sherwood Brewer, Piper Davis, Walter Burch, Ulysses Redd, Abe Saperstein (owner), Johnny Markham, Jesse Owens (part owner) (courtesy of Ulysses Redd).

throw what they called the hesitation pitch — lob it up there — and Welch used to tell us, "Don't try to hit it outta the ballpark. Stand up there. If he's throwin' fastballs, try to bunt it. If he's throwin' that junk up there, try to tear it up." That's how we beat Satchel that game. I remember gettin' one hit off of him. It wasn't much of a hit, though — just over the second baseman's head. [Laughs]

I got two hits offa Hilton that day. That was a great day for me because I was afraid of Hilton, I'll be frank with you. He could throw hard and then he had such a delivery for a righthander, and I hit from the right side, too. It looked like he's comin' right at you all the time. I think he belongs in the Hall of Fame. Nobody ever says much about him, but I think he should go.

Did you have any racial problems on the road?

A few. I had my wife with me one time when I was with the Harlem Globetrotters baseball team. Satchel was with us at that time. I think it was Dodge City; we had played out there and we slept at a motel just outside of Dodge City in Kansas.

I told my wife, "We're gonna beat everybody else to the cafe because it takes so long to get served." We walked in the cafe up there and the people wouldn't serve us. If my wife hadn't been with me it would've been okay, but that hurt. When she got back to Kansas City, she decided to come on back home after that. We was on the way to Kansas City then.

Most of the time we knew where to go and who to see, like some places we played in organized ballparks when the home team was

Ulysses Redd (center) presenting his uniform to the Negro Leagues Baseball Museum with Don Motley (left), Buck O'Neil (right) (courtesy of Ulysses Redd).

outta town playin'. Like in Chicago and in Memphis and Shreveport and Birmingham. We played in the same ballparks even though they were minor league teams at the time. They would have most of the lockers locked; the home team players had left a lot of their stuff and they didn't want us to bother it, but we didn't need a locker anyway. Go in there and change clothes and play and come back and take a shower and leave. That was never a problem there.

A lot of those cities we went to at the time, they had colored restaurants, and they had better food than the white restaurants I'd been in. We would always know where to go to eat.

Do you have any regrets from your baseball career?

None whatsoever. I enjoyed every minute of it. I loved to play ball and I would stop doin' *any*thing to go play ball. I never had any

regrets even though we wasn't makin' any money.

The first contract I signed with Birmingham, Welch had to coach me in when they started off on the contract. I was willin' to take anything. Playin' baseball, I'd play for nothin'. Welch was the one coached me through my contract.

The average contract at that time was $75 to $85 a month. When the man told me $85, Welch shook his head. He was sittin' kinda on the side behind the man and he shook his head to me. And I didn't know what was goin' on. The man was goin' crazy. [Laughs] I thought he was doin' that because he wanted me to stay there in Shreveport with him.

So when the man got up to 90, that's the most money I'd *ever* heard of to play ball. He ended up payin' me $110. Man, I was *some* happy about that! [Laughs] I kept tellin' him no until Welch bowed his head. When Welch bowed his head, I accepted. The man had everything written up in the contract but the amount. He wrote that on there — $110— and I hurried up and signed it before Welch could shake his head again. [Laughs]

Would you play baseball again?

Oh, yeah, but I could've done a lot better when I was out there. I've thought about that a lot of times. I was just playin' for the moment. I don't know. I don't think I would've done anything different, though.

BATTING RECORD

Year	Team, League	Pos	G	AB	R	H	2B	3B	HR	RBI	SB	BA
1940	Birmingham, NAL	s-2-3										
1941		s-2-3										.271
1942-46	military service											
1947	Harlem	ss-2b										
	Globetrotters, ind.	s-2-3										
1948		s-2-3										
1949		ss-3b										
1950		s-2-3										
1951	Chicago, NAL	s-2-3										
1952		s-2-3										

Tommy Sampson
"All-Star Second Baseman"

BORN AUGUST 31, 1912, CALHOUN, AL
HT. 6'3" WT. 180 BATTED AND THREW RIGHT

Negro Leagues debut: 1940

Tommy Sampson must have been a pretty good second baseman. For one thing, he was selected as the second baseman for the Negro American League in four consecutive East-West games. For another, while Sampson was still with Birmingham, Piper Davis played shortstop and first base, and there is ample evidence that Davis was a great second baseman.

While he was with Birmingham, the club won its first two NAL pennants ('43 and '44). The team lost the World Series to the Homestead Grays both years, but the '44 Series may have turned out differently if Sampson had been able to play. He was severely injured in an automobile accident shortly before the Series began and was laid up all winter.

Sampson recalls the 1943 East-West Game as the highlight of his career. He had the first hit and only RBI for the West squad in their 2–1 victory over the East, and he took away a base hit that would have been the tying run (two batters later, Buck Leonard homered) had the batter reached safely.

But, most importantly, Sampson's mother was in the stands.

I was born in Calhoun, Alabama, August the thirty-first, 1912. My mother carried me away from there when I think I was five years old. We went to Majestic, Alabama; that's about 18, 20 miles from Birmingham. I stayed there until I was 14 and she carried me to Scarborough, West Virginia, about 50 miles from Charleston, and I was raised there.

I started playing baseball in Alabama when I was 12, just playing with the kids. From there, I went to West Virginia and I started to playing with the men when I was 15. Sandlot. From there, I just developed.

I just played around there in the coal fields after I grew up. We got up a team there and I just kept playing. I was pretty good and finally I hooked up with a team in Raleigh, West Virginia. Teams came out of Virginia and North Carolina and a team from down at Portsmouth — the Portsmouth Grays — played against them [the Raleigh team] and that was when Birmingham saw me. That was in '38.

At that time, you were in your mid 20s. What had you been doing for a living?

I worked in the coal mines. That's the first job I had. I went in the coal mines when I was 17-and-a-half years old. It was work, but, listen, that was all the work that was out. My mother told me if I wasn't going to school, I had to go to work, so I went to work.

I liked it. Wasn't nothing else to do and I didn't figure baseball was going to ever amount to much, but I *loved* to play. Baseball was my ambition, to conquer it. During that time, they had nothing but the black leagues, you know. I used to take and pick up the paper and read about the guys and I said,

Tommy Sampson (courtesy of Tommy Sampson).

"Well, maybe one day I'll play with some of those guys."

During that time, when we had that team — it was a pretty good team — we used to play the Homestead Grays, the Chicago American Giants, and Newark Eagles. They used to barnstorm all down through there. I remember my manager and the manager of the Black Yankees knew each other. My manager talked to him, said, "I got three guys I'd like for you to take a look at." That was a big thing.

He had a pitcher, myself, and an outfielder to try out with 'em. Everybody looked at everybody and the guy — Tex Burnett, I never will forget this guy. I was a third baseman at the time. I went out there and the guy told me to throw overhanded. Well, my arm was a little sore, so he told me, said, "You can't play no ball."

After he told me I couldn't play, it didn't discourage me any. He carried off Reginald Timbers and the outfielder and they kept 'em

'bout a week and came back. The pitcher couldn't break a egg when he got back. They had pitched him too much and made his arm sore. This was in '36, I think.

I still stayed on the team and we played the Homestead Grays in '37. I hit two home runs off of 'em. The pitcher's name was Trees. Wade Trees. Pepper Bassett was catching. They had Josh on the team. Buck Leonard was there, Jelly Jackson was playing, [Lick] Carlyle was playing second base, Boojum Wilson was at third. I never will forget the whole team. When this happened, my name kind of flourished out a little bit, you know.

I played with another team. I went to spring training with the Bellville Grays in 1939 in Portsmouth. It was a Christian organization. After the season was over, we barnstormed down through Georgia and to Florida. We played a team out of Birmingham — the Birmingham Stars — and they told me they was gonna have a team in Birmingham in 1940 and they asked me would I come down and join 'em. I said, "Well, I don't care. I'm not doing anything."

So they sent a car up there to pick up a bunch of us: Buster Haywood, James Mickey, Gentry Jessup, myself, and a boy named Rogers. We went down to Jackson, Mississippi, for spring training for Birmingham.

All of you were with Bellville? That must have been some team.

Oh, we had a good team.

That was spring of 1940. Jim Taylor was the manager. You remember Candy Jim Taylor? We made up a team and after spring training, he was still trying out guys; they was going and coming. I never saw so many ballplayers; they'd bring a carload this week and next week they're shipping out a carload. [Laughs] I didn't know whether I was gonna make it or not.

To me, I just played the same way I always did, so when they picked the team, I was one that stayed there, and I stayed there for years.

You made the East-West All-Star team there for several years.

I was All-Star four years. I played the whole game in '43. I was chosen every year from '40 'til '43. I did pretty good.

You managed the Black Barons for a couple of years.

I managed in '46 and '47. See, I had the car wreck in '44 — I broke my leg — so I came back in '46 as the manager. Me and Tom Hayes [Birmingham owner] had a falling out at the end of '47. I went to New York Cubans in '48. In '49, I played with Chicago American Giants. I did all right with them and I retired in '49.

Your sore arm when the Black Yankees looked at you, did it come back around?

Oh, yeah. It came strong. When I went to Birmingham, it got strong.

As a young man, you were a third baseman. When did you switch to second?

I did that myself. I caught myself helping my arm out, so I switched over to second. That was a harder position, but it was closer to first base. That's the reason I changed.

I understand you had very good power for a middle infielder.

Yeah, I could hit. I really don't know how many home runs I hit, but I had *great* power. Remember the Senators in Washington? I hit 'em up in that center field stand. Boy, I used to wear that ball out.

Joe Lewis, my manager when I was playing at Bellville, he used to tell me, "Don't swing for the fences and start hitting that ball to right field." I started hitting it to right field.

You were a big man for a middle infielder.

Yeah. I weighed about 180 or 190 pounds. I was about six-three-and-a-quarter inches. Piper [Davis] was about six-three. Our whole infield at the time Piper came was six-footers. Lester Lockett was the third baseman, Piper was the shortstop, I was the second baseman, and we had a boy named Sloppy Lindsay playing first. We had [Lyman] Bostock, too, you know.

The owner didn't like Lyman. Tom Hayes didn't like him. See, when Lyman came out of the Army, I was managing in '46. I gave him a job and he was kind of muscle-bound when he first came out and I kept him because he was a good ballplayer when he went in. All he needed was to get hisself in condition.

Me and Tom used to fight about it all the time. "I don't see why you play that guy. Every time I see him, he's on his face."

So I said, "Mr. Hayes, just let me run the team. Let me take care of Bostock. Bostock's a good ballplayer. Keep him."

The next year we let him go, he got in condition, and he could hit. He went to Chicago.

Maybe you won't want to answer this. Who was the better second baseman, you or Piper?

Well, everybody rated me over Piper. I'll tell you the truth, I didn't have no problem with it. He was a shortstop and I was a second baseman at first. We played together as a combination, he and I. When they take him off that team there in Birmingham at the pipe shop, they brought him as a shortstop. I was the second baseman and nobody moved me the whole time I was there.

When Art Wilson came in, Art and I played together and Piper was the first baseman.

Wilson was a fantastic shortstop. Why didn't he get a better shot with the New York Giants?

You know the reason why? He couldn't hit the ball to right field. That was his problem. You throw the ball and he's gonna hit it to left field anyway, or he's gonna hit it to the shortstop. He was always running from the plate; he hit running. That's the reason why he didn't stay up. He could *field*. He was a good shortstop.

Who was the best player you saw?

There was *so* many I used to admire. I used to admire a lot of infielders because I was an infielder. Dick Seay was my idol. He and I used to talk a lot because I had a lot of confidence in him. I used to ask 'bout pointers playing second base, and he and I were very good friends. He really was a nice person.

We had a lot of good infielders. We had a boy named Sam Bankhead. That was Dan's brother. He [Sam] was a guy I used to admire because he could play anywhere. See, Dan and I went up and came in together. Sammy, boy, he could play! He could play anywhere. That's the reason why I admired him so.

He had one brother play with Memphis. Sam was the oldest. Then you had Fred; Fred played with Memphis.

But the one that I admired was Dick Seay. I liked the way he played and he was very easy to get along with. He wasn't one of those pop-heads, you know, who get mad if you talk to 'em.

When I was about 18, Homestead Grays had got another kid — George Griffin — and myself. He was a first baseman; he was about 23. We started together up in the coal fields and they sent a guy to pick he and I up in 1932 and this guy that they sent, he went down to Virginia and picked up two other guys. I was supposed to have went up the Grays at 18. They picked up the other guys. That's why I didn't make it when I was around 18.

Who was the best second baseman in the league? If it was you, say so.

I'll tell you the truth: I didn't rate myself. How they rated me, I don't know, but I was a pretty good second baseman. I didn't get the swell-head. To me, I was playing every day and that's all I wanted to do. When they picked me to go to the All-Star games, I topped the tally sheet.

At that time Kansas City had a good second baseman. He was [Bonnie] Serrell. And Cleveland Buckeyes had one named Johnny Cowan. He was good.

[Junior] Gilliam, he was good. I played against him when he was about 16. He played with Nashville. We were playing Baltimore and they had him in there. [Laughs] I hit a ball down there and they took him out 'cause, boy, I *hit* that ball down there. Next inning, they took him out the game because he was young and they didn't want him to get shell-shocked.

Sammy T. Hughes was a good second baseman, Ducky [Mahlon Duckett] was a good second baseman. I remember playing against them.

The Cubans had some good ballplayers. See, I played with Minnie Minoso and the catcher that went up with the [New York] Giants, [Ray] Noble, and I played ball against Luis Tiant's daddy. Boy, he had a good screwball, I ain't kidding you.

Verdell Mathis said he patterned himself a lot after the elder Tiant.

Oh, buddy, he was a good one. When we played Verdell, they used to wake me up when he was pitching. [Laughs] They'd say, "Verdell's pitching." I could hit him if you'd wake me out of a sound sleep. [Laughs] I used to tell him, I said, "Verdell, when you're pitching, I can wake up out of my dreams and hit you." Boy, I could hit him!

While we're on pitchers, who was the best?

Well, Satchel rates over all of 'em, but you had some pretty good ones other than him. The Buckeyes had some good pitchers. They had [Gene] Bremmer and they had two brothers; they were good pitchers [Big Jim and Schoolboy Tugerson]. Kansas City had some good pitchers, too. They had loads of 'em. They had [Jack] Matchett, they had Booker McDaniels, they had Hilton Smith and Connie Johnson and Jim LaMarque. These are guys I used to play against.

Which pitcher gave you the hardest time?

[Bill "Junior"] Savage. Memphis had a kid named Savage. He didn't play long. He was a pitcher used to give me a lot of trouble. Righthander. He didn't play but a couple years.

Then I'll tell you who else. The Jacksonville Red Caps — you know, they were in the league at that time — they had a guy named Preacher Henry.

Does one game stand out?

You know the game I really cherish and thought so much of because my mother was there, the 1943 All-Star Game. I performed well.

I was living in Chicago. She had been living in Alabama and I brought her to live with me in Chicago. See, I lived in Chicago ten years.

I drove in the first run. I think they [the East] brought Jerry Benjamin up to pinch hit for somebody [Horacio Martinez] and he hit that ball across second base and I went in behind second and threw him out. It was one of those bang-bang plays. The next guy was Buck Leonard, coming up behind him, and he hit a home run. That's the only run they got.

You wouldn't believe. There was 51,000 in that stand and I could hear my mother's voice over everything. [Laughs] That was the biggest thrill I believe I got in baseball. That's the thing; I always wanted her to be happy about me. See, I was her only boy she had and I was the baby. Yeah, that's the biggest thrill of my life.

What were your salaries when you first started and then later, after you were an established player?

Ninety dollars a month when I first started. At that time, we got 60 cents for meals. My salary ran $600 a month later, and we got three dollars for meals.

The conditions for a black man in the South were less than ideal then.

Well, the thing about it, you still had to go to those fleabag hotels. They wasn't so hot and that's where we had to sleep. We never slept in real nice hotels.

Did you enjoy the travel?

The only way we had to travel was in buses. Either you go that way or you wouldn't go at all. Every team owned their own bus.

When I got hurt in an accident, we were traveling in cars. I got hurt the week before the [1944] World Series. I think we had played in Louisville, I believe, and we was on our way to Birmingham when we had the accident. I was out 'til that next spring. I was in the hospital, I think, almost 13 weeks. I had a broken leg, head busted, and everything.

That spring I went to Hot Springs for the baths and I came out in '45 and managed a team out of St. Louis. [Abe] Saperstein had the team and he sent me out with that team. That's before I started managing [Birmingham]. I was out with that team until the next year. In 1946, I came in and managed Birmingham. He sent me out to let me kind of feel the waters of managing.

W. S. Welch was the manager of Birmingham. Winfield Welch. He told me not to take that job of managing, but I told him the guy hadn't did nothing to me. I said, "Look, as long as he treats me okay, what you and him did I have nothing to do with."

I took that job in '46 and it worked out all right. In '47, it worked all right until the end of the year. I had an operation. My appendix ruptured on me going to play in Knoxville. I had to go in the hospital for an emergency operation and when I came back to Birmingham after I got out of the hospital, he had a stoogie around there. I bought a filling station there in Birmingham and I used to go down there and sit around the station all day and he was telling him that I came down every day and when it was time to pay, he deducted $125 out of my salary. That's when me and Tom [Hayes] fell out. I told him to take his job and stick it.

I enjoyed managing. It was a headache at first. See, I had too many guys from Birmingham on the team, the home-town boys, and they were hard to handle. At first, I said, "I'm taking the job. I'm the same guy you played with, but I can't run around with you guys every day. We'll do it like a team. If I ask you to do something, I want you to do it."

But they had some guys. Newberry, Jimmy Newberry — he was the main one. He was the hard one to handle. He drank a lot. You give him an hour to go out and eat when we're in town and he may come back two hours later.

I had a good team in Birmingham and I enjoyed it.

Talk about Willie Mays.

Listen, I found that guy and, do you know, I got no credit for it. I found him out there playing with a little sandlot team. That was 1948 and Harry Barnes and myself went over there and I met him and I talked with him and I asked him, "Would you like to join my team?"

He said, "Yeah, I'd love to."

I said, "Can we talk to your mother?"

He said, "I stay with my aunt." See, his aunt raised him.

Harry and I went over and talked with her. We had to beg her and finally she gave her consent that he could go with us, so I said, "I'll take care of him."

I bought him spikes and everything. He was just a kid. I carried him down and the first place we played was in Macon, Georgia. We played the Newark Eagles and they only beat that team I put together, 2–1. Newark had all them good ballplayers. [Monte] Irvin was playing with 'em at that time, and [Leon] Day and all them, and they only beat my team, 2–1.

They tried to get me to come [to change teams], and Willie Mays. I told 'em, I said, "I couldn't let you have that kid. I just picked him up."

This guy out of Chattanooga was down there and he asked me could we come next Sunday in Chattanooga. We went in there and we played, and that's when I broke the team up. This guy promised 'em salary; I told 'em I couldn't pay salaries, I don't have that kind of money. I just had a percentage team, so he took the team.

I took the rest I had and went on the road. When I left to go on the road, I had seven ballplayers and Saperstein had me booked all out in Texas. [Laughs] I picked up a couple more and we went out there and played, then we left there and went into Canada. When I broke my team up, that's when I went with the Cubans. I think I was in Iowa when I met 'em, and I sent the team back to Birmingham and I went with the Cubans.

When you finally left baseball, what did you do for a living?

I did a little bit of everything. I painted, I plastered, I did construction work. The thing about it, when I went out of baseball, I said, "I think I had enough of it."

Any regrets from baseball?

No. I don't have any. Just like I said, things is going to happen and happened afterwards, but I don't regret a day of it. I never regret any of it.

I remember in 1939, when Joe Gordon came up to the Yankees, we was in West Palm Beach, Florida, and, oh, I was catching everything that was hit that way. Sliding over catching and all and people in the stands say, "I thought the Yankees had Joe Gordon. We got him right here." [Laughs]

Would you do it again?

Yes, I would. I wouldn't change nothing. I enjoyed the game.

BATTING RECORD

Year	Team, League	Pos	G	AB	R	H	2B	3B	HR	RBI	SB	BA
1940	Birmingham, NAL	2b										
1941		2b										
1942		2b										.354
1943		2b										
1944		2b									16	.272
1945		2b										
1946		2b-1b-m										.205
1947		2b-1b-m										.272
1948	N.Y. Cubans, NAL	2b-1b										
1949	Chicago, NAL	2b										.252

PART TWO
The 1940s

There was probably no better baseball played anywhere than in the Negro leagues during the first half of the 1940s. This did not go unnoticed by the white leagues and only the "unwritten rule" kept integration at bay. Finally, in 1946, a new commissioner and a forward-looking team brought it to pass. Jackie Robinson was signed by the Brooklyn Dodgers and several others were picked up by other teams.

Men such as Robinson, Larry Doby, Roy Campanella, Don Newcombe, and the ageless Satchel Paige, among others, showed that they could hold their own, and then some, in major league competition. This marked the beginning of the end for the black leagues. The Negro National League folded after the 1947 season, but the Negro American League played on, still producing talented ballplayers.

John Gibbons
"Little Man on the Mound"

BORN APRIL 16, 1922, MILLARD, GA
HT. 5'9" WT. 140 BATTED AND THREW RIGHT

Negro Leagues debut: 1941

There is a stereotype that comes to mind when one thinks of a pitcher: tall, perhaps a little on the lanky side but solid and well-muscled. The Boston Red Sox, for instance, for years went for young pitchers who may have been better suited for basketball; they signed the likes of Frank Sullivan, Tracy Stallard, Dick Radatz, and Roger Clemens. (Look up their sizes.) I myself made teams as a kid I maybe shouldn't have because I "looked like a pitcher."

If a boy was smaller, he had to be *good*— real good — because of the bias — unconscious in many cases — against small pitchers. There have been some great small pitchers, though: Bobby Shantz, Roy Face, Carl Erskine, and Leon Day are just a few.

And John Gibbons, while perhaps not an Erskine or a Day, was a good pitcher who made it all the way to the major leagues available to him, in this case the Negro National League. He stood 5'9", but the real problem was his weight, 140 pounds, which he could not increase no matter how hard he tried. In fact, when he wasn't careful, his weight would go the other way.

Even so, he pitched for the Philadelphia Stars for three years, barnstormed with Double Duty Radcliffe and with Jackie Robinson, and even was chosen to go to South America to pitch. A dead arm led to his premature retirement in only his mid–20s, but he showed the doubters that little men can pitch.

I was real small, about 140 or so. Oscar Charleston used to tell me all the time, "You better quit out there runnin' so much. I'll be able to read a newspaper through you after a while."

When did your baseball career begin?

I played right here in Tampa with a team by the name of the Pepsi-Cola Giants. We started playin' on the sandlot and we growed up until the Pepsi-Cola Company bought us a lotta uniforms, then we started playin' teams around here from Bradenton, Tampa, Orlando and we named it the Florida State League.

Every year, the big league teams would

come down, like the Black Yankees and all the teams. We played against 'em and we used to beat 'em, and that's where a lot of us got jobs. They'd wanna carry us back with 'em. That's where I got my job with Oscar Charleston. He come down with the Toledo Crawfords. This was around '41.

We played 'em out to Plant Field — the Toledo Crawfords out to Plant Field — and I pitched four innin's and I beat 'em. [Bernard] Fernandez came in after me and relieved, but I beat 'em and that evenin' after the ballgame, he [Charleston] asked me if I would come. I told him, "I have to go and ask my mother."

She didn't want to, but she decided to let me go and I went from Tampa to Indianapolis

John Gibbons (courtesy of John Gibbons).

with him. We didn't stay there long 'cause Charleston got a phone call from Philadelphia and they wanted him to come to manage the Philadelphia Stars. He left a day ahead of us and he said, "As soon as I get there, I'm gonna send for you."

Soon as he got to Philadelphia, next day he sent for me and Fernandez. I played for Philadelphia for two or three years.

I know I started one ballgame and won that one; the rest of 'em I would relieve — come in and pitch two or three innin's. But I beat Newark one night. I gave up a home run — to Johnny Davis, the center fielder — the longest home run I've seen hit yet. [Laughs] I beat 'em, 6–5; they got about eight hits.

That night I didn't know I was gonna pitch. We got over there and Charleston said, "Little man, you got it." I said, "Huh?" He said, "You got it." [Laughs]

It was cold. I put on my jacket under my sweatshirt. He said, "How you gonna throw the ball with your jacket under your sweatshirt?"

I got out there and started throwin'. I didn't think I was gonna get by because I'd never pitched to a team like Newark, but I pitched pretty good ball. I know they got eight hits. I didn't pitch but seven innin's. I don't

know whether Fernandez came in or Henry McHenry. He might have. He was a good pitcher.

I pitched a good ballgame against Asheville, I think, in Buffalo, New York. It was so cold we put a fire in there in the dugout. It was *cold* that night. I didn't pitch but three innin's, Fernandez pitched three, and somebody else pitched three. You shouldn't play ball when it's that cold.

I pitched my best ballgame, I would say, when we played the Jacksonville Eagles. I pitched against Preacher Henry. He was one of Jacksonville's best. I beat him, 2–1, in ten innin's. That's the greatest pitchin' game I ever had and I pitched all that one. That was the greatest thrill of my life. I was 19 then.

We got our runs on a bunt — bunt the ball with a man on third — and the next run come on a fly ball.

Preacher's ball looked like it was goin' up in the air and it would come down — dropped down. He had a good pitch. I had a good dropball, too. I didn't throw but about 85; I never did hit 90.

[Leo "Preacher" Henry was shorter than Gibbons (5'4") but weighed the same (140 pounds). He was a top pitcher, Jacksonville's ace, and enjoyed a lengthy career (from the late '30s to the early '50s) in the Negro leagues.]

When did you leave baseball?

In '46. I barnstormed with Double Duty Radcliffe in '46. Double Duty had the Globetrotters. We barnstormed with the House of David. Those guys had beards all around their face.

We barnstormed to Chicago, all out through Minnesota, California. We barnstormed all around the country for three weeks. Double Duty did everything. He used to catch me when I pitched, but he pitched, played third, did everything. That's the reason they called him Double Duty. He was somethin' else.

Who were some of the players you came across?

On my team we had big Shifty [Jim] West, we had Chet Brewer, had [Mahlon]

Duckett, we had [Bill] Cash. [Stanley] Glenn wasn't there then; he came later. I was too early for Glenn.

One of the best players I've seen was maybe Monte Irvin, but I've seen two good boys. I've seen Marvin Williams and I've seen Austin. Frank Austin, the shortstop. They were somethin' else, both of 'em; they were the best two ballplayers I've seen. They were leavin' Philadelphia. As soon as I got there, they were leavin' goin' somewhere.

Then there was a couple more good ballplayers. There was those Bankhead brothers — they were good ballplayers — and Larry Doby and Monte Irvin. I played against them; I was with Philadelphia, they were with Newark. I barnstormed with 'em, too, with Jackie.

It was '40-somethin'. He [Jackie] came to Tampa and he took me, Billy Felder, my brother — we barnstormed to Miami. Down to Miami, Daytona, Lakeland, Jacksonville. It was really enjoyable.

Who was the best pitcher you saw?

Satchel was the best one I've seen, him and Hilton Smith. Satchel pitched four or five, Hilton Smith come behind him and there wasn't no difference. Hilton Smith oughtta be in the Hall of Fame. That man could *throw* that ball. He could throw it outta sight.

We traveled in buses — it wasn't a big bus; it was a little bus. We played mostly teams around Philadelphia, New Jersey, New York. Every night we'd go and play the local teams and on Saturday and Sunday we'd play mostly league games.

Then we'd go to Washington [D.C.], go out to Chicago, Kansas City. We had to play the teams out that way. They'd come our way and we'd go their way.

Did you encounter any problems?

Well, they had eatin' problems, sleepin' problems. We had that. Some places we couldn't get nothin' to eat, some places you couldn't sleep, so we'd just ride all night. Don't have to worry 'bout tryin' to get nowhere to sleep. If we'd get in a town, you know, a big

colored town, sometimes you don't wanna stay in some of them hotels 'cause they ain't worth stayin' in.

The problem we had 'bout gettin' somethin' to eat, though; we'd just go to a grocery store and get somethin'. [Laughs] We ate a lotta sandwiches.

How much were you paid?

When I first went up, I made $90 a month. That was a lot of money durin' that time. Later I wound up gettin' $150. [Laughs]

We could live on it and bought some clothes. All the ballplayers bought their clothes at the same place in Philadelphia: Ben the Tailor. We all went on South Street and bought clothes at Ben the Tailor's. They were good clothes.

What did you receive for meal money?

Two dollars a day. Charleston got me a gal and used to keep my money. He said, "I'm gonna get a gal. She's gonna cook for you every day." He kept my two dollars. [Laughs] She'd cook for me and he'd keep my eatin' money.

What did you do when you left baseball in '46?

When I left baseball, I went to work. I come here and went around and then I started to work at the bars. I did that up until 'bout '94. It got too bad. I couldn't handle these young boys so I got outta there.

My arm got slow. I couldn't throw the ball hard enough. It happened in South America. I went down there and they took me straight to the ballpark and let me throw. I was throwin' the ball pretty good for about four weeks, then it looked like somethin' happened. I don't know, but I slowed up. Once you slow up and you can't throw the ball hard enough, you're gone. They ain't gonna hold you one day; you're gone the next day. They put you on a plane and you're gone. Twenty-five little kids by the hotel, flappin' their arms like they're wounded. [Laughs] I was down there in South America in '46.

Any regrets?

No. Only thing I had, I started too early.

I was 19, I think I started playin' too early. I didn't get strong enough and then I couldn't get no weight on me. That's the thing. I couldn't get no weight until I got to be a old man. I picked up all the weight and I didn't need it then. [Laughs] When I needed some weight, I couldn't get some. It just didn't come. I didn't wanna get out there and run; I didn't have nothin' to give away. I used to go trottin' and Charleston would get after me. "Don't do it too much. After a while I'll be able to read a newspaper through you." [Laughs]

Would you play baseball again if you were a young man?

Oh, man! I would play. I would be *glad* to play. The same thing, the same way. I enjoyed it. I didn't make no money, but I had a lot of fun. I would go through the same thing again, the same way.

PITCHING RECORD

Year	Team, League	G	IP	W	L	Pct	H	BB	SO	ERA
1941	Philadelphia, NNL			2	2	.500				
1942				1	0	1.000				
1943										

Napoleon "Schoolboy" Gulley
"Nap"

BORN AUGUST 29, 1924, HUTTIG, AR
DIED AUGUST 21, 1999, SKOKIE, IL
HT. 6' WT. 170 BATTED AND THREW LEFT

Negro Leagues debut: 1941

Nap Gulley began playing professional baseball at the age of 16. He began as a left-handed pitcher and 16 years later ended as an outfielder with a career .320 batting average in organized ball. He played from Canada to Mexico and from New Jersey to California. It was "the most fun you could think of havin'."

But Gulley had always had interests outside of sport, and chief among them was reading.

"I'm a high school person," he volunteered, adding — when goaded — "I'm pretty well-read. I've read Spinoza and Schopenhauer. On the road, when the guys were reading funny papers and playin' cards, I was reading classics."

After nine years of being a pitcher who played some outfield in the Negro leagues and Mexico, he entered organized ball, where he became an outfielder who pitched a little. With his hitting ability, it's too bad he didn't come along a decade later.

You began playing professionally at the age of 16.

Yeah, somewhere along there. I was with semipro teams before that around Arkansas.

Did the Monarchs find you or did you find them?

I think I found them. It was a combination of things. [Dizzy] Dismukes, who was the general manager of the Monarchs and secretary of the ballclub, asked me to meet them in spring training. I don't really know how the discovery went about.

You weren't with Kansas City long. Where did you go from there?

I went to Birmingham. They needed a lefthanded pitcher in Birmingham; they didn't have any. In Kansas City, we had three or four pitchers that were lefthanded and were more experienced so for me to gain more experience, they sent me to Birmingham. They

asked me if I would go and I went. I was there about two years.

After Birmingham, I came to St. Louis, where I had a sister and brother. I spent the winter there. I got to know some ballplayers there, like Pete Fields and that group. Wilbur Hayes was on the Cleveland Buckeyes, which had just become the Cleveland Buckeyes from the Jacksonville Red Caps; they had just entered the league. He had seen me pitch in the spring; I pitched against them before. He came to St. Louis lookin' for ballplayers in the winter months and he asked me how I would like to go to Cleveland and play for the Buckeyes. So I signed a contract with him and went to the Buckeyes from there. I was there three or four years.

Were you with the Buckeyes when they won the championship in 1945?

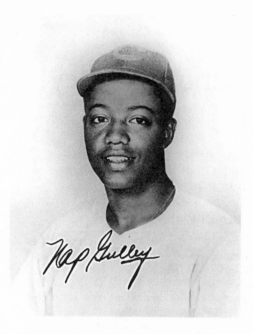

Nap Gulley (courtesy of Nap Gulley).

I was with them until about a month
before. Quincy Trouppe was managin' the
ballclub at the time. We had been playin'
under Parnell Woods and I wasn't gettin'
enough work and I was unhappy there. In
those times, they pitched lefthanders against
lefthanded-hitting ballclubs mostly and I
asked to leave.

[Double Duty] Radcliffe had a team that
was formed by [Abe] Saperstein called the
Harlem Globetrotters, so I left there 'bout a
month before the season [ended]—maybe a
month and a half—to go with Radcliffe,
which was the happiest time of my life. I had
a chance to tour the West—Montana and
Idaho and see Yellowstone. I'd been worn out
with the cities. We had a nice young ballclub
and most of us knew each other, like Ziggy
Marcel and guys like that.

We toured the country, all the way into
Canada out to Vancouver, and then back to
California and then back across the states
again.

I didn't know that the Buckeyes had won
the championship until the spring. I was so
happy and had so much fun and made more
money, and I wasn't even interested in what

Cleveland was doing. Somebody told me
about them having won the championship. I
was happy for [Archie] Ware and the guys. I
knew everybody over there. I was never
unhappy that I wasn't there.

We played teams like the House of David
and we played them daily and we played local
home teams, like Pocatello. We played some
of the farm teams of the major league clubs.
Billings, Montana. It was a kick, man, like
every day you're in a different city in the West
that you read about when you were in school
or you heard about. And now you're here.

They [the Globetrotters] continued, but
Radcliffe left. After Radcliffe left, players were
not together like they were before. Paul Hardy
became the manager—the catcher for the
Birmingham Black Barons. I stayed with them
a little while, wasn't too long.

There was a league formed in California,
Oregon, and Washington—the Negro West
Coast League—so I played for Seattle for
about a month and then there was an opportunity for me. The Chicago Brown Bombers
were barnstormin' out West and I had a
chance to go to the American Giants, so I went
with them for a while.

How did you get to Mexico?

They recruited me to come down. They
had the best players down there, except Stan
Musial and Ted Williams. They had Vernon
Stephens and Roy Zimmerman, Danny
Gardella, Sal Maglie. Maglie wasn't the pitcher
then that he turned out to be. No reflection
on Maglie; Maglie could pitch. He was one of
the great ones.

One man owned the league. He had mil-
lions of dollars and they formed a pretty good
association. We had several clubs in the league.
The salaries for the major leaguers was sky-
rocketing—they were high—and Negro league
ballplayers were making more money there than
they ever dreamed of making in the Negro
leagues. We had [Ray] Dandridge and we had
Cool Papa [Bell] down there and [Andy] Porter
and Roy Campanella and Monte Irvin. We had
all kinds of ballplayers that you could talk about
today. Josh [Gibson] was down there, too.

You had to cut the mustard. If you couldn't cut it the first day out there, well, they'd usually give you a ticket and send you home 'cause they had so many good ballplayers that wanted to come they didn't have to hang on to would-be ballplayers.

I worked at Tampico and I worked at San Luis Potosi. They had Pueblo and Monterrey and that was full of Cuban ballplayers mostly, and Venezuelans. Carrasquel — Alex Carrasquel — was on that ballclub from the Washington Senators. And Chili Gomez from the Washington Senators. You had *strong* competition. You don't see that kind of competition today.

The ballplayers had a different desire to play ball than they do now. They came to play for the love of the whole thing; they loved the game and they loved the country they played in. A lot of the guys was goin' to Cuba, Venezuela, Puerto Rico in the winter time anyway, from Mexico they were goin' and comin' like a shuttle service. They were very happy with the money they were makin' and they were happy with the people. They had no discrimination or anything to do with hotels and accommodations. You'd think you were in another world compared to your own country.

Most of the players I've spoken with have told me the conditions in Mexico were so much better they couldn't even compare them to here.

Oh, there's nothin' to compare to. Compare to what? [Laughs]

You didn't have to go through any stigmas like wondering if I can eat here or can I go in the back door there or can I sleep in this place. That's quite a burden for a ballplayer or anybody to carry around and still be able to produce without anger.

I know that was a serious problem in the South, but how did you find it in other parts of the United States?

I found all parts alike, basically. In the South, in Birmingham, we had Rickwood Field as our home ground when the Barons were away. We played the away schedule of the major league and high minor league ball-

Nap Gulley, 1998 (Lisa Feder photograph).

clubs. We couldn't use the clubhouse; we couldn't shower. You'd go from the hotel. You couldn't even use the water fountains. [Laughs] We'd get through with the ballgame and we'd go back to the hotel and there'd be enough hot water for two people to take a bath and that's about it.

At least in Birmingham there were black hotels. Many places didn't have them.

A few black hotels but some you wouldn't put a ballclub in because they were too rickety. Or they had shady reputations; they were houses of prostitution or whatever under the guise of being a hotel. Transient hotels with all kinds of squalor and everything goin' on.

Most times we lived in the houses of families that would take the ballplayers in. Run a shuttle service the next mornin' to try to get the ballclub together so we could travel.

Even in St. Louis we couldn't use the clubhouse. Kansas City was a good place we could use because of Satchel probably. We could use Blues Stadium's clubhouse. Out East we could, like Newark. I played in Newark in '47; that was right after [Larry] Doby left. And we had Jersey City and the Polo Grounds and Ebbets Field was our home ground. We had all the facilities at Yankee Stadium, all the showers and everything.

There were nice hotels there [in New York]. The musicians, like Count Basie and [Duke] Ellington and the bands, lived in the Woodside Hotel. They kept 'em clean and had plenty of good food, but once you left there and you went to Niagara Falls or other places you didn't have the facilities. Buffalo wasn't too bad; you could use the clubhouses and get a hotel room for ballplayers. We're talkin' about 20 or 25 ballplayers per crack.

Eventually you left the Negro leagues and played minor league ball in California. How did that come about?

On the recommendation of Roy Campanella and Jackie. I was on Jackie's first barnstormin' tour and they offered me an opportunity: If I would come with them, they would send me to Hollywood in the Pacific Coast League. They knew I could play in the PCL; they'd seen me pitch in Los Angeles all during several winters.

Fred Haney told me, which was very honest, he said that he knew I could play in the Coast League but if he hired me he would be the first person to hire a black ballplayer and he wasn't goin' to do that because Bob Cobb was his friend. He owned the Brown Derby. He'd [Haney] rather that I go to Santa Barbara, which was the California League, a fast, fast league. Like the Eastern League — Scranton and those.

You moved to the outfield there and you hit everybody.

When I was with the Globetrotters, Radcliffe gave me a chance to play outfield. The days I wasn't pitchin' I was playin' left field. He tutored me and helped me to become an outfielder and I'm very thankful to him today 'cause I think I became one of the better hitters in baseball at the time.

Your stats bear that out: a .320 average in organized ball. Why did you not advance? You were still a young man.

I was more like a gate attraction. They had those workin' agreements and I didn't belong to a major league club, so the home clubs always held my contracts. Basically, I could put a few thousand people in the seats every night. Sometimes I'd pitch one game and play outfield the next.

I didn't want the credit for the victory; I just wanted to play. When we were losin' like 12–2, 12–3, to rest the pitchin' staff I would

finish the game from the third innin' or sixth innin' or whatever it was. I became something like a valuable person, I guess, not sayin' so myself, but seemingly valuable to a ballclub.

There wasn't but two ballclubs takin' blacks at the time, anyway. That was Cleveland and Brooklyn. I'd had enough of the Dodger organization because I'd been called that magic word by Bill Hart, the manager of Santa Barbara. That caused me to leave. I wrote to [George] Trautman, the president of the minor leagues, tellin' him the story of what happened and the names he had called me and I told him I was unable to continue with this organization and I wanted 90 days deferment. Retirement, they called it.

So when the 90-day retirement thing came, I went and signed with the [Visalia] Cubs. Nobody ever asked me anything about it, nobody ever said anything about me signing in retirement. [Laughs] I was supposed to wait 90 days before I came back and let them know whether I was ready to play or not. To beat that, I went to Mexico for about 60 or 70 days and when I came back I signed with Visalia team. They kept me there three or four years. They wouldn't let me out of there.

The only year I hit less than .300 was my rookie outfieldin' year. I should've been the Rookie of the Year 'cause I hit .288 hitting eighth and drove in 88 runs hittin' eighth. They gave that to some other little rookie that came that hit like .270 or something like that.

But I was accepted in all the cities by the fans, except Bakersfield. I'd catch more hell there than anyplace. They let the black cats out on the field and that kind of stuff. You can't let that annoy you; you just go ahead and play.

I couldn't stay in the hotels in Bakersfield, so they wanted to move the team on the outskirts of town in motels and I wouldn't let 'em because the players would be angry with me because they had girlfriends and places they wanted to go. They didn't have their own transportation so why move way out on the outskirts of town just to satisfy me because I couldn't get a hotel room? I had former ballplayers that were friends, like Mark Lewins and guys like that who had played for old, old teams like the Zulu Giants and they let me stay in their homes. We had a lot of fun that way.

Who was the best ballplayer you saw?

Oh, man, what a question. *What* a question. Who was the best ballplayer.

Well, I've seen 'em all. I saw Martin Dihigo, who could play most every position well with authority, but the best all-around ballplayer — geez. I'd have to put Dandridge in there. What was he — 33? — when he won the Most Valuable Player in the American Association? The Giants could've used him. If they'd used him, they'd have probably won the World Series.

What about Wild Bill Wright?

Wild Bill, he had no one else in his category. He was a big man, could run like a deer, and he could do everything. Switch hitter. Played outfield, played infield.

I liked Willie Wells for an all-around ballplayer. We're talking about positions now. For his position, he was the best shortstop we ever had. Nobody ever seen anybody like Willie Wells. And will never see anybody like him.

I was talkin' to Lou Boudreau the other day; we were talkin' about those times. Boudreau and I have been friends a *long* time. They used to come to the ballpark in Cleveland when they had days off and watch us play and we watched them play, too.

We had so many great ballplayers. Younger ballplayers like Monte Irvin, who came up, could do it all. Cool Papa — they held high esteem for Cool Papa. Josh was a good catcher. You couldn't run on him at will; he'd throw you out just like that.

Was he the strongest hitter you saw?

Oh, man. Yeah. The only thing, the balls didn't go over the rooftops. [Henry] Kimbro, whom I was with in Milwaukee, is the only person to hit a ball out of Briggs Stadium in Detroit. He was a good ballplayer. We saw him goin' out and he was one of the best then. Kimbro could do it, too.

He was a lifetime .320 hitter with a reputation as an outstanding fielder and leadoff man. Does he belong in the Hall of Fame?

I would think they're 30 years too late with him. Kimbro should be in the Hall of Fame and should've been there already. He wasn't known as a home run hitter; if you happened to get the ball in the wrong place, you could forget about it 'cause he'd hit the ball out of the ballpark. But not on a consistent basis like Josh.

Every time Josh swung a bat, you could more or less expect a home run. And he didn't have a lot of effort in his swing. You know, like guys go all the way around and swing from the heels — no. He'd just stand there like a statue and the ball would jump off the bat.

Who was the best pitcher?

Ohhh, man. Oh, wow! Just say Satchel and stop. [Laughs]

Hilton Smith, Chet Brewer — you can go on and on, but I would take Satchel over *all* of the pitchers.

Hilton Smith was on the same ballclub; he was *really* somethin' else. And Raymond Brown, who was with the Grays — knuckleball artist and a great hitter. He encouraged young pitchers to be hitters. Chet Brewer was one of the tops in his day.

Hilton Smith wasn't very tall — about 5'11" — but Satchel was above six feet and so was Chet Brewer — like 6'5". When they were throwin' hard in their hard-throwin' days, it was like they were shakin' hands with you. On some days it was almost impossible to get anything. If you got one run or one hit, you were very fortunate.

What about Verdell Mathis?

We left out the best young ballplayer of our time. The best pitcher in our time was Verdell. He should've been in the Hall of Fame. The team he had wasn't too much offensively, but they had some good hitters over there, like Neil Robinson and Nat Rogers. They were home run hitters.

But Verdell could win. Just give him one run and he wouldn't have a problem. He beat Satchel more than Satchel beat him.

Would you go back and do it all again?

Oh, of course. Sure. In spite of the difficulty. It's the most fun you could think of havin' on a day-to-day or night-to-night basis.

It's kind of lonely out there on the road but you have to produce, but you get over bein' homesick when you can send a few dollars home to help out. Money's not the objective, really. I think if the money wasn't out there now like it is, not even one-third of what it is now, ballplayers would be more willing. They'd be ready to play a better brand of baseball because they'd have to worry about their jobs. Multi-year contracts. If he's got a three-year contract he doesn't have to produce this year because he's got to play next year. It's terrible. You don't have to produce.

They're stronger today. They've got their weight lifting and all that. Their heads are not in the park, though.

The fundamental thing about the ballplayer of today, he's thinkin' about his yacht and his ranch and his house. I could walk through the dugout and ask them how many men are out and I imagine maybe one or two guys could tell me. They're not payin' any attention to what's goin' on around them.

And the manager can't fire 'em. The manager could hire and fire you when I was playin' ball.

When I played, if you got hurt badly it was all over for you. There wasn't any disabled list. You were disabled 'til next year and there wasn't any insurance when you went home. You were all on your own. It made you tougher. You played hurt. You had to put a headache away.

You should see Radcliffe and those guys' thumbs and fingers today. Like [Biz] Mackey—I played under Mackey. His thumb was turnin' almost back to his wrist.

Does Mackey belong in the Hall of Fame?

Yeah. A gentle giant and one of the finest managers I had the privilege of playin' for. He could help a ballplayer to become a better ballplayer. Without him, Larry Doby, Monte Irvin, Don Newcombe, and those guys would have never seen the major leagues.

He taught Campanella. He went to Campanella's father's store and asked his father to let him come with the team. He was just 15. He was a good guy. Campanella got what he deserved, bein' in the Hall of Fame. He could do it all. He was rough and tough. He was a high ball hitter—up about the waist.

BATTING RECORD

Year	Team, League	Pos	G	AB	R	H	2B	3B	HR	RBI	SB	BA
1941	Kansas City, NAL	p										
	Birmingham, NAL	p										
1942	Birmingham, NAL	p										
1943	Cleveland, NAL	p										
1944		p										
1945	Harlem Globetrotters, ind.	p										
1946	Chicago, NAL	p										
1947	Newark, NNL	p	6	28	2	10	2		0		0	.385
	San Luis Potosi, MxL	p										
1948	Newark, NNL	p										
	Tampico, MxL	p										
1949	San Luis Potosi,	p	10	8	1	3	0		1	3	0	.375
	M.C. Reds, MxL											
	Chicago, NAL	p										
	St. Jeans, ProvL	p										
1950	Santa Barbara, CaL	of										
1950	Visalia, CaL	of	106	383	73	112	22	4	14	83	7	.292

Year	Team, League	Pos	G	AB	R	H	2B	3B	HR	RBI	SB	BA
1951	Visalia, CaL	of	123	427	67	123	27	3	13	88	3	.288
1952		of	103	393	74	131	43	6	8	82	7	.333
1953	Victoria, WIntL	of	28	89	19	24	6		4	23	2	.270
1954	Visalia, CaL	of	124	446	77	141	27	3	14	81	12	.316
1955	Spokane, NWL	of	127	478	88	173	26	2	18	126	11	.361
1956		of	71	263	41	83	19	3	3	35	5	.316

PITCHING RECORD

Year	Team, League	G	IP	W	L	Pct	HO	BB	SO	ERA
Records are listed only for the years in which records are available.										
1943	Cleveland, NAL	1		0	1	.000				
1945	Cleveland, NAL	3	6	0	1	.000	8	5	1	
1947	Newark, NNL	6	34	2	4	.333	30		24	
1948	Tampico, MxL	2	6	0	1	.000	9	4	7	4.50
1949	San Luis Potosi, M.C. Reds, MxL	10	15	0	1	.000	11	30	5	11.40

Larry Kimbrough
"Switch Player"

BORN SEPTEMBER 23, 1923, PHILADELPHIA, PA
HT. 5'10" WT. 195 BATTED AND THREW BOTH

Negro Leagues debut: 1941

There have been many switch hitters through the years and, occasionally, a player has come along who can throw both ways. Switch hitting is encouraged, but for some reason switch pitching is not. It's a lot more difficult than switch hitting, so perhaps that's one reason it's not considered an asset.

As the result of a childhood injury, Larry Kimbrough became both a switch hitter and a switch pitcher, and he carried those abilities all the way to the only major leagues available to a black ballplayer in the early 1940s: the Negro leagues. With his unique talents, he played everywhere: pitcher, infield, outfield, and even catcher on the sandlots after his professional career was over.

Had baseball not been segregated, a lot of major league fans would have paid good money to see Larry Kimbrough perform.

I was a natural-born lefthander. My mother had one of those old-time washing machines with the wringer and I used to watch her wring clothes. I figured, well, one of these days I guess I'd try it. She was out of the room one time — out of the house — and me and my little fresh self, I tried it, but when I put the clothes in the wringer I didn't turn 'em lose. I went right through with the clothes. I got pulled up off the floor a little bit — not much, just a little bit — but what most of the trouble was, all the blood was squeezed right up to my armpit and I had a bubble of blood under my arm 'bout the size of a baseball. I went to the hospital and they cast it up. I had a cast on for a little over a year.

That didn't stop me because I wanted to play ball. Back up there, everywhere you went was a ballfield and a team playing. Most players were much older than me, but I got in there and played with the cast on and every-

thing. Did pretty good. That's how I started throwing with my right arm.

I had a tough time with my left arm. I didn't think I'd ever use it again, but through my mother's patience and forcing me to do things that I couldn't do, it came around. Like picking up a teacup. She would put the handle on my finger and I couldn't hold it up — I'd drop it — and she told me, "The next one you let fall on the floor, I'm gonna beat your butt!" So I scuffled and scuffled and I got the arm strength back.

At that time, I was using my right arm more than I was using my left, so I just got to throw righthanded, too. I was seven or eight, something like that.

You signed with the Philadelphia Stars right out of high school. How did that come about?

My dad and Ed Bolden, the owner of the Stars, worked in the post office and so my dad was telling him, "Come on out. I want you to see my son."

I was playing a game one day—I don't know who it was against; that's too far back—and I happened to look up and I seen my father. I saw this fellow with him, but I didn't know who he was. That was Ed Bolden.

They sat around 'til the game was over and then he talked to me. My father was there to make sure everything was all right, I guess. He [Bolden] asked me would I like to play with the Philadelphia Stars and I told him certainly 'cause that was the major leagues at the time for the black ballplayers.

So I went to them in 1941 right out of high school. At first, I was just a batting practice pitcher, but in '42 I started playing and in '43 I went to the service and stayed in there and come back in '46 and played some more.

Then I went down there to Richmond and I was playing ball down there and I did pretty good against the Homestead Grays. I was pitching for the Richmond Giants. The manager of Homestead caught me after the game was over under the stands and said, "How would you like to come with us?"

That was the premier team in the Negro leagues, so I finished that season out with them. I pitched a half a season with the Grays—pitched, played outfield, played infield, everything. I did it all.

Did you play right- or lefthanded in the field?

Infield, righthanded; outfield, sometimes both.

We were in the Polo Grounds one time. I thought I'd get a chance to catch up there because they batted for the last catcher we had. He was taken out for a pinch hitter and I was down in the bullpen warming up the pitcher, and we didn't tie the game up so I didn't go in, but I might've had a chance to catch in the Polo Grounds. I was ready.

I caught everything in the bullpen but you know that's a lot of difference behind the bat. I wound up catching anyway out in the sandlots. We had a fellow, he went over to the Washington Senators one time—he could throw hard, his name was Charlie Drummond—I used to catch for him all the time. In fact, I had a team when I finished playing professional ball—we would play semipro ball and they would book us in different towns. I was the catcher, the only catcher on the team.

How was your throw to second?

Just like a bullet!

When you pitched, was it left, right, or both?

Let me tell you how this started. I played at Ben Franklin High School. We were playing the powerhouse of the school league, Northeast High. I started the game and pitched righthanded; 'long about the middle of the lineup, a lefthander comes up. I called time and I told the coach, "Throw me my other glove, will you?" The guy was a lefthander, good power hitter. So he threw me out my glove and I got him out on a deep fly.

They couldn't understand. "Is he pitching lefthanded and righthanded?" I was practicing all the time and this was a good time to try it. I went on to beat 'em that day.

Everybody complained. "You can't do that." I said, "Why can't I?" There was nothing in the rules that said I couldn't. There was

Larry Kimbrough (courtesy of Larry Kimbrough).

nothing in the rules that said you couldn't switch hit, was there? I switch hit, too. First game I ever played [in high school], I think I hit two home runs — one left and one right. I was the talk of the town then, you might say. Everybody wanted to see me.

Did you pitch left and right with the Stars, too?

Yes, but not much. They wouldn't allow me. At that time, I was using my right arm more and I had better control. I could throw just as hard lefthanded as I could righthanded, with a better curveball lefthanded.

I pitched left and right in some games. The first game I started for the Stars was up in Niagara Falls, Canada. It was misty up there and none of the old guys wanted to pitch 'cause it was cold and they didn't want to hurt their arms. I told 'em, "Give me the ball. I'll pitch." I was a youngster then, about 18 or 19 years old.

I started the game righthanded and the guy I beat — listen up — Max Manning! The score was 4–2. I pitched the whole game, part of it lefthanded and the other righthanded.

You also played in the field. How good a hitter were you?

I did pretty good. I wasn't no distance hitter. I got my shots — line drives. I didn't get a chance to hit too much 'cause I was pitching and I was down there at the bottom of the lineup.

But then, when I went over to Homestead, I played infield and I batted second, third, maybe sometimes fifth. I got in my shots over there. The supporting cast was a little stronger than in Philadelphia at that time, so they let me play as much as I wanted to.

My best position was shortstop and second base, but I played mostly shortstop.

You played professionally through 1950. What then?

I went to the post office. I started in 1950; I was a letter carrier. I worked at the post office until I retired in 1981.

By being active all my life, I just couldn't sit around. Someone told me that an insurance company in town was hiring, so I went down to see them and I answered the questionnaire. They asked, "How come you quit?" I said, "I retired." "And you want to go to work?" I said, "Yeah. I couldn't stay at home. I'm used to going to work."

Two days after I retired from the post office, they wanted me to come to work. [Laughs] That was on a Monday. I told 'em, "No, I want to take a couple weeks off before I go to work." They told me they'd give me a week off, so I took a week off and went to work and I worked there eleven-and-a-half years before I retired again. [In] June 1992 was my last working day. That made 44 years — 33 and 11. I'm taking it easy now.

Who was the best player you saw?

We had a meeting recently and we had the same thing asked. Seven Philadelphia Stars are left living here in Philadelphia and we all see each other once in a while, so they had invited us up to Beaver College and we had a question-and-answer thing for WHHY-TV. They asked that same question and every one of us gave a different answer.

Here's what I said. The best hitter I ever saw was Josh Gibson. Bar none. He was the best *hitter* that I've ever seen. Following him would be Ted Williams. They're the two — left and right.

Now for the best pitcher. Everybody said Satchel Paige. Satchel Paige was great, *but* he had a teammate that followed him to the mound named Hilton Smith. He was as good or *better*. Like I told 'em, "If you didn't get any runs off of Satchel, you wasn't going to get any off of Hilton. That's for sure."

I threw another sucker in there that just made the Hall of Fame and passed away: Leon Day. Leon could do *any*thing. Everything but catch. He could pitch, play the outfield, play the infield, and *could* hit.

There were many other *good* ones. I dare say I don't know how to pick 'em apart. There were some *great* ballplayers in our day. There's too many to say who was the best.

That's one of the problems today. The casual fans — or even some not so casual — have heard of Josh and Satch, but for all they know those two played ball by themselves.

The back-up crews they had or the teams — we had some *amazing* ballplayers.

One of the fellows that played with us was Marvin Williams. Man, he could hit. Didn't much get by him, either. I hope in my day I'll see some of these go in the Hall of Fame.

That's a farce. I read a lot. I belong to SABR and I go through the books they send me and the names they write about I haven't heard of. They've got guys in there that I don't think belong in there. I don't know how these guys vote.

I was up there one time when we was trying to get Webster McDonald in. Willie Mays was there; it was the same time he went in. We had a meeting and all they said was, "Show me stats. Show me stats." See, we didn't keep stats. We kept scorebooks; in fact, I used to keep 'em sometime when I wasn't playing. But when it was filled up, we threw it away. We never figured this would happen. There would be stats in there that would raise your eyebrows.

Josh Gibson hit one out of Yankee Stadium, and he hit it to right field instead of left field. First time I went to Yankee Stadium Bill Dickey was injured and he was in the dugout. He said, "You see up there? That's where Josh hit one. *Out!* Not up there. Out." Yankee Stadium was a triple-decker at that time.

We played in '44 at Parkside. In today's terms it was a bandbox, but it was a nice field. It didn't hold too many, but that's all we had. The field was nice; it was soft.

Josh come up one day and hit one going to left field and when it left here, Bus Clarkson [playing shortstop] jumped and tried to stab it. That ball kept rising and rising. I guess if it hadn't hit some of the trees over there it would still be going. That thing left the ballpark so fast you couldn't hardly follow it. Still rising as it went out, just like an airplane taking off.

He hit a ball at Washington's Griffith Stadium; that's one of the biggest ballparks ever. Left field was about 400-and-some feet and then they had a fence where they had a Coca-Cola sign on top. He hit the Coca-Cola sign. That's a *long* way. He hit one into center field; it hit the wall and bounced back and he got a single out of it. It hit so hard it bounced right back.

I'm just telling you what I saw and what I know. Josh hit more than 72 home runs in a season. He hit 'em everywhere, and when I say home runs, they were *home runs.* He had 90-some one year, I think. Buck Leonard coming up behind him hit damn near 70 himself. That was a tandem there. You talk about a powerful team, that was more powerful than the Yankees were.

When I got to 'em, most of those guys were old as the devil. They'd been around. I was more or less a utility to help some of the guys when they got tired. "Put Kimbrough in!" and I'd go on out there and play. [Laughs] I started games, too, but that was the team. That was something to see.

Would you play baseball again if you were a young man?

I certainly would. I lived to play ball. My mother had to look for me to eat dinner every night 'cause there was a field not too far from us. That's where I was, me and my brother. My brother never went anywhere; he was a footballer. She had to look for us every night 'cause we were out on a field kicking a football or throwing a ball or something.

The kids don't play baseball now. I belong to an American Legion post up here. They wanted me to coach a team; they wanted me to put a team in the American Legion league. I told 'em anytime. They were going to buy uniforms and all the equipment. Do you think I could get nine players? Everybody said, "I ain't got no time for no baseball." They all want to play basketball, so consequently that idea fell through. They never had a team.

Any regrets from your career?

The only regret I have is I couldn't make it to the major leagues. That wasn't a regret; that's the way it was. That's the only thing.

I did have a tryout with the old St. Louis

Browns. The day that I had my tryout — I forget what town it was — it rained like the devil, so they called it off.

My next shot was with Cleveland. They used to have a team at Reading; it was the Reading Indians at that time, now it's the Phillies. I did have a tryout up there. They gave me the ball and they said, "Okay, Kimbrough, you pitch batting practice."

It was terribly hot and I labored out there for about a half-hour or so and I was soaking wet when I came in. Nobody could touch me; I figured it's you against me and I want to try to do the same thing you're doing, I said to myself.

I was just firing the ball straight in. I didn't give 'em no curveball or nothing like that — just straight fastballs — and no one hit it. At that time, they had a guy out there — Rocky Colavito — he was back with Reading to rehab, so they called him in to hit and he didn't do no better than any of the others. I blazed it right by him.

After that was over, they said, "What kind of pitches you got?" I told 'em, "A curveball and a knuckleball." That knuckleball danced crazy out there; the catcher couldn't hardly catch it. My curveball was just fair, but I guess it would've gotten better if I'd've stayed with it, but I used to use my fastball and my knuckleball most of the time.

Practice was over and they took a little kid up there — a lefthander, couldn't've been more than 16 or 17 years old. Lefthanded, about the size of Bobby Shantz or even smaller. They took him and told me I was too old. That's the only regret that I have.

George Susce, the catcher, he was the guy that was running the camp. I said, "Too old!" Well, I was 28 years old at the time, but I told 'em I was 22 'cause I was young-looking. They said, "By the time we put you in the minor leagues you'll be too old." So they took this youngster.

There was another guy with me; his name was Leon Miller. He didn't go anywhere. Me and Miller was the only two blacks up there. Miller played shortstop and I want to tell you, you never saw a vacuum cleaner clean up better than Miller did. He picked up everything — in the hole, back, and everything — and threw guys out at first. They didn't take him, either. We were both too old.

How it came about, we had a field right down the street from me. It was an insurance building and they had a field down there. It was about three or four blocks. I'm standing around — we wasn't playing, but I'd always go down and watch the other teams play on our days off; it was a league down there — and I heard these guys ask, "You guys know a fella by the name of Kimbrough?" He didn't know who I was, but I heard him say that. "We'd like to see him."

So naturally I figured I'd better identify myself. I told him, "I'm Kimbrough. What can I do for you?"

He said, "You got your glove and shoes?"

I said, "No. I only live right up the street." So I drove up to the house and got 'em and went back down there.

They said, "We want you to throw some."

I got a catcher and we tossed on the sideline for a while. That's how I got a chance to go to Reading 'cause I had my stuff that night. They told me to meet 'em there at a certain time on a certain night and that's what happened to me. George Susce turned me down. I was firing, too.

PITCHING RECORD

Year	Team, League	G	IP	W	L	Pct	H	BB	SO	ERA
1941	Philadelphia, NNL									
1942										
1943										
1943–45	military service									

Year	Team, League	G	IP	W	L	Pct	H	BB	SO	ERA
1945	Philadelphia, NNL									
1946										
1947										
1948										
1949	Homestead, ind.									
1950										

Kimbrough also played infield and outfield throughout his career.

Herb "Briefcase" Simpson
"Integrating Albuquerque"

BORN AUGUST 29, 1920, HORNVILLE, LA
HT. 5'9" WT. 170 BATTED AND THREW LEFT

Negro Leagues debut: 1941

In the current Negro leagues literature, there is as little information on Herb Simpson as there is on anyone, yet he played through the 1940s and half of the 1950s and he compiled a batting average well above .300 in a career split between the Negro leagues and white baseball.

A southpaw all the way, he was a first baseman–outfielder, but foremost he was a hitter. Small (5'9") by baseball standards, he didn't hit many home runs, but his line drives repeatedly fell safely, and his speed stretched many of them into extra-base hits. His ability to produce runs kept him in the heart of the order, usually batting fourth or fifth.

In 1952, he broke the color barrier in the West Texas-New Mexico League when Spokane (Western International League) sold him to Albuquerque. His play there in the Southwest was so appreciated that the team invited him to have his wedding at home plate and even brought in his family for the occasion.

His career ended shortly thereafter, though, when he was called back home to New Orleans twice, once because of his father's death and once when the highway department had to build a road through his home. The latter problem took a long time to resolve and he got out of shape. Rather than not play up to his accustomed level, he chose to retire.

How did you get with the Birmingham Black Barons?

I started off as a pitcher as a youngster and then first base and then outfield. I played outfield off and on.

I got with the Black Barons through Wesley Barrow and Winfield Welch. The Barons came to New Orleans to play and I was a youngster in school, just comin' outta high school. Then I started playin' semipro and that's when the Barons scouted me. I joined 'em in '41.

When I started playin' pro ball, I didn't pitch. I pitched in semipro. I played first base and outfield. I batted about .3-2, .3-5 [.302 and .305], somethin' in there. I used to hit more line drives. I wasn't a guy that golfed the ball over the fence. [Laughs]

I played with the Black Barons through '42 and then I went in the service. I played on a service team and we played in Oklahoma City. I was stationed there at Will Rogers Field. We played down in Hattiesburg Air Base, Laurel Air Base, then I went overseas. I played in England, I played in France.

When you left the service, you didn't return to Birmingham. Where did you play?

I started off with the Seattle Steelheads in the Negro Pacific Coast League. From that team, the Cincinnati Crescents was picked at the end of the season. They had guys like Luke Easter, Piper Davis, Paul Hardy, and John Markham; Lefty McKinnis, Goose Tatum, and Ulysses Redd; Sherwood Brewer, Collins Jones, Joseph Wiley, and a couple of others.

Green Beverly, Lester Burch, and Mike Berry. We was on the team that went to Hawaii. Jesse Owens was our business manager and we stayed over there 25 days. We played 16 games; we won 15 games. We returned to the States in San Francisco; we played the major league All-Stars in San Francisco and Oakland and then we returned back home.

I played pretty good. [Laughs] I think the only person that outhit me on that trip was Luke Easter. He was 'bout three points higher than I was.

I got a thrill outta this. We was in Hawaii and the people wanted to see Luke hit those home runs — you know, he used to golf 'em so far and all — and that afternoon he didn't hit any and I was lucky — I hit one. [Laughs]

He was a nice guy. He was big and strong and I was about 175 [lbs.] and 5'9". They call that small, you know. They had me hittin' in fifth place and Luke was hittin' fourth, and the teams like the Bushwicks in New York and the New York Cubans and a couple other teams, they would walk Luke to pitch to me.

Luke said, "You gonna let them walk me to pitch to you? Show 'em you could hit the ball."

Sometime I'd triple or double, and Luke told Welch, the manager, he said, "Look. You take this man and put him in third place ahead of me. *Every* time they walk me to pitch to him, he would triple and he'd be right on my heels. I'd be puffin' and blowin', tryin' to get around the bases. Put him in front of me and if he's lucky enough to get a single or get on base and I hit a home run, he can walk around." [Laughs]

So they did change it and one afternoon Luke hit a home run and I was on first. He said when he came by, "Now how do you like that? You could walk around. You didn't have to be runnin'." [Laughs]

I went to the Harlem Globetrotters the followin' season. They had a schedule! [Laughs] They played everybody in the league; every pro team or semipro team that wanted to play them, we played them. We went to Mexico, Canada, all over the United States; sometime we played three games a day.

Herb Simpson (courtesy of Herb Simpson).

On the Globetrotters team we had, the manager was Paul Hardy, and we had Julius Haddan, Sherwood Brewer, and Sam Wheeler and Howard Hay; Rogers Pierre, Louis Hutchins, and Alphonse Dunn. Arthur Morris and Eugene Harden, and we had Carswell. Frank Carswell, he came from the Cleveland Buckeyes. And [Laymon] Ramsey and we had Jesse Williams, came from the Kansas City Monarchs. He was playin' shortstop. That was the guy they went to see when they picked Jackie Robinson. [Laughs] And they had Andy Anderson, Winslow Means, Ameal Brooks,

1949 Harlem Globetrotters infield (l-r): Ulysses Redd, 3b; Sherwood Brewer, ss; Jesse Williams, 2b; Herb Simpson, 1b (courtesy of Herb Simpson).

another Jesse Williams from the Buckeyes, Boots Moore, Ulysses Redd, Sonny Smith, Jim Fishback.

When I left the Globetrotters I went to Spokane Indians in the Western International League and I played over there. Boy, it was cold over there! It was too cold.

We had another guy named Morris Burleson, a white boy, and they sold Morris Burleson to Albuquerque, New Mexico, and he told me, "I'm goin' to Albuquerque, New Mexico. If they need somebody over there, I'll tell 'em to please send and get you. I know you don't wanna stay in this cold."

You know what happened? The first baseman in Albuquerque broke his ankle. His name was Tony Munez. The first baseman before Tony Munez was Jim Marshall. You remember big Jim Marshall? Jim Marshall had played a couple of years there, then Munez went there and then Munez broke an ankle.

I was over there in Spokane and they had a guy, Ed Bouchee, and he had signed a contract to play major league baseball — to play pro ball — and in college you couldn't participate in any sport after you signed a pro contract, so the Phillies had bought him and they sent him over there to Spokane and the manager had me teachin' him how to shift around the bag — you know, move around first base.

When this boy broke his ankle in Albuquerque, they called Spokane and asked 'em if they had a Herb Simpson over there they would like to sell. They said, "We have a Herb Simpson but we didn't wanna sell him." They asked how much they wanted for him [Simpson] and they put me up for sale and they sold me to Albuquerque. I flew down to Albuquerque and it was much warmer down there and I enjoyed it.

I hit .342 down there the first year and the followin' year, guess what? [I hit] .372.

[Laughs] The third year I was doin' better than that; I was hittin' about .4-1 [.401] up until around about April. They called me and told me my father had just passed. They got a ticket for me and sent me home to the funeral, and after the funeral I returned back to Albuquerque and I played. My average started droppin'. I couldn't get that off my mind 'bout my dad 'cause he used to play ball. I ended up hittin' about .3-5 [.305].

The next year I went back and I played and I had a phone call to come back again. [Laughs] The house that I had, the highway was buyin'. They was gonna run a highway right straight through my livin' room and dinin' room. [Laughs] I had to go back home and take care of that business and they kept foolin' around and foolin' around. You know how it does, negotiatin' and all.

So after that, they sent for me a couple of times and I said, "No, I've stayed out so long I don't know if I could go back again." Come up to par, you know.

But they helped me a lot before I left there in '55. They let me get married at home plate. The manager and the owner said, "Herb, you've been playin' good ball. You're a single man. Why don't you get married? We know you have a good girlfriend. We'd be glad to let you get married at home plate. Why don't you call her and ask her if she wanted to do somethin' like that?"

They sent for mother and the girl that I married and her brother and my two young nieces. They [the nieces] were just gettin' ready to enter college. I was still in my 20s, my late 20s. [Laughs]

I came back after the weddin' and we went all through spring trainin' and the season opened up and they called me 'bout that highway.

Was that when you retired?

Yeah, right. They kept after me so long I said I probably can't get back up to par, so I stayed home.

I played softball around here three times a week. I played first base and did a little pitchin'. We used to throw it like they'd throw a baseball; we'd curve it and throw it hard. I did that for a couple of years and I was workin' at this plant, Johns-Manville. I worked there for about three, four years and then they started layin' off and I said, "Well, I think I'll get somethin' else now."

I started workin' for the Orleans Parish school board as a head custodian. I did that for 20 years. I retired from the school board in '78.

When I left the school board I had a better job offered to me. I was workin' for the state of Louisiana and they offered me a little bit more money than I was makin' after 20 years with the school board. [Laughs] I worked for the state ten years.

Who was the best player you saw?

I got a chance to play with the old man Willie Wells. I played with Piper Davis, Art Wilson.

I played against Satch. The first time I met Satch, I didn't do too good. A guy told me, he said, "Don't worry about that. That's your first time meetin' him. You'll get used to him; you'll hit him just like you hit the others."

Finally, like he said, it started comin' around. I started hittin' Satch pretty good. Satch came to me one day and he told me, "You know somethin'? You're gonna be a hell of a ballplayer." [Laughs] He told me that.

I played against so many good ones. All the guys on the New York Cubans: [Louis] Loudon, [Dave] Barnhill. I played with Jesse Williams, Paul Hardy—he used to catch Satchel a lot in those All-Star games, and he used to catch for Birmingham when we were there, and they had a lotta others I played with. Willie Lee. I played against Cool Papa Bell. He was still fast.

Was Satchel the best pitcher you saw?

I don't think so. I liked this guy used to pitch for the Homestead Grays and one with Kansas City was real good, too—Hilton Smith. And another was Theolic Smith. And Verdell Mathis. Ray Brown was the one with the Grays. And ol' [Roy] Partlow. Gentry Jessup, Mike Berry. They were great pitchers.

I'll tell you what Satchel did one time when I played. Paul told him — him and Paul was good friends, Paul used to catch him — and Paul told him, "See that kid there? That's a fine young man there."

Satch said, "Where's he hittin'?"

Paul said, "He's playin' first base. I had him hittin' in fourth place."

"Oh, that's your bad man."

"No, he's not bad, but he's a good hitter."

We had a guy hittin' behind me that I always thought shoulda been hittin' fourth. I didn't mind hittin' fifth or third. This guy — his name was John Miles, not Zell Miles — and he could hit a ball a country mile. That night we played against Satchel and Kansas City, Satch said, "Little fella, they say you hit in that fourth place. What you like to hit?"

I told him, I said, "I like to hit the fastball."

He said, "In or out?"

I said, "It don't make no difference." [Laughs]

And he throwed me three good fastballs right down the heart of the plate. I didn't hit any of 'em. I just went zip-zip-zip. [Laughs] I went on back then and throwed the bat down and a guy told me — Jesse Williams — "Don't worry about it. You'll get him later. Wait 'til he's pitchin' one afternoon somewhere and the sun's shinin' nice. Anything he throw up there, you gonna hit it."

I said, "You think so?"

He said, "I know so."

We played 'em in Houston at the old ballpark in Houston. They didn't have no top on it, you know. Satchel was pitchin' and I came up and I got a double. I was surprised. And next time up, I singled. A guy told me, "See, it's comin' around. You were playin' under those lights the other night when he was pitchin'. It's daytime now and you can see a little better." [Laughs] From that day on, I always got me one or two hits off Satch.

Did you have any problems when you traveled about the country?

Not on the colored teams because we always stayed in colored hotels, but I did out in Albuquerque. Not *in* Albuquerque. I was the first Negro on the Albuquerque team, I was the first Negro in the West Texas–New Mexico League. We went to Amarillo and we had a little trouble. Just one guy.

Buck Faucett was my manager. He told me, "Don't worry. We'll clear it up." A guy — one person — he told Buck, "Buck, why you so red?" And he said a lotta stuff and Buck told him to keep quiet.

So you know what happened? Two of those guys — I didn't know what had happened 'til after it was all over — they called this one man outta the grandstand and they went up under the grandstand and they gave him a lickin'. He came runnin' back to the grandstand and he said, "Oh, they hit me!" And the grandstand of people was so quiet you could hear a pin drop. No one said nothin' else. And I never had any more trouble anymore.

The only other place I had a little somethin' happen was in a little town called Borger, Texas. Borger was in the league, and we was in the hotel and we was gettin' ready to go to the ballpark. Buck Faucett's room was next to mine and my roommate and I was layin' across the bed when the phone ring. I answered the phone and they said, "Mr. Simpson?" and I say, "Yeah." She said, "I'm sorry, but you're gonna have to move." I said, "Well, okay. Mr. Faucett is next door. Call him and tell him."

One big Texan didn't want his wife sleepin' in a hotel where they had a Negro, so Buck said, "If my ballplayer can't stay in here, my whole ballclub's goin'."

A colored lady. Mrs. White, had a motel — a nice motel — and a big restaurant. A lotta white and colored would go there 'cause it was so nice and clean. They had barbecued ribs, some of the best barbecue in Texas.

They took the ballclub over there and the lady said, "Yeah, I have room for all of you all. And I guarantee you, you'll get you three meals a day." That word got around to all the ballclubs in the league and do you know all those ballplayers started comin' over there?

Later on durin' the season. Albuquerque added another colored and one or two of the other teams had one. Remember Jonas Gaines? Well, Jonas Gaines used to pitch for Baltimore. Baltimore Elite Giants. He came over to play with Pampa in that same league. And they had Quincy Barbee and they had a Harrison and a Williams. They all played for Pampa. I think it was Marvin Williams. Some of the other teams, they had Sad Sam Williams — used to play with Birmingham — and a couple other guys that played in the league, like Eddie Locke. Amarillo had Eddie Locke. And Albuquerque had about three more. Oh, we had about four or five over there. When I left there, the whole league had about 30.

Before I left Albuquerque, Albuquerque sent me to Oakland. Charlie Dressen was the manager over there, and Cookie Lavagetto. They sent me over and I went over there the whole spring and played. Piper was on that team, Billy Martin, also, and Allen Gettel. I played over there in the spring. And Jim Marshall was over there, also.

Charlie told me one day, he said, "You know somethin'? I *love* the way you play." [Laughs] I said, "Oh, thank you." He said, "I'll tell you what. Would you like to stay here and play every other day or so like that, or would you rather go back to Albuquerque, where you can play every day? Think about it. Take your time; don't rush."

I told him, "I think I would rather go to Albuquerque where I could play every day." And they sent me to Albuquerque.

I used to like to play in that ballpark in Emeryville [Oakland]. When I was with the Globetrotters, we used to play the House of David in there and we played the Hawaiian All-Stars in there. That's where I broke my ankle, slidin' into third base in 1948. I got caught in that bag.

Any regrets from your baseball days?

No, I got no regrets. I enjoyed it.

Would you do it again?

Yeah, sure. [Laughs] I would love to.

BATTING RECORD

Year	Team, League	Pos	G	AB	R	H	2B	3B	HR	RBI	SB	BA
1941	Birmingham, NAL	of-1b										.305
1942		of-1b										
1943–46	military service											
1947	Harlem	of-1b										
	Globetrotters, ind.	1b										
1948	Chicago, NAL	of-1b								4		.308
1949		1b-of								1		.290
1950		1b-of										
1951		1b-of								2		.330
1952	Spokane, WIntL	1b										
	Albuquerque, WTNML	1b										.342
1953	Albuquerque, WTNML	1b										.372
1954		1b										.305
1955		1b										
1956		1b										

Wesley Dennis
"Doc"

BORN FEBRUARY 10, 1918, NASHVILLE, TN
HT. 6' WT. 170 BATTED AND THREW RIGHT

Negro Leagues debut: 1942

One of the many really good ballplayers to come out of Nashville, Tennessee (others include Henry Kimbro, Wild Bill Wright, Butch McCord, and Jim Zapp, to name only a few), Doc Dennis enjoyed a very productive 14-year career in the Negro leagues. He divided his time fairly evenly among the Baltimore Elite Giants, Philadelphia Stars, and Birmingham Black Barons, spending either four or five years with each club.

The stereotypical first baseman is big and slow and often in the lineup mainly for his bat, but Dennis was far from the stereotype. He must have been a heck of a first sacker, because he was agile enough and had the range and the arm to be a regular middle infielder, which he was early in his career.

But he *did* hit like the stereotype: a lifetime batting average near .300 and home run totals in the mid 20s year after year. He hit more than 200 round-trippers in his career in the Negro leagues. He was considered by his teammates to be the best hitter on the Birmingham Black Barons in the 1950s.

Here are a couple of little-known facts about Wesley Dennis: the nickname "Doc" was given him by childhood friends and it has stuck with him throughout his life. And to illustrate just how good an athlete he is, after his baseball days were over, he became an outstanding golfer.

Where did you start playing baseball?

I started in the sandlots around the Nashville area as a kid. Some of the players off other teams recommended me to play with them.

The owner of the Baltimore Elite Giants lived here and they decided that they wanted me to try out for the team. I was 18, I think. I started out as a shortstop, but at that time I was playing second base.

I'd been with the team just about a year and the fella they had playing second base, I don't know what happened but they got into it. He lived in Puerto Rico. They let him go and had me to try out at that position. I was about 21 or 22; it was 1942.

From there, I went to the Philadelphia Stars. At that time, a fella named Johnny Washington, he'd been in the Army and he got out and he come back to the team [Baltimore] and they let me go then.

When did you become a full-time first baseman?

At that time I did, when I went to Philadelphia. I was there 'til '49, then I went to Birmingham.

Some of your teammates told me you were the best hitter on Birmingham. Is that true?

[Laughs] Yeah, I'd say that.

What was your best season?

I batted about .325 one year with Philadelphia. My lifetime was 'bout .300. I hit 'bout 25, 30 home runs a year. Every year I hit at least 20 home runs.

How good a fielder were you at first base?
I was a pretty good fielder. You know, I moved from shortstop over there, and second base. I was a pretty good fielder.

Who was the toughest pitcher for you?
A guy named Henry Miller was one of the toughest pitchers. He was with the Homestead Grays.

Who was the best player you saw and who were the best players on your teams?
I think the best was Josh Gibson. He was great. The best I played with were Roy Campanella, Junior Gilliam, and Henry Kimbro. He [Kimbro] was sort of gruff, but he wasn't nasty.

You played for several managers. Who was the best?
A guy named Felton Snow. He was my manager with Baltimore.

Which of the teams you played on do you consider the best?
I imagine the Baltimore Elites was the better team during that time.

Did you play with Wild Bill Wright in Baltimore?
Yeah. He was real good. Real fast. He was a big fella, but he was real fast. He belongs in the Hall of Fame. They mention his name and he'll probably be selected. Some of the black players during that time got selected to go to play over with the teams in Puerto Rico and like that. He went to those places.

Did you ever go to Latin America?
No. I was supposed to have gone over there, but I never did go.

You guys traveled everywhere.
Yeah. The only mode of travel we had was riding the bus, sleeping in the bus. Sometimes we took long trips — real long trips. Like we'd travel from Philadelphia, we'd travel for 'bout half a day and then have to jump out of the bus and play. [Laughs]

Doc Dennis (courtesy of Wesley Dennis).

We were segregated, you know. Some places had pretty fair hotels, some places wasn't. They were mostly clean, but convenience wasn't what it should be. We had to eat segregated, too. We had to eat where you could, a lot in the bus. [Laughs]

Everything was pretty good during that time. We knew what we had to do. It wasn't as bad as it looks now. That was just the way it was.

Sometimes we had our wives with us. We were staying at different homes, so we had 'em with us for a while. Sometimes a half a season they'd be with us.

What were your salaries?
I started out at 300-and-some a month. It was about 400 with Birmingham.

You were about 30 when Jackie Robinson went to Brooklyn. Was there an opportunity for you?
I imagine I was too old. During that time, the name Jackie Robinson was something. He had a name, you know; he wasn't noted for being just Jackie Robinson then. They picked him from Kansas City and they

"DOC" DENNIS

Doc Dennis (courtesy of Wesley Dennis).

gave him a chance and he made it after he played with Montreal. If it hadn't been for him, we probably wouldn't been in there now. [Laughs]

What did you do when you left baseball?
I had a trade that I'd do in the off-season before I'd go to play baseball and I'd come and take it up again. I was a stonemason. My father was a stonemason. And the whole family.

Any regrets from baseball?
No, none at all.

If you were a young man again and it was the early '40s, would you be a ballplayer again, knowing what it would be like?
Oh, yeah. I imagine I would. I'm pretty sure I would.

BATTING RECORD

Year	Team, League	Pos	G	AB	R	H	2B	3B	HR	RBI	SB	BA
1942	Baltimore, NNL	inf-of										
1943		inf										
1944		3b										.285
1945		1b								16		.232
1946	Philadelphia, NNL	1b										.288
1947		1b								22		.247
1948		1b										.325

Year	Team, League	Pos	G	AB	R	H	2B	3B	HR	RBI	SB	BA
1949		1b										
1950	Birmingham	1b										
1951		1b										
1952		1b							28			.318
1953		1b							23			.311
1954		1b										
1955		1b										

Ralph "Big Cat" Johnson
"500 Club"

BORN NOVEMBER 24, 1924, BARTOW, FL
HT. 5'11" WT. 180 BATTED AND THREW RIGHT

Negro Leagues debut: 1942

Let's run down the list of players who have hit 500 home runs. We start with Hank Aaron. And there's Josh Gibson, Babe Ruth, Willie Mays, Mike Schmidt, Sadaharu Oh, Mickey Mantle, Frank Robinson, Jimmie Foxx.

That's just a partial list, of course, but those are well-known names. The point is, the names of the men who have hit 500 home runs are names all baseball fans know. Or thought they knew.

How about Ralph Johnson? How many 500-home run lists have his name on them?

Johnson was primarily a third baseman, but he also played a lot of shortstop and a little bit elsewhere. His career was neither long nor celebrated, but it was productive.

How did you get into professional baseball?

I finished high school in '38. I was in Miami, Florida, and I started playing with the Miami Giants, which was associated with the Negro leagues. During that time, the Indianapolis Clowns came through, but they wasn't the Indianapolis Clowns then; they was the Ethiopian Clowns. They picked me up and I started traveling with them. This was in '42. I traveled with them for a while, then I got me to New York. That was how I got into the Negro leagues.

My main position was third base, but I did play shortstop, second base, outfield. I was kind of a utility guy, but third base was my main position.

What was your main team?

The *big* name team was the Indianapolis Clowns, and I went to the New York Black Yankees, then to the New York Cubans. Then we hit the road and I wound up with the New Orleans Creoles. During that time, when I got

to the Creoles, they had a girl by the name of Toni Stone.

I played with them for a while, then I went to the Dominican Republic, out on the island. I went down there for a couple of years and then came back to Birmingham. That was in '49. Willie Mays was there; he was in the outfield. I played with them until '50, then I went to Kansas City to be with the Kansas City Monarchs. I was there until '55. That's when I stopped. Twelve years.

Do you know any of your career numbers?

I got a book right here with it in it. I averaged .296 for my career. I tell some guys about that and I say, "Man, look what the guys are getting now for .250." [Laughs] And I think I hit about 600 home runs. Man, I could've been in the money.

I was a power hitter. They talk about this guy McGwire. The Big Cat. That was my name when I was playing. I'm the original "Big Cat." [Laughs] I think it says 540 in the book. I was an old slugger.

When I started out, when I went up there, that's when I started seeing the curveball and all the other balls up there. A guy named [Roy] Partlow played with the Baltimore Elite Giants: *good* lefthander. After we left New York, we stopped in Baltimore and I hit two home runs off of him that night. Boy, that went 'round the league just like hotcakes. Everybody knew about that because Partlow was a *good* lefthander.

And then I batted against Connie Johnson and [Dan] Bankhead. He was over there at the Baltimore Elite Giants at the time. I think Partlow was the best pitcher. He was good.

But, man, I'm telling you. We had some good pitchers. We had some good ballplayers. Just like Joe Black. He was pitching in our league. We had Don Newcombe and Sad Sam Jones. He was with Cleveland. Bankhead was good, too.

I'll tell you another guy you probably hadn't heard of, a boy out of Winter Haven, Florida. They called him Schoolboy. Schoolboy Tugerson. It was two brothers: one of 'em was named Leander [Schoolboy] Tugerson and the oldest one, I forget his name [Big Jim]. The oldest one, he was about 6'2", 250 pounds. He was a *big* guy, boy.

Buck O'Neil was the manager when I was in Kansas City and we were playing in a little small town and playing the Clowns and Schoolboy was pitching. He hit Buck O'Neil the side of the head and I thought he [O'Neil] was dead. You could hear it all over the park. *POW!*

The thing about it, I was playing in the Grapefruit League down in Florida with Schoolboy during that time. I was with the Lakeland Tigers and he was playing with Winter Haven. After that, I wasn't too sure I wanted to go up there and bat. [Laughs]

Does one game stand out?

The best game that I remember was when we played the Jackie Robinson All-Stars. It was in Miami, Florida. It was an All-Star team that traveled around together. Jackie was playing second base. To me that was the best game I ever played in.

Ralph Johnson (Ben Darmer photograph).

They had some good ballplayers on there. They had Campanella, Junior Gilliam, Joe Black. That was it to me 'cause I was a little country boy. Within two or three years' time, I was playing ball with those guys. That's what made it such a thrill to me.

I'll tell you something that was exciting to me, too: when I went to New York, I got to New York on a Thursday and I couldn't sleep. I wound up in the Yankee Stadium. Man, that was something because I'd heard so much about the Yankee Stadium and Babe Ruth and all those big guys. The Yankees was out of town and the way they did that, the Black Yankees, whenever the New York Yankees leave, then they would book the Black Yankees out there to the stadium. Oh, man, that was exciting for a country boy. [Laughs]

Of all the teams you played on, which one do you consider the best?

The best team I played with was a semi-pro team called the Panama City Blue Sox. This was in '41 or '42. I was just 17, 18 years old. That was a good team.

We was booked to go out to Arizona for a tournament. If our team could've made it out there I'd've been into the majors, but something happened — I don't know what it was — and we didn't make it. It was bad. We had a *team* there.

Did you ever have an opportunity to go into organized ball?

Yes, I did, with the St. Louis Cardinals' chain in Hamilton, Ontario. I remember one summer — it was the beginning of summer in '44 — I was in Tampa at the time and the team from Ontario was doing spring training down there. They took me up there and I hurt my arm and had to come home. It come back, but not like it was in the beginning. I can use it, but that's what hurt me up there.

The same thing happened to me down in Dominican Republic, too. Down there, I went after a fly ball and I hit one of those concrete walls. They didn't have doctors down there the way they had here in the United States. I set there and my arm got big as my body.

You saw a lot of ballplayers. Who were the best ones?

Ralph Johnson (Ben Darmer photograph).

During that time, Willie Mays, Hank Aaron, a boy named Willie Wells, Buck O'Neil. I could just name a whole lot of good ballplayers then. The best ballplayer was a man named Archie Ware. I loved that ballplayer. He was a first baseman. He was with Baltimore and then he went to Cleveland. Oh, boy, that was a sweet ballplayer. Field and hit. He could do it.

And then they had another boy who played for the Newark Eagles. His name was Jimmy Hill. He died a few years ago. He was a lefthander; he weighed about 160 pounds. And was about five feet tall. [Laughs] [Hill actually stood 5'5" and weighed 140.] He could bring it, man, I'm telling you. He come out of Florida, too, because he was playing on the Lakeland Tigers team that I was playing on in Florida.

You played with a lot of teams and traveled all over the country. How was that?

Did you see the picture, *Soul of the Game*? Before the show started, there were about 15 or 20 reporters around talking to the guys down there. They said, "We'll cut off now and after the picture we'll talk some more." After the picture, I went down in the auditorium. About ten of 'em come up to me. I said, "They just fucked that up!" [Laughs] "They should've got me to narrate that thing 'cause I was there."

I was on the road all night long, sweaty uniform, nowhere to eat or sleep, get up the next morning and sometime play two baseball games. We got 75 cents a day, then it went up to three dollars a day for eating money. Got paid $290 a month. Wasn't none of that kind of stuff in there. They only talked about three guys.

In '92 or '3, we went to the Hall of Fame. They put 26 guys in the Hall of Fame, not for playing baseball but what they contributed to the game. They give me a medal — a bronze medal — that said, "Negro League Baseball Hall of Fame." I think as much of that as if it was gold. I really do.

Ever hear about the boy named Chico Renfroe? He was down on the island when I was down there. From '46 up until '89, he was here in Atlanta and he's the one that got this thing going, him and Southern Bell and the Atlanta Braves. They brought it out.

The first time when they got all these guys together, there was about 250 of 'em. All of 'em wound up right here in Atlanta for a whole week. We had a ball around here. And that got the ball to running.

The girl Toni Stone, when we were playing with New Orleans one night, we were playing in Council Bluffs, Iowa, right across the river. The lights up there were dim. The ball was hit to me and I threw it to second base for a double play. Back then the gloves wasn't made too good. I threw that ball from third base to second base and the ball went through the glove and hit her in the forehead. Knocked her out. Laying on the ground. A guy was yelling, "Get the water!" They poured the water on that girl and she jumped up. "Let's go! Let's go!" [Laughs]

I didn't see her no more 'til the Hall of Fame. I was walking around asking, "Has anybody seen Toni Stone?" "Yeah. She's over there." I looked all over the place and all the time she was about eight or nine feet from me.

I'm calling, "Toni! Toni!" and she told 'em not to say nothing. I got right there by the lady in the wheelchair. I looked down at her. She said, "Ralph Johnson, you looking for me?" I said, "Toni!" She said, "Yeah. You tried to kill me, didn't you?" [Laughs]

Were there many problems?

There were a lot of problems, man. A lot of problems. Especially in the Southwest and in the South. Mostly in the South, like Mississippi, Louisiana, Florida, Georgia — places like that. It was tough on us.

I really got scared with the Clowns. We were playing right out of Mobile there, in Pritchard, Alabama, I think it was. We got to the ballpark and there was a sheriff out there; he was the umpire. He said, "You boys ain't gonna beat our niggers here in town, now."

Our manager said, "Don't pay that man no mind. Y'all go play ball."

'Bout the fifth inning, we had about ten runs. He come in our dugout. "I told y'all, you ain't gonna beat my boys." [Laughs]

So after a while, we started taking that thing seriously. He had two guns on his side. He started calling balls strikes. A man'd be safe on base and he'd call him out. 'Bout the eighth inning, our manager come and said to us, "I'll tell y'all something. Y'all better start losing this damn ballgame." [Laughs] "Boy, if it's hit to you, either you better miss it or throw it away or something. Let these guys get some runs."

About the last of the eighth inning, them guys had caught up. I think we was tied up. In the last of the ninth inning they won that game and that umpire looked at us, said, "I *told* you, didn't I?" [Laughs]

I remember another time I got scared. We was going on the highway and we was hungry. We didn't have no more canned goods in the bus to eat, and we found a little grocery store on the side of the road. Two men come with a shotgun. "Two of you boys come in here at one time. The rest of y'all stay out."

Man, I was *scared!* I really was scared. That's the truth.

Didn't nobody never get hurt, but we got to some hell of damn places.

What did you do when you left baseball?

Went about driving a truck. I had moved to Tampa from Bartow. I started playing baseball in the summertime; in the winter time I had this job driving this truck for a piano company. I did that for about six years. I'd go play ball and come back and I'd have a job.

In '58, after I got through playing baseball, I went back to Miami and started driving a big 18-wheeler all over the United States. I drove from '58 up until '83. The thing about it, wherever I was going in the truck, I had been there before and that made a whole lot of fun out of that. Every time I'd go to Kansas City, I had a whole lot of people there that knew me.

You see the world being a ballplayer. I'll tell you something else. When I started playing for the Indianapolis Clowns, you *saw* the world then. [Laughs] The Indianapolis Clowns went *all over* the United States playing baseball. The people didn't like us as a person, but wherever we went, there was more white people to the ballgame than there was black folks.

We'd be going to like North Dakota and South Dakota out there; the people'd be so glad to see Negroes out there. One or two families might live within a hundred miles and when a ballteam come to town, man, the people were so *glad* to see us. I mean, invite us to their homes and everything.

Do you have any regrets from baseball?

I do not. You know, the reporters asked me that. They said, "What about these guys making all this money, buying all these nice cars, nice homes, and things?"

I just told 'em, "I don't have no regrets 'cause I loved what I did. I loved the game of baseball." They could wake me up at three o'clock in the morning and say, "Let's go play a game, man," and I'd go play. The little bit of money we got, it was good money for us at the time, and that's the way it was at that time. We had good times.

They'd give us three dollars a day for eating money. You know what we would do? We could eat all day off about a dollar and a half. The other dollar and a half we would save until the weekend. 'Bout four or five of us would get together and we'd pool our money together. Every Sunday we would be in a major city because that was a league game in a major city. New York, Chicago, Cleveland, Kansas City.

After the ballgame that night, we four or five guys would get our money and count it up. We'd have about $30 or better. We would have us a hell of a good time. We'd get about five or six girls, you know, and get in a corner and get some wine and some beer. We would have a damn good time. [Laughs] It was good!

No. I did not have no regrets from it.

Would you do it again?

I sure would. If I was able to get out there and play it now, I really would.

I got a little eight-year-old boy. I adopted him at two-weeks-old. Right now he can play baseball. I'll be out there in the yard with him and he hits the ball, he throws the ball. He takes off on David Justice and Deion Sanders. He says, "I'm gonna get my education, make a lotta money, and buy you a house and a car." [Laughs]

In '95 or '96, I put him in school, and at this school the people voted me in to be the PTA president. I gave them all my background and everything and they found I played Negro baseball. They put that in the paper and they came out to the school and they took me and my little boy's picture where I was helping him with a baseball bat. The reporter put in there, said, "Mr. Johnson, a Negro baseball player, is now beginning to play baseball again with his son." [Laughs]

That went over here in this city. I got calls and people come in and invited me to all kind of programs around here.

I hope you can keep up with the boy.

[Laughs] That's the damn truth. I was in the house here from '83 up until '90 by myself. The walls was coming in; I couldn't sleep at night sometimes, so he's put ten years on my life.

BATTING RECORD

Year	Team, League	Pos	G	AB	R	H	2B	3B	HR	RBI	SB	BA
1940	Eth. Clowns, ind.	inf										
1941		inf										
1942		inf										
1943	Lakeland, NFlStL	inf										
1944		inf										
1945	Panama City, NFlStL	inf										

Year	Team, League	Pos	G	AB	R	H	2B	3B	HR	RBI	SB	BA
1946		inf										
1947	Santo Domingo, DR	inf										
1948		inf										
1949	Birmingham, NAL	inf										
	New Orleans, NSL	inf										
1950	N.Y. BlkYanks, NAL	inf										
1951	Kansas City, NAL	inf										
	N.Y. Cubans, NAL	inf										
1952	Jackie Robinson All-Stars	inf										
1953	Kansas City, NAL	inf										
1954		inf										

Annual statistics are not available, but Ralph Johnson reportedly hit about 500 home runs and had a career batting average of approximately .296. These statistics are for all levels of competition.

Jim "Lefty" LaMarque
"Dizzy's Boy"

BORN JULY 29, 1920, POTOSI, MO
DIED JANUARY 15, 2000, KANSAS CITY, MO
HT. 6'2" WT. 182 BATTED AND THREW LEFT

Negro Leagues debut: 1942

Jim "Lefty" LaMarque was a member of what may have been the greatest pitching staff in all of baseball: the Kansas City Monarchs of the 1940s. During that decade, the Monarchs' staff consisted of such as Satchel Paige, Hilton Smith, Connie Johnson, Booker McDaniels, Jack Matchett, Gene Collins, Gene Richardson, Theolic Smith, Ford Smith, Frank Barnes, and Eddie Locke, in addition to LaMarque himself.

Generally regarded as one of the two or three best southpaws in the Negro leagues during the '40s, LaMarque pitched in two East-West All-Star games and led the Negro American League with a 1.96 ERA and 15 wins in 1948, while losing only 5 games. From 1945 through 1949, his record was 55–19 in league play. And in 1951 with Mexico City, he led the Mexican League with 19 wins.

Had you played professional ball before you joined the Monarchs in 1942?

Just sandlot ball and baseball with a team that was from where I was from. It was a white team.

I was born in Potosi, Missouri. That's 73 miles southeast of St. Louis. We had a black club and a white club. The white club's pitcher hurt his arm some kind of way, so they asked me — a black boy — if I would pitch for the white club. We only played a few games a season, but I played two seasons with them and we won most of our games.

The Kansas City Monarchs heard of me and they wondered why a black boy would be pitching on an all-white team, so they got in touch with me and I came to the Monarchs in 1942, I guess, and I left them in 1950. Then I went to the Puerto Rican League, the Mexican League, and the Cuban League with the help of a man from the Monarchs named Mr. Dismukes. I did pretty good over there.

From there I went all the way to Tokyo, Japan. I wasn't playing with the Monarchs then; I had finished with the Monarchs and I came to Fort Wayne, Indiana, where I played in the Southern League of Indiana on an independent team sponsored by the TV company, Capehart-Farnsworth.

I played with them and we won the championship, which they had every year in Wichita. We won that, which sent us to Tokyo, Japan, where we won that entire thing. I'm the only pitcher that lost a game. I lost after I pitched 13 innings, and today nobody goes 13 innings, but in my day, as a pitcher, we hated to come out because we wanted to go all the way.

We came back here and I went to work for Ford Motor Company in Claycomo. I worked 30 years and a half. I'm retired now; I live by myself. I have a daughter who is 24 and my wife was 19 years younger than me. My daughter comes by as often as she can because she has jobs that keep her on the go.

I depend on my social security and my retirement money from Ford. We were getting money from the majors, which was supposed to come the first of every quarter — every three months.

I have a good friend named Herman ["Doc"] Horn. He's one of the ex–Monarch ballplayers. He comes by to see me pretty often — well, damn near every day — to take me to the store or wherever I want to go. We get along real good.

How did the players receive you when you joined the Monarchs?

I've got to thank Mr. William Dismukes again.

Maybe I ought to tell you this. You see, Mr. Dismukes scouted me. When I went to the Monarchs, there were two older ballplayers — I won't call their names 'cause they've been gone a long time — who would always refer to me as "Dizzy's boy." I think that made Mr. Dismukes feel, "I'm gonna make something outta him if it's the last thing I do."

He had been a pitcher like this pitcher that the Royals had — [Dan] Quisenberry. Came from way down. He was a very, very smart man. They say that he would be in a ballgame and be pitching and keep score on the scorebook between innings. All the records that we had with the Monarchs were kept by him. They're still somewhere now. I think the paper here in Kansas City may have them.

Mr. Dismukes ran the team. He was the trainer, he handled the money, he was the traveling secretary, he figured up the earnings. Mr. Dismukes handled just about everything, even the spring training.

Mr. Dismukes would take us pitchers down weeks ahead to where the team was going to train, down South somewhere. How he trained us pitchers, we would get in the bus, he would drive us five miles from town, put us out, and he just said, "Start walking." And each day he'd let you walk a little farther. He said, "If you get tired, slow down but don't sit down."

I don't remember a year that any pitcher we had was bothered long with a sore arm.

Jim LaMarque (courtesy of James LaMarque).

And in the hottest summers, he would make us pitchers wear sweatshirts, keep that shirt on the pitching arm. I never had a bad arm.

They put us in shape in spring training. Instead of running around, we went through physical stuff. I mean, we had to run around the park so many times. As time went on, spring training got tougher and tougher. We'd have to take exercises, I mean the roughest kind. You'd take them until you got so sore it would hurt you to raise your arm to try to comb your hair. That's a fact. But the soreness would finally wear off. I was a young man and I knew I was healthy, but after spring training was over, the soreness left out of your body.

You were regarded as one of the top pitchers in black baseball.

Well, some said so. People seemed to think I was pretty good.

Was there ever an opportunity to go into white ball?

There was a time. I used to belong to the

1949 Kansas City Monarchs pitching staff (l-r): Hilton Smith, Jack Matchett, Booker McDaniels, Jim LaMarque, Connie Johnson, Satchell Paige (courtesy of James LaMarque).

Monarchs, which was owned by a man named Wilkinson at first, and his partner was named Tom Baird.

I had talked to the chief scout of the Yankees at that time. He was named Tom Greenwade. After Tom Baird found out that they might want me, he hiked the price on me, so Greenwade told me, "At your age, I can't pay this kind of money." So I didn't go with him.

Is there one game from your career that stands out in your memory?

The most disappointing game I've ever had in my life was in St. Louis in Busch Stadium — the old one. It has to do with a very important man here, Mr. Buck O'Neil. Buck was my manager and the first baseman at that time.

I was pitching in St. Louis and I lived in Potosi, Missouri, where I was born, and everybody from far and near came to see me.

I had two outs in the ninth. Goose Tatum, who was one of the [Indianapolis] Clowns' ballplayers and one of the basketball players for the Globetrotters, hit a slow roller which bounced back to me. He had given up coming to first; he was just trotting. I tossed it to Mr. O'Neil, my first baseman, and he just stood straddling the base. He never did touch the base; I don't know what got on his mind. Anyway, he [Tatum] was safe.

The next man came up and really hit a shot towards the third baseman, which I would say was a hit 'cause I don't know who would've caught it because it was a bullet. I lost that game on account of that. I have never mentioned that to Mr. O'Neil, but that's the worst thing I had happen in baseball. I still remember it. I've never mentioned it to him 'cause he might have forgotten it by now.

That was a loss, but overall you did very well.

1949 Kansas City Monarchs. Back row (l-r): George Walker, Jim LaMarque, Frank Barnes, Connie Johnson, Elston Howard, Nat Peeples, Frank Duncan, Jr., Jeff Williams. Front row (l-r): Tom Cooper, Mel Duncan, Curt Roberts, Buck O'Neil (manager), Gene Collins, Herb Souell, Creshan (only name given) (courtesy of James LaMarque).

I won most of my games. I learned to have real good control. I guess my top speed was maybe 80 or 85 miles an hour. As I was in baseball, I was learning more how to pitch, but my fastball always moved. I couldn't throw a straight fastball, it just moved. I guess just the movement on the ball kept the hitters from hitting it as well as they could if it came straight at them. I think I was a pretty fair pitcher. Well, most people said I was.

I hit fairly good as a pitcher. I don't have but three home runs in my whole life, but I remember where I got 'em at, but my lifetime was .333.

One [home run] was in Mexico, one was in Fort Wayne, Indiana, and let's see, one was in Marshall, Texas. That was when I was still with the Monarchs. That was against the Memphis Red Sox.

Who was the best pitcher you saw?

Satchel Paige was the pitcher they said he

was, and he got most of the publicity, but there was a pitcher named Hilton Smith who was a very good pitcher who got no recognition, no publicity. He didn't do nothing but pitch. He kind of felt bad over the years because he didn't get any recognition. One of the reasons was 'cause Satchel Paige was the drawing card.

But Hilton was a friend of mine and he was as good a pitcher as I've seen then *and* now. He was a *smart* pitcher, he had good control, he had everything.

He was as good as Satchel and way back then he was throwing that forkball they talk about now, and he had a knuckler and everything. And was a good hitter. I have seen him pinch hit and he could hit the ball a long ways and you couldn't hardly strike him out. He was just an outstanding ballplayer who got no recognition whatsoever.

Who was the best player you came across?

There were some players who were out

of baseball when I came. Jackie was one of the best. Jackie Robinson. Josh Gibson — of course, he was a great home run hitter. You just had a bunch of 'em. You had Willie Mays. Mays started playing with the big team when he was no later than 15.

We had one man named Bonnie Serrell who was a very good ballplayer. He could play *every*where. I mean, he just could play. He didn't feel very good because he thought *he* should've been the first one to go to the majors, other than Jackie.

Now here's how I feel about that. Mr. [Branch] Rickey knew who to send because he knew this man had to take all the abuse and all the other bad things that was happening between the races at that time, and I think that Jackie was the right pick. He was the best man for the job, I'll say that.

Willard Brown was a teammate of yours.

Willard Brown was as good a ballplayer as I have ever seen *if* he would have played as good as he could have. I guess you would call him just lazy. He loved the game and he could hit that ball out of any park as many times as you'd get it in there wrong. And he had speed on the bases, but he wouldn't slide sometimes. I have seen him steal second base and try to stop on the base and his foot come off the base and they'd hold the ball on him and he's out.

He loved to be around women. He wasn't trying to go with women, but he just loved to be around 'em. I knew him pretty well and I knew his wife. He was as good a hitter as anybody — if he wanted it. Brown had the power, too, and they would always keep the ball away from him. He was a righthanded hitter. We finally got him to hit the ball where it was and it'd go out of the park just the same. He was a good ballplayer.

How were the travel conditions?

According to the history before me, it was on trains and buses. My owner was named J. L. Wilkinson and I guess he had a little money. He was able to get us where we wanted to play. At my time, we rode in an ordinary school bus like you see going up and down here now — a yellow bus. Then as time went on, we got a flexible, which was a pretty nice-looking bus. It was more streamlined. We traveled in that quite a bit.

Mr. Wilkinson would not let us miss a ballgame. I remember one time we wrecked the bus slightly — we were in Pennsylvania — so Mr. Dismukes got us on a plane to be sure we got to the game.

What was your best salary?

My best salary was at the end of my playing time with the Monarchs. I made $125 a month when I first started; when I got out with 'em, I was making $500 a month. Mr. Wilkinson gave me a $500 bonus.

How much meal money did you receive?

When I came to the team — that was '42 — we got a dollar a day, then it was raised to three dollars a day. Mr. Dismukes was the traveling secretary and trainer, also. A lot of times he would give us *all* of our money at the same time and that'd be a pretty good lick — about $25. A lot of 'em just blew it all.

We were disciplined not to be going out at certain times. After we'd been riding and we got to the hotel or places where we were going to stay, we were not allowed to sit downstairs or be seen in our riding clothes after an hour after we stopped at any hotel or motel. It would be summertime, so you'd put on a nice shirt and pants, or if you wanted to put your suit on, you could.

If you were a young man again, would you be a ballplayer?

If I was young enough, yes. I believe I'd have made it, too.

PITCHING RECORD

Year	Team, League	G	IP	W	L	Pct	HO	BB	SO	ERA
1942	Kansas City, NAL			1	1	.500				
1943										

Year	Team, League	G	IP	W	L	Pct	HO	BB	SO	ERA
1944		8	44	2	3	.400	48	18	27	4.50
1945		12	83	8	2	.800	75	23	70	3.04
1946				7	3	.700				
1947		19	133	12	2	*.857	141	43	99	3.79
1948		25	*170	*15	5	.750	128	44	109	*1.96
1949		27	*196	13	7	.650	*187	39	96	3.08
1950		16	119	6	7	.462	105	29	53	3.25
1951	Kansas City, NAL									
	Mexico City, MxL	46	233	*19	6	*.760	279	93	72	4.17
1946–47	Havana, CWL	21		7	6	.538				
1947–48		32		11	7	.611				

* Led league

Ray "Junior" Miller
"Cleanup"

BORN OCTOBER 11, 1927, LEBANON JUNCTION, KY
HT. 5'8" WT. 180 BATTED AND THREW LEFT

Negro Leagues debut: 1942

Ray Miller was a .300 hitter with power who dominated the upper Midwest with his batting in the late '40s and early '50s.

His power shows attracted a Cincinnati Reds' scout and Miller signed with that team in the '50s, but subtracted a few years from his age. After a few years, he wearied of travel and returned to Michigan, where he continued to hit home runs for several more years at the semipro level.

Born and raised near Louisville, Kentucky, he returns there every May for Derby Week.

The way I got started was with the family. My father loved baseball and formed a club with family members. My dad played as pitcher; the rest of the team was made up of my three uncles on my mother's side, my brother, myself, the local schoolteacher, and my sister. When my sister started courting, her husband-to-be joined the family team. I was about 14 or 15 when my dad started to let me play.

From there I played with a team there in Louisville, the Louisville Black Colonels, and also with the Zulu Cannibal Giants. The Zulu Cannibal Giants was where I really got started. The manager was a tall, thin man from Africa by name of Charlie Henry. Charlie Henry was quite a character. He played a heck of a game; he played it like a showman. He was the one who knew how to draw the crowds. Charlie was from everywhere—New York City, Boston, Washington; there's no place Charlie hadn't been.

I stayed a while at my grandmother's while I worked in Louisville. Charlie knew my grandmother. He had seen me and knew I could play, so he asked my grandmother if I could travel and play with his team. I was 16 or 17, so he promised her he would take care of me on the road.

Both the Zulus and the Black Colonels was at the same place and if I wasn't playing with one, then I'd be playing with the other club. It was a chance to make some money.

That was still during the war. How were the conditions for a ballplayer during that time?

There wasn't too much money. You passed the hat and see what you could pick up and you rode around in cars. We had three cars at least. Then later, around '46, they had a bus to take us around.

In Knoxville, Tennessee, we had the bus—we called it the Blue Beetle, one of them small buses—and the motor went out. It happened about 12 o'clock that night, I guess, as we were traveling through Knoxville.

I worked on it 'til about 12 o'clock. I went on in and laid down and another boy was trying to get it straightened out and he got hit by a cab. The fellow that owned the cab line, it was his son-in-law was driving and he told us he'd get us a bus, said, "Don't worry about a bus." And he did; he got us a larger bus. That made it pretty nice.

One guy got his leg broke and another one got his arm messed up. They had to stay in Knoxville 'til they got straightened out, but we kept on going. They didn't rejoin the team. When we left there, we didn't have over about seven men. When we played with the Zulus, we'd go into a town and see if we could find some ballplayers, somebody who liked to play and could play ball and they'd join right in with us.

Did you ever see a plaque of the Zulu Cannibals? We had our pictures taken and we'd put it on a post — a light post — and people would see it all around and they'd come to the game. Then we'd have our little grass skirts on and, quite naturally, our wigs and swimming trunks and all that stuff. We'd really draw 'em in.

We used to play serious even though we dressed up in outfits like clowns. We did a lot of what they called "shadow ball" before the games. It was our warm-up and it would throw the other teams off. They didn't think we could play as good as we did after all our fooling around. That Charlie Henry, he knew how to draw the crowd.

When you entered the service in 1945, were you drafted?

No, I volunteered. My mother and dad told me they were out of money and couldn't send me to high school like they had done my older sister and brother, so I went into the service. My brother and uncle were in there, so I thought I could join them, but they got out as I was going in. But it was okay; I learned a lot and traveled, too. I was in the Navy.

I got to play ball, too. I'd go look for games in the parks or lots. I played ball at Lane Field in San Diego. That's when I met and played with Satch, back in '46.

How was he?

Damned good. I played with him before I went in the service and I played with him there. Excellent. I got a finger hurt; when I

Ray Miller (courtesy of Ray Miller).

look at it now I think of Satch. I was catching him there in San Diego and I'll be damned, he threw a fast one and I was thinking he was gonna throw a curve, and that thing was up on me before I knew it and I reached out there and it hit me on the end of my finger. It made it raise up and as the years passed, it hasn't gotten any better. It isn't crooked; it's just a knot where it swelled up.

He threw as hard as he wanted to. I wouldn't be surprised if he wasn't throwing a hundred miles an hour — when he wanted to turn one loose.

That's when him and Josh Gibson had it. Josh was just like Babe Ruth in the black teams. He could throw him a couple, but then he better look for that pea — that fast one. Josh's trying to get ready for it and that daggone thing was by him. He [Paige] was a heck of a ballplayer.

He had that hesitation pitch and they wouldn't let him throw it in the major leagues. They outlawed it. They couldn't hit it. He was a good man. He was the best pitcher, ain't no doubt about that.

Isaiah Harris from Memphis, a left-hander, he was good. He could bring it in

1950 Grand Rapids Black Sox. Back row (l-r): Joe Drake, Smith, Herman Purcell, Jelly Taylor, unidentified player, Henry Saverson, Sammy Robinson. Front row (l-r): Reuben Smart, Eddie Perry, Robert Norman, Ted Rasberry (owner), Lord Cannimore (also known as Cannibal), Ray Miller, Jake Robinson.

there. Come from the side and straight over. They say now he's sitting around his home, not doing much. He was the tough one for me. He was about the onliest one I know of was a good lefthander. I hit 'em just about the same, right and left; there wasn't too much difference.

What I would like to do if I could is get enough young fellows and teach them the game. It doesn't seem like baseball is appreciated like it was in my day. There's a lot of talent out there if a fellow can just get to the young people and get them started. It would help keep them off the streets and away from drugs, maybe.

When I was coming up, that's all we thought of. We used to get in a truck and travel. After they'd get through hauling the freight through the week, on Saturday and Sunday they'd let us have that truck to haul the baseball players and various different ones — Mom, Dad, and whoever wanted to go out to the games. We'd make a big lunch and just have a nice time.

When you returned from the service, what did you do?

I got in touch with the Zulu Cannibal Giants. This was in '46. I played with them in '47 and then we got a team up and played all down through North Carolina and Alabama, and we wound up in Grand Rapids, Michigan.

Then we got with the [Grand Rapids] Black Sox club — Ted Rasberry's club — and I played with him from '47 for about six or seven years. We had one of the best clubs up this a-way. Then I played with Sullivan's for a while. That was an all-white team; I was the only black that was on it.

With Rasberry, we had Roscoe Price, a boy named Peanuts, LeRoy Levinson, Herman Purcell, Jake Robinson, Sammy Robinson, Joe Smith. That's about it; I can't think of any others right now.

Where did you usually bat in the order when you were with Grand Rapids?
Fourth.

So you carried a big stick.
All you have to do is come up here in Grand Rapids and get the paper back from '47 up and you can read all about it. You can

also just ask anyone from back then still around here. They'll tell you all about me.

You mentioned Josh Gibson. Who was the best player you saw?

Oh, boy! That's kind of a tough one. I can't say myself. [Laughs]

Sure, you can.

I'd always get the runs in, I can say that. We didn't lose no games up here in Grand Rapids with the Black Sox. We had some good players.

Doc Dennis was a first baseman, and a good one. I used to use his bat 'cause he had a heavy bat. When I played against him, I would use that bat; he'd let me use it. He was a good man.

With Sullivan's, we used to go down to Wichita, Kansas, where they have that big tournament. In fact, that's where I got signed with Cincinnati. It must've been in the '50s, and we got beat out by a team named Kelly Homes out of Flint. I had hit two or three home runs against Kelly Homes and he wanted me to go down to Wichita with him. They had another boy that was a good home run hitter.

So I got with him and went down there. After I'd hit about the second or third home run, a fellow — a scout — come out and asked me was I ready to sign 'cause he'd already talked to me. So I said, "Probably." After the games was over, I signed.

They sent me over to Havana, Cuba, for my training. Then we went to Yucatan, Mexico, for training, too.

I only played a few years with the Cincinnati organization because I was about getting washed up. You know, a lot of times you put your age down and it might be less than what you are, but after you get older you get tired of traveling. I've traveled ever since I was a kid.

Traveling was a way of life in black baseball.

The conditions wasn't too awful good. Like you might play half the night and it'll be 12 o'clock when you get through playing and you don't know where you're gonna get to wash up. You may have to ride another hundred miles or so to wash up, unless they got some creek down around there, or river, where you can go and wash up. 'Course, we carried our soap right around with us.

Very seldom could we find hotels. Didn't have many black hotels at that time. In Memphis there, they had the Travelers Hotel; I remember staying there. We usually stayed in the bus or go in some boardinghouse. Usually you'd find most of the black people down around the railroad tracks. We'd look for that and then maybe we'd rent the rooms.

We had to get some food, but you couldn't go in the front door. You'd have to go around the side and have 'em to pass it out to you. The stores and restaurants, too. We ate a lot of meals on the bus. Most of our meals were baloney, cheese, onions, and bread or crackers. Charlie Henry used to pass the bottle of castor oil sometimes before the games to unbound us for the game. [Laughs]

Back in the '50s when I was with Sullivan's, we went to Wyatt Earp's hometown going to Wichita, and in the cafe I seen 'em keep looking back at me. I was the onliest black on the club, see. Then he told Sullivan he could serve everybody else, but he couldn't serve me. So Sullivan said, "Come on. Get up, fellas; we're gonna leave outta here." So we got up and went on 'bout our business. This was Dodge City. Sullivan is a good man.

You played under a lot of managers. Which one did you prefer?

Ted Rasberry was a good manager. He knew the game very much, there ain't no doubt about that. Sullivan was a good manager, too. And Charlie Henry of the Zulu Cannibals. We used to do all right, but, 'course, we had to pass the hat to get paid.

We played that shadow ball with the Zulu Cannibals. I've still got my grass skirt and my sweater, wig, and the whole ball of wax. I'm gonna take it down to the museum in Kansas City.

How much did you earn?

Oh, it wasn't much. It was mostly passing the hat. We made enough to kinda survive, that's about it. I would make about 300 a month on some of those clubs, but mostly we was just having fun. Some fellows would get paid according to what they could do. Some didn't get too much.

Does a game stand out?

Yeah, in Michigan City, Indiana. I hit three home runs, a triple, and a double. The guy had a duck farm up there in Michigan City and he told Rasberry, "Take the boy home before he has my duck farm." I hit two righthanders out and a lefthander. I was playing with the Black Sox and we was playing against the House of David.

We used to have the Grand Rapids Jets here back in the 1940s. That was a farm club for black teams.

You played a long time. Do you have any regrets from your baseball days?

I can't say that I do 'cause I enjoyed every bit of it. That's what we did; we played it for fun.

We'd get in one of them trucks that delivered stock and stuff around this little country town in Kentucky and, boy, on Sundays, they started making them potluck dinners and then we'd head out for the ballpark. I had three uncles that played, my dad played, my brother played, I played, and my sister's boyfriend and his brother played. [Laughs] We had a family club. That was every weekend we did that. Every little country town had ball.

What did you do when you left baseball?

I settled down and got jobs. I finally settled to work with Meijer store. I also used to coach the company team. That was a lot of fun, too. I worked there over 30 years and never missed 30 days of work other than vacation. I worked there until I retired in '92.

Would you be a baseball player again?

I'd do every damn thing just like I did it before. I loved the game of baseball.

BATTING RECORD

Year	Team, League	Pos	G	AB	R	H	2B	3B	HR	RBI	SB	BA
1943	Zulu Cannibals, ind.	1b										
1944	Zulu Cannibals, ind.	1b										
	Indianapolis, NAL	1b										
1945	Zulu Cannibals, ind.	1b										
	Louisville, NSL	1b										
	Birmingham, NAL	1b										
1947–54	Grand Rapids, Detroit, Kansas City	1b*										
1955	minor leagues in Cincinnati system											

*These teams were all owned by Ted Rasberry and players were shifted back and forth between them.

Marvin "Tex" Williams
"Hitter"

BORN FEBRUARY 12, 1923, HOUSTON, TX
HT. 6' WT. 195 BATTED AND THREW RIGHT

Negro Leagues debut: 1943

Marvin Williams was a hitter. In a 19-year professional career divided between the Negro leagues, Latin America, and the minors, he posted averages such as .338 and .393 in the Negro leagues; .321, .362, and .393 in Mexico; and .328, .360, and .401 in the minors. At various times, he led his leagues in runs, doubles, triples, home runs, runs batted in, batting average, and slugging average. All together, he clubbed more than 300 home runs and compiled a career average in the .320 range.

He hit so well, in fact, that he was invited to Boston for a Red Sox tryout in 1945. Invited with him were Jackie Robinson and Sam Jethroe. It has been written that this was only a token tryout. Williams says it was fair, but fate must have intervened, because none of the three was signed at that time. History tells us that the two men who accompanied him on that Boston trip were eventual National League Rookies of the Year, so one has to wonder what Williams might have accomplished had he been signed by a major league club, but arm problems incurred in Venezuela made him less attractive as a prospect.

Even though he never made it to the majors, he enjoyed his long career and would do it all again.

You joined the Philadelphia Stars in 1943. How old were you?

I was 23. I'd been playing around here [Conroe, Texas] — semipro in sawmill towns. They're all close together — Houston, Baytown, all the sawmill towns. There wasn't no league or nothin'; just every little ol' town had a team and that's how we played.

Two players, Red Parnell — he was from Houston — and Pat Patterson, who played third base, both played for the Philadelphia Stars. We picked the All-Star team between Conroe and Houston and Baytown to play the Negro league All-Star team. They were barnstormin' and I had a pretty good two games with 'em and they thought I could make it up there.

They asked me if I wanted to go and I said yeah. They said, "Now you know it's gonna be different." I said, "I know it's gonna be different. Those guys up there, if they can make it, I can make it." So they said, "All right, we'll give you a try."

So I went on up — the twenty-third of June, 1943. I had luck enough to finish the year good enough and got that contract for the next year and so I didn't stop 'til '62.

You were a heck of a hitter.

Yeah. That's what kept me up there.

I went up to play shortstop — that's what I was down here — but they had a boy — you might remember him, he passed, he went to the Pacific Coast League — named Frank Austin. He came up in '44 and he couldn't play nothin' but shortstop. We both could hit

Marvin Williams (courtesy of Marvin Williams).

pretty good. They asked me to move to second base because Austin couldn't play nothin' but shortstop.

You played in the East-West All-Star Game in 1944.

I pinch hit in that game and flied out. I was supposed to play the whole game but [Junior] Gilliam, with the Baltimore Elite Giants, had been a regular second baseman so they let him start it and I pinch hit for him against Satchel. I told 'em, "If I pinch hit I wanna pinch hit against Satchel." [Laughs] I was just glad I made the All-Star Game.

You hit more than 300 home runs.

Yeah, I think so. I had 45 in one year. I think I won everything that year. I hit .401. Triple crown. Spaulding Sporting Goods offered me $50 or either a set of golf clubs, and I took the golf clubs.

You mentioned Satchel. Was he the best pitcher you faced?

That was the best. A Cuban boy called Martin Dihigo was good. And I'll tell you who did me bad but he slipped off to the major

leagues before I could catch up with him was Bob Gibson. He was with the Birmingham Black Barons. He struck me out *four times* one night. I said, "I'll get even with you!" But he slipped off and went to the major leagues and I couldn't get even with him. [Laughs]

In 1945, you, Jackie Robinson, and Sam Jethroe were given tryouts by the Boston Red Sox. How did it go?

I would say it went as well as any would have went. I wouldn't say anything bad about the tryout. Let me try to explain it to you. During that time, they were travelin' by train, the major leagues were. When we got there, we were supposed to try out three days. Now, the Red Sox were leavin' that first evenin' and we tried out at 10:00 that mornin'. There wasn't any of the real regular players out there — you know, Bobby Doerr, [Johnny] Pesky.

A lot of people wouldn't understand that, but you had to play ball to understand. If I'm gonna leave at 1:00 that evenin' to catch a train to go somewhere to play, well, I don't think I'll be feelin' good to go out there that mornin'. So that's why I wouldn't say anything bad, 'cause the regular players, they were leavin' that evenin'. Joe Cronin had some players there but there wasn't the big stars. You know what I'm talkin' about — the regulars, the big boys.

Now, we were supposed to have a tryout the next day when the Braves was in town. They was comin' in that night and we were supposed to practice the next day. I think we woulda had a better tryout, but President Roosevelt died that night and that stopped everything. He died that night while we was there.

What did they have you do in the tryout?

We took infield practice and battin' practice — just like we would with any team. They had relief pitchers throwin' to us — long relief pitchers. They had about three of 'em; I don't remember their names. They didn't have their stoppers, but they was still major league pitchers.

And they had guys that wasn't playin' every day with the Red Sox — they had them out there. I wouldn't say anything bad about 'em.

Joe Cronin told us, he said, "No doubt that you guys can play major league baseball." He said, "I've seen all of you play and I know you can play it. You can play better than some here, but what owner, what manager is gonna have the nerve to put one on a team?" That was his worry. He said not that he don't want to sign us — I'm just tellin' you what he said. He said, "Because if *one* is signed and don't make it, you'll hurt the rest of 'em." We understood it.

Our biggest problem was there when we got to Boston. We had reservations at the hotel, but they couldn't find 'em. One of the newspapers — a black paper — had a fit.

A guy was in the hotel — he was white — and he had a big home and he knowed we was comin'. I don't remember his name; he was a track man back in college — way back. He said, "Don't worry about it. Come on, I got plenty of room." And we stayed at his home.

That was the only problem we had — they couldn't find the reservations. When President Roosevelt died, we had to stay two extra days. There wasn't *nothin'* movin'. Cab drivers wasn't even workin'. Everything stopped.

In 1950, you played in the Pacific Coast League.

I went to Venezuela and we had a black guy in Oakland who was pushin' for the Pacific Coast teams to get blacks on the teams out there. He recommended me and a boy called Walter McCoy, a pitcher. So they come back to me in Venezuela and I said, "Yeah, I'll be there." I went on and finished the season with 'em.

You can't live on the Coast on $600 a month. [Laughs] I was stayin' in a private home; it was reasonable rent, but I didn't have anything left after that. That's why I didn't go back to Sacramento.

In 1954, you played for Vancouver in the Western International League.

I was playin' in Mexico City and a doctor owned the team there. He told me, "I think this league in Mexico is gonna break up and they want you in Vancouver."

I said, "How much they gonna pay?"

He said, "I'm gonna talk with 'em tonight."

I said, "You tell 'em I'm not comin' up there for nothin', not less than $700."

He said, "I'll let you know somethin' tomorrow."

Bill Brenner was the manager and the third baseman was Richardson. Good third baseman. I don't know if he played in the majors; if he did, he didn't play too long. We had played together in Mexico and he was up in Vancouver and he told Bill Brenner, "Yeah, get him 'cause he can really hit." So he gave me what I wanted and I caught the plane and went on up there.

I had to spend two days in Great Falls, Montana. We got snowed in. [Laughs] We was flyin' — we flew in from Wyoming into Great Falls and it was snowin' when we got there. The airline took care of the hotel and everything, so they checked us in but they wouldn't let us out for a couple days.

It was cold! It didn't seem like it bothered them; I guess they was used to it. I called Vancouver, I said, "Look, man, it's too cold here. I'm gonna come on the bus." [Laughs]

He said, "Just wait for the plane. You got plenty of time."

You led the league in hitting at .360.

Yeah. We won the championship.

The next year you played in Columbia, South Carolina.

Yeah. Me and Frank Robinson was on the team together. The Sally League, they called it.

You hit everywhere you went. Did you ever think you'd get a chance to go to the major leagues?

I thought the year they signed Jackie I might. We was in Venezuela together; we took the All-Star team down there. Jackie told me, "Come on back. I know they're gonna sign you. I'm pretty sure."

What happened, I hurt my arm down there and I didn't throw too good, so Eddie Gottlieb, the owner of Philadelphia [Stars] sent me to Laredo, Mexico. You remember Connie Johnson? They sent him down there to a doctor, got his arm straightened out. That's how he got back into the major leagues. The worst part about it, when I got there, the guy had left Laredo and went to some other part of Mexico and didn't nobody know where he was.

We worked on my arm and worked on my arm and worked on my arm and didn't nobody know what they was doin', and I never did get to throw like I did before I hurt it. Gottlieb called me up in the office and said, "The Yankees is behind you and the White Sox is behind you." But that throwin' is what I think kept me out of it.

Another thing, [Joe] Gordon or [Jerry] Coleman was the Yankee second baseman then. I think I'd've went to the Yankees, but Gottlieb said, "The way you're throwin', they're not gonna move him. You can outhit him." You know, it was gonna be hard for me to move anybody then, there was too much prejudice and racial stuff. That was part of it, but I think throwin' handicapped me more than anything.

You played on until the early '60s. Does one game stand out?

Yes. The year I hit 45 home runs, the first three times I was at bat I hit home runs. We was playin' in Phoenix, Arizona, and just like in Colorado, the air's thin. The first three times I hit home runs and they walked me the fourth time so I wouldn't hit another one. This fan — a white guy — come out of the stands and wanted to jump on the pitcher. [Laughs] "Give him a chance! Give him a chance!" he yelled. I was gonna try to hit four. He put me on intentionally. That's what got the fans so mad. That's the game that stands out.

What did you do when you left baseball?

I had a bad case of sinus trouble. I had a problem stayin' in different climates and I was plannin' on stayin' in Tulsa; I played with Tulsa in the Texas League and they had got me a job up there, but that sinus was so bad on me that I couldn't stay there.

I went to two German doctors in Mexico and they told me, "We can operate on you.

There's two little holes in your nostrils that are stopped up. We can operate on it and get it out and you'll be all right for a while, but you get in the wrong climate you'll still have this problem. What you're gonna have to do is find a climate that don't give you no problem, and that's where you better stay."

I played in Victoria in the Texas League and this millionaire, Tom O'Connell, lived there and I told him I wanted to get me a job down there. They had three big factories. He said, "I'll talk to some people."

So I put in an application for Sears and Roebuck and Tom O'Connell come into Sears and Roebuck and I was workin' part-time. He talked to me and the manager saw him talkin' to me. Tom O'Connell had a great big ranch and he had quite a few Spanish people livin' on it. He come up to me and said, "You workin' here?"

"Yeah, but I ain't started regular yet."

So he went to the manager; he told the manager, "I'll make a deal with you. I got five families on my ranch. They live out there. I will buy five freezers, five refrigerators, five washers and dryers, and you hire Marvin regular and let him take 'em out there."

The manager said, "You got a deal."

So I worked 20 years for Sears. I worked ten in Victoria and got transferred here in Conroe. That's where I retired at, right here.

Would you go back and be a ballplayer again?

Yeah, I'd go back and do the same thing over and over.

Any regrets?

No. I don't even feel bad 'bout not makin' the major leagues 'cause there's so many others didn't get a chance and I *did* get a chance.

When I went up to Philadelphia, Parnell told me, "Now, the only way you're gonna be able to stay up here — you got to learn to hit."

I said, "There's a lot of 'em up there ain't hittin'."

He said, "But they ain't gonna be up here long."

We played some teams and next time we played 'em some of 'em be gone home and they wanted to know why. They just couldn't hit up here.

I thought I was a pretty good hitter here but, you know, it's different up there. Different pitchers and everything. I think what give me the confidence is when I met Satchel Paige for the first time. They told me that the way he made his money, he pitched mostly every night—five innin's or so. And the first night I met him we was playin' in Shibe Park. They named that park three or four times. I got two hits off of Satchel. I told Parnell, "Well, I think I got it made."

He said, "What do you mean?"

I said, "What I done read about Satchel and heard about Satchel—I got two hits off him. Other pitchers don't mean nothin' to me." [Laughs] I said, "I done hit the best."

So nobody else bothered me much. Martin Dihigo did.

After I learned, I kept tryin' to learn to be better. When a guy was gettin' me out, I would go in the hotel that night and they didn't have any videotapes like they do now. I would say, "There's somethin' wrong. I know somethin' is wrong." I'd go to Parnell and I'd say, "Parnell, did you see what I was doin' last night?"

"Yeah."

"Well, what was I doin'?"

"You wasn't hittin' strikes."

I said, "I thought—"

He said, "They wasn't strikes. You was swingin', hopin' you'd hit it, but you got to hit strikes and they got to be out in front of that plate. You remember that." He said, "Don't worry about curveballs, changeups—nothin'. It's got to be over that plate. Every pitcher in this world is gonna throw it over that plate sometime. You just got to be patient to wait 'til he get it over that plate and you got to hit it out in front of that plate."

I kept that in my mind and I practiced, and I think that's what made me be lucky and successful as I was. Sometime I would chase a bad pitch, but when they got me out I didn't feel bad 'cause I hit a strike. It wasn't because I hit a bad pitch.

I told Frank Robinson when we was playin' together, I said, "Frank, strong as you are, you don't have to be reachin' for no balls. You learn to hit strikes, hit the ball, and let it go wherever it want to. But just hit it out in front of the plate and hit it solid. Sometime you will and sometime you won't."

I said, "There ain't no such thing as a good curveball," and it was a good while 'fore I could make him understand that.

He told me, he said, "Why do you say that?"

I said, "You make it a good curveball. Get in the box and I'll show you. Take your position. Kinda crouch over like you're gonna hit." And he did. And I said, "Now stay right there. Don't go down, don't reach out. Don't swing at no balls. Just let 'em pass by and see where they're goin'. Just watch the ball go in the catcher's glove. Don't swing." And he did that.

I told the guy throwin' battin' practice to throw him some curveballs. As soon as he got out of the box, he said, "I know what you mean now."

I said, "Explain it to me."

He said, "That curveball comes at you to get you to straighten up. If the curveball breaks out over the plate, that means you straightened up."

That's what makes it look like it's a good curveball 'cause you're pullin' yourself off it. You gotta hit a curveball after it breaks; you can't hit a curveball until it breaks. After that curveball breaks, it ain't gonna do nothin' else and if you're down in your position when it breaks, if it's a strike you're there waitin' for it. And he thought about it.

He learned well.

[Laughs] Yeah, I think he did. But he did it on his own.

When he was managin' in Frisco—he had Jack Clark and a bunch of 'em with him then—I went down there in Houston to see him. Soon as I walked in the clubhouse, he said, "Here's the man showed me how to hit." [Laughs]

But no. No regrets. I'd do it all over again.

BATTING RECORD

Year	Team, League	POS	G	AB	R	H	2B	3B	HR	RBI	SB	BA
1943	Philadelphia, NNL	2b										
1944		2b	40	154	30	52	8	3	4	32	2	.338
1945	Mexico City, MxL	2b	51	221	53	80	18	6	10	51	7	.362
	Philadelphia, NNL	2b	15	56	15	22	1	3	4	13	1	.393
1947	Pastora, VenL	2b										
1948	Mexico City, MxL	2b-1b	78	302	69	99	13	*11	14	57	8	.328
1949	Jalisco, MxL	2b	3	12	4	7	1	0	1	4	0	.583
	Philadelphia, NAL	of										
1950	Cleveland, NAL	2b	22	84	14	21	4	1	0	10	1	.250
	Sacramento, PCL	2b	38	120	18	30	4	1	6	21	3	.250
1951	Mexico City, MxL	inf-of	80	296	58	95	18	5	12	64	8	.321
1952	Chihuahua, AzTxL	2b-3b	117	397	136	159	27	9	*45	*131	10	*.401
1953	Laredo, GCL	of	23	86	14	24	7	3	3	14	0	.279
	Mexico City, MxL	2b	40	153	37	53	12	3	2	29	11	.373
1954	Vancouver, WIntL	2b	119	456	114	164	32	9	20	90	15	*.360
1955	Columbia, SAtL	3b	97	351	70	115	18	7	16	84	1	.328
	Seattle, PCL	1b-2b	35	117	20	27	6	2	5	22	1	.231
1956	Tulsa, TxL	inf-of	144	534	102	172	38	7	26	111	1	.322
1957		inf-of	134	466	53	118	23	3	8	76	2	.253
1958		1b	144	524	76	154	33	3	19	88	2	.294
1959	Mexico City, MxL	1b-of	109	378	76	117	14	2	*29	*109	1	.310
	Victoria, TxL	ph	5	5	2	2	0	0	1	2	0	.400
1960	Victoria–San Antonio, TxL	1b-3b-of	94	297	52	83	13	2	17	54	0	.279
1961	Victoria, Rio Grande Valley, TxL	3b-1b	116	354	55	98	16	2	10	71	2	.277
1944–45	Ponce, PRWL	2b		90	17	34			1	13		.378
1946–47	VenL	ss			*29		*13			*41		
1947–48	Leones, CubaL	2b		42	5	12	1			4	2	.286
1949–50	Ponce, PRWL	2b		183	31	44	8	1	2	25		.240
1957–58	Vera Cruz, MxWL	2b		232		77			11	57		.332

* Led league

Maurice Peatros
"Baby Face"

BORN MAY 22, 1927, PITTSBURGH, PA
HT. 5'11" WT. 230 BATTED AND THREW LEFT

Negro Leagues debut: 1944

Maurice Peatros first began playing professional baseball while still in high school, with the reincarnation of the Pittsburgh Crawfords in his hometown, in the short-lived United States League. He was so young that his father had to sign the contract for him to be able to play.

After an interruption for time in the service, he returned to baseball but the USL had died an early death, so he joined the great Homestead Grays, also his hometown team. There he came upon the first obstacle he had ever encountered in athletics: the first baseman, his position, of the Grays was Buck Leonard, known as the Black Lou Gehrig and one of the finest hitters in the history of the game and *the* man the fans came to see.

Still, Peatros's ability remained. None other than Hall of Fame third baseman Pie Traynor encouraged the Pirates to sign him, but they refused. However, after a brief try-out, the Brooklyn Dodgers did and he bounced around the minors for a few years before a growing family caused him to reevaluate his priorities and he retired, still in his 20s. He could have played on; his batting averages that we know today ranged from the .290s to .316. Also, in each stop along the way, he was the league's leading fielder at first base.

After spending his life in places that have long, cold winters (Pennsylvania, Michigan), he now lives in Las Vegas, where "it's even warm in February."

The Crawfords. That was my first professional team. In '43, I'd played semipro ball in Pittsburgh while I was still in tenth grade. In '44, Gus Greenlee decided to reorganize the Crawfords and he got me for that. I was still in school in the eleventh grade when I went to the Crawfords in '44. I was playing first base all the way.

The Crawfords were in the United States League, and unbeknownst to a whole lot of people — unbeknownst to us for a while — it was financed under the table by Branch Rickey.

With the United States League as it was, we won it both years. The Boston Blues, they were pretty formidable, as I remember. Gus

saw to it that we were loaded. Catching was Euthumn Napier, pitching staff had one of the Walkers from the New York Cubans and Bill Pope from Pittsburgh — Willie Pope; we had Dave Pope playing the outfield. He was signed by the Indians; he went to Reading and then he played left field in Cleveland. Eddie Dean was at second, Jimmy Johnson was at short, Joe Atkins was the big third baseman. They billed us as the "Dream Infield" and I was the original "Baby Face," the kid first baseman with the dimples. I was this guy taking down everything they hit, called Baby Face.

I was the original Baby Face in baseball and that was a come-on because of a tie-in with young Baby Face Nelson, the young killer. He'd look at you and smile and all of a sudden you were lying there getting ready to die and you never knew what happened. That's how they were billing me, this guy with the smile—you try to hit the ball by him and you can't do it, and you try to pitch to him and you can't get him out. He kills you a lot of different ways and he runs. At first, I was going to be "Lefty" and Lefty was very ordinary, so they tried a whole bunch of things. Harlan Kelly was the guy who was the advertising man; he wrote for the [Pittsburgh] *Courier* and Gus hired him as his publicity agent and Kelly said, "Let's go with this: 'Young killer.' The girls would come out to see the dimples and everyone else would come out to see if he can live up to the publicity." That was where the nickname came from.

You were a baby—18 at most.

I was younger than that. I was 16. My dad had to sign the contract; I couldn't sign it. Like I said, I was in eleventh grade in high school.

Do you know your batting average?

I was about .316, something like that, for what records they kept as best they could.

What happened when you left the Crawfords?

I had to go in service. Gus tried to keep me out because the war was over, but they said, "He's well-known in the Pittsburgh area. If we do that, there's going to be repercussions." You know, shielding an athlete, a celebrity.

Gus said, "If you're not here, you can't go in," so Gus made some arrangements for me to go to Mexico to play in the winter league so I would be out of the way, but I guess it only worked for a little while—three weeks—and my dad said, "You better get back here." I was playing ball in Mexico and then I had to come back and go in service in January.

I was in Army Air Force and while I was in the Air Force, I made the Air Force traveling All-Star team. We were based out of Mitchell Field. That's where everyone met to

go play. My job was an athletic instructor at West Point. I was up at Stewart Field. I was there at the time of the great Army team— [Doc] Blanchard and [Glenn] Davis, all of those guys.

The athletic instructors, we doubled as assistant trainers so we did the rubbing-down of the players and stuff like that at games at Michie Stadium. At the Army-Navy game at Yankee Stadium—nothing–nothing—I was there at that.

What we used back then to rub the guys down when they got cramps was Coke bottles. They had the curvature. That's what we did on the sidelines; when guys got cramps, we jumped right in. We had the bottles filled with hot sand. Take the baby oil or olive oil or mineral oil and spread it on the leg or arm or whatever it was and then massage them with these bottles of hot sand. [Laughs] That was in '46.

At the end of '46 I got moved to Enid Air Base and I was the athletic director for about 700 of the black troops. It was still segregated then. I set up all the intramural programs to keep everybody busy because all they were doing then was taking apart planes and scaling down. I basically ran the athletic department for all the black troops. Then they said we're going to deactivate the [Army] Air Force and everyone got discharged.

So I went back home in the spring of '47 and that's when I went with the Grays. They knew everyone was being scouted by that time and See Posey, he wanted to corral especially all the younger players in the Pittsburgh area. He didn't want any of the Pittsburgh players to get away from the home team, which would be the Grays. The United States League had folded then and all the teams became traveling teams. The Grays, though, were in the majors, so naturally everyone who had a chance would jump to a major league team, especially if it was in your town.

I was with the Grays. Buck [Leonard] was still playing. I didn't know the deal—how they were going to use me. I said, "Hey, Buck is here. He's the greatest that ever did it. What am I going to do?"

Well, the way it was laid out to me, "Buck had leg problems and back problems, but Buck is the drawing card. We only have a few. Buck is not going to be picked up by the major leagues." He was about 42.

The deal was, "Buck has to play because we have to keep our superstars active in order to have the crowd." So Buck would play seven innings — we were playing our eight games a week, doubleheader on Sunday — and then they'd say, "Hey, kid, better get loose." I would usually play the eighth or ninth inning at first base. On real cold nights, Buck would play like for two at-bats and we knew if he got two good blows early on, I knew I was going in. They got to see Buck Leonard hit. That was the deal.

Buck and Josh. Josh wasn't there. Josh died. I was an honorary pallbearer at Josh's funeral in early spring of '47. You know, he was a Pittsburgh guy, too.

Anyhow, they were there to see Buck, and after Buck did his thing, I would come in and pick up the pieces. When Buck would play the whole game, Vic Harris — he was the manager — would use me in the outfield during the end of the game 'cause Jerry Benjamin's legs were going on him. So what happened, Bob Thurman — you remember him? went to the Cincinnati Reds — Bob would move to center field and I would go into right. And when we played the Sunday doubleheaders, I knew I had the second game. I knew I would be in the second games on Buck's second time at bat. That is where my playing time came in with the Grays.

In spring training [1947], we went to Atlanta. Atlanta was like an unofficial farm club; they were in the Negro Southern League. All those teams like that had working agreements basically with Negro major league teams. We were playing an Easter Sunday doubleheader and I got hit in the head. Back then, they didn't carry you around and nurse you. If you got hurt, the team got you to the hospital and when you were okay to travel, they made arrangements.

Since it was spring training and everybody was still trying to get in shape, I wasn't

Maurice Peatros (courtesy of Maurice Peatros).

going to get in shape, so they wanted me to stay there in Atlanta and play myself into shape with Atlanta Black Crackers. That was okay because I had relatives there. My cousin lived there and had a restaurant, so I stayed there and played.

Just as I was getting ready to catch up with the Grays, the manager there — Bill Perkins, the catcher; he was one of Satchel's first catchers — Perkins and his wife had a little restaurant in Birmingham — that was his home — and somebody leaked word to him that the guy that had a barbershop next door was getting close and cozy with Perkins' wife. Perkins told John Harden, who owned the Black Crackers, "I'm leaving. I'm going home. I've got to go straighten something out. I'm either going to straighten it out or kill it out, one of the two."

And John Harden looks around and say, "We've got to have someone manage this club. Hey, kid, you're the most educated. You've been telling people what to do while you were in service. You know all the signals, you know how to make out a lineup." So John Harden appoints me playing manager 'til Perkins gets back. [Laughs]

That's great for the experience, but I'm saying, "Now I'm in Atlanta. When will I ever get back with the Grays?" [Laughs]

I was the youngest one by far [on the team]. Phillie Holmes that played with the Indianapolis Clowns was there and there was a bunch of guys. [Jim] Zapp was the left fielder. They had this little guy — Early Bird — who was catching and Dude Richardson at shortstop. I forget a bunch of the other guys, but I'll tell you who we *did* pick up in Longview, Texas, while we were traveling. Charlie Neal of the Dodgers. His mother didn't want to let him go; she said he's too young to go. We had a catcher from the New York Black Yankees that had broken his leg and he had a real stiff leg. He went by the house there and explained to them that, "The man that's leading us, he's a kid himself. He's been on the road and he's giving us directions."

So she said if we would sign a thing saying that we would be protective of Charlie Neal, she would let him play with Atlanta; however, we had to take his brother with us. His brother had to come, too. His brother was an outfielder; I really forget his name, I think it was Bobby. That's how we got the Neal brothers into baseball out of Longview, Texas. He was playing second base and I was playing first, and that gave us a brick wall on the right side of the infield. The Atlanta players wanted to give a prize to anyone that could hit a ball between me and Charlie Neal. [Laughs]

Me, Hank Aaron, Charlie Neal, Lino Donoso with the Cubans, Josh Gibson, Jr. — we were the babies. Willie Mays. We all met together at Rickwood Field when Willie Mays first signed with Birmingham Black Barons. The Grays and Birmingham that played the World Series in '46 had like an exhibition tour set up in spring training. Everyone that didn't get to see the World Series, here's a rerun of it and that's where Willie Mays first came in. Willie Mays was in the outfield. We were playing them. He would run around catching balls one-handed. We were the babies.

The guy that took me under his wing with the Grays was Sam Bankhead, the shortstop. Sam was like in my ear hole constantly 'cause he knew my dad and the idea was "Look out for my son."

And Napier also came from the Crawfords to the Grays. We also had Cecil Kaiser, pitcher, and Luis Marquez was with us. Luis Marquez was playing third base. The Braves drafted him. And my roommate was Luke Easter. Luke was not playing first base with the Grays. Everybody thinks he was the first baseman; he was the first baseman with the Cincinnati Crescents in the United States League. He had the same thing as me; they had Buck Leonard at first base. They put Luke in left field. He was big and he used a 34-inch bat. It looked like a toothpick in his hands. A very little bat. It was unreal. Thurman was just the opposite; Thurman used a 36-inch. [Laughs]

After I left the Crawfords, the word was out — being signed, being signed, being signed — and we said, "Yeah, right," but the money was offered up in the Canadian league. What opened up the Canadian league was when the guys jumped the [New York] Giants — Max Lanier, Adrian Zabala, Castleberry, Mickey Owen. When those guys jumped and went to Canada, our guys had been playing with them in South America and our guys had gotten them off-season jobs in South America, so when they signed them up there, they said, "Hey, payback time."

And they said yes and they started recommending guys out of the Negro leagues, so a *whole herd* of guys went up there to play in Quebec. That was a powerful league. Then we got the word, "You guys have been scouted." And I was contacted: "Come to Ebbets Field for a tryout."

The story on that was, I wanted to play with the Pittsburgh Pirates, naturally. I'm from Pittsburgh and Pie Traynor had a show on radio — KQV in Pittsburgh — and he was the Pittsburgh scout. Pie Traynor kept saying, "Sign him. Sign these two guys, Maurice Peatros and Joe Atkins. They're young, they're powerful, they're local. We'll make a ton of money."

Bill Benswanger was the owner of the Pirates and he did not want to be in the vanguard. He was just like [Clark] Griffith in Washington, D.C. The Senators could've been the most powerful ballclub for a decade in major league baseball because they had first choice of all the Homestead Grays. That was one of our home fields. When we played in the South, we were known as the Washington Homestead Grays. He could've had Josh, he could've had Buck, he could've had Bankhead, he could've had the Walkers, he could've had Thurman, he could've had Easter, Jerry Benjamin; he could've had a franchise right there, but he drug his foot on everything. He didn't want to be bothered. You pay the rent and use the ballpark and that's it.

I did three interviews with Pie Traynor on KQV in Pittsburgh on the 6:30 sports thing and the letters began to come in 'cause the *Pittsburgh Courier*, the black paper, they were writing about it. Bill Nunn was writing about it. Mel Goode was writing for the *Courier* and he had the radio station and he's the one that came up with the phrase, "The walls come tumbling down."

So with all the pressure on him, they got to Pie Traynor. Pie told me himself, he said, "If you talk about it, I'll deny out loud and I'll never speak to you again, but they threatened me with my job and pulling my radio station job if I continued to promote you and more-or-less bad-mouth them for not signing you."

So to shut Pie Traynor up, they signed a guy named McGee from Detroit, a little basketball player. [Laughs] He was a second baseman and he could run real fast. They signed him and sent him somewhere and that was supposed to shut up everybody. "We've got a black ballplayer." He was the first black ballplayer signed by the Pirates.

People went crazy 'cause they wanted me and Joe Atkins to be the first signed by the Pirates, and a lot of people said they would boycott and they weren't going to see any more Pirate games. The hell with it. They had a big thing in the *Courier*, "To hell with the Pirates. They turned their back on their home-grown own."

Joe was well-known for his basketball in high school and I was well-known for baseball and football in high school, so the two families were well-known, and the Pirates, they turned their back on us.

Then all of a sudden the phone rings and I guess what the *Courier* did was call Branch Rickey. They said, "One of the guys that you were scouting back in the United States League with the Crawfords is being given short-shrift by the Pirates." Next thing I know I got a thing in the mail when I was getting ready to go to spring training that said come to Ebbets Field. There would be a three-day tryout. Rex Barney was there with his wild-throwing self and they wanted him to have more work. They kept Rex Barney there to throw the batting practice.

We were there for three days. Dick Williams that managed Oakland — I used his uniform. Number 18.

Then they sent us to different farm clubs. I went to Geneva, Twin Falls, Fargo, North Dakota — places like that. One of the farm clubs I was with was Erie. Will Grace was there. He'd played with the Cleveland Buckeyes. I stayed at his house. We won everything there. God, what a powerhouse that was! That was unreal. On that team, Ollie Echeverria was catcher — went to the Senators; Dean Stone, big lefthanded pitcher, threw real hard — he went to the Senators; and we had a little guy — I forget his name, little short guy — went to Rochester Redbirds in Triple-A.

After a while, I said whoa. I was married, second child was on the way, so I went back to Pittsburgh and managed the Greater Pittsburgh League. My dad was business manager in the league and all the ex–minor leaguers were there. Eppy Miller, the Miller brothers from Lawrenceville that played with the Braves, they all played in the Greater Pittsburgh League and I was managing my dad's team here in the Village. It always ended up a big shootout with us and Honus Wagner's team for the championship every year.

Joe Schmidt played when he was in college — the linebacker with the Detroit Lions. He played with North Pittsburgh. Mike Ditka played with Bellevue. There was a lot of good athletes in the Pittsburgh area. This was all before Dorsett and all those other guys came. They could've matched up with Double- and Triple-A teams 'cause they knew how, and that's who they were: ex–major leaguers and minor leaguers. Paul Waner and Lloyd Waner played. Jeep Handley, the third baseman. The league was loaded; it was the cream of western Pennsylvania.

At the end of baseball I went into sales in Pittsburgh for a couple or three years. I had the Crayton Sausage franchise here — frozen food distributorship with headquarters in Cleveland.

Then we moved to Michigan 'cause they sort of wanted me close to my brother, who was the first black high school athlete from Pittsburgh to get a scholarship to Michigan State. Willie Thrower, the quarterback, remember him? He was the first black player out of Pennsylvania to get a scholarship there but he was from New Kensington. My brother Bill was the first out of Pittsburgh. My family wanted me to be close to him. We had relatives in Michigan, so we moved to Michigan and one thing led to another and I went into civil service.

I was in boys' training school as a supervisor and counselor for 20-something years and then I switched over into Management Budget and I managed eight office buildings for the State of Michigan up until retirement — May 30, 1997.

What level of education do you have?

High school. Everybody swears and be-damned that I went to college. [Laughs] What I do, I read everything that doesn't get out of my way. They still kid me about it because I go through two papers a day: The Las Vegas paper and *USA Today*. I make it a point to stay on top of everything and be well-versed. A lot of people ask me questions and I never did get caught off base but two or three times in baseball, and I'll be damned if I'm going to get caught off base now. [Laughs]

I cut things out of the paper and I've got a scrapbook and people say, "You have all this!" I say, "Yeah. I learned very early on,

you've got to be able to back up your lies." [Laughs]

I've got pictures and stuff back from when I first won little awards in high school in the inter-class things. The guys say, "Damn, man! You got a picture of me doin' this?" I say, "Yeah."

I got a picture of Willie Pope scoring on a home run in Yankee Stadium and stuff like that. I would make copies of things so the guys could have them 'cause they never had anything. They just played; they never thought in terms of keeping anything. I've got my original contract from the 1944 Crawfords; I've got stuff that's all packed away because we haven't been able to really unload everything yet because in the houses here there are no basements, there are no attics, so if there's something you don't want to put your hands on right away, you keep it in boxes.

Any regrets?

Not really. I've said this on television and everything: What we were doing was hard but you didn't look at it as how hard it was because that's all there was and as hard as it was, it was better than what anyone else had. We were professionals, we were celebrities, we were in the limelight and people paid money to come see us do what we did. So to that extent, it would be the same as today: Show business is our life.

The only difference was there wasn't any money in the damn thing. Gosh, my first contract with the Crawfords was $250 a month and a dollar and a half a day meal money. That's why you made friends with all the waitresses, so they could help, put something in a bag for you, when no one was looking, to have on the bus.

That was one thing: We knew we were going to eat because we were in a different town every night, and after you made the circuit you went to the same restaurants and the same barbershops and everything, and you were known. Like I say, it was a form of like living off the land in addition to your salary.

The accommodations could have been better, because if you weren't in a hotel you'd be in a boardinghouse and the men would all be on one floor. There would be entertainers — all the bands and everything: Billie Holiday and Count Basie and Duke Ellington and Jimmy Lunceford — they would all be there and their vocalists and all the women stayed in one room together. The ballplayers and the band were on another floor. It would take two or three boardinghouses to put up the traveling people coming through town.

But that was it. That and the bus was our life.

Would you go back and do it again?

No, not knowing what's available now, because if you had to do the exact same thing again, no. Now you would know how hard it is.

Your roommate was your trainer, your doctor, and everything else. You looked out for his body and he looked out for yours.

Luke Easter and I, we broke a couple or three beds right off the bat early in '47 'cause he was 260 and I was 230. We weren't going to buy beds because we'd replace furniture all over the country, so we had an alarm clock. Luke would sleep in the bed for half the night and the alarm would go off and he'd get out. We had a pallet so either him or I would be on the floor the first part of the night, then we'd switch. We both couldn't be in the same bed.

But if the same situation came up and you didn't know and thought that's all there was, and you knew you could do it, that's what you would do.

I had scholarship offers in high school, but if you could make a buck — and this is wartime, remember; no one is thinking about going to the great hereafter; it's like, *live now* — so if there's a chance to make a buck and you're the young high school kid who could go down the hall and every head in the hall would turn, including teachers, you'd go for the buck. I was making what teachers were making and I was in their class and my name was in the paper. [Laughs]

The question was, "Is he a good influence on the rest of them?" It's like they say today, "Everybody can't go to the majors." That's for a select few at any level. That's what they were trying to tell the kids. "You've got to admire Maurice, but you're not going to be a Peatros, so turn the pages in the book."

BATTING RECORD

Year	Team, League	Pos	G	AB	R	H	2B	3B	HR	RBI	SB	BA
1944	Pittsburgh, USL	1b										
1945		1b										.316
1946	military service											
1947	Homestead, NNL	1b-of										
1949	Geneva, BordL	of	16	53	5	11	2	0	0	4	2	.208
1950	Fargo-Moorhead, NorL	1b	87	285	56	90	11	5	1	52	8	.316
1951	Erie, MidAtlL	1b	121	472	103	141	27	10	3	57	11	.299
1952	Magic Valley, PioL	1b	132	469	86	135	26	2	4	75	9	.288
1953	Drummondville, ProvL	1b	36	124	27	36	3	1	2	17		.290

Jim McCurine
"Big Stick"

BORN MAY 8, 1921, CLINTON, KY
HT. 6'2" WT. 190 BATTED LEFT, THREW RIGHT

Negro Leagues debut: 1945

Big Jim McCurine was a slugging outfielder who spent the better part of a decade playing semipro ball around Chicago, but eventually his team played an exhibition game against the Chicago American Giants. American Giants manager Candy Jim Taylor was impressed — so impressed, in fact, that he kept after McCurine until he convinced him to join his team.

It was a good move. With Chicago, McCurine teamed with John "Mule" Miles to give the American Giants a very formidable power duo, perhaps second only to the Homestead Grays' pair of Josh Gibson and Buck Leonard in all of Negro baseball.

Organized ball took notice, and in 1949 the Boston Braves invited McCurine for a tryout. His throwing arm was shot, though, from trying to pitch years earlier, so the Braves tried to make a first baseman out of him. They wanted to send him to the low minors, and he saw this as a step backwards from the level of play with Chicago, so he rejoined the American Giants for one last season, one in which he could no longer play every day because of his arm.

Eventually, he entered the insurance field and has done well. He summers in Chicago and winters in Florida.

You began playing professionally in the 1930s.

Well, yeah, I guess so 'cause I was playing with semipro teams around Chicago. I don't know if you can call it professionally. I traveled with 'em when I was around 15, 18 years old. They used to give my father money to let me go play. [Laughs] When I was 16 and 17 years old, I would go up to Wisconsin and Iowa and downstate Illinois with the semiprofessional teams, like the Hartford Giants and the Brown Bombers, and then later with the old Lincoln Giants.

So your father was being paid and you were playing.

[Laughs] It wasn't so much that. It was that my father was very religious and he didn't want me to play on Sundays and he would let me play on Sundays, if they gave him $25. [Laughs] I still got my portion of what I was supposed to get.

How did you come to join the Chicago American Giants?

More or less from word of mouth, and then the team I was playing with — the Lincoln Giants — played the American Giants in an exhibition game up in Racine and Candy Jim Taylor was very elated with the way I hit the ball. He left no stone unturned 'til he got me on that team.

How much were you paid by the American Giants?

They started me out with 375 a month.

It wasn't bad; that wasn't bad for a start 'cause a lot of guys didn't make that much to start out with. I was with the American Giants from '45 to '49.

I was an outfielder but I used to pitch a little bit. That's what ruined my arm. When I was playing semipro ball I used to pitch and play outfield, play first base, play everything, but the worst thing in the world for me was to fool around with pitching, and that's what ruined my baseball career.

I had been invited by the Boston Braves and I couldn't even throw from the outfield when I got up to Boston. I couldn't comb my hair with my right hand. [Laughs] It was that bad. They got the soreness out of my arm, but when they got it out I couldn't throw from the outfield anymore. They wanted me to come up as a first baseman and I just decided to go back home. Being a young fella, prejudice was still out and we'd been prejudiced against so much, I just figured why did they want me to go back down to Class C when I'd been playing in the Negro league, which was almost equivalent to the major leagues themselves.

I just went home. Sometimes I regret it and sometimes I say I didn't make a bad move. I did pretty good from a financial point of view. Playing in the big show really would've been a great thrill for me. I really would've loved that. That's the one thing in my life that I missed.

I had a tryout with 'em, and I went to spring training. I was only down there maybe about a week or so, but my arm was so bad I couldn't throw. That was '49.

You're a big man. Were you a slugger?

Yeah. I batted third position with the American Giants the first two years I was there and the other years I batted in the cleanup position. On the average, I hit between 20 and 25 home runs a year. I didn't hit all that many in Comiskey, but I hit that fence out there a lot of times. I really don't have the count of how many I hit in Comiskey Park. I did hit a few.

You traveled all over the country. How was it?

Being a young man as I was in that day,

Jim McCurine (courtesy of James McCurine).

it was really thrilling to me. I look back on it now under the conditions and the stress that we played under, it really wasn't so good. But it didn't make any difference to me 'cause at that point that's all I had ever experienced.

When we played in the North and in the big cities, it wasn't bad anyway. It was just when we got away from the big cities and ventured into the Middle West and South. All the prejudice and everything rose and we had to be segregated and pushed around. Most of the time, as ballplayers, we weren't pushed around as much as if we had been just public people, civil people.

If we were playing *in* that town, we were treated royally, but it was the time when you were traveling through the cities that you weren't playing in. That's where you got a lot of the crap from like when you stopped to eat or something like that. You had the problems, but when we played in the town itself, they kind of rolled out the red carpet to you. They were highly elated over the Negro league base-ball players. When they'd [the team] come to town, the people would come from far and near. I don't think we ever played in any of those small towns without it being standing room only. They came in droves.

That was big entertainment.

In those days it was. We played in towns like Birmingham and Memphis and New Orleans; those ballparks would hold 15- 18-, 20,000 people, and they all would be packed. Standing room only.

They were good fans and in the South you'd be surprised that the majority of the people there were white people. They had the stands segregated and they filled up their side and would be sitting on the side with the blacks. That'll show you how foolish it is. All they wanted to do was see a ballgame.

Does one game stand out?

There's several, but one that I think still stands out in my mind that I got a great bang out of was one in Birmingham. At the time, I was having problems with my arm and I wasn't playing. That was the same year I had the tryout with Boston.

We were playing Birmingham, and I was on the bench because my arm was sore. We went into the seventh inning and Birmingham was leading us, 4–1. The bases got loaded and Candy Jim Taylor called me to bat. Jimmy Newberry was pitching; he was a righthander. When they saw that I was a lefthander coming up, they took Newberry out and brought Jehosie Heard in there, a little lefthander.

He came in there and he worked the count to 2–2 and I hit him on top of that roof in right field with the bases loaded. [Laughs] We won that ballgame by the score of 5–4.

The thrilling part of it was when I went to right field to play the next inning and they held up the ballgame for almost 15 minutes 'cause people were throwing dollars and quarters to me out there. That's the way they did in those days. That was one of the biggest thrills I've had. There were others, but I thought that was a real thrilling moment. The

fans' response was really something. I will never forget that. [Laughs]

Everywhere we played, the fans were that way. We did a lot of barnstorming with the Kansas City Monarchs up through Wisconsin. Basically, your fans were like 98 percent white, and the people were so appreciative it wasn't even funny. Again, you were playing to whatever the ballpark held 'cause they came out to see Satchel and all. It was just a lot of fun.

I remember a game we played with the Clowns that went 23 innings. I don't think there's any game been played in the Negro leagues any longer. They called it after 23 innings because of dark.

I hit a triple to score Bernell Longest to tie the ballgame. I should've got a home run inside the park, but Mule Miles was coming up behind me and Candy held me up at third base and I didn't score. That ballgame went tied up to 23 innings and they called it. I think we eventually played that thing off later in the summer, but I don't see anything about that. It was 3–3 when it was called. I hit this triple to tie the score. We were losing, 2–1, and I hit it against that left-center field scoreboard in Comiskey Park. Anyplace else, it would've been out of there.

Candy held me up. I could've scored 'cause I was getting around there, but Candy held me up at third base. They said, "Well, Miles is gonna bring him in," but ol' Peanuts Davis struck him out. [Laughs] Miles was a big hitter anyway, a free-swinger, and those kind of guys are easy to strike out.

He's my longtime friend. I just talked to him by long distance. He's trying to get me to come to San Antone and I'm trying to get him to come down here.

You mentioned Satchel. Who was the best pitcher?

[Laughs] You know, Satchel gets so much credit. You can't take nothing away from Satchel. He was a great pitcher, but there were some guys I thought was just as good as Satchel.

Verdell Mathis was one. Hilton Smith

was another one; he was a very good pitcher. Jim LaMarque from the Kansas City Monarchs was another one. And [Gene] Collins from Kansas City. All those guys I thought was very good pitchers.

Satchel, when you talk about pitching, you just put him off to the side and talk about the others. He was outstanding and you had to give him credit. He was unique in every aspect of his pitching. I guess his life, too.

Gene Collins could throw about 150 miles an hour, but he had no idea where the ball was going.

No. He was a hard thrower. It was terrible standing in against him. [Laughs] The first time I started playing against him, I was afraid of him, but it so happened — I guess maybe it was in my first year with the American Giants — we were playing Kansas City and I was batting third position. He struck me out about three times and Candy said, "It don't make sense, you walking away from that ball the way you are."

We had a big ol' boy by the name of Jim Bumpus from Kentucky and he said, "Tomorrow morning, I want Earl Taborn and you and Jim Bumpus to go out to the ballpark and you stand up there and hit that hard-throwing lefthander." [Laughs]

We went out there and had batting practice for almost a half-an-hour or better. Jim Bumpus was a *big* boy. He was much larger than Collins: he was about six-foot-two and weighed about 230 pounds and he could throw through a brick wall. Again, he was another one who didn't know where it was going half the time. [Laughs]

That took all the fright out of me about lefthanders. From that time on, lefthanders were nothing to me. I ate 'em like a piece of cake and I never tried to switch hit. I was hitting 'em good.

I know we played in St. Jo one year right after that and I can't think of the fella's name now, but he had pitched for the Philadelphia Athletics and he was on his way out. He was an old-timer but he made a heck of a career in the major leagues. He pitched that night

Jim McCurine, 1999 (Lisa Feder photograph).

and I think I got three out of four hits on him. He wanted to come into the clubhouse. "I wanna see that lefthander. I ain't ever had that much trouble out of no lefthander." He couldn't get me out.

It's mental. I found out that to be the case and it doesn't make sense, but if you never experience it you just accept it and keep going. But I found out. I didn't care anything about lefthanders after that particular incident. Candy Jim Taylor told me that.

Who was the best ballplayer you saw?

There's quite a few. I never even thought about picking out any particular one.

I thought the little boy that played shortstop for Birmingham — Art Wilson — was an outstanding little ballplayer, for a little man. He was a good fielder, good hitter. I thought that Piper Davis was another *excellent* ballplayer, all-round. So was Renfroe, Chico Renfroe. Very fine athlete.

A guy like Buck Leonard and Josh. Josh was really my favorite, I guess, because of the experience I had with him. I thought so much of him. He was one of the most outstanding ballplayers I've ever seen.

Jim McCurine, 1999 (Lisa Feder photograph).

The first year I was with the American Giants, we played the Homestead Grays in Dayton, Ohio, and I had a pretty good night that night, so he came in the clubhouse afterwards and told Candy, said, "Candy Jim, that right fielder you got out there. He's a hell of a good ballplayer for a rookie. I know y'all ain't paying him no money. I'm gonna take him out for a steak dinner tonight." [Laughs] You know he was making good money in those days. He did a lot of exhibitions with Satchel and they made a lot of money.

He did. He took me out for a steak dinner that night and we talked for several hours. I got to know him very well and, ironically, the very next winter he passed.

The year I played against him, he was one of the most outstanding ballplayers I've ever seen. I've seen him play in the All-Star Game. I've seen him hit that ball in those speakers in Comiskey Park on a line drive.

The most astounding thing I thought about him was, we were playing in Welch, West Virginia — that's a coal-mining town in the mountains — and the ballpark was built like the old Polo Grounds was. Center field was straight across and it was about 400 feet to the fence and behind center field was a highway — a two-lane highway — and then

straight up from that, the mountain went up. I'd say about 100 feet above the street level they had a big rock up there and they had painted a Kelvinator, which was a refrigerator, sign. Josh hit a line drive off of Gentry Jessup into that rock and it bounced back to our second baseman, Bernell Longest. [Laughs] That's how hard he hit that ball. That ball just leaves the ballpark like a jet plane.

He had become a very good catcher. I understand when he first come up he wasn't the greatest, but when I met him he was a real good catcher, as good as any. He was as good as Campanella, or better, at that point. It was just too bad he had that little incident about his health.

What did you do when you left baseball?

I went back to Chicago and I didn't know what I wanted to do. I really couldn't figure out what I wanted. My cousin was working for the Chicago Transit Authority and at that time he was driving streetcars and that kind of enthused me. [Laughs] I went to work for the C.T.A. I worked for them for about three or four years.

That was really not my cup of tea, and a friend of mine introduced me to the insurance business. I didn't know whether I wanted to do that or not, but I worked for about, I guess, six months as a part-time agent before I left the C.T.A. I did so well with it I decided I might as well make a livelihood out of it, and that's what I did for the next 32 years.

Would you do it all over again if you were a young man?

Oh, yes. I have no regrets of the times that I spent in the Negro league. It was one of the great things of my life. I'll always cherish it.

It's amazing how here in later years I get so much of a thrill from people who were not even born during those days. It's amazing the letters I get and the requests for autographs. Many times people send me two or three dollars to sign a 3 × 5 card.

You take the first 40 years I was out of baseball, you heard nothing about it. A couple of books was written, I think, that really did the job: the Negro legends book and *Only the Ball Was White*. That's where a lot of this stuff has come from.

I get these requests from people all over the world. "I read about you," and such and such. I answer all I can. I feel very elated that these people think that much about Negro league baseball after all the years. I thought people had forgotten we even existed.

BATTING RECORD

Year	Team, League	Pos	G	AB	R	H	2B	3B	HR	RBI	SB	BA
1945	Chicago, NAL	of										
1946		of							26			.296
1947		of										
1948		of							20			.257
1949		of										

Eli "Eddie" Williams
"A Career Too Short"

BORN 1916, CAMDEN, AL
HT. 6'3" WT. 200 BATTED LEFT, THREW RIGHT

Negro Leagues debut: 1945

Eli Williams is a big man (6'3", 200 pounds) and had a tremendous arm, which he was able to use for only one year in the Negro leagues. His career might have been longer, but a back injury incurred while playing winter ball after his year with Kansas City caused him to be unable to perform at that level any more, although he was able to play on with local teams.

That one year, though, was a good one. It was 1945; he batted .300 and was a teammate of Jackie Robinson, whom he calls one of the nicest people he ever met. Williams says he got along well with his teammates over the years and after speaking with him, it's easy to understand why.

When I came up in the Negro league, Kansas City was my team in 1945. I was playin' with the Miami Giants, and the manager, he knowed all those people. I think he got some money out of it, but I don't know. [Laughs] He recommended me to Kansas City.

I didn't play [with Kansas City] but a year. I got hurt. I was playin' with the Miami Giants; we played winter baseball down here in the winter league. I came back and played with them. We played a team out of Spartanburg, South Carolina, and I hit a double. I went sliding into second base on my stomach and the guy on second base went to tag me and his elbow hit me right in my back, right in the center of my back. That's what knocked me out. I was in the hospital. I recovered, but I still have back trouble. I had to give up playin' with Kansas City. I played a little around Miami later on.

How many years did you play altogether?

I played a lotta years. First, when I was in Alabama, President Roosevelt had a camp for young guys called the TC Camp. That's where I started playin' at. I was about 16.

Then I left that and played with a local team in Alabama. I played there for a few years and then I come on to Miami. Then I went on from Miami to Kansas City. I enjoyed it. I got along with everybody on any team I played with.

Do you recall any games with Kansas City?

Yeah, I remember a lot of games. One against Newark Eagles — we were playin' in Newark. V.J. night and Joe Louis was there — first time I ever seen him — and I hit a home run. I hit it a pretty good ways. I bat left but the guy throwed me a fastball outside and I hit it to left field. Not too many guys bat lefty and hit a ball that hard that far [to the opposite field]. I'll never forget that. Newark had Monte Irvin and Larry Doby. It was a good team. There was a lot of good teams.

I hit that home run that night. I was happy about that. I didn't hit too many home runs. I hit more doubles; I hit a lot of doubles. I batted around .300.

I could throw the ball from left field — one hop to home plate. I'm not braggin', but I could do it.

Jackie Robinson was a teammate of yours.

Jackie was as nice a guy as I've ever met. He had a good education; he was, I think, a lieutenant in the Army. He had finished college. He was nice, you know. Some guys like that, they kinda look over you, but he was a very nice guy, a good man.

Could you tell at that time how good he was going to be?

No, I couldn't tell, but I knowed he was good, but I didn't know he'd do as good as he did when he made the major leagues. [Laughs] He was pear-toed — you know, his feet went thataway — but he could run. He could steal bases and he was a good ballplayer. He could do 'bout all of it. Steal home. Not many guys could do that.

Who were some of your other teammates?

The guy that played shortstop was Jesse Williams. Me and him were good friends. And the first baseman was [Lee] Moody and left field was my roommate Chico [Renfroe]. I was friends with most all of 'em.

Who was the best player you saw?

The best hitter was Josh Gibson. [Laughs] He could hit 'em outta any park, but he was hardheaded. I think he drank a lot. He thought he was supposed to be the person before Jackie, but he was too hardheaded. But he could hit 'em. He could *hit* 'em. Any park, he could hit 'em outta there. Oh, he was somethin', let me tell you.

Who was the best pitcher?

There was a lot of 'em along in there. There was [Dave] Barnhill; he played with the Clowns and New York Cubans. He was from Miami. You know Satchel. There was a lot of 'em.

What did you do when you left baseball?

Eli Williams, 1998 (courtesy of Eli Williams).

My brother was a longshoreman on the dock in Miami, and that's where I retired from. I retired in 1981.

Would you go back and be a baseball player again?

If I was a young man? Yeah, I'd be glad to do it. I loved it.

Do you attend any of the Negro leagues gatherings?

Joe Robbie Stadium in Miami — they changed the name to Pro Player Stadium — they have a lotta things there for the Negro leagues. Every time they played the Dodgers they had a Negro league thing. They wanted me to throw out the first pitch. I was the only one on the team from Florida when Jackie was there. I explained to them I couldn't throw it 'cause I just had a stroke, so they asked me would my wife throw it out. [Laughs] I said, "Sure. If she wants to throw it out, let her throw it out."

They asked her and she said, "Yeah, I'll throw it out." And me and her went out there halfway to the pitcher's mound and she

throwed it to the mascot; she throwed a perfect strike. They said [to her], "We should sign

you up." You know, they're teasing. That was
a big thing.

BATTING RECORD

Year	Team, League	Pos	G	AB	R	H	2B	3B	HR	RBI	SB	BA
1945	Kansas City, NAL	of				8		3				.300

Jim "Zipper" Zapp
"A Temperamental Natural"

BORN APRIL 18, 1924, NASHVILLE, TN
HT. 6'3" WT. 220 BATTED AND THREW RIGHT

Negro Leagues debut: 1945

As a boy, Jim Zapp attended a private Catholic school. Facilities and enrollment both were limited and, as a result, there was no baseball program.

Come World War II, he entered the service without ever having played baseball, but he tried out for the black baseball team on his base in Hawaii. Not only did he make the team, his play was so good that the manager of the white team on the base decided to integrate and did so by picking up Zapp.

Once out of the service, he entered Negro leagues ball and eventually white baseball. Hitting for average and power, there's no telling how far he may have gone, but he was his own worst enemy. When things didn't go his way, or when he felt he was being slighted, he would quit his team. His talent always allowed him to get another job in baseball, but word of his temperament spread, and this undoubtedly prevented him from advancing farther than he did.

He now believes his temper held him back, and that's his only regret from baseball.

I didn't play baseball until I went into the Navy. I was stationed in Hawaii at Aiea Naval Barracks right outside of Pearl Harbor. I went in in '42 and I started playing ball, I guess, the following spring—'43.

As a boy, I played just a little softball around town. Everything was segregated then; we didn't have a baseball team, especially where I went to school. I went to school at a private Catholic school in Nashville.

I started playing over there [in Hawaii] and we had two teams: a black team and a white team. Both teams were called Aiea Naval Barracks. One day we were playing and the manager for the white team was watching us play. I was playing third base at the time. His name was Edgar—they called him "Special Delivery"—Jones. He was an All-American football player from the University of Pittsburgh, and after he got out of the service, he

went to the Cleveland Browns and played quite a few years. He was a half back for Paul Brown.

Anyway, he saw us play and he integrated the white team at that time. He took me and the first baseman. The first baseman didn't stay long, but I stayed with them until we moved away. The first baseman's name was Andy Ashford. He died not long ago up in Port Huron, Michigan. I stayed with him [Jones] until our outfit moved to a place called Manana Barracks, which was about five, six miles from Aiea, so I lost contact with them after that.

I think in about the first part of April of '45, I came back to the states. It was getting towards the end of the war and I was stationed at Staten Island, New York. They had a baseball team there so I went out for the team and the manager of that team was a fellow by the

Top: Jim Zapp, 1948. Bottom: Jim Zapp, 1954 (courtesy of James Zapp).

name of Larry Napp. He umpired in the American League for a long time. At that time, he was in the Dodgers organization, but he got out and it didn't seem like he was going to make the majors, so he turned to umpiring.

A fellow was playing right field for us from Baltimore. I can never remember his name — a white boy. We only had two blacks on the team, another first baseman. He asked me one day, "Jim, if I recommend you to the Baltimore Elite Giants, would you go down and play with them on weekends?"

I told him yes. I'd heard of all these guys, but I didn't know any of them. [Henry] Kimbro, he was playing, but I never did know him. And Doc Dennis, he was playing, but I didn't know him until I played with the Elites on weekends. That started my baseball career right there.

My biggest problem was I was very temperamental. I think that's one thing that held me back. That's why I didn't advance further. They called it temperamental, but I didn't call it temperamental. If I didn't think the owners was treating me right, I'd quit, ask for my release, or whatever, as long as they didn't give me enough money. Sometimes they did not.

I went to spring training in '46, trained in Nashville. You know the Elite Giants originated in Nashville. The owner of the team was Tom Wilson. They had a lot of old ballplayers playing for years. I played in spring training with them, then they sent me to Nashville, which was their farm team. Nashville Cubs.

I stayed all year with Nashville, and the following season I was still with Nashville, so they traded me to the Atlanta Black Crackers. I stayed there a half a season and when the team went to New York to play — you know we traveled all over the country — my mother and sister were livin' in New York, so I quit the team right there because of the owner of the Atlanta Black Crackers; you had to almost *fight* him to get your money.

Then I went back to Nashville that winter and I was uptown one day, standing in front of a nightclub, and a fella from the Memphis Red Sox, T. Brown, was coming through Nashville and he saw me. He said, "I heard you quit playing baseball."

I said, "Yeah, I'm giving it up. I can't stand it no more."

He said, "Would you go back to playing

if I recommend you to the Birmingham Black Barons?"

I told him, "Yeah, I'd go to the Black Barons."

I went to spring training with the Black Barons and stayed with them all year—1948. That's when Willie Mays joined the team full-time in May, after school was out. He and I played together that whole year.

After the season was over, they were going to barnstorm against Campanella and Jackie Robinson's All-Stars and against the Indianapolis Clowns. They were going to pick two teams: a team that goes with the Indianapolis Clowns and a team that goes with Campanella and Jackie Robinson and you're playing on percentage. So who would you think was going make the most money?

So they picked all the boys from the Birmingham area to go with Jackie Robinson and Campanella and they put me with the Clowns. I got upset again, so I told them just give me my release. And they did, they gave me my release. That's probably one of the biggest mistakes I ever made in my life.

Piper Davis always said I was the only man he ever saw in his life to leave a championship team. [Laughs] Anyway, that year they were playing split seasons and we won the first half, or maybe it was the second half. Kansas City won the other half, so we had to have the best-four-out-of-seven playoff for the championship.

We beat them two straight in Birmingham and played them in Memphis the third game. In the third game, they were leading us, 2–1, going in the ninth inning and I came up with one man on and hit a home run and beat them, 3–2.

Buck O'Neil always said I never should have come to bat because they had two outs and whoever was batting in front of me hit a

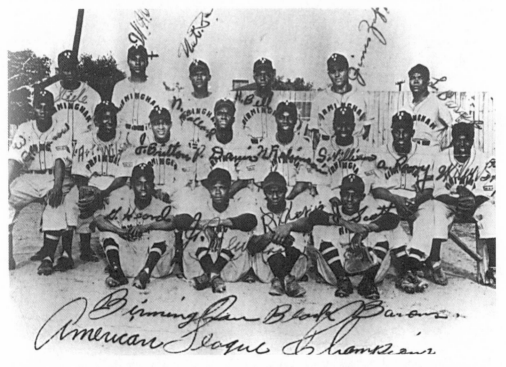

1948 Birmingham Black Barons, champions of the Negro American League. Back row (l-r): Ed Steele, Bill Powell, Nat Pollard, Herman Bell, Jim Zapp, Pepper Bassett. Middle row (l-r): Bill Greason, Art Wilson, John Britton, Piper Davis (manager), Norman Robinson, Sam Williams, Alonzo Perry, Wiley Griggs. Front row (l-r): Jehosie Heard, Jimmy Newberry, Roosevelt Adkins (trainer), Joe Scott (author's collection).

ground ball to [second baseman] Curtis Roberts, who went to the Pittsburgh Pirates right after that. And he made an error, so that let a man on first base and I hit the home run and beat them, 3–2.

We went on to Kansas City and they beat us three straight. In the seventh game, we beat them. I think it was 4–1. Bill Greason pitched the seventh game, so we won the [Negro] American League championship. I left the Birmingham team after that.

Everyone who saw you play says you were a tremendously powerful hitter.

[Laughs] Yeah, that's what they all said. Some of the guys said I hit the ball as far as Josh did. Not as consistent. They didn't keep good batting averages in the Negro leagues, but after I went in integrated baseball I had good batting averages.

I guess my temper got the best of me in Paris, Illinois, too. Butch McCord had recommended me to Paris, Illinois, and the owner of the team was a guy by the name of John Gibbons. He called me and asked what kind of salary would I want and Butch had already told me what to ask him for. He said, "That's above our limit, but Butch says you can play, so we'll take his word for it and that's what we'll pay you." And they did.

I think I hit about .330 and led the league in home runs, had an RBI record that's still standing in that league. The league now is called the Midwest League. Something happened during the season that they didn't like about my personal life, so they gave me an unconditional release during the winter.

I always think about what could have happened if I had stayed with the Aiea Naval Barracks team. You see, before I left the Aiea team, all these major league ballplayers came in to Aiea, and it turned out Barney McCosky was our manager. Detroit Tigers. *Great* guy.

We had McCosky and John Lucadello, Hugh Casey, Bob Usher — all major league ballplayers. I wasn't playing too much but I was there. I was 19 or 20 at the time, but I enjoyed all of them. I really enjoyed McCosky. He could *play*. I thought he was the best

ballplayer I'd ever seen. I don't know why they don't mention him for the Hall of Fame.

Does one game stand out?

That's it, against Kansas City. I hit a lot of home runs in Texas, also, when I went out to the Longhorn League. I didn't report to the team until June the sixth and hit 32 home runs. That was the Big Springs record.

Who was the home run against Kansas City off?

Buck [O'Neil] has always said Gene Collins; Gene Collins just passed and he knew better. It was off of their best pitcher, Jim LaMarque. Roberts was the second baseman, a boy named [Tom] Cooper was playing first base.

Who was the best player you saw?

I played against all those major league ballplayers overseas. Johnny Mize and all those guys. And [Joe] DiMaggio. You understand, DiMaggio was great, but Johnny Mize was hitting them tape measures. [Laughs]

All the great ballplayers were in Hawaii during the war, all major league ballplayers. Bill Dickey, his brother Skeets Dickey — all the guys were over there. Phil Rizzuto, Pee Wee Reese. Reese played with Aiea Hospital, right up the hill from us. Since that time, he and I were in an old-timers game in Louisville.

Willie Mays was a scrawny kid when you played with him.

In 1948, this guy wasn't a good hitter, but he could go get 'em and he had a sweet arm.

Were you surprised when he turned out to be as great as he did?

I was surprised. [Laughs] I guess all the guys were surprised. It was a treat to watch him get in a hot box. It was a *treat* to watch him get out of the hot box. We still stay in touch.

When I was out in Texas after I quit baseball, me and my family would always go down to Houston to see him when he came in. He never forgot to leave our tickets on the gate.

Piper [Davis] was a great ballplayer. He was a good all-around hitter, a good hitter and the best guy in the world to play for. Best manager that I ever played for. They say his best position was first base, but I think he's the greatest second baseman I've ever seen. [Laughs] I said, "If he can play first base better than he can play second base, I don't know." [Laughs] He didn't play first base when I was there in '48; we had Joe Scott playing first base. He was playing second and Artie Wilson was playing shortstop and on double plays, it don't seem like the ball would ever stop — on that pivot — and zip to first base. That was the best double play combination I ever played with.

In '51, I played with the Elites again. Here's another quitting deal. I played with the Elites in '51. I was playing for a man by the name of Sue Bridgeforth, who bought the team. In mid-season, they had the East-West Game. I should have been in the East-West Game unanimous, but they took me off the team and replaced me with somebody else, so I quit the team and went on to New York. That was my best year in Negro league baseball. It was politics.

So I quit again, went to New York, and then I came back and quit baseball, until Butch McCord recommended me to Paris, Illinois. That's when I got into integrated baseball. I said I'd never play in the Negro leagues again, which I didn't. Well, I played a few more games with them in '54, but I went out to Big Springs, Texas.

I went to spring training with Lincoln, Nebraska, and we were spring training in Corpus Christi, Texas, but at the end of spring training they left me there to play with Corpus Christi. I was there about three or four days and Corpus Christi came up with the idea that they weren't ready for a black ballplayer yet, so they optioned me to Odessa, Texas, and I'd never heard of Odessa, Texas. [Laughs]

I inquired about Odessa from some of the guys in a barber shop and they said, "Man, you don't want to go to Odessa. That's nothing but sandstorms, tumbleweeds, and rattlesnakes."

Jim Zapp, 1999 (Lisa Feder photograph).

[Laughs] So I took my train fare and instead of going to Odessa I came back to Nashville.

I couldn't get a job or nothing, so I called them and told them I'd better report to Odessa. They called me back and they said Odessa had their roster filled, but they would recommend me to Big Springs, Texas. I'd never heard of it, either.

What they wanted to do, they wanted to send me out to Big Springs on what they called a 24-hour option, whatever that is, but the guy who owned the team was the manager, also. Pepper Martin. Not the old man. He said, "Well, I won't take him on that deal without taking a look. If I like him, I'll buy him."

They went for that. I went out to Big Springs; Pepper met me at the train station and everything — the team was out of town — found me a room — a place to stay. It was segregated; I had to stay in a black private home.

The team was in San Angelo. He took me on down to meet the team. I was out of shape and fat. [Laughs] The sun was hot. It was hot in San Angelo and it was a day ballgame and, you know, the first time up I hit a ball over the center field fence for a home run.

We went on back to Big Springs and the first game we played there, I did the same thing. Out in west Texas, you know, they give you cash money through the screen and I collected $200 through the screen. I actually made close to a thousand dollars hitting home runs that year.

I had 31 home runs by the last day of the season and I was warming up on the sideline and one of my own ballplayers — a pitcher warming up with somebody else — hit me in the eye. Closed my eye. [Laughs] They knew I was going for the record, so Pepper said, "Yeah, you're going to play." So I played with one eye closed and hit a home run to set a new record. Thirty-two home runs.

You know, they had another great home run hitter out there at that time. Joe Bauman. [Laughs] The followin' year, I had 29 home runs and I was close to Joe, and Pepper upset me — moved me to first base. I couldn't catch nothing on the right side — I was used to playing the left side — and I was ready to quit again. [Laughs]

So he traded me to Port Arthur in the Big State League. Joe Bauman had recommended to the general manager out there to get me and they did. I went out there and played at Port Arthur the last month of the season. I think I hit eight home runs, eight doubles I believe, and one triple and drove in 29 RBIs the last month of the season.

I'm 31 years old. At the end of the season, they released everybody on the team but me and another boy, who happened to be from Nashville, named Jim Kirby. They were going to cut my salary, so instead of me playing, well, I just quit. I had a chance to go to work for the Air Force, and I went to work for the Air Force out there in Big Springs.

You hit for power and average, so you feel it was your temper that kept you from advancing.

I think so. My personal life, too — after-hours life. I wouldn't say I was wild but I stayed out late a whole lot when I should have been in the bed resting. I know some guys who had the same or worse reputation than me; they went on. Hank Thompson had a worse reputation; he and I turned out to be great friends. [Laughs] Isn't that funny now enemy ballplayers turn out to be great friends? He was a great guy, I'm telling you.

Hank Thompson — he didn't take care of himself. Couldn't adjust to life again after he left the majors. He couldn't adjust to the middle-class life. He'd drink, drink, drink.

Buck [O'Neil] and I became great friends in the last 25 years. We always stay in touch. Buck's a fine guy.

Let me tell you about Buck. I had not seen Buck in years and I went to work for the Air Force, and after the base in Big Springs, Texas, was closed, which was a pilot training base, I transferred out to Fort Rucker in the Army, so I saw in the paper where Tennessee State University baseball team was going to play in a tournament up at Tuskegee, so I went up to see if I'd see anybody I know.

I went in the ballpark and the first guy I saw was Buck sitting behind a screen. That was the first time I'd seen him since 1948. I'd gotten big and had a mustache. I walked up behind him and hit him on his back and he looked around at me and I said, "Hey, Buck, how you doing?"

He said, "Fine. You?" He turned around and watched the game.

I said, "Buck, you don't know me?"

He looked around. "Your face *does* look familiar."

He had another scout sitting there with him by the name of Scott. I saw him at one of the baseball games I'd been in and he knew who I was. I said, "Buck, you don't remember me?" He kept on looking.

He [Scott] said, "Buck, this is Zapp."

He said, "How in the hell can I ever forget you!" [Laughs]

Buck and I have been friends ever since.

My wife and I, we go to baseball spring training every year. We've been going to St. Petersburg, Florida, but we're going to Orlando this year. We became very close to Brian Jordan. He calls us his adopted grandparents. Brian Jordan — I wish I'd had his personality. He's the sweetest guy you'd ever want to meet. He's always the same Brian every time

Ron Jackson, Marquis Grissom, Jim Zapp (Lisa Feder photograph).

you see him. We'll be going to Atlanta back and forth quite a bit.

Who was the best pitcher you came across?

I didn't see Satchel but a few times in 1951; he was with the American Giants then and he'd only pitch the first three innings each night. He was great, but I'm thinking in the Negro leagues, Sam Jones, and we had another boy, I think played for Asheville and he never did play in the Negro leagues, by the name of Bob Bowman. He came from the side with everything — hard from the side like Ewell Blackwell. I think he and Sam Jones are the hardest pitchers I ever faced.

During that time I was a good fastball hitter. You could hardly get a fastball by me. And most of the time, Sad Sam Jones would not throw me a fastball for a strike. He'd show it to me, but he had a good curveball, too. I could get around on the fastball when I was young.

You say your temperament hurt you. Is that the only regret you have from your playing days?

Yes, it is. I never should have quit the Birmingham Black Barons. One time Piper mentioned during the season — not to me but I was told he said it — that I was the best prospect on the team at that time. I don't know why I didn't stay with the Black Barons.

Would you go back and do it again?

The first thing I would do is what my high school basketball coach told me: Get my education first. But I wanted to play baseball, so I did not get an education. If I had to go back over it again, that would have been my first thing. I could have gotten it free — the G.I. bill — but I didn't do it.

When I came out of the service, this basketball coach wanted me to go to Tennessee State to play football without ever playing football, but I did not want to play football.

Jim Zapp, Marquis Grissom, Mrs. Zapp, and Ron Jackson at Milwaukee County Stadium, 1999 (Lisa Feder photograph).

The school I was going to didn't have a team and my mother would not let me go to city schools because she did not want me to get hurt and I'm glad she did not now. I see guys walking around now, including Butch, can hardly walk. Football did it.

But I would have played baseball. That was my love.

BATTING RECORD

Year	Team, League	Pos	G	AB	R	H	2B	3B	HR	RBI	SB	BA
1945	Baltimore, NNL											
1946												
1948	Birmingham, NAL	of	61	221	36	53	11	5	1	26	1	.240
1950	Baltimore, NAL	of										
1951	Baltimore, NAL	of										
1952	Paris, MoVL	of	122	467	85	154	31	9	*20	*136	7	.330
1953	Danville, MoVL	of	11	42	11	12	3	0	1	10	0	.286
	Lincoln, WL	of	3	7		1						.143
1954	Big Springs, LghnL	of	90	341	76	99	18	1	32	86	5	.290
1955	Big Springs, LghnL	of-1b	89	334	74	104	15	0	29	90	4	.311
	Port Arthur, BgStL	of	39	129	20	37	7	1	8	29	0	.287

* Led league

Benny "Billy" Felder
"Or Is It Benny?"

BORN DECEMBER 9, 1926, TAMPA, FLORIDA
HT. 5'9" WT. 170 BATTED AND THREW RIGHT

Negro Leagues debut: 1946

Check the existing Negro leagues literature and you'll find a listing for William Felder. But there's a problem with that: his name is not William. It's Benjamin.

As a small boy, his playmates called him Billy, and it sort of stuck. As he grew, people came to believe his name must be William. As a result, he was called Billy by some and Benny by others, but for the record, his name is Benjamin.

He was a good fielding shortstop who was equally at home at second and third. Existing Negro leagues' statistics, which are incomplete and quite possibly inaccurate, suggest he wasn't much of a hitter; but perhaps a better indicator of his ability with a bat is his average from two years in the minor leagues. He batted a composite .301 with good middle infield power.

I started playing baseball right here in Tampa for a local team here. We had a real good independent team, the Pepsi-Cola Giants, and I started with them. I really just got out on the field when I was around 13, 14 years old. I played with Pepsi-Cola about three or four years.

The old Negro league teams used to come down and play the Pepsi-Cola Giants in Tampa. On Easter Sunday and Monday, we played the Newark Eagles down in Port Tampa. We had a good series that Sunday and Monday and I had a pretty good couple of days. Leon Day, he pitched one game, and Rufus Lewis pitched the other. Pretty good pitchers. I think I got a couple of hits each day, and I had a good fielding day.

Abe Manley was the owner of the team [Newark]. After the game, he asked me if I wanted to go with them, so I told him that they would have to ask my mother. I was 18.

So they did. They went out to the house and asked my mother after the game that Monday afternoon. They took me home and asked my mother if I could go with them. You know how it is. You want to get away to see how things are. Abe told her to let me give it a try 'cause I wanted to try it anyway, so she agreed. That night, she made dinner for the whole ballclub. They came to the house and had dinner, and after dinner we left on the bus to go to Jacksonville.

I started a few games, but you get excited and until you get used to it with the older guys it's tough. They had some good ballplayers, too, that year. Newark was always strong.

Did the veteran players give you a hard time?

No, not really. I got used to them. I started playing shortstop and Larry Doby was playing second base at the time. We got along real good.

I was with Newark two years. From there, I came back home and Newark traded me to

Benny Felder with nephew Freddy Felder (courtesy of Benny Felder).

a team out of North Carolina. Jim Williams had a team and he got me from Newark to go with him. I went down there to spring training, but I didn't stay. I didn't like it.

I came back to Tampa and started playing back with Pepsi-Cola. I stayed there, and in 1948, Oscar Charleston had a team in Baltimore. They started a team in Baltimore, so a group of us from Tampa went to Savannah, Georgia, for spring training and then we went to the Raleigh Giants.

I didn't stay there. Dirk Gibbons, he had gotten on with the Indianapolis Clowns. Walter "Dirk" Gibbons. He came to Baltimore and got me to go back with him to the Indianapolis Clowns. I went to the Clowns in '48 and I stayed with them the rest of that year.

From there, I came back home and I didn't go away anymore for a while. I got a tryout with the Florida International League here in Tampa. There was Tampa, St. Petersburg, Fort Lauderdale, West Palm Beach. I was one of the first ones in the league. I went with Fort

Lauderdale and they moved to Key West. I played the rest of 1950 with Key West. Havana, Cuba, was in the league and we played over there.

I went to Texas in '53 in the West Texas–New Mexico League. I played out there two years for the Pampa Oilers. I played shortstop, second base, sometime third base. In two years at Pampa, I hit .301 one year and .302 one year. We won the championship out there in '53. We beat Clovis, New Mexico.

You played professionally about seven years. Does a game stand out?

One game I will always remember. You know how integrated it was out in Texas. We were playing in Lubbock, Texas, one night and I got hit in the head by a *hard*-throwing righthander — a tall white boy — and I had a concussion. I had to go to the hospital.

I stayed in the hospital two weeks. When they took me to the hospital, I was from the South and I knew what to expect at that time and I didn't let it bother me. They put me down in the basement of the hospital in a little room to myself. I couldn't do nothing for myself for a couple of days but just lay there 'til they came to see 'bout me when they got ready. That kind of got next to me.

My first game back, we was playing the team in Lubbock. Ted Powalic was the manager of our team; he was an ex-catcher. The bases got loaded that night and he asked me did I think I could swing the bat.

I said, "Yeah, let me try it."

And the Lord helped me. I hit a grand slam home run that night and that was one of the best feelings that I had in baseball.

I usually hit about 12, 13 home runs a year. In that league, whenever you hit a home run, the people call you when you walk by the fence and they just stick dollar bills through it to you. Whoever hit the home run, well, they would have to buy the beer that night after the game.

Were there other blacks on the Pampa team?

Yeah, it was more black than white. That's what made it so good. The people in the stand would call us "niggers" and "burrheads." "Hit that burrhead in the head!" and all that stuff. The only way you can get back at 'em is by going out there and beating 'em. That's what we did. We had a *good*, good ballclub. Good hitting ballclub.

Who was the best ballplayer you saw?

There's quite a few. [Laughs] Satchel Paige was one. Josh Gibson. My first year at Newark was Josh Gibson's last year.

I *never* will forget in Ruppert Stadium in Newark when we were playing the Homestead Grays. Josh was at bat and I was playing third base this day. Everybody would say, "Back up!" because he would pull the ball down third base line a mile a minute. And sure 'nough, I played right at the edge of the grass — the outfield grass — whenever he would come to bat 'cause he hit that ball through the infield so fast.

He hit one down that line, but I happened to gobble it up and throw him out.

There was some good ballplayers back in those days.

How much were you paid?

When I first went away, I was making $245 a month. That was good money at that time. I would send my mother money home and I got along pretty good.

I was sending money home for her to use, but when I came home, my mother gave me *every* penny of the money that I had sent her. I was able to go and buy me a little car.

We was getting $2.50 a day for meals. I learned how to eat pork and beans and sardines. A lot of times, like when we were playing with the Clowns, the Clowns played *every* day, sometimes two and three games a day, and you didn't get a chance to stop to eat. You got to run in a grocery store and get a loaf of bread and lunch meat or stuff like that to eat.

The Clowns were *always* on the go. They went all over the world. I remember we played in Chicago one Saturday night and had to ride all night long to the Yankee Stadium to play the next day. We had to change clothes on the bus and get right out of the bus and go right on the field. Tired, tired, but we still played good ball.

I enjoyed the travel. I sit down and think about it now and I wish I was able to do it again. I would do it all over. I enjoyed it. I didn't make no money, but I got a lot of experience.

Who were the managers you played under?

Oscar Charleston was a good manager. He was kind of mean, but he was good. He knew baseball. He was good for young ballplayers. He could teach you a lot.

And my manager at Newark was real good. Biz Mackey. He was a real good guy and he was a great ballplayer. With the Clowns, Buster Haywood was my manager. He was a good guy, too. Mackey and Buster was catchers. And Ted Powalic was a catcher, also. Catchers study the game; they know how to study ballplayers. I guess they knew how to handle ballplayers from having so many different pitchers they had to work with.

You left Pampa after the '54 season. What did you do then?

My family was brick masons. They'd build homes and I did that. I also bought a service station and I was in that business up until '97; December 31, 1997.

I got these bad legs now. I had vascular surgery. They removed a vein from my left leg and put it in my right leg because they wanted to cut the right leg off. I wouldn't let 'em do it and I got a second opinion. I went to my heart doctor and he told me no, that's the last resort. He got a team of doctors and they saved my leg.

Do you have any regrets from baseball?

No, I don't. Only thing I hate now is the way they're *giving* money away up there now. Ballplayers are not *near* as good as the ballplayers was back there in those days. We played for the name of the game because we *loved* the game, but now they're playing for that money.

We didn't know anything about no relief pitching and all this kind of stuff. When a pitcher went out on the mound, he was out there for nine innings. The only way he would come out is if he got in real trouble. Now they got a different pitcher for every batter that comes up.

BATTING RECORD

Year	Team, League	Pos	G	AB	R	H	2B	3B	HR	RBI	SB	BA
1946	Newark, NNL	inf										
1947		inf										
1948	Indianapolis, NAL	inf										
1950	Key West, FlL	inf	77	245	13	43	5	1	1	14	2	.176
1953	Pampa, WTNM	2b-3b	128	522	113	157	32	6	5	73	15	.301
1954	Artesia, Longhorn	3b	23	95	18	28	3	0	2	18	2	.295
	Pampa, WTNM	ss-3b	95	377	62	114	21	4	6	69	3	.302

Dave Pope
"Victim of a Youth Movement"

BORN JULY 17, 1921, TALLADEGA, AL
DIED AUGUST 28, 1999, CLEVELAND, OH
HT. 5'10" WT. 170 BATTED LEFT, THREW RIGHT

Negro Leagues debut: 1946

Dave Pope could hit. Along the way in a 14-year professional career, he had averages of .361, .352, .345, and six other seasons above .300. In four years as a Cleveland Indian, he batted .294.

Dave Pope could run. Bases weren't being stolen very often in his playing days (basically the 1950s), so look at his triples. Five times he led his league in those, baseball's most exciting play.

Dave Pope could field. In 165 major league games in the outfield, he made only three errors and compiled a .991 fielding average.

Dave Pope was tough in the clutch. In 1955, he was second in the American League in pinch hitting with an average of .387 (12-for-31).

There was only one thing Dave Pope couldn't do: get back to the major leagues after being sent down in 1957. There were reasons, of course. Cleveland was not the team it had been, and over the next few seasons the slide continued. Rather than trying to win an extra game or two with a proven quantity such as Pope, whose playing days were approaching an end, the club tried young players in an attempt to regain its prominence in the AL. As a result, several young outfielders were tried over the next few years: Rocky Colavito, Roger Maris, Gary Geiger, Tito Francona, Carroll Hardy, Marty Keough, Walt Bond, and others. Some worked out, others didn't, but they all had one thing in common: they were five to ten years younger than the Indians believed Pope to be.

So Pope, a World War II veteran and a Negro leagues alumnus, played out his career in the minor leagues with major league production. He should have had another shot.

You began your professional career in 1946 with the Homestead Grays at the age of 20.

No, a little older than that. The records are not correct as they stand, but I have not bothered them. I entered with the Grays at 24. I was born in 1921.

I came out of the service. I didn't play semipro until after I left the Grays. I only played about two-thirds of a season and then I went to the Pittsburgh Crawfords, who, at that point, were a semipro team in the league that was initiated by Branch Rickey — the United States League — in 1946.

I played in Canada a couple of years in the Provincial League — the old Provincial League. I believe it was '48 and '49. Then, of course, I signed with the Indians in 1950.

The Provincial League pitchers didn't seem to hold many secrets from you. You had a two-year average there of .334.

No, I did all right up there. Of course, it was a good time and I had a good record up there, but even in organized baseball, pitchers have not been too much of a problem. Even the records we look at have some provisions that should be looked at if we're talking about official records, which should include, of course, the opportunities that were presented to play.

For instance, in the big leagues with the Cleveland Indians, two years of .294 were not really demonstrative of anyone's ability in my position because of the way I played — filling in here and there. I think one year there was less than a hundred appearances. That record means this is what you do when you get up off the bench and are asked to do something. That's a part of the game, also, but it is not a part of the game that demonstrates a person's total ability.

I listened to Hank Aaron and I didn't think that anyone else had even experienced what I did in my young days — in my childhood days — and that is hitting bottle caps with broomsticks. I listened to him and he said that he did, that's the way he learned to hit, also. Hitting was not really a problem. It was a matter of getting the opportunity to play and I guess, at that time, the opportunities were not as good because baseball was not situated like it is now. Baseball has changed a lot now, which gives a lot of other players an opportunity which they would not have gotten when I was playing. The nine-inning pitcher, the nine-inning player — all of that kind of stuff. Everything has changed. More teams.

In 1954 in Cleveland, there may have been a better starting first three outfielders, but you guys had six outfielders who would probably have been regulars almost anywhere else in baseball.

That's true. I say a lot about Casey Stengel and the New York Yankees over that dynasty they had. Stengel had two ballclubs where he could just close his eyes and pull off the bench and say, "Go ahead in there." Well, in '54, Cleveland was much similar to that. We didn't have *two* ballclubs, but we had a lot of extra ballplayers who were performers. Al Lopez had not too much of a problem that year with doing things because whoever he called on went in and performed up to a standard

where the team didn't lose that much. Guys like myself, like Sam Dente, Wally Westlake, Hank Majeski — some of them had been regulars and stars before but they were on their waning years and some of us had never reached that level of stardom, but that year every one had a good year. It didn't matter what happened, if Lopez needed a pinch hitter or if he needed a shortstop to play or whatever he needed, it was there. The players produced for him.

I've always held that I think a manager's biggest asset is keeping 26 ballplayers inspired over the period of 154 or 162 games, whatever it's going to be — keeping those guys hungry and wanting to win. The other thing is, of course, the knowledge of pitching and when to make changes in the pitching rotation and on the hill. I think that that is probably the manager's biggest concern because if you look at the situation, professional ballplayers know their job, they know what to do, and they do it. The biggest job for the manager is keeping them inspired and wanting to do the job and knowing when to change pitchers and alternate players here and there.

Again, we have to go back to Stengel. How much did Stengel have to do to manage the New York Yankees over a period of ten years? Not much.

Both managers had excellent pitching coaches. Stengel had Jim Turner and Lopez had Mel Harder, so the pitching situations for both teams were in good hands.

It was. I think that, too, is probably a great asset to a ballclub. In fact, in Cleveland in 1954 and in all of the years that I played there — 1952, '53, '54 — I think that the guys who made that club were the coaches: Tony Cuccinello, Red Kress, Mel Harder, and Bill Lobe, and guys like that who kept the team on the prod and kept 'em loose, so to speak. I think that the coaches contributed much more than people give them credit for doing, as far as the morale of the ballclub and so forth.

We had some excellent people. Red Kress really was a guy who was loosey-goosey and he kind of kept the ballclub that way. Tony Cuccinello was a knowledgeable person, knew the game, knew how to coach, all of that. Mel Harder was the same way with the pitchers. Bill Lobe had the bullpen and he kept us going a little bit, too. I think the coaches deserve a lot of credit that they don't usually get.

Coaching staffs have really expanded recently.

Everything is specialized now, that's why. Everybody has a special coach for a special reason. We've got body builders, we've got weight coaches, we've got finesse coaches, we've got basic fundamental coaches. Since the game is so specialized now, we also have specialized coaches.

In Game One of the 1954 World Series, you were out there in right field when Dusty Rhodes hit what would have been a routine fly ball anywhere else in the world. Did you think you had a chance at it?

Yes, I did. In fact, there's a picture of me jumping up beside the wall. There was just a slight breeze out there that day towards the stands. If the wind had not been blowing, I believe I would have caught the ball. After all, the ball just hit on top of the cement. It was a cement wall — I would imagine it was almost a foot thick — and the ball hit on top of that wall. But I thought it was coming down beside the wall. Had it not been for that little breeze, I think I would have caught the ball.

Did you think that Willie Mays was going to catch Vic Wertz's ball?

No, I didn't. I guess we've heard a lot of talk about that catch and some people claim it was easy, some people claim it was hard, but Willie was playing a pretty shallow center field at that time and I didn't think that he was *ever* going to catch the ball. He caught it over his shoulder, but I think that the most important thing about that catch, too, not only did he catch the ball, but he was able to turn and throw before the runners could advance on the bases. I think that that was a great part of it, also. He forced the runners to remain on the bases.

Dave Pope (author's collection).

It had to be demoralizing to you guys — a ball hit five miles for an out.

Yes, it was. I think that that was probably the turning point in the Series itself and in the feeling of the ballplayers, also. I thought that we had the game, I thought we could *win* the game, and then when you look at a hit like Dusty Rhodes's, which was what — 200-and-something down the right field line? And when you think of a 250-foot home run and you think of a 410-foot out, it's just something that doesn't seem to match. But that's the way the game goes.

You were very fast — you had a lot of triples everywhere you played — but back then, bases weren't stolen. Would you have been a base stealer today?

Yes, I'm pretty sure I would. I could run and I think that I had the ability to analyze pitching, also. That was one of the assets for my hitting — the fact that I could pick up different types of pitches earlier and then hit the ball wherever the pitch was, rather than struggle to manufacture directions. I'd just hit the ball where it was. Yes, I would have liked to have been a base stealer, but in those days there was not a whole lot of base stealing. There was hit-and-run and you didn't have to steal a base.

You spent four more years in the minors after you left the majors.

Yes, I went two years to San Diego, one year in Houston, one year with Toronto.

By this point, you're pushing 40 and still hitting. Did you think you'd get another chance in the major leagues?

Yes, I did. I always did, especially the first two years that I left here. I left Cleveland in '57 and I certainly thought that I was going to get another chance in the big leagues because the way I left was rather disappointing. That year I think I had an excellent spring training. In the first place, I didn't feel that I should have been the person to go to the minor leagues, because I felt that I had performed as well as any of the outfielders on the ballclub. I didn't understand all of that other stuff about opportunities to play in the big leagues, how many years you had in the big leagues, the seniority system, and all that kind of stuff. I just felt that the best ballplayer ought to be out on the ballfield, and that wasn't the case; but I did have a good spring training, and I felt that I should not have gone to San Diego that year. However, after going there, I still had two good years there.

Two outstanding years.

Well, they were not outstanding for Dave Pope. I will say that, too, because I knew what I could do. The years at San Diego were not outstanding. I think I had an outstanding year at Indianapolis in 1952. That was outstanding, but I don't think the other years were outstanding. Not for me because, like I said, I knew what I could do and I had confidence in what I could do.

Although, in my eyes, they weren't outstanding, they were still the best production that was in San Diego and partially in the Pacific Coast League in those years, After I

didn't get the opportunity to come back after the first year — that was '57 — and winning the Most Valuable Player Award for the San Diego club, also, I began to get a little frustrated at that time because I felt that, if the Cleveland Indians were not going to bring me back to the big leagues, that I should have been released or sold to some other ballclub. Later, I found out that there were opportunities for that to happen, but they didn't sell me. In fact, Hank Greenberg [Cleveland general manager] came out there and we had a talk about that and he told me that he had an opportunity to sell me to a couple ballclubs but he felt that he didn't want to get rid of the best ballplayer in the Pacific Coast League. [Laughs] I couldn't understand his reasoning there, so we got into a little heated conversation about that.

I think that the fact I was not recalled in '57 and '58 sort of developed, in my mind, some kind of psychological effect, and that's why I'm saying to you that those years were not exceptional years for me. I know they could've been much better, but there was a psychological effect because I didn't go back to the big leagues.

You were only in the Negro leagues a short period, but who was the best player you saw there?

That *is* kind of hard because there were *so* many guys there, but the guys that I knew best, of course, were the people on the Grays. I would think that Cool Papa Bell was probably the best ballplayer I've ever seen. Josh Gibson and Jerry Benjamin, Buck Leonard, Sam Bankhead —*all* of them were exceptionally good ballplayers, but I think that Cool Papa was probably the best all-around — and when I say that, I mean as far as his personality, his baseball expertise, and all of those things. I think that he was probably the best.

Who was the best pitcher you saw in the Negro leagues?

The one that stands out in my mind most is a guy for the New York Black Yankees called Neck Stanley. I think that he had more tricks than most pitchers that I've ever seen, and I thought that he was probably the toughest. But there were *many* that were excellent pitchers.

The talent that most of the country never got to see must have been amazing.

I always say, and I hope that it will have some kind of effect — or at least start people to thinking — it's too bad that the American people were denied the opportunity to see those great ballplayers. I just came back from Kansas City and I visited the [Negro Leagues Baseball] Museum and they had about 200 of us there, former Negro league ballplayers. The stories that I heard and the people that I talked to, even I, who had been in baseball almost all my life, didn't know the things that had gone on and the good ballplayers that they were. I met guys who had played before I was born. It's too bad the American people did not have an opportunity to see those guys in action.

I had a meeting with George Shuba in one of the meetings here for the Ohio Hall of Fame and he made a statement that I'm sure was true, but he said when Jackie came up to Brooklyn, they were all surprised about how well he could play and how many positions he could play so well.

I said to him, "Yes, that's true." They would have been surprised because none of them had ever had the opportunity to see the Negro leaguers perform and to know that they *had* to perform like that and to perform in more than one position. That's why Jackie was so good, because he had had that experience.

Who was the best you saw in the major leagues?

Oh, gosh. [Laughs] I would have to take Mays as one of the best hitters. Hank Aaron, Mickey Mantle. Ted Williams, of course. Those stand out in my mind as excellent hitters.

Those years that I played, Cleveland and New York probably had the best pitching staffs in the world, guys like Allie Reynolds, Bob Lemon, Early Wynn, Bob Feller — those guys.

Is there one game that stands out in your memory?

No, not really. In fact, you know, strangely enough, I never remembered games like that. I hear people talk about great feats that they've done; I never remembered those. My wife kept all of the records. I didn't keep any. I never bothered about statistics, I never bothered about batting averages or anything. When I read the paper the next day, I read the important parts about winning and losing and that was about it.

Any regrets or disappointments from your career?

Disappointments — no, I don't think there were very many disappointments. I was doing the things that I loved to do.

Of course, there were a number of things I felt should not have been. In spring training, for instance, when I first joined the Indians, the integration had not really caught on at that time in sports and a very disappointing situation was in spring training. There were two separate buildings for players to live in, one was for the white ballplayers to live in, one was for the black ballplayers. That would not have been so bad, but the place that the black ballplayers lived in was an emptied tool shed. We had spring training on an Air Force base, an empty Air Force base, and there was a small tool shed, maybe about 30 × 30 or something of that nature. There were eight of us and we were in double bunk beds in that building while the other ballplayers had — they weren't luxurious but they were facilities in what they called the "Wigwam." We were in the teepee, they were in the wigwam. [Laughs]

Another thing is that we couldn't even eat together. That was in Daytona Beach, Florida. You know how they rope the tables off in restaurants? That's what we had. I couldn't imagine doing that with an organization that was a private organization and had its own organizational structure, yet those kinds of things were going on down there.

The Indians were one of the more advanced teams in integration and race relations. Can you imagine what it must have been like with the Yankees or Red Sox or some of those? The black player in the early '50s was in limbo. The black leagues were dying and the white leagues weren't really ready for him.

That was one of the real detrimental things as far as black ballplayers were concerned. There was just not enough room for *all* of them and, as you say, with black baseball dying, it just left a lot of them out in the cold.

Would you be a ballplayer again if you had it to do over?

Yes, I would certainly be a ballplayer. With my experience now and looking back at circumstances, I think that my pattern of life would be different as far as doing things. I happen not to be one of the assertive-type ballplayers and, I guess you could say, mouthy or self-assertive. I think that that would not be the case if I would do the whole thing again. That doesn't mean that I would be a boisterous type guy, but I would certainly make the most out of the opportunities and

the doors that opened by virtue of being a professional ballplayer.

Do you get much fan mail today?

Yes, I still do. I get quite a bit. It's *very* nice to be remembered. Sometimes, with the letters that I get, I just feel like writing back and throwing my heart out to people for those kind of letters and sometimes I do respond like that.

Most of the names mentioned by Dave Pope in this interview are at least familiar to the baseball fans of today, but one may not be. John "Neck" Stanley was a lefthanded pitcher in the Negro leagues from 1928 to 1949, primarily with the New York Black Yankees. His best pitches centered around the use of saliva and emery boards, and in exhibition games versus white major leaguers he was extremely tough. He shut out Babe Ruth's All-Stars, 8–0; Dizzy Dean's All-Stars, 6–0; and Bob Feller's All-Stars, 4–0. The latter game, in 1946, so irritated Feller's players that they refused to continue the tour unless Stanley was dropped from the team. His nickname came from the fact that he had a very long neck.

BATTING RECORD

Year	Team, League	Pos	G	AB	R	H	2B	3B	HR	RBI	SB	BA
1946	Homestead, NNL	of										
	Pittsburgh, USL											
1948	Farnham, ProvL	of		313		113			23	72		.361
1949		of		304		93			19	77		.306
1950	Wilkes-Barre, EL	of	120	403	74	108	13	*18	8	71	7	.268
1951		of	138	512	*113	158	27	*13	15	95	8	.309
1952	Cleveland, AL	of	12	34	9	10	1	1	1	4	0	.294
	Indianapolis, AA	of	126	475	77	167	29	7	13	79	4	*.352
1953	Indianapolis, AA	of	154	600	101	172	33	*14	24	88	3	.287
1954	Cleveland, AL	of	60	102	21	30	2	1	4	13	2	.294
1955	Clev., Balt., AL	of	121	326	38	86	13	4	7	52	5	.264
1956	Balt., Clev., AL	of	37	89	7	20	3	1	0	4	0	.225
	Indianapolis, AA	of	100	367	66	111	18	9	25	76	4	.302
1957	San Diego, PCL	of	129	460	74	144	21	6	18	83	8	.313
1958		of	142	545	88	172	31	7	19	96	11	.316
1959	Toronto, IL	of	129	455	62	125	30	3	16	69	5	.275
1960	Houston, AA	of	135	498	61	138	33	5	12	62	9	.277
1961	Toronto, IL	of	30	50	8	12	2	0	2	5	0	.240
1951–52	San Juan, PRWL	of		111		29			2	17		.261
1952–53	San Juan, PRWL	of		18		9			0	5		.500
1953–54	Gavilanes, VenzL	of	78	275	57	95	*22	*6	9	52	12	*.345
1954–55	Santa Maria, VenzL	of		171	*32	55		*6	5	25		.322

* Led league

Bill Powell
"250 Wins?"

Born May 8, 1919, West Birmingham, AL
Ht. 6'2½" Wt. 195 Batted Left, Threw Right

Negro Leagues debut: 1946

Bill Powell was a big, hard-throwing righthander who pitched for 22 years. We don't know his complete record, but counting the Negro leagues, the minor leagues, and Latin American winter ball, he may have won 250 games.

For three seasons in a row, he won 21 games a year with the Birmingham Black Barons. He won in double digits several times in the minors. He pitched ten seasons in six different countries in the winter leagues. It may not all add up to 250, but it should come close.

He has a great East-West Game record. He won the 1948 game and saved the '50 contest. His ERA for his All-Star appearances is 1.50 (one run in six innings).

He played with Willie Mays. He played against Hank Aaron. Like them, he enjoyed a long and successful career, but unlike them, his is not a household name. A 250-game winner should be better known.

I got into baseball when I was playing in what we call a YMCA league here in Birmingham. I was about 15. I started playing around. We had what we called semipro teams in Birmingham and I started playing with them and working at a pipe shop — metal cast iron pipe shop.

We worked at three in the afternoon and the name of the team was the Twenty-Sixth Street Red Sox, and from there I went to American Cast Iron Pipe and I played with them until I went in the Army. I was in the service a little bit better than four years. I played ball in the service, too.

When I got out of the service, I joined the Birmingham Black Barons. I was 25.

How did you make contact with the Black Barons?

They come to me when I got out of the Army. All teams wanted me when I got out of

service 'cause they knew me before I went in service. After I got out, they were waiting on me, but I joined the Birmingham Black Barons in 1946. I played with 'em five years, from '46 to '50, and me and the owner fell out.

In 1951, I went to Sacramento, California, in the [Pacific] Coast League. That was better than the majors. It was just like a minor league, but it was better. You'd meet good players.

When I joined up there, they optioned me out to a team called the Colorado Springs Sky Sox. I played that year and I won 15 and I lost 8 with them.

Getting back to the Barons, in '48, '49, '50, I won 21 games three years in a row. That's the year Cincinnati and Chicago and all of 'em was after me, but, I don't know, they just looked me over. Campanella was trying to get the Dodgers to sign me. It was tough

Bill Powell (author's collection).

then, man; segregation was *bad*. It's still there now. Good ballplayers in the minor leagues and they won't bring 'em up. It's rough. You have to be almost perfect.

After that year in Colorado, I went to play winter ball. Cincinnati signed me in 1951. I went to spring training with 'em and broke spring training, but they optioned me out. They had a boy lost 15 games and won 5. I had won 15 and they took him up. [Laughs] That hurt me, you know.

They sent me out to Toronto, Canada — International League — and I was winning for that team there 'cause we was on top. Me and Luke Sewell, the manager — he was from Birmingham — we couldn't set it, so they shipped me over to Havana, Cuba. They was in the league, too.

I finished that year up and the next year, I went to Charleston, West Virginia, and I stayed with 'em two years. The last year I was with Charleston I had another 15–8. That was best in the league, the American Association. That was a good league. I was the best pitcher

in that league and Cincinnati still wouldn't call me up.

That's all the teams I played with in America, but I played a lot of winter league ball. My first year in winter ball was '48. I went to Mayagüez, Puerto Rico; '49 I went to Havana, Cuba; in '50 I went back to Cuba with Santurce; and the next year I played with Ponce. I played three years in Cuba.

Then I played in Caracas, Venezuela; I played in Santo Domingo; played in Colombia, South America; and I played two years in Mexico. My last year, when I was 42 years old — I played 22 years, I was playing manager in Canada — that's when I hung 'em up. I had a good career and I went everywhere. [Laughs]

How many games do you think you won in those 22 years?

Oh, man. I was the winningest pitcher just about everywhere I went.

In winter ball, the seasons was short. I'd say if you win six or seven games, you had a good season. I won on the average — in Puerto Rico and Mexico and Caracas, Venezuela, and Cuba — I'd say I'd average out about six or seven games a year with those teams. But in America, like I say, I won 21 three years with the Birmingham Black Barons, I had a 15–8 with Charleston, West Virginia, I had a 15–8 with Colorado Springs. And I played with the Negro leagues when I left and had about a 8–3 or something like that in part of a season [1952].

See, if you're a good pitcher, they get you in the winter time to play overseas. I won a lot of games staying in baseball 22 years. I went to Knoxville, Tennessee, as a pitcher's coach — that was in the Baltimore organization — and there I pitched — as a reliever and a starter — in 70 games. We only played a hundred-something games and I set a record in that league that year. That was '58 or '59; I was 40 then. [Laughs] I played 'til I was 42.

Did you ever have any arm problems?

One time I had a little arm trouble and stayed out about a week. I pulled a ligament in my shoulder and the chiropractor told me, said, "When I get through with you, you'll be as good as new. Better than you was when you first came to me." He said that. I stayed out a week and then went on and pitched then 'til I retired.

That's what makes me mad. I set there and watch these pitchers on television and somebody picks 'em up in five innings. That's bad. That makes baseball bad. So many of the guys don't watch the ballgames no more. They don't like to watch it. We aren't mad with 'em making their money, now. I'm for 'em making their money. The guys that are doing the hitting and the pitching, they deserve it because they're the ones putting the people in the park. Everybody says they make too much money; no, they don't make too much money. Owners are making all the money. Don't you think owners don't make any money.

Talk about the conditions in the Negro leagues.

We rode in a bus from Chicago to Memphis, Tennessee — we didn't have no four-lane highways then — and we were late coming through that evening traffic. We pulled the shades down and changed clothes in the bus and we got out to the ballpark and throwed two or three balls and went to playing ball.

They asked, "Where did you all come from? Where'd you change clothes at?" We did that a lot of times — ride the bus all night, half of the day, jump off the bus and run right in and change clothes, eat sardines and cheese and crackers. We eat out of the bus, eat out of the can.

I ate out of the can for a long, long time. It was good food, but we couldn't get nothing in the white restaurants. They wouldn't let us eat in there.

But, when we'd get in a town — like in the afternoon — they had all those places called, you know, a mom's restaurant. And here's what those people would do if they knowed we was coming. I don't care how much food they had to sell, folks'd come in and they'd say, "We don't have any more food. I got to save my boys some food."

And she'd save all her boys some food. She did all the teams like that. Every team,

she's going to save her boys some food. That was good food, buddy. [Laughs] You're talking about black-eyed peas and butter beans and red beans and roast beef and chicken. I mean, good home-cooked food.

I don't know how we made it, eating out of a can. Most of the time — like we'd leave Birmingham going to Memphis — we know we won't have time to eat when we get there. The manager would try to let us stay at home with our wives as long as we could and we'd leave 'bout nine or ten o'clock. It's a pretty good drive going to Memphis and we'd stop and buy sardines and cheese and stuff like that. We'd try to buy wholesome stuff.

But you know one thing that made it so great with our team, we were all like brothers. Just like a bunch of brothers. They asked us out to the ballpark if we had to do it all over again, everyone of us said we'd do the same thing over again. I loved it. I wouldn't change nothing. We had fun, but we had fun playing for nothing. And we could play.

During my time, Birmingham white Barons wasn't drawing anybody 'til they had

Bill Powell (courtesy of William Powell).

[Walt] Dropo down here. We used to put 15-
and 16,000 in that park every Sunday. Maybe
20. Stack 'em all out in the outfield. They
would take our money; they'd count the money
and give us what we wanted. We were paying
for the park. They couldn't pay the salaries.

Is there one game that stands out?

Oh, yeah. In Memphis, Tennessee, we
was playing the Kansas City Monarchs for the
World Series. All they had to do was win one
game and we beat 'em two in Birmingham.
Piper told me that night, "I'm gonna let you
pitch in Memphis under them dark lights."
[Laughs] I could throw *hard*, man. I don't
know if I threw as hard as Satchel, but I was
in the range.

That night I pitched and I won that
game. I beat Kansas City, 3–2. Boy, you talk
about some big games. They come to us with
just *one* game to win and I beat 'em, 3–2, and
there went the championship. My picture
right now is in Rickwood Field [in Birming-
ham] on the wall with the rest of the guys.
They put me up there. [That was] 1948. Zapp
hit a home run, and, boy, he hit it, too. Willie
Mays was on that team.

You've seen guys fight off pitches. This
guy kept throwing Zapp fastballs, fastballs —
and he wasn't getting around. He was getting
under 'em or over 'em 'cause the ball was moving. So the manager called him from the
bench, said for LaMarque to give him a breaking ball. Zapp was looking at him or something and he guessed with him. [Laughs] It
didn't break enough. He hit that ball!

That was my game. That was one of the
best games I think I ever pitched.

I knew everything must come to an end.
I played 'til I couldn't play.

I'll tell you another great game I pitched.
It was against the major league All-Stars and
I beat 'em in Atlanta. I think I beat 'em, 3–0.
I beat Larry Doby, Campanella, Al Smith,
Junior Gilliam, Suitcase Simpson — all of 'em
barnstorming through here, and I beat them
that night and I didn't give 'em but three hits.
Doby didn't get nothing. I've pitched some
pretty good games in my life.

A guy in Memphis asked me, "Mr. Powell, how do you pitch at 40-some years old?"
I try to tell him, "The only way to be a good
athlete of any kind is eat good, train good,
and get your rest." If you don't do those three
things, you're through. I tell some guys I'm 79
years old and they don't believe it. You got to
rest, eat good, and I train *hard*. I ran 15 minutes a day for almost 22 years. When I wasn't
pitching, nobody told me to run. Every manager I've had said I was the workingest pitcher
they ever had on their team.

They would call on me any time for a
tough game. I've pitched with three days' rest.
I pitched 19 innings one time. Everybody
wanted to know how. "What kind of arm you
got there?" And the next day I went over and
throwed batting practice. There was a guy
named Joe Becker from Cleveland. He was my
manager.

I'll tell you who could've gotten me —
the Cubs, Cincinnati, the Dodgers, and Milwaukee [American Association] was going to
sign me. The Brewers. One night in Memphis, they watched me. They wanted a package: Bob Boyd and me, for roommates. Boyd
could hit that ball.

Tom Hayes, my owner, wanted a $30,000
package deal for the two of us, but they only
wanted to give 15,000, so Tom Hayes wouldn't
sell us. We got messed around; I could've been
in the majors.

The team I played with, for pitching we
had myself and Sammy C. Williams, Bill
Greason, Jimmy Newberry, Jehosie Heard, a
lefthander, a little boy named [Curtis] Hol-
lingsworth. We had four of the toughest
righthanders in that league.

Our infield consisted of catching was
Herman Bell and Pepper Bassett and first base
[Joe] Scott and second base after [Tommy]
Sampson left, Piper went to second base, and
Art Wilson and [Jack] Britton. Norman
Robinson, Ed Steele, and sometimes Zapp
would alternate. Then we had Willie Mays;
when he got there, he just took over. That was
a ballplayer. You couldn't hit nothing up the
middle. Art Wilson was one of the best shortstops ever put on a glove.

Some have said that Wilson and Davis were the best double play combination ever.

It was. It was the best you could see. Piper — the reason they didn't sign him in the majors, they say it took him too long to get rid of the ball. He had long arms. Unh-unh. He would cheat a lot; that ball would hit the glove and he'd get it to first base. They just didn't want to sign him. Boston brought him up there and he hit .3-something [for Scranton] when Dropo wasn't doing nothing, and when Dropo started hitting, they released Piper.

But we had a *ball club!* I was the best pitcher on the team, though, and I was the hardest-throwing pitcher on the team. I was one of the hardest-throwing pitchers in the whole league. Didn't nobody want to hardly bat against me at night, especially them cool nights.

One night, I pitched against Doby and them, and Birmingham was cold. Doby took hisself out of the game. [Laughs] I had a heavy ball. My ball moved all the time.

You talk about great catching, that boy Herman Bell was a *cat!* We made people happy then. You know what? When, like, these catchers now ain't hitting, they're standing behind home plate. You hit a ball to the infield, that catcher should be behind first base before the ball gets to first base. There was a rhythm to it. You don't see that now. They don't whip that ball around the infield; they throw the ball slowly and then drop it over to the pitcher. They used to whip the ball around the infield and it was good; the fans liked that. They used to come out to see us take batting practice. The people had their mind on what we were doing. But, you know, everything changes.

Where I'm sitting right here now, I bought my home out of baseball. I was married 47 years when my wife passed two years ago. We bought this place when we was married and I added something to it. When I bought this house, I bought it for $3,000. Know what it's worth now? I'd say $70,000, but I couldn't get it in this neighborhood I'm in. Neighborhood used to be fine.

I have had the great Lord to bless me. I had a great, great career and now I'm retired from my job in '84. I was lucky enough to come back here and get a job with a beer company. By me being an athlete, and the people knew me here in Birmingham — that really helped me 'cause I got a job with Schlitz as a sales rep. They weren't doing nothing. Schlitz was raising sand all over the United States, but Budweiser was killing 'em here.

I went around and let everybody know that I worked for Schlitz, and in one season, we went to number one. I took 'em to number one. Yes, sir.

I went out there with the right approach. Everybody knew me from playing baseball, but my personality, the way I dressed, and you can't beat a smile. I'm a natural smiler. That's something you can't beat — a natural smile. That'll do more for you than anything in the world.

And a good handshake. I learned how to shake hands and smile from the man that trained me. I'd been a very quiet guy all my life, but after I got in baseball and got around the guys, then I started to open up.

Hardship causes some guys to be what they are. I come a hard, hard way in life. I been ornery, naked almost — it just make you different from what you're supposed to be. That wasn't me and after I got my wife, I wouldn't've been nothing if it hadn't been for her. She made me. You won't see two people married like we were. She was a teacher and I had no kind of formal education.

She could've married in college. A lot of guys — doctors and everything else. Most folks that send their girls to college are professional people. She used to come to the ballpark with Piper's wife 'cause Piper was her brother-in-law, and when she came home from school breaks she watched me *two* years. I said, "You been sittin' in that ballpark watchin' me for two years." I said, "What did you want with me out of *all* them fine doctors and lawyers?" She said, "I don't know. I loved you." We stayed together 47 years.

People say love ain't all of it, but it makes a big difference. If you love somebody, you can keep a whole lot of things together. You can have a dollar or don't have a dollar, but love will keep things together if you really love each other. Me and her saw some tough ways of going, but we pulled it through. You can't stay together having hardships if you don't love each other.

And put the Master above everything. I'm a Christian man and believe in the Master. That'll see you through a lot.

We didn't have any kids. It was just one of those things. You know what? That used to hurt me so bad, but I found out there's thousands and thousands of women don't have children. I would've liked to have myself a little boy. [Laughs] I wanted a boy, but my wife loved little girls. Either one would have been all right.

We couldn't adopt. We were getting older and we didn't have the money. She was working and I was working; they ain't going to let you adopt a child.

Who was the best hitter you faced?

Hank Aaron. He's one of the best in baseball. I faced him in the minor leagues.

One of the best hitters I've ever seen was Josh Gibson, but I never pitched to him. I was going to pitch to him one night, but Piper took me out and put somebody else in, a good curveball pitcher. He hit a line drive to cen-

ter field like a bullet. [Laughs] He was something. He hit a home run in all parks.

Who was the best pitcher?

Oh, Satchel Paige. We played against his team, but I never pitched against him.

You saw Willie Mays in the beginning. Could you tell then that he would be as good as he turned out to be?

Oh, yeah. We knew he was a natural from the time he joined us. Only thing he couldn't do was swing the bat, but after he stayed with us — I think he stayed with us one year — he started swinging the bat. One year he had a batting average about .400 'til he went to New York to play.

He was a better ballplayer than Aaron. Better hitter than Aaron. If he'd've not went in the Army, he'd've beat Aaron. He stayed in the Army two years. A lot of them pitchers went to school on him and then he just couldn't hit nothing. He come back hitting about .200 on that trip. But he was a good ballplayer.

Willie Mays could do *everything!* Hit, run, throw, catch — everything. They stood at the ticket office and asked people what did they come to the ballgame to see. They said, "I come to see his cap fall off," or, "I come to see him hit a home run." They came to see him do something in *every* ballgame.

PITCHING RECORD

Year	Team, League	G	IP	W	L	Pct	H	BB	SO	ERA
1946	Birmingham, NAL									
1947		10	70	5	0	1.000	55	25	34	2.96
1948		19	130	11	3	.786	133	40	103	3.81
1949		*32	182	11	11	.500	189	56	124	3.61
1950		26	162	*15	4	.789	164	68	110	3.00
1951	Col. Springs, WL	33	188	14	8	.636	189	107	157	4.69
	Sacramento, PCL	5	9	0	1	.000	6	13	6	7.00
1952	Birmingham, NAL									
	Toledo, Charleston, AA	31	175	5	15	.250	205	88	88	5.09
1953	Charleston, AA	33	215	14	9	.609	187	85	121	3.06
1954	Toronto, Havana, IL	31	151	10	8	.556	145	97	76	4.23
1955	Charleston, AA	31	131	3	10	.231	152	58	59	5.15
	Havana, IL	13	46	3	4	.429	55	27	17	5.28

Year	Team, League	G	IP	W	L	Pct	H	BB	SO	ERA
1956	San Antonio, TxL	16	47	1	3	.250	52	45	19	5.74
	Savannah, SAL	25	175	8	12	.400	153	80	71	3.14
1957	Nuevo Laredo, MxL	17	84	3	7	.300	82	62	52	3.96
	Savannah, SAL	3		2	0	1.000				
1958	Knoxville, SAL	*70	141	7	8	.467	127	57	58	3.70
1959	Asheville, SAL	1		0	0					
1961	Charlotte, SAL	16	23	1	1	.500	30	13	15	6.22
1949–50	Marianao, CWL10		1		4	.200				
1952–53	Cienfuengos, CWL	11		3	2	.600				

* Led league

Note: In 1948, 1949, and 1950, Powell won 21 games each season when non-league games are included.

Marvin Price
"Move Over, Joe"

BORN APRIL 5, 1933, CHICAGO, IL
HT. 6' WT. 190 BATTED AND THREW RIGHT

Negro Leagues debut: 1946

Ask any baseball fan, "Who was the youngest person to play in the major leagues?" and you will be told "Joe Nuxhall." Nuxhall was 15 years, 10 months, on that day in 1944 when he took the mound for Cincinnati. But Joe is not even the youngest white major leaguer.

There is some debate over who the true youngest was (in white ball). I believe it was Fred Chapman, who pitched one game for Philadelphia in the American Association (then a major league) way back in 1887 at the age of 14 years, 8 months.

A problem here is the definition of "major leagues." If the definition is "American or National League since 1900," then it's Nuxhall. If the definition extends back to the 19th century and encompasses all leagues then classified as "major and white," it's Chapman.

But if the definition includes *all* leagues that were "major," the answer becomes Marvin Price. Price played briefly (but longer than either Nuxhall or Chapman in their debut years) in 1946 with the Chicago American Giants of the Negro American League, a major league by anyone's definition. He was barely 14 and, unlike the other two, whose only appearance was in a single home game, he traveled with the team.

Like Nuxhall, Price returned to play high school ball after his major league fling, and, also like Nuxhall, he again played professional baseball after graduation. (Chapman never played in the major leagues again.)

Eventually signed by the Baltimore Orioles, Price's "manners" apparently cost him a shot with the parent club, but he played on at the semipro and amateur levels until he was in his 50s. He loved the game and holds no bitterness.

I was playing ball with some grown men in Washington Park in Chicago and a guy that used to play with the Chicago American Giants saw me play one holiday. [Jimmie] Crutchfield was his name; he was center field for the American Giants before my time. He said, "You're pretty good." I was about 13 years old and I was playing with grown men. He said, "How old are you?" I told him I was 13 and he said, "I want somebody to look at you," and he took my telephone number.

I thought it was a joke when he called. [Laughs] He said, "I want you to get in touch with the league president. He's the owner of the club."

That was Dr. J. B. Martin, and he called and said, "How would you like to work out with my ballclub? Somebody said they saw you and you looked pretty good. How old are you?"

I said, "I'm almost 14." So that's how I started.

I waited for the club to come in on Sunday. Quincy Trouppe was the manager — it was 1946 — and he said, "I don't need a batboy."

I said, "Hold it. My name is Price."

He said, "But you're nothin' but a baby." But he said I could work out.

Dr. J. B. Martin and my family was out there before batting practice at Comiskey Park and I put on a show for 'em.

That year, he took me South when they were playing games down there and he told me not to tell anybody. He wanted to see what I could do in league games, and I did pretty good. I doubled and got hit in the side of the face and got right back in there and doubled again. He told me I had a lot of nerve and guts, so just keep playing.

My mother wasn't all that glad for me to go, but my father knew a whole lot of guys in the Negro league because when they formed the club they were just a bunch of guys in the Sunday school league. They formed the American Giants in 1920. My father played with Double Duty Radcliffe when they first started. He was the captain of the team.

I think I played about a week with 'em and I came back home because I didn't want to mess up my school standing. I thought it wasn't right to play and I might get caught and I'd be kicked out of school.

They let me work out with the team when they came in to Chicago when the White Sox was out. I graduated from high school at 16 because I skipped some grades. I was kind of a student at one time.

I loved the game and I played when I got a chance. A college coach saw me play and he wanted me to come to college in Chicago. It was the Teachers' College then before they made it Chicago State College. I told him I'd work out with him and help him all I could, but if I got a chance to go away I would.

When I was about 17, I went South in the spring and hooked on with one of the ballclubs. That was 1949; I played with the Cleveland Buckeyes. The next three years, I played with the Eagles. The first year, they were out of Newark and then they moved to Houston.

Then I had to go to the service. I came back and started playing again, and the Orioles and Kansas City and I think it was the Yankees was all after me. I was playing first

Marvin Price (courtesy of Marvin Price).

base in the Negro league and I moved to shortstop.

We had a team that didn't lose a game that year. When Baltimore signed me, we were 32–0 and I was hitting the ball at .700 or better. It was a semipro club; they called themselves the Chicago Monarchs.

Baltimore signed me to Double-A and I went to San Antone. I wasn't at San Antone too long before I was moved up to Baltimore.

Lum Harris thought I was a sensation and told Paul [Richards] to take a look at me. I was hitting the ball in another land, you know.

But me and Paul didn't get along. He didn't understand me, I didn't understand him. He thought I should've bowed and scraped. We was always on the wrong track together. He told me I didn't have no manners.

The guy that struck out Babe Ruth and all those guys in the All-Star game, the left-hander—[Carl] Hubbell—he was the manager of Jackson. Willie Mays was my buddy—we played against each other in the Negro league—and he tried his best to get me with them before Cepeda *or* McCovey. Then Aaron tried to get me with the Braves and Ernie tried to get me with the Cubs. I don't know what he [Richards] told 'em, but they said, "No dice."

I was tearing up the Grapefruit League. I did quite well against major league ballclubs. I don't understand it; he said I didn't have no manners. I didn't understand what he called "manners." I didn't even know what he was talking about.

The guy that signed me to a contract was

Marvin Price (Lisa Feder photograph).

Tony Piet—played second base for the Chicago White Sox—he asked Paul, "What can't this man do?"

"It's got nothin' to do with baseball," he said. "He just don't have no manners."

I think he was trying to tell me I didn't have manners with white people. Most of the guys that played for him that were black were kind of humble toward him, like, "You're my boy." But I don't know where he got the idea I didn't have no manners. We only had a few conversations. I guess he thought I had a little too much education. I don't know. Brooks Robinson was the first one to say, "He belongs here more than I do."

Charlie Grimm [Cubs manager] didn't even give me an answer. Willie Mays begged Durocher, and Durocher said he couldn't do nothing about it. Aaron and a guy named [Jim] Pendleton went there with me to the Braves and they said they can't do nothing for me. I was blackballed and I knew it, but Ernie said, "Don't even think about it no more. It ain't worth it."

I'm really not that bitter. I didn't understand what I did.

I kept playing ball. I played ball up to past 50 years old on the weekends and whenever I got a chance. Everybody knew me in the Chicago area.

I talked to Buck O'Neil in '95 at our reunion in Kansas City. He said, "If I ever call you by your first name and I haven't seen you in 35–40 years, something was instilled in my mind about you." He came down that morning and he sat down at the table and he called me by my first name. He said, "You know what? You could hit." He said, "Personified. You carried them guys in '51 on your back to the championship."

We never did know what we were batting, but the *Pittsburgh Courier* and the *Chicago Defender*, they put a cumulative thing from '49 to '52—those four years—and they said I hit .297. In 1951, I must've hit about .390. I was really tearing the cover off the ball. One of the catchers on our team called me "the Thumper," like I was hitting the ball like Ted Williams.

A thing I didn't like about the league, if you were young they'd try to push somebody older. They'd say, "You got a lot of time." They sometimes might take some of your hits off your hitting and put 'em on somebody else.

I started watching the clubhouse man on our team keeping batting averages. Bob Boyd — he was with the Memphis Red Sox — he told me, "Gee, we're hittin' tit-for-tat." We were up less than 30 times at bat in a week and we both had over 21 hits. His were more like line drives — some were out of the ballpark — but I was hitting the ball *way* out of the ballpark.

I hit a ball in Joplin, Missouri — and this is the God's truth — it was a prison and they had a guy up there on the spotlights and I hit the ball over the little place where the guy stayed. We were playing the Memphis Red Sox and it was off Sam Harris. It went over 500 feet before it hit the ground. The warden said nobody had ever hit the ball that far. I must've been about 18.

When I started hitting home runs, it was just a flick of the hand. I think the first year I hit 13, then I just stopped keeping up with 'em. I didn't think in terms of home runs; I was just hitting.

We opened up in Birmingham in '50 and I hit two that day against [Bill] Greason, Willie Mays's buddy, and then I hit another on Tuesday. I must've been up about six times and I hit three. I just started popping the ball and it just started jumping.

Most of the guys in the league that seen me, like Buck O'Neil and Buster Haywood, the manager of the Clowns, they couldn't understand. The ball just started jumping. Haywood said, "Put the cat on." We was playing for the championship in the last game and he said, "He just doubled off you." One of the Tugerson boys was pitching — I don't remember which one — and he said, "No, I don't wanna win like that. I wanna pitch to him." And I hit one above the flagpole.

There was a guy named Beverly that played on our team — Fireball Beverly — and a guy was showing him a bat that a very wealthy guy had that was in gold casing and

Beverly looked at it and said, "That bat ain't no good."

He said, "Why?"

"You don't have Price's name on it."

He came all the way to Chicago and got my name on the bat. And a year later, he brought his son back to meet me.

I didn't really play baseball to be exonerated by white people. I played ball with my own and I really started out that way, and when guys like Aaron, Mays, and Banks thought I was a ballplayer, I thought I reached the pinnacle anyway.

You mentioned those great players. Who was the best player?

I never saw this guy play, but everybody said that Oscar Charleston was the greatest ballplayer that ever lived. My daddy saw him play.

In my time, Willie Mays. I thought the best hitter I ever seen in my life was Ted Williams. I seen him and he's a regular dude. I got to give it to him. I didn't ever see Josh; I know he hit thousands of home runs, but I never saw him. The one I saw was Ted Williams.

I almost got put in jail trying to see him. I was trying to sneak in the ballpark and a police officer said, "Where you going?"

I said, "I hitchhiked all the way out here to see Ted Williams."

He said, "You sure?"

I said, "Yeah. I just wanna see him."

He said, "You sit here and when I come back I want you to be sittin' here."

And I saw Ted. For just a pure hitter, he was the purest hitter I ever seen. He could swing a bat. I had a chance to talk with Ted, and I think he was one of the squarest shooters I ever met. He made an impression on me.

Who was the best pitcher you saw and who was the toughest on you?

Satchel Paige. Both of 'em. I hit Satchel hard, but he got a curveball up on me and I was lucky enough to get around on it. I thought it was luck and we were riding the bus and he wanted me to ride in his Cadillac with him. I called him "Mister"; he said,

"Don't call me 'Mister.' You're a ballplayer; you call me 'Satch.'"

Satchel could throw the ball as hard as anybody. I faced major league pitchers. I faced Herb Score and he was throwing it hard, but Satchel—I swear the ball got halfway up to the plate and took off. His hands were so long and lean. His curveball would break a foot and a half. There was something on it all the time and he had the same expression on his face. He would pitch three innings every night. I saw him when he was older and they say when he was younger he was a lot better.

I don't know whether this is true or not. He stole an apple in Alabama and they put him in jail because he couldn't pay the fine. Somebody saw him pitching in jail and they got him out. [Laughs]

Here's something else you've got to understand about baseball. You've got to *believe*. Just like Dizzy Dean said: "We weren't the best ballplayers." He said it himself. They used to barnstorm on the [West] Coast. Ted Williams said, "I feel so humble going into the Hall of Fame and guys like Josh Gibson and Satchel Paige ain't there. I don't feel like I'm the best."

And guys like Babe Ruth wouldn't even face Satchel. What does it say? Is it the color of their skin, or they might make 'em look bad?

In the off-season, they played against each other in California. Dizzy Dean faced Satchel Paige for 19 innings, and Dizzy Dean got a lucky hit down the right field line. He got to third base and Satchel Paige walked over to him and said, "In nine pitches you'll still be sittin' here."

He struck out Rogers Hornsby in 19 innings *five* times. Hornsby said, "I wasn't tryin' that hard 'cause he was black."

It almost turned me off of baseball when I was a young kid. I saw where the Cubs was holding a tryout camp between here and New York, so I jumped out there at five o'clock in the morning trying to hitchhike a ride. I was about 12 or 13.

A guy gave me a ride right to the place and I walked up there and Rogers said, "What you want?"

I said, "I want to try out." I knew I was too young.

He said, "You can't. You're not wanted."

So I was walking back across the field getting ready to get another truck going back the other way. Phil Cavaretta was the captain of the Cubs at the time and Andy Pafko was with him. They said, "Where you going?"

I said, "Mr. Hornsby told me I couldn't work out. I couldn't go up there and dress."

Cavaretta said, "Don't worry about that. Just dress in the weeds and come on."

I told him I was just 13 and he said, "Just keep playing ball." That was about '44.

There's always somebody to take up the slack and find out skin ain't nothing but a color.

Here's the way I feel. I just know guys like Oscar Charleston, Josh Gibson, Buck Leonard, Cool Papa Bell—them kind of cats—would've been *super, super* stars if they had played.

Jackie was no star. What people don't understand, Jackie Robinson was a utility man. Somebody was hurt; that's why he was playing when Brooklyn saw him.

I'm not saying Jackie wasn't good, but he had something different the white boys didn't have. He had "knack" speed—he didn't have real speed; he had *knack* speed. He knew *when* to run, and that just blew their minds. He knew how to jump up and down, act like he was going. He just messed up their minds 'cause they was playing straight baseball: ground ball to second base, over to short, short to first. He was stealing bases and stealing home, and guys didn't know what was going on. He just changed the game.

I have *never* thought of an athlete by the color of his skin 'cause I don't feel like that, *but* I'll tell you what. My father was a hell of an athlete, and he said that the greatest ballplayer he ever saw play the game was Oscar Charleston. For 20-some years, that man hit over .360, he had a hell of a throwing arm, played in the Mexican and Puerto Rican leagues in the winters and come back and played here. My father said he was six-feet and better and could *fly*.

If they start talking about ballplayers now, if they don't say Griffey, Jr., they made a mistake. He's the best ballplayer in baseball now. Twenty or 30 years ago, it was Willie Mays. If you want to go back and talk about ballplayers, you have to go back to the black ballplayers. They played against each other, but when they had a chance they would play against whites.

First of all—and let's give credit where credit is due—black athletes are gifted more with strength, with speed, and whatever else. And more desire. And they show it when they play.

A guy saw me playing ball in the alley one day. I was in the alley 'cause we didn't have no place to play. I was about eight years old. The guy walked by and said, "Hey, young man, you're pretty good."

I said, "I don't know. I just like to play."

He said, "How'd you like to play with my ballclub?"

I said, "I don't know. I'll have to ask my ma and dad."

So he said, "I'll ask 'em for you."

He bought me a glove and he bought me some shoes. [Laughs] He said, "That was the cheapest buy I ever got in a ballplayer."

All my friends I was growing up with on the block, they started talking and saying, "You think you're better than we are." There's always a drawback when you think something is good. There's always a drawback and you have to live with it.

We're in the greatest country on earth and if we let bullshit that don't mean nothing divide us by the color of our skin, we're pretty sick. People look at this country and they say, "How great are they? They're not all that great. They can't even keep law and order in their own country."

When I went off to war, I didn't know what I was doing, and I guess the average guy that goes in the service don't know what he's doing, but he thought it was the right thing to do. That's the way I look at life. I didn't have a bad living—I was the boss of the post office over 23 years, I worked for the park district—and I don't feel bad. Kids have a lot of respect for me 'cause they know I tell 'em the truth. I've been a lucky man. I'm still alive.

BATTING RECORD

Year	Team, league	Pos	G	AB	R	H	2B	3B	HR	RBI	SB	BA
1946	Chicago, NAL	1b					2					
1949	Cleveland, NAL	1b							13			
1950	Newark, NAL	1b										
1951	Chicago, NAL	1b										.390
1952	Chicago, NAL	1b										
1953–54	military service											
1955	San Antonio, TxL	ss										

Bob Scott
"Child Prodigy"

BORN JUNE 22, 1930, MACON, GA
HT. 5'11" WT. 178 BATTED AND THREW RIGHT

Negro Leagues debut: 1946

At the tender age of 10 in 1941, Bob Scott began his baseball career. At that age, he joined the Macon Braves, a local team coached by his father. It was not, however, a children's team; it was made up of adults. Nor was Scott a batboy; he was a playing member of the squad.

At only 13, he moved up to the Macon Cardinals, a semipro team and the cream of Macon, Georgia, baseball. From there, he took the big step to the New York Black Yankees, where he was both a pitcher and a first baseman. Later, he played with the Memphis Red Sox, leaving the Negro leagues in 1953, still only 23 years old.

Primarily a relief pitcher, he had a career record of 35–25, and as a batter, he hit a solid .278.

He has some marvelous memories of his days in baseball, but some are not so great. Once, they traveled more than 600 miles to play a doubleheader. The bus needed gas and they pulled into a station in Pine Bluff, Arkansas, but the attendant refused to sell them the gas they needed to continue their journey.

Among his fonder memories, though, are the times he played with Jackie Robinson's All-Stars and later with a very young Willie McCovey in the minor leagues. The good outweighed the bad, and it was a life he would relive with pleasure.

Talk about your pitching.

I was used mostly as a relief pitcher, and I played first base a lot. One year I went about 5–3, one was 10–2. And I had some starts.

I remember one of my starts. [Laughs] Buck Leonard took me out of the yard twice. He could really hit. They beat us about 8–5 that game. We was playing 'em in Raleigh, North Carolina.

I pitched a real good game against the Memphis Red Sox. They beat me, 1–0. That same day they took that picture after the game. We played a doubleheader; the first game was 1–0 and the second game was 4–3.

Casey Jones, he got a double, and Bob Boyd come up and hit a line drive to right field and that's how they got that run. They only got about three hits 'cause I had a live fastball that day. I think we come up with about four hits, but couldn't get no runs.

The pitcher was a lefthander. It was either Mathis or Charlie Davis. Charlie was a good pitcher. Nice guy.

You began playing when you were only 10 years old.

Oh, yeah. I was very young. I was playing against guys 25 and 30 years old. I was playing first base and I was learning how to pitch. I had a good live arm and my father, he didn't want me to lose it, so he wouldn't let me pitch too much back then.

I moved up to the Macon Cardinals around '43 or so. I stayed with them about two years. I volunteered to go in the service, but just before they swore me in my mother got me out of service. [Laughs]

You played with the Boston Blues in the United States League for a short time.

That was a few games. We were barnstorming. They needed a couple of players, so I played a few games with them. That was back during the time, I'm pretty sure, when I came to the Black Yankees. I went to Boston when I was up there for a couple of weeks and they needed a player, so I filled in for 'em.

How did the Black Yankees find you? You were still just a kid when you joined them.

I was about 16 years old. I'll tell you what happened. My hometown of Macon, Georgia, was a live baseball town. They had the Sally League there. My cousin — he's a minister now in Detroit, Michigan — he tried to play a little baseball, too. He was a catcher. As a matter of fact, he tried to catch me a lot and I was too fast for him. [Laughs]

He took me down to the game. The Black Yankees was playing the Baltimore Elite Giants at the Macon ballpark. I think they called it Luther Williams Field. He asked the manager — the manager's name was Hack Barker — to give me a tryout and see if I could make that team. So he did.

Those guys was pretty good scouts. They knew whether a guy was able to make the Negro league. They gave me a chance, looked me over. Then about me being so young, they wanted to know if I could leave home. Back then, you had to get permission; you couldn't just jump up and leave. So I got permission from my mother and that's the year I started with the Black Yankees: 1946. I stayed with 'em for four years.

I didn't really see too much action that year because at one time I was getting ready to leave and come back home. [Laughs] What they was doing, they was like taking me to school, letting me learn. But I got into quite a few games 'cause I had a live arm. And I think I was a kind of favorite of the manager. [Laughs]

Bob Scott (courtesy of Robert Scott).

He also wanted to take me to South America. I had a chance to go to South America in 1949. I was young and foolish and didn't go.

Also, I was signed by the Pittsburgh Pirates. George Sisler signed me when I stopped playing in 1950 with the Black Yankees. The Negro league was folding up. I went back home to Macon and I was playing sandlot ball. The Pittsburgh Pirates give a tryout camp and I went down to try out and they signed me up for Grand Forks, North Dakota. I was going to play there, but people would tell me it's cold up there and it don't get hot until July.

I said, "Can't you guys send me no place else?" [Laughs] They didn't have another place they wanted to send me and I blew that.

I think I did have a chance 'cause George told me that the scouts there were high on me when they were sitting around the table discussing the players. When they signed me, there was about 1100 ballplayers down there and they only signed five ballplayers out of that 1100.

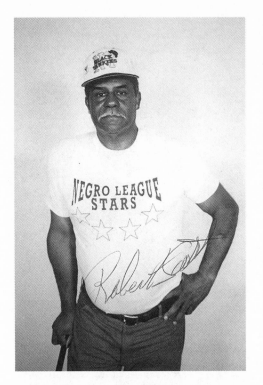

Bob Scott, 1997 (courtesy of Robert Scott).

George was a nice man. I had a chance to meet his wife. As a matter of fact, he came all the way down there to Macon to sign me.

You left the Black Yankees after 1950.

In 1950, the Black Yankees didn't play no more. That was the end. I went down to Memphis. Memphis played on 'til around 1955 or '56. Goose [Curry] was our manager; he was some kind of character.

Jackie Robinson picked an All-Star team in 1950. He picked guys from the Negro league to play against the Negro league. We barnstormed across America. I was one of the guys that he picked. I think Joe Black was the only one from the [Brooklyn] Dodgers wasn't there. I know Don Newcombe was there, Campanella, and Larry Doby from the Cleveland Indians, and I can't remember whether we had Dan Bankhead. I think we had him for a while.

The experience that I had with Jackie and Campanella and Doby and Newcombe and

Suitcase Simpson and all those guys, it was great. A great experience. They was impressed by me. I pitched quite a bit on the tour and I did real good. I also played first base, too, for Jackie's All-Stars.

Suitcase Simpson was a darned good ballplayer who never seemed to quite get it all together.

Suitcase was, like, happy-go-lucky, like a lot of ballplayers. They take the game serious, but they don't play it like they do. He was that type of ballplayer. He was a *good* ballplayer and he was a nice guy. And real loose, what we call in baseball "loosey-goosey." He could hit and he could run. And he was a good outfielder.

They called him "Suitcase" because they kept trading him. But he had that reputation for not being serious, and when you get a reputation like that, it's hard to get over it. A lot of ballplayers get a reputation like that, but they're good ballplayers.

When these guys make an error, it goes like, "Well, he didn't try. He didn't care about it," and that's what happens. They just play loose, some of these guys. Baseball is a pressure game and some guys don't show it.

My favorite ballplayer was Jackie. I thought he wasn't only a good ballplayer, he was a real gentleman. He was fit for the role that he was in. And he did a good job.

I'd put Aaron there with Mays. He was the type of player that played the game *for* the game, and Mays also played it because he loved it. Aaron was a great ballplayer, and he was just as good off the field as a gentleman as he was a ballplayer.

Now that we're talking about players like Aaron and Mays, who was the best ballplayer you saw?

During my time playing? Josh Gibson was sick; he was on the team, but he wasn't playing much.

That's a hard job for a ballplayer to say: Who was the best ballplayer he ever saw. I saw Willie Wells play. To me, he was a great ballplayer. Playing your position would make you be a good ballplayer, and know how to play it — where you should be on all plays, you know. We always said that Wells was the guy that was always there.

I saw Bob Boyd. As a matter of fact, I played on a team with Bob Boyd. I thought he was a good first baseman. I thought he was about the best in the Negro league. He was up in his 30s when he got signed by the major leagues.

I got a chance to see my man, Ernie [Banks]. He was great. He hit a home run off me. [Laughs] Every time I see him, I say, "Hey, wanna take another shot at me? I'll make you tap dance a little bit." [Laughs] Ernie was a good shortstop; he was one of the best I ever saw at that job until [Derek] Jeter come along.

Who were some of the best pitchers you saw?

When I was coming along as a young guy, I used to love Bob Feller, I guess because he pitched mostly in my style. I tried to style myself off him because I had a live arm. I thought Bob Feller was good. He's a nice guy, but most of the ballplayers are nice to ballplayers, but he's nice to all people.

We had a good pitcher there named Stanley, used to pitch for the Black Yankees. Neck Stanley. He was great. He helped me a little bit, too. He was one of the greatest pitchers I ever saw.

And then you had a guy down there with Memphis, a lefthander. Mathis. He should be in the Hall of Fame. He was a great pitcher.

And, you know, those guys didn't walk nobody. The guys today, they walk the bases loaded. They don't throw strikes. I don't understand why they're afraid to throw strikes. You just can't do that.

You know what we used to do. We used to be up at eight o'clock in the morning out to the ballpark. We had a four-string box with two posts on each side and make a box with string and we'd throw through 'em, through those strings. That's in order to make you learn how to throw strikes.

You couldn't get a pitcher up at eight o'clock in the morning to go out there to

throw strikes now. It's a terrible thing. If I was a manager, that's what they'd be doing. They'd be out there for two hours a day and they'd learn to throw strikes. That's what you call "pitching," when you pitch a ball where *you* want to pitch it. You just don't throw the ball where the batter can hit it.

Who was the toughest pitcher on you?

Mathis was a pretty good pitcher. Then there was a pitcher that played for the Clowns. He threw a screwball and he threw a change-up. He had a *good* changeup. I would be *always* out in front of that guy. Jim Cohen. He had my number.

What did you do when you left Memphis?

I went back home and in 1955 I played in the Georgia State League. There was a team called the Sandersville Giants in Sandersville, Georgia. They belonged to the New York Giants. Carl Hubbell, he was the main head of the Giants' farm system. They asked me to come over and play the rest of the season, so I played the '55 season with them down there. As a matter of fact, I played outfield for them. I didn't do no pitching.

We won the playoffs. We had Willie McCovey there; he could hit. We had a good team. I'm pretty sure I batted about .260 or .259. I hadn't been playing for a while.

The Negro leagues were almost forgotten until recently.

Parents — white parents — bring their kids to card shows for autographs and they ask questions about the Negro leagues. They want their kids to know about it.

But I don't see nobody in line with the black kids to let them know about the Negro leagues or to let them know they *had* a league. It's a terrible thing to not tell kids about their history because, if they know about their history, that begins to make them be better kids and make them feel that they can do something, too. But it's all up to the parents.

How did the fans treat you?

When we played baseball, we never got mad if people called us names. We took it as fun. It was fun to us. [Laughs] We'd kid one another. "Hey, did you hear what that guy called you?" [Laughs] "Why don't you go up there and hit a home run and let 'em know you know what you're doing." We had a lot of fun.

We didn't take things like that to the heart. We knew that things were going to get better, but it didn't make things better by being bitter. You didn't make things better by talking back to somebody or calling them names or wanting to fight. You didn't do that.

We were playing upstate New York — Cooperstown — and we had a few ballplayers that were called the "N" word. Right there in New York State. I never heard that name called when I was playing down South because most of the people in the South, they loved baseball and they wanted to see the game be played.

One of the things I remember playing in a ballgame, I think we was down around Tupelo, Mississippi. The policeman was always at the games and one of the guys hit a guy in the head, the batter. The guy fell down at home plate. Everybody run up there to assist him. The policeman come out there, says, "All right. You boys get him off the field and get another boy in there. Let's get this game going." [Laughs] He was okay, but the policeman wanted to see the game. He didn't say, "Let's take him to the hospital." He said, "Get this boy outta here. Let's play the game."

Were you able to get meals as you traveled?

In some towns, like Jacksonville, we had a nice restaurant there; it was run by blacks. And, also, we had pretty good eating in Memphis because Doc Martin owned the Memphis Red Sox and he had a restaurant at the ballpark, so we had good food there. And we had a good restaurant in Birmingham; we had good eating in Birmingham. I remember all the good places that we had to eat.

Most of the time, in other places, we called it a "Dutch meal." We'd get together and go into a store and buy different stuff and we ate on the bus. In small towns, we didn't have no place to eat. We ate a lot on the bus.

I can remember back in '55, when I was playing down in the Georgia State League, the white guys used to bring us sandwiches. When they'd go in the restaurant, me and McCovey, we used to sit on the bus for these guys to come back and bring us a sandwich.

There were only three of us. The other guy's first name was Ralph. It could be Ralph Johnson. He was a third baseman. He was a good little ballplayer.

Do you have any regrets from baseball?

I only regret one thing, that I didn't go to play in the major leagues. I had the opportunity. That's the only regret that I have.

And after I left baseball, I didn't return back to baseball. After 1955, I didn't return to baseball until 1995, or maybe it was '93, when the New York Yankees give me an award at Yankee Stadium. I just couldn't bear to watch the game from the stands. [Laughs] I figured I'd be running out there on the field.

Would you do it all again?

Would I do it again? Before the guy could ask me. I'd say, "Where you want me to be?" [Laughs] "When do we start?"

It was fun. I loved it.

A young lady came from CBS down here to interview me. I told her, "A ballplayer always say he don't care about the game, but once the spring air is here and the sun shines and he gets back to the baseball diamond, he just can't help but stop and look. He wants to go over there. It really grabs you. It's something that you just can't get out of you."

PITCHING RECORD

Year	Team, League	G	IP	W	L	Pct	H	BB	SO	ERA
1946	N.Y. Blk Yankees, NNL									
	Boston, USL									
1947	N.Y. Blk Yankees, NNL			5	3	.625				

Year	Team, League	G	IP	W	L	Pct	H	BB	SO	ERA
1948				10	2	.833				
1949										
1950	Memphis, NAL									
1951										
1952										

Bob Scott's career won-loss record in the Negro leagues was 35–25. In addition to pitching, he also played first base at times and compiled a .278 batting average in the Negro leagues.

MINOR LEAGUE BATTING RECORD

Year	Team, League	Pos	G	AB	R	H	2B	3B	HR	RBI	SB	BA
1955	Sandersville, GaStL	of										.259

Walter "Dirk" Gibbons
"ManDak Moundsman"

BORN OCTOBER 13, 1928, TAMPA, FL
HT. 5'7" WT. 185 BATTED LEFT, THREW RIGHT

Negro Leagues debut: 1947

Walter Gibbons was probably destined to play baseball. His older brother, John, played in the Negro leagues in the early '40s, and Walter came along to play in the late '40s. And in between, they played together on a semipro team in their hometown of Tampa. Walter, however, had his greatest successes neither in Florida nor the black leagues.

The old ManDak League was made up of teams in Manitoba and North Dakota, places with cold weather and short summers. That area has been described as having two months: winter and August.

Because of the weather and the short summers, baseball seasons up there are, of necessity, short, roughly four or four-and-a-half months, compared to the six-month or longer seasons normally played elsewhere. Walter Gibbons won 18 games up there one year in that short season. That's the equivalent of 25 or more wins in a regular-length season.

But he really didn't choose to go up there to play. The Indianapolis Clowns sold him to Brandon, Manitoba, and that's how he got there. It was generally accepted that if a Negro league player was sold, the player would receive a portion of the sale price. And some did. A whole lot, however, never saw a dime of the deal. Walter Gibbons was one of them.

But while with Manitoba, he was the dominant hurler in a league that also boasted Leon Day and Satchel Paige. Twelve of his 18 wins were consecutive, and he tossed back-to-back one-hitters at one point.

I started playing baseball here in Tampa on the sandlots when I was about eight years old. We didn't know anything about Little League; we'd just find a field and clean it off and start playing. During my time, also, we didn't play baseball in school, so it was a sandlot thing we just did on our own.

My brother started way ahead of me, back in '41; he went to the league in '41. He started playing ball much earlier than I did; I used to be batboy for the team that he played with here in Tampa.

We ended up playing together. See, we started with the Pepsi-Cola Giants and I was the batboy, and we formed a team called the

Pepsi-Cola Juniors for younger guys. It ended; the Pepsi-Cola Company wouldn't sponsor us anymore, so a newspaper guy here that owned the *Florida Sentinel*, called Andrews, sponsored us. It was a little local paper here and we named the team the Tampa Rockets.

That's how me and my brother got playing together, with the Tampa Rockets. We traveled all through New York. We had a league here called the Florida State [Negro] League and we traveled to different places. This was in the middle '40s.

All the Negro teams — the Indianapolis Clowns, the Cleveland Buckeyes, all the teams — used to come down South to barnstorm. We'd play against them and they'd ask some of the ballplayers if we was willing to go back with 'em. That's how we got with 'em, all the guys that played against the teams here in Tampa. The ones that they liked, they asked us to go back with 'em. Naturally, we had to get permission from our parents. I left to go with the Clowns to Chicago when I was about 16 years old.

They signed me up around the last of '46. My first full year was '48. I was with 'em about two-and-a half years: '47, '48, and '49.

A lot of people wouldn't remember this, but Goose Tatum was our first baseman. Sam Hairston was there. Later, Hank Aaron came in, but at that time I think they had shipped me out to Canada. Hank Aaron didn't stay with the Clowns too long.

The league was beginning to fold. After Jackie Robinson was picked up, the ballplayers started going different places. Money was being offered to Negro ballplayers to come to Canada, Mexico, and different places. I chose to go up to Canada and I played up there in the ManDak League. That was good ball. A lot of the guys from the league was there with me. I played out in Brandon, Manitoba, then from there I went to Winnipeg, then I finished my season in Minot, North Dakota.

Being a boy from Tampa, you must have frozen up there.

Well, yes and no. I made the best of it. I always prepared myself for cold weather. I didn't like it, but I enjoyed it. [Laughs]

Willie Wells was the manager up there in Winnipeg. Leon Day, we played together in Brandon. Satch played in that league, too, you know. He was down in Minot. There was a guy there that I didn't know anything about, but I know he was an ex–major leaguer. Roy Weatherly. He was there with us.

Do you know any of your stats with the Clowns?

You know, to be honest with you, that's something I didn't keep up with. I don't know why. I was just a young kid excited to be up there.

You take the Clowns. They played every day. We played league games on the weekend.

Walter "Dirk" Gibbons (courtesy of Walter Gibbons).

We used to play all the factory teams all around New York and different places. A lot of people didn't recognize the Clowns because of the name they had and the entertainment they had on the field, but they was about the drawingest team in that league. People was excited with that team. The Clowns played every city in the United States, and that was another thing I enjoyed.

I know some of my records in the Man-Dak League. They sent me all my clippings recently. A lady came down here from Winnipeg and she's writing a book about us, about the ManDak League.

We knew that all the [Negro league] players wasn't going to the majors — wasn't no doubt about that — and after the stars started leaving and they started going to better places — money-wise — the [ManDak] league turned out to be a *very* good league. I'm sorry that it didn't continue.

Are there any games that stand out?

I've pitched games where I've pitched one-hitters. To be honest, most of my best pitching was done in the ManDak League and I had three or four one-hitters and two hitters. I was an 18-game winner. I didn't realize that I did that myself until I looked at the clippings. I didn't believe it because I didn't keep up with those clippings myself.

In the Negro league, I didn't pitch as many league games as I would've liked. Being a young kid, I really didn't get the chance. My manager was Buster Haywood, and in the Negro league, if you're a real young player, they don't give you the opportunity to really prove yourself. Buster mostly used us young guys for these factory games, and the league games, he had all the old-timers pitching them.

I'll never forget. Me and Billy Felder was on the same team and we was the only two guys at that time from Tampa. He made us send our clothes home. At that time, we was traveling with foot lockers and he said, "You Tampa boys always want to be good dressers." [Laughs]

Now, on the Clowns, the ballplayers didn't clown. We just had people on the sideline. King Tut and Bebop and those. Goose Tatum — he was a *good* ballplayer. The Phillies wanted him, but he was in love with basketball.

You saw some great players in two countries. Who was the best?

To be honest with you — and it's something I've never done — I put myself in that category. I felt that I was better than anybody, and I really dominated that league when I first went up there — to Brandon and then to Winnipeg and Minot. I can say that. I didn't think nobody was better than me. I don't want to take nothing from nobody.

I have *all* these clippings and I take 'em when we go to signings and schools and different things. People are surprised. "Who is this Gibbons?" I say, "It's me." Our manager's wife — she still lives in Brandon, Manitoba — she sent this stuff to me.

How much were you paid along the way?

When I first started, I got $200 a month. When I went in the ManDak League, they gave me a thousand dollars. You see, they were just beginning to play, but when they started getting the ballplayers, they got their head on right and started paying the guys 350 and 400 and 500 dollars because they couldn't survive with that big money. See, they didn't know what they was getting into. Each city wanted to get the best ballplayers, but they couldn't afford that big money at the time. That thousand dollar salary didn't last long; they got us all together.

I still believe 'til this day that I was *sold* to them, but wasn't no money came my way.

Compare the conditions between the U.S. and Canada.

I've come to a conclusion. It was much different than being in the United States, but you still have that little fuel that brought that segregation there. They didn't have segregation [in Canada], now, but they still had that attitude about blacks. Everywhere you go, you're going to have that; it's always going to be a fuel.

But we got along so good. There wasn't no problem with living conditions or anything. We was accepted. In my town, it was a little different than being in Winnipeg 'cause Brandon was a smaller city and people hadn't really been too close to blacks. They'd see 'em come by on the trains — the porters or something like that.

I'll never forget a little incident. They got a place they call Clear Lake right outside of Brandon where everybody goes on the weekends to enjoy theirself. I had this kid walking behind me, walking around me. I asked him what he was walking around me for. He said he wanted to see did I have a tail. [Laughs] But I was brought up to overlook stuff like that. I never would fault the kid for that; he wasn't taught any better.

I had always read about Canada. Oh, it was God's country, you know, but I don't care where you go, that stigma is always there. There's always going to be somebody there that don't like you because they don't know nothing about you.

My main problem about being segregated

wasn't in the Negro league. I had to go to the Korean War and when they found out I was a baseball player, they sent me to Fort Riley, Kansas. I went overseas and didn't take no kind of training. They used to come out on the bivouac course and get me for baseball practice, and when I went to Korea, all I knew how to do was pull a trigger and shoot a rifle. I didn't know nothing about breaking a rifle down, which they teach you in basic training.

We were going to Fort Leavenworth to play the prison, which meant we had to change clothes and everything. We couldn't take nothing in; we had to change outside the prison. They furnished us our bats and balls; all we could take inside was a glove, and that was examined.

But on our way there, we stopped on the road — now this was the Army — at a cafe to get us a sandwich. I got up and some guy from New York said, "Walter, I hate to say this to you, but they're not gonna allow you in there. If you want me to stay out here with you or bring you something back, I will."

I said, "Oh, no. You guys go on and eat."

Like I say, I was taught the do's and don't's, but I figured if I was in the service I'm going to fight for my country. I'm training to go overseas and I'm with a baseball team right outside the base and I can't get a sandwich? That was real bad.

I could understand that and live with it. I put it in my head, if you don't want my money, I don't want to deal with you. I'm not going to hassle or stand up and argue.

When I was in the Negro league, I enjoyed it. We all knew the do's and the don't's, but we wanted to prove to ourself that we was good ballplayers, and we did that. We didn't have no such thing that they got now, a guy coming in as a relief pitcher and pitching one inning. If you're good, you go nine innings. I don't think the pitchers today are as tough as the guys when I was coming up. You know, pitching is a mind game anyway. You're setting up there figuring what you can do to get the batter and he's figuring what he can do to get you.

I know, in the Negro league, we figured

Walter Gibbons, 1999 (courtesy of Walter Gibbons).

we can challenge anybody. We didn't believe in throwing at you. We'll ease you back a little bit if you're giving me a hard time, but we believed we could strike out *any*body.

They're not playing baseball like they should today. They're not playing for the fans. We used to play for the fans and because we loved the game. The guys today, it's big business. I don't condemn the money they're making, but it's not the same game anymore.

What pitches did you throw?

Oh, I had a *good* fastball and I had a *good* curveball. We used to call it dropball. I used to have a pitch that I'd throw sidearm and it went in and out. They call 'em sliders now. I threw my curveball about as fast as I did my fastball. I wish we'd had a timer during that time.

I'm one of those guys didn't brag about what he did. I just went out there and pitched the game. My son said, "Daddy, just talk about yourself." He's the reason why I'm talking today.

Any regrets from your baseball days?

Oh, no. No, no. To be honest with you, I'd do it again. I'd go through the same things that I went through before. I don't know if I'd go through that Army thing again, but being in the Negro league and the excitement, yes.

Being in the Negro league taught me how to eat sardines and pork and beans. [Laughs]

We used to dress on the bus and we traveled so much and we wasn't allowed in cafes, so that's what we used to eat. Goose Tatum taught me how to eat. He said, "You won't be able to eat in these cafes, so you get you a can of sardines and pork and beans and mix 'em together and a loaf of bread and lunch meat." I loved it! [Laughs]

PITCHING RECORD

Year	Team, League	G	IP	W	L	Pct	H	BB	SO	ERA
1947	Indianapolis, NAL									
1948										
1949										
1950	Brandon, MnDkL			18	2	.900				
1951	Winnipeg, MnDkL									
1952	Minot, MnDkL									

John "Hoss" Ritchey
"The Call Never Came"

BORN JANUARY 5, 1923, SAN DIEGO, CA
HT. 5'9" WT. 180 BATTED LEFT, THREW RIGHT

Negro Leagues debut: 1947

The interview that follows is very short. John Ritchey had a stroke several years ago and his speech was affected, making answering questions difficult for him, but with the aid of his wife we got a few questions answered.

Ritchey was a catcher, but mainly he was a hitter. He spent only one year, 1947, playing Negro league ball, but he led the league with a .382 average. (Not bad for a rookie.) Some claim that his average was inflated due to the loss of the top pitchers to organized ball, but that is an invalid argument for two reasons: (1) in 1947, Jackie Robinson's rookie year with Brooklyn, relatively few blacks had been signed, and (2) if his average was inflated, why weren't everyone else's?

The next year, 1948, he signed with his hometown team, the San Diego Padres, and became the first black to play in the Pacific Coast League, which, in those days, was almost of major league quality. As a rookie there, he batted .323. All together, in a nine-year minor league career spent mainly in the tough PCL, he compiled a lifetime batting average of an even .300.

In '48 at San Diego, he played for Hall of Fame manager Bucky Harris. Harris said that Ritchey was better than anything the Yankees had and that he would soon be called up. But he wasn't. (One of the Yankees' catchers that year was a kid named Larry Berra, later to be called "Yogi".)

The reason given for not promoting Ritchey was that his arm wasn't of major league quality. His contemporaries, however, will tell you that his arm was fine, and the pitchers he caught all found him to be a fine defensive receiver who called a good game.

The Yankees, it must be remembered, were among the slowest to integrate and did it then only to appease the fans they were losing to their National League rivals, the Dodgers and the Giants, both of which integrated early and successfully. Had Ritchey been white, he would have been in New York in 1949 or '50. Today, black or white, he would be in New York.

An easygoing, soft-spoken individual, he accepted with class his burden of integrating the Padres and the unfairness of being overlooked by the majors. As in the cases of so many, he was the victim of his time.

How did you come to join the Chicago American Giants?

A friend of mine played with them and he got me a look-see.

You were an excellent hitter and a good catcher.

Why do you think you never got a chance in the major leagues?

[Laughs] I don't know.

When did your interest in baseball begin?

Oh, at about nine or ten.

239

John Ritchey with Sacramento (PCL), 1954 (courtesy of John Ritchey).

You were 24 when you joined the American Giants. Where were you before that?

I was in school. San Diego State.

Is there one game that stands out?

There was no game that really stood out.

Who was the best hitter you saw?

Jack Graham in the Pacific Coast League. [Graham was a slugging first baseman/outfielder who, in 1948 as Ritchey's teammate, led the PCL with 48 home runs and was named league MVP. In '49 with the St. Louis Browns, he walloped 34 home runs, but his batting average was too low to keep him in the major leagues, even with the Browns. In 1950, he was back in San Diego, where he hit 33 more home runs.]

Who was the best pitcher?

Gentry Jessup. He befriended me when I came to the American Giants. I caught several of his games and he congratulated me on the way I caught. He was a very particular type of pitcher. He was sure of himself. After I played winter baseball with him, we heard from him one or two times, but that's been years.

How much were you paid with Chicago?

Four hundred dollars a month. That was good pay for then.

In the Coast League?

Somewhere in the 800 range.

What did you do when you left baseball?

Through the Urban League, I got a union job with Carnation Dairy as a salesman. It worked out well. Since I was in the union, I got a recommendation to go to Continental Baking Company, which is Wonder Bread and Hostess. The money in those types of jobs was very good. I stayed with it until I retired.

Any regrets from your baseball career, other than not making it to the majors?

There was so much pressure in being the first black [in the PCL]. I was easygoing, but it bothered me. But I have no regrets.

What did you think of Emmett Ashford, the first black umpire in organized ball? He was in the Coast League when you were there.

He gave the people a laugh, but I have no other opinion of him.

Would you play baseball again if you went back?

That's a hard question. Guys like Tony Gwynn didn't have the things to go through because the path had already been cleared for them. But I would go and do it again.

BATTING RECORD

Year	Team, League	Pos	G	AB	R	H	2B	3B	HR	RBI	SB	BA
1947	Chicago, NAL	c	58	176	42	67						*.381
1948	San Diego, PCL	c	103	217	35	70	10	2	4	44	2	.323

Year	Team, League	Pos	G	AB	R	H	2B	3B	HR	RBI	SB	BA
1949	San Diego, PCL	c	112	327	29	84	10	1	3	35	12	.257
1950	Portland, PCL	c	107	241	32	65	8	4	2	46	1	.270
1951	Portland, PCL	c	1	3	0	0	0	0	0	0	0	.000
	Vancouver, WIntL	c	137	451	91	156	26	5	7	86	20	.346
1952	Vancouver, WIntL	c	137	443	96	152	24	8	2	76	27	.343
1953	Sacramento, PCL	c	147	454	62	132	28	8	5	55	10	.291
1954		c	94	283	24	77	6	2	0	23	5	.272
1955	San Francisco, PCL	c	139	375	52	107	15	1	6	41	10	.285
1956	Syracuse, IntL	c	19	54	6	10	2	0	0	7	0	.185
1948–49	Magallanes, VenL	c			30		14						

* Led league

Raydell Maddix
"Lefty Bo"

BORN OCTOBER 7, 1928, TAMPA, FL
HT. 5'9" WT. 150 BATTED RIGHT AND THREW LEFT

Negro Leagues debut: 1948

Tampa, Florida, was apparently a veritable goldmine of baseball talent back in the 1940s and early '50s. Coming out of there were the Gibbons brothers, Benny Felder, Quack Brown, and Lefty Bo Maddix, among others. They all went on to success in the Negro leagues.

Possibly the most successful of them as a Negro leaguer was Lefty Bo Maddix, a true power pitcher who occasionally wasn't sure where the ball was going when he turned it loose. He led the Negro American League in strikeouts for two consecutive years, something done only rarely.

His playing was interrupted by the Korean War, and he didn't play long professionally after he returned, but he played on at the semipro level until he was nearly 40. Along the way, a lot of batters returned to their dugouts shaking their heads.

After his playing days, a veteran newspaper columnist in Tampa was asked, "Do you think Beau Maddox [sic], the former Pepsi-Cola Giant lefthander, could have made the majors?" He answered in his column: "Beau would have made it for sure. He had a great fastball and knew how to keep it low and away. His curve was not too good but he could have been taught how to throw it."

I was just a little skinny, raw-boned kid. I was just about 16, 15 really, when I started playing. Still growing.

I played 'til 1967. That was in the Michigan City, Indiana, league, and I played first base and led the league in hitting at .412. That was the first time I ever switch hit because I bat cross-handed and when I was playing in the Negro league, they wouldn't let me, talking about how I might break my wrists. Left-handed I batted cross-handed, righthanded I didn't.

I never would have won the championship if I don't bat that way because this boy, Ron Reed, he was in there. He was going to Notre Dame then and, boy, he was firing that ball in! You better cross over back then because

he had a hell of a deuce. He was *really* bringing it.

He was a crybaby. I think the first time we played him I had a cold or the flu or something and he struck out about six or seven in a row. Everybody was telling him, "If Lefty Bo was in the lineup, you wouldn't've had that success." He talked a lot of trash. He was cocky.

But I hit him up. Stole second, third, home on him. You could run — oh, man! You could walk on him down to second base, at least when he was in college. He learned later on to cut down on his stride.

I started playing on a local team here called Tampa Rockets. The first time I ever played in the Yankee Stadium — it was in

1947 — I played against Asheville, North Carolina, Blues. I was pitching against an old man, a submarine pitcher, and I lost, 2–1, on an error. I was real young and it kind of broke my heart.

From that point, I went down to Panama [City] and I played with Panama Blues for that whole year. We had a good team down there and I was 24–2 and I pitched back-to-back no-hitters in Luther Williams Stadium in Macon, Georgia. One was against the best lefthander I ever seen named Lefty Bronson, the other was against Tuskegee Bombers.

I lost track of Bronson. That was the only time I ever met him and I didn't want to ever meet him again 'cause he was twice the pitcher I was. He was much older, but, boy, he had everything in the world you need to be great. I pitched a no-hitter against him and that's the only way I could've beat him 'cause the score was 1–0. He was really something.

Quite a few Negro ballplayers went through there and heard about him 'cause he never did leave. They say some woman took care of him, had a bar, and he wouldn't go nowhere, just drive 'round in a new car. You know, one of them kind of deals. They tried to get him to go with us.

From Panama City, I came back to Tampa and then Indianapolis came down here to play us. I beat them and they asked me did I want to go with them up North to play in the Negro league for 250 a month, so I signed a contract and went on up there and started playing with the Indianapolis Clowns.

I know I led the Negro league in '48 and '49. I went to Korea in '50 and I led the league in strikeouts in '48 and '49. That's when Ernie Banks was getting ready to go with the Cubs, and Willie Mays. Hank Aaron came to the Indianapolis Clowns when I was in Korea 'cause when I came back my buddies told me, said, "Man, you missed Hank Aaron."

I wasn't even aware that I had led the league in strikeouts 'til I read the clippings from Kansas City they sent me. It said a young southpaw was returning from Korea and that I had led the league in strikeouts.

Tampa's Negro Leaguers (l-r): Benny Felder, Walter "Dirk" Gibbons, Bob Mitchell, Sr., Raydell "Lefty Bo" Maddix, Leonard Wiggs, John Gibbons, Clifford "Quack" Brown (courtesy of Raydell Maddix).

I was in service for two years, from '50 to '52. I didn't do but 21 months because I volunteered for front line duty if they'd knock three months off. I was crazy and dumb 'cause the first night I went up on the front line, all that incoming fire — oh, man, I liked to have a heart attack. [Laughs] I was trying to get back to play baseball, you know. I loved the game just that much, but if I had known what I was doing, I wouldn't've volunteered for no front line. [Laughs] I was just 22.

I came back in '52 and I played one more year. I played '53 and that was the last year I played with Indianapolis Clowns. I left there and stopped playing for a few years and then I went to Indiana and started playing there until '67. I won that batting championship in '67 and that was my last year of baseball.

Juan Marichal played in that league at one time. Sad Sam Jones played in that league. I had some hell of duels with Sad Sam Jones in Orlando, Florida, and beat him, 1–0 and 2–1. They called him "Hard Luck." He was supposed to be a hard-luck pitcher all his life. He used to carry a toothpick in his mouth the whole damn time.

I barnstormed against Jackie Robinson. He had an All-Star team. And Satchel Paige's team. I remember in Montreal, I pitched the second game of a doubleheader. Satchel would pitch only 'bout three or four innings and he was telling me, "Little Lefty, you throw hard as lightning bump a stump." That's the first time I had ever heard that. But he knew how to hit me and I just bust out laughing 'cause Satchel couldn't hit. [Laughs]

You know the guy I want to mention to you? Goose Tatum. He was playing first base during this time when I was there. That was the best gloveman I ever seen in my life. You know, the two years I played with him, I never seen him make an error. But they'd practice like that; they'd throw the ball over there in the dirt, one hop, two hops, skip, skid. That's the way he practiced every game. He don't want you to throw the ball in the air.

I got a picture here with Verdes Drake, the boy that used to play with me from Cuba, and Goose Tatum is on this picture, and Sam

Hairston, my catcher. He signed with the White Sox.

In the Negro league, if you couldn't go nine innings you'd get a ticket and go back home. Wasn't no relief pitchers. What the hell is a pitching coach? You had to learn the hard way on them old bad-ass diamonds. You'd have to pick rocks all night.

We had a pitcher named Peanuts Nyasses Davis, a knuckleball pitcher, and you couldn't even play catch with him unless you had a mask on. The ball'd hit you in the mouth. He could throw it with *control* and throw it hard!

Leon Day, he was a good hitter. He was a pitcher with Baltimore Elite Giants with Campanella, and Junior Gilliam was there. Peanuts struck him out three times. The last time, on the third strike, he caught the ball in his hand and throwed it in the dugout he was so damn mad. [Laughs] I never will forget that. In Baltimore.

A black pitcher had little chance to progress in organized ball back in your day.

You know what hell Satchel had getting to Cleveland. Wasn't no pitcher out there as great as him, and if he couldn't get 'em you know 'bout what the rest of the black pitchers faced. It speaks for itself.

I know some pitchers who would set the major leagues on fire just like Satchel in his day. Chet Brewer was one. They were not only major leaguers, they were *superstars.*

Jackie fought that for a long time. We all know what the real deal is. Some people don't believe that these guys was good enough to play because of that myth, and then some people really want to know the truth.

Buck Leonard. Man, I never saw a guy could hit like this guy and it's *so sad* that the people didn't get a chance to see him hit.

And when you saw him, he was in his 40s.

He should've been barred out of the league then. Rookies like me shouldn't have to pitch against old men like that. [Laughs] Man, he could hit curveballs going away from him — going down a mile a minute, pull 'em 400 feet!

Was Satchel the best pitcher?

Satchel was the best that I ever came in contact with, and I watched 'em all. I know all about Koufax and Bob Feller and them. You had to see this man to really appreciate him and know for yourself and compare his pitching to others. He could do things that the average man couldn't even think about doing. You know what I mean?

He'd load the bases and then pitch three straight balls to your cleanup hitter and come back and throw three of the damnedest strikes you ever seen. [Laughs] Oh, man, that man had some ability!

The second best was this guy I told you: Chet Brewer. In my estimation, I would pick him. Brother, he had control just like Satch and he had a curveball just like Satch. He could make you duck your head and break it in the strike zone. You got to get good rotation on that ball to do that.

You heard about Joe Williams. There was a lotta guys even before my time that Satchel Paige was telling me about that was great ballplayers, too, you know. Those three just dominated; they could do damn near whatever they wanted to do. And they didn't give a damn who was hitting. That's what I like about those guys. There's certain guys that couldn't get certain guys out, but these guys could get anybody out and brag about it and prove it.

We had a old long-haired boy named [Honey] Lott. Every time we played in New Orleans, he hit two home runs, so we were playing Satchel Paige All-Stars and he say, "Where's this guy Lott, this long-haired boy you're telling me hit two home runs every time he come here? You tell him that I will throw him three fastballs down the heart of the plate. If he tip one, he can have a home run."

He ain't tipped one yet. [Laughs] This boy was a notorious fastball hitter and he couldn't even *tip* the damn ball Satch was throwing so hard by him. He had to be 'round that 100 [mph] mark, and by him having such pinpoint control and could change speeds, it looked like he's throwing *twice* that hard when he cut loose.

Who were some of the best players you saw?

The best defensive guy with the glove at first base — digging stuff out of the ground — was Goose Tatum, but he wasn't that good a hitter.

Buck Leonard was the best hitter I've seen from the left side. I would have to give to Hank Aaron even over Willie Mays 'cause I could get Willie Mays out throwing fastballs away from him. He hit one homer off me in my career.

The same way with Ernie Banks. You couldn't throw him nothing low; he was a notorious low-ball hitter and I used to fire the ball in on his wrists. He had that loop swing and he hit a home run off me in an exhibition game one time, but other than that, he wasn't no trouble. The guys that gave me trouble was Willard Brown and they had a guy named Bonnie Serrell.

Bob Thurman I think faced me 50 times and struck out 45. He say he couldn't pick my ball up to save his soul. He got about ten watches for hitting balls out of the park over a certain sign. [Andy] Porter — our ace right-hander — he [Thurman] could hit him. He could even hit Peanuts Nyasses Davis, but he couldn't hit me. I guess I was one of the kind of lefthanders who could pitch and wherever the ball was going, I didn't know then, either. When he [Thurman] went to Cincinnati, they used him as a pinch hitter against righthanders.

Did anybody have your number?

That little S.O.B. played third base for Kansas City. I called him "Baldy." He was something like Nellie Fox. He may have hit a double once, I don't know, but little ol' stuff over third, little stuff over the infield. Boy, he used to break your heart. Even Verdes Drake couldn't get that little stuff he hit. Ol' Baldy weared me out. Herb Souell, that's who he was.

Earl Taborn was catching for Kansas City then and Elston Howard was there. Elston Howard hit the longest foul ball that ever been hit off me in my life, but I come back and throwed a third strike by him. Elston Howard used to catch for the Yankees, but I never seen him catch when he was with Kansas City. He must've been third-string catcher because Earl Taborn was the first catcher and then a boy name Johnson, I think, was the second. He played outfield. I never seen him catch in my life and I look up one day and he's catching.

Souell used to just kill me, but I got him once. I throwed that sucker a sidearm pitch one day with the bases loaded and he swung and missed it. That was the happiest day of my life. I struck him out *one* time! He was a tough little out; he would choke up and half swing. He was one of those little banjo hitters.

He was good with the glove, too. He used to pray to these boys who pitched: [Frank] Barnes and [Gene] Collins and [Gene] Richardson and [Jim] LaMarque and Connie Johnson. I couldn't hit Connie Johnson, but the other ones, he'd pray to 'em don't pitch nothing in on me 'cause I'd *kill* him down there with those shots. [Laughs] I used to pinch hit a lot and I used to play outfield some and pinch run.

You were a power pitcher. Seeing the pitchers today, how hard do you think you threw?

I don't have any idea 'cause they didn't have no guns back then, but compared to what I see now I got an idea of what I was throwing. To throw that ball by Willie Mays and Ernie Banks and them — I'm talking 'bout just a *fast* dead-red ball — you got to be up in the 98s, 97s, or something like that. Them guys light a damn fastball up, but I used to throw three by 'em, zip-zip-zip.

Like I told you, I led the league in '48 and '49, and Junior Gilliam and Elston Howard, Willie Mays, Ernie Banks — all them boys was in the league. Joe Black, I out-dueled him for the championship in '49.

Do any games stand out?

That one in New York. The first time I ever played at Yankee Stadium and I lost, 2–1. I think I had 14 strikeouts, but, hell, that submarine pitcher was pitching against me, he had 16. [Laughs] That's the first time I'd ever seen him; he was 40 years old. We got maybe three or four hits. I know I got a hit, a guy

named Gerrard ["Gerrard" appeared in several box scores; his correct name was Alphonso Gerald] — played outfield, a Cuban boy from Havana — he got a couple of hits. In fact, he was the only one I know that could really do anything with him 'cause he hit some line drives that would've been homers but they went foul. The rest of us — righthanded guys — oh, God! [Laughs] We was real young, you know,

The two no-hitters back-to-back in Luther Williams Stadium stand out. I'll tell you a game that stands out in Denver, Colorado, against the Kansas City Monarchs. I had a 4–0 lead in the ninth inning and Ernie Banks hit a ball that the third baseman should've got but he didn't and they got one run.

Then the next three guys was LaMarque, a pinch hitter, pitcher for Kansas City; I throwed him three drop balls. And then a Cuban boy come up to pinch hit and I throwed *him* three drop balls. Then Buck O'Neil came up to pinch hit and Buster Haywood, the manager of the Clowns, come and told me, "Don't throw Buck O'Neil nothing slow. Just throw fire and if he hit it, he just hit it." I throwed him three strikes. That was in the ninth inning and I was getting a little weary. I read in the paper about that game later; they said I pitched a superb game.

We had a game in Birmingham against the Birmingham Black Barons. There was two girls in the stands and one of 'em give me a note to give to Willie Mays. She wanted a date with him and the note said to meet her at Ma Perkins' Restaurant, where we used to hang out. I give the note to him and he asked me which girl it was and I pointed to the one next to her, who wasn't as pretty. Well, we went there after the game and I went with the pretty girl and he got the other one. [Laughs] She was mad 'cause he didn't date her.

How did you find the conditions?

The conditions was terrible because we had to Dutch; that's how we eat. We called it Dutch and we had to go to the grocery store and get sardines and baloney and crackers and stuff like that. And if we do find a place where we could get a hamburger, we had to go to a little back window and they'd hand it out to you.

It was really embarrassing, but even in the Army I ran across that. They wouldn't serve us on my way to Korea. We had vouchers and we stopped at a place to get a steak. They said, "We can't serve the black guys. We'll fix a place back there in the back." I said, "I'm not going back and eat a damn thing. Just give me my voucher and let me go over there and eat some real soul food anyway." So we went over there to eat. Segregation was the thing.

We even had to change clothes on the bus sometimes. [Laughs] It was rough.

I'll tell you something else; I'm glad you made me remember. I beat [Jimmy] Newberry with Birmingham Black Barons, Mays's team, in Cleveland. I beat him the second game of a doubleheader and that night we went to play a white team and I had to come in in the second or third inning and finish that game. I pitched 15 or 16 innings. I remember Syd Pollack, the owner of the Clowns, say he was gonna give me a bonus. He ain't give me nothing. [Laughs]

In Panama [City], I pitched a shutout, then that Tuesday night I relieved my buddy, Deke, in the fifth inning. The next night, I relieved Snake in 'bout the sixth inning. Then we go all the way to Miami and this boy goes all the way up to the seventh or eighth and I had to relieve him. I relieved *five* times in one week and had to pitch my own ballgame. I could do that and never had a sore arm or was weak. Every time I go out there, it was just fire-fire-fire. It didn't bother me one bit, and we did it for years.

Looking back on how often we pitched, on a 30-day tour with Satchel, he pitched *every* night. People talk about rubber-arm pitchers, this guy Peanuts Nyasses Davis I was telling you about, he could come in and relieve you with the bases loaded with three balls and no strikes and throw knuckleballs and get the guy out. I never know a guy could have control like that and throw it that hard. Lord, he had a good one. If he could have played in the majors — man!

He showed me clippings where him and Satchel Paige would hook up 14 innings, 18 innings — and nothing–nothing.

This relief specialists that have to pitch one inning, that's all, I say, "Good God Almighty. You make that much money and pitch one inning?" Can you imagine Satchel pitching just one inning? [Laughs]

What did you do when you left baseball?

I got married in '57 — July the second, 1957. Still married to the same lady. I worked at Continental Can in New York. I moved to New York from Indianapolis. I worked there until '73, then I came back here to Tampa and I worked at the University of Tampa 18 years. That's where I retired from. When I was 62 I called it quits.

Looking back on your baseball days, do you have any regrets?

Yeah, I have regrets. I feel that what we did wasn't really appreciated; it wasn't even discussed, really. We had to hang in there to keep baseball alive. It was ridiculous that we wasn't compensated. You never made any money, you never complained, and we gave the people some great baseball. Old-timers will tell you in a minute 'bout some games they've seen that we played and they wish that they could see some of those games now. [Laughs]

Would you go back and do it again?

I'll tell you what. I love baseball, but knowing what I know now, I don't think I would. I couldn't accept that treatment. I always did have a lot of pride, but sometime I would just swallow it and go on because you had to survive. You *knowed* you was a hell of a man and you *knowed* you deserved better and you *knowed* you shouldn't been treated this way and you're still just going on to keep the peace.

Jackie Robinson wasn't near the best ballplayer, but I knowed guys who carried a razor in their back pocket and you couldn't call them no nigger and get away with it. They had to pick somebody who wouldn't lose his temper. I can understand that.

Willard Brown wouldn't accept it. Cool Papa Bell wouldn't. They were great ballplayers, but they wouldn't accept that. That's something like this boy Belle now. Albert Belle. It's not really as bad as the media build it up.

Same way with Sad Sam Jones. I remember one time, Sad Sam Jones was wild as hell and he didn't have a curveball. The umpire would call close calls and he'd kind of over-react. He was so quiet; he could drink a pint of hundred-proof [Old] Granddad and pitch a shutout the next day.

When we were playing Tuskegee when I pitched that no-hitter in Macon, Georgia, I had struck this guy out three times and I had two strikes on him. I throwed a ball and it got away from me and sailed under his chin. He made two or three steps out to the mound and swung that bat and I ducked and that bat went over my head. When I come back up, he was laying flat out on the ground. My catcher had run behind him and hit him in the back of the head with that iron mask. [Laughs] My catcher took care of me.

We played hard and we just loved the game. We would've played under any conditions, anything just to play baseball.

PITCHING RECORD

Year	Team, League	G	IP	W	L	Pct	H	BB	SO	ERA
1948	Indianapolis, NAL								*	
1949									*	
1950–52	military service									
1953	Indianapolis, NAL									

* Led league

Hank Presswood
"A Late Start"

BORN OCTOBER 7, 1921, ELECTRIC MILLS, MS
HT. 5'11" WT. 150 BATTED AND THREW RIGHT

Negro Leagues debut: 1948

Hank Presswood enjoyed a five-year career in professional baseball with the Cleveland Buckeyes and Kansas City Monarchs. The key word there is "enjoyed." He loved every minute of it.

And it was a career that almost never happened. Content with working and playing sandlot ball, Presswood did not pursue professional baseball. His friend Willie Grace, who played for the Buckeyes, came and got him when the team was barnstorming through the South in 1948, and even then he wasn't sure he wanted to go.

But he did go, and he's very glad he did. Very few men speak as enthusiastically of their playing days as he does.

Your first year with the Buckeyes was 1948. Where had you played before?

I had been in the city league in Birmingham and different places like that. We used to call it sandlot baseball, you know. A fellow named Willie Grace, he had played sandlot baseball and he went to the Buckeyes, and when he got there he told the owner about me. That's how I got in. He came and got me; I was workin' in this place called Canton, Mississippi, then.

How old were you when you joined the Buckeyes?

Oh, let me think. [Laughs] It's been so long. I was in my 30s, I think. That's the reason why, after so long, I wouldn't keep on. They tried to get me to keep on, but after I went to Kansas City I found out some balls were passin' me at shortstop that hadn't been passin' me. You know when you done slowed down. [Laughs]

But anyway, I was in my 30s. I don't remember exactly. What happened, Willie

Grace came to Canton, Mississippi, and he came after me. They was in Memphis to play the Memphis Red Sox and so he came down there to get me to go and my bossman at the plant there said, "Go ahead on. Anytime you come back, Hank, you got a job." I told him I didn't wanna go right then, but I went on anyway and I'm glad I did.

I went to Memphis and played the Memphis Red Sox, and we played 'em throughout the South and then we went back to Dayton, Ohio, to play against the Kansas City Monarchs.

I played with Cleveland from 1948 to 1950 and Cleveland went outta the league in 1950, then I went to the Kansas City Monarchs from '50 to '52.

Were you always a shortstop?

I was a shortstop and sometimes I had to play third base when I went to the Monarchs. In fact, I was an infielder. You can put it like that.

Hank Presswood, 1999 (Lisa Feder photograph).

Willie Grace says you were a very good shortstop.

[Laughs] Thanks, Grace. I never did pat myself on the back about it, you know. I had a job to do and I wanted to do it well. I did the best I could.

Do you know any of your seasonal batting records?

One time at Cleveland, I was battin' .287, I think it was. .287 or .274, somewhere up in there. And the time I was with Kansas City I wasn't playin' as much and so I had a .194 there.

You traveled all over the country. How were the conditions?

We had a nice bus, sorta on the Greyhound style. It was very comfortable and everything. We enjoyed it; there wasn't no problem there at all. We didn't have no problems whatsoever. I can't tell you we had problems in different places. No, we did not. If we did, you couldn't tell it. We wasn't lookin' for no problems and we didn't have 'em.

We'd go in and wherever we had a game we always had a reservation. Everything was all set up whenever we got to these different cities. You know, we played different towns; for instance, Birmingham Black Barons — we'd play in Birmingham, Memphis Red Sox, Kansas City for the Monarchs. And we played a lotta other teams outta the league — exhibition games.

We played the New York Black Cubans. When we didn't have no league games, we played exhibition games. I don't know the purpose of it 'cause I didn't ask no questions. We was always on the move and we had nice places to stay. I really enjoyed it.

That Father Time caught up with me. When the ball started passin' me at shortstop, I knew the time had come. [Laughs] It was really wonderful, you know; I just wish that I could've stayed just a little bit longer. They tried to get me to stay. Buck O'Neil — John "Buck" O'Neil — he'll tell you about me. That was the skipper for the Kansas City Monarchs. He called me "Baby."

How much were you paid?

I had $300 a month, plus expenses. At that time, $300 was a *whole* lotta money. [Laughs]

See, things was very cheap. For instance, you could take a little money and eat. As far as eatin' was concerned, it wasn't no problem because you could take five cents and buy you five slices of baloney — one cent each slice — and the same way with wieners or whatever. And get you a big bread and a pop and you're ready. Then you could get some beans or somethin' else like that. [Laughs]

I would get six dollars a day for eatin' money, and I never was a drinker or smoker so that was big money to me. I had a money belt with my money in it.

One thing about it — I can say this — I *loved* the game. I still love baseball. Not only me, we all really loved it.

We might play ball here — play the Chicago American Giants today — and we ride all the way to New York to play the New York Black Yankees tomorrow afternoon. Sometimes they'd send a squad in on the plane and the rest of us'd come in the bus.

We had two shortstops. Othello Renfroe — we called him "Chappy"; if Chappy flew, then I'd ride the bus. If I flew, Chappy would ride the bus. Then sometime both of us would go at the same time.

It was really exciting, I'm telling you the truth. I loved it, so when I started workin' at the steel mill I played softball. Fast pitch. I got trophies on toppa trophies and jackets on toppa jackets where we won championships. They said they couldn't fool me with that ball and they couldn't. [Laughs] We won championships and everything there at the plant. I worked at Inland Steel in East Chicago, Indiana.

Who was the best pitcher you faced?
Satchel Paige. [Laughs] Satch was tough on *every*body.

I'll tell you a story. We went to Kansas City to play the Monarchs and when we got there we was in the hotel with the Monarchs. They left and went out and took the field before we did.

About an hour later I guess it was, we got in the bus and went on out to the ballpark. We got there and you could hear some "Poom! Poom!" Alonzo Boone was the manager of the Buckeyes and I said, "Hey, Skip. Man, why in the world is they shootin' fireworks? It's not July the Fourth."

He said, "Man, they ain't shootin' no fireworks. That's ol' Satch warmin' up in there." [Laughs]

Our hitters wasn't sayin' nothin'. Sam Jethroe — Jet — was our lead-off man, went with the Boston Braves. So, anyhow, we got our equipment and went on in. "Poom! Poom!" The poundin' like that kept up.

We walked through a little hall and went upstairs in the dressin' room. There's Jethroe, big Tom Harris, Big Joe Greene, Joe Caffie — all the heavy hitters; they wasn't sayin' a word. It was *quiet*.

We dressed out and went on back downstairs and went through the tunnel to the dugout. So we're sittin' there in the dugout and we looked 'cross on the other side of the playin' field and Satch was warmin' up. Earl Taborn — he was the catcher — he had a new mitt. He was a little bit farther than the

Hank Presswood, 1999 (Lisa Feder photograph).

[normal] distance from the pitcher to the catcher. He said the reason he was that far off, Satchel's arm was so strong he couldn't get in the regular position. [Laughs]

Satch got through warmin' up and he put on a blue warm-up jacket and he wore a number 13 shoe, I believe it was.

He come over to our dugout. He walked down to the end of the dugout lookin' down. He'd get to the other end and turn around. He paced there about a couple of times and then he reached in his back pocket and got the ball. He started pitchin' it up in his right hand and he told us, "Boys, I got that ball today." That's what he told us.

When the game started, I was the sixth man to come up. When I come up, Satch said, "You know, Hank, I been hearin' you're hittin' them low line drives. You ain't gonna touch me today."

I said, "Man, I'm gonna take this 34-inch bat and I'm gonna whip you today."

When the big Bailey told me to come to bat, I reached in the bat rack and got that 34-inch bat and went on out there and dug in. You didn't dig in on Satch. I dug in and he reared up and shot one in and I hit the dirt.

I got right back up, saying, "You can't scare me."

So he wound up and threw his curveball and I hit a long foul outta the ballpark. I got back in and he reared up again and he throwed me a aspirin tablet. [Laughs] He wound up with a baseball and throwed a aspirin tablet.

He got two strikes on me and I'm tryin' to outguess him, you know. I said now he's probably gonna try me with another fastball and I'm gonna be waitin' on it, and if he don't do that he's gonna throw me his curveball and I'm gonna sure-'nough be waitin' on that one.

And he reared up and he had that hesitatin' pitch and he made that step and he threw me one of the worst knuckleballs I ever seen in my life. It was just dancin' and I swung and pulled a muscle in my side. [Laughs]

It was an excitin' time. I had a good time.

Who was the best hitter?

Josh Gibson's the best hitter. Big Josh. He could snappy hit that ball. No doubt about it, Josh was a good hitter. He could hit that ball and hit 'em a long ways, too. He was a pretty good-sized guy, you know. Ol' Josh could hit.

Who were some of your teammates?

We had Willie Grace and Jethroe and we had George Jefferson, had Al Smith, Sam "Toothpick" Jones — Sad Sam played with the Cubs — and, let's see, Big Joe Greene and I think Sherwood Brewer was with us then and Caffie, Willie Reynolds. I can't name 'em all. We had a murderers' row up there with ol' Jethroe on there. All those guys was heavy hitters, but I could hit them low line drives and run like a deer. That was my thing.

Did you steal many bases?

No, I wasn't too much of a base stealer. Jet would steal 'em, you know; Jethroe was real fast. Sammy Jethroe.

If you were a young man again, would you play baseball?

So help me!

I do walkin' for my exercise now, but I see some things happen and I say, "Oh, my goodness! I believe I could do just as good as that now." Maybe I couldn't, but you always have that belief that once you played baseball and you loved it, you always believe that you can still do it. Being the age I am now, I *still* think I can do some of it.

I walk four to five miles a day and I jog. I used to go swimmin' with my friend, but he gets up a little bit too early for me. But I do do my walkin'. I stay in good condition. Now I'm at 178; I usually be right in from 180 to 175. I was 155, 160 when I played and about 5'10".

BATTING RECORD

Year	Team, League	Pos	G	AB	R	H	2B	3B	HR	RBI	SB	BA
1948	Cleveland, NAL	ss										.198
1949		ss										.287
1950		ss										.238
1951	Kansas City, NAL	ss-3b										
1952		inf										.194

Mickey Stubblefield
"Mayfield Moundsman"

BORN FEBRUARY 26, 1926, MAYFIELD, KY
HT. 5'9" WT. 150 BATTED AND THREW RIGHT

Negro Leagues debut: 1948

Kentucky is known for several things — horses, basketball, tobacco — but has never been rated high on the baseball scale. Through the decades, there have been professional teams in the state, but Louisville is the only city that ever held on to a franchise for any length of time, and even that city was without a team for a number of years.

But some good ballplayers have come out of Kentucky, although not as many as from most other states. The Bluegrass State has produced Earle Combes, Pee Wee Reese, Ray Chapman, and, more recently, Willie Blair, among others who have played in the major leagues.

Then there were also such as Ray Miller, John Beckwith, and Mickey Stubblefield. These fellows also played in the major leagues — the black major leagues.

Mickey Stubblefield, from Mayfield in western Kentucky, played only two years in the Negro leagues, during which time he was a member of one of the best pitching staffs in all of baseball: that of the Kansas City Monarchs. Joining Stubblefield on the mound for the Monarchs in 1948 and '49 were such as Jim LaMarque, Ford Smith, Hilton Smith, Theolic Smith, Connie Johnson, Frank Barnes, and several others who could help almost any team today.

The '49 season was Stubblefield's last with Kansas City because he began playing in the minor leagues the next year, but his arm gave out on him and he left professional baseball after the '51 season.

How did you get started in baseball?

I got out of the Navy in 1946 and I fooled around here with the local ballclub. In 1947, a friend of mine was playing in Nebraska and he called me and asked me did I want to play ball and I told him yes. He said that they would send me money for a ticket, so I got the money and I went to Omaha, Nebraska. I played with a team called the Omaha Rockets, owned by a black guy.

In 1948, I went to Kansas City with the Monarchs. I spent two years there. In the book, they only have a year, but it's two years.

What kind of record did you have?

It's been so long, I done really forgot so we can just probably put anything down. [Laughs] The first year I played in Omaha, I played three or four positions. I played shortstop most of the time with Omaha and pitched, also. With Kansas City, I just pitched only.

I was maybe 15–10 for the first year and maybe 12–6 for the next year, or something like that. I was fair, not bragging.

What pitches did you throw?

A lot of junk stuff. Curveball. Drop, we called it at the time — overhand drop, sidearm, underhanded. I could curve it either way.

Throw it overhanded, we called it a drop; now they call it a slider. We used to throw it sidearm and we called that a inshoot.

I played two years with Kansas City and from there I played one year in the Kitty League here in my hometown. I was the first black to play in that. I played one year here and from here I went to the Northern League in Duluth, Minnesota, and I played a year there.

From there, I went back to Nebraska and I stayed there in a town they called McCook. I played there, played third base, played anything there. 'Course, I was on my way out then. I was about 33. I played 'bout ten years altogether.

In the Kitty League, I won most all of my games; in the Northern League, I had 'bout 10–8, something like that. I left because my arm got bad. I run out of gas.

I played with Cool Papa Bell and Satchel Paige. The best player probably was a guy by the name of Willard Brown. He was a home run hitter. They had a guy by the name of Hank Thompson. He and Hank, at the time, went with the old St. Louis Browns in '48. They didn't stay long, maybe a month or so, because they weren't ready for blacks at the time.

Mickey Stubblefield (courtesy of Mickey Stubblefield).

The best pitcher at the time, there was a guy by the name of Connie Johnson. And we had Lefty LaMarque and Gene Collins. We had some good ballplayers there.

Most of 'em are gone now. I guess the good Lord leaves me around here for something. I take pretty good care of myself. I didn't drink a lot or nothing like that. I never smoked. Then I'm a good guy. I think by being good, you live a long time.

What were you paid with the Monarchs?

Four hundred dollars a month and two dollars a day for meals when we was on the road.

I got married the first year I played with the Monarchs. I have 11 children now, but I had five anyway when I was still playing. I was on the road when I had three. I got eight girls and three boys. I lived in Nebraska for 17 years after I quit playing ball. My family — most of 'em — are in Nebraska. My wife and I, we divorced in 1970, so I came to Mayfield. I got so many grandkids I'm afraid to count 'em, and I got some great ones, too, at least five great-grandchildren.

The Monarchs franchise was one of the better ones in Negro baseball, and the conditions for Monarchs players were better. What problems did you encounter?

Well, eating and sleeping. Staying in the hotels and things like that. During those days, it just didn't happen. That was probably the most problems. You'd be called names — *nigger* — which that didn't bother me. I've been called some of everything. [Laughs] It didn't bother me; I felt sorry for the guy that was calling me that. [Laughs]

Traveling, it was rough and we'd sleep on the bus sometimes, but in those days we stayed mostly in the black hotels. Sometimes we'd be in a white town, so we would sleep on the bus or sometimes they'd let us have a motel or something. I guess that was probably the worst part about it.

We bought food and kept it on the bus. Like I say, I rolled with the punches, so it wasn't all that bad anyway because we didn't know any better.

What did you do when you left baseball?

I went to work for a Chevrolet garage in Nebraska. Hormel Chevrolet. They also owned the meat place in Austin, Minnesota — Hormel Packing. He was a very good friend of mine and he did a whole lot for me and my family. He helped me to get a G.I. loan back in those days. I always will remember him because he was really a good guy.

The little town that I lived in was all white. We was the only black family there and I never knew I was black 'til I looked in the mirror. That's how good they were.

When I worked for the Chevrolet garage, I started out washing cars and I ended up installing radios and working on the heating systems and hooking up truck beds. From there, my wife and I, we divorced, and I came back to Mayfield in 1970 and I went to work at General Tire — they build tires — and I was lucky to get a job there. I worked there 22 years. In 1992, I retired.

When I got out of the service, I went to trade school on the G.I. bill and played ball in the summer. Things were rough back there in those days, too. When you first got out of the service, you couldn't find a job. You'd draw more money drawing the rocking chair money than you could working, and that wasn't but $20 a week. If you worked, you couldn't make but about ten dollars a week.

Had you played ball in the service?

Yes, I played in the service. Mostly I played sports, so I guess that kept me from going overseas. I wanted to go when my friends went, but I never got the chance. I stayed in the service two-and-a-half years.

Does a game stand out?

I remember one time we was in a little town in Kansas and we played a white club. I think there was a Western League pitcher pitching against us. We went 16 innings and I won that game. That was one of the games that I will always remember. Back in those days, you had to go all the way. [Laughs] It was not like it is now. I was with Kansas City then.

When you look back on your days in baseball, do you have any regrets?

Well, yes. I was too old to cut the mustard when I started out. [Laughs] I wish that I'd've been a lot younger, but it had to be like that. That's the way the ball bounces.

I had a better arm when I was young, but when you get older, you get smarter. You use your muscles when you're young. But now, I look at the games now and look at those guys; they throw 'em outside and inside. You know, you don't have to put it down the middle all the time. Back in those days, I tried to throw it down the middle and throw it by 'em.

Would you be a baseball player again?

Yes, I would. I loved it. I loved it more than I loved my wife. [Laughs] That's how much I loved it.

I'd like to mention a couple of things. I played with a lot of guys that was 'round here on this local team that could've played. We had a pretty good little team here. I believe that we could've beat some of those teams in the black league after I got out of the Navy. A very good friend of mine — he's still living; most everybody that I was raised up with around here is dead — a guy by the name of A. J. Lawson, he was a heck of a ballplayer. 'Course, he batted cross-handed. He could hit it over the fence, but he walked like he was a turtle. [Laughs] A guy by the name of Ezell Hayes — he was an older guy — he gave me my first ballglove. Life's been bad, but it's been good 'cause I didn't know any better.

PITCHING RECORD

Year	Team, League	G	IP	W	L	Pct	H	BB	SO	ERA
1948	Kansas City, NAL			15	10	.600				
1949				12	6	.667				
1950	Mayfield, KittyL									
1951	Duluth, NorL			10	8	.556				

Josh Gibson, Jr.
"A Hard Act to Follow"

BORN AUGUST 11, 1930, PITTSBURGH, PA
HT. 5'10" WT. 170 BATTED AND THREW RIGHT

Negro Leagues debut: 1949

Following in the footsteps of a legend is hard, as any number of hard-luck players, black and white, will tell you. But when that legend is your father, who may have been the greatest hitter in the history of baseball, it has to be even more difficult.

Josh Gibson, Jr., played his professional baseball career during a time—1948–51—when black men could play in white leagues, and that's where he started, but while he held his own, the team didn't. It folded, so he joined his dad's old team, the Homestead Grays, where he played two years, then went with his late father's friend, Sam Bankhead, to Canada to play one year in the Provincial League, where his career was ended by a broken ankle.

Altogether, the younger Gibson had a four-year professional career. It wasn't like his father's, but few, if any, were.

I guess to say, "You were born to baseball," is an understatement.

Yeah, really.

I want you to look this up. In 1937—I got the actual copy of it from the *New York Times*—Cumberland Posey and Gus Greenlee and Dr. [John] Martin, who had the Memphis Red Sox, and the Manleys, who owned the Newark Eagles, they all met in New York. The New York reporters was callin' Cumberland Posey a tycoon because he bought my father off of Gus Greenlee for $2500. Ain't that somethin'? And the headlines of the article called it "the biggest deal in baseball." Not the biggest deal in black baseball—the biggest deal in baseball at that time.

Were you at the ballpark with your dad essentially from day one?

Well, not from day one. I started travelin' with him when I was about 11 years old, and when I was 14 years old I had been in 24 of the 48 states. I used to count 'em as a kid. And it was only two weeks out of the summer that I would go with him. I'd been to all the major league ballparks that they'd let us play in at the time. We couldn't play in Boston; we had the All-Star Game in the Chicago White Sox park; [P. K.] Wrigley wouldn't let us play in the Cubs' park; we played in the Polo Grounds, New York Yankees Stadium; they didn't let us play in Detroit; we played in Forbes Field here in Pittsburgh, also in Philadelphia and Cincinnati.

There wasn't no teams on the other side of the Mississippi, so what people was actually seein' was good baseball as far as the public was concerned, but it was black baseball. The Grays, durin' the Second World War, they actually outdrew the Washington Senators. That was Mickey Vernon's era. When we went to D.C. to play, my father and them wore a "W" on their sleeves. They were the Washington Homestead Grays.

Josh Gibson, Jr. (courtesy of Josh Gibson, Jr.).

You may have been too young to notice, but how was the team accepted by the Griffith family?

I don't know. It must have been all right because durin' that era the groundskeepers in Griffith Stadium was black. It must've been the money [Clark] Griffith needed because from '41 to '44, the Grays was adopted there by the community and they outdrew the Washington Senators.

Is it true that you played in organized ball before you played in the Negro leagues?

Yeah. When I got outta high school, I was playin' with the Youngstown Colts, Class C ball [Mid-Atlantic League], and I stayed there that one year, then the league went down.

So you only played the one year in organized ball?

Yeah. There was no other opportunity.

Youngstown was kinda tough. I had to play with the nails comin' up in my spikes. I didn't say nothin' to nobody. At that time we didn't have no fountains in the dugout; they didn't want me to drink outta the water pail. They gave me cups.

When I first hit Youngstown, we had a road trip up to Uniontown, up to the Summit Hotel there. They had to have a meeting to see who I was gonna sleep with. There was four guys in a room. I was the only black on the team. I can't remember the name, but there was one guy — he was an older guy — and he told 'em that I could stay in the same room with him 'cause he once played against my father.

As far as my relationship [with the players] was concerned, I don't know. It was all right. Only when Al Ott — no relation to the great Mel Ott — he was the manager of the team and he came over and told me, "Here's some cups, Josh, 'cause the rest of the guys don't wanna drink outta the water pail." There was a dipper and ice and water.

When you were with the Grays, were there any social problems?

No, 'cause we knew where to go. We used to stay at the Dunbar Hotel in D.C. — 114th and U. In some places, we had to stay at roominghouses or people's private homes when we went down South.

Your father was a catcher, but you were an infielder.

I was a third baseman. I played a little second base in Youngstown, but I was a third baseman. I could run, as we say, "fly."

Now Sammy Bankhead — in '49 and '50 I played with the Homestead Grays and he was the manager, the brother of Dan Bankhead of the Brooklyn Dodgers. Sam was actually the first black manager in organized ball, but it was in Canada. We played 40 miles from Montreal. Joe Black and Junior Gilliam was playin' with Montreal; we used to go over there and hang out with 'em on our off days. That was B or A ball up there, I forget which. That was the Provincial League. They had older guys, especially guys that had played in the Negro leagues. Leon Day and Lester Lockett. Wilmer Fields played up there — pitcher and third baseman.

You said you were fast. Were you allowed to steal?

On my own? Playin' underneath Bankhead, yeah. Any time I got on. And the same way with the Grays. It was '49 and '50 with the Grays and '51 in Canada. We played in the smallest town in the league. We didn't have but 5,000 people — half English, half French — and 40 miles from Montreal. Farnham.

You were hurt badly there.

Yeah. Slid into second base, broke my ankle. That, plus the high blood pressure that runs in my family, caused me to retire. I never had headaches or nothin', but I know like in high school I had a hard time passin' physicals. A couple doctors just gave me a break. My father died of a brain hemorrhage and me and my sister, we have high blood pressure. My mother died at childbirth. I've never seen my mother. My mother's mother raised us.

You were 16 when your father died and Bankhead was pretty much your surrogate father.

Yeah. Even when we got out of baseball and started workin'. I worked with him. I listened to him still, like playin' baseball. He was one of the smartest guys 'cause he read all the time.

You played four years professionally. Is there one game that stands out?

Yeah, when I hit a home run and stole three bases down in Griffith Stadium. That was against the Newark Eagles; the pitcher was [Lenial] Hooker. He used to rock; he used to have a windup and bring his leg up and just rock back and forth and then pitch the ball.

Do you receive a baseball pension?

The league was still goin' on then, but here's what happened. These older guys — now I'm talkin' like Double Duty [Radcliffe], he's 95, and Bobby Owens is 95 and most of the guys that's still livin' is in their 80s. They get $10,000 a year. We're tryin' to argue that now. Joe Black and Peter Ueberroth, what happened was they claim that when they signed Jackie Robinson that was the end of the Negro leagues. They wasn't prejudiced no more. They don't wanna pay the guys that kept goin', like out there in Kansas City. The Indianapolis Clowns kept on playin'. But the teams in the East, people lost interest in 'em on account of Jackie.

When I was a kid I never heard none of them guys say nothin' about playin' ball in the major leagues because they was just playin' ball. The stars of the league played all year 'round. My dad went to the Latin countries. Satchel and my dad.

I had a chance to bat against Satchel. I didn't get a hit. [Laughs]

My father and [Roy] Campanella were the only two American baseball players in the Mexican Hall of Fame. Me and Campy and Campy's wife and my wife, we went down there and got the plaques. My father was the Most Valuable Player in Puerto Rico, too.

Them guys went out West when there wasn't no big-time baseball. There wasn't nobody marchin' up and down the street for the Negro leaguers to get into the majors, there wasn't no NAACP, there wasn't no drive to get Josh Gibson or Buck Leonard into the majors. They just kept on playin'. And, see, down in the Latin countries my dad and them made good money.

You spoke of Satchel. Who was the best pitcher?

Number one is Satchel, then Ray Brown. I watched Ray pitch as a kid, but I batted against Satchel. Maybe I got a little prejudice there, but, damn, Ray Brown was good.

I got a picture here — got four Hall of Famers on it, 1936 — them guys went up in the *Denver Post* tournament and the Negro team ended up winnin' the tournament. My father was the Most Valuable Player; he got a $150 watch. Some guy from Denver sent me that information, so I had the pictures made up. He even sent me the box scores.

Who was the best player you saw, besides your dad?

They had quite a few players, in my opinion. I liked Bankhead 'cause he could play anyplace. He could pitch, he could catch. He was chewin' and spittin' tobacco all the time. I'm tellin' you, that tobacco juice! I've seen Bankhead pitch, I've seen him catch. He was a regular shortstop, but when we got Dude Richardson outta Decatur, Georgia, he played short and Sam played second base. I played third and Buck [Leonard] played first. Buck was a good ballplayer, too. Line-drive hitter.

When you look at those records that those guys are goin' for today, they use those muscle-builders — you know what I mean. That right field 344 [feet] in Yankee Stadium — Babe Ruth hit many a home run over that 344. And Roger Maris. And nowadays that's a pop-up. Mark McGwire so far is a nice guy; he gets on well with the public, but America ain't gonna never forget Babe Ruth. I'm includin' McGwire, I'm includin' Michael Jordan. You know they don't talk about Hank Aaron.

I got a 8 × 10 picture with me, Willie Mays, and Bill Cosby. We're all in tuxedos in New York City in 1971 or '72 at the Black Hall of Fame.

They put my dad in the Hall of Fame in '72. Thanks to Bowie Kuhn, Monte Irvin, who worked for Bowie Kuhn at the time, and Willie Stargell, they put a headstone on my father's grave in Pittsburgh.

Who would be on your all-time All-Star team?

Oh, man. I'll give you some names, but that's hard. Some people would call me prejudiced, but my father is the number one catcher.

The way McGwire has hit the ball the last three years, him and Buck Leonard at first base. Second base — Junior Gilliam was nice in the Negro leagues and he played good ball in the major leagues, and Junior didn't have a strong arm, but he always made the double play. And I liked Pete Rose. He didn't have the arm, either, but he had good baseball sense, especially at the plate. A lotta baseball is out-guessin' the pitcher as far as battin'. But Satchel would tell you what was comin'. You didn't have to outguess him.

Marty Marion and Ozzie Smith at shortstop. Third baseman — George Kell. You remember George Kell? I used to like him. He could hit the ball better than Brooks [Robinson], along with fielding. And Jud Wilson. Strong, and very quiet in the dugout.

Satchel Paige, Ray Brown — pitchers.

Wasn't no such thing as stoppers. A guy would relieve a guy, but there wasn't these special pitchers and everything they've got. Cecil Kaiser was a nice lefthander. Cecil's about 90 now; I ain't seen him in a couple years. He played with the Detroit Stars, then he came over with the Homestead Grays. He lives in Detroit now.

Outfielders. Larry Doby didn't play outfield in the Negro leagues. Larry Doby played second and Monte [Irvin] played shortstop and they were thinkin', beautiful players that could make that double play. And both of 'em could hit the ball.

The other outfielder, as far as hittin' the ball and runnin' it down, I'd take Wilmer Fields. To me, he was a better outfielder and a third baseman than he was a pitcher. The only thing about him, when Wilmer was pitchin', he threw a *fat* fastball — you know, where some guys throw what we used to call "peas" up to the plate. He could hit the ball.

Would you go back and be a ballplayer again?

Yeah, if I could get healthy. You know, the high blood pressure and the leg injury.

What do you think of the game today?

Baseball is comin' back with the home run race. And you're seein' good baseball, too, but there's some expansion teams — well, you know, you've got to crawl before you can walk.

The most disappointing thing to me was that guy that owned the Marlins. I don't understand that.

I have got adapted to the fields, because all I knew is dirt fields and grass. By watchin' it on TV, I got adapted to it, but it gives a lotta hits that shouldn't be. [Laughs]

And why do they have to have aluminum bats?

Baseball back in those days, includin' the major leagues and the Negro leagues and all baseball, was no irons, no steroids — just milk. [Laughs]

BATTING RECORD

Year	Team, League	Pos	G	AB	R	H	2B	3B	HR	RBI	SB	BA
1948	Youngstown, MAtlL	inf	8	23		3						.130

Year	Team, League	Pos	G	AB	R	H	2B	3B	HR	RBI	SB	BA
1949	Homestead, NAL	3b										
1950		inf										
1951	Farnham, ProvL	3b	68	187	35	43	8	0	2	20	20	.230

Neale "Bobo" Henderson
"From SD to KC"

BORN JUNE 24, 1930, FORT SMITH, AR
HT. 5'9½" WT. 170 BATTED BOTH, THREW RIGHT

Negro Leagues debut: 1949

The San Diego area has produced some fine ballplayers. None other than Ted Williams is a San Diego product, and the Splendid Splinter is a hard act to follow, but through the years many other very good baseball players have come out of the southern end of California. The Boones — all three generations — Mark McLemore, the Coscararts, Cecil Espy, Deron Johnson, Mel Nelson, and Thad Bosley are just a few who come to mind. They all played in the major leagues.

There are others from that area who may have been just as good as or even better than those guys (well, maybe not as good as or better than Williams, but we'll never know). These players, however, never played in the major leagues. Why? Baseball wouldn't let them. They were black and they played at a time when blacks were barely accepted by organized ball (and not at all by many teams).

Without belaboring the situation by creating another list, two of them tell their stories in these pages: John Ritchey and Neale Henderson.

Henderson was born in Arkansas but spent his developing years in San Diego and played with and against many of the top white ballplayers in high school (he and his team defeated Don Larsen and his team in a tournament in Pomona in 1947) and in winter leagues, but he and the other young blacks had no recourse but to play in the Negro leagues if they wanted to pursue baseball professionally.

The belief that baseball was "integrated" the day Jackie Robinson signed with Brooklyn is a myth. It was "integrated" just as the ocean would be red because a drop of blood fell into it. Robinson's signing, of course, was one of the most important events in the history of both the national pastime and the nation, but anyone even remotely familiar with the situation knows that it was still years before baseball was truly "integrated."

For those such as Henderson and Ritchey, the door was still closed in the late '40s and early '50s. It's a shame they never had a chance.

I played outfield, but, you know, we played mostly anywhere. I played shortstop and outfield.

How did you come about joining the Monarchs?

My high school coach had dealt with the Kansas City Monarchs. He got Gene Richardson. Gene Richardson and I, we played together in high school and my coach told them that I was a hell of a shortstop.

I played with 'em from '49 and I played up until '53. From there, that was it. After I didn't make it to the major leagues, I left. After they folded up, I just folded up with 'em.

Back in '38, down in Arkansas, the Kansas City Monarchs came through and they played. I was the bat boy when Buck O'Neil first started out. I took infield with Cool Papa Bell. He gave me some pointers and I stood right there on that field and I said, "One of

Neale Henderson (courtesy of Neale Henderson).

these days, I'm gonna play with these guys." The pointers Cool Papa Bell gave me helped me throughout my career.

Who were some of your teammates in Kansas City?

Gene Richardson was a hell of a pitcher. Barney Serrell, he played second base. Ernie Banks. Elston Howard played outfield and did a little catching. Ol' Willie "Fireball" Beverly. All of 'em were just a hell of a bunch of baseball players. We just had a hell of a team.

In 1951, a young man came up by the name of Milt Smith. He was a hell of a shortstop. With Buck O'Neil coaching, everything just formed and fell in line and we just played ball.

Most of the country never got to see 'em. I just hate that it was that way, but I've found a lot of persons right here in California, even in high school, that had the same problem. We ran into the same thing out here. Even when we would go over and play in Arizona, it was the same thing.

But we enjoyed playing around for different people, even when we went over into Mexico. We played in Abilene against Pepper

Sharpe. Robert "Pepper" Sharpe. He was a hell of a pitcher.

Who was the best player you saw?

I have to tell you Satchel Paige. [Laughs] Also, I'm not going to throw my buddy out of it. Gene Richardson. Gene was a hell of a pitcher, but the best that I really met was Satchel Paige. I didn't get to barnstorm with him; I came a little bit after him. I got to meet him, but I didn't get to play with him.

Is there one game that stands out?

When we played Memphis down in Abilene, Texas, and Robert Sharpe, he pitched and I went 3–4 on ol' Pepper.

I was a line-drive hitter. That's all I did. I was mostly triples, doubles. I was inside the park and I've gotten inside-the-park home runs. I was pretty fast. I couldn't say I was fast as Cool Papa Bell, but I bet I could almost equal him for speed.

I had an excellent arm and I was quick. My coach from out here in California, he told me I was one of the best that ever came out of San Diego High School. He told many people that. My lifetime batting average with them was .351.

We did real good in the little world series. We came in third. That's the time that I met Babe Ruth in 1947, just before he died. I have pictures taken with Babe Ruth. I cherish that. Somebody stole my baseball. I had a baseball signed by him and it's worth $12,000 now.

I used to do a head slide. I used to be like Jackie Robinson; I'd get on third base and worry that pitcher to death. I have stole home about three times when I was in the old Negro league. I could steal home and I could steal second. Go in head first and come up and still be running to go to third. [Laughs]

I was a hell of an outfielder, too. I had a good, strong arm. I could go back against the wall; a lot of us used to go *on* the wall. [Laughs] They called it "walking the fence."

Do you know any of your seasonal batting averages?

[I hit] .325 in 1950. I was a good little hitter. Baseball, no matter how good you are, there's going to be ups and downs.

I played against Ted Williams out here during the winter months — winter league baseball. When I was playing with General Dynamics, each team could have four major league baseball players on it.

When Negroes first broke into professional baseball — just like St. Louis picked up a lot of us, a lot of my old teammates — and they put 'em on the farm. They put 'em out on the farm and wouldn't bring 'em up. A lot of us, if they'd have give us a chance, we could've maybe been a Willie Mays or a Jackie Robinson or anybody, but they just swept us under the carpet and forgot about us. It's a shame that things were like that because it wasn't meant to be, but that's just the way it was.

When I came up, Gene Baker and I, we took infield, so the Birmingham Black Barons' coach noticed me and he tried to buy me from the Kansas City Monarchs, but the Monarchs wouldn't let me go. I had the opportunity to go with the Birmingham Black Barons, but I played with the Monarchs until July and they farmed me out to Abilene, Kansas, and I finished 1949 out there with the Abilene Ikes. I think they were a Boston Braves farm team or something like that and I was the first black to ever play with the Abilene Ikes. We won the championship.

I won the championship for 'em. When I first got down there, they was only pulling in maybe like a hundred people. Not even a hundred maybe. But after I started playing with 'em, they started winning and got up to 700-and-some people. That just shows you there that I had to be something to pull 'em in.

I spent the last half of 1949 there. I think I ended up at .285 or .290. I was 19 years old. On Junction City in that same league was Earl Woods, the father of Tiger Woods.

Then, like I was saying, I pitched and I did a little bit of everything. We won the championship. That was the first time they ever won it.

You mentioned Ernie Banks a while ago. Could you tell then that he would be as good a ballplayer as he became?

Yes! But definitely! I was with Ernie in '95 when we had our reunion and he still remembered me. We're real good friends. He's a fine person. He don't care what color you are; Ernie Banks is Ernie Banks.

Who was the best hitter you saw?

The best hitter I saw was Elston Howard. He could swing that bat.

Any regrets?

The color barrier is the only thing I have regrets about. That, and the Korean War came along. That really knocked a lot of black ballplayers out of it, also.

The only real regret I have is that I didn't make it to the majors. That was my life's dream, to play in the major leagues. Out here in California, I played with mostly all whites. There wasn't no prejudice out here, so I felt like I could've played with anybody. Mostly all the guys that played with the Dodgers, I played against them in high school and beat 'em. I played against Eddie Mathews and we beat them every year. Mathews was just one hell of a ballplayer. Boy, that boy, he could hit that ball!

Also, Jim Marshall. I played against him. We all made the Foundation team out here in California. And Dave Salazar. Those were some of the guys I played against, and we all made first team out here in California.

It was just a shame. I was just as good as the average one of 'em, but they just didn't choose me.

Neale Henderson mentioned the name of Gene Richardson several times. It's a name not widely recognized out of Negro league circles, but Richardson, who passed away in 1987 at the age of 69, was a top lefthander who pitched primarily for Kansas City from 1947 through 1953. Also, the Boston Braves and Chicago White Sox scouted him in the early '50s.

In 1946, Richardson's senior year at San Diego High School, he won 14 and lost only one, and in the state playoffs that year, he struck out 54 batters in 27 innings (a school record 19 in one game) and was named California High School Player of the Year.

San Diego High was loaded. In addition to Richardson and Henderson, both Curtis Everett and Hank Wallace also went on to play in the Negro leagues.

Those latter two, as well as Richardson, Henderson, and Ritchey, played on the semipro Gibson Tigers, which was also a loaded team. Other members of that team were Earl Wilson, Jr., a future 20-game winner in the major leagues, and Walter McCoy, a top Negro leagues pitcher who also pitched in the PCL. The Gibson Tigers attempted to schedule exhibitions against the San Diego Padres, but the Padres' management refused to play them for fear that a loss would lower them in the eyes of the fans.

BATTING RECORD

Year	Team, League	Pos	G	AB	R	H	2B	3B	HR	RBI	SB	BA
1949	Kansas City, NAL	of										
1950		of										.325
1951		of										
1952		of										
1953		of										

Merle Porter
"Fancy Dan"

BORN JANUARY 19, 1921, LITTLE ROCK, AR
HT. 5'11" WT. 170 BATTED AND THREW LEFT

Negro Leagues debut: 1949

Merle Porter's big brother Andy was one of the best pitchers of his era. Andy is 13 years older than Merle, and his tales of professional baseball made the younger Porter want to play professionally, too. A decade later, Merle might have gone into organized ball's minor leagues, but this was in the 1940s. The color line was being broken, but it was a selective and slow break; many teams were waiting for the novelty of the black players to wear off and some were waiting, even hoping, that the chosen few would fail.

And, too, major league teams were signing very few young blacks in the late '40s. Mainly, if they signed anyone at all, it was a veteran who had proven himself over a period of years. Look at the early signings: Sam Jethroe, Dan Bankhead, Roy Campanella, Larry Doby, Satchel Paige, Monte Irvin. These guys had been around for a long time, but it was their success that finally led the major league teams to sign young, unproven players, such as Willie Mays, Hank Aaron, and Ernie Banks, in the early 1950s.

So Merle Porter was right in the middle. He was young and unproven in the late '40s when the older players were being signed, and he was in his late 20s in the early '50s when the young players were being pursued.

Still, he spent two years (1949–50) playing first base for the Kansas City Monarchs, the cream of the Negro American League. The Monarchs always had good players; it is probably safe to say if a man could play for them, he could have played in "organized" ball.

How did you start in professional baseball?

First, I started off in the Negro Southern League. I started off with the New Orleans Creoles; Cool Papa Bell was the manager. I played with them for a while — a couple of years — and then I went from there to Kansas City and played with Cool Papa Bell and Satchel Paige with the Kansas City Stars throughout the West Coast and Midwest, on up through Canada.

Then after that I went over to the big team — the Kansas City Monarchs. I was there for two years.

Why did you leave?

Baseball started folding up then, more or less. Guys were leaving, guys were going to get jobs. They had a chance to go to work. I had a chance to get a job, so I just stopped. I went to work in a Uniroyal factory — automobile tires.

Is there a game or games that stand out?

All of 'em were good games. Some of the games that were funny were against the [Indianapolis] Clowns, against Goose Tatum and King Tut — that group of guys. I liked those guys because of the funny games. That's the most memorable because of the way they acted, King Tut in particular, with his antics

Merle Porter (author's collection).

as a clown. They were something to see, and they were good athletes, too.

Who were the best players you saw?

The best player I think I've seen was Herb Souell, played third base for the Kansas City Monarchs. He could hit and he was a good third baseman.

Who was the best pitcher?

My brother was good. And I played with Satchel Paige; he was good.

Who was the best pitcher you faced?

The best pitcher I faced, the guy that gave me the most trouble — we used to play a team out of Asheville, North Carolina — his name was Bowman. I couldn't hit him for nothing. He played with the Asheville Blues in the [Negro] Southern League. They were a good team. He was a good pitcher.

You came from a good baseball background.

Yes, I did. That's what got me into baseball, wanting to be like my brother.

How much were you paid?

We weren't paid very much. As much as I made was 450 a month. In that day in age, it was good money. We didn't get but three bucks a day for meal money.

You and Buck O'Neil shared first base. How were you as a first baseman?

I was as good as I wanted to be. They called me "Fancy Dan."

What about your hitting?

I could hit good. I hit about .265.

How was the travel?

Oh, I liked to. We traveled by bus. It was an experience because we could go from city to city, town to town and watch the people as we go through the towns. It was real amazing. I traveled all over the country, coast to coast and all up through Canada.

Throughout the South, the fans were real good. Anywhere we played in the South, they were real good. We had a few problems in the South because that was during the time of segregation. It was real bad in some places, but when we had trouble the manager was the only one would speak up. We wouldn't say too much. We were told not to say too much.

There was one incident that was real funny. We were out of Gulfport, Mississippi, and our bus broke down. We were sitting on the front drinking pop. We were all nice and clean; we had just left New Orleans going to Gulfport. It was in the summertime and we all had on nice clothes — nice white slacks and everything.

The cops went down the highway and they saw us sitting out there drinking and all clean and everything and they immediately turned around and came back and asked us what we were doing out there. The manager spoke up and said, "Officer, we're baseball players. Our bus broke down and it's being fixed in the back." That's what Cool Papa Bell told them.

So the older officer — a big man — sent the young one back there to see if he was telling the truth. He came back and whispered in the big man's ear and the big man got mad about something. He looked at all of us and the young man said, "Look. They all got their shoes shined."

We did. We had just left New Orleans and we were dressed real nice. We had black and white shoes and some brown.

He said, "Let me tell you one thing. Goddamn it, get up from here — all of you! Get in the back. If I come by here and catch you again, I'm gonna put you all in the field and put you to work."

That was comical. We had to get up and get in the back. We all were mad, but we did it. We knew not to say anything.

If you were to be a young man again, would you be a ballplayer?

Yes, indeed! I would play again.

BATTING RECORD

Year	Team, league	Pos	G	AB	R	H	2B	3B	HR	RBI	SB	BA
1949	Kansas City, NAL	1b										.272
1950		1b										.264

"Jumpin' Johnny" Wilson
"Athlete"

BORN JULY 7, 1927, ANDERSON, IN
HT. 6' WT. 170 BATTED AND THREW RIGHT

Negro Leagues debut: 1949

Every now and then an *athlete* comes along. By *athlete*, I mean a man who is not just a good baseball player or a good football player; I mean a man who can and does excel in all sports.

I guess the prime example is Jim Thorpe, but there have been a few other, less-heralded men. Red Badgro was one, Jackie Robinson was one, and Irv Noren was another. Recently we have seen the likes of Deion Sanders and Bo Jackson.

Johnny Wilson was one, too. That's a name not immediately familiar to most sports fans of today, but John did everything — football, basketball, track, baseball — at the college level and went on to play baseball and basketball professionally.

John is black, though, and during the years he was playing, blacks were still not properly accepted in professional sports, so he played on black teams, baseball with the Chicago American Giants and basketball with the Harlem Globetrotters. Tell me anyone who can play with the Trotters couldn't play in the NBA.

They called him "Jumpin' Johnny" because of his leaping ability. His high school coach would put a quarter on top of the backboard and tell him to get it.

John left professional sports in his 20s because he got married (he didn't think he could be a good husband while on the road half the year) and entered teaching and coaching. It was education's gain. Today, in his 70s (he looks to be about 45), he is still doing both. He is the coach of the girls' basketball team at his alma mater, Anderson High School.

I started playing [basketball] in grade school. When I was a third grader, I was playing with the sixth grade team, and then when I was a fifth grader our team went undefeated, won the city championship, and I was the center on the team, although Carl Erskine, the ex–Dodger, was on the team. He was taller than me, but I still played center.

When I was a sixth grader, I broke the city scoring record, scoring 248 points, I think, in 13 games. I had 29 [in one game] for the city record. That got people to start thinking possibly that they had someone that could come to high school to be a basketball player.

At the same time, I was playing park league baseball. They didn't have Little League at that time. All the schools were integrated, but as far as the summer program was concerned, it was completely segregated. We had our own league. We had an eight-team league that we played in, but Carl Erskine and another fellow that ran around with us — Carl was a pitcher, Jack [Rector] was a catcher, I was a first baseman — and I decided that I was going to play with them, so I jumped the league and went to their league and we won the game [the only contest, as it turned out, the trio would play in], 22–0. The next day, they made Carl's team forfeit the game 'cause I played.

268

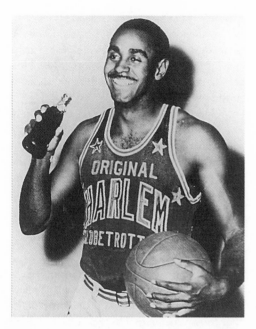

Jumpin' Johnny Wilson with Harlem Globe-trotters basketball team, early 1950s (courtesy of John Wilson).

He was a year older than me, but I left the park league a year early and went to Junior Legion baseball when I was 12. Junior Legion is 13 to 15. I played first base and batted third in the batting order.

I played that during the summer and in the school year I didn't play baseball. I ran track. I wanted to do them both, but the track coach was about 4'8", 4'9", the greatest track coach in the world, and he would not *think* about letting me do both. And then the baseball coach was the athletic director, also, *and* the basketball coach, and he didn't pressure, so I didn't play baseball. Only in the summers.

Then, as I got into high school, I was faced with a situation. See, at Anderson [High School] for about, oh, a ten-year period, there'd only been three blacks that played basketball. They were three brothers, the Clemons brothers. Frankie Clemons was the first one. Frankie played on the '37 state championship team, and he was one of the guys that I tried to copy off of. Another brother, Lee, was a great athlete but dropped out of school after his sophomore year, and

then the last brother was Clarence, who played on up until — well, he was a senior my freshman year in high school.

When I was getting ready to come into high school as a freshman, I came into high school in midterm in January but wasn't able to play then. That fall, they brought a new coach in and the new coach had been coaching at Crawfordsville, Indiana, but was originally from Webb City, Missouri. I saw this in the paper and said, "Oh, there's just no way. This guy from Missouri coming in, there's just no chance that anything would change in Anderson." I condemned the man, you know.

But, later, as life went on, he is responsible for me being where I am today. As I tell any- and everybody, he's probably the greatest man that I've ever known, other than my father. Not only did he coach me in basketball and football, but he made me take courses that would get me into college. Once he had me take a literature course and an algebra and an advanced history class, and my counselor, who was a woman, said, "Oh, Johnny, you don't want to take those courses."

I said, "Look, I'm going to college." She said, "Oh, you don't want to go to college. You just want to go out and get you a good job after you get out of high school." And the only job then would've been a janitor.

So I said, "No, I want these courses." So she excused herself and went out of the room and came back in about ten minutes and signed me up for the courses. I found out about five years later, in talking with the coach — Charles Cummings — he asked me if I remembered that day and I said, "Oh, yes. How could I ever forget it?"

He said, "She came down to me and said, 'Mr. Cummings, what are we going to do? John wants to take literature, algebra, and some advanced history. He may not pass those courses and can't play basketball.' And I said, 'If he fails, he just won't play basketball 'cause those are the courses I told him he had to take.'"

He stuck with it. He wouldn't let me come in the gym for practice without bringing my books. He told me, "I can make you take 'em home, but I can't make you study.

But one day, you're gonna sit down and wonder what's in that book and you're gonna find out it's pretty interesting once you get inside." This is the kind of guy he was.

As I came into my sophomore year — at that time, freshmen didn't get a chance to play varsity — the first four games I started with the reserve team and they won the first four games. Then, the next game, he put me in as a sub starting the second half of the varsity game. I played half the reserve game and then played the second half of the varsity game. The following game I started, and I started all the games after that.

My sophomore year was the best team I played on. The first game I played in as a sub we lost and the first game I started in we lost, and then we won all the rest of the games for the rest of the season. Then we got to the semi-state and we were playing Aurora, Indiana, and I went up for a shot — I took off in back of the foul circle floating toward the basket — and this kid ducked his head and ran at me and hit my ankles. I turned a flip and landed on my back and tore two ligaments in my back.

The next week at the state tournament, I would grab the rebound but I couldn't turn and get out on the fast break. That's what we ran. I would rebound and lead the fast break on the dribble, but I couldn't get out and we lost to Kokomo in the afternoon game of the finals by four points, I think it was, and we'd beaten them by 13 points on their floor right at the end of the season, so that cost us a state championship.

We had a great team. The team, was rated number one in the state and *Look* magazine did an article on it that year. My brother, Ray, was starting guard on the team; he got drafted in December of that year. And then, in the summer before school started, we lost Bob Hutton, who was 6'5" — he was the center — and we lost a kid named Bob Smith, who was a guard who started. These guys started the year before. They were drafted. So we lost them off the team, three people that were starters, yet we turned out the number one team in the state.

Were the teams you played integrated?

Muncie Central had one black kid on the team that year, my sophomore year. And I don't think I played against another black kid all that year. I hadn't even thought about it until just now.

The following year, Fort Wayne had several black players. Fort Wayne Central. Richmond had a black kid, Lafayette had a black kid, and Marion had a black kid. Shelbyville had three black kids on the team, including Billy Garrett, who was the first black to play in the Big Ten, at Indiana University. But that was pretty much it.

Some of the teams, like Indianapolis Tech, which was in our conference and the largest school in the state of Indiana, had no black students, period. They all went to Crispus Attucks. All black kids in Indianapolis at that time went there. Crispus Attucks, along with the parochial schools, was not allowed in the high school athletic association tournaments until 1942. They were barred from playing in the tournaments.

In my junior year, we had a good ballclub but we didn't do well in the tournament, and then my senior year was the year that we ended up winning the state tournament, but we lost seven games during the season. The next-to-last game, we lost to Kokomo and we led, 27–14, at the half and got beat, 31–29. We only made a free throw in each of the last two quarters. We just went flat.

The next week we played Newcastle and lost by 12 points. We only scored 21 points in the whole game.

The tournament started the following week and we had two meetings. We got together and talked about the problems and one of the kids said, "Coach, you yell at us too much." The coach was a big guy, but he was very soft inside. It really hurt him when the guy said that. He said, "If that's what the problem is, I'm sorry." And the meeting was over.

Two other players and myself went into the office where he was. He was sitting there with tears in his eyes 'cause he felt that he had cost us a chance, so we told him, "Coach, it don't matter what the guy says. That's not the reason. We're gonna win the state tournament."

He said, "All I really wanted was for you guys at least to win one game and show people that you could play."

And we really put it together and had a *great* tournament. Fort Wayne, who had beaten us by 27 points during the season, we met them in the final game and, 'course, all the papers were saying Fort Wayne was going to blow Anderson away, and we beat them by 13 to win the title.

Then I was named Mr. Basketball for the Indiana All-Stars, becoming the first black to play in the All-Star game against the Kentucky All-Stars. We won the game and I set a scoring record with 27 points, but they gave the Star of Stars award to Sonny Allen of Kentucky, who scored 18 points.

Then I went on to Anderson College. I wanted to go to Indiana University, but, at that time, the Big Ten were not giving black scholarships, but the next year Bill Garrett *did* go. The reason he got to go was because an insurance agent in Shelbyville paid his way through.

But I went on to Anderson College and we had real good ballclubs the three years that I played. I played basketball, baseball, football, and ran track. That's when I really got a chance to play a lot of baseball in the spring besides just playing in the summer. I led the team in hitting for all three years and I led in home runs and stolen bases. I had pretty good running skill; I was a dash man and high jumper in track. In basketball, I broke the college scoring record for three years in a row.

The coach, he was the basketball coach, football coach, athletic director, track coach. We had a track meet and I was ill and I told him that day that I didn't feel like going to the meet, so he told me, "Come and go along. If you happen to feel better when you get there, you can run."

I said, "I'm gonna stay around home 'cause I'm gonna be baptized tonight into the church, so I'm gonna make sure I'm feeling better."

He convinced me to go. He said, "I'll get you back. I'll send you back with one of the other fellows who drove his car down." The team went on a bus.

I didn't run. Coming back, I told the bus driver I had to get back, so he said, "Don't worry. I'll get you back. I'll drop you off a block from your house instead of going on to the college."

So we get 19 miles from my home and the coach told the bus driver to stop, we're going to eat. That's something we hadn't been doing at all. We get off the bus; he looked at me, said, "Come on, you can eat with us."

I said, "No," so I walked down the street to the bus station and there was no buses. There was a cab out there and I asked, "What'll you charge me to take me to Anderson, which is 19 miles?"

He says, "Aren't you Johnny Wilson?"

I said, "Yeah." He said, "You got five dollars? I'll take you for five dollars."

He got me there and I was baptized into the church, and the next day I went to the college and turned in my stuff and told the coach I was through, that I could not play for him when he would take an attitude that would prevent me from doing something I felt would change my life completely.

I wouldn't take my final examinations, either, which was dumb on my part. I didn't take them 'cause I told the head of the education department, who came out to my home on three occasions to try to get me to take them, I said, "No. If I take them I'll be eligible, then maybe somebody would come and talk me into playing again."

So I didn't take them and I had a tryout with the White Sox. This was in '49. They didn't think I was good enough and that's when the American Giants asked me to come back for a tryout with them. The next weekend I had the tryout and made the team and started playing baseball.

At the [White Sox] tryout, there were two people at each position, with the exception of catcher and pitcher. They had several people on those. We had two intersquad games, but before that, we had foot races. I outran everybody in the camp, and then we had throwing from the outfield and only one guy could out-throw me.

The intersquad game was shortened by rain, but I went to bat two times. I had very good running skills—I was clocked in 9.9 in the hundred-yard dash, which at that time was pretty good—and I hit a ball to the third baseman and he threw me out before I got halfway down the line. It was hit that sharp. The next time, I hit a ball into left center field that the center fielder went over and made a circus catch of it.

When I went back in to dress, the clubhouse manager for the White Sox asked me, "What did they tell you?" I said, "No one said anything." He said, "I'll go find out."

He went down and came back up and told me, "They said you did everything well, but you couldn't hit." [Laughs]

Even before that, probably the most disappointing time came when the St. Louis Cardinals had a tryout here in Anderson and I tried out. They had the same thing—running races and I outran everybody and outthrew everybody but one fellow, and he had the same name I had, John Wilson, a big, blond-haired kid from up in Alexandria, which is nine miles from here.

Then we had intersquad games for two days. I went to bat 11 times, I had nine hits—four home runs, three triples, and two doubles—and when the camp was over they didn't even ask me my name. That kind of bothered me a bit. I wondered what chance I would have.

And the Yankees invited me up to Michigan City for a tryout, but I didn't hit the ball well up there. I think the big reason was I spent the night sleeping in a car and we got our sleep interrupted 'cause we were parked across the street from the state penitentiary. [Laughs] I didn't deserve a shot with them 'cause I did not play well, but the others I felt that I played pretty well.

What did the American Giants tryout consist of?

I went through batting practice and fielding practice and all that. They had a doubleheader with Philadelphia and in the tenth inning of the first game, there was a man on second and, to my surprise, he put me in as a pinch hitter and I hit a sharp single up the middle to drive on the winning run. The second game I didn't play at all, but then the next morning they signed me to a contract, a big $200 a month. [Laughs]

Also, the same day, Winfield Welch, who was the manager of the American Giants and also the business manager for the Trotters, took me over and I signed a contract with the Globetrotters.

I was with the Trotters five years. My first year was the fall of '49. I went in in October when they started training camp. I was a little leery 'cause I had never been away from home except when I went to baseball, but I got off to a pretty good start because I had the fellows watching 'cause I would dunk. None of them were actually dunking the ball; they were capable of dunking, but they just didn't do it until after they saw me dunk.

The first tryout there was probably eight players, and Clarence Wilson from Horse Cave, Kentucky, and Bobby Milton from Fort Wayne, who I played against in that state tournament and also he played half a semester at college before he flunked off, were there. We were three rookies on the team along with Goose Tatum, Sweetwater Clifton, Marcus Haynes, Ermer Robinson, and Babe Presley.

I got a chance to start a lot of ballgames that first year and with the travel, which was far more extensive than the American Giants, the living conditions were much better. In most places, we had better hotels than we did with the American Giants and we made a little bit more money.

After I played about two or three weeks— 'course, we had different little skits we did— and we had the football skit and Marcus Haynes was the kicker. One day, we were in the gym early someplace and I told Marcus, "I can outkick you." I was placekicker in college in football.

We started just horsing around out there kicking and that first day I guess I kicked in maybe 13 out of 25. Marcus, who didn't have to, said, "Hey, man. that's your job. You do the kicking now."

In about the fourth game in which I kicked, we were playing in Marion, Indiana, and it was the first game that my mother had watched me with the Globetrotters — she had watched me in high school and college — and we went to the football skit and — Boom! — I kicked it and — Swish! — nothing but net. That really made me feel great.

The next night we got to Cleveland and [Globetrotters' owner] Abe [Saperstein] is in Cleveland and he tells Lou Groza, who's the kicker for the Browns at the time — and I'd played with his brother, Alex, in the All-Star basketball game — he told Lou, "Hey, this man is gonna steal your job. He drop-kicked the ball for a basket last night."

So in Cleveland, they snapped it back to me and — Boom! — I kicked it and nothing but net. Two nights in a row. The Sandusky paper played it up — we were playing in Sandusky the next day — so I kicked it and it falls in the foul circle. [Laughs] I really blew it.

But over the course of the years I played, I guess I kicked in something like 60 or 70 of them. You only got one a game. I kick more now than I did when I was playing ball. I'm the assistant at the high school and the coach and I, we have a little game. He'll toss the ball one-handed underhanded and I'll drop-kick.

I was at a church camp in Decatur, Illinois, and the minister there was a guy I'd gone to college with, so he told the TV people that I can drop-kick the ball in the basket. They came out to film it. I hadn't kicked all that day, so I said, "I'll tell you what now." For film, you've seen guys make all kinds of crazy shots, but what usually happens, they will shoot the ball and the camera will take it up so far and then somebody will toss that ball in and they'll splice it together. "You just line up back here and we'll see what happens." And I made it.

Then last year, I was running the in-school detention at one of the middle schools and one of the ladies was an Anderson Indians fan and she wanted to know if I would let her film me kicking the ball. So I said yeah

and she came down and got the audiovisual camera and set it up. I guess I kicked about seven or eight before I kicked it in. I kicked it from where the midline meets the sideline. Then I walked back to the free throw line extended at the opposite end and kicked another one and it was nothing but net from back there.

Going back to playing with the Trotters, after my first year I got drafted in the service, so I played part-time with them — whenever they would come in my area. I had a chance to play, in those two years, probably 50 to 75 games.

In the Army, I was player-coach at Fort Lewis, Washington — a team that didn't have any big names but we had a tremendous ballclub.

When I got out of the service, I went back with the main unit, which was the Eastern unit with Goose Tatum and Marcus. I had another good year and then we went to Europe that summer, but before we went to Europe they made the movie *Go Man Go*, which I had a chance to play in. About three days into the shooting, I had to be vaccinated before going overseas and the vaccinations made me sick, so I missed three days of the shooting and I missed out on the skit of kicking the ball and some of the lines I was supposed to have.

Then we went over to Europe and it was a great experience — to travel all over Europe and then to North Africa. I finished up that year, and the next year I didn't get to camp 'til two or three days late because that was the year that the Dodgers and Yankees were in the World Series. I'm a Yankee fan, but I had to cheer for Carl [Erskine] when he pitched. That was the year [1953] he struck out 14 Yankees for a new strikeout record.

I got a call from Welch asking where I was, and I told him I'd be in. He said, "Get in tonight," but I didn't leave for three more days so I could see the rest of the Series. I caught the train and went on up, and when I got there and started working out, Welch said, "You should be going with us this year." I said, "Where are you guys going?" He said, "We're going to the South Pacific." I said, "Get me on that unit!"

He said, "Nah, you wanna be back here with Goose." I said, "They want me to play backcourt and not play inside."

Elmer Ripley, who used to coach Army, used to coach Notre Dame, he was going to be the coach over there, so I said, "I can get with the Rip and pick up on my guard play." So we convinced Abe and he let me go. I had a chance to go to Australia, Asia, South Pacific. It was a tremendous trip.

But I made my mind up the first year I went out on the road that after being out there for a while to see what life was like, that if I ever got married I would quit 'cause the temptations are just too great — for me — to be a married man and out on the road. There's no way that I could be true to a wife with the temptations out on that road.

That summer of '54 I decided to get married, so I wrote Abe and told him that I was quitting. And I did.

My marriage only lasted 13 years, but, as I tell everybody, I had a successful marriage because I had three wonderful kids and from that I've got five tremendous grandkids. It worked, but it just didn't last. But if I had to do it over again, I'd do it the same way.

My baseball, the reason I gave it up was that basketball was going to go summer and winter. Sweetwater had gone with the Knicks and I just felt that here was going to be my chance to possibly go to the NBA.

I talked with Abe and asked him, "What is the chance of me going back and trying to hook up with Indianapolis in the NBA?" It was the Indianapolis Olympians at that time. The guys from Kentucky had already been banned, so they were needing ballplayers.

I had just gotten out of the Army and I went down and talked with the business manager of the Olympians and he just told me no. The thing about it, the players that he had on the team, all, with the exception of Arnie Rizen, I had played against in high school and college, and I outplayed them every inch of the way. He gave no reason.

I got married in August and moved to Kokomo, where my wife lived, and I took a job in a factory 'cause I still had to finish up my schooling. I talked with an insurance agent up there who was going to form a basketball team and play against some of the traveling teams. I told him, "I need a job." He said, "If I get you a job, will you play for my team?" I said, "Definitely."

So he got me a job at Pittsburgh Plate Glass Company, who had not hired any blacks since about 1938, I think. I played ball for him and I also played ball for the team at that plant. I was going to school at Indiana University Extension at Kokomo, at which I picked up just around 12 hours during that year to make up for the hours I'd lost that one semester.

The following year I decided to go back on campus, but my classes were during the day and that's when I was working, so I talked to the people at Pittsburgh Plate Glass and they set up a special night shift so I could work and go to school. They kept that shift going up until February, when things started really slacking off. They told me I'd have to come back on days, but I was one semester away from my degree so I got another job at a glove factory for a while and it went down, so I had to draw unemployment compensation until school was out in June.

It was a scuffle because I was driving 52 miles each way to Anderson. The night I got my degree, my wife and my son, who was about three months old, my mother-in-law, and one of my sisters-in-law, were together, so the first place I went was by Mr. Cummings' house — my high school coach — and I knocked on his door. His wife came to the door and I said, "Mrs. Cummings, I need to talk to Mr. Cummings." I went in, took my family and introduced them to him, and then I pulled out my diploma and said, "Coach, I made it!" [Laughs] I think he was happier than all of us because he wanted it so bad for me.

I had a teaching degree in history and health and physical education, so the latter part of that summer I went to Indianapolis 'cause there was no chance of getting a job in Anderson or Kokomo as a teacher. They were not hiring black teachers. I went to Indianapolis and I went to the superintendent's office and they told me the assistant superintendent handled the hiring.

I went to his secretary and I said, "I'd like to see Dr. Olsheimer." She said, "Do you have an appointment?" I said, "No, I don't, but tell him it's Johnny Wilson from Anderson."

She went in and I heard him talking to her. He said, "Oh, yes. Tell Johnny to come in between appointments."

He said he remembered me from high school, running track and playing basketball. He said, "What can I do for you?" I said, "Dr. Olsheimer, I have my degree and I want a teaching job."

He said, "I don't have anything right today, but you've got a job. I'll call you."

I didn't even fill out an application; I just left my phone number. About three days later, he called and told me he had a job for me and for me to send him my credentials, which I did.

I went down and looked at the school where I was going to be teaching. It was a nice school. About two weeks later, he called me back and said, "John, I want to send you to a different school." He sent me to a school on the west side of Indianapolis. I liked it; it was a smaller school, but in the school — I didn't know it then, of course — George McGinnis was a second grader.

At the end of that year, Ray Crowe, who was coach of Crispus Attucks, retired from coaching, and Bill Garrett, who had been the freshman coach at Wood High School, was given the job. Dr. Olsheimer called me and asked if I wanted to go to Wood High School and replace Bill as track coach and freshman basketball coach, which naturally I would take.

After two years there, the principal called me in and told me that the head [basketball] coach, who was the A.D., had to give up the coaching job because he couldn't hold both jobs, and he gave me the job. At the time — that was in 1959, the fall — that made me the first black head basketball coach in an integrated high school in the state of Indiana. My first year we were 11–9. That was the worst year we had; we got better each year.

It was a school right downtown, five blocks south of the Circle, and it had been Manual High School. They built a new Manual High School a little farther out and they closed the school. They opened it back up as a special school mainly for slow learners and then the principal got them to put in kids from the neighborhood. We had kids that came to us from all over the city because we offered [courses] other than the regular academic courses. We had shoe repair, barbering, cleaning and pressing, pre-nursing; we would bring kids in from all over the city.

I was fortunate enough to get pretty good kids to come in, such as a kid named Greg Northington, who we called "Poncho." He ended up being 6'11" and broke all of Oscar Robertson's scoring records for the city while in high school.

I had another kid named Kenny Morgan, who was about 6'6". He ended up going to Indiana University. Now Kenny is back and he was head of the redevelopment of part of the west side of Indianapolis. You can go to the Walker Building, the Lockeal Gardens, all around there. In the area there is a hospital. It's one of the real big areas of Indianapolis where IUPUI [Indiana University–Purdue University at Indianapolis] holds the amateur track and the tennis and all that. He developed all that area. And I had Bill Smith; he later coached Broad Ripple High School to a state championship.

Here was a school where a lot of the kids were rejects and a lot of people used to talk about the kids because they went to Wood, but yet, during my eight years that I was head coach and 13 years altogether teaching there, we had 37 of my ex-athletes ending up getting a four-year degree.

In the school system in Indianapolis, there's probably no less than, I'd say, 50 kids that have gone to Wood High School that are teaching. The kids have done very well; a lot of them were very, very, very poor, but they saw a chance to get up and move another step and they really worked at it. What helped is we had a tremendous faculty and a tremendous principal who cared about kids. It just made a difference. A lot of teachers today, all they worry about is first and fifteenth [paydays].

I finished up my master's at Indiana State and while there, in one class — Administration of High School Athletics — I was very outspoken. At that time, I wasn't coaching basketball and there was no black coach at an integrated school; there was no black athletic director in the state of Indiana, other than at Crispus Attucks.

At that time, the blacks were beginning to dominate the game, but then after their playing days, they no longer had that leadership ability to be coaches 'cause they just didn't get jobs. That's how the school boards felt.

Dr. Stebbins was one of my professors; he called me in the office one day. He'd already told one of my friends I was too militant, which I wasn't. I was not militant at all, just outspoken. He called me in and showed me a letter and it was from the vice-chancellor at City College of Chicago, offering him, Dr. Stebbins, a job as Director of Athletics, head of the P.E. Department, at this junior college that was changing its name from Crane to Malcolm X.

He could not afford to leave Indiana State for a position in a junior college and he asked me if I would be interested. I said I might be, so he got ahold of the vice-chancellor and the vice-chancellor wrote me and told me to come in for an interview.

They set it up for the nineteenth of July, so I went up there then and went by the school. Nobody. The school was closed. I went back to my hotel and I went through my things and finally found the vice-chancellor's number and I called him. He told me the schools are closed today because this is Moon Monday; that's the day they walked on the moon.

He called the president, who at that time was staying at a hotel on the Loop, and they told me to meet them there. I went by the hotel and we met in the dining room and talked and went over some things. They said they'd give me the job if I wanted it.

Then we started talking finance. I was making 7-5 [$7,500] in Indianapolis and he offered me 15, so I told them, "Let me think about it and I'll get back to you." I came back home and talked it over with my mother 'cause I was divorced at the time. She always told me, "Whatever you think is best, that's what you need to do."

I called them back and asked the president, "What is the chance of 16-5?" He said, "No. I've gone the maximum." So I took the job and when I got there and got a copy of my contract back, the downtown office had crossed out the 15 and put 14-5.

I went to the president and talked to him. He said, "That's the doing of administration downtown. Just stick with me and I will handle things." So at the end of my first year, he told me in a meeting the last week of the semester that I would be put on full salary during the summer. And all I had to do during the summer was go to meetings maybe two times a week.

When my contract came up for the fall, he gave me a double increment. Instead of getting a $500 increment, I got a $1,000 increment on my pay. At the end of that spring semester, he put me on the payroll again during the summer and then a double increment again.

He talked to me a little later and said, "Coach, are you satisfied? Did I take care of you?" [Laughs]

Going up there at first was really an experience. Playing ball for the Trotters and the American Giants was my first true contact with an all-black situation, with the exception of when I was a little kid playing park league baseball. Even then, all my running-around was with Carl Erskine and another kid named Jack Rector. We were together every day.

I had not really been in a situation like Malcolm. It got a little hairy at first because the Black Panther Party was strong then and a couple of their leaders had been killed by the police in Chicago, and that was only a few blocks from the college.

One day they had a meeting and I never heard such language in my life between them and the president. They said, "Everybody come to the meeting," and I was sitting in my office on the third floor and they came and got me. They always carried rifles, you know, so I definitely went to the meeting. [Laughs] I'm standing there listening to them and I'm saying, "Ohh, let me get out of here! I'm gonna call Mama. I'm goin' home." [Laughs]

I went back to my apartment and thought about it. I didn't call her 'cause that would've upset her, so I went on. It was one of the best things I've ever done in my life because I got an education in blackness and I got a real chance to take leadership, as far as an athletic program, as far as a physical education program — something I never would've had a chance to do in Indianapolis.

And I had a chance to meet some of the pro athletes in Chicago. Pat Williams was the general manager of the Bulls when I got there and whenever I wanted tickets for myself or for my team I could get them. When I wanted to go see the Cubs play, Jack Brickhouse took care of me on tickets there. It was a real experience for me in that I felt that I grew up, truly became a man, because I was in a new area, and things were tough in Chicago at that time as far as gangs and things.

In coaching, I had a chance then to start trying to give back to the young people what I had received from my coaches, like giving them a chance to see things and do things. See, I had probably the toughest junior college schedule in the country because we played about 31 games but only ten of them would be at home. We went to Washington, D.C., we went as far as Florida, we went to Oklahoma, we went to Texas, went to Arizona, went up into Calgary, Alberta. We played in probably 12 states — 12 to 14 states — and before I left I scheduled games in New York and California. The year that I left they went there.

The first year we went to D.C., I told the fellows, I said, "Now, when we get to D.C., we'll go down and see the White House and see the Capitol Building." They'd say, "Aw, we don't wanna see that stuff. That's a white man's world." This was in 1973.

But then when we got there, we checked into the hotel and we were going to go eat, but the driver took us down to the area down Constitution Avenue, down to the Congress Building. The same kids that were telling me they didn't want to be a part of it, they jumped off and said, "Take my picture! Get my picture!" [Laughs] All of a sudden they realized there was something else in the world besides Chicago. From then on, that's when I started traveling all over the country because it was an education for those young people.

I tried to dress my teams just like when I played high school ball. My coach said, "If you're gonna be a champion, you gotta dress like a champion." We had seven sets of game uniforms; we had two reds, two blacks, two whites, and a silver uniform. We had warm-up suits for each of those uniforms. We were the only school that provided shoes and all the equipment. It gave them a chance to see some better things. Of that, I had 27 of our kids who played at Malcolm who graduated and left us and went on to a four-year school and many of them got a degree.

I gave them a chance to venture out and see something different. We'd take a train. We went on a train to Arizona and Charles Kuralt was on the train. He was doing a thing with the conductor, who was making his last run on this line. Mr. Kuralt came in and interviewed some of our kids.

Jamie Farr was on the train and they got to meet him. It was great for these kids out of Chicago who had never been anywhere and probably would never go again. They had a chance to see and do things.

After I finished up at Chicago, I ended up coming back home. The mayor talked me into running the community center. When they built the gymnasium for the community center, they put my name on it — the Johnny Wilson Provilion. I worked in that area for three years before I went back into teaching again.

I was also assistant coach at Anderson University, but then after four years there I decided to go back and be assistant at the high school, which I'm still doing now. I like it better working with the younger kids.

I've always told people God blesses people, and I just felt like He picked me and gave me a special blessing because I have so much to be thankful for over the years from where I started. We were, as a family, a very loving family — everybody cared for everybody — but we were very, very poor. We had beans five days a week and for breakfast, if you didn't eat oatmeal, all we had was syrup and biscuits. We very seldom had milk.

We didn't have much, but the family stuck together and cared for each other. There were ten kids altogether and now there's only two of us left. I was the seventh. I was born on the seventh month, the seventh day, the 27th year, at seven p.m.; I weighed seven pounds, and I was the seventh child.

When I played ball in high school after my brother went to the service — I'd worn number three at first — when new uniforms came out at Christmastime, number three was too tight for me then, so I moved up to number seven, at that time not even thinking about the sevens in my life. I wore that right on through high school and college. And this past season [1997-98] they retired the number seven and it hangs in the high school gym, called the Wigwam.

My father passed when I was 13, but my mother took charge and she raised everybody and she lived until she was 90. It was a true blessing to be able to have a mother that many years.

Now I'm still hanging around coaching, but I go around to see my grandkids. My grandson plays [high school] football in Pennsylvania; he's a super athlete. He's big and strong and providing everything goes right — no injuries or anything — he could have a professional career in some sport.

Who was the best basketball player you saw?

The same guy that was the best basketball player that ever played the game: Oscar. These guys now get a triple double three or four times a year and people talk about it; Oscar had triple doubles for the whole season.

Another thing I like about Oscar — I don't know some of the guys now, but I've watched some of them in crowds, I've heard comments about some of them — but Oscar Robertson is the same guy that he was when he was playing high school basketball. He never changed. He's a guy that cares about people and takes time for people. The year before last he showed how caring he was when he gave up one of his kidneys for his daughter.

The last time I had a chance to talk to him was about three years ago at the Hall of Fame banquet. He was talking with some bigwig people and I walked in; he saw me and excused himself from those people to come over to talk to me. I love the guy. The one thing I was glad about was he came along ten years after me. [Laughs]

Who was the best baseball player you saw?

My best player is Joe DiMaggio. You had guys that were better fielders, such as Willie Mays; you had better hitters, like possibly Ted Williams; but I thought for the complete ballplayer on the field and off the field that he was the greatest.

My next favorite was Mickey Mantle, but he wasn't as great because of his leg problems. I'm a diehard Yankee fan. If he hadn't been hurt, he would've been the greatest ballplayer that ever lived.

I got really hurt. There was a clothing store here owned by a friend of mine. He had refereed some games when I was coaching. He had a Mickey Mantle clothing store in Indianapolis and I bought clothes there. I was living in Chicago and he called me and told me that Mickey was coming to the store. It happened that I couldn't make it down that night, so I called my ex and asked her to take John, Jr., over there. The guy told me he was going to have Mickey pose with John, Jr., and take a picture and then send the picture to Mickey for him to sign it for him. And my ex couldn't take him.

It hurt me deeply because I felt this was something that John would've liked. When John came up as a little kid, I had him a baseball uniform made up — the Yankees' road uniform. Gray, with "New York" on the front and number seven on the back. The day John was born, in the paper they had listed his birth and right underneath of it, it had "Mickey Mantle hits two home runs in spring training." The 22nd of March, 1956. He kept that quite some time.

If you could go back to 1949, would you be a professional athlete again?

Yes. I would've still gone into pro sports.

Although things were tough and there was a lot of discrimination, I still think it gave me an opportunity to see the world. It gave me an education. When I came back to teaching history, I think that my travels did more for me than the books I studied out of.

The people I had a chance to meet in college are a good example of being an athlete. The popularity came. At Anderson College, when I got there in the fall of '46, probably 60 percent of the students were white Southern students and members of the Church of God. These people turned out to be my best friends.

When I'd traveled with the Trotters and gone to places like Alabama and Georgia and West Virginia, Virginia — these guys and young ladies would come out to the ballgame. At that time, the games would be segregated as far as the crowds were concerned, but that didn't matter to them. Like in Birmingham, we were playing and there was about 8,000 people there and this fellow and his wife came down and both of them embraced me right there in front of the crowd.

These people lived the life that they were preaching. It gave me a chance to see that no matter where people were from, it was individual and not the location.

We went to Dallas, Texas, and a buddy of mine I played baseball with in college — Tex Litton — came and got me and took me to Sunset High School. At that time, there was no integration and he took me through all the school and introduced me to all the teachers. Then afterward he had to go to a meeting and his wife and I went to a supermarket. Just watching her, you'd never know that I was black and she was white.

What athletics did for me was it gave me a chance to see people for what they really were and not for what you read about or hear about different sections of the country. It really helped me to become a better person in life.

I don't understand the attitude of some athletes. Like today, the coach wasn't feeling well and I subbed for him — taught his classes — and three kids asked me for autographs. The saddest day of my life will come when no one remembers. [Laughs] But players today won't take the time.

I'm always willing to give out information because some little kid may read it and say, "Hey, I can do that!" and get him off the street or keep him from going to prison or whatever. If it's just one person, it's worth it.

BATTING RECORD

Year	Team, League	Pos	G	AB	R	H	2B	3B	HR	RBI	SB	BA
1949	Chicago, NAL	of							3			.312

Johnny Wilson also played basketball with the Harlem Globetrotters from 1950 through 1955.

Clifford Brown
"Quack"

BORN DECEMBER 9, 1930, TAMPA FL
HT. 6' WT. 175 BATTED LEFT, THREW RIGHT

Negro Leagues debut: 1950

Rarely does a man who played in the Negro leagues have regrets. That in itself is remarkable when one considers what these players went through in the face of old Jim Crow himself.

Several of the later players, however, have a regret: they stopped playing too soon. Those who played in the decade of the '50s could have been — and were — signed by teams in white baseball, but the conditions there for a black man many times were worse than they were with Negro teams.

A white minor league team in that day may have had one or, at best, two black players. These fellows had to wait outside restaurants while white teammates brought them sandwiches. They had to stay at hotels or boardinghouses completely across town from where their white teammates stayed. They were often shunned or ignored by their fellow players. At least in the Negro leagues, the whole team ate and slept in one place and there was companionship.

Clifford "Quack" Brown's regret is that he left baseball too soon. He was signed by the St. Louis Cardinals and told to report to a small town in a class-D league in Mississippi. Imagine how it would be for a young black man playing on a white team in a small Mississippi town in the early 1950s. He chose to retire then, only 22, but even at that age, he had already played three years in the Negro leagues. And he says he would do it again.

First, how did you get the nickname "Quack"?

[Laughs] Everywhere we go, people want to know. When we were little kids, we used to play stickball in the street and we hit the ball in a lady's yard. They had ducks. I jumped the fence and I fell over and all the ducks hollered, "Quack! Quack!" All the guys begin to call me that. Everywhere we go, that's the first thing everybody want to know.

How did you get started playing baseball?

I started in Tampa, Florida. We had a team here called the Pepsi-Cola Giants and the Pepsi-Cola Juniors. Semipro teams. I was real young; I guess I was about 14 or 15 years old. We had guys grown, 30 and 40 years old. We played teams that come down, like the Negro league teams.

I left from the Pepsi-Cola Giants and I went to Richmond Giants in about '47, '48 — something like that. That was a Negro team in the [Negro] Southern League. When I left there, I came back home and went with the Philly Stars. Oscar Charleston was the manager. That had to be around '50. I was with the Stars a couple years.

My teammates was Carl Dent, Wilmer Harris, Adam Young, Billy Felder, [Robert] Schoolboy Griffith, a pitcher, and Ben Littles.

I think my batting average was around

.280, but I mostly was a good glove man. Oscar Charleston told me, "Boy, you can pick up the earth and throw out reindeer!"

Mays and I, we ended up playing against each other. He was in the service when I was in the Army. I played against his Army team and I played against him when he was with Birmingham.

After Philadelphia, I came back and I went with the St. Louis Cardinals Triple-A team. It trained down here in Florida. After that, they wanted to send me to some little small league — a D league, I think it was — in Mississippi, me and another fella. We refused to go because we figured that we should be playing with the Triple-A team. This was about '51 or maybe '52. Harry "The Hat" Walker — you remember him? — was the manager then.

After that, I came back home and after I come back home, I just played ball right around here, got married, and got a good job and that was it. I was real young when I retired.

Was there a special game along the way?

With Philadelphia, I remember we played three games one day in Virginia — different towns in Virginia — and I was lucky enough to hit a home run in each one of those towns that day. That was my first home runs. [Laughs] I played three games that day; I never will forget it. We played against local teams and we won all three.

You were a very good fielder. Does a game stand out from the standpoint of your fielding?

Yes. When we played Willie Mays in Birmingham, we was leading 'em and he came up in the ninth inning with one out and one on. He hit one 'cross second base and everybody thought it was a base hit to tie the game up. I went across second, picked it up, touched the base, and then I threwed him out by 'bout a step. That ended the ballgame. I always remember that. We beat 'em, 8–7.

I seen him a couple times after he was in the majors and I actually told him 'bout that and he remembered.

We was in the Army and Mays was com-

Clifford "Quack" Brown (courtesy of Clifford Brown).

ing around in the chow line to eat and I told a guy from Palmetto, Florida — he didn't know who Mays was — I said, "See that fella right there? When he gets through, tell him to pick that tray up and empty it like everybody. He ain't playing no ball now."

The guy went and did it and what happened, Mays had a sergeant, something like a bodyguard, and when he went up there and told Mays, that man jumped all down him. [Laughs] Ol' Mays was laughing.

I was stationed in Fort Jackson, South Carolina, and he was in Virginia, I believe. We used to call him "Buck," you know.

In your playing days, people say there were no good players left in the Negro league, but there were still guys there like Mays and Aaron and Banks. Who was the best player you saw?

The best player I saw was a guy named J. B. Broome, and the best infielder was Willie Wells. Oh, I played with the Black Yankees for a half a season, too; I forgot to mention that. That was before Philadelphia. That's when I played with Wells. Oh, man, he could pick it!

"Just in time." He'd throw the ball and he'd holler, "Just in time!" The guy'd be running down to first and he'd flip it over there just in time. [Laughs]

Clifford "Quack" Brown (courtesy of Clifford Brown).

I'm not familiar with Broome.

No, you won't know that name. He played 'round here in Tampa with us, and when all the teams come down — I mean, *all* of 'em tried to get him to go with 'em. He decided to go up there with the Black Yankees. He went up there and stayed a half-year and the time he was there, he was leading the league in hitting. He was *good!*

After that, you know, he came back home and he ended up killing him and his wife. He had a brother used to pitch for the Jacksonville Red Caps; they were in the Negro leagues long ago. I guess J.B. was about in his 30s. We were fixing to go play baseball that day in Bradenton. That was Sunday and they said J.B. had killed hisself.

Who was the best pitcher you saw and who was the toughest on you?

The best pitcher that I batted against was Toothpick Jones. You remember him? What happened, he was stationed in the Army down in Florida and he used to pitch in the Florida State League where we was at. He pitched for a team out of Orlando and we used to play against them. Sam Jones. Oh, he was tough!

And I played against a guy in the Army named Carlton Willey. He ended up playing with Milwaukee [Braves]. He was tough, too, but we always beat him in the Army. We had a good team in the Army.

What was your best salary?

Salary was 280 a month. I think we was getting three dollars a day to eat.

The conditions were changing when you played.

You know how we traveled — by bus. We played two or three games a lot of days. Some of the fields were in bad shape, but we played on some of the major league fields. We played on some good fields, but some of 'em wasn't. It was pretty rough, but if I had to do it again, I think I would because I had a lot of fun. I didn't make much money, but it was fun.

Your career was short, but you obviously enjoyed it. Do you have any regrets?

Yeah, I guess a regret was when I left and didn't go back. That's the only thing.

Other than that, it wasn't too bad on me. I was real young, but I had guys from Tampa who was on this team — about five guys from Tampa — and that's why it wasn't too bad on me, see. We played together in Tampa and we went up there.

I was too young to see some of the greatest ballplayers there was, like Josh. I seen Satch, but he was way up in age. I wish I had seen Josh 'cause I heard so many good things about him.

BATTING RECORD

Year	Team, League	Pos	G	AB	R	H	2B	3B	HR	RBI	SB	BA
1950	N.Y. Blk. Yanks, ind.											
	Philadelphia, NAL	inf										.280
1951		inf								4		.270
1952		inf										

Granville "Granny" Gladstone
"Panamanian Import"

BORN JANUARY 26, 1925, PANAMA
HT. 5'11" WT. 170 BATTED AND THREW RIGHT

Negro Leagues debut: 1950

One of the most vivid memories of my youth is listening to the public address announcer for the Oakland Oaks in the early '50s when the Portland Beavers were in town. One of my favorite players played for Portland and whenever he came up, everyone in the old Emeryville ballpark knew it because the announcer would say, much louder than normal, "Now batting for Portland, the center fielder, Grrrrrranville GlllllllaaaAAADDD-STONE!" I loved it.

I was just a kid and I knew very little about Granville Gladstone except that I liked his name and I liked his hustle. He was 5'11" tall, but he looked smaller down there on the field as he ran down fly balls or tried for an extra base.

Especially impressive was his fly-chasing. Playing right field for Portland was Joe Brovia, a marvelous hitter and one of the nicest guys who ever lived, but he had the feet and glove of a designated hitter, so Gladstone had to play not only center field but most of right field as well. I recall once when Oaks first baseman Jim Marshall (I think) hit a long fly almost to the fence in straightaway right field and Gladstone came over from his center field position to make the catch. (In fairness to Brovia, Marshall was being played to pull the ball, and Brovia was way around toward the line.)

I also knew that Gladstone had played in the Negro leagues, but I didn't know with whom or when. Later I learned it was with the Indianapolis Clowns in 1950, when he led the Negro American League in triples with 13 (in only 64 games).

Gladstone spent six of his ten years in white baseball at the Triple-A level. Today he would be in the major leagues.

Why did you come here from Panama?

I came to play ball. First, I played in the colored league for the Indianapolis Clowns under Syd Pollack, that owned the team. I played one year and while I was playing, a lot of major league clubs was interested in me, and I got to find out that when I went back to Panama. While I was playing winter ball in Panama, Syd Pollack sent me a contract in December for me to return and play for him. He got to find out that many teams was interested in me; however, he got to find out that I was going to Portland Beavers through

Frankie Austin. Portland asked me to sign a contract and I told them no, and then I came to play ball with the Portland Beavers through Frankie Austin. He was playing with the Beavers and he recommended me, and I decided about going that way.

I got a lot of offers to go to Canada to play. I turned it down and I had offers to play with the St. Louis Cardinals organization. I didn't go; that's when I went to Portland.

How did you come to join the Clowns?

A guy named Buster Haywood, he came

Granville Gladstone with Portland (PCL) (Doug McWilliams photograph).

to Panama to play. Buster Haywood, he was the manager of the Indianapolis Clowns and he recommended me to Syd Pollack. On that team [in Panama] we had Sam Jones, too. Haywood seen me play in Panama and asked if I cared to go. I said, "It's up to you. I'll go."

Who were some of your teammates in Indianapolis?

A guy named Verdes Drake; he was a Cuban. Buster Haywood, he was the catcher. Ray Neil played second base; [Jim] Britton played third base. The outfield was a guy named [Henry] Merchant, Drake, myself. When I leave, a new guy came — [Hank] Aaron. He came after I leave. A guy got killed in a plane going to Venezuela, he was supposed to go to the Cardinals — Charles Peete. He was a good ballplayer; he could hit the ball a long ways. He used to play outfield, too.

How was your year at Indianapolis?

It was good. I played good ball and a lot of people was after me and looked at me. The major leagues at that time was looking for colored ballplayers and I was told that they were

interested in me. San Hairston went to the White Sox, was a catcher, and they was interested in me.

Mays was the same year as me. Willie Mays was playing with the Birmingham Black Barons and I was playing with the Indianapolis Clowns and we started at the same time. I had a good year there.

I was with Portland in 1951. I been with them up and down — I played one year with them and then I'd leave and they sent me to Victoria [Western International League] the following year. I played there at Victoria and I was called back up to Portland. I was up and down.

Eventually you became the property of the Brooklyn Dodgers. Did they buy your contract?

They didn't buy my contract. I signed with the Brooklyn Dodgers through Jim Russell. You remember when Jim Russell was playing at Portland? While I was at Portland, Jim Russell was playing with me, so Jim recommended me to the Dodgers organization. He got in touch with me and told me about it, so I told him okay, I'd do it. I had to leave Portland then. I went to St. Paul.

You were fast, but Portland never stole a lot of bases. Why?

They don't play to run or nothing like that. The manager was Sweeney. Bill Sweeney. He tell me that I got the job in spring training. He saw me play and saw what I did in spring training and how fast I was, so he said, "You're my center fielder."

The following year they had Clay Hopper; he just came from Montreal or one of those clubs. At that time, Jim Russell was there, also. He was some kind of manager, I don't know. He wasn't a good manager. He just played what he liked and knows. He didn't get the best for his ballplayers.

During the off-seasons, did you remain here or go back to Panama?

I remained here. I go back to Panama and played, but I played in Venezuela in winter ball.

I played up to when the Mets came into

the league [1962]. Buzzy Bavasi recommended me to them, said get in touch with them.

They were looking for me while I was here in New York. They sent a contract to San Francisco, where my wife was, and she didn't send it to me 'cause she was mad at me. She didn't want me to play no more ball, thought I was gettin' hurt. I got in touch with Buzzy to find out what happened, and Buzzy told me that he was looking for me all over. I tell him I was here in New York and he told me to get in touch with George Weiss. Weiss was the general manager for the Mets when the Mets started to play.

He told me I must pay my way to spring training to make the club. I said, "For what?" I didn't get back to him at all. I decided to give it up then. I was 35, 37.

Who was the best player you saw?

There was a lot of good players I've seen. I can't just name one because they was a lot of pretty good players. We had a lot of good players in the Coast League. They wanted to make it the third major league, but it didn't go through.

Joe Brovia was there with me. He was a hell of a ballplayer. He always tell me, he said, "Get on. I'll hit you in." He used to bat fourth and I'd bat third. Sometimes I bat fourth and he'd bat fifth. We had a good lineup.

Artie Wilson was there. Second base. We had [Eddie] Basinski; he played third base. Austin played shortstop. Joe Lafata was our first baseman. We had two first base guys — Joe Lafata and another guy.

This guy Jim Rivera used to play center field for Seattle. He belonged to the White Sox. The guy who was the manager was Rogers Hornsby. They had good ballplayers. We had a good league.

Who was the best pitcher you batted against?

The hardest throwing pitcher I met was Sam Jones. He used to play for the Cleveland Buckeyes, then he played in Panama with me — the same club, Spur Cola. He was a nice guy; he was my good friend. The times I went to hit against him, he'd look at me and laugh and say, "Hey, you ain't gettin' no fastballs so just forget about it."

I hit against Paige. Satchel Paige. He was old, but he could still bring it. We played against the [St. Louis] Browns in spring training and he was there. They had a pitcher who used to throw hard; he went to the Yankees. Bob Turley.

We played in Pasadena against the Browns and I hit a ball a long way. Bases loaded, everybody tagged up, and the guy scored from second base. I don't forget that.

Vic Wertz, he hit a line drive off the fence and it bounced back to the shortstop. I mean, the ball was traveling. That ball went by me and hit the fence and went by me and went back to the shortstop and he fielded the ball.

We played against the major league clubs. We played against the Chicago Cubs, we played against the St. Louis Browns, the Indians.

Is there a game that stands out?

There's a lot of things we did. I remember one thing that we did. I was playing against Seattle and this guy was with the Yankees, Tommy Byrne — you remember him? I came up and I hit a home run off him in the first inning. Next time I come back up, Jim Russell was at second base and another guy was on first and Clay Hopper gave me a bunt sign and we was ahead in the game. I bunt a perfect bunt down the third base line and Jim Russell, he was surprised; he didn't move.

I saw Tom Byrne again in Seattle and he said, "What kind of manager you all got? You're always hittin' the ball good and you just hit a home run and this man has you bunt."

I said, "Well, he's the manager. What can I do?"

I remember, I was slumping. A lot of clubs was after me — major league clubs — and we played a series in San Francisco, played a lot of doubleheaders. Maybe eight games or six games in San Francisco and he had me on the bench. Everybody wanted to know what's wrong with me. I said, "Ask the manager." That's when Jim Russell told me, "I can get you out of here." That's when I went to the Dodgers.

In that series, all he did was brought me

in to pinch hit twice. He put me in to pinch hit and I hit a ball over the center field wall. Only three guys hit the ball that far. A guy said, "That's a long way to hit the ball." I said, "Well, the wind was blowing out."

If you were a young man today, would you be a ballplayer?

With what these guys are getting? [Laughs] I say, the kind of money they get, yes.

It must be frustrating when you think there are players in the major leagues today who couldn't have carried your glove.

It is. I look at guys sitting on the bench and getting that kind of money — that big money. I couldn't sit on the bench. I wouldn't like to sit on the bench 'cause I come to play. I love to play to win.

A guy tells me the other day, says, "Didn't you play ball?" I said, "Yeah." "What do you think of all these guys makin' that kind of money and they couldn't carry your shoes?" What can I tell you? They're lucky.

The ballgames that I've seen played today, they're always squawking. We never looked at an umpire. When you go up to hit, you're going to hit. You ain't going to look at an umpire.

And another thing, these umpires got some *wide* strike zones. That's ruining the game right now.

Speaking of umpires, do you remember Emmett Ashford?

Yeah. He was good. They had good umpires in the Coast League. [Chris] Pelekoudas, all of them.

BATTING RECORD

Year	Team, League	Pos	G	AB	R	H	2B	3B	HR	RBI	SB	BA
1950	Indianapolis, NAL	of	64	192	40	46	6	*13	4	23	9	.240
1951	Portland, PCL	of	90	161	31	37	6	1	1	14	2	.230
1952	Portland, PCL	of	10	42	10	11	2	1	3	8	0	.262
	Victoria, WIntL	of	143	550	81	162	40	6	15	126	19	.295
1953	Portland, PCL	of	69	244	21	60	9	1	5	33		.246
	Victoria, WIntL	of	85	310	72	108	23	2	19	93	5	.348
1954	Portland, PCL	of	123	392	47	86	11	4	10	54	3	.219
1955	Eugene, NWL	of	98	352	76	106	22	6	11	88	12	.301
1956	St. Paul, AA	of	130	393	71	109	22	2	12	59	5	.277
1957		of	83	254	34	64	15	3	3	32	3	.252
1958	Amarillo, TxL	of	3	5	0	0	0	0	0	0	0	.000
1953–54	PanL	of		117		36			4	27		.308
1958–59	Azucareros, PanL	of		136		37			1	24		.272

* Led league

PART THREE

The 1950s and the 1960s

The NAL continued to play, but the schedules were loose and the play was of a lower level than in earlier times. Some have said the play was "inferior," but it was not unlike expansion. There were more opportunities for black players, even though many of the white teams were still reluctant to sign them, but to make up for those who did go into white ball, the black teams signed players who may well not have been signed ten or twenty years earlier.

But "inferior" is hardly a label for baseball that produced players such as Henry Aaron, Ernie Banks, Connie Johnson, Elston Howard, and many others, all of whom played in the NAL in its waning days.

Those days were numbered, however, as fan support diminished. The Negro leagues' fans were watching their favorites in the major leagues now and television enabled them to do it without even leaving home. A few teams kept barnstorming into the '60s, but by 1961 or '62, true black baseball had gasped its last.

Gordon "Hoppy" Hopkins
"Bunny's Boy"

BORN JUNE 30, 1934, OLNEY, MD
HT. 5'9" WT. 165 BATTED SWITCH, THREW RIGHT

Negro Leagues debut: 1952

While still in high school in 1952, Gordon Hopkins was introduced to McKinley "Bunny" Downs by a family friend. Downs at that time was the business manager of the Indianapolis Clowns and Hopkins was a very good high school first baseman, and it proved to be a fortuitous meeting for both man and boy.

Downs had been associated with black baseball as a player, manager, and executive off and on for nearly four decades at that point and had been a top-notch second baseman in his playing days. In the young Hopkins, he saw a second baseman rather than a first baseman, and the conversion was made successfully.

Hopkins played a solid second base for the Clowns through the 1954 season and was preparing for winter ball in Puerto Rico when military duty called. He served in the Marine Corps through 1958 and was an All-Star second baseman on service teams, but his professional career was over. As short as it was, it's something he would do over again the same way.

I was born in Montgomery County, a place called Olney, Maryland, and I was reared in Montgomery County. I went to elementary school in a place called Norbeck and a lot of my relatives are from the Norbeck, Sandy Spring, and Olney area. I started high school in Rockville. I played baseball when I was 14; I made the varsity team at Lincoln High School.

I wasn't on the regular team, but I had a pinch hitting role and I came through every time I was put in. I did play one night in that league in 1950 in May, during the spring season. That was the ballpark in a place called Emory Grove, Maryland, where the old Elite Giants used to play and the Raleigh Tigers and teams of that caliber. There were traveling teams, also, that played in that ballpark. The Frederick Hustlers was a white team out of Frederick County.

What really got me started playing baseball, I really got fascinated by baseball when I was a little boy about five years old. I had an uncle named Everett Holland who was a very avid baseball player and fan and he loved baseball and he was very good. I used to watch him in the yard and he had a pair of spikes and a glove and what he used to do, he used to run around the house with these cleats on and he would have dirt flying up in the air. I got so excited I said, "Wow! That's exactly what I want to do. I want to be a baseball player."

And I had that set in my mind from day one, and I never let it go until I got into the pro baseball ranks. I really had my mind set as to what I wanted to do at a very early age. I loved it; I ate and slept baseball. When I would go to practice, sometimes I'd take a lunch. [Laughs]

I played a lot in the sandlot areas around the Washington, D.C., area and Montgomery County. We used to play a lot of little teams coming in from different places and we had a lot of boys. It seems like a lot of the kids my age didn't have the interest to play ball. I tried to make everybody a ballplayer. I don't know why, but some of them didn't have the coordination. I was a young fella trying to make other boys interested in the game. We were in a rural area and the kids lived so far apart and it was hard to really try to get a team together to try to play ball.

We finally got a little team together and we played, and as I got older I couldn't see myself making any progress, so I had to go to a better team. I started playing on sandlot and semipro teams around here in the Washington area, and I played with one semipro team called the Ivy City Giants out of Washington, D.C. I was playing first base and we played quite a few good caliber teams around this area.

Then in 1950—the early part of '50—I went on to New York and I enrolled in high school in New York City and I got on the baseball team there. I played first base and didn't have much problem there. I was given a lot of opportunity to play sandlot ball around there, and semipro ball. We played a lot of teams out of Jersey and we played some teams on the road. I hooked up with the House of David several times during the summer months, and then sometimes we played on the road.

Gordon Hopkins (courtesy of Gordon Hopkins).

I later hooked up with Bunny Downs. A friend of mine from the D.C. area was up visiting his uncle, which was Bunny Downs. His name was Cliff Meade. Bunny Downs was the business manager of the Indianapolis Clowns at that time. Cliff Meade came by our house to see us 'cause he knew my mother from when I was real little. He came by to holler at us and he saw my trophies and my baseball and all these letters on the wall in the house and he said, "Wow, Gordon, I didn't know you played baseball." I said, "Oh, yeah, I play baseball."

He said, "My uncle is the business manager of the Indianapolis Clowns. I think you ought to give him a call. Maybe he can do something about you."

So I took his number and I decided to call him. When I finally called him, I was playing with the George Washington High School team and that summer he sent a guy out there to look at me. We were playing a team from the Bronx called Gompers High; it was like a Catholic school. I had a good day that day and he went back and gave a report to Bunny Downs. He told him, "He can play."

Next thing I knew, Bunny had signed me. This was '52. He sent me out to different places. He said, "The club is real crowded right now and I got to find somewhere to put you 'cause I don't want to lose you." So he did; he hooked me up with the House of David and teams like that. We played on the road different places.

There was other places he could've sent me, too. There was a team in Canada, but Canada always started late. Up in Brandon they never started 'til way up in May. It was almost June before they even got started up there.

I went with the House of David and we trained down in Norfolk at the same field that the Clowns trained in. We had quite a bit of experience with them, and I learned a lot playing with them. But it was really rugged. We didn't have the same kind of facilities that we had with the Clowns. The team was really just like a minor league to the Clowns. [Laughs]

Finally I got hooked up with the Clowns and I was really happy about that. I didn't care how I made it. I was mostly used as a utility infielder, but second base was my bag. I really liked my second base.

When I really got my real shot was in '53. The Clowns put a team together — a second team which was like the "B" team — to play in the post-season All-Star barnstorming tour. We had fellas like Jimmy Robinson. It seemed like everybody played a different position. Jimmy Robinson was a shortstop and they put him on third base. We had Bill Holder playing shortstop. They put me on second, I had never played second before but I had learned how to play it, but I had played some third base a long time ago. Junior Hamilton was about 16; they put him on catching. He was very good, but he lacked a lot of experience, but he could catch and he could hit pretty good.

The oldest fella on the ballclub at that time a boy named John Parker out of Rock Hill, South Carolina. He was a lefthanded glove man, but he batted righthanded, and he was a real powerful long ball hitter. He was one of the assets we had on our ballclub. We had another fella named Rufus McNeal; he was a part-time outfielder when he wasn't pitching.

And we had Jim Tugerson, who had some controversy with the Hot Springs team down there in Hot Springs, Arkansas, in the early '50s. There was a big controversy and it was all over the papers all over the nation at the time and he wasn't allowed to play down there. He played with us as a pitcher and he played the outfield when he wasn't pitching.

We played the Clowns all through the South and Southwest and the North and everything. We really had a good team put together, but we lacked teamwork — getting synchronized — and when the team got synchronized the team we had was really something else. I never will forget the teamwork we had; we had really a dynamite team put together out of a bunch of young fellas their first time together.

There were several nights we played that we had three-hit nights. Me and Jimmy Robinson and Rufus McNeal. Rufus McNeal

really hit the long ball, and Parker could hit the long ball, so we really had a powerhouse.

I batted third 'cause I was very fast. I used to run the hundred in about 9.8, and I guess that's good for a number three hitter. I was a good stick man. I didn't hit the long ball, but I could hit the doubles and singles and triples. That's one of the reasons [Frank] Carswell, our manager, was gonna put me in the three spot.

Our manager was Carswell and the Clowns' manager was Buster Haywood, but we were all under the Clown regime. This was like the second team — like the rookies — and they figured they weren't going to do much and we would make them look good. [Laughs] Before that tour was over — about halfway in that tour — we were kicking butt so great that it was unreal.

One night I was with Bunny. After each game, he makes his report on the gate receipts and his commentary on the game and the scores of the game. He called Syd Pollack in New York and he relayed it to him. Syd asked him, "What was the score tonight?" I think we just finished playing a game in Chattanooga.

Bunny said, "It was 14–8."

"Them Clowns are really hitting that ball, ain't they?"

"It was 14–8, All-Stars."

He said, "What!?" [Laughs] "What the hell's going on down there?"

Bunny said, "Them boys can play ball." [Laughs]

A lot of those boys really got a lot of exposure from that and the fans were going crazy. I mean, it really was fantastic.

Carswell was a good manager. I liked him. He was one of the Clowns' old pitchers and he was taking care of managerial things for the All-Stars. He was a wonderful manager; he wasn't too hard on the guys. He gave us a lot of flexibility, but he just wanted to see what everybody could do.

I don't know exactly how many games we won, but we won quite a number of games out of that tour. The Clowns, they still won more games than we did, but we let 'em know that we were out there. I batted .400 and

Jimmy Robinson and Rufus McNeal, every time I was on base, they were on base, too, so they must've batted close to .400, too.

Rufus McNeal, one game he hit two home runs. He just could hit the long ball; he was powerful. And when he pitched, he throwed the ball hard, too. His pitching arm was not as accurate as his throwing arm from the outfield. [Laughs] He wasn't really that tuned-in with the pitching thing, but he could throw hard and he could get the job done. He would keep the guys on their toes. He was a very good ballplayer, and he was from A.&T. College out of North Carolina; [North Carolina] A. & T. University they call it now. And Jimmy Robinson was from A. & T. They graduated I think the same year.

And Erwin Ford was with us; he graduated from A. & T. Erwin Lee Ford. He was a center fielder. Now that rascal could fly! He run past me; I mean, he was one of the speed demons. He'd do the hundred in about 9.4. He was something else. He used to run like slew-footed. He had broken his leg in the early '50s and then he came back, and when he came back, he still could fly.

I've never seen a guy run so fast looking back over his shoulder in my life, and he ran slew-footed like a duck. [Laughs] That guy could fly, man! He'd run rings around me, and I knew I could move. That guy could really move. They talk about Cool Papa, but I'm going to tell you something: I've had fans come up to me, like in recent years, and say, "You played for the Clowns? I know a fella named Ford. Man, that guy could fly!" I say, "Yeah, I know Ford. And he *could* fly!" [Laughs]

And he could hit that ball, too. When he'd be swinging, he'd be moving around in that box. Oscar Charleston was our manager with the Clowns and he'd say, "Ford, be still in that box! Every time you get ready to hit the ball, you're moving your feet. You'll never hit nothing like that." Finally, he said, "Just keep your feet still and just swing. Don't worry about nothing else; just stand still and swing the bat."

Next thing I know, Ford went on a home run–hitting streak. [Laughs] We played in a game in Buffalo one Sunday. The Buffalo stadium — Offerman Stadium, where the Buffalo Bisons played — it had a real high fence — it must've been about 30 feet — in left field, and this Sunday a strong wind was blowing in and Ford hit one out of there. [Laughs] He hit it over a sign — a clothing sign or something — and I had to go with him to pick up his clothes that the merchants give away to whoever hits the ball over the sign.

He learned a lot from Oscar Charleston. Oscar Charleston taught you something if you played with him. He didn't let you constantly be making mistakes. He'd stop you and say, "Look. You're doing this all wrong. Stop this. Do it this way." Then he'd say, "I don't care what you're doing wrong. This is the way you do it."

He helped me with my batting. I used to be a switch hitter when I started with the Clowns; I was a switch hitter all through high school and when I first started out in pro ball, and even when I went in the military I was switch hitting. I put all this together when I was with Oscar Charleston. He told me, "You're going to have to open up there a little bit, open up that stance, and let him bring that thing on in there, and bend that back leg a little bit, get some power."

One time we were playing Kansas City one night. This lefty — he wore the cap on the side of his head — he threw one in there. I hit one of the hardest balls I've ever hit in my life, but it was right at the guy and he hauled it in. I felt so good, though. It was something that he told me that came in view and it happened. What he told me, I made it work and I give him a lot of credit for that, you know.

Then, too, there's a lot of other things going along with hitting. He didn't have the time to tell you all the elements and everything at the time you're going up to bat, so sometimes he'd tell you some of the most important things and then you're able to put it in play right away.

Then after I left the Clowns, I went in the military and I played against Johnny Podres. I run into him in the locker room one day and I asked him, I said, "Johnny Podres, look here. How the hell does a guy hit you?" [Laughs] He was lefthanded.

First thing he told me was, "Hop, the first thing is that you know, if you're batting lefty and he's a lefty, three-quarters of the time he's going to throw you that big curveball and it's going to back you away from the plate. You know you're going to get that one; you're just going to have to wait a little longer. Wait a little longer for that pitch."

I put all this together with Oscar Charleston and Johnny Podres and after I talked to him, I didn't switch anymore. It took me two years to really get it hooked up right, to really make it a part of me. You could take this point here and that little point, also, from this angle, but still, you've got to make it a part of you. Then when you're able to do that, and execute, I didn't care who was pitching after that. I would take care of business. I was a terror when that guy was coming inside with that stuff. He was in a world of trouble. I didn't care who he was.

I did play a little ball in Puerto Rico while I was in the military. A guy that played in the Puerto Rican League came over there and played against us one Sunday. I come up to bat and I was watching him warm up. I started off the inning and I watched him warm up. Man, he was throwing balls so hard and so close to the ground, I said, "Good God! This guy's been down there somewhere." He's a lefty, too, now. Man, he was throwing that ball so hard, the ball was coming around my knees. I'm just trying to time him while he's taking his warmups. I said, "This is my chance to find out what I can do with these lefty pitchers."

This guy threw me some balls and I swear I fouled everything that he threw in there 'til finally he come in there again and I hit this ball to the sugarcane field. [Laughs] And then they were afraid of me. They started walking me every time I came up there after that. I mean, I lost that ball, man; I hit that thing *out* of there. That ball was gone. I wasn't a powerful hitter, but if he'd throw it inside they could forget it. I would knock the first baseman

or the second baseman down because I was hitting with a lot more power when I was in the Marine Corps. I was about 22 years old, going on 23.

But when I was 18 — young — I was taught by Bunny Downs to hit it where they ain't. He told me, "Always hit it where they ain't," and I kept a better batting average when I was doing that. I owe that to Bunny. You were more of a threat when you could hit the ball and you were more reliable up at the plate when you hit the ball where it's pitched.

Sometimes what I used to do in the later part of my playing career, I'd start off by hitting it where they ain't — try to get a hit the first or second time up — and then I can go for the long ball. [Laughs] Then I spread my wings a little bit. If I got me one hit, I'd say, "Well, shucks, I can go for the long one here."

A lot of guys never did a lot of bunting, so I also had a drag bunt that I used a lot. I used the drag bunt a lot when I was playing with the Clowns in the Negro league. I used the drag bunt and I had a lot of speed.

But first, I had a problem with my sliding when I first got in the Negro league. I used to run so fast and I'd be halfway running over the guys on the base before me, so Bunny told [Dewitt] Smallwood one night, he says, "Man, that Hop is so fast he's running over everybody. We gonna have to throw a lasso on him to give him some brakes 'cause he's gonna kill himself. He's gonna break his ankles or something."

So he told Smallwood to take me out there and teach me how to slide to save me. Smallwood did just that — took me out there one time before a game, about three or four hours before the game, and had me working in the sliding pit and taught me how to do that fallaway slide. After I got that down, boy, I was terrible on the bases after that. [Laughs] There was no stopping me after that. I was really tickled pink then. I said, "Oh, man, I'm on my way now!"

It was hard when I was playing and I couldn't slide. I got on base all the time; I was always on the bases. A lot of the times, some of the teams that you'd play were not that kind to you when you come down there. They wouldn't tell you to hold up; they'd let you go on and slide anyway. They wouldn't tell you there was no play or the ball wasn't coming or something like that. Everybody wasn't like that, but some guys were like that.

We were playing a game one night on the barnstorming tour in '53. We were playing in Chattanooga in Lookout Stadium down there. No, they called it Joe Engel Stadium. That was the Washington Senators' farm club. The bases got drunk and I hit a triple. They had a thing like a manicured area in center field where "Lookouts" was manicured in the grass up by the left–center field wall and I hit one right up in there. That ball was bouncing around and by the time they got it, all them guys had scored and I could've almost scored if the guy in front of me wasn't so slow. Junior Hamilton was the catcher and he was in front of me and he was so slow! I kept hollering at him while I'm running around the bases, "Junior, move up! Move up!" and he was running fast as he could, but he was carrying a lot of baggage. [Laughs]

Jimmy Robinson came up behind me and drove me in. We had a great big inning there; we had a lot of runs that inning.

When I got back in the dugout, somebody called out and said, "Where's that number eight? Where's number eight?" and so, finally, Carswell, my manager, told me, he said, "Hop, go out there. The people want you." So I went outside the dugout and the guy called me over there and said, "Congratulations! That was a nice hit you hit there, number eight. What's your name?" And I told him what my name was and the guy gave me ten dollars. Man, that was the biggest thrill I ever got. [Laughs] I thought the world of that. I felt like I was appreciated out there. That was a big thrill, plus I was broke at the same time. [Laughs] He was a mind reader.

My after-baseball thing was very interesting. After I got out of baseball, I did do a little coaching and played a little sandlot ball and played with quite a few of the major league ballplayers, too.

But when I played in the military, I

played against so many major league ballplayers. I felt like I was at my high point because we played against Vinegar Bend Mizell of the Cardinals, Taylor Phillips — he played with the Braves — and then Billy O'Dell was playing with 'em. Billy O'Dell with Baltimore. Then you had a boy named Quackenbush, who was with the Cubs, and Frank Bolling of the Tigers. He hit one out the day we first played 'em. And Al Spangler, Norm Siebern. They had a hell of a team.

We played like a three-game series, and we'd usually get one out of it. We also played Eddie Lopat's boys down there, the Richmond Colts [International League]. I think it was the Colts at that time. We played like a three-game series with Richmond and we got one of them, too.

In '56 in Camp Lejeune, we had a hell of a team down there. We won the All-Marine championship that year. We won the Fleet Marine championship, also. That was '55. In '56, I did get voted for All-Navy All-Star shortstop in the Fleet tournament. I played short in 1956, but I did play mostly second. We had a shortstop at the time and he was short-legging so many balls, that's why the man put me in there. He'd be going after the ball and he'd be doing like a mark-time and then reach out after the ball instead of getting on over there and getting the ball. Sometimes that ball'd be hit too hard and he didn't want to have it.

Then I went to Parris Island and played. I played two years at Camp Lejeune and one year at Parris Island. We run into a lot of guys like Eli Grba — they was at Fort McPherson in Atlanta, Georgia — and Marv Breeding out of Baltimore and Jim Owens of the Phillies. Man, they had one hell of a team that year.

We had one boy was pitching for us and he had 'em going for about three innings. He had 'em shutout for about three innings and them boys was sizing him up. Next thing I know, the roof fell in. [Laughs] It reminds me of the big pros like DiMaggio and Williams. You might get 'em the first two or three times at bat, but, buddy, believe me. They're analyzing your case and by the time their third or fourth time comes up, they're going to put something on you.

And that's exactly what these boys did. Man, them bats swole up! [Laughs] I felt so sorry for my man. I tried to keep going out there talking to him and they had to take him out of there. *All* them bats got fat. We were playing 'em down at their field down at Fort Mack. Boy, they really had a heck of a team down there.

They had boys playing like A-ball in that camp that couldn't even get on the team. That's how good they were. They had guys that played A-ball and Double-A, couldn't even get on the ballclub 'cause they had so much talent on it. Every year we played 'em, they had so much talent — '55, '56, and '58.

But they weren't that great as fielders, though. They just wanted to come to bat. [Laughs] Some of 'em could knock four or five runs in and let three in.

That was a great experience for me, just to play with those guys. You know what it did? It made you play better. Playing with all those pro guys that had been up there in the majors, it really made you play ball. I mean, you're the underdog almost automatic. We had one guy on every team that could always say that this guy's a bonus baby, etc. Mel Roach, too. He's still living in Richmond, I believe. He plays golf and I see he's playing in that Chesapeake Golf Association. I've seen his name in the paper. I'd like to run into him again.

I've got a scar right now beside my elbow on the back of my arm where he hit a drive to shortstop and I fell out on the grass trying to pull it in. I skinned my arm up. I never forgot that. It was in that Fleet tournament game and we lost it to Little Creek. He was at Little Creek. He was an ensign in the Navy. He was a fine guy — always friendly, polite. He was not rowdy. But he could hit that ball.

Remember a guy named Mickey Harrington? Played with the Phillies. He could hit that ball, too. Whew! Man, it's really a treat to see them guys hit that darned ball.

Also, there was a football player that was one hell of a ballplayer, too, when it come to baseball, out of Michigan State. Earl Morrall.

Played shortstop. The college used to come down South in the spring to play us and that's where they'd get their spring training down through there.

There was just such a group of good teams coming through at different times, like in the spring. East Carolina, Furman out of South Carolina, and the University of Miami. We even played on their campus. Them guys had some good teams; they had some good players. They had some Cuban boys on there, too. They had a good ballclub down there.

I'll tell you what. I run into more segregation when I was in the Marine Corps than I did when I was playing ball. There was more of a segregation problem than I had when I was playing with the Clowns.

I played two years at Camp Lejeune. When I was first sent down to Parris Island, when I got there I was working out and I never got out of my sweat gear and this coach — his name was Captain Floyd Johnson — tells me that he's got a crowded infield and he can't use me. I said, "Look, you guys sent for me. They sent me down here to play ball. Plus, that guy over there played second string behind me last year." But that didn't cut no ice, so I got my gear and went on back to my company. They had me in service company at the supply depot.

What happened, when I come home for my Christmas leave I told the story to Bunny. I went over to Bunny's house in downtown New York, down on 133rd Street, and he said, "We gotta sit down and write this letter."

So he set down and wrote a letter to the general down there in Parris Island. That's like December. He mailed that letter to the general. The general got that letter and it was in January when we got some sort of response. The letter went something like this: "You have a player in your camp by the name of Pfc. Gordon Hopkins. He played with the Indianapolis Clowns on a professional level and with the Camp Lejeune team for two years. We think he should be playing and he was denied playing there in 1957. We want to know why. Please return a response."

Next thing I know, I was down working

at the clothing issue where they bring the recruits in. I was giving out gear to the troops at the time I got the phone call. They said, "Hop, you got a phone call." I said, "Who is it?" "I don't know."

So I went to the phone and it was Captain Floyd Johnson, the baseball coach. He said, "This is Captain Floyd Johnson. I got a call from the general. He got a letter from the Indianapolis Clowns, somebody saying I didn't give you a chance to play ball in 1957."

I said, "Skipper, let's not kid each other. I've been playing baseball since I was knee-high to a duck. Now you know you didn't give me a chance. I didn't even get out of sweat gear; how the heck did you give me a chance?" And I hung the phone up.

There hadn't been a black boy to play on Parris Island, that's what it was. They used to have guys try out for the team, but what would happen, they would cut the guys before they even had a chance to look at 'em good.

When the spring training got started, another boy came out for the team. He had been in the Giants' chain; he was a pitcher. I took my own good time; I said, "I'm gonna play it for all it's worth." [Laughs] Training was supposed to be a certain time; I didn't even go out for the team. I waited for about two weeks before I even showed up. [Laughs]

What happened, the general wrote Bunny back and said, "Mr. Downs, you don't have to worry. Pfc. Hopkins will play in 1958." That's what he told him. Bunny showed me the letter.

When I finally showed up for practice one day, the skipper saw me out there in the fieldhouse and he called me into the office. He shut the door and said, "I don't know what this is about that I didn't give you a chance, but I'm gonna give you a chance."

That particular season — '58 — we trained near Miami, Florida, down in Opelika at the Navy base down there. That was nice to go down to that warm climate. He said, "We're going to train down in Florida. I'm gonna give you a uniform and I'm gonna give you a chance."

I said, "That's all I ask."

I tell you what, when I left that ballclub in 1958 at the end of that season — what happened, the thing broke out in Lebanon, I got called back to my old engineering outfit — and he came to me and told me, "Hoppy, you are one hell of a ballplayer." I said, "Thank you, skipper," and he shook my hand. That made me feel a ton.

I was on a hot streak, too. In July and August, I'm always hot with the bat. I don't care who's pitching, he's in trouble. Most good hitters usually get hot around July and August. That's when your eye's sharp. In the springtime, you're not all that coordinated.

As a matter of fact, the game before that night, we played Fort Gordon and they put this guy in that pitched in the Texas League. The team had got into a rally and they hadn't seen me play too much. I hadn't done much that night; I think I had popped out. We had got a rally going and they brought this dude in and I checked him over and he started firing that ball. It looked like it was low to the ground around my knees.

They brought him because they thought they was gonna get me out, so what I did, I went into a crouch — like I'm trying to lean over the plate to hit some of his curves. I hit everything that guy threw; I fouled it off and next thing I knew — I leaned over the plate like I'm waiting for a curveball and I want that fastball so bad I can taste it.

And here he come! I almost undressed him! I hit one back through the box, man, and he just barely got out of the way. [Laughs] I was hot!

After I got out of the military, I had an aunt that was very sick in Philadelphia. That's why I moved to Philadelphia, to live with her and try to assist her.

That's where my sons were born. I got married in Philadelphia. I met my wife there; she was born in Philadelphia and all my boys were born in Philadelphia. I spent 12 years there and then in 1970 my wife passed. That changed my whole life — my thoughts and all my goals and everything else. I always had goals in mind.

It seemed like I'd been waiting all my life

to have a wife and kids. It seemed like all my props got knocked out from under me. My wife was young; she was only about 29 years old and she had a cerebral hemorrhage. My boys were so young. My youngest boy was two years old, going on three.

I didn't know what to do. I was so confused. I didn't know how to handle it. I was really in a confused state of mind. I did the best I could, but I could've done better had I had somebody that could give me some good advice. I even had to go to counseling and everything else.

Just prior to that, I did go to school for cabinetmaking and carpentry at the Bok Vocational in south Philadelphia, and that's what I did on the G.I. bill. That was one advantage of going in the military; you do have some kind of rights, as far as G.I. benefits and school benefits. That helped me quite a bit.

While I was going to school, I got married and then my status changed and then the twins were born a few months later. Then my status changed again and they put you on a different pay scale.

The twins were about eight years old when my wife died, then I moved back to my home area in Maryland and my aunt helped me out so much. From that time on, I took some of my skills that I learned at the Bok Vocational Trade School and I got in with some of the big builders around in this area, and some of the leading contractors. I was building new homes and remodeling and then sometimes putting in kitchens. I did work for Sears and Roebuck and the Hechinger Corporation, which is one of the big lumber supply places in the Mid-Atlantic and down in the Southern area.

Later on, they were starting to give so slight a piece of the action that I started saying, "Well, look. I'm doing all these good chores for these people and they're giving me such a small piece of the rock that it's time for me to start springing out on my own." What I started doing was working out of my own basement and doing my own thing on a part-time basis.

So in 1976, I was working over at Mary-land University with a contractor and they laid me off, and I haven't looked back since. I'm still working for myself now. I'm thinking about retiring now and just doing some small jobs just to keep myself active.

I do play a lot of golf, so that's going to keep me pretty busy. I love my golf. I try to keep myself in fairly decent shape.

And I play a saxophone, too, on a regular basis, just for my own entertainment. I have played in some groups and I studied it in school and I played in the school bands. It was a toss-up between baseball and music and my music teacher begged me not to go play baseball. [Laughs]

You had some female teammates on the Clowns.

Toni Stone was the first one on the team. Toni was a second baseman and she was very intelligent and she was very pleasant to be around, but she didn't fool around. She was very sharp; she didn't go for no foolishness. She was strictly business and she knew what her role was there, and that was very important.

Bunny Downs was one of the men that really had all this hooked up properly. As a matter of fact, he was really the coordinator and he lined up the booking engagements and all this type of thing all over the country and in Canada. Also, he made arrangements for their billeting, their lodging, This was something that he took care of before we even hit the road because Bunny Downs used to play with the Indianapolis Clowns and also he used to play with the Lincoln Giants, the St. Louis Giants, and Hilldale.

He was so much on the road that he knew all the ins and outs. It was so important that he was the man that could put all this stuff together and hook it up. He knew the places to go and this eliminated a whole lot of problems that a newcomer would have if he was into just booking and that type of stuff. He would not know where to start from, whereas Bunny knew the places to go plus he had his contacts — the booking agents and promoters and all those guys. He knew just about everybody and if he didn't know 'em he knew *other* people who knew who to get ahold of.

Mamie [Johnson] and Toni was there, so Mamie and Toni had special arrangements. Sometimes we stayed in a hotel and sometimes we stayed in tourist homes, private homes, things like that. Maybe the girls might've stayed in private homes if they were crowded at some other place. They ate with the family and that was provided for by Bunny.

They were well respected and the ballplayers also respected the girls. The players treated them well because they knew better than to do otherwise because Bunny would always tell 'em when they'd get up there, he'd say, "Look, I may as well get everybody told. If y'all think you can't handle that, we'll take you down to the bus station tomorrow and we'll get you a ticket home. We'll get somebody who can go along with this program. Now, these girls are gonna be here. Whether you're gonna be here or not, that's up to you." [Laughs]

We had several occasions when things would get a little rough, but basically the guys were okay. There were some guys who really weren't too fond of the program, but Bunny told 'em, "These girls are putting money in your pocket. You can act like a horse's rear, but you gotta use your head. Before, what kind of money were you making? Think about that. We got a pretty good card here now and the girls can play, so treat the girls right. Treat 'em like they're one of you. That's all I ask you to do."

We didn't have no problems but one or two times. One of the guys might make a throw that would almost endanger Toni at second base. One of the guys pulled that one time and almost got Toni spiked and Bunny chewed him out, believe me.

I didn't care. I figured, "Who the hell am I? They can do without me."

Bunny helped me *way* before I even got there 'cause I had been over to his house. I would be there *every* night and he'd tell me what's going on and I respected him. I respected everything he believed in and he

didn't pull no punches with me. He told me like it was and he trusted me and he would tell me things that would help me further my playing ability out on that field, so the least I could do was show him some respect as to what he was operating on.

He was operating a nice program with these girls. They were trying something to try to keep everybody going out there and it was working because the girls could play. They could play ball. They weren't all that great, but I mean they were good ballplayers. I'm not going to try to compare them with anybody else 'cause that's not my job. That's not for me to say. Who the hell am I to be comparing anybody, you know what I'm saying? But I know they could play. They did their job.

Just like I saw a whole lot of other players out there playing, but I can't say so-and-so was better than so-and-so. That's not my place to say that, but the only thing I can say is this: Every player I ever saw play had some good days and some bad days. That's everybody's case. Some of the players only tell you some of the good days, but like I just said, I had some bad days out there, too.

I remember one day I had a bad day. I made two errors. I never did forget that. I couldn't shake it off. Oscar Charleston said, "Shake it off, boy!" For some reason, I couldn't. [Laughs]

I remember when I had some good days, too, but I also remember that bad day I had. I never did forget that.

I remember one time, Pancho Herrera was playing and the pitcher got caught on to where he likes his pitches and, man, he couldn't get nothing. I have seen him strike out three times in a row. But he knowed that somebody found his weakness. And I have seen him hit three out of the ballpark in one day.

We had a boy named Wannamaker. One time we were playing somewhere in North Carolina. George Wannamaker was our third baseman and Pancho was their first baseman — Kansas City — and they had a home run battle going that night. Boy, the people just about tore the stands up. Pancho, when he come up, he'd hit one out. Wannamaker come up for us, he'd hit one out of there, too. [Laughs] This Wannamaker was something else, I'm not jiving, man. And he wasn't big as no Pancho, now. He was about the size of Jim Wynn, but he weighed about 185 pounds and he was solid as a rock. They picked him up in a place called Spartanburg, South Carolina. Man, that guy could hit!

I don't know if you know Kansas City's old ballpark, where the Kansas City Blues played at. We were playing in Kansas City one day and Wannamaker, the first time he hit it over the right field fence and they're saying, "Aw, hell. He lucked up and hit that one." [Laughs] This was a Sunday, too, now. So the next time up, he hit one over the left field fence. [Laughs] This day he hit three home runs. The next time up, he hit it over the center field fence. They used to have another little fence back behind the new fence. The old fence was behind and that's the one they said that Oscar Charleston hit one over in that same ballpark when he was playing. Bunny Downs showed me that 'cause he seen him hit it over there.

And I had to go with him just like I did with Ford in Buffalo. I had to go with Wannamaker to get his stuff. I think he got one of these transistor radios and some clothes, and I had to help him go to some club up there and help him bring the stuff back to the bus. He hit the ball over so many signs with them three home runs. [Laughs]

And, also, he had a weak spot, too. But I'll tell you one thing: you better not throw it up in his face 'cause he'll lose it. Outside, too; he'll hit it out. He didn't have a specific strike zone; he stepped right up to everything. All the time. Boy, that boy had some power. He went to Puerto Rico that year and won the batting title down there. That was like '54; he went down in the '54 season. I was following him in *The Sporting News* and I seen his name in there and I was so tickled. He used to be my roommate at different times and him and I got pretty close. He was all right. Good ol' dude, but he passed away back in '75, I think it was. He was 25 in '54.

A friend of mine out of Texas, Dr. [Layton] Revel, got ahold of his sister and found out where he was living and his sister told him that he had passed in 1975. He got back to me on that and told me. We usually try to keep up with the fellas.

Any regrets?

I don't really have any regrets because I learned a lot, and if I had to do it all over again I think I'd do the same thing. Really. Even if the situation was the same as it was, even with as much as I know about life now and people and all that and if the conditions was the same, I think I'd go back and do it because I liked to play ball. I'd do the same thing because I think I'd have a better chance to hit a bigger batting average. [Laughs]

I have dreams now about playing ball. I had a dream the other night where I was playing somewhere and a guy was hitting me some infield practice. I happened to wake up and messed up my dream. [Laughs] I was getting warmed up, too, man. I have 'em all the time.

Bunny's wife used to tell me when I used to come over there to visit and see Bunny. He may have been in the other building 'cause he was the superintendent to the building next door to where he was living, and sometimes I'd come over to the house and I would have to wait until he got back over there. His wife was named Nanny and she was saying, "You know, some nights Bunny'd be running the bases — his feet was kicking and he'd be saying, 'Throw the ball!' He'd be playing ball in his sleep." [Laughs] I'd say to myself, "I don't think that'll ever happen to me." And believe me, I told a lie. It has happened to me and I dream about it, I'd say, three or four times a month. I'd dream that I'm at a game or I'm playing a game or something. I'm playing shortstop or second base or hitting the ball or running bases.

Bunny Downs wasn't the only guy that really helped me to get my little act together to go play with the Clowns. Bunny was a very unselfish individual. When I met him, the first thing he tells me, he said, "I want you to go meet Dewey Creacy." Dewey Creacy used to play with the old St. Louis Stars, a bad third baseman. He had a lifetime batting average of .300 back in the early '20s and early '30s. Bunny said, "You go to see him 'cause this guy is something else, and I want you to know something about what he knows."

I used to go over to his house every Sunday at one o'clock. I'd show up on his doorstep and he'd let me in and I'd be writing down everything. He'd tell me how to play hitters and how to shift and all this kind of stuff and how to take care of my arm and what kind of liniment to use. He told me how to shower down and rub my legs down and all that kind of stuff. He told me all kind of things and how to handle yourself out on the road. I really appreciated him for that.

And I'll tell you, the first time I hit the field, I was *ready!* That made me feel so good. I didn't feel like I was at a loss, so to speak; I felt like I'd been there before. That's the kind of feeling you get. First time a guy hit the ball to me, I shifted like he told me and it worked. [Laughs]

I remember one night we were playing a team that was in the Piedmont League, a team called the Portsmouth Merrimacs. This guy that used to play with the Kansas City Monarchs named Quincy Barbee — he was one of the first blacks to play with the Portsmouth Merrimacs down there, he was a big first baseman — hit one to me the first time up. The guy threw him a fastball and I had just shifted for him and here it come right across the bag like it was going into center field, but I had cheated at second — he was a right-handed hitter — and I'm right close to the bag and here's the ball coming right to me and I throwed him out. Next time he come up, same thing. [Laughs]

The guy asked Bunny, "Who is that little cocky guy down at second base? He gets everything I hit down through there." Bunny said, "He was a hot item. He's got a magnet in that glove."

Bunny used to talk a lot of trash. I don't know whether anybody ever told you that, but the guys had so much respect for him because he wasn't all business. He could play with you,

he could get your humor and anything else. He knew how to do it and he did a perfect job about it. He would tease you a little bit but just a good-natured kind of thing. That's why everybody was crazy about him, but nobody better not mess with him. He could get real firm with somebody if they messed up.

His right forefinger, he had it knocked out of place so many times when he was playing ball that it was crooked and when he'd point that crooked finger at you, you better look out. [Laughs] You was in trouble. When he'd point that crooked finger at you, you done messed up somewhere down the line. He was in your corner 'til you messed up. *If* you messed up with him, not just any kind of ordinary mess-up. He'd try to help you, but don't mess up with him or try to upstage him, now.

Bunny used to have a little thing. He used to tease the guys about this ballclub he was gonna get together. He called it the "Lee" team. That's where he would get the guys going with this "Lee" team. Ug-Lee. Everybody that ever played around Bunny Downs knows about the "Lee" team. I'd ask guys that played around before me, "Did you ever play on the 'Lee' team?" They'd say, "Oh, my God, yeah. You know Bunny Downs." [Laughs]

Like a new guy would just come on the ballclub — it could be Kansas City, it could be Birmingham or Memphis — and Bunny would take one of the boys over there and say, "Hey, Home!" "My name ain't no Home." Then Bunny'd get him then; he'd say, "Well — Cokey, then." "My name ain't no Cokey, either."

Then he'd say, "Well, what's your name — Lee? I know your name is Lee." "My name ain't no Lee. My name is so-and-so."

He'd look over there and he'd say, "Merchant, look here. You think that boy could make the team?" Merchant'd say, "Oh, yeah. He'd be a cinch." [Laughs] Bunny would say, "I don't know. I don't know whether he could make the team or not."

And the guy'd say, "Man, I can make any team, man." He don't like for nobody to tell him he can't make a team.

Bunny would say, "I don't know. You're going to have to prove it to me. You think he can make the team?" "Yeah, Bunny, he can make the team."

"Well, next thing I'm gonna tell you, your name is Lee. Ug-Lee." [Laughs] "You can make the Ug-Lee team."

The guy would say, "Aw, man, you're crazy."

That's the team that Bunny always used to talk about. He'd get a guy going good with that. We used to crack our sides because the guy would be so befuddled he don't know what's coming off. He'd say, "What team?" and Bunny'd say, "We're gonna have a game at Memphis stadium and we're trying to get enough players for this Lee team. We're gonna have to play the Baltimore Orioles." [Laughs] "We're running short of players. We're gonna need a few more." And the guy'd say, "Count me in, man! Count me in!" [Laughs] I used to crack my sides every time because it was really so funny.

One time we had a college guy — Willie Brown, played shortstop for the Clowns around '53 or '54. He was a switch hitter, too; he'd bat right- and lefthanded and he was a good hitter. All of a sudden, he just went into a slump; he couldn't hit his butt with a tennis racket. He'd go 0 for 4, 0 for 3, and all like that. He went to Bunny. "Bunny, what am I doing wrong? Seems like I can't get nothing to go right." He really was a clutch hitter; he really could hit that ball.

Bunny told him, "Look. I see what you're doing wrong." "Wh-wh-what am I doing wrong?" He used to stammer a little bit. "First thing, you ain't holding your mouth right." Now this guy is a college guy; he graduated from Tuskegee. This is no lie; it just shows how Bunny could get your brain.

He said, "What you mean, I ain't holding my mouth right?" Then he had the nerve to ask Bunny, "How do you hold your mouth?"

Bunny showed him. He put his tongue out of the side of the mouth and turned his mouth to the side, said, "That's how you hold your mouth. You do that when you go up

there and hit that ball and I bet you come out of that slump."

You know what? Next thing I know, Willie Brown had come out of that slump. He started tearing that ball *up*. He was on top of the ball for the next couple of days and he come up to Bunny — he was sitting in the dugout one night — and said, "Bunny, man, since I started holding my mouth right, I've been wearing that ball out." Bunny liked to fell out in the dugout and I did, too. [Laughs]

We talked about it afterward. When he used to call Syd I used to be there with him 'cause I was like his shadow. They didn't mess with me too much. The guy'd be messing with me — they didn't know who I am — pulling them little games like Bunny played on the other boys and Oscar Charleston would say, "Look. You don't want to mess with Hoppy, now. That's one of Bunny's boys." And they'd back up a little bit. [Laughs]

There were a lot of other guys that helped me out: Buck O'Neil, Buck Leonard, and Leon Day. I got a lot of savvy from those guys, too, when I was playing ball. Johnny Hayes up in New York. A lot of those, they'll find out that you're a hot item. Alex Pompez was one, too. Matter of fact, if I hadn't went in the service that fall of '54, Pompez was going to get me in the winter league down there. I'd've been down there with Wannamaker.

What happened during that time, the major leagues just dominated that. The black boys was going down there from the Negro league, then after a while they started going on down there. We had two connections down in Venezuela and down in Mexico, but in Puerto Rico, man, they [major leaguers] had went down and flooded Puerto Rico. But I was selected to go down there in '54, but I got called in service. I went in in November, '54, right after Oscar Charleston died.

That was a big blow to us when he passed. I didn't expect that to happen that soon, I mean. He was a tough manager, but he was a very good manager. He was the type of fella that didn't play around. When he was out on that ballfield, he was all business. Believe me, he was.

He would kid around with me. I was the guy that used to rub down Oscar Charleston every night, and I'll tell you why. He used to fungo the balls to the outfield and he would be stiff and sore afterwards. When the thing was over, he'd say, "All right, Hop. Come on." Somebody told him I used to do massages.

That man — he might look fat, but believe me, that was not fat. That was like hide. That was some tough flesh 'cause I had to massage him. That man's meat was tough, and I had to massage around by his shoulders and back. All that was not fat. I don't know what they call it, but it sure wasn't fat.

BATTING RECORD

Year	Team, League	Pos	G	AB	R	H	2B	3B	HR	RBI	SB	BA
1952	House of David, ind.	inf										
	Indianapolis, NAL	2b										
1953	Indianapolis, NAL	inf										
1954	Indianapolis, NAL	inf										

Carl Long
"He Didn't Survive"

BORN MAY 9, 1935, ROCK HILL, SC
HT. 6'2" WT. 180 BATTED AND THREW RIGHT

Negro Leagues debut: 1952

Walter Masterson, a very good pitcher in the 1940s for the very bad Washington Senators, once said, "The best ballplayers aren't in the major leagues. The survivors are in the major leagues."

That was never more true than it was in the case of Carl Long. Long was a five-tool guy: hit, hit for power, run, throw, and field. He once batted over .400, he hit double figures in home runs year after year, he stole bases handily, he once threw out Larry Doby at third by daylight, and his stellar plays in center field pushed Henry Kimbro, one of the greatest center fielders in Negro leagues history, to right field. And he played in the All-Star game at the age of 18.

In spring training of 1958, Long was working his way up through the Pirates' chain (Pittsburgh had purchased him from the Birmingham Black Barons at the end of the '53 season) when he injured his shoulder, ending his very promising baseball career. He was not yet 23 years old.

We'll never know what would have happened if Long had not been hurt, but he could do it all. He proved it at every stop in the Negro league and the minor leagues.

Being born in Rock Hill, South Carolina, to Willie H. and Ella G. Long, we didn't have any balls. I had two brothers and we used to play baseball in the street. It wasn't baseball; we used to hit tin cups, milk cans, and rocks. That's how I learned to play baseball.

My brothers couldn't get me out, but I could always take them out. I was the baby. They used to get mad because they couldn't get me out.

In the evening, we used to go play softball at the school, the West End School there in Rock Hill. The girls played the boys, and I used to get mad because we had to quit when dark come. [Laughs] I loved the game so.

I used to play football at Emmett Scott in high school. I was a good football player, but I *loved* baseball and they didn't have baseball there in the school. We used to play softball at lunch time and I'd get mad when the bell rang and we had to go in. [Laughs]

I could hit the ball a long way, and could throw. I could do it all. My father saw me playing ball out there in the yard. He said, "Let me see you hit a ball. I got you a ball here and I want to see you hit it."

And I lost the ball I hit it so far back in the woods. [Laughs]

My father was a big man; he weighed 350 pounds, and when he spoke, *every*body listened. My father saw me play one time professionally.

In 1951, I left home. John William Parker came and got me and said, "You want to go play baseball?" I told him yeah. He asked my father and my father told him, "Take him on." I was fifteen and a half.

I left and went to Nashville and played

Carl Long (courtesy of Carl Long).

4, 5 for 5, and 0 for 4. [Laughs] But I was up there trying.

We played in coal towns in West Virginia; down in Greenwood, Mississippi; Bluefield — all these little towns. North Dakota. People were hollering for baseball and we went in there and we played and we beat just about everybody we found. That's how good we were.

In North Dakota, conditions were *so* much better. People were so friendly up there, and South Dakota. Mississippi was a terrible place. I was king in Mexico. They treated me with a whole lot of respect in Mexico. They used to come and get me, take me out, feed me, take me to the bullfights. Wouldn't let me spend no money. They respected you and everybody wanted an autograph.

I got fined for signing an autograph. I went to the outfield and signed an autograph. The guy got ready to throw the pitch and, "Hey, Carl! They're ready to throw the pitch!" And they fined me. [Laughs] They said, "We'll take $25 from you." I said, "For what?" "You're out there signing autographs when the game's getting ready to start."

Every ball hit to me for a third out, I'd take it and throw it in the stands. They said, "That ball's gonna cost you." I said, "How much?" They said, "Five dollars." I said, "Okay," and I kept throwing 'em in the stands. [Laughs]

When I was at Birmingham, Hank Aaron was playing shortstop for the Indianapolis Clowns. We played 'em. Ernie Banks was playing shortstop for the Kansas City Monarchs. That's just some of the big names that I played against.

In 1953, when I went to Birmingham, 52,000 people was in the park in Kansas City, Missouri. We played 'em Opening Day. I'd never seen so many at one time in all my life in one place. Doc Dennis told me, said, "You're gonna have to go out there and play. Don't worry about those people." Really, I got nervous, there was so many people.

Doc Dennis was a good hitter. I'll tell you. He played with the Baltimore Elite Giants, but he was a better hitter when he was with Birmingham.

with the Nashville Stars. Doctor Jackson was the owner of the team and Oscar Charleston was the manager. I started playing with them and did pretty good. Oscar Charleston taught me a whole lot about baseball, things that I didn't know, that I found out. He told me, "You're goin' somewhere, son." I could throw, I could hit, and I could run. I wasn't as good a hitter as I become.

At the end of the year in 1951, Dr. Jackson told me, "I'm gonna sell you to Birmingham. You're gonna be playing with the Birmingham Black Barons." I thought I was in heaven then.

Before I went to Birmingham, we used to play three ballgames a day, and after playing three ballgames a day, I still didn't want to quit. [Laughs] We played at ten o'clock that morning in one town, two o'clock in the evening in another town, and eight o'clock at night in a third town. Sometimes I went 2 for

Buck O'Neil was playing first base for the Monarchs. Banks was the shortstop. That's just some of the guys that I remember that the Monarchs had on their team. We beat them, but we didn't beat 'em Opening Day.

Birmingham had a good team. Doc Dennis was playing first, [Eddie] Brooks playing second, Pee Wee Butts playing short. I don't remember who was playing third [Irwin Castille], but I was playing center, Kimbro was playing right. Lloyd "Pepper" Bassett was playing catcher. Otha Bailey catching. And there was a long, tall righthander, Menske Cartledge — called him "Rabbit" — was pitching. He made Buck O'Neil look foolish. [Laughs] I often tell Buck about that; he say he don't want to talk about it.

We had a good time there in '52. In '53, I went right back to Birmingham. I had a good year; I don't know what I hit — they didn't keep the records — but I know I did real good. At the end of the season, they said, "There's a scout in the stands wants you to join the Pittsburgh Pirates." I said, "You mean to tell me I'm going to the Show?" "No, you're going with the Pirates. You have a chance to go to the Show."

I was a young fella, not quite 19 years old, and I don't know nothing about this. The money I got, I didn't need because my father took care of me, but I was getting five dollars a day and $150 a month. That was a lot of money to me. I'd never seen that kind of money because I never wanted for anything. My father was a bootlegger. [Laughs] He owned a restaurant; they called him Big Bill Long and everybody loved him to death.

When Birmingham sold me to Pittsburgh, I went to St. Johns, Quebec, Canada, and I hit 20 home runs my first year. Branch Rickey, Jr., he said, "Son, the guy throwed you a changeup and you had strided and come back and just dropped your wrist and the ball went so far out of the ballpark. That's the furthest I've ever seen a ball hit in my life. Off a changeup!" He said, "That's natural power. You can't stay down here."

I was just hoping he'd take me back with him right then. I had a *tremendous* year up there in St. Johns in 1954. In a short season. *Cold!*

The following year, they sent me to Billings, Montana. Forty-two inches of snow when we landed in April. I did real good up there and they needed some help down in Waco. They took me from Billings and sent me to Waco. I went down there and they didn't have no place to put me on the roster. They was in first place and beating everybody. I said, "Why did you send me here? They don't even let me get in the lineup." But when I got in the lineup, I showed out. [Laughs]

They flew me right back to Billings. I finished the season there with 18 home runs. They had Dick Stuart there. Every time Dick hit a home run, I got knocked down. [Laughs] I didn't mind it so bad because when I got knocked down, I stole second and third. [Laughs] I got so I would tell the guys, "I'm gonna steal second now. You hit me; I'm gonna take second." And there I'd go. Even off a pitchout, there was no play.

The following year, 1956, they sent me to the Carolina League, being the *first* black ballplayer in the league for Kinston. I was playing against guys like Willie McCovey, Curt Flood, Leon Wagner. They were so good in the Carolina League. I was leading the league one time and Curt Flood took over. Leon Wagner was hitting the ball out of every ballpark he went in, but I was on the last-place team. I carried the Kinston section of the league and made the All-Star team. McCovey didn't even make it. Flood, Wagner, myself made it. Outfielders.

Wagner was a butcher outfielder. He could *hit* that ball, but he wasn't a good outfielder. He didn't have the arm and he misjudged a lot of balls. Curt Flood, he could do it all. He could do *every*thing. He could do it just like I did it. I hit more home runs than Flood.

After leaving here, I went to Mexico City and batted .407. Branch Rickey say, "You cannot stay here." Everything they threw me, I hit that ball. We played in Monterrey, Yuma,

Yucatan, Mexico City, Laredo; I forget where else.

I hit a ball in Yuma. It was over the scoreboard. I hit it so doggone far, the people from Mexico didn't do nothing but stand up there and clap their hands. [Laughs] I didn't even see the ball when it was hit until I looked around and saw where everybody was looking, then I saw the ball. [Laughs] I put something on the ball there in downtown Yuma.

I left Mexico and went to Beaumont. This is still '57. I started getting sick in Mexico City. I did well in Beaumont. While I was in Kinston, I married Ella Smith in '56. My wife came to Beaumont in '57 after our son was born. My roommate was named Mike Sotello, so I named my son Sotello. Sotello Long. Then we left and came back to Kinston, North Carolina; that's where my wife was from.

In 1958, I went to spring training and tore a muscle in my shoulder. Branch Rickey said, "You're gonna have to go back home because your shoulder is giving you a whole lot of trouble. You're gonna have to have surgery."

I told Branch, I said, "No, sir! I cannot have surgery. I don't like no knives."

He said, "We're gonna have to do something with you." So he sent me back home and I become the first black deputy sheriff in the state of North Carolina.

I want to get back to something I missed. My father saw me play the first time when I learned all the major league ballplayers, barnstorming with Birmingham in 1954. Jackie Robinson, Campanella, Larry Doby, Don Newcombe, Minnie Minoso, Luke Easter, Joe Black, Bob Trice, Hank Thompson, Junior Gilliam — we were all barnstorming together. We played a game in Charlotte, North Carolina.

I forget who was pitching for the Campanella All-Stars, but my father was there to see it. I got up there the first time at bat against them guys and I hit a double off the left–center field wall.

My father stood up and said, "Hey!" He was a big man, got a big voice, and everybody was listening. He said, "That's *my* son!" And everybody fell out.

When I got up to the bat next time, I struck out. [Laughs] A guy told him, he said, "Hey, whose son is that?" My father got up said, "Damned if I know." [Laughs]

I got back up there the next time. I said, "My father's here and I can't disappoint him," so I had another double off that doggone left–center field fence. I tried to get it out of there. I hit it so hard they almost throwed me out going to second. [Laughs]

Larry Doby tried to go from first to third on me — I was in center field — and that ball passed him so fast, he just turned around and looked at me and put his hand on his hip and shook his head. [Laughs] You talk about Mays had a gun, Mays couldn't touch my arm. Roberto Clemente couldn't touch me. I told Branch Rickey I was the best ballplayer he had in his organization.

Playing against the Campanella All-Stars, Don Newcombe wouldn't pitch to Pee Wee Butts because he knowed Butts would hit him. He said, "Let's try to work that young fella," talking about me. Mistake. [Laughs] Don Newcombe fired that ball in there and I hit him a ton. [Laughs]

Campanella said, "I *told* him to go on and pitch to Butts and leave you alone." [Laughs]

Campy said, "Young fella, you got everything that you need to go to the majors. Keep a cool head."

I didn't drink, didn't smoke. I went out a lot, met a lot of people, did a whole lot of things. *Good* things. I just had a good time. The main thing — my concern — I just wanted to play baseball. I loved that game so doggone much.

When I tore my shoulder, it was a cool night, raining, and taking infield and throwing. I made a quick throw and I could hear something when I did it. Never did come back. I could swing the bat, but I couldn't throw, so I come back here and played with a semipro team. All I did was just hit.

All the guys knowed about me. They said, "How's that young fella doing?" They *knowed* I was going to the majors.

I had already become the first black

baseball player here and I become the first black deputy sheriff here and then I become the first black city detective. This was 1971. I left there and become the first black bus driver from Kinston for Carolina Trailways. [Laughs] That's what I'm doing today; I've been doing it ever since then. My wife's been trying to get me to retire and I just won't. My head's too hard. I said, "No, honey, I'm just getting away from you." [Laughs] I love it because I travel a lot. I go to Las Vegas and California — all over the United States. Canada. Get paid to do it, meet a lot of people. I carried the president — Mr. Clinton — all over the state. Smartest man in the world.

You've mentioned some great ballplayers. Who was the best one you saw?

I'd say the best hitter I saw was Hank Aaron. We used to try to get that guy out and we couldn't get him out. We'd try to knock him down and we couldn't hit him.

Ernie Banks had some great wrists, but for somebody hitting the ball, Hank was hitting the ball everywhere — to the right, left, center. I didn't know exactly where to play him. I tried to look in to catch the signals of what they're going to throw him or where they're going to try to throw it to; that was the only way I knew how to play Hank. I'm sure he caught what I was doing out there; when I moved to my left, he knew it was going to be a curveball. [Laughs] I just tried to play him straightaway when I found out what he was doing.

Curt Flood was a *good* ballplayer. He didn't do that great in the majors like he did in the minors, but I said, "This guy here is going." And Willie McCovey — he could hit that ball. Yes, sir! We called him "Stretch."

We called Willie Mays "Buck." He come home from the service — he was stationed in Virginia — he come home to Birmingham and Hoss [Walker, the manager] come to me and told me, "You wanna take the night off?"

I said, "For what?"

"I wanna let Mays play center field."

I said, "No, I don't. You better get Kimbro or somebody. I wanna be out there with him." [Laughs]

Carl Long, 1999 (Lisa Feder photograph).

Kimbro was evil! He was evil all his life. [Laughs] Mean and evil. Kimbro was something else. I played beside of him and I *know* him.

There was a heck of a good hitter used to play with Birmingham. I played against him down there in Mexico City. Alonzo Perry. He bent in a crouch — *way* down in a crouch — and he come forward. I just played deep and deeper. [Laughs]

Which pitcher was toughest on you?

Turgeson was one of the tough pitchers on me. Not Schoolboy, his brother [Big Jim]. They was playing with the Clowns. He was a big, tall righthander, real heavy. He was tough on me. He could throw so hard and he come from the side, too. His motion was getting me, but the rest of them guys I could hit. I didn't worry about them.

Bobby Boyd — he was tough sometimes when he wanted to pitch. Memphis Red Sox. And this guy used to pitch for the [San Francisco] Giants, called Jones. Toothpick Jones. Sam Jones. He was a superb pitcher.

At the time you played in the Negro league, blacks were starting to be more accepted, but only a little. How did you find the travel and the hotels?

We couldn't stay at the white hotels. We couldn't eat at white restaurants. We had to find places to eat, but it didn't take much for us to start with. We went to Memphis, we had a place to stay there; went to Birmingham, there was Bob's Savoy—places like that.

The guys just had a good time. In Kansas City, I had a chance to meet Louis Armstrong. He stayed the same place we stayed, on the hill in Kansas City.

Chicago was a little bit better. So many people around Chicago, all they wanted to do was see the ballplayers. New York—same thing. We stayed in the Bronx. We didn't have no problems. We played in the Polo Grounds, played in Chicago in Comiskey Park, in Philadelphia. We had a good time playing all around.

Was the game your father saw your biggest thrill?

My daddy was something else. [Laughs] I'd give anything if he could've seen me play more ballgames. But that's the closest place we got to South Carolina and that's the only time he got the chance to see me play. I was sure that he was going to see me when I went to the majors, but it wasn't to be.

My biggest thrill was playing in the Carolina League when I drove in six runs, hit two home runs, and we beat Greensboro, 18–3. They was calling us everything. "Knock that nigger off his feet!" "Hit that coon up side of his head!" They was calling us everything.

A little old white lady come out there and said, "Why don't you all shut up and leave them boys alone? Every time you open your mouth, they hit the ball outta the ballpark." [Laughs]

I went 4-for-5. Hit a grand slam. Another black guy, Frank Washington, he drove in five runs, and the pitcher—he was a black guy, Cleo Luright—he drove in two runs.

We was in last place because only a few guys was hitting. When they'd get somebody there to help the team, Branch Rickey would come and get 'em and take 'em out.

Other than the injury, do you have any regrets from your baseball days?

No, sir. If I had to do it all over again, I'd do it the *same* way, other than get hurt.

I sure would have *loved* to have went to the majors so the people could see what I was all about. It was some kind of thrill to be affiliated with just *any* team playing ball.

BATTING RECORD

Year	Team, League	Pos	G	AB	R	H	2B	3B	HR	RBI	SB	BA
1952	Birmingham, NAL	of										
1953		of										
1954	St. John's	of							20			
1955	Billings, PioL	of							18			
	Waco, BigStL	of										
1956	Kinston, CarL	of										
1957	Mex. City, MxL	of										.407
	Beaumont, TxL	of										

Jim Robinson
"In His Blood"

Born January 21, 1930, New York, NY
Ht. 5'9" Wt. 165 Batted and Threw Right

Negro Leagues debut: 1952

It seems as if everyone who knew Dizzy Dismukes had a great deal of respect and affection for the man. It was well founded; he once gave a player money out of his own pocket because the player had to go home for the birth of his son. And that was not an isolated incident.

Jim Robinson played under Dismukes with the Kansas City Monarchs in the mid to late '50s, and he shares the same warm regard that everyone else feels for the thoughtful manager.

Dismukes probably had some good feelings about Robinson, too, because Robinson was an All-Star all three years he played for the Monarchs. College-educated and therefore quite able to make a living in other fields than baseball, he stayed in the game because, as he says, "Baseball was in my blood."

Did you ever hear the name John Beckwith? He had retired from the Negro leagues, but he had a bunch of Negro leaguers who lived in New York City, and they played on weekends. I would consider that my first experience in baseball because we played teams like the Bushwicks, the Union City Reds, and the Patterson Silk Sox. That was back in the late '40s and early '50s. That was a team called the Brooklyn Royal Giants and I guess I was 19, 20 years old — something like that.

I had gone with my father to see Negro league games and these were the guys who had finally given it up, but they were playing on weekends. I guess I was the rookie there.

I was away in college down in Greensboro, North Carolina — North Carolina A.&T. — and Oscar Charleston came through with the Philadelphia Stars — this was in '52 — and I was supposed to join him in May of that year. Unfortunately, I broke my arm in April

[laughs], so I didn't get to join them until very late in the season and only played a few games right before the season ended. That was 1952, which turned out to be the last year the Philadelphia Stars participated in the league.

So I went back to school to finish up and found it kind of difficult hooking on with anybody. In fact, I called the owner of the Philadelphia Stars, and *that's* how I found out they weren't playing anymore. [Laughs]

At mid summer, or maybe August, I was able to catch on with the Indianapolis Clowns. Even though it was late season, they were going barnstorming, so I got a chance to play 40 or 50 games with them.

At the end of that tour in '53, Quincy Trouppe, who was working with the Cardinals, signed me to a minor league contract with the St. Louis Cardinals. At the time, I was only the third or fourth black signed into the Cardinals' organization. The guy who was the first was a roommate of mine in college, Tom Alston. Eventually, in 1956, the Cardinals let me go and Quincy Trouppe was able to hook me on with the Kansas City Monarchs. I played three full seasons with the Monarchs: '56, '57, '58.

During this period, the only teams left in the Negro leagues were in the West. They were no longer in the East; there were about six clubs in the West, and the Monarchs, of course, was one of them.

With the Cardinals, I was originally assigned to Lynchburg, did a little stint in the service, and I came back and was with Allentown — that was the Eastern League — and they released me. I didn't really play enough to talk about it. [Laughs] They released me in the spring of '56 from Allentown, and that's when I hooked on with the Monarchs.

I was really a second baseman–shortstop. I played second base and shortstop in college. I played third [as a professional] because that was the position that was open, but eventually I ended up playing second base. In my last year with the Monarchs, I played a full year at shortstop.

After '58, I came back to New York City, got a job in city government. I had my bachelor's degree and eventually earned a master's degree in social work. I worked for the city government for about 30 years here. Most of those were with the New York City Housing Authority.

I retired from there and then I took a new job for six years down at South Carolina State University in Orangeburg and put the baseball program together there and I taught criminal justice. I was there from '88 to '94, and in May of '94, I finally hung it up.

Was anyone helpful or influential along the way?

Two people in particular: Joe Echols, my college coach, and my manager with the Monarchs, Dizzy Dismukes. Dizzy was a fine gentleman. What a beautiful guy. He had to be in his 60s; he had played back in the teens. He was just the calmest guy I ever met in my life and he was so supportive, and he just provided an excellent example of what a leader should be.

I really didn't know much about his background until the last 10 or 12 years. I've been reading the stuff and I see his name, I see his picture. He was with that group that went over to the Dominican Republic when Trujillo got that team together to play in the Caribbean championship. I'll never forget that guy as being, to me, not only a great manager, but very influential in terms of how one should handle life.

He would sit up in that bus and he would *never* lean back. He'd sit straight as an arrow in the front seat of the bus. You couldn't tell whether he was asleep or not; he would never change his posture. It was amazing. [Laughs]

Do any games stand out?

What stands out is that in '56, at the end of the season with the Kansas City Monarchs, a group of Negro leaguers were chosen to play against the Willie Mays All-Stars. We played about 35 or 40 games. They had Willie Mays, Hank Aaron, Monte Irvin, George Crowe, Joe Black, Gene Baker, Brooks Lawrence, Toothpick Sam Jones — people like that. To me, I loved the idea of playing against those guys for about 40 games. We started after the World Series and we played all the way into November, mostly down in the warm weather — Louisiana, Texas.

We did okay. I think we won about four or five games out of the whole batch. [Laughs] I did well; I didn't feel out of place. We hung in there, but eventually their talent was just a little bit too much. That was a great team and it was a great experience.

We were playing at that time on percentage, and we would have capacity crowds wherever we played. It was a great time.

Also, I was selected to the Negro League All-Star team each of my three seasons with the Monarchs.

Do you know any of your seasonal stats?

My last year with the Monarchs, I hit .310. I don't know exact figures before that, but I was always around the .300 mark.

How much were you paid?

My top salary was $300 a month. That

was my last year with Kansas City. Meal money was two, three dollars. When I was playing, it didn't seem like such a bad deal. It only seems like a bad deal now when I compare it with what the guys are getting today. [Laughs] Mediocre guys are getting a million dollars, and look at the earned run averages.

Who were the best players you saw?

Willie Mays and Hank Aaron. They would stand out.

How about in the Negro leagues?

There were some good guys there. A couple of 'em made the majors. In '56, Walter Bonds was on my team. He was a good friend of mine. When he was with Houston [Astros], he used to come and eat dinner at my house. All the way to the end, he really denied that he had leukemia. He was such an imposing guy physically — he was like 6'6" — and up 'til right before he passed away, you couldn't tell that he was sick.

Another guy I found to be a really *good* ballplayer was John Kennedy. He passed away a few months ago. In fact, I had talked to him about five days before he passed away. He was a really solid ballplayer, really a good, hard-nosed ballplayer. He could hit well and he was a good fielder.

There was a guy who played third base for us with the Monarchs in '57 and '58, I think. His name was Harold Hair, a great defensive third baseman. Harold and I were teammates in college. He was a *strong* hitter, really, really hit the ball hard. Really a good hitter.

And then we had an outstanding catcher, a guy named Ira McKnight. He was a fine catcher. He had a good arm and was really a great defensive catcher.

Which pitcher gave you the hardest time?

Just about all of 'em. [Laughs] Right-handers and lefthanders.

There was a couple of guys with Birmingham. One guy ended up in the majors; his last name was Smith. Willie Smith. He was always tough; he had a great curveball. He was quite a hitter, too. They moved him to the

Jim Robinson (courtesy of James Robinson).

outfield. He was a guy who really gave me a hard time. He was an outstanding pitcher.

You remember John Wyatt? We played with Indianapolis together and then I played against him when the Monarchs played against his U.S. Army team. He was sort of a smart pitcher and moved the ball around a lot. He was tough for me, anyway.

Charley Pride was with Memphis in '58, and he was tough for everybody. Kelly Searcy came like a year or two behind me at North Carolina A. & T. I saw him pitch in college. He had a great curveball. He really had a live arm. He was some pitcher.

Who was the best defensive player?

Kennedy was one. He was a fine shortstop. I played second base with him.

Then there was a center fielder with Birmingham. Jessie Mitchell. I saw him at a reunion about a year ago. He was one of the finest center fielders I've ever seen in my life. He was smooth; he reminded me so much of Paul Blair. He used to play right behind second base and

JIM ROBINSON IF
NEGRO LEAGUE *53-'58
K.C.MONARCHS '56-'58

Jim Robinson (courtesy of James Robinson).

Jessie Mitchell was the same kind of center fielder. I always admired the way he played; he was so graceful.

The travel was different in the '50s from what it had been like earlier, but did you still encounter problems?

Oh, yeah. No question about it. We still were restricted in terms of where we could go, and there were very few hotels, so we spent most of the time in the bus.

It was a pretty good bus. We had a good bus. A guy named Murphy used to drive. It amazed me how he could drive all night. We didn't have that much trouble as far as the bus breaking down.

You were only 28 when you left baseball. Do you have any regrets?

I had a shot at doing something I really like. To be able to play ball *every* day was great. I just felt so grateful because baseball was in my blood. It's still in my blood. [Laughs]

The main regret might be that I didn't get a chance to play through. I lost about a year and a half in the service, and I think that somehow my skills might have been diminished somewhat. Just to stop and not play on a regular basis was unfortunate, I think.

At that time, I knew what to expect. We're talking about the '50s. I had gone to college in the South, so I knew. We just dealt with it. Funny thing, when you're in it, you sort of deal with it on a day-to-day basis. I guess you kind of overlook some things. Of all the experiences of my life, it was certainly one that I will never forget.

Would you do it again?

Under the same conditions? That's a weird question. Would I do it again knowing what the alternative is? Yeah, I'd do it because I'd be doing something I like. I loved playing baseball. There was nothing better than going to the ballpark.

The fact that I had been able to carry that over after I had finished and after I had retired from the New York City Housing Authority and was able to go to South Carolina State, that was really something that was exciting to me.

They had dropped the program. The last guy to play there was a guy named Willie Aikens, and then they dropped the program. As result, having met guys like Mookie Wilson and [Herm] Winningham, who were from that area, they had to go somewhere else to play ball. Mookie went to the University of South Carolina, and Winningham went to some small college because the South Carolina State University dropped the program.

And, believe it or not, they dropped the program again. [Laughs] That's why I left.

BATTING RECORD

Year	Team, League	Pos	G	AB	R	H	2B	3B	HR	RBI	SB	BA
1952	Philadelphia, NAL	3b										
1953	Indianapolis, NAL	3b-ss										

1956 Kansas City Monarchs. (l-r): Tidmore, Townsend, Hubbard, Jim Robinson, Bill Washington, A. Jackson, Willie Lee, Self, unidentified, unidentified, Dizzy Dismukes (manager), Jarvis, John Winston, Dewitt White, A. J. Jackson (courtesy of James Robinson).

Year	Team, League	Pos	G	AB	R	H	2B	3B	HR	RBI	SB	BA
1954	Lynchburg, PiedL	3b										
1955	Allentown, EL	3b										
1956	Kansas City, NAL	inf										.302
1957		inf										.295
1958		ss										.310

Juan Armenteros
"Import"

BORN JUNE 24, 1928, SAGUA LA GRANDE, CUBA
HT. 5'10" WT. 185 BATTED AND THREW RIGHT

Negro Leagues debut: 1953

In the 1950s, more and more promising young black ballplayers were being signed by clubs in integrated ball. Selling promising prospects to major or minor league teams was, in fact, one of the ways the remaining Negro league teams made money. Hank Aaron and Ernie Banks were produced this way, being sold by Negro league teams in the 1950s.

The Kansas City Monarchs were leaders in this new marketplace, and they came upon an almost untapped (at the time) source of talent that they found they could hone and pass along for a handsome profit to organized ball. This source was Cuba. (It's still a great source of talent, but not one that baseball in the United States can routinely utilize, unfortunately.)

On the Kansas City rosters in the early to mid '50s were such players as Pancho Herrera, Dagoberto Nunez, Juan Armenteros, Enrigue Maroto, and Miximo Diago, as well as others. These young men were discovered in Cuba and brought back to the States by the Monarchs. Some played a year or so with a Monarchs' farm team, but all eventually played well for Kansas City, and most were later sold to organized ball for a profit necessary to help the Monarchs stay afloat. (As well as these Cuban ballplayers, K.C. continued to develop and sell homegrown talent, too.)

Juan Armenteros, by all accounts, was a heck of a catcher. There was no question about his bat; his three-year batting average with Kansas City was .327, and he was an All-Star all three years.

Sold by the Monarchs to El Paso (Texas League) in 1956, the St. Louis Cardinals bought him for '57. He may have made it a lot further than he did, but he got married after the '58 season and did not want to subject his wife to the conditions he found as a black ballplayer in this country, so he chose to retire.

Today, his love of baseball is as strong as it ever was. His wife says, "He doesn't speak too much English, but he knows *every*thing that's going on about baseball, not only the home team, but every team. He memorizes *every*thing about baseball."

The English language is not his forte, so in the interview that follows, his wife served as interpreter.

Did you come to the United States to play baseball?

Yes, I did.

Did you play in Cuba?

For a little while.

What was your first team?

Almendares.

I came here with a branch of the Kansas City Monarchs. They brought us over from Cuba. I played with the Monarchs' branch for a year, and then I went to Kansas City for three years—'53, '54, and '55. I was always a catcher. I was an All-Star all three years.

314

Do you know your batting averages with the Monarchs?

.330, .340, and .309.

Did you play minor league ball when you left Kansas City?

Yes. The Monarchs sold me to El Paso, Texas, in 1956. I played there one year, then the St. Louis Cardinals bought me and sent me in 1957 to Winnipeg, Canada. I was there one year, too, then I was sent to York, Pennsylvania, in 1958. Later the same year they sent me to Winston-Salem. That was the end of my career. I played six or seven years.

In that time, who was the best pitcher you caught?

I caught Satchel Paige for a month.

Who was the best ballplayer you saw?

Ernie Banks. I played with him in 1953 — the whole year.

Pancho Herrera was with the Monarchs when you were there.

Yes. Buck O'Neil wanted him to pull the ball to the left, and he used to make his home runs to the right.

What problems did you have coming to the United States and not having a good background in English?

I didn't have that many problems due to the fact that I had John O'Neil — Buck O'Neil — right next to me all the time. He helped a lot.

Have you been back to Cuba since coming here?

Once, for a week in 1979. I have family there; I know about the struggles. They got good baseball players there.

Who was the best ballplayer you saw in Cuba?

Juan Armenteros (courtesy of Juan Armenteros).

Oh, wow. It could be Minnie Minoso, but there were a lot of them.

There was a great deal of travel with the Monarchs. Did you encounter many problems?

I didn't understand at that time what was going on. I had to sit in the back of the bus. As a matter of fact, I stopped playing because I got married in '58 and I didn't want her to go with me because of the situations I saw.

If you were young again, would you be a ballplayer?

Yes. That's been my life.

Is there one game that was special?

For me, every game was special.

BATTING RECORD

Year	Team, League	Pos	G	AB	R	H	2B	3B	HR	RBI	SB	BA
1953	Kansas City, NAL	c										.330
1954		c										.340
1955		c										.309
1956	El Paso, TxL	c										
1957	Winnipeg, NoL	c										
1958	York, NYPL	c										
	Winston-Salem, CarL	c										

Mamie "Peanut" Johnson
"A Winning Woman"

BORN SEPTEMBER 27, 1932, LONG BRANCH, NJ
HT. 5'4" WT. 120 BATTED AND THREW RIGHT

Negro Leagues debut: 1953

Let's begin by dispelling a couple of baseball myths. Myth number 1: Randy Johnson is the tallest player in baseball history. Myth number 2: Ila Borders is the first woman to pitch and win a professional baseball game.

No. 1. Johnson is 6'10" tall, but not one but two Negro leagues players were reported to be seven feet tall. One of them was Cuneo Galvez, who pitched for the Cuban Stars from 1928 to 1932, and the other was Bill "Big Boy" Pryor, a pitcher and occasional outfielder for the Memphis Red Sox in 1927 and the Detroit Stars in 1931. Neither approached Johnson's success, however.

No. 2. Ms. Borders won a game in the independent Northern League in 1998, but she was 45 years too late to be the first. Mamie Johnson won 33 games from 1953 to 1955 for the Indianapolis Clowns in the Negro American League.

Mamie Johnson, called "Peanut" because of her size (5'4", 120 pounds), was a righthander who could throw as hard as most men, and with better control. And she could hit; she often filled in at second base when not on the mound. If one was to examine the records, it would appear that she is the most successful woman ever to play professionally.

Peanut was one of three women signed by the Clowns in the 1950s; the other two were Toni Stone and Connie Morgan, both second basemen. Ms. Stone has been called the first woman to play professional baseball in a men's league, but that distinction actually goes to Pearl Barrett, a first baseman who played with the Havana Stars in 1917.

Today, Mamie Johnson operates the Negro Leagues Baseball Shop in Mitchellville, Maryland (2100 N. Crane Highway, if you want to visit). She carries a whole line of Negro leagues memorabilia.

How did you become an athlete?

Where I come from, down in the country, you had nothing else to do but play baseball. That was our main pastime. When you got big enough to do something or play or whatever — when you got big enough to play any kind of sport, baseball was it. That's how I became a baseball player.

How did you get the attention of the Indianapolis Clowns?

I knew a fellow — his name was Mr. Bish

Tyson — that played in the Negro leagues some time before, and he'd seen me pitching and at that particular time I was playing semipro ball, and that's how I became known, through Mr. Tyson. He knew Mr. [Bunny] Downs [Clowns business manager], and he introduced me to Mr. Downs and I got a tryout.

I was pitching semipro on a men's team. I never really played with girls; I played a little bit of softball, but I was busting up fingers and things and I just didn't want to play. It just wasn't my type of sport.

When I was in junior high, one of the best athletes in our school was a girl. She wanted to play basketball and baseball, but she was discouraged by the coaches. Did you find this?

Oh, no. This is what I've thought about some young ladies. They won't be persistent about it. I was persistent. I said, "You're gonna let me play."

I found after you show them that you are a ballplayer, then they say, "Hey, if she can play, she can play." And it doesn't become a thing that you have to struggle with, but the fellows have to find out that you can play. If you be persistent and go out with the idea to let them know "I can play," then it's really not a problem. It wasn't for me.

I was told you could throw as hard as most of the men.

Oh, yes. And I was accurate. At one particular time, I was taking rocks and knocking birds off the fences. It wasn't a problem with me because where I come from I didn't come up off sandwiches. I came up off greens and cornbread and buttermilk. I was just a strong person, and where I got it from I don't know.

Were any of your brothers or sisters athletes?

No. I'm the oldest of 13 half-sisters and [half-] brothers. I've got six on one side and six on another, and one on another, and I didn't grow up with them. I grew up with my uncle.

Little girls are often told not to go out and play with the boys.

See, I was not told that. This is something that I'm very, very proud of, as far as my mother and my grandmother was concerned — my uncles and all — anything that I wanted to do, they encouraged me to do. They always told me to be the best at what you can do. It wasn't that I had to go play with a doll because that's not what I wanted to do. What I wanted to do was play baseball and this is what they encouraged me to do.

Do you know your record with the Clowns?

Let me see. I can tell you; I've got it on a baseball card. In 1953, it was 11–3; in 1954, it was 10–1; 1955 was 12–4. Average was .262

Mamie Johnson (courtesy of Mamie Johnson).

to .284. I pitched and played utility second base, but pitching was my thing.

Like I said, I was throwing, knocking birds down, so it really wasn't a problem. It was something I wanted to do and I put my mind to do it, and anything I wanted to do, I wanted to do it well. I wanted to be the best. I want to be the best at anything that I attempt.

Do you have any idea how fast you could throw?

I'd say maybe between 80 and 85 miles an hour.

You traveled by bus. Did the Clowns have a good bus?

Oh, yes. Yes, we did. We had a gorgeous bus and it was very comfortable on there. In fact, we stayed on it more than we stayed anywhere else. We slept on it most of the time. We covered the whole country. And Canada.

Mamie Johnson, 1998 (author's collection).

Who was the best player you saw?

You know, I'm going to tell you the truth. I wouldn't want to crown anybody with that. I'll tell you why: There were some of the best ballplayers that ever picked a glove or a bat up. I wouldn't want to say anybody was better than another, other than Mr. Paige. He was the best pitcher out there. And other than Josh Gibson, which I didn't see. He was the best hitter, so they say. I don't know, I wasn't there, but I must believe that. Other than certain outstanding persons, like Josh Gibson, I can't say that this one was better than the other.

Who were some of the ones you felt were out-standing?

Hank [Aaron], he played with us. He was a good ballplayer at that particular time. He left us and went to the major leagues. Mr. [Buck] O'Neil. There was a gentleman that played with us — Ray Neil, the second baseman. He was a tremendous second baseman. There was also a young man, a lefthander, by the name of [Ted] Richardson. He was an outstanding pitcher; in fact, he helped me a whole lot.

There were some good ballplayers on the Birmingham team that I knew. There's *so* many gentlemen that were outstanding ballplayers, so you can't name any particular one.

What was the general feeling of the other play-ers on the team when this little girl showed up?

At first, they looked at me real strange because I was so little, and, like I said, after you prove yourself, then everybody gets real friendly, and after you get friendly, you begin to talk to each other. It was a good experience for me.

Was there any sexist behavior?

No. We didn't have that.

Was there any overt animosity?

No. Back then they were gentlemen. I mean, if they felt that way you didn't know it.

Do you remember your first game with the Clowns?

Yes. It was in Virginia. We spring trained in Norfolk, I think it was, and we had to go over the water to Richmond to play. We went on the ferry over to Richmond. I won it. That was the first game I ever played in the major league.

When you left the Clowns, what did you do?

I went to nursing school. I became a nurse.

If you were a young woman today, would you try to play baseball?

Yes.

PITCHING RECORD

Year	Team, League	G	IP	W	L	Pct	H	B	SO	ERA
1953	Indianapolis, NAL			11	3	.786				
1954				10	1	.909				
1955				12	4	.750				

BATTING RECORD

Year	Team, League	Pos	G	AB	R	H	2B	3B	HR	RBI	SB	BA
1953	Indianapolis, NAL	p-2b										.262
1954		p-ut										.284
1955		p-ut										.271

Eddie Reed
"Bad Boy"

BORN OCTOBER 12, 1929, SPRALIN COAL MINE CAMP, AL
HT. 6' WT. 150 BATTED LEFT, THREW RIGHT

Negro Leagues debut: 1953

Some folks are their own worst enemy. Eddie Reed sure was.

He jumped his contract with the Memphis Red Sox twice. The first time, he signed with the Cleveland Indians and was sent to Keokuk, Iowa, where he played in the same outfield as Roger Maris. For two weeks. That's when Memphis complained about his jumping his contract and the Indians were told to return him.

The next time he jumped (the next year), Memphis let him go. Then the Dodgers signed him and he hit well for them — far and often. There was little question that he was a legitimate prospect.

But spring training was not his favorite thing. He would report late and didn't let them know where he was. They would fuss at him, so he rebelled further by not showing up at all.

This obviously held him back. A discipline problem is rarely promoted, and he was a discipline problem. Reed himself knew it. "I was a pretty bad boy," he says today.

How did you start in baseball?

I was playin' sandlot with the old men. I was a batboy at first, and then, after one guy got hurt, they wanted me to go out and play outfield for 'em and I did. I started to playin' regular then. I was 16, I guess.

I went to the tryout for the Birmingham Black Barons. They cut me when we was playin' a game in Memphis, and Memphis said, "No. We'll take him." I was there three years.

I batted second most of the time and then I went down to fifth. I could play any outfield position, but I played right field most 'cause I had a good arm. I could throw that ball from home plate to center field, out of the ballpark. And I was fast.

Do you remember one game in particular?

The only one that stands out was when

we played in the East and West Classic in Chicago. I hit a home run. It was July the 31st, but I just don't remember the year. I don't remember who was pitchin', but Satchel Paige pitched for us. I was young then. [Laughs]

Who was the best ballplayer you saw?

Well, Satchel was the best pitcher I ever seen. The guys that I know that come out to be super good, there was Hank Aaron and Ernie Banks. He [Banks] was with the Monarchs.

They were very young when you played against them. Could you tell then how good they would be?

Yeah, you could tell 'cause they hit the heck out of the ball. [Laughs] They was doin' like me, hittin' the stink out of the ball. Yeah, they was gonna be good. [Laughs]

In fact, I was sold before either one of

those, but I sold myself and I got caught. [Laughs] When I jumped the league, the manager of the Memphis Red Sox looked me up. I went to play with the Cleveland Indians and they sent me to Keokuk, Iowa. Me and Roger Maris was together.

Then the guy that had my contract, he called the head of the minor leagues and told 'em to look me up. They found me and told me I had to go back to Memphis. [Laughs] I was there [Keokuk] about two weeks when they run me down. [Laughs]

Then I went back to the Memphis Red Sox and I finished that year out and then I jumped the contract again and went down to [Carlsbad] New Mexico. I was a terrible guy. That's the reason I didn't make the majors. [Laughs]

They didn't send me back again. The Dodgers picked me up and they sent me to Great Falls; that's how I'm in Montana now. The Dodgers bought me from the Carlsbad Potashers. I was a pretty bad boy. [Laughs]

I did good for the Dodgers. I hit home runs and everything else here. I started here in '58. Great Falls Electric. I got a clipping when I hit a tape-measure home run. They found it over the fence; it was 509 feet. I was a power hitter, but I was a hitter, period. I could hit the ball. [Laughs]

I didn't advance because I had a hard head and I wouldn't go to spring trainin' on time. When I did go, they'd chew my butt out, then I wouldn't go next time. [Laughs] I was terrible, I tell you. My brain was off in the left side. [Laughs]

Have you mellowed with age?

Oh, gosh, yeah. I guess I had to. [Laughs] I'm all settled down now.

What did you do after you left baseball?

I went to work out to the Air Force base. I was blowin' snow and stuff like that in the trucks. I worked for the Paris Department Store, designing the windows, then I went to work at Town and Ranch; I was there for about 25 years. I was deliverin' furniture. I loved it there 'cause I liked to get out of the building. I don't like to stay inside.

Top: Eddie Reed, 1959. Bottom (l-r): Raymond Haggins, Eddie Reed, Willie Sheelor; Memphis Red Sox, 1954 (courtesy of Eddie Reed).

You've been in Montana a long time. You must like it.

Eddie Reed, 1958 (courtesy of Eddie Reed).

I do. I been here 40 years. The cold doesn't bother me. [Laughs]

You traveled a lot when you were with Memphis.
Yeah, that's all we did. It was good. I enjoyed it. Different states, different towns. Shoot. Lotta gals. I wasn't married then, you know. We saw the whole country.

Where was your favorite place to go?
All of 'em. I enjoyed everywhere I went.

What was your salary with Memphis?
I wasn't makin' that much money. 'Bout 250 bucks a month. Everything was cheap then and I was livin' by myself.

How were the conditions in the towns you went to?
Oh, to me it wasn't bad where we stayed, but it wasn't no king's place. It was just a regular old hotel. We'd get good food all the time 'cause we went to cafes.

Any regrets?
No. Why should I? I enjoyed myself. If you're gonna do somethin' and you show ability to do it, do it. If you don't have it, then you don't get angry with nobody else.

If you were a young man again and it was 1950 or so, would you play baseball?
Heck, yeah. I'd play it now if I could. [Laughs] What are you talkin' about. It was fun.

BATTING RECORD

Year	Team, League	Pos	G	AB	R	H	2B	3B	HR	RBI	SB	BA
1953	Memphis, NAL	of										
1954		of										
1955	Keokuk, IIIL	of										
	Memphis, NAL	of										

Year	Team, League	Pos	G	AB	R	H	2B	3B	HR	RBI	SB	BA
1956	Carlsbad, WTNML	of										
1957		of										
1958	Great Falls, PioL	of										
1959		of										

Enrique "Ricky" Maroto
"Workhorse"

BORN SEPTEMBER 7, 1932, HAVANA, CUBA
HT. 5'9" WT. 150 BATTED AND THREW LEFT

Negro Leagues debut: 1954

Enrique Maroto took the scenic route to the Kansas City Monarchs. He began his professional baseball career in his native Cuba, then in 1951 he went to Canada to play. From there, he came to the United States, but played on the Cuban traveling team.

In 1954, the Monarchs acquired him. With them, he divided his time between the mound and the outfield, but he was still primarily a pitcher. Both seasons ('54, '55) he was with Kansas City, he was selected to play in the East-West Game, and one year he played both outfield and pitcher in the classic.

Possessing a strong left arm and sound mechanics, the Monarchs used him in an unheard-of manner in 1955. When the team played doubleheaders, Maroto would start the first game and relieve in the second, if needed. On May 22 of that season, he pitched a five-hit, complete game victory over the Detroit Stars in the first game, then worked the final seven innings of the second to win that one, too.

Then three weeks later, he defeated the Birmingham Black Barons with a four-hit shutout in the opener and came back to win the nightcap in relief.

In an article in the *Chicago Defender* of July 2, 1955, headlined, "Maroto Top Pitcher in NAL Loop," it stated, "It's now standard operating procedure for the Monarchs to work Maroto in the first game of a twin bill and then have him ready for relief in the nightcap."

While in Cuba, he won two games for Cienfuegos over Marianao in the championship series, the first game with a three-hitter. At this time, Cuban rosters were dotted with major leaguers or future major leaguers.

Did you play ball in Cuba?

Yes. I played for Marianao and Cienfuegos. I played two year for Marianao, one year for Cienfuegos — the last year after the revolution with Fidel Castro. [It was] 1959, I think.

I went to Canada in 1951. I played for Brandon in Manitoba. I was a pitcher. I played in Canada one year, and then I played in United States; the Cuban traveling team come over here. I think they once belonged to the Kansas City Monarchs, and I played for that team as pitcher and outfielder.

Then, in 1954, they trade me to the Kansas City Monarchs. I was pitcher and outfielder — '54 and '55. Both years I went to the All-Star Game. There were write-ups in the *Chicago Defender*.

After '55, I played for Charlotte [South Atlantic League] in Charlotte, North Carolina. I played two years for Charlotte. I was a pitcher there.

Then I went back to Cuba and played for Marianao two year, but they don't give me too much a chance to play. Then I went to Nicaragua. I won 12 and lost five in Nicaragua. [That was] 1958 or '59. I played to 1961 or '62. I went to Mexico. I played for Monterrey, I played for Mexico [City] Reds. I play for Cuban Sugar Kings in '59 or '60.

Do you ever visit Cuba now?

I just came back from Cuba. I went there for two week. Vacation. I got family and my wife's family there. We had a good time. I played ball with the children. They got real bad fields; they don't got no balls, they got no gloves. The same thing when I was young, so don't blame Castro. When I was young, we don't have nothing. My first glove I make myself. We were so poor we could not afford a glove.

Is there one game — anywhere — that stands out?

In Nicaragua, I was pitching a no-hitter to the eighth, and the worst hitter — the *worst* hitter on the other team — was the one that got the hit on me. In the eighth inning with two out.

If I could run over there and get the ball before he hit, I would because it was a fastball letter-high. If a good hitter hit me, okay, but it was the worst. I think he was the eighth hitter before the pitcher. And I know him; he was from Cuba, too. He was a bad hitter; he had good hands, he was a good shortstop. He couldn't hit a watermelon.

Then another game I played for Charlotte. I pitched on Thursday; I win, 1–0. Then I pitch Monday and win; it was 5–2. Three days' rest. Complete game both times.

What I hate about the Negro leagues, they have no records. One time I pitch nine inning and win the first game and go relief in the second inning in the second game and win both games. I pitched 16 innings. With the Kansas City Monarchs.

How did you feel after that?

I was 22 year old. After that you can go dancing. [Laughs]

You saw baseball all over the Western Hemisphere. Who was the best player you saw?

To me, the best player is Willie Mays. He's complete: he can throw, he can catch, and he can hit, he can run, he can stole bases. Like Hank Aaron — he was a good hitter, but he can't stole no bases, he no have that great arm. Clemente was super, too.

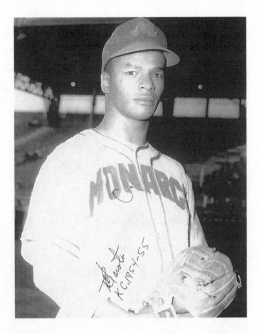

Enrique Maroto (courtesy of Enrique Maroto).

As a pitcher, which batter gave you the most trouble?

When I pitch in the Negro league, I think I was so good nobody give me no trouble. When I play here in the All-Star game in Chicago, I play outfield and I got two doubles. Then I pitch seventh, eighth, and ninth inning. I think I struck 'em out. The first six inning I played center field and I hit those two doubles, then I pitch. I feel so good, I have so much confident in me.

Then the Chicago Cubs, they want me, but I think the owner of the team [Monarchs], he asking for too much. We stayed over in Chicago for six hours because they were negotiating. [That was] 1955.

I never had that big body that they looking for. They never believe a man 5'9", 150 pounds can play a whole season, you know. If you're not 6'0", 180 pounds in that time they look down on you.

Who was the best pitcher you saw?

I played with Jim Bunning. I got a picture [of] me, Jim Bunning, Minnie Minoso, Charlie Lau, Mike Fornieles, Julio Becquer — played first base for the Senators — and [Jose] Valdevielso, shortstop.

Top: 1957-58 Marianao, Cuban Winter League. Back row (l-r): unidentified, Charlie Lau, unidentified, Orlando Lerux, Connie Marrero, Enrique Maroto, unidentified, Rene Friol, Raul Sanchez. Middle row (l-r): trainer, unidentified, Mike Fornieles, Juan DeLis, Aldo Salven, Alberto Alverez, Bob Shaw, Jim Bunning, Jose Valdevielso, unidentified, trainer. Front row (l-r): Quintana, Minnie Minoso, Rodolfo Arias, Julio Becquer, Juan Isaquirre, Napoleon Reyes (manager), Jose Maria Fernandez, unidentified, Aldrual Baro. Seated: batboys. Bottom: 1956 or 1957, Charlotte, South Atlantic League. Enrique Maroto is third from left in the front row (courtesy of Enrique Maroto).

I wish they'd let me go back to 20 years so I can do it again. [Laughs]

As a batter, did one pitcher give you a hard time?

I was a good fastball hitter. I hit pretty good. I never like to hit against a lefthander. [Laughs] I was a lefthanded hitter, and if a lefthander threw sidearm, I hate it. [Laughs]

You played in a lot of countries. Did you enjoy the travel?

I loved it. I love to travel. The worst thing was here in the Negro league where we had to travel 3-, 400 miles every day. We got dressed on the bus. Sometime the other team was waiting for us on the field and we had to get dressed on the bus and went out from the bus to the field. You know, after you traveling 400 mile, you have to do a little running so your legs aren't stiff. It was terrible, but when you're 20 years, you think everything's okay.

What was the situation with the hotels and the restaurants?

It was a problem for everyone. We black; there wasn't many we can go. You can go to movies sometime. It's a long history; the young people, they don't know about it.

In Cuba, if you got the money, you can go everywhere. But here, I remember one time I want to go to movie; I had to wait outside and see if any black goes in, then I go and get my ticket.

When I play for Charlotte, same thing. We live in one hotel, the other white ballplayers live in another one. Same thing when you go to the field. You got your teammates against you, the other team against, the umpire, and 20,000 [fans]. It's not the same thing playing as the white ballplayers.

That's the reason I say Willie Mays is the best because he got everything against him. Even in the big league, they were separate at that time. They go to different hotels, different restaurants.

Sometime we go to a hotel where the people, they fight and everybody have their face cut with the knife, and drinking, and prostitution. Sometime you don't sleep the whole night, especially when you're Cuban

and you don't understand what they're talking about. You're even afraid to get out of the room.

In Canada, we have no trouble, but it was so cold. I don't think it's the place to play baseball. In Brandon, Manitoba, it was so cold! Man! I can't even concentrate on the plate. I feel so cold, shaking all over. I want to go back, only I no have a warm home waiting for me. [Laughs] Even in May, it was so cold. It snowed there.

What was your best baseball salary?

Oh, never more than $500. With $500, I make more money than everybody in my neighborhood. [Laughs] Not my family, my *neighborhood*. At that time, it was a lot of money. I remember American $500, I give my mother $200 every month.

What did you do when you left baseball?

I learn how to be a carpenter. I went to Cuba in 1962 from Mexico. I was supposed to stay in Cuba for 12 days to get papers for my wife and my son — I want to get them out of Cuba — and it take me four year to get out. I lost all my ability to play. I had to go to my brother; he had a carpenter place. I went there and learned how to be a carpenter. I do it here for 30 years. I still do some little work.

I used to have a restaurant in Dominican Republic in 1979. I see all those ballplayers, but I was looking for somebody to support me, you know, like a major league contract. I could be a millionaire by now, but I never had a good connection. I see a lot of good players, but they need money.

Any regrets from baseball?

No, I don't have no regret. I'm happy and got my family. Everything okay. My children, one gonna be a doctor; the other is a contractor, like me. He learn to be a carpenter and he's in Denver, Colorado, and he got 450 apartments to take care of. He bought a house for $150,000. My other son, he's in Louisiana in the university; he's a teacher there. I can't complain. To me, everything's beautiful.

Like I tell my wife, I say, "What are you complaining about? You should be happy. Our

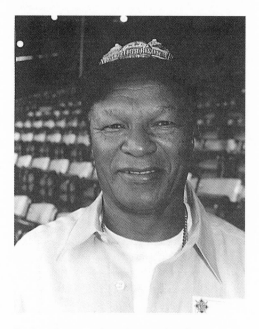

children, they got good health, they don't give no trouble." She got a job, I got a job, and we built this house. We're gonna sell it for $220,000 and go to Miami and buy a house and with the retirement money we get, we can live like kings.

You know how much the people make in Cuba now? My wife's sister — she's retired — you know how much she get? Fifty cents Cuban peso. [That's] $3.30. She don't have no clothes. Everything she got are the clothes we give her two years ago when we were in Cuba. When we there this year, everybody dress with the clothes we give 'em. We take clothes and money and shoes and underwear. Last time we went, we pay $300 overweight. We bring clothes for everybody.

No, I got no regret.

Enrique Maroto, 1999 (Lisa Feder photograph).

PITCHING RECORD

Year	Team, League	G	IP	W	L	Pct	H	BB	SO	ERA
1951	Brandon, MnDkL									
1954	Kansas City, NAL									
1955										
1956	Charlotte, SAL									
1957										
1958	Marianao, CubL									
1959										
1960	Cienfuegos, CubL									
1961	Mex. City Reds, MxL									

Maroto also played outfield while with Kansas City.

Bob "Peachhead" Mitchell
"A Latter Day Monarch"

BORN NOVEMBER 18, 1932, WEST PALM BEACH, FL
HT. 5'11" WT. 162 BATTED LEFT, THREW RIGHT

Negro Leagues debut: 1954

Bob Mitchell was a righthanded pitcher for the Kansas City Monarchs from 1954 through 1957. Although his career as a professional baseball player wasn't long, his career as a fighter for the rights of black Americans has been. And it's still going on.

And now, in addition to attempting to correct injustices to the black population in general, he's working on a more specific cause.

Major League Baseball decided several years ago that segregation in baseball officially ended when the Brooklyn Dodgers signed Jackie Robinson. From that day on, they maintain, all players, regardless of color, were treated equally by the major leagues. Of course, if one looks at the rate of integration of both the major and minor league clubs, it's apparent that that is untrue.

As a result of this decision, blacks who played professionally *before* Robinson's signing are given a pension today by Baseball, and deservedly so; but blacks who played *after* he signed are not, even though some remnant of the invisible barrier — racism — that kept them out of organized ball still existed. Eighty-five percent of living former Negro leagues players fall into this latter group.

Mitchell is campaigning heavily to correct this. He believes that players who participated in recognized black leagues in the more than a decade after Robinson's signing deserve something.

He has the experience, the facts, and the ear of the right people. And with his track record, if it can be done, he'll do it.

How did you come to join the Monarchs?

I was playing with a team called the Florida Cubans, an all–Cuban team here in Florida. The Monarchs were scheduled to play them and one night they started me against the Monarchs here in Lakeland, Florida — Henley Field, where the Detroit Tigers have spring training.

I pitched against them that night and they had good players. They had [Ernie] Banks and all them guys. He had just come back from the Army; this was in '53. After the game was over, I went in and took a shower

because I was disgusted with myself. I couldn't find the plate, and I retired one man by the strikeout route. He happened to be a good home run hitter, good average hitter, too, named Ernie Johnson. He went up to Triple-A after that.

I went into the dressing room to take a shower a little bit disgusted and Buck O'Neil saw me and he asked me did I know Hopp. I said, "Yes. Hopp was my coach down in West Palm Beach."

He said, "Hopp told me to get you away from up here." I said, "What's the offer?" He

Bob Mitchell (courtesy of Robert Mitchell).

said, "I don't know. It's spring training now; I don't know whether you'll be able to make it or not. We'd like to have you, though. Are you always that wild?"

I said, "No, no." He said, "Good curveball and all that?" I said, "Yes. Everything you see is what I have." He said, "We'd like to have you. I'll tell Mr. Baird." Tom Baird was the owner at the time; he lived in Kansas City, Kansas. He said, "Mr. Baird will get in touch with you."

I went with the Florida Cubans a while, traveling up through the South, playing in Mississippi, Alabama, Georgia, and various places. Then I came back before the season was over; I didn't go into Canada with them. I went back to West Palm Beach to a team called the Lincoln Giants; that was in the Florida State Negro League.

A counsel from South America was brought up here by the owner of the Miami Giants, a fellow named Roderick Silva, and he was looking for pitchers. That Sunday I was laying on the bench with my glove over my face shielding the sun out of my eyes and he asked for pitchers. A guy said, "Here's a pitcher here."

Back then I was number one 'cause every Sunday they started me and every game I played down there with the Palm Beach Lincoln Giants on Sundays I won. The Hispanic counselor from South America said, "No, no. I do not want a high school pitcher." One of my teammates said, "He's a league pitcher."

Well, he offered me $350 a month and offered to pay *all* my expenses, to go somewhere in South America because a lot of players went down there already. He said, "I'll get in touch with you in a week or so."

So I waited around about a week and in between that week the owner of the club, Bill Elam, had worked out an option for me to try out with the West Palm Beach Indians, which was the only all-white team in the Florida International League. I went down there and went to the office there and talked with the general manager, named Bruce Henry. He said, "You think you can play this kind of ball?"

I said, "Sure, very emphatically. The only difference is these guys are white and I'm black."

He said, "All right, all right," and sent me to the dressing room. I suited up and I heard some racist remarks, particularly by their long-ball home run king. Butch Lawring was his name. Three or four of the other players were sitting close to me and they were talking to me, trying to make me overlook that.

I went out and pitched to about three batters. I think Bucky Harris — he was a catcher, he'd been with the Cubs or somebody — he was the manager at the time and he caught me and warmed me up.

Butch Lawring was one of the main ones who came in to bat and he hit a shot back to me and if I wouldn't have caught it, it would've torn my head off. I pitched to two other batters and came in and sat down and they started the game. I watched 'em use that night seven or eight pitchers and I wanted to be under contract so bad. Oh, goodness! But nothing happened. They lost bad to Tampa — Smokers, I think it was. A big ol' boy named Claro Duany, a Cuban boy, hit that ball *way* over those very tall telegraph poles — way over those lights onto Okeechobee Road in West Palm Beach at Wright/Connie Mack Field.

I went out there twice, and one morning I saw in the *Palm Beach Post* that Robert Mitchell would not be signed by the local Indians but into a league of lower classification, so I said to myself, "To hell with that."

I stayed around a week and I went to Philadelphia. When I was in Philadelphia, I received a letter from the Kansas City Monarchs in the winter, from Tom Baird, saying Buck O'Neil is high on me and he wanted me. He offered me $250 to start and [asked] how did I want to come, by plane or train. Well, I'd never flew so I said train.

So I took the TRR, the C&O, the B&O, and everything to get to Newport News, and that's how I got with the Monarchs.

How old were you?
About 20, I guess.

How did you do?
I was in the rotation. We started off in spring training. We played the Indianapolis Clowns. I had heard about these guys when I was young and I'd heard of Ray Neil and all the heavy hitters they had. I think it was in Newport News, Skip started me out the first three innings. Boom-boom-boom. Strikeout, swinging. Boom-boom-boom. Strikeout, swinging. Boom-boom-boom. Strikeout, swinging. Boom-boom. Strikeout. Pop-up over the infield. I went through three innings that way. Struck out most all of 'em in three innings. About eight strikeouts.

That was my three innings. I said, "Skip, these are my boys." He said, "All of 'em are your boys." I said, "Can I have another inning?" He said, "Yeah, go on in and get another one." So I went in and it wasn't no difference. It *wasn't* any difference. I had a pretty damn good fastball and my ball would rise—it'd run, a natural slider.

Do you know any of your seasonal statistics?
One year was 7–7. I believe that was the ending. One was 6–7. I can't remember the others, but I remember vividly the 7–7 'cause I won more games with less rest than I did

with having four days' rest. I was more effective on three days' rest.

I discovered that running was the best thing for your arm when you're a pitcher. And the main thing is to always keep something on your arm. When you're sleeping, have a clean undershirt and sleep in it. You've got to protect your arm. But running was one of the main things to give you a good fastball; it makes your arm better. It not only keeps the soreness out, it makes it better. It helps your legs; it builds stamina.

Why did you retire when you did?
Good question. When I was in LaCrosse, Wisconsin, my fiancée was pregnant with my child and she wanted me to come home because she was getting near that time. So that day I went up to the manager's room—Dizzy Dismukes—and I said, "Skip, my wife sent me a telegram." I told her to send me a telegram; I said, "The only way Dizzy's gonna let me go is if you send a telegram." So within the hour I had the telegram and I took it to show it to him.

He said, "You'll do more good here than you can there. You'll be working." I said, "Yes, but you know how a woman is when she's having her first child." Mine, too.

He said, "Okay, you can go. I'm gonna have to give you what you had made." I think I had about three weeks coming, but he gave me some of his own money along with it and arranged for me to catch a train out of there.

I went back to Philadelphia, back to a job that I had in the off-season and told 'em I was back. They told me, "You can start now." I said, "No, I can't start now. I got to get married." They said, "Well, when you get married, come on back to work."

The very night I got married was the night Randy Turpin and Sugar Ray Robinson were fighting. Robinson beat him that night and got his title back from Randy Turpin. And, also, we went to the movie *Something of Value*. It was about a Mau-Mau secret order of Kikuyu tribesmen tired of the white minority rule.

Did you try to go back to the Monarchs?

Bob Mitchell, 1955 (courtesy of Robert Mitchell).

Not with them. I made an attempt to go with a new club that was being formed in Newark. I went there and I stayed about a month until I discovered that these people wasn't properly funded, so I left and went back to West Palm Beach, my hometown.

I was a shipping clerk in Philadelphia, and when I went back to West Palm Beach I was working in a home furnishing store. I worked at Burdine's, too. Then I got a job with Palm Beach County in juvenile detention, but most of my activities centered around civil rights. That was my real work; my livelihood was my job. My real work was working — civic and political — in the community and parts of the state.

I was chairman of the Florida Black Republican Council. I organized the first council here in Florida in 1975. A fellow named John Wilkes — he used to be Assistant Secretary of Defense for Contract Compliance — asked me when I was in Washington would I organize something, so I said, "I'll see what I can do, John," so I came back and I organized it.

From there, I was elected to the Palm Beach County Republican Executive Committee and I stayed on there 15 years. Everything else is history. You go to West Palm Beach now and call my name to most people, they would know who you're talking about.

Are there games that stand out?

The games that stand out would be the tough games, like I was pitching against Kelly Searcy, Birmingham's ace lefthander. Me and him locked up one night and I think he beat me, 2–1 or 2–0. We had it going down to the wire.

Another time I was in Chattanooga. Sometimes you get rabbit ears and you can hear the fans hollering: "Come on, Youngblood! Come on, Youngblood!" I had 'em going. That was at the Lookouts' place, where they've got the big words "LOOKOUTS" written with big rocks in giant letters in the outfield.

I had some outstanding games. A lot of games I pitched sometimes they'd get no runs for me. Some of the players commented about that: "Bob, we can't get no runs for you. For Cardenas [a Cuban lefthander], we get a lot of runs and he was just walkin' the ball up there."

In '56 — it wasn't a league game but we had to travel about 358 miles from Buffalo to St. Thomas, Canada. We had one of the best bus drivers in the country, Sylvester Murphy, who's not living now. He used to be the bus driver for the Harlem Globetrotters.

We were still on the highway about eight o'clock for a 7:30 game and still about 15 miles from the ballpark, so those guys who had their suit rolls inside the bus on the rack, they start pulling down the shades and start dressing on the bus. We got there, we hurried up and dressed, and I had to warm up on the sideline by going to first base and running from first base to the outfield fence pretty fast and walking back. I done that for about five minutes and then I got a ball and started playing catch with any infielder that would catch me. I just threw the ball back and forth, back and forth. I did that for about five minutes and I was ready.

I went in that night — it was an all-white team — and I struck out 13 and beat them, 2–0.

We ran into some little racist stuff. The kids don't know any better 'cause they're taught that way. Near the dugout, one of the kids said, "Aren't you niggers?" I said, "Hey, you better get him away from here!" Some of the women fans told him to go away and don't do that.

In LaCrosse, Wisconsin, I don't think they'd ever seen too many blacks there. We saw some Indians there, but I don't think the kids under ten years of age had ever seen any blacks. They looked at us very strange as we were going into the supermarket one day, and I knew that they had never seen us before.

I just got through reading a story about Jackie Robinson, when him and his wife came down to Florida and they were headed to Pensacola. Before they got to Pensacola, they'd gone to New Orleans and they couldn't go from there because the airlines said they had to take some people off the plane so they could get more fuel on, and the weather and all that, and they had to stay back. It took them 36 hours to get where they had to go. His wife ran into this Jim Crowism, and she was the one that couldn't handle it. She was the one that was ready to fight it, but because of Jackie she kept her cool as much as she could because she knew what he had to do.

The Florida Humanities Council had me to go to the 1998 Cleveland Indians camp two days after the Indians had left, to speak to a group of people concerning the Negro leagues and my experiences. And, also, they had me at the Holocaust Museum over there in St. Petersburg where I spoke on the same thing before 25 or 30 teachers about the Negro leagues and the problems we were having and things that I went through, etc.

Talking about going through things, how bad was it as you traveled through the South?

It wasn't too bad for some people if you stayed in your so-called place, but, see, I didn't necessarily stay in my so-called place. It wasn't that important to me to be able to sit down on the toilet or next to a white person — that kind of little simple stuff like that.

All I knew was that it was wrong; I knew what it could create with myself. It was something that you had to cope with. In my town, one day going to lunch I said I was going into this Woolworth's and I'm going to order me a hot dog and a drink and I'm going to stand right there at the counter and eat it. *Stand,* not sit.

So I ordered it and I stood right there and ate it. The woman said, "You can't do that." I said, "Why not? I just bought it." I stood right there and ate it, drank my soda and everything.

While I was there, some wannabes from the black community was coming through the store. Roderick Stevens — he runs a funeral home — he looked through the counter, through all the goods on the counter, and saw me doing that and he carried it back. He carried it back to the community and some of the white liberals there in town heard what I'd done.

When I got through, I walked out of the store. When I walked out of the store I saw a man, looked like he was following me. Tailing me. He looked to be in his late 50s. I saw him out of the corner of my eye — peripheral sight, you know.

I walked a little fast and I spotted him again out of the corner of my eye, so I crossed the street and went into Montgomery Ward. I walked *fast* in the store, went upstairs where they keep the appliances, and I got behind a refrigerator and there he come. He stood in there looking all around, but he didn't see me. I just went out the back way.

They used to refer to me as a firebrand. If you would go to the morgue [the archives] of the *Palm Beach Post Times* and the *Miami Herald* and Channel Five and Twelve, you'll see what I contributed.

One time I came home from work and my brother told me, "Bob, the FBI called here about you." I said, "For what?" See, I was with the NAACP and they didn't like the idea that we was too militant for the old crew.

I went down to talk to him and he asked me, "How many members do you have?" I said, "Those who know don't say and those who say don't know." He said, "Okay, you don't have to tell me." Then he said, "Do you know Stokely Carmichael?" I said, "I know him correspondingly." "That's all we want to know."

"Don't get in no trouble." I said, "It depends on how you find trouble." The agent's name was Kellogg.

About eight or nine years later, he ended up in the same party. He's a Republican. He saw I had some influence.

The feeling of many is that the caliber of Negro league ball was inferior during the time you played. Who were some of the players you played with and against?

There was Banks. There was a lot of good players that had major league caliber and high caliber potential to shortly advance to the major leagues and high classification minors.

I'm going to give you a good example. Look at John Kennedy, how late they got him. He went to the most racist team in baseball, which was the Philadelphia Phillies. He burned up the Grapefruit League. His sister's going to send me some clippings so I can show them to Bud Selig. He never got a chance; he played in five games and they sent him back.

Hell, we had Hank Mason with the Phillies, Francisco Herrera with the Phillies. Every time I see [Sammy] Sosa, I think about Herrera. Had Herrera been given a chance to go up there and swing at that type of pitching, God knows what he could've done. I've seen Herrera hit back-to-back home runs in St. Louis at Busch Stadium. That's when they had the eagle flying in the A. I saw when he had three home runs back to back in Columbia, Mississippi, one night when they was broadcasting a game.

The same night, Dagoberto Nunez, one of our hard-throwing pitchers who had a good bat, hit three home runs. I saw that. I wasn't working that night and I went into the bus to hear the game because I couldn't believe that in Mississippi they was broadcasting the game. That was the first time I heard a broadcast of a Negro league game.

Larry Lester, a Negro leagues researcher, asked me did I know of any broadcasts and I told him, "You call the people there and they might be able to run it down."

I remember one time I was sitting in the dugout in Cincinnati and Gabe Paul came in the dugout. He was looking for players. Buck said, "See that guy out there around second base and shortstop?" I think it was Jess Williams. "He's ready now." That's what Buck told him.

We had some good players and quite a few of them had major league caliber. If they didn't go straight to the majors, wherever they went they'd have been up within three years. One to three years.

A lot of young black talent's being lost today the same way 'cause they have nowhere to go. Scouts are not going to come out there to the black parks. They didn't when I was playing. When I was in high school, I was doing just as good as Ken Johnson, who was at Palm Beach High School about three miles south of where I was going to school. Herb Score was in Lake Worth, which is about ten miles south of where I went to school, in the next town.

I used to go out there and watch them pop the mitt. Scouts went there, but they didn't come down to Lincoln Park, which is only about two-and-a-half or three miles north of where Ken Johnson was playing.

Right now today, they're not getting American black players. They're going down to South America. It's the economics — anything those guys can get, I don't blame them at all. If they can make just $30,000 a year, that's a fortune compared to what they're getting down there.

Would you play baseball again if you were a young man?

Oh, yes. Sure. I love it. I used to eat and sleep it. In fact, I wanted to be an artist, I wanted to be a writer. That went on 'til baseball knocked out art.

My greatest thrill was to have the great Leroy "Satchel" Paige as a teammate in 1955.

One night in Dothan, Alabama, the Monarchs' third baseman, Hank Bayliss, told Satch that I "thumb-cocked" the ball; it's why my fastball took off like a slider.

Satch told me after demonstrating his chewing gum wrapper home plate pitching, he said, "Bob" or "Mitch," I forget which one, "Don't press. Just pitch to get the ball over." Satch told me that if my grip was comfortable, don't change it.

One night we were playing the Memphis Red Sox in Saginaw, Michigan. Satch was to pitch only the first three innings. Satch left the game scoreless. I went in and completed the remaining six innings, winning, 6–3.

Baseball was good to me — the game, I mean. As I've said, I ate and slept baseball since I was about 11 or 12 years old.

But today baseball needs to get its respect back from the black fans by righting the 78-year injustice created by the infamous "Gentlemen's Agreement," which kept blacks out of organized ball.

PITCHING RECORD

Year	Team, League	G	IP	W	L	Pct	H	BB	SO	ERA
1954	Kansas City, NAL									
1955										
1956				6	7	.462				
1957				7	7	.500				

Ted Rasberry
"He Did It All"

BORN OCTOBER 8, 1913, WEST POINT, MS
HT. 5'6" WT. 140 BATTED AND THREW RIGHT

Negro Leagues debut: 1954

It has been said of a lot of men, "He did it all." Well, it was never more true than in the case of Ted Rasberry. He is probably the only man in history who was, at the same time, owner, manager, player, traveling secretary, booking agent, and everything else of a major professional team. And he also served as vice-president of the Negro American League.

Born in Mississippi in 1913 with a love of baseball, Rasberry played for and organized several teams over the years, beginning in elementary school and culminating, first, with the rebirth of the Detroit Stars, and finally as owner of the greatest franchise in the Negro leagues, the Kansas City Monarchs, a team he still technically owns today.

Today, more than three decades after the Monarchs played their last game, he is still involved in sports. He promotes the Harlem Travelers, a touring basketball team whose exploits on the court are well worth the price of admission.

I started in baseball when I was very young. Don't know why, didn't have anyone in the family that had participated. Somehow or other, I fell in love with the game.

When I was about 12 or 13, I was going to a little country school—one building, everybody in the same room—and I built us a baseball park. The schoolhouse was in the woods, so I cleaned off a space out there large enough for a little baseball diamond. When I got the bushes and things all cleared away, in the afternoons we'd go out there and play baseball. I don't know why, but that was my love.

A couple years ago, I was down in Mississippi and my cousin took me by this little school. It was Rasberry School in Clay County. The building was still standing there; it looked so bad I was really afraid to go on the inside—like it was ready to fall without wind. I could look out there to the left, just south of the building, and see the shape of

that baseball diamond, where I cut and had that baseball diamond. That form and everything was still out there.

I used to make my baseballs out of my mother's stockings. I could unravel those stockings, put a rock in it, and make a ball. I made my bats back in that time. My dad, he was a blacksmith and he had a shop, and I would cut down small trees, like hickory and ash. Those were my two specialties. I would make my baseball bats out of those timbers.

I went to high school and college. I started in high school in seventh grade and I was probably the youngest kid around that liked baseball, but they had a baseball club. I went out—anybody said "baseball," I was there—so I went to the baseball diamond and worked out with the team. Guess I was about 15 then and they said I was too young to play, but I could do it all, some better than some of the guys that they had.

I remember on one occasion — probably the next year — I was working out with the team. I was working out at shortstop. I looked real good. They couldn't play me with the team, but they finally let me hit during batting practice. They let me hit last. The pitcher couldn't throw the ball by me. Couldn't none of 'em throw the ball by me. I could always hit. I could just hit anybody.

When I would come home after MIC College, I'd bring some of our baseball regalia with me — the catcher's mitt and the mask and a couple of balls or whatever I could get out of there without them stopping me — and we organized a team in my hometown — not town, my home country, out there in the country where we lived. We called it the Rasberry Quicksteppers. We stepped pretty fast. We beat most of the teams that had been playing — little country teams — that had been playing for quite some time.

My uncle was playing on a team called Griffith. They had some good ballplayers. They came up and played us and we beat them. I was pitching at that time, my brother was catching. We had guys at the different positions; couldn't any of 'em play too well. My brother and I would win the games 'cause I was an extremely good pitcher at that time. I never admitted it after I hurt my arm. When I came up here I never admitted I had ever pitched because I knew I would hurt it again. I knew I didn't have the kind of stuff I had then. I could throw as hard as I wanted to, had a good curveball — what we called "outdrop" — and that kind of stuff, so we just beat everybody.

After that, I came to Grand Rapids. When I came to Grand Rapids, I was teaching at Hopewell School. I left a teaching job to come here. What really brought me here was to bring my uncle's family up here. I was boarding with him where I was teaching. He came up and found out that he liked Grand Rapids and he wanted his family to come to him. After the school season ended, then I agreed to bring his family up. We came up on the train.

After we was up here — well, before the next school season started — I had decided that I wanted to stay, so I wrote 'em and told 'em that I wouldn't be back and they could get another teacher. I stayed in Grand Rapids.

First team that I saw working out, I was out there. That was Charles Taylor's team. Taylor's All-Stars or something. I played with them and a guy named Jesse Elster, who had been around some time — Jesse Elster's Athletics, he was well known and he always put together a pretty good team — saw me playing and he wanted me to play with his team.

I joined them and they were playing weekends in these little towns around Grand Rapids. Every little town had a ballclub. We'd play Holland, we'd play Muskegon — all these little towns on the weekend we'd go play 'em. This is mid '30s. I came here in '35. This was '36, '37, and '38 — along in that area.

I played with Jesse Elster until about '42. In '42, I had become first his manager and then his business partner. I helped to sponsor the team and we had the Jesse Elster's Athletics and some of the Negro league teams would come here to play us. We had that type of a team; we had a good team.

We played out at Bigelow Field. That's the place where they had lights in Grand Rapids. They had a professional team here once called the Grand Rapids Jets; that's where they played.

In about 1946, I wanted to get into the Negro league. Jesse Elster, he was an older guy; he was satisfied at what we were doing. I was happy at what we were doing, but I wanted to move up. That was my destiny.

I started working with some of the guys I got in touch with in the Negro league and that created my interest. I decided that I'd organize a team that would be good enough to go in the Negro leagues. I had a guy working with me at that time called Frank Lamar. We put this team together and Captain Walter Cole was with this team. We got players from all over the country, put 'em on a salary, brought 'em here to Grand Rapids, and they were known as the Grand Rapids Black Sox.

After the first year, Mr. Lamar and Captain Cole quit. Mr. Lamar said that he didn't

Ted Rasberry (courtesy of Ted Rasberry).

want to go the next year; he wanted to fold the team. I said, "No, I'm going to keep it going."

The next year, I kept the team going and we just got better and more popular and I wanted to get into the Negro league, but Dr. J. B. Martin, he was the president of the league, they had a meeting and he said, "No. Grand Rapids ain't big enough. You got to get yourself something larger than Grand Rapids to come into the Negro American League."

I still was determined to get into the Negro league. We got into the Midwest League; that was played out of Chicago. South Chicago and two teams in Wisconsin — one of 'em was Kenosha, the other one was Racine — and the Grand Rapids Black Sox.

We won the championship in that league, then we got in the little leagues around here, these cities around here like Holland, Grand Haven, Muskegon, South Haven. We had a league that we organized in this area. We won the championship in that league.

Then I decided that I would organize a team out of Detroit, 'cause Detroit had discontinued in 1950. All those teams folded after Jackie Robinson went into the majors. The

[Negro] National League folded. The [Negro] American League kept struggling, so in 1954 I had organized a team known as the Detroit Stars. We got a franchise in the Negro league. We played our games out of Tiger Stadium.

That was my beginning and I continued on after I got in the Negro league with the Detroit Stars and in 1955, Mr. Baird decided that he would discontinue because he was getting old. He wanted to fold the Kansas City Monarchs. The Kansas City Monarchs was really the life of our league 'cause the Indianapolis Clowns had pulled out the year before. We wanted Tom Baird to sell the team to somebody else so we could keep the league going. We only had four teams left now: Detroit Stars, Kansas City Monarchs, Birmingham Black Barons, and Memphis Red Sox.

He wouldn't sell to anyone else. He said, "I only want to sell to one guy, and that's Ted Rasberry."

I already got the Detroit Stars, but they're not going to do any good without the league, so now I've got to try to keep the league going by buying the Kansas City Monarchs.

I had a guy in New Orleans said he would go part-interest on the Detroit Stars and he only lasted a year. We called 'em the New Orleans-Detroit Stars for that year and then I still had 'em back in my lap. Some wonder why I had two teams; it was to keep the league going.

I purchased the Monarchs after the season in '55, and in '56 I had charge of the Monarchs and we trained in Hattiesburg, Mississippi. Mr. [Dizzy] Dismukes, who had been with the Monarchs for quite some time, was my manager. He came over when I bought the Monarchs.

One of the things that convinced Tom Baird that I wouldn't run the team down — the Monarchs had been the tops all the time; they was the main attraction — we played the Kansas City Monarchs for the Negro World Championship in 1955. We'd only been in one year — we beat everybody else out — and that second year we played for the championship.

In that championship, we almost beat the Monarchs; I think they'd won about 26 of 'em.

I just have to mention how the thing ended up. The reason we didn't beat 'em — they probably was the best — my reason is, I made the wrong decision. We was leading 'em by one run — I think the score at that time was 1–0 — and they had two men on and there was two outs. I went out to talk to my pitcher and he said, "I got 'em." You know that conversation that goes on between the manager and the pitcher.

I said, "We can't let nothing go here. We gotta have it." He said, "Okay, I got him."

So I turned and came on back and they substituted Buck O'Neil. I'd never seen Buck; I had heard about him, but he had never played in any of the games when they were playing us and we played 'em a whole lot. He was kind of like I was; he'd only come in to pinch hit only when he was needed in those desperate situations. I did the same thing.

He came in to pinch hit. I went back out to my pitcher and said, "Look here, now. You got a pinch hitter." I didn't know really that much about Mr. O'Neil at that time. I thought he was dilapidated. The pitcher said, "I got him, I got him. I can get that old man." He was John Winston; he later went on to the Cleveland Indians organization. He was good, but wasn't good enough.

Buck came on up and before I could get back to sit down on my seat in the dugout, the ball was rattling on the housetops out of the park. [Laughs]

I just mention that to let you know that Tom Baird knew that I put a pretty good team together and that I wouldn't run it down. If anything, I would keep it moving with the same kind of respect that it had in the past.

I never have disclosed what I paid for the Monarchs. It was quite a price and I'm ashamed to expose it. It was a nice sum. I bought the Monarchs, I bought the bus. I *thought* I was buying the team, but before I got ready to go to training, I started checking for the players. Mr. Baird had sold all the players to the majors. [Laughs] All I got was the bus and one player stayed with me. He was a home run hitter, but he was too old; they wouldn't take him. I think it might have been

Jackie Robinson (left) and Ted Rasberry (courtesy of Ted Rasberry).

[Willard] Brown. He came out and played with me a while.

I put the team together. I had letters from guys from all over the country wanting to go to spring training. I sent those guys to the Monarchs and Detroit. Detroit trained in Birmingham and the Monarchs trained in Hattiesburg, Mississippi. We came out of there with a good team.

That was one of the things I was going to specially do, keep that Monarch name up because it was good for all of us that the Monarchs was that good drawing card. That's how I ended up with two teams. After the guy in New Orleans dropped out, I ended up with two teams.

I had a niece that was interested in baseball; she tried out. Her name was Minnie Forbes. She and my wife played on a softball club I had here and I picked a couple of my best girls with the intention of playing them with the Monarchs, like Toni Stone and Miss Mamie Johnson, who was playing in the Negro leagues and was quite a draw. I picked me a couple of ladies that would add to the attraction.

(L-r) Sharon Robinson (Jackie's niece), Ted Rasberry, and Larry Lester, Negro Leagues historian (author's collection).

My niece bought an interest in the Detroit Stars. She was part owner for, oh, I'd say probably a year. They didn't make the team, though. They just worked out. Good softball players, but there's a difference. [Laughs]

The Detroit Stars didn't fold. The Detroit Stars, the Kansas City Monarchs, the Birmingham Black Barons, and the Raleigh Tigers played in the last East-West Negro American League Game in New York City at Yankee Stadium in 1961. That was it for the league. I barnstormed with the Kansas City Monarchs for a couple of years after that.

Satchel Paige was the feature attraction for this East-West Game. He was already playing with the Kansas City Monarchs ever so often. I don't guess nobody could keep him too long. He would play for me ever so often. I'd book some games with him; I booked him two weeks up in Minnesota, in that area, and we had a ball.

I used to travel with him for several reasons; the most important reason was to be sure he was at the game on time. [Laughs] When I had him for this tour, I stayed with him. He had his car and his wife was there, and he had

his boat on the car and he'd go fishing. He had his rifle in the car and in the evening we'd go out and shoot some game and come back. His wife would cook it. He enjoyed that.

I discontinued the Stars after 1963, '64. Like a lot of teams, they just fell by the wayside. I kept the Kansas City Monarchs.

People don't realize how good the players were [in the Negro leagues]. They've heard of Satchel Paige and Josh Gibson, but I hate to say how good some of those other players was because it sounds like I'm just running off at the mouth. Jackie Robinson wasn't the best shortstop in the Negro leagues; we had several shortstops who was better. Them guys could play. We could pick stars out of the Negro league who could play as well or better than the superstars today in the major leagues.

Satchel Paige was the greatest pitcher, not only in the Negro league but in the major leagues, too. And Josh Gibson got the best record in the Negro league. He was the greatest. He and Satchel Paige hung up several times.

Satchel was crazy, anyway. He'd tell Josh what he was going to throw him. [Laughs] If

I was hitting and a guy told me what he was going to throw me, I definitely wouldn't be looking for it. [Laughs] He'd tell Josh, "Navel high and a little faster," and that's what he would do. I know Josh figured he was going to try to trick him with a curve or something, but he struck him out. [Laughs] In the World Series!

Several times he'd call the men in in tight games — the outfield — say, "Y'all come in. I don't need you." He'd set 'em down and strike out the side. He did that a lot of times when he was playing with me.

Way back, when I had the Grand Rapids Black Sox, I used to have him come up and pitch some games for me. I had him in Elkhart one night, and I had a pretty good little ol' team. He was to pitch the first three innings. The first inning, the guy hit the ball to short-stop and the shortstop missed it. The guy got on first. He throwed another pitch; the catcher missed it and the guy went to second. Then he walked the next guy. Then there was a ball on the next guy that came up and I started warming up my pitcher.

He stopped me. The umpire called time and Satchel met me halfway, called me in. He said, "I'm gonna put these guys on where I know where they is." So he loaded the bases and struck out the next three men. [Laughs] I'm telling you, man, he was something else. That guy was *better* than they said he was. Anybody ask me, "Was Satchel as good as they say?" and I say, "He was better than that."

John Winston was the most talented ballplayer that I not only had, but ever seen.

I kept the Black Sox here for a farm system and we'd put 'em here and try 'em out and they'd tell me when they're ready on the road. They'd say, "We got one ready up here." They told me that about John Winston.

He had as good a curveball as I've seen, and I've been around baseball all my life. And he could throw it with the same motion that he throwed his fastball. He had one we called "falling off the table," it was such a good drop. And his fastball moved.

He signed with Cleveland. They had managers in the minor leagues that was *awful* rough on us; some was as prejudiced as any-body you've ever seen. John Winston told this manager, "I can play first base," so he let him play first base. He played first sometime for me. And the manager let him play other posi-tions he said he could play, and they played him 'til it was his time to pitch. When it came his time, the manager said, "You're pitching tonight."

He talked back to the manager — I guess he thought he was still in our league — he said, "No, I ain't pitching tonight. I just got through playing third base the night before." So he [the manager] told him, "Yeah, you're pitching tonight." They got in a little dispute about that and they sent him home.

That's it. That's the story of me and base-ball.

Ted Rasberry owned the Detroit Stars, which entered the NAL in 1954, and in 1955 he purchased the Kansas City Monarchs. He operated both franchises until Negro league baseball play ended in 1961. At that time, he continued to operate the Monarchs as a barnstorming team. He is still the legal owner of the Monarchs.

Pedro Sierra
"An All-Star at 18"

Born July 26, 1938, Havana, Cuba
Ht. 5'11" Wt. 165 Batted and Threw Right

Negro Leagues debut: 1954

Some people say the Negro leagues died in 1946, the year Jackie Robinson entered organized baseball. Others say 1950 was the last true year of Negro leagues play, with black baseball played beyond that year being of inferior quality. But many black teams played on through 1960 (and a few beyond), and theirs was definitely not an inferior brand of ball.

For proof, 60 former Negro leaguers joined the major leagues *after* 1950 and dozens more played in the minors. Some of them are among the greatest players in history. Here is an All-Star team of former Negro leaguers who debuted in the majors in the 1950s:

St. P	Sam "Toothpick" Jones
Rel. P	Joe Black
C	Elston Howard
1B	Bob Boyd
2B	Gene Baker
SS	Ernie Banks
3B	Jim Gilliam
LF	Al Smith
CF	Willie Mays
RF	Henry Aaron

And speaking of All-Stars, Pedro Sierra was a Negro league All-Star in 1956 against this kind of company. At the age of *18!* And later he enjoyed a long career in integrated ball, consistently winning in double figures all the way up to Triple-A. His career, which began in 1954 at the age of 16, ended in 1976.

Today he is a recreation director and guides young people on the right path via athletics.

When did you come to the United States?

In 1954. I was 16 years old when I came over here. I went back home in '58 and came back here in the middle of '59. I've been back a few times but I've lived here since.

I came to play with a contract [in '59] but I came too late — almost in the middle of the season — and there was no slot there for me, so one of my, like, we call "play uncle," that lived in Washington, asked me to come over with him, so I did and I stayed with him.

Do you still have family in Cuba?

Yes. I have a brother and a sister and an aunt and some cousins. My dad just passed away four years ago.

How did the Indianapolis Clowns sign you?

There was this guy, like a bird-dog scout, back home. He had seen me play in the sandlots at a Legion-level type of baseball and he thought I could play. He approached my dad and said, "Give him a chance. Let him go play.

He can make some money." Coming from a poor family, that's a great way to get some financial gain, so that's when I went.

What problems did you encounter?

I did know English. My dad had made it a point early when I was growing up, he said the more educated that you get the better, other than life and home education. He said I should try to learn English because one day I wouldn't regret it. I used to go for a couple hours every day for four-and-a-half years to learn English in school. When I came here, all I had to do was adjust the ear to the pronunciation because you learn what we'll call the English English, not with all the slang. It was not that much of a problem.

There was an adjustment because I didn't have the idea that it was barnstorming type of baseball. I thought that you would go for a couple of days here, a couple of days there like I heard a couple of the other guys say. I always hung around guys that played professionally, even guys that played with the New York Cubans. They say we travel here or there, but I didn't imagine playing here today and tomorrow in New York and the next day from New York to Miami, Florida, and from there to Wyoming.

Me and this other guy from my neighborhood that went with me, being the rookies on the team, we had to sit in the back seats and we couldn't lean back. And then we had to eat on the bus and maybe change our pants on the bus and go out and let somebody else change. We had to sleep sometimes in hotels where there were four guys to a room and one bed and a cot. It was a big adjustment.

We ate baloney sandwiches and chocolate milk and Lorna Doone cookies. I remember that 'cause that got to be my favorite. It was a challenging adventure that I think prepared me for a lot of things in life.

When you went from Birmingham, Alabama, to Wyoming — you know, the different cultural shock. Go one place and see all the cowboys and play in a rodeo grounds, then you kept going. It was a great experience.

What racial problems did you encounter?

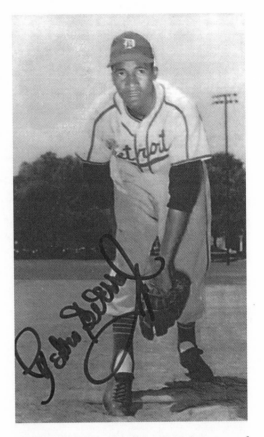

Pedro Sierra, Detroit Stars, 1956 (courtesy of Pedro Sierra).

The problem to me was the adjustment to seeing the signs at that time, "For Whites Only." I didn't expect to see that vivid, although I had an aunt who was a maid who came to the United States and had traveled to the South, and she had said that this is what you see there.

But I guess a lot of times, funny enough, when people knew that I wasn't a black American they talked to me differently. They wanted to know more about Cuba because Cuba has always been a country I guess everyone wants to visit. They would ask me how it was and everybody would talk about the beautiful beaches. I would start a conversation with them and all at once I was just a human being.

Very few things I remember that were a personal attack on me. I heard some slurs and then I had to learn what did they mean. If

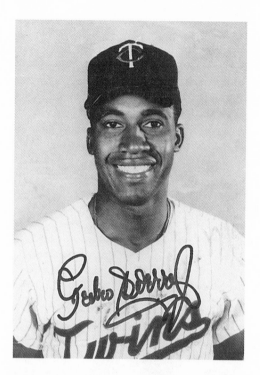

Pedro Sierra, spring training, 1965, Minnesota Twins (courtesy of Pedro Sierra).

somebody called me black, so what? We heard the "n" word and all of that and you wonder why people are so narrow-minded at times, but then with the excitement of baseball you hardly have any chance to think about it. You say, "Well, you know you are now accepted," but you are cautious of things. We weren't afraid of the big Klan or the hangings and all that stuff and we thought, "Aw, come on. That doesn't happen," but then when you go to bed, you start thinking, "What if it happens?" So you don't put yourself in a position to create any attack. I always tried to be polite with everybody and present myself like that.

In areas of North Carolina I had trouble. I played there in High Point–Thomasville in 1965-66. There was this family, they would go out of their way. It was a white family and there was only three black guys on the team. They would do anything for us and when people would get like a little rough with racial slurs they would speak up.

Even the chief of police came one time. Me and the other guys were at their house watching the All-Star game and the chief of police came with some complaint and he said a racial slur about us and that woman, she bawled him out completely. She said, "We gotta make these young people welcome here. It's an embarrassment."

We didn't encounter that with the fans — slurs or anything. Once in a while, you'd find one guy that'd try to get smart, but you overlook it. He's like the ugly duckling in the whole pond and everybody's looking at him.

I had an experience. It was in '65. We were playing in Shelby, North Carolina, and I was with High Point, a farm team of the Minnesota Twins. We went there and I was a relief pitcher at that time. I went to the bullpen and we had powder blue uniforms with the names on the back.

This kid had been playing catch with me for a couple of days and I gave him a ball. His grandfather came over and I was sitting in the bullpen. He was sitting across the fence right next to me. He was like what you'd call the typical redneck guy with a red bandana and overalls and the shoes and a railroad hat and all that.

He looked at the name written on the back of my uniform: "Sierra." "What kinda name's that for a nigger?" And his grandson said, "Grandpa, don't say that! He's a nice person. He gave me the ball." He said, "He did?"

It surprised me; the guy said, "Thank you. How do you pronounce your name?" So I told him and he said, "Where're you from?" I told him and he didn't know where Cuba was from Adam. I explained it to him and he said, "Oh, you're from that Castro island." I said, "Yeah, something like that."

What was rewarding to me was he felt embarrassed by saying something like that because I had been nice to his grandson and his grandson made him feel embarrassed.

Let's talk about your performance. How did you do as a pitcher?

I didn't do bad, but I guess I didn't develop to be a better pitcher until '56. When I went to the Detroit Stars, I made the East-West All-Star Game, and that was exciting.

I look back in retrospect on my career and every year I played I learned more or I got smarter pitching or something, and you learn how not to be a thrower — to be a pitcher — and how to do certain things and how not to do certain things. I think I did well. I'm sad that [Negro leagues] records were not kept, and if they were the only one that I have is of me making the East-West All-Star Game. I pitched one inning but I didn't do very well. I know I won more than I lost otherwise in the Negro leagues.

Some people say the Negro leagues were dead by then, but there was still a good level of ball being played in the '50s.

I think it petered out in '60, but we had some good players, very good players. Ed Steele, who was my manager; Buddy Ivory; John Kennedy; Ira McKnight, a catcher with Kansas City Monarchs; Herman Green; Harold Shade; Charley Pride with Memphis Red Sox. Ike Brown was there, George Altman, Willie Lee. There was a number of guys.

Then after, I ran into them in organized ball. I ran into Ike Brown in '63; he was playing for a farm team of the Detroit Tigers in Duluth, Minnesota. I ran into Willie Lee later. The league had some caliber. If there had been more [major league] teams like there is right now — expansion — a whole bunch of those guys are going to the big leagues.

How did you get into organized ball?

What happened is that when I came back here in '59 to go to an organized baseball team, which was too late, I came to Washington. I knew Camilo Pascual and Pete Ramos and guys from Cuba — [Minnie] Minoso and Julio Becquer, who was a first baseman with Senators in '58-'59.

I started working construction with a friend of my dad and I said, "No, I'm not a construction worker. This is not for me." I saw those guys and they said, "What are you doing here?" So I said, "I wonder if I can get a tryout." So they got me a tryout with the Washington team then and they signed me and they sent me to a rookie league in Lynchburg, Virginia, that year.

What had happened, the years before when I was with the Negro leagues, somehow they had made me register in the Selective Service. I don't know why, but to me it was great because you always have the dream of being a hero from seeing war movies. So I registered and, Lord and behold, when I got there to Virginia I got the famous "Greetings" saying that I had to go in the Army.

I had a great season in Lynchburg but then I went in the Army for two years. They sent me to Fort Hood, Texas, and I played ball while I was there. By that time, the Senators had gone to Minnesota and become the Minnesota Twins. I became the property of the Twins, and the Senators came up with another team.

How high did you reach in the minors?

I went to spring training with the Washington Senators in 1970, and I stayed there almost to the last week of spring training and I got sent to Double-A baseball. I played there a couple of years and I got called back to the big leagues. All I did was just pitch batting practice with them.

When they moved to Texas I got sent to Mexico, which is Triple-A baseball. I played there from '72 to '76.

What were some of your best records?

In the Army we won the Fourth Army championship; I was 17–5 with the Fort Hood team, and I even threw a no-hitter there.

When I was in the Twins organization in 1966, I led the league in relief appearances with 54 games out of 120 scheduled. Then in '67, I wasn't making progress with the Twins and we got into an argument, so they released me. I went to play independent ball in Canada in the Provincial League. The first year I was 11–3 with a one-point-something ERA. The second year I was 10–7 and the third year with them I was 14–3 and I was my team's Most Valuable Player, I was runner-up to the league's Most Valuable Player, and I had the most wins in the league. That's when Washington signed me upon Zoilo Versalles suggestion.

After that, I would say my last year with

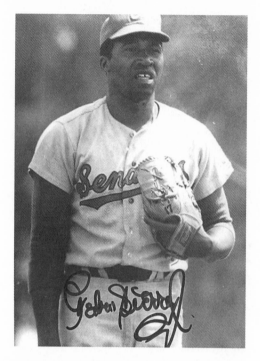

Pedro Sierra, Washington Senators, 1970 (courtesy of Pedro Sierra).

Vera Cruz I was 12–3, 12–4 — something like that. With Washington, I had a good year in Pittsfield with 10–6. Those are the ones I remember.

Those records today, with expansion, would get you a shot on a major league roster.

Oh, I say that myself without trying to brag too much. I had some good earned run averages. The worst I had was my first year in Mexico when I was 14–12 or 14–10 and it was a matter of adjustment in the league — traveling and all that. Other than that, I had good earned run averages through my career.

Who were some of the best players you saw along the way?

The hardest guy for me to face was a guy in Mexico named Miguel Suarez. He was so hard for me to get out and I have faced guys like [Greg] Luzinski in the Eastern League, Mike Schmidt, Bob Robertson, Cecil Cooper, and I had success with those guys. They were great players — great hitters — but I had success against them. Rico Carty — I guess I'd go

50–50. He hit me fairly well at times but it was even.

Zoilo Versalles was a great guy, an outstanding person. Brooks Robinson, Clete Boyer — guys like that. Silent players. Cal Ripken — if he hadn't broken this record for continuous playing people wouldn't even notice because he's unnoticeable. But those who know baseball, if you look you see his accomplishments, his style of playing, his personality, his attitude. He's not a dramatic player like Billy Martin or somebody like that.

Who was the best pitcher you saw?

I would say Bob Gibson because he had so much determination and he wouldn't give an inch to anybody.

I would say that Jim Bouton was good. Camilo Pascual was an unlucky guy. Should he have been with a better team he would have been great. Luis Tiant — to see how much he could get out of the style of pitching that he was a master at. Juan Marichal.

Denny McLain was great. He had a great year but his following got him into a lot of problems. In 1963, I was with the Twins farm system. I was playing in Bismarck, North Dakota, and he was playing in Duluth, Minnesota, and we faced each other.

I caught a cold in my arm and I pinched a nerve. I guess we were traveling from either Bismarck to Duluth or Aberdeen or someplace like that. It was really cold and I sat on the right side of the bus and I caught a cold in my arm. I don't sit there anymore from that day on.

I was pitching against him and Calvin Griffith had come to the ballpark to see me pitch 'cause I had pitched a couple shutouts in a row and there was a big move to get me up to Denver, which was Triple-A, or to the big leagues. I couldn't even break an egg with the cold in my arm that day.

I was warming up and the game started, and by the second inning I was taking a shower. My manager said, "What's wrong with you? You're trying to make me look bad!" and all that.

Then when he [McLain] got traded to

1956 Detroit Stars. Back row (l-r): Pat Patterson, Frank Evans, Willie "Bud" Ivory, Abduhl Johnson, Herman Green, Peaster Mumford, Willie Harris, Pedro Sierra. Front row (l-r): Juan Soler, Ray Richardson, Harold Shade, Henry Saverson, Ed Steel (manager), Johnny Winston, Herbert Howell, Eugene Scruggs, Joe Mims (courtesy of Pedro Sierra).

Washington, I saw him here. He was playing the organ at the Sheraton Hotel. I went over there and we talked a little bit. I haven't seen him anymore.

If you were back in Cuba and 16 years old again, would you do this all again?

I think I would. It was a challenge and an experience for me. Everything that I do right now is still mentally challenging.

I went back almost ten years ago. I was invited by the government to go down and do some baseball clinics. I had this kid [Orlando] Duque Hernandez; I had him aside and I showed him a few things about mechanics and things like that. I didn't know his brother [Livan] but El Duque was a great prospect at that time. The next day we told the rest of the

players — the pitchers — to come into the ballpark and the only one that showed up was him. That was great determination on his part. I refined a few points with him and then I learned that he had become such a great pitcher in Cuba prior to coming here.

Yes, I would do it again the same way. I would go back because there was the excitement of going away from your country as a player and making your family look good, saying I'm doing something for my country. I'm going to be another Minnie Minoso, another Camilo Pascual. That's something that's great. It was big excitement to be a professional athlete at that time. I think even right now it is something that the young people, and everybody, look up to.

PITCHING RECORD

Year	Team, League	G	IP	W	L	Pct	H	BB	SO	ERA
1954	Detroit, NAL									
1955										
1956										

Year	Team, League	G	IP	W	L	Pct	H	BB	SO	ERA
1962	Erie, NYP	23	151	8	11	.421		59	107	4.02
1963	Bismarck, NoL	29	125	7	7	.500		42	80	3.96
1964	Wisc. Rapids, MWL	37	159	8	10	.444		66	90	3.68
1965	Thomasville, WCarL	40	65	4	2	.667		20	45	1.62
1966		*52	90	8	13	.381		51	56	3.70
1967	Coaticook, ProvL	19	141	11	3	.786		42	92	*1.76
1968	Sherbrooke, ProvL	25	170	11	7	.611		62	86	3.43
1969		22	147	*14	3	*.824		47	100	3.26
1970	Pittsfield, EL	37	123	10	6	.625		43	65	3.66
	Washington, AL	On roster, did not appear in a game								
1971	Burlington, CarL	3	11	1	0	1.000		0	4	3.27
	Pittsfield, EL	11	38	3	2	.600		15	24	5.68
1972	Puebla, MxL	41	205	14	13	.519		88	67	4.13
1973	Puebla, Tampico,									
	Chihuahua, MxL	32	128	12	1	*.923		49	42	4.57
1974	Chih., Vera Cruz, MxL	27	174	10	2	.833		57	63	3.64
1975	Aguascalientes, MxL	1	2	0	0	.000		1	0	0.00
	San Francisco de									
	Macoris, CuL	5	36	2	3	.400		24	17	3.95
	Puerto Plata, CuL	18	125	8	4	.667		47	89	3.03

* Led league

Jim Cobbin
"From Short to Center"

BORN DECEMBER 27, 1934, MONTGOMERY, AL
HT. 5'10¾" WT. 183 BATTED AND THREW RIGHT

Negro Leagues debut: 1956

At one point in the 1950s (with proper trades) a Hall of Fame outfield of Monte Irvin in left, Mickey Mantle in center, and Hank Aaron in right could have been fielded, and it probably would have been the best in baseball. And to back up those three, you could have Al Smith.

But what besides the outfield do these three Hall of Famers, and Smith, have in common?

They all began their professional careers as shortstops.

Look around and you'll see many outstanding outfielders who started out at short. In recent times, there have been All-Star center fielders Robin Yount and Eric Davis, for instance.

Another young shortstop made the successful switch from the demanding infield position of shortstop to the demanding outfield position of center field: Jim Cobbin. If luck had been with Cobbin, today we might be writing about him in a different context, but the luck wasn't there and what may have been was derailed by the Army. He might have been alongside Aaron in Milwaukee, but instead the only thing they have in common is the Indianapolis Clowns, for whom they both played in the '50s.

Today, in addition to being a successful businessman, Jim Cobbin serves as vice-president of Yesterday's Negro League Baseball Foundation, an organization working for the benefit of former Negro league ballplayers.

I originally started as a shortstop when I was signed by the Pittsburgh Pirates. I was 19 or 20 years old.

The Cincinnati Reds and the Pittsburgh Pirates were interested in me as a ballplayer. I played in Youngstown, Ohio, where I had lived since age three. I was playing for a Class-B team which won the regional championship in Altoona, P-A. Many of the players were being scouted by a number of major league teams. I personally was scouted by the Pittsburgh Pirates.

While still in high school, the Cincinnati Reds' scouts had been talking to me and

I had considered going to their spring training camp. But, when I got out of high school, I received a scholarship to Allen University. A full scholarship. That scholarship was a bittersweet accomplishment. It was bitter because I really wanted to play baseball, and sweet because I was the first in my family to have the opportunity to go to college. My family was elated. They told me that I should go to college. I'll never forget my uncle saying, "If they want you now, they'll want you later." It's too bad that he didn't really know the reality of the situation, because I believed him and left for Allen University instead. I went

Jim Cobbin (courtesy of W. James Cobbin).

in '53 and '54 and I just couldn't take it any longer. I just made a decision to follow my dreams.

I had maintained a relationship with the scout from the Pittsburgh Pirates. I had told him that I was going to leave school to play baseball. He set up a tryout for me at Forbes Field. After a two-day successful tryout, they assigned me to go to Brunswick, Georgia, for spring training.

Can you imagine the excitement of a 20-year-old kid being signed up by a major league team? It was probably the happiest day of my life. I couldn't sleep, couldn't do anything. It was just a happy day.

I arrived in Brunswick, Georgia, and saw all the guys that were meeting there; they were coming in with their bags. It was just so exciting—*super* exciting—to think that I am finally living my dream!

The staff was counting out and assigning rooms and giving keys to all these ballplayers. However, Reggie Howard, another black guy—he and I hadn't been assigned to a room, nor had we received any keys. We approached the coach and asked, "Coach, where's our keys?"

Just then, a truck drove up and there was a black guy in this truck and he told us that we have to go with him. He said we were going to stay with him and to throw our stuff in the back of the truck. At that point I realized what was happening. I was totally disenchanted. I found it hard to believe that because we were black, we were not included in all of the activities. I think a team has to be a team. Separation has no place within a team.

In the mornings, the black man would bring us back to the field. But in the evenings when we had to leave again with this man, the other players had the privilege of pursuing the informational bulletin board, special announcements, meetings in the hotel about the game, about what's going to happen. We did not get the opportunity to get to know the other players; we knew the names of a few. You just felt like an outcast— no, we *were* outcasts. I don't know how a ballplayer could adjust to that sort of racism and be expected to perform at his highest level. That's an awful lot to ask, I think. That's a hell of a lot to ask.

We tried to endure it. After preliminary cuts we began to get into the serious business of baseball. After four or five days, the coach called the four guys left for the shortstop position and he said, and I quote, "Any one of you guys can play on this team and play this position, but we're only going to need one." I guess at the end of this exhibition period, he was going to make his selection as to who that "one" was going to be.

Unfortunately, I knew that I wasn't going to be the "one." [Laughs] You don't have to be a genius to understand the process of racism. It was a sign of the times.

Somehow, Ed Hammond from the Indianapolis Clowns heard about us. He wanted to know if we wanted to play in the Negro league — Negro league baseball. Reggie and I looked at each other and said, "Let's get out of here." [Laughs] I wanted to play, so Reggie Howard and I left and we went to the New York Black Yankees. We left Brunswick, Georgia, and went down to Tampa, Florida, where they had their spring training — the New York Black Yankees and the Indianapolis Clowns.

Ed had told me that the Milwaukee Braves had an interest in the Indianapolis Clowns for additional Negro talent. In 1957, when we left, I had the impression that Jim McCoy, Verdes Drake, and myself were going to the Milwaukee Braves to try out for center field. I can't remember the center fielder, but he had got hurt and I guess they were going to pull somebody up from the minors to take his place.

At that point, I was sure that center field was going to be my position. With the Clowns I had led in RBIs, home runs, stolen bases — I had led the team in all areas. I was confident that I was going to get that shot. But in January of 1958, Uncle Sam called, believe it or not. I'm thinking I'm just about ready to get to where I need to be in baseball and they call me.

I left for the service in January of '58 and they really tried to get me out of the Army. Some players had been excused using whatever strings they could pull. My departure was stalled. My unit went to Germany and I was still in Fort Knox for two months after my unit was gone, until one day the sergeant came in and said, "It doesn't look like it's going to happen, Jim. You gotta go." And I was off on the next plane to Europe.

What frightened me a little bit was when I got to Europe, there's colonels and generals waiting to transport me back to the base. [Laughs] I didn't know if they were going to put me in jail or what they were going to do. I didn't know what was going on.

It was apparent that they had been waiting for me. I believe that my reputation preceded me; they definitely knew who I was. I went to the base. I didn't go to the Army barracks; I went to a special barracks where the ballplayers and the special duty people stayed. From the day that I got there, I don't think I ever put a uniform on.

The Fifth Corps was in the European Baseball League and I guess it was a real big deal. Some of the players in the league were minor league ballplayers. And a few had played in the major leagues. They were playing on various teams around the European

Jim Cobbin (courtesy of W. James Cobbin).

League. The Fifth Corps wanted a championship in the worst way.

We played baseball there, and for two years we had one *heck* of a tour. In fact, we won the USAREUR World Series. We were the champs. That was really a big deal.

I was a very accomplished ballplayer. I had 49 stolen bases out of 50 attempts. I was stealing home and the whole works. The European tour is where I got most of my newspaper clippings; the guys would clip them out for me. I accumulated quite a bit in that tour. I played center field for CPA Scorpions and had a batting average of about .317, and I think I was number two in the whole league for RBIs.

We had a real good year over there, and a good time. In fact, I was faced with the opportunity to play for a team in El Paso, Texas, when I left the Army.

When I did get out in 1960, believe it or not, I went back to play with the Clowns with the hope of getting that Milwaukee shot again, However, those kind of opportunities are not there waiting for you.

After that disappointment, I had a pivotal

Jim Cobbin with service in Europe (courtesy of W. James Cobbin).

talk with Alberton "Smitty" Smith. He was an older guy who had been playing Negro league baseball for I guess 15 or 20 years, and he said, "Jim, I don't want you to get locked up. You're a good ballplayer and you've been around, but I'm telling you. You're 25 years old and they're not interested in guys that are 25 and 26 years old."

I talked to Ed and he said, "You've got a place on this team for as long as you want, but you realize the older you get, the less chances are to make it."

I had some soul-searching to do. I played a couple months and then I decided I better go lay some concrete. [Laughs] I better get something a little more solid than baseball.

I had missed two years of baseball while in college and two years while in the Army;

that's four years out and that's tough to overcome, especially being a Negro ballplayer.

While you still played, do any games stand out?

Well, I guess there was a game in Columbus, Georgia; I'm not sure if we were playing the Birmingham Black Barons or some other team. I was thinking about this when I visited the Louisville Slugger Museum because I had to have a big-handled bat. My grip is big and the little skinny bats I just couldn't hold tight enough.

The bat in Columbus, Georgia — I'll never forget — that bat was crooked. [Laughs] It was not straight and I bet you I hit 20 home runs with that bat. In Columbus, I hit three home runs off the top of the scoreboard in that one game. That bat was great and the pitchers were great, too.

In Europe, I played against this team in the USAREUR World Series. It was known around the league that you don't throw me a high fastball. Forget about it if you do. Well, this guy — he knew me well because we had played against them in the regular season — let a ball slip out of his hand to the extent that, when they looked at some of the movies that they took, this guy had thrown his glove in the air before the ball even got to the bat. [Laughs] It was a high fastball and away it went. That was a great time. That game in Europe and that one in Columbus, Georgia, are just two games I remember.

Oh, one more. In Italy, during the World Series, high fastballs are what I hit. Curveballs — I don't recall ever trying to power a curveball. I'd try to hit them to right field if I could.

Well, this ball — the bases were loaded — and this guy threw me a ball, a slow curveball, and I'm impatient but it seemed like this time I just stood there waiting. At first, I was not even going to swing at the ball and then, all of a sudden, I said, "This ball ain't got here yet." [Laughs] And I swung on that ball and I bet you — if I'd've been home I'd've got a tape measure 'cause that ball went over the left field fence, and the left field fence was 385 feet, I think, and it looked like a mile high as it was going over the fence. It just went out of sight.

Jim Cobbin stealing second base. Shortstop is Jerry Ducharme (courtesy of W. James Cobbin).

After that whole thing was over, I was told that place was much like Denver. It was high altitude and the ball will carry. [Laughs]

Those are three times that I don't think I'll ever forget. A lot of games I'd steal home but that wasn't a big thing. I'd do that in a minute. If you get a team that's not familiar with me in base running, there's a good chance I'll be able to steal home.

I did not steal bases in the traditional style. The way that you can really steal is the untraditional way. That's what I used to do all the time. For instance, if I'm on second base, I'd drift halfway down the line after the pitcher made his pitch. And I'm just standing there, halfway down the line.

If a catcher sees me and tries to throw it to second, I'm at third before the ball can get there. And if he gets really lackadaisical and he lobs it back to the pitcher, you can go home.

Those are ways that I stole and, of course, after a while I gave pitchers a fit in terms of trying to pitch and watch where I was. I really had fun with that.

Who was the most helpful player to you?

Verdes Drake taught me how to play the outfield. It was one very little simple thing that I was doing that really turned my whole thing around with the outfield and Verdes Drake taught me how to chase down a long fly ball.

In Europe, they referred to me as "Ohio State Patrol" because I was very fast and I could get to any field, but Verdes Drake taught me how to get there and catch the ball. When you run and try to chase a fly ball, the ball jumps. He taught me how to run without the ball moving. You could run on your toes and the ball will not move, will not jump; it will be just as smooth as smooth could be. Run on your toes. When I learned that, I was getting all over the place. It's easier to judge because nothing is moving; you've got good concentration on the ball.

Remember, I was a shortstop when I started. When I moved to the outfield and learned how to play it, I knew this was my best position because I had the speed and I had the arm.

Jim Cobbin's first team. He is 9 years old and middle of first row (courtesy of W. James Cobbin).

Of the people I knew, I thought Verdes Drake was a tremendous center fielder, too. He was Cuban. He would catch the ball and you would sit there wondering, "How'd he do that? He's not that fast. How'd he get there?" He had the ability to move off the ball. When a guy plays outfield, when a guy swings and even if he misses the ball, you're moving. The way he swings gives you a jump on the direction the ball is going.

What did you do when you left baseball?

I went home and took up accounting in college. I decided I wanted my own business, but I was undecided on exactly what kind of business.

In the meantime, I started doing tax accounting and insurance. I did business with some of the local doctors. I wanted my own business, but I just didn't want to get into doing the kind of businesses that blacks customarily do, a barbecue house or maybe a restaurant or something like that. I wanted to

do something in the area of business that would be attributed to all people.

After doing tax accounting for a while, I decided I was going to do office supplies. I opened up an office supply store and I sold office supplies and office furniture. The name of it was Ivy Supply.

I did that for three or four years and it was going fairly well, but I just wasn't satisfied so I went into the travel industry. I became a travel agent and then I bought buses and I did ground transportation. From then until now, that's what I do. We do coast-to-coast charter work.

Would you go back to the mid '50s and play baseball again?

Sure. Yes, I would. Absolutely. In the short time that I had, I had some tremendous times in baseball.

That was my life when I was small. I cried when it rained because I couldn't play baseball. We had regular backyard games with a broomstick and some socks tied in knots until we learned how to put a golf ball and put some tire rubber around the golf ball and tape it real good. Electrician's tape. And then we found out a broomstick wasn't heavy enough — wouldn't get enough power on the ball — and then we started using sledge hammer handles for our baseball bat.

I found, not long ago, a picture of the first organized team I played for. It was in 1944; we played on the 11-and-under. I was nine years old. The team we played for was Driscoll's. Driscoll's Ice Cream or something like that. Mr. Driscoll saw me — it must have been 15 or 20 years ago — and he had a picture and he had a copy made for me.

But baseball was gone until I got renewed here with [Dennis] Biddle and those guys and I started thinking, trying to come up with all of my stuff and I found that picture.

BATTING RECORD

Year	Team, League	Pos	G	AB	R	H	2B	3B	HR	RBI	SB	BA
1956	N.Y. Blk Yankees, NAL	of										
1957	Indianapolis, NAL	of										.316
1958–59	military service											
1960	Indianapolis, NAL	of										

Eugene "Dick" Scruggs
"From the Mound to the Mortuary"

BORN MAY 17, 1938, HUNTSVILLE, AL
HT. 6' WT. 155 BATTED BOTH, THREW RIGHT

Negro Leagues debut: 1956

The early life of Eugene Scruggs wasn't easy. His mother died when he was 12. His stepfather was a sharecropper, and when young Eugene was old enough to work in the fields, his education was placed second on the priority list; he attended school only on those days when field work was not possible. The future was bleak for a black teenager in the Deep South in the 1950s.

But Eugene Scruggs could throw a baseball, and this talent took him away and gave him a new perspective on life. Baseball showed him the country and made lasting friendships for him, and most importantly, gave him memories for a lifetime.

The people in his hometown called him "Dick." His uncle Dick died when Eugene was born, and his name was unofficially given to the youngster. When he played, however, his manager and teammates named him according to his size. Tall and thin, he was usually called "Pee Wee," but sometimes it was "Puny" or even "Wee Wee." But the opposing batters didn't find him puny, as shown by his three-year pitching mark, which, according to records that can be found today, was 28–13.

Scruggs recalls that he first heard the people of his hometown talking about black baseball players such as Josh Gibson, Jackie Robinson, and others when he was a small boy attending first grade at Meridianville Bottom School. His teacher that year was Mrs. Sadie Kellam, and many years later, his daughter, Sabrina, attending Calvary Hill School, also had Mrs. Kellam as her first grade teacher. Mrs. Kellam sent the accompanying photo of first-grader Eugene to him via Sabrina.

I started playing baseball in the sandlots when I was 14 years old with a team called Moore's Mill Red Sox. I started out as an infielder until I was hit between the eyes. I was not able to hit the ball very well, so I started pitching. [Laughs] The school I attended didn't have baseball so I started out playing with grown people. They didn't have Little League baseball.

My mother died in 1951 and I was 12 years old and the mortician who funeralized her was Mr. R. E. Nelms. I started going around him at an early age; whenever I went downtown I would go see him. I enjoyed talking to him.

When I was 16, I was pitching for the Moore's Mill Red Sox and I can remember I was on the average of 17 to 18 strikeouts per game at the age of 16. I had a curveball and a pretty good fastball. I struck out 20 once in a game.

At that time, blacks wasn't allowed to

play in the Southern Association; however, when I was working for Mr. Hubert Ray, owner of Ray Auto Ford, he introduced me to Mr. Jim Talley. Mr. Ray asked him to see if I was good enough to play organized baseball.

I went out there and threw approximately ten minutes and he reported back to Mr. Ray that I had a good enough curveball, but I needed weight and size. He said I had a pretty good fastball, but I needed more zip on it. He stated by the time I turned 17 or 18 years old, he would like to take a look at me again.

However, I went to Mr. Nelms and he called Mr. Ted Rasberry, who was the owner of the Kansas City Monarchs and the Detroit Stars. I was given the opportunity to try out for the team when they came to Decatur, Alabama. Mr. Nelms drove me there where I met the manager, Mr. Ed Steele, and the team. I made the team, and started traveling across the country, especially around Memphis. Mississippi, and Arkansas.

The first game I played was on a Sunday afternoon in Memphis, Tennessee, in 1956. I won that game against Memphis; however, I really didn't know the fundamentals of baseball like the other players on the team, who were trained through the ranks of baseball.

I was sent up to Grand Rapids, Michigan. Ted Rasberry had a team called the Grand Rapids Black Sox. I played with the team for two months because I was too shy for the large crowds and the noise from the fans. I met and played with and became friends with Willie Lee and James Ivory, who were from Birmingham, Alabama. When I came home in 1958, I did not see them again for almost 40 years.

When I started traveling around signing autographs, I saw my old friends again who had returned to their home city and only lived a hundred miles from me. The last time we saw each other we was young boys and it was the greatest moment of my life when I saw them again. It was like we had died and been born again: all broke down and hobbling. [Laughs]

While I was in Grand Rapids, I got a chance to meet a lot of other players who went

Eugene Scruggs (courtesy of Eugene Scruggs).

on to play in the minor leagues, like Herman Green and Ray Miller. John Kennedy, he was on the team that I played with and he went on to play with the Philadelphia Phillies. In the mid '50s baseball was a good game to play.

As a young man growing up with no hopes, I was proud because I had the opportunity to play organized ball. Before my mother got sick and died, I told her I was going to make her real happy. I said, "I believe I'm going to play organized baseball one day." When I turned 12, she died and that made me more determined to meet my dreams, and that's what I did.

When I was 15 years old, I thought I had hurt my arm because my shoulder would jump out of place, but after I turned 16 I did not have this trouble anymore. I think I started throwing too much at a young age and my arm had not developed.

Let's go back to Grand Rapids. I stayed around Mr. Rasberry a lot. He was a fine businessman who you could learn from. When I was there, I went through training and learning the fundamentals of baseball and getting used to large crowds and the noises of the fans. He made me feel good about myself. I really can't say enough about him because he was a great influence in my life.

I had other ambitions in my life, and one was to be a surgeon; however, that did not work out because I was not able to continue with my schooling. After I returned home, I went to see Mr. Nelms and I started working at the funeral home. I became a mortician just like my mentor and I still do mortician work on a day to day basis. I ended up under the grandfather clause for people who did not have a chance to attend school. I am certified through the state of Alabama as a licensed mortician.

During this time, the funeral home provided ambulance services to transport patients to the local hospital. One Sunday afternoon while I was working, a call came in that a car had hit my son. I was at the point I did not want to do this for a living, so I found another job as maintenance worker at the Central Bank Building in downtown Huntsville. I have worked there for almost 32 years.

Since I have started going to baseball reunions and gatherings, it has made me feel good to be able to look over my life and reflect on what I did in my younger years. I played three years beginning with the '56 season. My first year, I was 8–4 with the Detroit Stars. If I count the games I played with Grand Rapids, I think I won five games there. The next year I had about the same. In the '58 season, I started playing with the Kansas City Monarchs, and halfway through the season I went back to the Detroit Stars. Mr. Rasberry owned both teams and sometime they would get unbalanced and we would transfer to the other team.

Does one game stand out?

Yes, the first game that I pitched, which was in Memphis. When I left home at a young age, it was very hard and I did not have any encouragement that I could make the team. I was not large enough or strong enough in my mind.

The score was 6–3. I think I gave up like five hits. I think I had nine strikeouts. It could have been more than that, but I can't remember.

Another good game was in North Carolina. I lost the ballgame in the last inning. The score was tied up, 2–2, and a player hit a home run in the bottom of the ninth inning with two outs. It was against an independent team that the Army had there. I had struck the player out like two or three times. [Laughs] I remember shaking the catcher off and he hit the home run. Mr. Steele, the manager, told me that night the longest day I live, *never* shake the catcher. [Laughs] I knew I had made a mistake because he hit a fastball. Since I was small, I got weak in the last inning.

My next good game that I played in was in Grand Haven, Michigan, outside of Grand Rapids. I pitched a three-hitter there.

Who was the best player you saw?

There were a lot of them. However, if I have to choose one, it would be a player by the name of Juan Soler, was the second baseman of the Detroit Stars. The Chicago White Sox had signed him; however, he never did get the chance to play because he died that fall. Otha Bailey, Willie Lee, and James Ivory were good and all of them made it.

Who was the best pitcher?

Willie Smith. I would pick him over anybody; he was major league material who did get the chance to play in the major leagues. He could hit, also.

There were a lot of good ballplayers in the league then. However, when they started integrating the teams, a lot of these players were too old to play. Buddy Ivory, he went on with the Dodgers. That's James Ivory's brother.

I disagree with some of the old players about how everything ended in 1950. Look at Ernie Banks and Gene Baker. There were ballplayers that could still play in the Southern Association even then. I think they are wrong for saying that because I feel the ballplayers in the '50s and into the late '50s were just as good as the players in the '20s and '30s.

Why did you leave baseball when you did?

In 1958, the civil rights struggle was going on and all sorts of things were going on, including bombing of buses. We did not have anything like that happen to us; however, I did not want to be involved in any trouble. I just decided to come home and would stay off a year until things was better. In the 1957 season, I was either in Birmingham or Mobile and this man was pushed or made to jump off a bridge between Montgomery and Birmingham. I started thinking that I should be at home.

Do you have any regrets from baseball?

No, I don't. It was a great opportunity for me because when I started playing, the only places I had been was like Chattanooga, Nashville, and Birmingham. I had the chance to travel *all* over the United States. I do not think this could happen if I had not played baseball. I cherish all these memories about the towns I traveled through, including Canada. It was worth playing.

If you were a young man in the '50s again, would you do it all again?

I sure would. I would play again. As far as the bus riding, that was just part of life.

I will not forget about all the guys that was on the team with me because it was just like we were a big family living together in the same house. I'm looking at a picture now with all these guys and it is bringing back a lot of memories that I have of each of them.

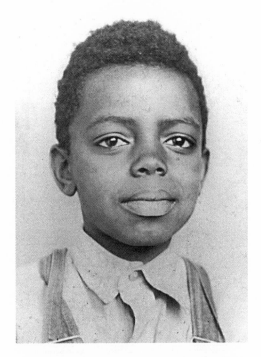

Eugene Scruggs, age 8 (courtesy of Eugene Scruggs).

When I hear music from the '50s, it brings back a lot of memories of the entertainers we saw, such as Ray Charles, Little Richard, and Little Willie John. When I was in Grand Rapids, we would go down to the center of downtown and we'd hear music like this song called "You Give Me Fever." [Laughs] Do you remember that? I don't hear it much now, but every now and then I will hear it. It was a lot of fun.

PITCHING RECORD

Year	Team, League	G	IP	W	L	Pct	H	BB	SO	ERA
1956	Grand Rapids, ind.			5	0	.667				
	Detroit, NAL			8	4	.667				
1957				8	5	.615				
1958	K.C.-Detr., NAL			7	4	.636				

William "Sonny" Webb
"Still Going"

BORN NOVEMBER 30, 1935, CINCINNATI, OH
HT. 5'11" WT. 180 BATTED AND THREW LEFT

Negro Leagues debut: 1958

Some baseball careers are short. With a little searching, one can find players who played one game and then were gone. There are even some who joined a team and *never* played.

Sonny Webb's professional career wasn't *that* short, but it was brief: spring training with the Cincinnati Reds' minor leaguers and then a short stint of barnstorming with Ted Rasberry and his teams out of Michigan, all in 1958.

But his overall baseball career has been long. Very long. He played with the famous and very high quality semipro Cincinnati Tigers before his venture into the professional ranks, and today, in his mid 60s, he's still playing in an over-30 amateur league.

I got my first training on Boone Street in Walnut Hills. They had a gentleman who lived up the street who had played in the old Negro leagues named Louis Dula. He would come home during the off-season and whenever he had a chance, me and some of the kids would be out in the street playing and we'd always get those kind of special instructions from him. He was kind of an icon in our neighborhood. I guess I was about five or six.

I was born and raised in an Italian and black neighborhood, and the Italians would always have a team. I remember the first time being asked by a good friend of mine by the name of Ed Lavatori to participate with this team. That was the first organized team that I played with. I guess I was about seven years old; we played in the Knothole [League] down at Deer Creek Park. That was quite a thing to be able to play down on Diamond Six; it had the concrete steps and everything and it was the best-looking field. Whenever you got a chance to play there, you were *really* happy

about it. Surprisingly, there would be a lot of people who would come out and watch these Knothole games on Saturday.

Then I went to grade school at a Catholic school called the Assumption School in Walnut Hills. They had a softball team; they didn't have hardball. I played Knothole ball all the way up. I played for the Junior Elks; I always played baseball and I played a couple of years in high school at Purcell High School. It was a Catholic school.

After high school there was a team in Walnut Hills called Whitlow A.C. It was run by a blind man, a Mr. Wren, and the manager's name was George Sparks. The ironic thing about it was, it was a fast-pitch softball team. We had a whale of a team there; our home park was Ashland Park and we played on Sundays. We'd play teams from Louisville or Indianapolis or from the area right there. Man, it seemed like there would be 4- or 5,000 people. They had a bar there on Chapel Street called the Stop Inn and people could get beer and stuff on Sunday; they'd bring picnic lunches and the police would allow 'em to double and triple park to see those ballgames. That was some great ball and I think it contributed in that it *really* quickened up my swing, because I had a quick bat.

I remember once [many years later] when Frank Robinson was the manager of the San Francisco Giants. At Wrigley Field, Frank let me put on a uniform and go to the field and shag flies during batting practice. Oh, what a thrill that was; I had my own little game going and I was enjoying every minute of it. He called out to me as I was in the outfield talking to Dan Gladden, who was a Giant outfielder, "Do you want to hit?" Man, I just took off running to that cage.

Someone threw a bat from the dugout; I didn't look at whose it was, but, boy, did it feel good. Don Buford was throwing the batting practice and Tommy McCraw, who was the hitting coach, was behind the cage. Buford was laying them in there and I was getting some real good cuts. I hit a line drive, you know the kind a lefthand hitter hits that dives and hooks to the right. That's when Bill Laskey said, "You got some quick hands!" I said, "Yeah, for an old man." They all laughed.

When I did get to look at the bat it belonged to Dusty Baker. Someone must have told him that I was using his bat, and you should have seen him rushing to get it. It was his gamer. He said, "I see you are using Old Betsy"; that's what he called it. "Yeah, and there's at least two hits in it today, Dusty." I guess someone threw his bat out there and my friend Frank Robinson, being the manager, said if this old man broke it, what could he say? Dusty got two hits and the Giants beat the Cubs, 5–2.

We even played against a team called the Compton Cuties; they were a derivative of the King and His Court, which we played over at the Covington [Kentucky] ballpark. That's how good we were. We won the ASA [Amateur Softball Association] championship and we went to Fort Madison, Iowa, to participate in the national championship. We didn't win it, but we represented well.

Sonny Webb (courtesy of William L. Webb).

Those were some good days. That's when I met Don Johnson, Bunny Warren, and all these guys. Hank Boston and Henry Merchant. We had a team that was run by Walter Banks — we called him Papa Banks — and he had the Cincinnati Tigers. That was a very famous team. They had me try out with them — they kept asking me to play; I guess they had seen me playing this softball. This was in 1955. I was 19 years old.

I tried out with them and they liked the way I played, but it was a while before they'd let me play. I'd make the trips and all that. My mother and father, they would pack lunches and get in the car and follow us to wherever we played. It was one of these type of teams that had *good* ballplayers. All the guys were good and they were close-knit. They'd been playing together a little while and you just didn't come there and take somebody's job. The first baseman was a guy by the name of Hank Boston — Henry Boston, Daryl's father.

I never will forget the first day when I got on the team. I was happy, so I got there early, me and this guy named George Thatcher, another infielder. We called him "Fish." We got down and got on the bus. Papa Banks had a restaurant down there on Fifth Street, so I went in and got me a couple of those little miniature sweet potato pies to carry on the road and jumped on the bus and just sat in a seat.

Here comes this Hank Boston. *Big* fella. He comes on the bus and he says, "Young man, can you read?" "Yeah, I can read." "Then what does that say up there?" I said, "It says 'Boston.'" He says, "Well, I'm Boston and that's my seat."

"Well, where am I gonna sit?" There's several other guys on the bus and they're looking at this and he said, "All these other seats got names on 'em, too, but that one back there don't have none." That was back there in the back, the very last seat across the back. That's where the bats and balls and all the bases and stuff like that were.

I said, "That's got equipment on it." He said, "That's the only seat I see available." So I went on back there; he was a big guy and he kind of intimidated me.

So I'm riding back there and bouncing on all this equipment, so finally I stood up and I said, "Hey! Mr. Boston!" He said, "Yeah, rook." I said, "One day, I'm taking that seat." He said, "Well, young man, that's what you'll have to do." And from then on, he and I had a real nice rapport.

He was a real good ballplayer. Left-handed home run hitter. I just watched him, but he never was as quick with his hands as I was. I mean, I could pick it and I had a move on ground balls. They barely hit my glove and — boom! — I'm to second base on the two. I was quicker and a little flashier than him. He couldn't make it fast like me.

I must've went three, four games before I got a chance to play, and the only reason I got a chance to play was because Papa Banks said, "Hey, son. We gonna play you today. You're gonna get some playing time. We're gonna see if you can play some ball."

My mother and everybody's there and I don't start, but finally he told Henry Merchant, who was managing us then, "You let the lefthanded boy play." Boy, you could just see the happiness on my parents' faces.

I never will forget the first time down at first base. This lefthander hit a ball inside between me and the bag and I shifted over there — I know I didn't look good doing it — and knocked the ball down and fell down, but I got it. I scrambled to get up and I did beat the guy to the bag. The pitcher came over to cover, but I just stepped on the bag.

I didn't look good doing it and I said to myself, "Man, you got to get yourself together. Just relax and play the game." From then on, I decided I'm going to look good playing this game because I've always been proud of the way I put my uniform on, my sanitaries; my shoes were always shined and I always had my uniform cleaned and pressed. I just believe in looking good and I always felt like, "If you're gonna be good, you might as well look good." People will see that.

The first time up in that game, I hit a line shot over the second baseman's head, so then I knew I could hit and then I got comfortable. First time up, I hit that rope. From then, it just like took off, so they started letting me share some time with Hank, and sometimes I'd get to play a little outfield.

Then Papa Banks started me doing a little pitching. When I didn't play first base, I pitched. Me and Don Oliver, Yado, and Charlie Frank. We had a fairly good little pitching staff and I was the lefthander. We ended up later getting a guy named Irvin McMurtry — we called him "Blackie" — and he was another lefthander. He was very smooth.

On that team, several guys had to play several different positions. We'd ride that bus to Racine, Wisconsin; we would go down to Paris, Kentucky, and Bluefield, West Virginia. We'd be all over with Papa. Indianapolis, Indiana. We played against the Clowns.

Later, I played briefly with the Cincinnati Reds. The Reds down at Crosley Field always held tryout camps, so a couple of friends of mine, George Thatcher and a guy named Otis Williams, who was also a singer that I used to be with [a group] called the Charms, would get their hair cut up at Bill's Barber Shop in Walnut Hills. Bill was an avid baseball fan and one day they were getting their hair cut and he told 'em that the Reds were going to have a tryout camp. George Thatcher called me and told me to come on down and go with them.

We go down to Crosley Field and we look and there's probably 4- or 500 guys. The first thing they had you do after they took your name and give you a number was line you up and make you run. They'd do dashes against different guys — maybe 50 in a line — and you'd take off and run 40 or 50 yards.

They started weeding you out. It was a two-day camp and they said, "If you hear your name, we'll let you know to come back the next day." The first day, they ran you and hit some ground balls, but no intersquad games. That first day, they just weeded 'em down; I guess it was down to about 70 guys for the second day.

I got invited back and that day they had intersquad games. Tommy Thompson, Phil Seghi, and a lot of coaches and scouts were there. They said, "You'll hear from us later on. We'll write you a letter. We're having spring training in Laredo, Texas."

Finally one day I got a letter from 'em. It said, "Spring training in Laredo, Texas, on March 1," and they would pay my transportation and my room and board and would I be interested in attending. Well, heck, yeah.

Me and George Thatcher and a guy named Grover Kilgore — his brother Myron was a big-time football player at Xavier University, and Grover was about 6'5", 230–35 pounds, a righthand pitcher, and, boy, he could throw. He could throw that ball hard. The three of us jumped on this train and went all the way to Laredo, Texas. That's the first time I'd ever really been away from home like that on my own. I remember my mother and brother and sister and the family taking me to the train station. The last thing I heard my mother say there was, "Now you take care of my boy."

We had to go through St. Louis and Little Rock, Arkansas. That's where I really found my first incident of racism, there in Little Rock. We get on the train there in Cincinnati down at Union Terminal and we just sat in the train anywhere we wanted to, you know. I wasn't thinking about this kind of stuff and we went on through Indiana and on through St. Louis and we get in Little Rock, Arkansas, and the train stopped there for a little layover, or we had to change trains, one or the other.

So I go in to the terminal. I'm looking around in the terminal — it's not very big — and I see this water fountain over there, and I walked over there and proceeded to drink. Didn't no one really jump on me right then or anything like that, but this black conductor — I guess he was changing trains — said, "Boy, can you read that sign?" I looked up and it said, "White Only." He said, "You got to drink over there, boy," and I saw a little further on down a sign that had "Colored" on it. And it was right in front of a "Colored Only" toilet, and they had white toilets. I thought to myself, "Man, is this the way it's gonna be?" That was a wake-up call for me.

There were certain things in Cincinnati that you couldn't do, isolated places you couldn't go to that you just accepted. You weren't allowed, but to be away from home and *see* the colored and the white signs, I never saw that in Cincinnati. That was the start of it because I saw it from then on. I really saw it.

We proceeded on down on one of those really nice trains, like a Vista View coach. We go to San Antonio and we had to change trains. We had to sit with a bunch of Mexicans and there was cattle cars on there. We had to switch and start sitting with them; that was cool, but why? We couldn't sit up there with the whites no longer. We had to ride in an isolated car on in to Laredo.

When we got to Laredo, that was something else. That was as far south as you could go. In one part of Texas we passed Charlie Neal's hometown. I believe it was Midland, Texas. When we got to Laredo, we checked in. What the Reds had done, they had bought or rented what used to be a hospital and they converted it into like a hotel. They called it Redleg Terrace. It was a very nice-looking building and it was very clean.

There were guys from everywhere that

they had signed and they were pairing people off to sleeping quarters. There was a lot of white guys there and we stayed in the same building, but they would have two white guys to a room, but all the black guys — the Spanish and the Puerto Ricans, I remember Vic Power's brother, and Venezuelans and Cubans, Afro-American blacks, "colored" then — were up on the top floor and they had this one big room — a big dormitory — and they had cots in there for us and like foot lockers. That's where I met Leo Cardenas, who became Cincinnati's starting shortstop.

All the blacks stayed together in this big room. The room was full, but not overcrowded. Now, I have to say, the room was nice. It was clean and everything, but I couldn't put it together why all the blacks were in this one room, and on the other floors there'd be two white guys to a room.

That's when I met John Ivory Smith and Eddie Moore and Eddie Locke and all these guys. They had played in the Negro leagues.

The first day, they had us out to the ballpark and we got assigned to different rosters. The first roster I played on was a roster out of Albuquerque, New Mexico; Phil Seghi had that. He went on to get big with the Reds, then he went over to Cleveland when my friend Frank [Robinson] became the first black manager in the big leagues.

I remember at Lopez Park down there we was playing an exhibition game and I hit a home run for him. I guess they used to kind of bet little steak dinners against each other. So I hit a home run for Phil Seghi down there off of this Mexican kid, a righthander. The ball went out of the park, across the street, and hit up on this roof. A woman had a tin roof; you could just hear it bang. After that, he'd always call me "Slugger."

When I hit that home run, it drew attention so they looked at me pretty good. It ended up I played for Dave Bristol down there and Dave wanted me real bad for Geneva, New York, in the NYP League. This was told to me by Henry Royer, a clubhouse attendant who sat in on the daily meetings.

I come to know blacks couldn't play — and this was news to me — in Gainesville, in the Florida State League, and places like that. Blacks couldn't play there. I think blacks were allowed to play up in the NYP League and you could play out in California, but places like Palatka, Gainesville, Douglas — you couldn't play down there.

I played well down there. Everybody knew that I could play the game, that I had some talent. But the elation I had being there, the prestige of it, the nostalgia — meeting guys over here from Cuba, Puerto Rico, Mexico. They said things like, "This guy Webb can play," and so on. Hearing this stuff makes you feel good. A ballplayer can't lie to himself; you know whether or not you belong. I could run good; I wore my uniform with a lot of pride. I had power, a good arm, and a love for baseball.

Eddie Moore slept right next to me and he would tell me, "Yeah, man, I heard about you today." We had a clubhouse boy by the name of Henry Royer — a white kid, very nice guy. After every workout, all the scouts and the managers would have a meeting. This was how they would vote. You know, "What do you think about him?" "We're gonna keep him around for more," and so on. And they would release guys 'til they would get down to what they needed.

Well, Henry Royer would always tell me what they were saying in there about me. The reports were great. He said, "Sonny, they like you." Bill McKechnie, the farm director, he'd be in on the meetings.

I got to feeling real good about that, you know what I mean? Playing ball and I'm gonna get paid. Although the money was no issue; just let me play.

But I had an incident that just turned me off. I'd accepted that big room we were living in all together; I was living with the black guys and we'd talk and laugh and have fun. Now, the Spanish guys — that was gibberish to me, but they were doing their thing.

But what got me was, there in Laredo I had went somewhere — I think it was the dry cleaners — with some guys and we come back, and they had this drugstore and they were selling hamburgers and malts and stuff like that. We really didn't have enough money to buy a whole lot of outside stuff, but we go over there to get us a hamburger and a malted milk. We was gonna sit down in there and these people said, "You're not allowed to sit down. You shouldn't come in here. You go around there and then we'll wait on you around there."

I'm saying, "What?" But you're in the South and that's the way it is. Ever since that, I had a problem. With my background — from Ohio where I was born and raised, they didn't have that racism like that — I wasn't used to it. I went to Purcell High School and I was the first black in the history of the school to play varsity football. It was my ability that got me there; I was the only black on the team. I saw little things of racism when they would try to take me certain places to play, like Kentucky, but never to the magnitude that was down South. Thank God for the blacks who stood up to this madness.

I met this one white fellow from Sun Valley, California; his name was Pat Mitchell. He and I became friends; he was a first baseman, too. We decided we were gonna go to a movie one night. We go down to town to the movie and we walk in. This guy was looking at me funny, so he says, "You can come in, but you got to sit upstairs."

I told Pat, "It's okay, man. Let's go in." I'm still trying to deal with this shit.

I go upstairs in this balcony and I'm the only son of a gun up there. I guess I wasn't there ten minutes when I hollered out, "Hey, Pat! Let's go." So we went on out of there and went on over into Mexico and kind of bummed around. But the thought stayed in my head: "I only wanted to watch a movie."

In another incident, I met Sammy Potter and some of his white friends. Mickey Owen brought them up from Springfield, Missouri. There were about four of 'em. One night, they asked me to go to a movie with 'em. They had a 1958 Plymouth and they asked me to go to this drive-in. This was the thing that broke the camel's back.

We get in this car and I'm sitting in the

Sonny Webb, 1996 (courtesy of William L. Webb).

middle up front. There's three of us up front and three in the back. We go on in this drive-in. I never will forget; it was a movie called *The Girl Can't Help It*, with Jayne Mansfield. It was a horrible movie, but they just loved her.

Everything's fine and we're having a good time. Intermission come up, so we had to go inside to go to the bathroom. We go on in and there's no "Colored" or "White" signs there, and I wasn't even thinking about that, anyway. I'm standing there, and all of a sudden I hear this shouting, "Where is he! Where is he!"

And this guy come over there to me, "Nigger, don't you know you ain't got no damn business in here!? What the hell you doing in here?" Just screaming. *Irate.* I look at this guy and I can see the *rage* in his face.

Then it dawned on me. I looked around and saw nothing but a sea of white faces. Not a black to be seen. And this guy's cursing still. "There ain't never been no niggers in this drive-in! You ain't allowed in here!"

I want to retaliate, but it's not the best thing to do. I never will forget; I said, "Oh, my God!"

The guys I was with, they come in and they want to take it up. I said, "Hold it! Hold it! Just let me out of here." And I turned around and all of these white faces were staring. At that point, I wasn't afraid, just mad, so I looked up and started walking and they started parting like the Red Sea. They were just looking at me and I walked on out. And this guy is still badgering and hollering and screaming obscenities and racial slurs.

When I got in the car, I started to shake. We get on back to the Redleg Terrace and I go upstairs and I'm sitting on the side of the bed, and I just went into an uncontrolled shake. Eddie Locke looked over at me and said, "What's wrong with you, man?"

I told him where we went and what happened. He said, "You went where!?" I said, "This guy come in there and he acted like he wanted to kill me."

"He probably did, man. Damn, don't you know where the hell you are?"

"What do you mean?"

"Man, you're in the *South*. You can't do shit like that!"

I guess I was naive. I should know better, but I *don't* know better and it's not my fault, because I didn't come up like that. It was frightening, it was insulting, it was demeaning. It was everything. That's why I *hate* it so much, because it didn't have to be. Look, I was *invited* there by some white guys who apparently didn't know, either.

As I look back, I can admire Jackie Robinson even more because, when you're tested — I'm not so sure if I'd've been the first I could've done it. Probably a lot of other guys would've failed. To me, he is an icon.

This guy named Edmund Snatch from Cincinnati — the Reds had asked him to do a documentary on the minor leagues — was getting a group of guys together to get on this documentary. They wanted to show a scene of some of the guys going to church. I was Catholic and they had a church down there. There was about six or seven of us who were

Catholic who were going to this Saint Andrew's Church. I'm the only black in the group.

We walk in and all these people are looking at me. There was no blacks in there. I took Communion and people looked, but no one said anything. He took pictures out in front of the church of me and the priest and the guys. No one ever said nothing, but there was no blacks in the church. It come to dawn on me that Laredo, Texas, was not a place to have blacks. There just wasn't any around there.

That started to eat on me. Being that far away from home and having to endure all this racism stuff — no one told me it would be like that and I just could *not* adjust to it.

But I had a great spring. Right at the end, Henry Royer told me, "The Reds want you, Sonny." I called my Uncle Garfield — Garfield Thompson — and said, "The Reds are ready to sign me." Everybody was elated.

The next morning we get up and we go over in this field and there's these people there to take pictures of us for these bubblegum cards. Then word come down that when I sign I'm supposed to go with Cardenas and them down in the Sally League. Savannah.

The next day camp's supposed to break and early in the morning they were calling some guys to come down there in front on the mail room. My name was called and I go down there and there's about three or four of 'em down there. I never will forget this, and I never will understand it, either.

The only thing I can attribute this to was something that happened. There was a fight. Leo Cardenas and some other Puerto Rican or Cuban boy were going out there to work out one day. Me and this guy, Pat Mitchell, the boy from California, were in the locker room and he could not find his windbreaker. This was getting close to cut-down day or shipping-out day. We go on out on the field to work out and he looks over there and he sees it. Leo Cardenas has got it on.

He goes over there and words are exchanged between 'em. Then they started fighting. Well, this other guy's ready to jump in it, so I got ahold of him to keep him out of it so that Pat Mitchell and Cardenas can go at it.

Pat showed him it was his. He pulled the label up and his name was there, so it was his jacket.

To this day, I think that was it. Cardenas lives up this way and he says, "Sonny, I thought you was scheduled to come to Savannah with us." Bill McKechnie, Jr., come up and he put his hands on my shoulders and says, "Son, you're a hell of a ballplayer," but they were releasing me. He said, "We're gonna send you home." And they never would tell me why. You know, I really believe — I can't say for sure — but I believe it was because of that, because Leo, he had a good year and they liked him and I think he complained about the fight. The Reds didn't really have anything invested in me, and I really believe that had something to do with it. I can't be sure, but I know it was not because I didn't have the ability; I proved that. Maybe it was because I got along with whites too well. Remember, it's 1958.

There was a guy who had played in the Negro leagues or knew something about 'em — I don't remember his name now — and he had seen me train down there and he says, "Give me your name and your number and your address." I did, and I was gone.

Then one day, I got a letter from the Kansas City Monarchs and Sputniks. It was from Ted Rasberry telling me his organization was a showcase for the major leagues; [he asked] what could I play for, and he said he normally started his players off at some amount of money. He said to let him know 'cause it would behoove me to go to as high class ball as I possibly could and stuff like that.

So I went up to Grand Rapids and they were having a tryout. I worked out for 'em and they liked the way I played ball, but I didn't want to sign a contract or nothing like that. So what I did was I joined 'em and they were going down to West Virginia. I still hadn't signed a contract, but I wanted to go and see, and it was something like a barnstorm.

What I really found out during that time, it really wasn't a league. They were trying to

hang on; there were only four or six teams that they were drawing from, and guys would be with this club here this weekend, maybe with another later — wherever they were trying to fill in. Basically, what they were trying to do was sell some ballplayers to major league franchises. From what I saw, there wasn't a whole lot of talent there and you're riding on buses just trying to make it, and I wasn't impressed with that. I was working at the General Electric Company then and I had a good, steady job, and a family to support.

It pisses me off that they would let something that was *so* good die like that. As much as I would have wanted to play ball and really would've been a guy to try to carry that legacy on, it was embarrassing. What you saw was some guys who had never done nothing else try to hang on and make a dollar here and there. The talent just wasn't there. As a kid, I saw the talent when the Negro leagues came to Crosley Field to play. I was in awe. I thank God that I got an opportunity to witness the Negro leagues at that time.

I have conversations now with Charlie Davis. Charlie was with the Memphis Red Sox. I think he quit along about 1955, and he was saying, "I agree. The talent had fallen off." It wasn't like it was in his heyday.

He talked about the guys. Guys could play, like Willie Wells. He played against guys like that, guys that I heard about.

Something I noticed, especially about black players, some of 'em peak late. They play for a long time. These guys were still, at that time, hitting the ball *hard*. They could field, they were playing a couple games a day. I can remember doubleheaders down there at Crosley Field and it was a *good* brand of baseball: competitive, emotional, enthralling. It was an event.

Like Charlie, I envy him so because we sit around and he talks about how he made contact with some guys that he thought was dead. Someone told him, "No, he lives —" here or there and gives him phone numbers. He was so happy to locate them.

I sit there and realize how angry I get because that's an institution that, for whatever reason — someone's greed or what — was allowed to die. I tell him, "That could still be going on." Maybe not to the magnitude that it was then, but they *could* be playing somewhere in these little towns. You know, that's a part of our history.

Now the whites want to put black history into schools. Well, how can you want that when you're part of stopping it? The league never should have died.

I live on a 38-acre farm here in Pleasant Plain, Ohio. There is one little section that is being made into a little ballpark, nothing fancy, but a place for little guys to play. They say that if you build it they will come and play. We'll see!

BATTING RECORD

Year	Team, League	Pos	G	AB	R	H	2B	3B	HR	RBI	SB	BA
1958	Detroit, NAL	1b										

Tommy Taylor
"The Dream Ended Too Soon"

BORN JANUARY 28, 1937, MADISON COUNTY, TN
HT. 6'2" WT. 180 BATTED LEFT, THREW RIGHT

Negro Leagues debut: 1959

Tommy Taylor had what every team today wants in a pitcher: size (6'2", 190) and a good fastball.

Back in the late '50s and early '60s, however, it was a little different situation. Sure, all teams were looking for big, strong pitchers. Big, strong *white* pitchers.

Yes, there were black major league pitchers in those days, but look at who they were: Don Newcombe, Bob Gibson, Mudcat Grant, Sam Jones, Juan Marichal. These guys have one thing in common: they were *great* pitchers.

There were a few others, but very few. Check over the rosters of, say, 1958 through 1963. How many black pitchers do you find? Sixteen to 20 teams means somewhere between 160 and 300 pitchers, and perhaps five percent of them were black. And of that five percent, maybe half of them were allowed to contribute.

Baseball executives of that day will deny it, but blacks were still being discriminated against, and especially black pitchers. A black position player had to be outstanding to make it, but a black pitcher had to be nearly perfect.

And Tommy Taylor wasn't perfect. It was his dream to play in the major leagues and it was a dream unfulfilled.

It was also his son's dream, and he lived it. Briefly. Terry Taylor pitched for the Seattle Mariners for a short time in 1988.

Tommy Taylor has stayed active in sports. He was the baseball coach at Lane College for eight years, and now he is a physical education instructor working with young children.

Ira McKnight was my catcher in Kansas City, and Sherwood Brewer was my manager. He was the one that got us a chance to play in the Western Canada League in the '60s.

I wasn't even aware until after I got the opportunity to get involved. After I got released by the Cincinnati Red organization, that's when I got an opportunity to go to Birmingham on a recommendation. That's when I got to play with the Kansas City Monarchs. We began to barnstorm.

Later on, as I got older and historically things would happen, then I heard this documentary on NBC. That's when I got a chance

to see Sherwood. They were talking, I guess, about five years ago. They were going ro remind America of the Negro leagues and how it was so important.

We were the younger guys and I think the people that paved the way were more or less the people for the people's choice. Later on, we still had carried the torch, in a way. Especially with the logos that we were wearing. Some of those previous ballplayers that we were following in their footsteps, we may not have been drawing as many crowds as they used to, but we were still symbolizing.

Jackie Robinson was the person that gave

(l-r) Bob Herron, Thad Tillotson, Tommy Taylor, 1960 (courtesy of Tommy Taylor).

me the courage, I guess. I started playing base-ball here in Jackson and everybody was say-ing how *good* I was. Then I went to several scouting performances that they would have here. The Cardinals would come here, and each time you would have like a three-day elimination. I would stick all the way through, but unfortunately I did not get signed. On the last day, they signed Walter Bond, used to play with the [Houston] Colts.

Bond and I, we used to play against each other here in Tennessee. We played like rural baseball. I think he played for St. John and I played for Blair Chapel.

After that, his father was wondering why they did not pick me up, but Buddy Lewis, which was the scout of the Cardinals at that time, said they were going to come back and try to get me the next year, but it didn't hap-pen.

I got interested in going to a few base-ball schools. I went to Jack Rossiter's up here in Springfield, Illinois. I went there for sev-eral sessions with Boom-Boom Beck, used to pitch for the Washington Senators.

During that time, I think there was still that color barrier. It was there because I rec-ognized that there were a lot of ballplayers, and I was the only black that they felt like had potential, but at the same time, they would always sign another player. Boom-Boom was telling me each and every year how good I was, and yet they wanted me to come back each session.

Finally, I just decided to go to Bill Vir-don's Baseball School. I went there and I got the attention of a scout. They wanted to sign me, but for some reason I didn't get signed. It was the Chicago White Sox.

Then I got an opportunity to get signed by Bismarck, North Dakota. I didn't do that because I played with another team, the Bradenton Nine Devils in Florida. This was about '59 or '58. It just so happened that we were playing a team out of St. Petersburg and there was a scout sitting out in center field. He begin to ask me if I wanted an opportunity to play pro ball and I told him yes. His name was [Paul] Florence, used to be with Cincin-nati. He fixed it up where I could go to Tampa; they wanted to look at me.

At that time, Johnny Vander Meer was coach of one of the Class-D ballclubs. I went over and I think I threw about 15 minutes on the sidelines and after that they begin to talk about my hands and how large they were and my height and how good a fastball I had. I guess it was about 15 minutes; they had a conference between Johnny Vander Meer and Paul Florence and they signed me.

After that, I played in the D league, in Palatka and in Hornell [Pennsylvania] and I played under Dave Bristol. Dave was my manager the first year I got into pro ball, along with Tony Gonzalez and Chico Ruiz. I played with some pretty good ballplayers during that time.

Then I played in Palatka under Johnny Vander Meer, but at the same time, it still was a struggle. I wasn't aware of it, but I was grateful, and it seemed like I was making a little progress of living out a dream.

Just before the season, they were going to promote me to Double-A, but they came in and I got released. At that time, Tommy Thompson was involved in the Reds' organization. When I moved to Cocoa, Florida, Dave Bristol was the interim Reds' manager and I was at the ballgame and he tried to apologize. He said he did not have anything to do with me being released because he felt that, in their organization, I had the best fastball for my age bracket. I told him it wasn't anything I could hold against anyone because I was too young. I was only about 20 years old or so at the time.

That's when I got hooked up to go to Birmingham through John Ivory [Smith], used to be in the Reds' organization. Piper Davis got a chance to talk with me, then I got a chance to play with Kansas City Monarchs. And I started barnstorming with them.

The guy that owned the team was from Grand Rapids, Ted Rasberry. It was still a struggle. We would be barnstorming; we would be in Chicago one night and then we would be in Yankee Stadium and so on. We also played in tournaments and we got a chance to go up in western Canada. I played against Saskatoon and some of the top-notch teams up in that area. There were some good ballplayers up there.

The manager for the Saskatoon Com-modores, his name was Spiro Leakos. Sherwood [Brewer] had been playing up in that Canadian league prior to that because they would allow two or three imports from the States. After playing in this tournament, we had not gotten paid from Ted, and when Sherwood got back on the bus, he said, "We have a decison to make here. There's ballplayers on this team Spiro Leakos would like to [have] help him in the playoff at the end of the season." He selected Ira McKnight; Nate Dancy, a shortstop; and me, so there were three of us.

We decided that we were going to stay because we had not gotten paid, so we left the team. They went on back and we stayed up in Canada. I guess we played with the Commodores for about a month and a half.

We played the best-four-out-of-seven series. We were playing against Lethbridge and we managed to end up with the series tied. I had pitched us into that game, and after that my elbow got stiff and I had to get a cortisone shot. We lost the game and they beat us, four games to three.

The last game went 12 innings. I have some clippings here. One says, "Taylor Baffles White Sox. Righthanded Tommy Taylor served up some crackling slants Tuesday night as he pitched Saskatoon Commodores to a 4–3 victory over Lethbridge White Sox in the opener of the best-of-seven Western Canada Baseball League final."

After the series, another one said that "an arm injury to Taylor was unfortunate because the Negro righthander might have been a savior in a relief role if he had been able to hurl."

Leakos flew each of us back to our respective residences. Ira went back to Indiana, Nate went back to California, and I come on back to Tennessee.

By touring with the Negro league, it actually got me an opportunity to go back and play in this Canadian league. I got a chance to play with Curley Williams. We played together in Lloydminister. Curley got me the opportunity to go back in about '61 or '62. I stayed in Canada until '64.

I thought I would get an opportunity to get back in organized ball, but it never did

Tommy Taylor graduating from Lane College, 1979 (courtesy of Tommy Taylor).

come about. Len Tucker, that had played up in the Western Canada League, put a recommendation through the Los Angeles Angels organization; I got the letter here in my scrapbook. Also, the Orioles were slightly interested, but I'm gonna tell you what they said. I was 23 years old, but they said they already had a pretty outstanding pitching staff where the people were already in the Trips [AAA] or Double-A.

I got a chance to get an opportunity with the Giants, but I had to go down in Sanford, Florida, and, man, that was a horrible experience. I had to stand by; when the bus driver let me out, he told me to stand under a light before I could get in. They had forgot to pick me up.

I got a history of trying my best to become a professional ballplayer. That was my goal in high school after I found out that God had given me this talent. People here felt like I had the makings of getting into the big leagues.

I was visiting my dad out in the rural area where we used to live and play and this man asked me, "What happened to you?"

I said, "What do you mean?"

He said, "Why didn't you get to the big leagues?"

I said, "It may not [be] meant to be, but I got a lot of experience."

He said, "Man, I used to sit behind and watch you. During that time you were playing, you had the *best* stuff. Everything that you threw moved."

I did have opportunities. I went to Jacksonville. I was about 24 and Cincinnati was thinking about signing me back again.

I thank God for the ride, though, you know.

Now, with our young kids that's coming up, they don't even know what the struggle was like. They don't even have an idea.

My son, Terry, played with the Seattle Mariners. Ironically, we've almost traveled the same route. He got picked in the fourth round [1982] by Seattle. I got a chance to see him when he played in the Southern League, and then when he got to the Bigs in 1988, he invited myself, his mom, his granddad, and his sister.

I started him in a way. I bought him a little bat and a whiffle ball at Woolworth and I started throwing to him. Even the neighbors would boast, say, "Come look at this little boy hit the ball!"

While we were living in Cocoa, I got a neighborhood team up and quite naturally I put my son in there. I put him in center field simply because I felt like that was the main territory, because not too many kids knew anything about trying to pull or go to right and I knew he could cover everything.

How was the travel with the Monarchs? It was pretty rough earlier, back in the '30s and '40s.

I think it had begin to improve slightly. Riding on the bus, running in and out, changing. We were in Grand Junction, Colorado; we played out in Iowa — we would beat some of these teams unmercifully.

You know, in the '50s, Doby was with the Indians, Jackie was in there, the McCoveys and all, and I think acceptance began to kind of sink in. Ted was struggling because he also had a basketball team, but we stayed in some pretty fair hotels. When we got to Chicago, Billy Williams knew our manager and we got an opportunity to stay in the Strand Hotel. It wasn't the best, but it was a good hotel. And we stayed in little motels and they were okay.

The best experience that I received was when we got a chance to play in Briggs Stadium [Detroit], especially recognizing that previous ballplayers had been there. And in Wrigley Field before 22,000-some people. We played in those places providing that the big league team was not there at that time. We got a chance to play in old Yankee Stadium. I remember pitching against Memphis and that's when they had that 290 [feet] down the right field line.

We also did a lot of tournaments. But the hotels were okay. But when I was with the Cincinnati organization, it was still split.

The thinking of the people there was sad. I'll never forget this. We were playing Fort Lauderdale. A guy threw a deep curveball — Johnny had me warming up on the sideline — and what happened, this guy's bat accidentally flew out of his hands. It flew right up in the stands almost where I'm warming up. It hit this white lady and it come from a black person's hands, but it was accidental.

The stands at that time was low; you were almost on 'em. This guy said the "n" word; he said, "You better not go down there 'cause they'll kill you." See, I had turned around to see what had happened, and that was yelled out.

We had a clash between us; Fort Lauderdale belonged to the Yankees and we were with the Reds and Johnny was the type of competitive manager that would actually have you to throw at certain ballplayers. This guy Gonzalez that played second base for 'em, he even tried to tell some of the guys that we're going in to try to take him out.

When I was playing, I felt *good* because it was a partial dream, especially coming from a town like Jackson, 'cause there wasn't too many ballplayers that had got an opportunity to play professional baseball. There's a lot of people right now, they do not understand the professional process. They don't understand minor league or either they'll say, "You were playing semipro." I say, "No, it wasn't semipro. I belonged to an organization trying to work my way up to the big leagues."

We have a Double-A team here now, the Diamondjacks, and they got a beautiful ballpark and there's a lot of people, they still don't understand what is going on.

People like you are trying to get people to understand the process. Eventually, it will even help some kids where they will understand, if their endeavor is leaning toward that way. It's not all peaches and cream: you got to go through something. You have to have a desire, but your ability has to merit a little above. You got to have good work ethics, and you also got to have some luck on your side. If you make it, it's great, but if you don't, you thank God for the experience. That's the way I did.

I got a chance to see Satch some up in the Canadian league. He called me "Big Pitch." During the time, he was going to try to get Willie [Mays] in the '60s to go on a barnstorming tour with him, like they used to do, but [Horace] Stoneham, he wouldn't permit it because Willie had played in those 154 ballgames. He had selected me to be on his team.

He gave me a few pointers. He said, "Big Pitch, you got good stuff, but what you need to do—" and he begin to demonstrate, show me how to kind of break the rhythm. Maybe a pause, not keep going straight through, kind of slow the speed down and not throw immediately. A delay. He said, "Maybe one time you'll pump one time, next time you'll pump two. Or next time you may not pump at all." It was exciting to just get an opportunity to see that.

I got a chance to see him in action, and Satch *had* to be near 70. They put a little kid out there about seven years old and he still threw knee-high strikes, but not real fast. But he still could throw.

He had a barnstorming team that come up there, too, to play in that Canadian league. I guess that was the most exciting thing that happened to me. Mac [McKnight] and I talked about it.

I started my scrapbook in '57 when I got signed with Cincinnati. I played two years in the Cincinnati organization, from '57 to '59.

I have the Geneva Redlegs' roster from 1958. I was 21, 6'2", 190 pounds, I hit from the left side and I threw righthanded. I have some of the players I played with at that time, like Dave Bristol, Harold Ruiz — Chico, he was my roommate; Vic Power's son, Ozzie. Ozzie Power. He was almost like his dad, the way he had that little low crouch and swung the bat kind of quick-like.

From there, I played for Kansas City from '59 through '61. Then I played for Saskatoon. I've got clippings from all those places.

Here's one. When I was with Kansas City, we played the Grand Junction Eagles. We beat them, 16–7. The clipping says, "Tommy Taylor went the route for the visitors."

Another one says, "Monarchs' ace no-hits Boosters. Tommy Taylor, the classy righthander who had pitched the Kansas City Monarchs to first place in the Negro American League, shut out the Danville Boosters with a no-hit, 6–0 triumph at Danville Stadium Wednesday night." [The article goes on to point out that only two balls were hit to the outfield.]

Here's one. "Losing streak ended as Redlegs win, 11–6, with homer barrage. Tommy Taylor, an 18-year-old kid from Florida, pitched all the way and showed a whale of a lot of courage when he survived a tough situation in the ninth. Tony Gonzalez blasted his twelfth and thirteenth homers."

Do you have any regrets from baseball?

Oh, yeah. I'm gonna be frank with you. I definitely do. See, I got an opportunity. At Bill Virdon's Baseball School, when they selected what they felt were the best prospects, I just could not believe that I was not good enough during that time where I could have gone much further in baseball.

When I was working at Lane, the president — we grew up together — he felt like it was just before my time. He said it was just one of those things where I was early and there was a lot of good black ballplayers in the big leagues at that time [when Taylor was at Lane] and he said, "Tommy, you were good enough

where you *should* have had the opportunity to go to the big leagues, but there was things against you."

When I was in Jack Rossiter's Baseball School with Boom-Boom Beck, Boom-Boom indicated how good I was. At that time, the old Washington Senators was in the league, and I think Jack was a scout for the Senators. During the selection out of the school, they sent guys home, yet they kept me and I made the All-Star team. Out of all the cuts, I was the only black. My son had gone through that same type of process. Many times, he was the only black —"the pea in the pod."

You can't understand if you were that good, why could you not go further? Why wouldn't they give you that opportunity?

I'm in my 60s now and, sure, I regret because I really put my all in it. Riding on those buses, going through all of the segregated type of situations, even in the Redlegs' organization. We played as a team, but when the game was over, I had to live in a different section of town. Even when we were traveling, I would stay in those little station wagons we were traveling in while they would go in and get a sandwich and bring it to me. Here I am in Cincinnati's professional organization and as a kid, 18 or 19 years old, it just didn't dawn on me what was going on.

I can remember a guy named Don Pray. He was from Buffalo, New York, and he was one of my teammates. There was a bonus baby that come in out of Georgia and we were traveling. During that time, Martin [Luther King] was marching and the radio was on and Don Pray asked this boy, he said, "What do you have against Tommy's race?"

He said, "I don't have anything against Tommy's race. I was brought up where there are differences."

Don said, "Tommy's a part of our team. Are you not aware, if he pitches and wins, we all win together?"

I can remember when I got signed. I was leaving Florida, and Cincinnati put me on the bus to get me to New York. Going from here to Birmingham, an incident occurred where the police come on the bus. I was asleep in the back part and they awakened me and outside there was about seven Doberman pinschers. It was right outside of Bessemer, Alabama, before we got into Birmingham, and they stopped the bus.

They got me up and had me to identify myself. I had a card that said I was a part of the professional baseball organization. This young cop asked me for my identification and I showed it to him and he said, "Oh, you're one of them."

They were looking for someone who had attacked a white woman. They wanted to know when I got on the bus, but a white lady told 'em I been on it the whole time.

Frank Robinson and Vada Pinson came over to our place in spring training near Tampa and they were talking to us. This particular incident, I happened to be walking down the street and it was at night. We had a curfew and we resided over a funeral parlor in the black part of town. That's where the black ballplayers stayed.

Approaching me, I saw this light coming. The police stopped me then. I told them that I was part of the Redlegs' organization. He said that he was looking for someone that been in someone's home. There was all kinds of incidents that I went through.

I met one of my better friends there in Cocoa. John Ivory Smith. Johnny was in Triple-A at that time and he got an opportunity for me to go and play in the Mexican League. Johnny sent this letter to the people that reared me. I was not at home and my aunt couldn't read very well. I was playing in Canada then.

I'm very satisfied that I got a lot of experience, but I had to endure all of the suffering. Some people are not aware of the segregated type of situation that blacks have gone through. We've made some type of progress, but at the same time, you feel that you were denied. You *were* denied.

It was a tough row to hoe, but would you go back and do it again?

Oh, yeah. Sure, I would. Certainly. I realize that God gave me a gift, a gift of being a pretty profound athlete.

I did not want to be a teacher, but now you see I wound up in that area. I'm still in the physical education department, where I deal with young kids. I'm trying my best to give some ideas about what it's like if you get an opportunity to become a professional athlete. It's not as easy as some people may think. You have to work, and then you have all the other difficulties. It's hard, yet you have to try to prevail.

Yeah, I would do it again, and I would do it over and over. Hopefully, someone would give me an opportunity to not say color is a barrier.

I made a little money, but I did not go up the ladder like I thought I should have. Even when I was released by the Cincinnati organization, there was so many of my teammates, they just could not believe it. When they came in and released me, I cried like a baby.

I remember Tommy Thompson telling me this; he said, "Someone else will pick you up." But the road at that time was still narrow.

I went to Cocoa. There was 12 ex-professional ballplayers — myself, Ira McKnight. There was a guy named Sylvester. And there was a guy that I played with in the Negro league that I thought could be compared to Mickey Mantle, 'cause he was one of the best switch hitters that I have ever seen. His name was Don Barner. He was on another team; I think he was with the New Orleans team.

There was about 12 of us who had congregated in Cocoa and we were trying to get the attention of other scouts so we could get ourselves back into organized baseball. It didn't happen, but we had enough guts to keep trying our best. It was a long road, but I'm grateful to the Almighty that I did get an opportunity to get signed by a professional organization; but I feel that I was denied the opportunity given some of the white ballplayers.

It was like a dream where you wake up before the dream is finished.

PITCHING RECORD

Year	Team, League	G	IP	W	L	Pct	H	BB	SO	ERA
1957	Palatka, FlStL									
1958	Hormel, NYPL									
1959	Kansas City, ind.									
1960	Kansas City, ind.									
	Saskatoon, WCanL									
1961										
1962										
1963										
1964										

Bibliography

Charlton, James, ed. *The Baseball Chronology*. New York: Macmillan, 1991.

Clark, Dick, and Larry Lester, eds. *The Negro Leagues Book*. Cleveland: The Society for American Baseball Research, 1994.

Echevarria, Roberto Gonzalez. *The Pride of Havana*. New York: Oxford University Press, 1999.

Kelley, Brent. *Voices from the Negro Leagues*. Jefferson, NC: McFarland, 1998.

Marazzi, Rich, and Len Fiorito. *Aaron to Zuverink*. New York: Avon, 1982.

Marshall, William. *Baseball's Pivotal Era 1945–1951*. Lexington, KY: University Press of Kentucky, 1999.

McNary, Kyle P. *Ted "Double Duty" Radcliffe*. Minneapolis: McNary Publishing, 1994.

O'Neil, Buck. *I Was Right on Time*. New York: Simon and Schuster, 1996.

Peterson, Robert. *Only the Ball Was White*. New York: McGraw-Hill, 1970.

Riley, James A. *The Biographical Encyclopedia of the Negro Baseball Leagues*. New York: Carroll and Graf, 1984.

Rust, Art, Jr. *Get That Nigger Off the Field*. Brooklyn: Book Mail Services, 1992.

Rust, Edna, and Art, Jr. *Art Rust's Illustrated History of the Black Athlete*. Garden City, NY: Doubleday, 1985.

Thorn, John, et al., eds. *Total Baseball*. 4th ed. New York: Viking, 1995.

Wolff, Rich, editorial director. *The Baseball Encyclopedia*. 9th ed. New York: Macmillan, 1993.

Index

Photographs appear on pages with italicized numbers.